Rural Employment

An International Perspective

Rural Employment

An International Perspective

Edited by

Ray D. Bollman

*Statistics Canada
Ottawa, Canada*

and

John M. Bryden

*Arkleton Centre for Rural
Development Research
University of Aberdeen
UK*

CAB INTERNATIONAL

*in association with the
Canadian Rural Restructuring Foundation/
la Fondation Canadienne sur la Restructuration Rurale*

CAB INTERNATIONAL
Wallingford
Oxon OX10 8DE
UK

Tel: +44 (0)1491 832111
Fax: +44 (0)1491 833508
E-mail: cabi@cabi.org

CAB INTERNATIONAL
198 Madison Avenue
New York, NY 10016-4341
USA

Tel: +1 212 726 6490
Fax: +1 212 686 7993
E-mail: cabi-nao@cabi.org

*Published in association with and available exclusively in
Canada from the:*
Canadian Rural Restructuring Foundation
c/o Rural Development Institute
Brandon University
Brandon, Manitoba, Canada, R7A 6A9
E-mail: rollheiser@brandonu.ca

A catalogue record for this book is available from the British Library, London, UK
A catalogue record for this book is available from the Library of Congress,
Washington DC, USA

ISBN 0 85199 198 X

Printed and bound in the UK by Biddles Ltd, Guildford and King's Lynn
from copy supplied by the editors

Table of Contents

Lifestyle Choice and Commuting

Rural Enterprises

Agriculture and Rural Employment

Rural Employment Policy

Preface

Rural communities desire sustainable or growing employment opportunities. This book focuses the research and policy debate on rural employment. To understand the issues, the annual rural policy conference of the Canadian Rural Restructuring Foundation was held in October 1995 in partnership with the community of Coaticook, Québec and the OECD.

Seven chapters are reports of international comparative analyses prepared for the OECD Rural Development Programme. Retaining and retraining rural youth is the focus of four complementary chapters. The roles of lifestyle choice, residential choice and commuting in understanding rural employment issues are addressed by six chapters. The roles of small and medium enterprises and independent entrepreneurs provide another theme grouping of five chapters. Six chapters on various aspects of rural employment policy coalesce the research findings into policy frameworks for proactive and practical rural policy initiatives.

Intellectual property rights, not the time spent working, are now the focus of development policy. Our partnership with the Coaticook conference local organizing committee amply illustrates this focus. Over one hundred individuals worldwide attended the Coaticook conference via the Internet. This global link (initially supported by Heather Clemenson, Rural Secretariat, Agriculture and Agri-food Canada) is now providing a platform for learning at the *Centre régional d'initiatives et de formation en agriculture de Coaticook.* You are invited to visit Coaticook at http://www.multi-medias.ca/MRC_Coaticook/index.html.

A report on the results of the OECD Project on Rural Employment Indicators (REMI) entitled **Territorial Indicators of Employment: Focusing on Rural Development** is being published by the Organization for Economic Co-operation and Development (OECD) and may be purchased at the OECD, 2 rue Andre-Pascal, 75775 Paris Cedex 16, France. Internet: Compte.PUBSING@oecd.org.

On average, "rural" areas perform at a lower level than more urban areas but some rural areas outperform the best urban areas. Thus, rurality *per se* does not necessarily cause lower performance. In addition, the mix of employment across industries is not necessarily a factor in determining performance. Rather, it appears to be something specific to a certain location. Understanding this intangible factor is one of the keys in furthering rural employment policy.

Leonard P. Apedaile
Canadian Rural Restructuring Foundation

Foreword

Employment Creation in the Coaticook Region

A community should take care of its interests and not rely on outsiders to take care of its concerns ...

The **International Symposium: Perspectives on Rural Employment**, held in Coaticook, Québec, focused on job characteristics and trends, the role and impact of employment creation policies in rural areas, as well as the actual experiences of rural communities. Among other things, the *Symposium* focused on communities that take charge of their concerns, that rally their strengths and bank on members of the community to pitch in to help each other.

Why Coaticook?

The region of Coaticook was chosen as the site for the symposium because it is a dynamic community which benefits from the concerted action of its various partners, its job development strategies as well as its cultural and birth rate policies.

The region of Coaticook consists of more than 16,000 people with 58 percent of the population living outside the City of Coaticook. Thirteen percent of the population depends on agriculture for its livelihood.

The region of Coaticook is known as the heart of milk production in Québec. The region is also involved in other types of production, ranging from pork to grain, including sheep, poultry, horses, Christmas trees, fruit, vegetables and many others.

The forest plays a significant part in economic activity with its cutting operations, sawmills and processing enterprises. Coaticook's industrial sector, undergoing constant change, represents an important source of employment for workers in the region. While initially based on textiles, significant diversification has taken place in the last few years. Finished wood, plastic, rubber and specialized products are now produced in the region.

There is positive interaction among municipal elected officials, economic development officers and members of social development agencies. Each one strives to understand the concerns and projects of the other. Often several actors are involved in the same project. Every idea is good until proven otherwise.

In 1992, the *Forum du développement du territoire de la Municipalité régionale de comté (MRC) de Coaticook* [Forum on Development in the Regional Municipal County of Coaticook] played an important role in encouraging coordination among the municipal and economic and social development agencies.

Successful local and regional consultation grew out of this exercise. The *MRC* of Coaticook became one of the first *MRC*s to establish a new development plan based on extended participation which included all possible actors.

Forum participants considered the strengths, weaknesses, threats and opportunities in each sector. Avenues of development were set out based on priorities identified for each of the sectors: agriculture, tourism, industrial development and training.

The *MRC* and local municipalities decided to assemble the elected officials of the fifteen municipalities by creating the *Assemblée générale des élues et élus* [Assembly of Elected Officials]. This group reviews projects proposed by local municipalities and economic and social development boards within the region. This type of assembly is unique in its kind. Obviously the municipalities are stronger together than if each one acted in an isolated manner.

Community Achievements to be Proud of!

Since the development of the agricultural sector is the top priority for the region, the *Centre d'initiatives en agriculture de la région de Coaticook (CIARC)* [Coaticook Regional Agricultural Initiative Centre] was created in 1990 to encourage coordination and development in the agricultural sector. The organisation was born out of the concerted efforts of agricultural producers and enterprises, municipalities, development organisations, businesses and many individuals from the region.

The *Centre régional d'initiatives et de formation en agriculture (CRIFA)* [Regional Agricultural Training and Initiatives Centre] was born out of an initiative of the *CIARC* and the Coaticook school board. It is a unique teaching institution, the product of an alliance between agriculture, educational (high school and college) and economic development interests.

A *Société locale d'investissement et de développement économique (Solide)* [Local Employment Investment Fund] was set up in September 1995 thanks to the involvement of development agencies, a group of businesses, the *Caisses populaires* [credit unions] of the region and the municipalities. This fund is a source of venture capital which is easily accessible to local business.

Each year, the MRC awards the *Prix de mérite régional* [Regional Merit Award] to honour individuals who have contributed significantly to the development of their region. In addition to this, the *Excel* competition is organised development of their region. In addition to this, the *Excel* competition is organised annually to recognise the efforts of the business of the year.

The Coaticook *MRC* was the first to set up a regional family policy to which all municipalities adhere. Each year the MRC holds a *Fête de la famille* [Celebration of the Family] to celebrate the arrival of newborn babies.

The City of Coaticook has devoted close to 2 million dollars since 1990 to support economic development, particularly in the industrial sector. The city has invested in new structures and a new road network. In 1992, the city bought and financed its first industrial complex. The city also purchased the building of one business in order to facilitate its relocation in a new building located in the industrial park. It was a strategy which allowed Coaticook to keep a business which had foreseen moving outside the region.

In 1993, the city undertook construction of a second industrial complex and attracted expanding new industries. In 1995, the city pushed ahead with the construction of a new business incubation centre.

The *MRC* of Coaticook was the first rural territory in Québec to proceed with a selective household waste collection system in each one of its municipalities. It was also the first to set up a master plan for waste management.

In 1995, the "single window" project, which aimed at putting all employment development services under the same roof, became a reality. The personnel of Human Resources Development Canada , the Coaticook Economic Development Corporation and the Community Futures Development Corporation now work in the same offices and share their resources.

The municipalities and other socioeconomic development partners agreed jointly to fund an Agricultural Development Officer and a Tourism Development Officer. These officers aid the economic development officers in assisting entrepreneurs with their commercial development.

Spin-off Effects of the Symposium: Coaticook Moves Forward

Job Creation Objectives

Following the *symposium*, the Mayor of Coaticook and partners in the community asked themselves what could be done to encourage job creation. They identified what entrepreneurs were lacking to encourage job creation and they conceived a program adapted to the needs of the local community. Different levels of government were convinced to contribute amounts from existing programs to a tailor-made program for the community. The community itself made a considerable investment to support this initiative. The *Fonds local de création d'emploi* [Local Job Creation Fund] was thus created. This fund assists entrepreneurs that create new jobs by granting financial aid to cover the cost of part of the salaries of the workers for the first year. It is a good example of what a local community can do to take charge of its situation.

into the region via the *Fonds local de création d'emploi*. More than $30,000 was redistributed in the community. This investment is in addition to the organisation of the symposium which provided jobs for five full-time employees for a 9 month period.

Gain for the CRIFA

To host the *International Symposium*, the *CRIFA* acquired equipment necessary for holding large events. The *CRIFA* is now prepared to accommodate other symposiums, seminars and conferences.

Seen Around the World

The symposium benefited from good press coverage. The symposium also enabled the *MRC* of Coaticook to be the first *MRC* in Quebec to display itself on the World Wide Web. This allowed participants to exchange ideas with people from all corners of the globe during the symposium.

Major Spin-off Effects

The symposium brought in more than $235,000 in economic spin-offs. The region directly benefited from this amount because almost all of the products and services necessary were drawn from within the territory of the *MRC* of Coaticook. On several occasions, participants had the opportunity to note the diversity of our regional products and services.

Conclusion

Job creation in rural communities is certainly a primary concern when confronted with the exodus of our youth toward large urban centres. The well-being of our population can only be achieved by forces from within the community working together. Development is a question of acting as equal partners. Our region is working towards this goal; as if in each one of us there was a Development Officer waiting to be discovered.

Paul Rouillard
Centre régional d'initiatives et de formation en agriculture, Coaticook, Québec

Acknowledgements

My attention to rural issues[1] started with the formation of the Agriculture and Rural Restructuring Group (now, the Canadian Rural Restructuring Foundation (CRRF)) in 1987. Numerous special colleagues have influenced and encouraged me over the past decade — to each I owe personal thanks. More recently, an advisory group to the OECD, the Steering Group on Rural Indicators has provided stimulus and focus. To support the work of both groups, I undertook to organize the program for a conference on international perspectives on rural employment. The conference in Coaticook, Québec succeeded thanks to the detailed work by a large group of community volunteers that was organised by Jean-Charles Blais and Rosaire Provencher. Je vous remercie pour votre dévouement et pour la confiance que vous m'avez témoignée en travaillant avec un groupe qui n'était pas bien connu dans votre communauté.

Thanks to Christian Huillet and his colleagues at OECD for their support and participation. The OECD's "patronage" of the Coaticook conference is gratefully acknowledged. Thanks to Ken Donnelly, Human Resources Development Canada, for loyal and proactive encouragement of all CRRF activities. Thanks to CAB International for partnering with CRRF to assemble this book. Once again, I have enjoyed working with Danielle Baum in Ottawa, who cheerfully and competently produced the entire manuscript from the scattered diskettes that I passed to her.

Statistics Canada provided the flexibility of work arrangements to allow me to organise the conference program and, subsequently, to edit these papers. My family, Betty, Eric and MifAnne must be thanked for allowing me to work numerous evenings on the project. Finally, the book happened because each author "came through". Each author receives my first and my final thanks.

Ray D. Bollman
Statistics Canada

---

[1] *My interest in rural issues has been long-standing. My masters thesis is one piece of evidence.*

The Canadian Rural Restructuring Foundation (and earlier, the Agriculture and Rural Restructuring Group) organises Canada's only national rural policy conference and provides an excellent opportunity to visit different parts of rural Canada and to meet with people from all walks of life. I have benefited greatly from participation at nearly all of these events since 1987. The explicit search for international comparative perspectives for the Coaticook conference, largely provided by individuals working on case studies for the OECD Rural Development Programme, represents an important advance. I am pleased to participate in the assembly of these papers addressing the employment nexus of rural policy.

John M. Bryden
The Arkleton Trust and
The Arkleton Centre for Rural Development Research
University of Aberdeen
UK

Chapter one:

International Perspectives on Rural Employment: Introductory Propositions

Philip Ehrensaft
Université du Québec à Montréal, Montréal, Québec, Canada

The following propositions offer an introduction to international perspectives on rural employment. To understand the place of non-metro labour forces in the new world division of labour:

1. There is **not** a labour force crisis at the world level. However, "western" countries are losing their privileged niche.

2. The non-metropolitan labour force is faring no better **and** no worse than metropolitan labour forces.

3. Enterprises are restructuring and we are seeing new forms of enterprises. Big firms predominate. However, there is a perceived increase in the importance of small firms because work that used to be done within large enterprise is now conducted via formal and informal alliances with smaller firms. The big firms are still drumming the beat.

Basic new perspectives to understand rural employment are:

4. Rural–urban has become metro–non-metro. The role of commuting has integrated the edge city into the metropolitan economy. The new separation is between the groups within commuting zones and the groups in the hinterland.

5. The paradox of globalization: location becomes more important. The national economy no longer exists as economies cross boundaries. Communities have personalities and communities determine the nexus of cooperation and work.

6. Rural Canada is not falling apart. The population is viable. Rural areas receive more (unintended?) transfers than they pay in taxes. However, they are susceptible to social policy cutbacks.

7. The new production paradigms are "flexible" production and service provision. Rural areas have relative advantages in flexible production and service provision. Smaller units can do this more easily and rural enterprises are smaller.

8. There is a segmented labour force. Labour market behaviour differs between the genders across urbanization classes. Age differences matter. Regional differences matter.

9. Beware of long movement fallacies. Some citizens feel that governments can do nothing — many feel they should merely wait for the next boom. However, analyses of the long run indicate that government policies are key. Also, technological innovation is irregular.

10. There is a convergence of "environmental" concerns and "rural" concerns. This should favour rural interests, relatively.

Many of these propositions have been developed in the literature on world labour market restructuring. They are summarized here as propositions or hypotheses for further research, debate and discussion.

Chapter two:

Rural Employment in OECD Countries: Structure and Dynamics of Regional Labour Markets

Heino von Meyer
Rural Development Programme
Organisation for Economic Cooperation and Development, Paris, France

Abstract

In most OECD countries, unemployment rates are higher in rural than in urban regions and labour force participation rates are lower in rural than in urban regions. In all countries, rural women are under-represented in the labour force. Rural areas of many OECD countries will be confronted with substantial increases in their working-age population. This will generate uneven territorial pressures for labour market adjustments that will require either creating additional jobs, coping with higher unemployment or facilitating migration flows.

Some rural regions belong to the most dynamic areas within OECD countries. They were more successful in generating new employment opportunities than were national economies as a whole. The dynamism of these regions shows that rurality in itself is not an obstacle to job creation. For lagging rural regions, dynamic rural regions probably provide a more realistic development model than do urbanized regions.

The success of the dynamic rural regions is not due to favourable sectoral mixes. Like most other rural regions, they tend to have shares in declining industries that are higher than the national average. The positive performance in creating rural employment results from specific territorial dynamics that are not yet properly understood, but probably include aspects such as regional identity and entrepreneurial climate, public and private networks, or the attractiveness of the cultural and natural environment.

Introduction

Unemployment problems and the potential for job creation have become key issues on national and international policy agendas. The OECD Jobs Study (OECD, 1994b, 1995a), like most other economic analyses, is based on comparisons of national economies. Too little is known about the diversity and dynamics of true labour markets which in reality are usually not national but sub-national, regional and local. This chapter:

1. argues that territory matters in understanding and influencing national economic development even in a context of increasing globalization;
2. describes the territorial scheme for sub-national data collection and rural analysis developed by the OECD;
3. analyses territorial disparities in unemployment and labour force participation rates;
4. provides an impression of the importance of different economic sectors for rural labour markets;
5. reveals the great diversity of territorial development patterns and dynamics in OECD countries; and
6. draws some lessons for future approaches to rural analysis and policy.

Territory matters

In the highly developed market economies that are members of the OECD, almost **35 million persons, more than 8 percent of the total labour force, are at present unemployed and searching for a job** (Figure 2.1a). Over the last two decades, the number of unemployed persons has more than doubled. In several OECD countries, every second unemployed person has been looking for work for more than 12 months. In some countries a quarter to a third of the young is unemployed.

No doubt, unemployment is causing serious economic costs and social hardship, problems that need to be addressed politically. It is often overlooked, however, that in the OECD area since 1975, not only has the number of unemployed persons increased by about 17 million persons but also **almost 100 million additional new jobs have been created**. This was not enough to absorb the total increase in the labour force. But the trend in unemployment rates appears much less spectacular than the trend of the number of unemployed persons. Over the last twenty years the average unemployment rate for the OECD area ranged in the order of 5 to 8 percent (Figure 2.1b).

Figure 2.1a.   In OECD countries, 17 million more persons are unemployed than in 1975

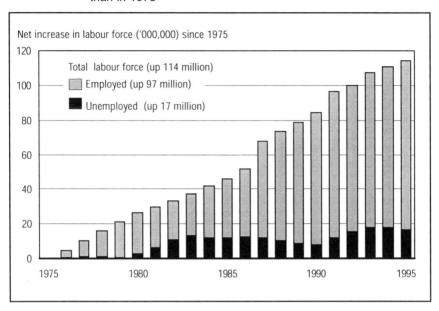

Source: OECD Labour Force Statistics.

Figure 2.1b.   The OECD average unemployment rate varies between 5 and 8 percent over time

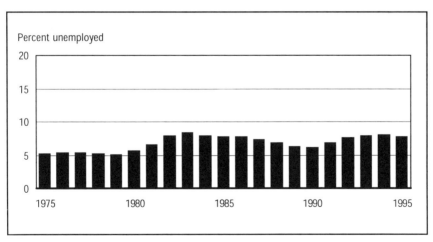

Source: OECD Labour Force Statistics.

Figure 2.1c.   The unemployment rate across OECD countries ranges from 3
to 23 percent

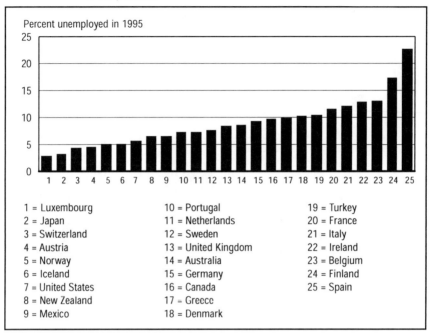

Percent unemployed in 1995

1 = Luxembourg	10 = Portugal	19 = Turkey
2 = Japan	11 = Netherlands	20 = France
3 = Switzerland	12 = Sweden	21 = Italy
4 = Austria	13 = United Kingdom	22 = Ireland
5 = Norway	14 = Australia	23 = Belgium
6 = Iceland	15 = Germany	24 = Finland
7 = United States	16 = Canada	25 = Spain
8 = New Zealand	17 = Greece	
9 = Mexico	18 = Denmark	

Source: OECD Labour Force Statistics.

Differences in unemployment rates over time are much less significant than
those across OECD countries. In 1995, **national unemployment rates ranged
from less than 3 percent (Japan) to over 23 percent (Spain)** (Figure 2.1c).
Thus, the relevance of (un-)employment issues can not be understood by looking
only at average figures for the OECD area as a whole. The originality of OECD
statistics and analyses does not primarily stem from the insights gained from
time series but rather from the comparison of differences and similarities among
OECD countries. **What is true for differences among OECD countries is even
more true for territorial disparities within countries.**

Conventional labour market analyses, however, tend to neglect this important
analytical dimension. While great efforts are undertaken to generate statistical
details about the sectoral mix by activity, or about employment by age, sex and
skill, no territorial breakdown by sub-national units is provided. This weakens
analytical capacities, since even in a globalizing economy, the relevant labour
market for most people and firms remains regional or even local in scope.

Although the *OECD Jobs Study* mentions that the burden of unemployment
is unevenly spread across the labour force, the analytical focus and the empirical
evidence provided concentrate on sectoral rather than territorial differences. The
sole references to territorial disparities are the following:

*Within countries, differences in the regional incidence of
unemployment have typically been higher and much more persistent
in Europe than in the United States. The regional distribution of
unemployment is particularly uneven in Finland, Germany (since
unification), Italy, Portugal and Spain. (OECD 1994b, p. 11)*

*Some countries also face the problem of serious regional differences
in unemployment. (OECD 1995a, p. 7)*

Of course, these results are strongly influenced by the **choice of the territorial
grid** at which the analysis is performed. Since for North America, "regional"
unemployment rates are calculated on the basis of US states and Canadian
provinces, disparities appear much lower than in Europe where less aggregated
territorial cuts are used to measure regional unemployment. If smaller territorial
units are used, disparities in unemployment, in fact, appear bigger in North
America than in most European countries.

Ideally, for territorial employment analysis the unit of observation should
reflect regional labour market areas. Thus, a comparison of unemployment rates
for more comparable regional units (see OECD, 1994a) leads to a rather different
conclusion:

*Not only are there large differences among national unemployment
rates, but also within countries territorial disparities are significant.
All OECD countries, including those with comparatively low national
rates, are confronted with substantial differences in unemployment
among regions. In most OECD countries regional unemployment rates
differ — on average — by more than 30 percent, in some countries
even more than 60 percent, from the national average.*

The territorial scheme

The previous section has shown that territory matters and that the choice of
appropriate territorial units for economic analysis and policy is crucial for their
success. On the other hand, detailed sub-national data sets as such, containing
information on thousands of places, are not very useful either. In order to
understand territorial diversity and dynamics and to draw policy relevant lessons,
it is necessary to be able to create meaningful classifications and typologies of
areas that allow analyses of similarities and differences among the various
territorial units. One important analytical and policy relevant dimension for
structuring territory is obviously the rural-urban gradient, describing different
settlement patterns.

In order to create a basis for quantitative territorial analyses the OECD
(OECD, 1994a) has established **a territorial scheme for sub-national data
collection in a multi-national context** which:

1. covers the **entire territory** of OECD countries;
2. distinguishes **two levels** of geographical detail (about 2,000 regions and 50,000 local communities); and
3. applies **practical definitions** for area classification and typology based on simple and intuitive criteria (Figure 2.2).

Figure 2.2.   Territorial scheme for OECD analysis

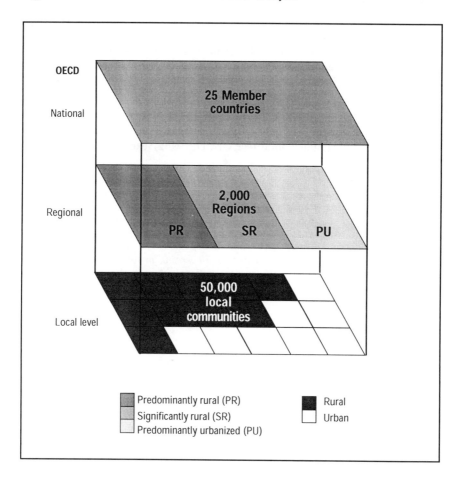

Only if information is available for the entire territory can meaningful comparisons be organized. Since territorial statistics involve huge amounts of data they should be structured as neutral and polyvalent as possible in order to enable not just rural but also urban, regional and local analyses.

The distinction of different hierarchical levels for territorial analysis is crucial in understanding the conceptual approach of the OECD work on rural indicators:

1. at the local level, the territorial grid consists of basic administrative or statistical units that can be classified as being either rural or urban; and
2. at the regional level, larger administrative or functional areas like provinces, commuting zones, etc. can be characterized as being more or less rural.

In **a first step, at the local level** OECD identifies rural areas as communities with a **population density** below 150 inhabitants/km^2. According to this definition, about one-third of the OECD population (35 percent) lives in rural communities that cover over 90 percent of the OECD territory. National shares of population living in rural communities range from less than 10 percent in the Netherlands and Belgium, to over 50 percent in parts of Scandinavia and in Turkey (see Gröhn, Chapter 5 in this volume, Figure 5.1). This does not mean that rural development issues are less important in some countries than in others. However, rural problems and perspectives, and hence rural policy issues and approaches will often be different.

In **a second step, at the regional level**, the OECD scheme groups territorial units according to their degree of rurality, measured by the **share of rural population** in the regional total. This is appropriate not only for reasons of data availability, but also because the development options and opportunities for local rural communities, to a large degree, depend on their relationship with urban centres, in particular those within their own region. Thus, in addition to and in combination with the local level, the regional level is of great importance for assessing rural development problems and perspectives. This is particularly true for employment issues.

To facilitate analyses, the 2,000 OECD regions can than be grouped into **three types of region** depending on the share of population living in rural communities: **Predominantly Rural** regions: over 50 percent; **Significantly Rural** regions: 15 to 50 percent; **Predominantly Urbanized** regions: below 15 percent. Thus each of the three types of region contains some rural and some urban communities although to a different degree. In total, about a quarter (28 percent) of the OECD population dwell in predominantly rural, often remote regions with a majority of people in sparsely populated, rural communities. At the other extreme, about 40 percent of the OECD population is concentrated on less than 3 percent of the territory in predominantly urbanized regions. The remaining third of the population (32 percent) lives in the intermediate category of significantly rural regions (Figure 2.3).

Figure 2.3.   Distribution of population in OECD member countries by type of region

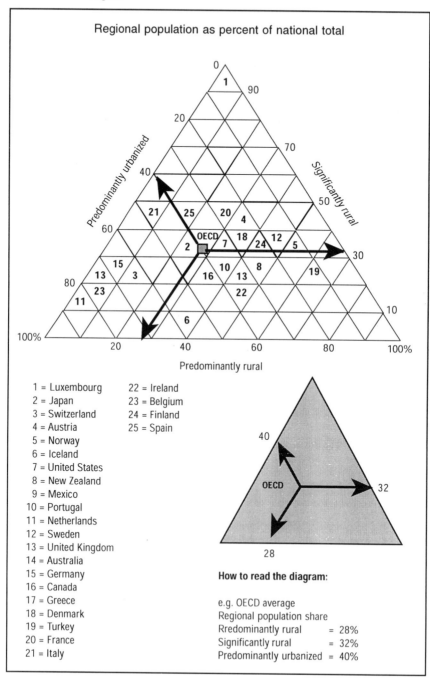

Regional population as percent of national total

1 = Luxembourg
2 = Japan
3 = Switzerland
4 = Austria
5 = Norway
6 = Iceland
7 = United States
8 = New Zealand
9 = Mexico
10 = Portugal
11 = Netherlands
12 = Sweden
13 = United Kingdom
14 = Australia
15 = Germany
16 = Canada
17 = Greece
18 = Denmark
19 = Turkey
20 = France
21 = Italy

22 = Ireland
23 = Belgium
24 = Finland
25 = Spain

How to read the diagram:

e.g. OECD average
Regional population share
Rredominantly rural   = 28%
Significantly rural   = 32%
Predominantly urbanized = 40%

The spatial organization of OECD countries is characterised by a **great diversity of territorial patterns**. Whereas for some countries — for example most Scandinavian countries — the population shares are descending from predominantly rural (PR) to significantly rural (SR) to predominantly urbanized regions (PU), while shares are ascending in others — such as Belgium, the United Kingdom, or Germany. Other countries are characterized by a dual structure with large proportions of the population at both extremes, predominantly rural and predominantly urbanized (e.g. Ireland, Greece, Portugal), while in France, Spain and Italy the largest share falls in the intermediate category of significantly rural regions (OECD, 1994a, pp. 89–92, Figure A.1).

Considering these different patterns, the following tables and graphs are not arranged by alphabetical order but in **clusters representing different national settlement patterns**. This is an attempt to better enable cross-country comparisons of rural issues. In addition European and non-European OECD countries are placed in separate clusters.

Unemployment and labour force

International comparison of territorial differences in the degree to which rural and urban labour markets are affected by unemployment must start from the fact that already national unemployment rates differ largely among countries. As noted earlier, national rates often differ by more than 10 percentage points.

In those OECD countries with the highest share of rural population, **the predominantly rural and often very remote regions tend to be more affected** by unemployment problems than the more urbanized regions (Figure 2.4a). Here, more than 50 percent of the country's unemployed labour force is searching for work in predominantly rural regions. Only in the most urbanized countries do the few predominantly rural regions have unemployment rates below the national average.

In total about one-third of all unemployed persons in the OECD area live in predominantly rural regions. Although unemployment is not specifically a rural problem, (inter-)national policies aiming at a reduction in unemployment could probably be more successful if they were based on a better understanding of the specific characteristics and dynamics of rural labour markets.

Unemployment rates are problematic indicators for assessing rural labour market conditions. They relate the number of persons unemployed to those participating in the labour force. Thus, rates differ not only due to differences in unemployment but also in labour force participation. In most OECD countries, **rural participation rates are lower than urban rates** (Figure 2.4b). Again, the most urbanized countries show some exceptions.

Figure 2.4a. Rural unemployment rates are generally above the national rate

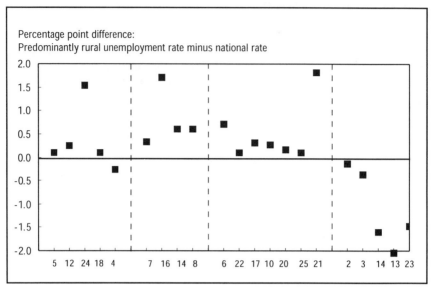

Source: OECD Rural Data Surveys.

Figure 2.4b. Rural labour force participation rates are generally below the national rate

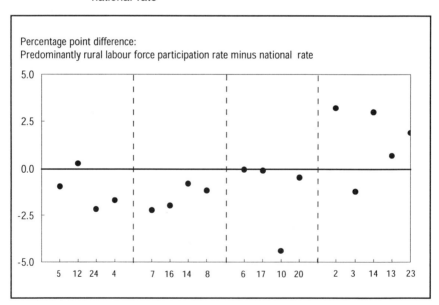

Source: OECD Rural Data Surveys.

Figure 2.4c.   Rural female labour force participation rates are below the national rate

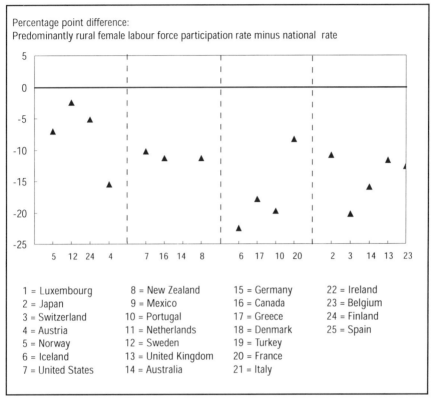

Percentage point difference:
Predominantly rural female labour force participation rate minus national rate

1 = Luxembourg
2 = Japan
3 = Switzerland
4 = Austria
5 = Norway
6 = Iceland
7 = United States

8 = New Zealand
9 = Mexico
10 = Portugal
11 = Netherlands
12 = Sweden
13 = United Kingdom
14 = Australia

15 = Germany
16 = Canada
17 = Greece
18 = Denmark
19 = Turkey
20 = France
21 = Italy

22 = Ireland
23 = Belgium
24 = Finland
25 = Spain

Source: OECD Rural Data Surveys.

In all countries, rural women are underrepresented in the labour force (Figure 2.4c). However, the gap between male and female participation rates is less pronounced in some of the more rural countries. For example, in Sweden or Canada, two out of three women of working age are actually employed or searching for a job. In Germany and Belgium, this is true for less than half the rural women.

Over the next decade rural regions in the OECD area will be confronted with an increase in working age populations. However, **demographic labour market pressures** will differ considerably. At the national level, pressure indicators are particularly high in North America and in some of the countries characterized by a dual rural/urban pattern like Australia, New Zealand, Iceland, Ireland and Greece (Table 2.1). In these countries every older person leaving the working age population will be replaced by almost two newcomers. For Germany, Italy and Luxembourg demographic labour market pressures appear to be rather low.

Table 2.1.   Demographic labour market pressure indicator by type of region, 1990

	National average	Predominantly rural	Significantly rural	Predominantly urban
	Population 5 to 14 years / population 55 to 64 years			
Turkey	3.70	..	..	..
Norway	1.36	..	..	..
Sweden	1.17	1.17	1.16	1.20
Finland	1.29	1.27	1.27	1.36
Denmark	1.17	..	..	..
Austria	1.17	1.25	1.16	1.00
Mexico	..	..	..	..
United States	1.67	1.69	1.73	1.58
Canada	1.58	1.76	1.70	1.38
Australia	1.76	1.84	1.75	1.73
New Zealand	1.82	1.87	1.64	1.89
Iceland	2.03	..	..	..
Ireland	2.41	2.43	2.30	2.43
Greece	1.52	1.50	1.51	1.55
Portugal	1.28	1.07	1.45	1.39
Czech Republic	1.45	1.54	1.48	1.34
France	1.28	1.16	1.35	1.34
Spain	1.27	1.11	1.35	1.26
Italy	0.97	..	..	..
Japan	1.11	1.02	1.12	1.15
Switzerland	1.10	1.36	1.27	0.98
Germany	0.93	1.12	1.00	0.88
United Kingdom	1.22	1.15	1.27	1.21
Luxembourg	0.98	...	0.98	...
Belgium	1.05	1.18	1.07	1.05
Netherlands	1.28	...	1.39	1.26

Source: OECD rural data surveys.
...   *not applicable*
..   *not available*
Note: The "demographic labour market pressure indicator" is an indicator of the change in the working age population between 1991 to 2000 (assuming no migration) and is the ratio of the population 5 to 14 years of age divided by the population 55 to 64 years of age.

Sub-national territorial patterns show interesting differences. For the least rural European countries, demographic pressures are higher in rural than in urban regions. This is also the case for the United States and Canada, but not for Japan, where pressure is greater in urbanized regions. In European countries with large shares of rural populations such as Sweden, Finland and Greece pressure indicators are highest in predominantly urbanized regions. Also in France, Spain and Portugal pressure is comparatively low in predominantly rural regions.

These results clearly demonstrate that it is impossible to assess **the importance of rural (employment) issues** for national policies just by looking at the overall degree of rurality of an OECD country. On the contrary, it is in some of the most urbanized countries where rural labour market pressure appears to be highest and vice versa.

Sectoral employment structures

For a long time, agriculture was considered the most important economic activity in rural areas. For most rural labour markets in the OECD area this is no longer true. **Agriculture is no longer the backbone of rural economies**. Today, the vast majority of rural employment opportunities is in non-agricultural activities.

The share of agriculture in national employment ranges from over 20 percent in Turkey, Greece and Mexico to less than 5 percent in Belgium, Luxembourg, the United Kingdom, United States, Switzerland, and Sweden (Figure 2.5). Of course, in all countries the share is higher in rural regions than elsewhere. But for most OECD countries, **even in the predominantly rural regions only one out of five jobs is in the agricultural sector**. Only in the predominantly rural regions of Iceland and Greece more than a third of the work force is still engaged in agriculture, forestry or fisheries. In Ireland, Spain and Portugal this is true for only about a quarter.

Not only is the part of agriculture in the total number of rural jobs smaller than often imagined, also **their number is shrinking**. During the 1980s in most countries, agricultural employment in predominantly rural areas declined by more than 10 percent, sometimes even more than 25 percent.

In addition to farm employment there are **many other activities up-stream and down-stream** that depend on primary agricultural production. In the end, however, this is true for most economic activities. What is even more important from a territorial development perspective, in many countries such activities — like farm machinery manufacturing, chemical industries or food processing — are not necessarily located in rural regions.

Even in the predominantly rural regions, employment shares of the **industrial sector** — including mining and construction — are higher than those for agriculture. In many OECD countries the shares of industrial employment are even higher for rural than for urban regions. They range from 20 to 35 percent. In Germany and Austria they are even higher. Compared with national averages, the predominantly rural regions in Spain, Portugal and Greece have relatively low shares of industrial employment. With 20 and 30 percent, however, they are still in the same range as those for the predominantly rural regions in Australia, New Zealand, Canada and the United States.

Figure 2.5.   Agriculture is not the major sector in predominantly rural regions

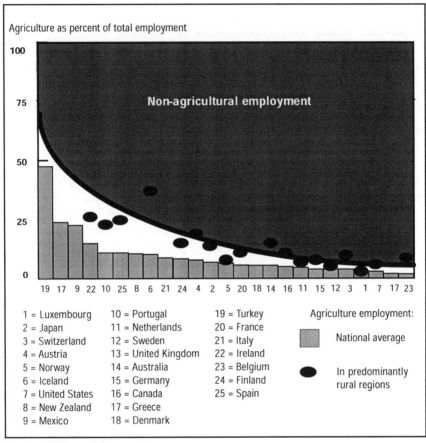

Source: *OECD rural data surveys.*
Note: *"Agriculture" includes agriculture, forestry and fishing (ISIC 1).*

In the predominantly rural regions, at least **every second job is in the service sector**. Only in Iceland, Greece and Portugal, countries characterized by a dual pattern of territorial organization, as well as in Austria and Germany are service sector shares in rural regions somewhat below 50 percent.

In all OECD countries, employment growth in the 1980s in the predominantly rural regions was primarily, if not exclusively, due **to substantial net increases in service sector employment**. Often increases were particularly high in public sector employment. In Norway and Sweden every third job in predominantly rural areas is in community, social and personal services provided mainly by the public sector. Given the need to reduce budget deficits in many OECD countries, such a strong dependency on public sector employment may in the future be an even greater handicap for rural areas than their dependency on agriculture.

Employment change

In the public debate there is generally great pessimism concerning the possibilities of creating new employment opportunities in rural areas. This is not justified. During the 1980s, in almost all OECD countries, **rural regions experienced a net increase in employment**. Rural employment increased despite the fact that all rural areas had to cope with often substantial employment reductions in agriculture, forestry and fisheries.

On average, non-agricultural employment growth, although positive, was not sufficient to maintain the share of the predominantly rural regions in total national employment. However, rural shares did not drop dramatically. In absolute terms only the predominantly rural regions in Finland and New Zealand experienced a net loss in the total number of jobs. Apart from Finland (- 6.7 percentage points), the divergence of rural to national growth rates was important also in the United States (- 5.0) and in particular in Japan (- 8.8). At the other extreme, the predominantly rural regions of former West Germany experienced growth rates much higher (+ 7.7 percentage points) than the national average.

Comparisons of employment change just among the three types of region do not reveal, however, the **territorial diversity in development dynamics**. The actual territorial patterns of development are much more complex and cannot be properly appreciated just by looking at average figures. Canada and Austria provide clear but not untypical examples. Cunningham and Bollman (Chapter 4 in this volume, Figure 4.16) have plotted each Canadian region according to its degree of rurality and according to its employment growth. For the Austrian case, see Schindegger and Krajasits (Chapter 11 in this volume, Figure 11.6). These examples show that there are many rural regions that have been much more successful in employment creation than the national economy as a whole. In fact, also in other countries many (dynamic) rural regions, although not the majority, perform better than many of the more urbanized (but lagging) regions. There is no straight forward correlation between the degree of rurality and the dynamics of employment change.

The **differences in employment creation dynamics among rural regions** are impressive. In 1991 in Canada, 19 percent of the total national employment was located in lagging predominantly rural regions (Figure 2.6 and Table 2.2). During the 1980s, employment in these regions dropped by 10 percent. At the same time, in the dynamic predominantly rural regions the number of jobs increased by 13 percent. These regions represent 11 percent of the national employment and cover more than a third of the national territory.

These results indicate that **rurality in itself is not an insurmountable obstacle for job creation**. Rurality is not synonymous with decline, as much as urbanity and agglomeration are not automatic guarantees for prosperous development. Not all rural regions are problem areas in need of support. On the contrary, some rural regions belong to the most innovative and dynamic parts of the OECD area.

Figure 2.6.   Employment change in dynamic and lagging labour markets, Canada, 1981 to 1991

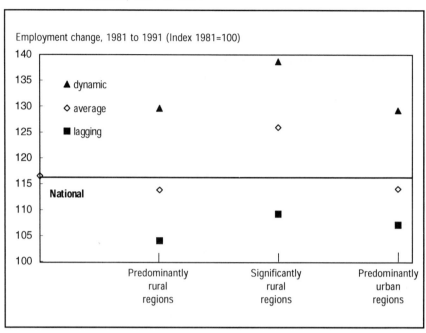

Table 2.2.   Employment change in dynamic and lagging labour markets, Canada

	Number of regions	Employment 1991 (%)	Employment change, 1981–91	
			Total 1981=100	Difference to national
National	266	100	116.5	0.0
Predominantly rural regions	209	30	114.1	-2.4
Dynamic	68	11	129.3	12.8
Lagging	141	19	107.0	-9.5
Significantly rural regions	38	23	126.0	9.5
Dynamic	21	14	138.6	22.1
Lagging	17	8	109.2	-7.3
Predominantly urban regions	19	47	113.9	-2.6
Dynamic	12	21	129.6	13.1
Lagging	7	26	104.0	-12.5

Source: *OECD Rural Data Surveys.*

Implications for rural analysis and policy

Obviously, this has implications both for rural analysis as well as for rural and other policies. It means that, in territorial analyses, in addition to the **settlement dimension** (rural vs. urban) regions should also be distinguished according to a **development dimension** (dynamic vs. lagging). Instead of focusing only on the differences between rural and urban, thus implicitly making urban the model for rural, one should also aim at better understanding the differences in development performance between dynamic and lagging rural regions. For the latter, dynamic rural regions probably provide a more realistic policy reference than do urbanized regions.

From this perspective it also becomes evident that **rural policies make sense not just from a point of view of equity and social cohesion,** but also in terms of economic efficiency and innovation by trying to take advantage of territorial development potentials not yet properly utilized. If the underlying characteristics and forces are better understood, rural development initiatives can be launched more systematically and with greater success.

It could be expected that the differences in development performance are due to the fact that the sectoral mix of economic activities in dynamic regions differs from that of the lagging regions. If this would be the case, regions with above national employment growth were successful because of higher employment shares in fast growing economic activities. This would provide a convincing argument for sectoral policies to speed up adjustment across sectors.

However, an initial empirical analysis does not support such conclusions. The importance of differences in the sectoral mix is high when disparities in rural to urban growth are to be explained. Over-representation of shrinking sectors like agriculture, under-representation of expanding sectors like services explain a great deal of these rural–urban differences. When it comes, however, to the disparities among rural regions — lagging versus dynamic — differences in sectoral mix are apparently much less important. In almost all OECD countries, the dynamic rural regions are equally faced with a handicap stemming from an unfavourable sectoral mix. However, this appears not to prevent them from mobilizing other development forces.

To a large extent, territorial development dynamics probably depend on **specific regional and local factors, structures and tendencies** which are often difficult to measure, such as entrepreneurial traditions, work ethics, public and private networks, regional identity and participation or the attractiveness of the cultural and natural environment.

Thus, instead of digging further into more sectoral detail in employment statistics, the Steering Group on Rural Indicators will aim at **extending the scope of the territorial indicators work**. Additional, territorially disaggregated information on productivity and investment, on social indicators concerning levels and distribution of income, education and housing quality, as well as indicators on environmental conditions and rural amenities will be collected. This should help to provide further information for a more accurate assessment of territorial development potential and performance.

Conclusion

In the OECD area, not only are there large differences among national rates of unemployment and job creation, but also within countries, territorial disparities are significant. In most countries, unemployment rates are higher in rural than in urban regions. Conversely, labour force participation rates are lower in rural than in urban regions. In all countries, rural women are under-represented in the labour force. Rural areas of many OECD countries will be confronted with substantial increases in their working-age population. This will generate uneven territorial pressures for labour market adjustments that will require either creating additional jobs, coping with higher unemployment or facilitating migration flows.

The vast majority of rural employment opportunities are in non-agricultural sectors. Agricultural employment is declining not only in relative but also in absolute terms. During the 1980s, rural economies managed to compensate for these losses in shrinking sectors, although in general at a pace below national growth. However, rural employment shares did not drop dramatically.

Some rural regions even belong to the most dynamic areas within OECD countries. They were more successful in generating new employment opportunities than were national economies as a whole. The dynamism of these regions shows that rurality in itself is not an obstacle to job creation. For lagging rural regions, dynamic rural regions probably provide a more realistic development model than do urbanized regions.

The success of the dynamic rural regions is not due to favourable sectoral mixes. Like most other rural regions, they tend to have shares in declining industries that are higher than the national average. The positive performance in creating rural employment results from specific territorial dynamics that are not yet properly understood, but probably include aspects such as regional identity and entrepreneurial climate, public and private networks, or the attractiveness of the cultural and natural environment.

Appendix 1. Notes concerning basic definitions and concepts

A **rural area** is a local community with a population density below 150 inhabitants/km² (500 inhabitants/km² in the case of Japan). **The typology of regions** is based on their degree of rurality according to the share of regional population living in rural communities as defined above: "Predominantly Rural" (PR) more than 50 percent; "Significantly Rural" (SR) between 15 and 50 percent; "Predominantly Urbanized" (PU) below 15 percent.

German employment data refer to the old *Laender* of the former West Germany without Berlin. The OECD Rural Data Surveys data generally refer to 1970, 1980 and 1990. For Australia, Austria, Canada, the Czech Republic, Greece, Ireland, Norway, New Zealand, Spain and the United Kingdom data refer to 1971, 1981 and 1991. For France data refer to 1982. Employment statistics are classified by major group of economic activity following the International Standard Industrial Classification (ISIC) adopted in 1968 by the United Nations Organization (Rev.2, Add.1, 1971).

Major group of economic activity:

Agriculture, hunting, forestry and fishing	ISIC 1
Mining and quarrying	ISIC 2
Manufacturing	ISIC 3
Electricity, gas and water	ISIC 5
Construction	ISIC 4
Wholesale and retail, restaurants and hotels	ISIC 6
Transport, storage and communication	ISIC 7
Finance, insurance, real estate and business services	ISIC 8
Community, social and personal services	ISIC 9
Activities not adequately defined	ISIC 10

In this report economic activities are aggregated to three sectors as follows:

Agriculture	(ISIC 1)
Industry	(ISIC 2 to 5)
Services	(ISIC 6 to 10)

References

OECD. (1993) *What Future for Our Countryside? A Rural Development Policy.* Paris: OECD.

OECD. (1994a) *Creating Rural Indicators for Shaping Territorial Policy.* Paris: OECD.

OECD. (1994b) *The OECD Jobs Study: Facts, Analysis, Strategies.* Paris: OECD.

OECD. (1995a) *The OECD Jobs Study: Implementing the Strategy.* Paris: OECD.

OECD. (1995b) *Creating Employment for Rural Development — New Policy Approaches.* Paris: OECD.

OECD. (1996a) *The OECD Jobs Strategy — Pushing Ahead with the Strategy.* Paris: OECD.

OECD. (1996b) *Better Policies for Rural Development.* Paris: OECD.

OECD. (1996c) *Territorial Indicators of Employment — Focusing on Rural Development.* Paris: OECD.

Chapter three:

Employment and Population Dynamics in OECD Countries: An Intraregional Approach

Eleonore Irmen
Federal Institute for Regional Research and Spatial Planning
Bonn, Germany

Abstract

Prospects for rural community development differ depending upon the degree of rurality of the region where the community is located. Rural employment has been declining in rural communities within rural regions. Within rural regions, urban communities as a whole are barely holding their own. In more urbanized regions, deconcentration appears underway with growth in rural areas peripheral to large urban centres together with decline in urban centres. The distribution of employment by sector is not a major factor in explaining employment change. Rural policy strategies should take into account the regional structures in which the rural community is located.

Introduction

Predominantly rural regions have population growth rates higher than urban regions in some countries (e.g. Belgium, Germany (the former Federal Republic), Great Britain) (OECD, 1994). Other countries (e.g. Canada, United States, France) show a continuing trend to urbanization as their predominantly rural regions are growing slower. However, within each type of region, development patterns differ between their rural and urban communities. The purpose of this chapter is to illustrate the different pattern(s) of intraregional change across different types of regions.

Background

The OECD territorial grid for rural analysis (OECD, 1994) is based on two levels: the regional and the local level. Therefore it enables a two-tier approach to rural analysis:

1. a regional level for regions with different degrees of rurality (predominantly rural, significantly rural and predominantly urban regions); and

2. a local level for sub-regional units of two types: urban and rural communities.

This study will provide additional insight into the intraregional employment structures, the structures within regions. Employment change between and within different types of regions will be used to characterize both the macro-spatial structural change and the micro-spatial structural change.

On one hand we want to understand more about the role of urban communities in the development process of predominantly rural regions. Is employment growth in rural regions based on employment growth in their urban communities? Seen from the location point of view, urban communities provide the opportunity for local agglomeration effects to develop and for other forms of synergy. They are also the connection points for the rural economy and the rural population to the national and international economy through transportation and communication systems, financial and governmental institutions and trading firms (OECD, 1995).

On the other hand, the future development of many urbanized regions may depend upon their internal spatial organization and on the relations their urban centres have to the surrounding rural areas. Is there a spatial labour division between urban and rural parts? Are urban or rural communities the "winners" of spatial structural change? Over-agglomerated regional centres may get strangled by increasing congestion and pollution, whereas urban communities with easy access to rural amenities may have much better development prospects.

The economic characteristics of rural regions in most member countries are a growing service sector and a relatively high share of industrial employment (OECD, 1994). Only in some regions is agriculture of significant importance as an economic base. In many countries the differences in the intraregional rural/ urban development pattern can be seen as a result of sectoral specialization. In these countries, the differences in regional employment development would reflect the impacts of the macro-spatial division of labour.

Analytical questions

The analysis will compare employment and population change in selected OECD countries to find the common development paths and to understand the differences among the development processes. Employment and population change serve as indicators — among others — which mirror the general objectives for regional development: growing population and more jobs. We wish to determine:

1. What role do towns and cities (urban communities) play in rural labour markets and in rural development?

2. Are there specific patterns of rural/urban differences in employment and population change?

3. What is the economic base of urban/rural structures? Are there significant differences in the economic base between urban and rural?

To get a more complex picture of the quality of development described below, more indicators would have to be taken into account. Employment growth in rural areas does not give information about the quality of the jobs or their importance for the adjustment of the regional economy. Employment growth also does not necessarily lead to labour market relief in the sense of a decrease of unemployment. Thus, the following analysis will give aspects of the spatial structural change and the gain or loss in importance of urban and rural areas during the 1980s. To evaluate future prospects, more rural analysis and the results of the other OECD case studies have to be taken into account.

Methodology

Seven OECD member countries are included in this study: Austria, Finland, Germany (only the former Federal Republic), Norway, Switzerland, United Kingdom and the United States.

Questions 1 and 2 above will be addressed by measuring the change in the national importance of each community group. To measure the change in national importance, we calculate the change in the national share of population and employment held by rural and urban communities within each type of region. This will prevent distortions due to factors that differ across countries such as differences in demographic profiles. A positive change represents a gain in national importance — note that both rural and urban communities within a given region will gain in importance if the region itself is gaining in national importance.

Results and messages

Decrease in rural employment is correlated with the country's degree of rurality

The countries with a **higher degree of rurality** show **employment losses** in their rural communities. In these countries, the share of employment between 1980 and 1990 decreases in rural communities and increases in urban communities (Figures 3.1a to 3.1d). In the United States and the Scandinavian countries (especially Finland), rural communities loose importance in employment and population and urban communities gain importance. In Norway, rural communities are not confronted with a decrease in employment but in population, which probably can be explained by a special economic situation during the 1980s (an expanding oil sector). Austria seems to face a different situation: rural communities loose importance in employment and gain in population, which obviously implies that commuting is an important structural explanation. People more and more prefer living in rural communities to enjoy their amenities — the missing rural jobs were compensated by commuting into the growing cities.

In countries with a **lower degree of rurality** (Germany, United Kingdom, Switzerland), rural communities **profit from a spatial structural change**. In Germany, the United Kingdom and Switzerland (for Switzerland only population data), rural communities gain importance in employment and population and urban areas loose importance in terms of population and employment. This result can be interpreted as a relative spatial deconcentration of employment and population. The picture for Germany however looks different if the German New Länder are integrated into the analysis. In these Länder, the conditions of restructuring and reorientation of the economy result in the urban communities being the most dynamic locations in terms of employment and population.

These basic development trends show that rural community employment and population development appear to be closely connected to the degree of the rurality of a country — countries with a higher degree of rurality are confronted with rural employment and population losses. This finding gives some indication that these countries have relatively larger development problems in their rural communities compared with other countries.

Change in the importance of RURAL communities

Figure 3.1a.   Employment

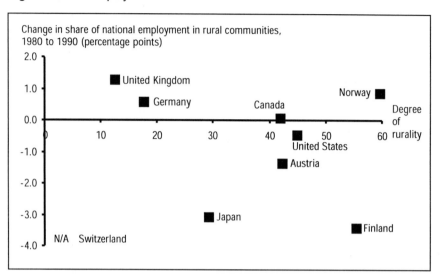

Figure 3.1b.   Population

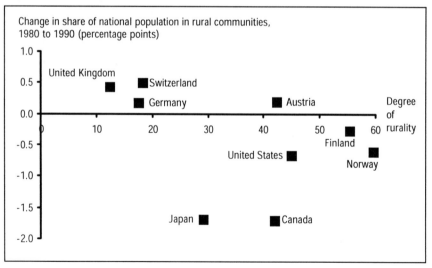

Change in the importance of URBAN communities

Figure 3.1c.   Employment

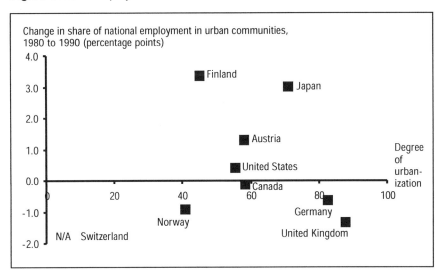

Figure 3.1d.   Population

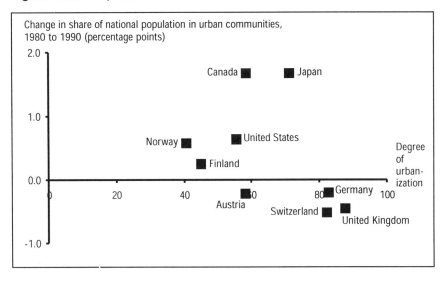

Urban communities play an important role in rural development

The picture becomes more detailed if one looks at rural and urban community change within each of the different OECD types of region: predominantly urban, significantly rural and predominantly rural.

The patterns of urban and rural community change depend upon the degree of rurality of the country: in the **more rural countries**, Austria, Finland, Norway and the United States especially, **rural communities within predominantly rural regions are the losers in spatial development** (Figures 3.2a and 3.2b). These rural communities lose population and employment, whereas the rural communities in the other types of regions (predominantly urban and significantly rural) gain in national importance. They seem to profit from spillover effects and suburbanization processes in urban development. In Norway, the difference between negative population and positive employment change in rural communities within rural regions again presumably depends upon the special regional location of oil extraction employment.

The urban communities within rural regions play different roles in the different countries. In Finland, Norway and the United States the **urban communities of rural regions hardly keep or even slightly lose** their importance in population and employment (Figures 3.2c and 3.2d). Winners are the urban centres of the urban regions and their rural communities (Finland, United States) or the urban centres of significantly rural areas (Norway). Austria again faces a special situation: the urban parts in predominantly and significantly rural regions gain employment, but hardly any population, which again points to strong changes in intraregional commuting flows.

The urban centres in rural regions of these countries obviously face a problematic situation. They can hardly keep up with the national rate of population or employment growth. Policy strategies should concentrate on supporting and strengthening their infrastructure, agglomeration and synergy effects to make them able to attract new employment possibilities. Only they seem to be able to give impetus to the development prospects of the rural region.

Deconcentration and suburbanization in countries with a lower degree of rurality

In the selected **countries with a lower degree of rurality** (Germany (only the Federal Republic), United Kingdom, Switzerland), **deconcentration processes of employment and population change** are characteristic of the spatial structural change — the large urban centres of urban regions experience the highest loss in importance concerning employment and population distribution. The gain of importance varies: in the United Kingdom, the urban centres of significantly rural regions and their rural communities gain the most while the rural and urban communities of rural regions keep their shares. Concerning population change, Switzerland shows a similar pattern. In Germany the development lines are much

Change in the importance of RURAL communities

Figure 3.2a.   Employment

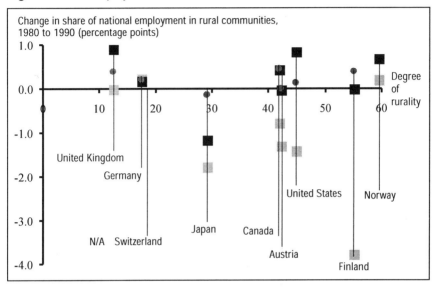

Figure 3.2b.   Population

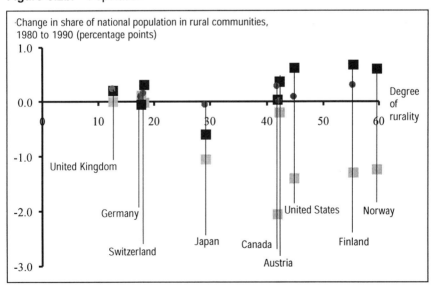

Change in the importance of URBAN communities

Figure 3.2c.   Employment

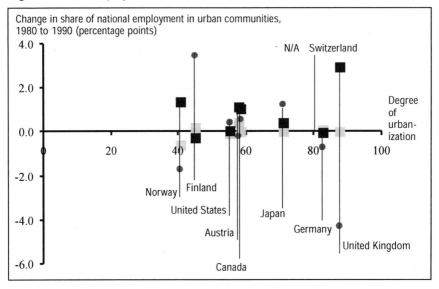

Figure 3.2d.   Population

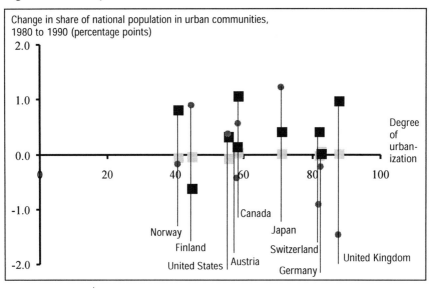

more balanced: urban centres in rural regions show a slight gain in importance but winners are all rural areas around the urban centres, which points to an intensive suburbanization process in the employment structure.

How can similarities among these countries be explained? One aspect is that Germany, the United Kingdom and Switzerland have a dense network of urban systems and a settlement structure with a more or less regular distribution of large and medium sized cities and city regions. They all have agglomeration and infrastructure advantages. As in the other countries included in this study, the large cities seem to suffer from over-agglomeration and constraints of traffic, pollution and high costs for living and working. Medium sized cities and their catchment areas seem to profit from this development. The few rural areas are more or less economically integrated into the urban networks.

The economic base of rural areas is more specialized than in urban areas

In all countries the urban/rural differences from the national sectoral structures are similar: rural areas in the three types of regions have a positive deviation in employment of the secondary and primary sectors — these sectors are over-represented — and a negative deviation in the tertiary sector (Figure 3.3). In the urban communities the secondary and primary sectors are under-represented and the tertiary sector dominates.

The strongest differences between urban and rural are to be found in the countries with a higher degree of rurality, Austria and Finland, but also in Switzerland. Their rural areas are much more intensive in primary sector employment than the other countries, as has already been illustrated by the OECD rural indicators report (OECD, 1994).

Smaller differences between urban and rural economic bases are to be found in Germany, the United Kingdom and the United States. These countries have a more balanced regional economic structure. Germany has a strong manufacturing base whereas the United States has a strong services based regional economic structure. Nevertheless their rural areas show similar tendencies of sectoral specialization.

Further and detailed information on the dynamics, the skill and qualification levels of the jobs in the different industrial sectors could give more insight concerning the quality of "modern" structures of service sector development. Jobs created in services during recent years often were low-skilled jobs so that growth in service sector employment did not always provide stability for regional development. It has also been mentioned that the industrial structure does not explain a region's economic performance. Often the reasons for being dynamic or lagging are to be found within the sectors due, for example, to the level of innovation of processes and products.

Figure 3.3.   Differences in share of employment by industrial sector
compared with the national share, 1990

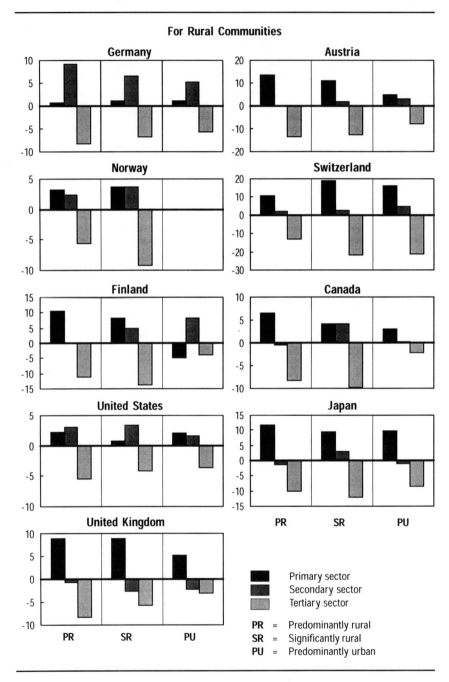

For Rural Communities

Figure 3.3. Differences in share of employment by industrial sector compared with the national share, 1990 (Concluded)

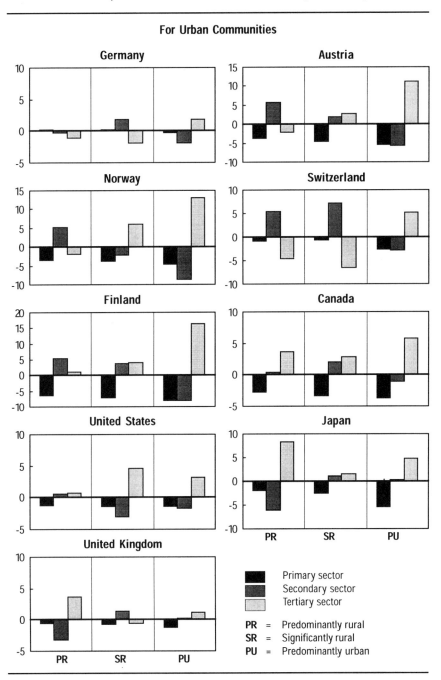

For Urban Communities

Summary and Conclusions

Apart from some difficulties in comparing nations on a subnational level, there are some systematic urban/rural patterns of change which can be derived from this intraregional analysis. The differences in the degree of rurality of the region **and** in the importance of medium and small sized urban areas are two important factors determining rural community population and employment change.

The United States represents a country with large rural regions where many have no urban areas with potential centres of gravity. Though the sectoral specialization between urban and rural is not very distinct, employment in rural regions seems to be more endangered. The Scandinavian countries have large rural regions, which seem to face different situations: on one hand a gain in importance with economic specialization (oil) in Norway and on the other hand, a general loss of importance in Finland. Economic specialization is no guarantee for regional stability.

These countries show the general urbanization processes of a gain in importance of large and medium sized city regions and their rural surroundings. The main tasks for rural policy are to find means to strengthen the rural regions and areas. Apart from activities supporting the labour market demand side (for example, education and training) and the labour supply side (for example, direct aids, indirect aids like access to technology transfer), from the location point of view, the small and medium sized cities must be made capable to create or attract new employment possibilities. This requires mainly good transport and communication accessibility.

The countries with a lower share of rural population (Great Britain, Germany (only the former Federal Republic)) show considerable similarity in their spatial settlement structure. Their rural areas profit from spillover effects and more or less take part in the national pace of development. Deconcentration of employment on a macro-spatial scale and suburbanization and dispersion on the micro-spatial level are characteristic of the urban/rural development pattern. It must be acknowledged that the general patterns of change hide some specific rural problematic situations. Besides supporting the special development potentials of the rural areas, rural policy in this situation is asked to consider much more the environmental aspects and the protection of natural resources.

Austria has a lot of similarities to both groups of countries — it has a decentralized settlement structure and, on the other hand, a high degree of rurality. The separation of population and employment change in rural areas seems to be a major characteriztic of rural development.

With the globalization and internationalization of economies, there will be winners and losers among communities and regions. This will not be determined solely by being rural or urban. It is a bundle of factors that determines development prospects. However, the probability of belonging to the losers is higher for those rural regions without any urban attractivity. Medium and small sized urban areas especially have the potential to combine agglomeration advantages and good infrastructure with the proximity to rural amenities. The development prospects of rural areas will be closely connected with urban areas and vice versa. Therefore, policy instruments facilitating communication and co-operation between rural and urban areas will become more important.

In general, differences in the situation and dynamics underlining rural communities should be addressed by policy strategies which are adapted to the particular regional structures in which the rural community is located.

References

OECD. (1994) *Creating Rural Indicators for Shaping Territorial Policy.* Paris: OECD.

OECD. (1995) *Government Measures for Rural Employment Creation.* Paris: OECD document for the Group of the Council on Rural Development.

Chapter four:

Structure and Trends of Rural Employment: Canada in the Context of OECD Countries

Ron Cunningham and Ray D. Bollman
Statistics Canada, Ottawa, Ontario, Canada

Abstract

In 1991, 33 percent of Canada's population lived in predominantly rural regions. Employment growth in rural regions averaged 1.3 percent per year over the 1980s, ranking fourth among OECD countries. In 1991, only 11 percent of the rural workforce in Canada worked in agriculture, forestry or fishing. Within rural regions, employment growth was highest in rural areas adjacent to metropolitan centres. Business services was the fastest growing sector in all types of regions, but rural regions received only a minor boost due to the relatively low share of their workforce in business services. On average, rural areas showed less growth — however, within rural areas, there were regions that showed more growth than urban regions. Rurality does not necessarily imply slow employment growth.

Introduction

The development of policy alternatives for stimulating rural employment requires benchmark information on the structure and trends of rural labour markets. Policy analysts need both:

1. an appropriate concept/conceptualization of the degrees of rurality; and
2. the collection and tabulation of relevant data within each degree of rurality class.

The objective of this paper is to use international comparative data to compare rural Canada with the rest of Canada and also to compare rural Canada with rural regions in other countries.

Background

Bollman, Fuller and Ehrensaft (1992) identified the following economic trends, structural changes, and employment trends of importance to rural Canada:

Fundamental economic trends

1. Due to advancing technology, capital is costing less relative to human time. Therefore, the substitution of capital for labour will increase (e.g. farms will continue to get bigger).
2. The real prices of resource commodities are decreasing.

As a result of the above trends, employment in resource-based industries will continue to decline, as will resource-dependent communities.

Major structural changes

3. Although Canada's rural population is increasing in absolute terms, its percentage of the total population has been declining. Previous to the 1931 Census, the rural population was in the majority. Since then it has been decreasing steadily, declining to just 23 percent in 1991 (based on the share of population in centres with a population less than 1,000)[1].
4. There has been a parallel and even more rapid decline in the farm population as a share of the rural population. The share slipped below 50 percent by the 1956 Census and was only 13 percent in 1991.

Trends in employment by industry

6. Agriculture's share of total employment is small relative to many other sectors, even in rural Canada.
7. The services sector is the biggest employer and is growing in both rural and urban Canada.

---

1. *This trend has not only been happening for a long time, but it is not unique to Canada. In 1893, G.B. Longstaff of the U.K. authored a paper entitled "Rural depopulation", in which he wrote, "The 'alarming depopulation of our rural districts,' has of late been the subject of many articles and even more speeches. Able journalists have discoursed on the causes, and ambitious politicians, anxious to catch the votes of an ignorant electorate, have vied with one another in suggesting remedies, but few persons seem to have had time or inclination to take a comprehensive view of the actual facts. It is the business of the statistician to clear the way by ascertaining and recording the precise state of the case, and so determine the geographical extension and numerical intensity of the phenomenon; when this has been done then, and then only, shall we be in a position to dogmatise as to causes and remedies." (reprinted in the* Journal of the Royal Statistical Society, *Vol. LVI (1993), p. 380).*

8.   Rural is sharing in this growth of services.

9.   The share for manufacturing is shrinking everywhere but not as fast in rural areas.

10.   "Rural-intensive" (resource-based) industries are maintaining their share of national employment in rural areas relative to urban areas.

11.   Rural areas' share is increasing relative to that of urban areas in some "urban-intensive" industries, such as manufacturing; finance, insurance and real estate; wholesale and retail trade; and government services.

What is rural?

International data previously compiled by the OECD had been published almost entirely as totals at the national level. In 1991, the OECD initiated its Rural Development Programme, of which the rural indicators project is an important part.

The OECD scheme begins with a distinction between two levels of geography: the **local community** and the **region**. A community is defined as a small basic administrative or statistical area, preferably as homogeneous as possible. According to the OECD design, a community is classified as **either** rural or urban. A region is defined as a larger administrative or functional area, providing "the wider context in which rural development takes place" (OECD, 1994, p. 20). A region can be described only as being **more or less rural**. The purpose of having the two levels was to accurately reflect the complexity of rural problems; "local and regional administrations perceive rural issues and implement rural policies . . . at the local community level," while national, "as well as supra-national administrations . . . deal with rural issues at the more aggregate regional level" (OECD, 1994, p. 21). All communities having a density of less than 150 persons/km^2 are considered as rural, the others as urban[2]. At the regional level, three possible types were defined: rural regions, intermediate regions, and agglomerated regions, the classification depending upon what proportion of the region's population lived in rural communities. A **rural** region has more than 50 percent of its population living in rural communities, **intermediate** between 15 and 50 percent, and **agglomerated** less than 15 percent. (This designation is identical to the OECD designation of "predominantly rural", "significantly rural" and "predominantly urban", respectively.)

---

2.   *Japan was the only exception on this point. Because Japan's farm structure, and resultant population distribution patterns in areas that are primarily agricultural, are so different from those of other OECD countries, the 150 persons per km^2 threshold produced "rural" areas very different from what was commonly perceived as rural. For this reason, a different threshold, 500 persons per km^2, was chosen for Japan.*

With this two-level hierarchy available, analysis can be done in three ways: at the community level (urban vs. rural); at the regional level (rural vs. intermediate vs. agglomerated); and at a combined level (six types of areas can then be compared: urban communities within rural regions, rural communities within intermediate regions, etc.)

For community-level statistics, Canada chose the census consolidated subdivision (CCS), which is a grouping of contiguous municipalities often having one large municipality totally or partially surrounding other municipalities, such as a township surrounding a town or villages. There were 2,628 CCSs in Canada as of the 1986 Census.

For the region, Canada chose the census division (CD), a subprovincial level of geography usually corresponding to a county or regional municipality. There were 266 CDs in Canada as of the 1986 Census. As mentioned above, the region is associated with the idea of a labour market area. An indication that the CD is an appropriate choice for the region is that, according to the 1991 Census, 82 percent of employed Canadians work in the same CD in which they live. Since this paper deals with employment data, most of the analysis will take place at the regional level.

In order to take account of the influence exerted on a region by the presence of a very large city, Canada made the following refinement to the OECD classification scheme: "If a region has a CCS whose population is over 300,000, it is classified as agglomerated, regardless of whether it meets the population thresholds established by the OECD." (Government of Canada, 1995)

The share of Canada's population in rural regions is near the median of OECD countries (Figure 4.1). It turned out that a few countries had no predominantly rural regions: Luxembourg, the Netherlands, and surprisingly, New Zealand. The latter can be explained by the fact that, though New Zealand has one of the lower population densities in the OECD, the mountainous, uninhabitable parts of the country are located in large regions which include a number of cities and towns along the coast; thus, even these most remote regions have the bulk of their population living in urban communities (i.e. communities with a population density over 150 persons per km^2).

Figure 4.1.   In 1991, 33 percent of Canada's population lived in rural regions

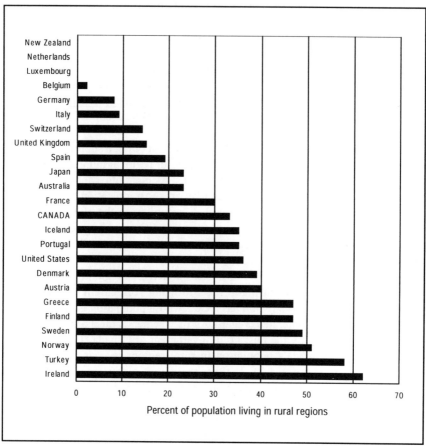

Source: OECD (1994).

How does rural Canada look compared to other OECD countries?

Canada had a strong rate of employment growth relative to most other OECD countries (Figure 4.2). For most countries, the rate for rural regions was slightly lower than the national rate, though this was reversed for two countries: Belgium (which actually had negative growth in intermediate regions and no growth in agglomerated) and Germany. Finland had a very polarised type of situation with the lowest (actually the only negative) rate of rural employment growth among all countries, but the highest rate for agglomerated.

Figure 4.2.   Canada's rural employment growth for 1981 to 1991 was 1.3 percent per year

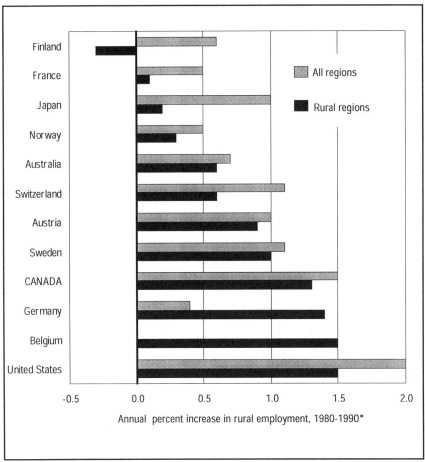

*   *Australia 1981–86; Austria 1981–91; Belgium 1980–89; Finland 1980–90; Switzerland 1975–85.*
Source: OECD (1994).

The share of the employed in rural regions who are working in a primary industry is much higher than the share at the national level for every country (Figure 4.3). The share of employment in the primary sector is decreasing in western countries generally, accompanied by a continuing increase in employment in service industries. The primary share in Canada is one of the lowest, while the services share is one of the highest, indicating Canada is well along the road in the transition to a services economy (Figure 4.4).

Figure 4.3.   In 1991, 11 percent of working rural residents in Canada were
employed in primary industry

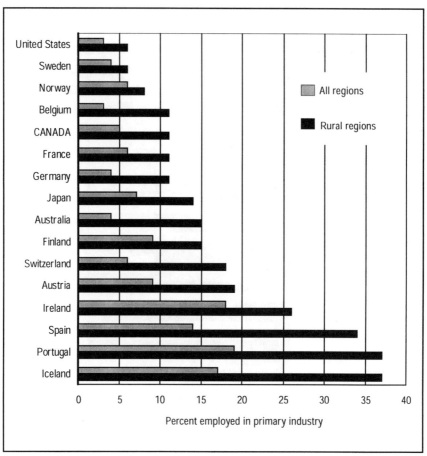

*   *Primary includes agriculture, forestry, and fishing (but excludes mining and oil extraction).*
Source: OECD (1994).

Figure 4.4. In 1991, 66 percent of working rural residents in Canada were employed in service industries

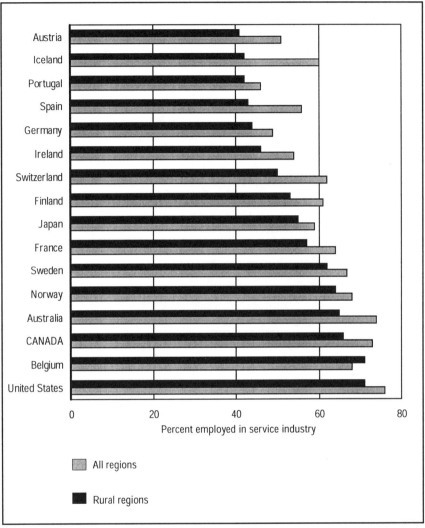

Source: OECD (1994).

Relatively high unemployment is often associated with rural areas. This is true for most OECD countries (Figure 4.5). Canada has one of the highest rates in the OECD, at both the national and rural levels. Thus, even though (or because) Canada is ahead of most other countries in its transition to a service economy, there is still a significant shortage of jobs accessible to rural residents.

Figure 4.5.   In Canada, 12 percent of the labour force in rural regions was
unemployed in 1991

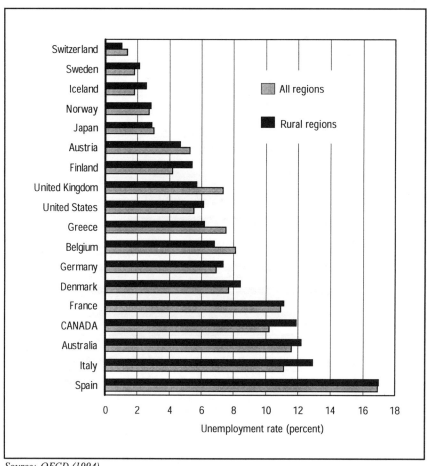

Source: OECD (1994).

Comparing Figure 4.5 with Figure 4.3, one can detect some relationship
between the unemployment rate and the share of employment in primary industry
(i.e. Canada is an exception). However, there is also an inverse relation between
employment growth and primary share (and Canada follows this trend), implying
that most of the new jobs in rural regions are not primary. This is in line with the
observations by Bollman, Fuller, and Ehrensaft (1992).

Table 4.1 provides a summary of how Canada compares to the other OECD
members for a number of population-related and employment-related indicators.
The next section will provide a more in-depth analysis of various employment-
related indicators for Canada.

Table 4.1.   How does rural Canada measure up?

Rural regions[1]	Canada	OECD median	OECD minimum		OECD maximum	
% share of population	33	35	0	(Luxembourg, Netherlands, New Zealand)	62	(Ireland)
Population density (persons/km²)	1	47	1	(Australia, Canada, Iceland)	124	(Japan)
Net population change 1980–90 (per thousand per year)	5.7	2.9	0.6	(Denmark)	14.8	(Australia)
Population dependency ratio (population 0–14 + pop. 65+)/ (population 15–64)	0.54	0.55	0.50	(Austria, Germany, Japan)	0.59	(Sweden)
Employment growth 1980–90 (percent per year)	1.3	0.8	-0.3	(Finland)	1.5	(Belgium, US)
Ratio of employment growth to population growth 1980–90	2.3	2.2	-3.3	(Finland)	7.1	(Sweden)
Unemployment rate	11.9	6.2	1.0	(Switzerland)	17.0	(Spain)
Sectoral employment share (%): Agriculture[2]	11	15	6	(Sweden, US)	37	(Portugal, Iceland)
Industry[3]	23	28	18	(Belgium)	45	(Germany)
Services[4]	66	54	41	(Austria)	71	(Belgium, US)

1   *Three countries (Luxembourg, Netherlands, and New Zealand) have no rural regions according to the OECD definition.*
2   *agriculture, forestry, fishing*
3   *mining, manufacturing, construction, utilities*
4   *all other*

How does rural Canada look to Canadians?

Before examining the employment-related data for Canada in more detail, it is necessary to return briefly to the question of geography. Is the OECD scheme, as described above, satisfactory for a large, diverse country like Canada? For example, should one distinguish between different types of rural regions? Is not a rural region located near a large metropolitan centre essentially different from a more isolated rural region? And what about northern Canada?

Above, we noted that 33 percent of Canadians live in rural regions. However, these rural regions represent 79 percent of all the regions in the country and 95 percent of the total land area. There is considerable variation within this vast area in terms of resources, population distribution patterns and accessibility. The internal variations are likely as great as the differences between rural, intermediate, and agglomerated regions[3]. Another dimension needs to be introduced to subdivide this area into areas that are "more rural" and "less rural."

Besides population size and population density, the rurality-related variable most commonly mentioned in rural geography literature is the notion of "accessibility" or "remoteness" in regard to large centres of population and services[4]. This notion has been quantified in a variety of ways:

1. Robin Armstrong (1993) developed an "accessibility index" for all municipalities in Canada, based on how big a circle you would have to draw, centred at that community, to include 100,000 persons.

2. Leon Arundell (1991) developed an "index of remoteness" based on distances to various cities weighted according to their populations.

3. Calvin Beale of the United States Department of Agriculture developed a coding system for US counties based on the presence of, or adjacency to, metropolitan areas of various sizes (Bender *et al.*, 1985).

Ehrensaft has said that "what it means to be rural in late twentieth century OECD economies" consists primarily of "low versus high population densities and distance from metropolitan labour markets" (Ehrensaft, 1994, p. 154). This is essentially the theory behind the Beale codes. Ehrensaft and Beeman (1992) assigned Beale codes to the 1986 census divisions in Canada. By combining this information with the OECD geography, it is possible to marry the fundamental notions of population density and accessibility.

Three basic groups of rural regions were identified: those adjacent to metropolitan centres ("metro-adjacent"), those not adjacent to metropolitan centres ("non-adjacent"), and the remote north ("northern"). Using this subdivision, Canada can be classified into five groups of regions, or degrees of rurality (Figure 4.6). Note the location of the agglomerated and intermediate regions, a relatively small number of regions having a large proportion of Canada's population. Taking into account the fact that the five groups of **regions** are composed of both urban and rural **communities**, Figure 4.7 shows how employed Canadians are distributed among the different types of regions.

---

3. *This is, however, how rural Canada has usually been treated. "Rural areas have traditionally been defined with reference to an urban benchmark. This process has tended to give the impression that rural Canada is one residual area largely homogeneous in its demography, employment base, income, culture and social infrastructure." (Bollman, 1994, p. 142)*

4. *"The requirements of simplicity and temporal continuity have produced, in all the western industrial nations, definitions of rural space based on population and related measures such as population density ... and proximity to major metropolitan centres" (Fuller, Cook, and Fitzsimons, 1992, pp. 18–19). These comments were actually framed in a rather negative context, in which the authors said that there are more meaningful ways of defining rurality, but they are not commonly used due to practical considerations.*

Figure 4.6.   The OECD regional geography applied to Canada

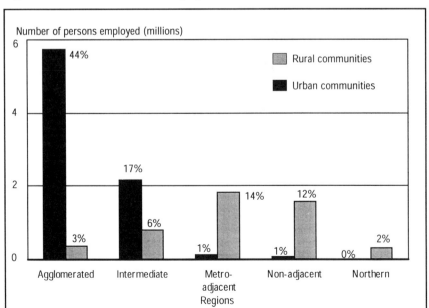

Produced by: *SAGA, Agriculture Division, Statistics Canada, 1996.*

Figure 4.7.   Where are the employed located?

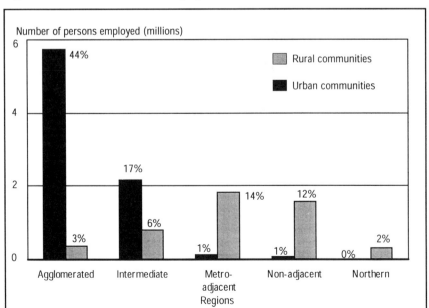

Source: Statistics Canada, Census of Population, 1991.

Employment-related data are examined under three main themes: **job growth** (expressed as percent increase in employment), **employment structure** (described by shares for various industrial sectors), and **unemployment**. The data shown have been taken from 1991 and 1981 census data tabulated for OECD's Steering Group on Rural Indicators.

Job growth

Between 1981 and 1991, the highest growth occurred in intermediate regions (Figure 4.8). Growth rates are less for regions with higher degrees of rurality. Note that intermediate regions largely refer to southern Ontario and Quebec: 34 of the 48 intermediate regions are located in those two provinces.

Figure 4.8.   Employment growth was highest in intermediate and metro-adjacent regions, Canada, 1981 to 1991

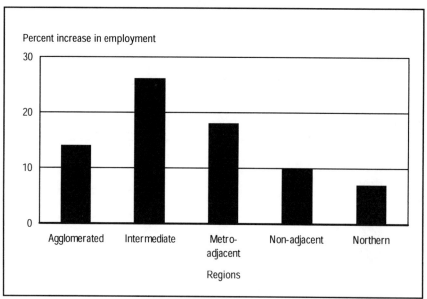

Source: Statistics Canada, Census of Population, 1991.

What type of employment is growing? Bollman and Biggs have noted, "Our natural resources are still rural-based, but the employment in resource-based sectors is not growing. In rural Canada, the broadly-defined service sector is growing in relative and absolute terms." (Bollman and Biggs, 1992, pp. 41–42) The services sector, however, is huge and diverse, encompassing both very high- and very low-skilled jobs, so specific categories of services have been examined. Table 4.2 shows employment growth rates by region for 14 industrial sectors[5]. Note the negative growth in all rurality classes for manufacturing and for primary industries other than agriculture. Although agriculture had positive growth in all classes, this growth was weak in the three areas where it has a significant share of employment: non-adjacent, metro-adjacent, and intermediate.

The three industries with the highest employment growth rates are in the business services, health services, and consumer services sectors (Figure 4.9). Interestingly, the same industries ranked first, second, and third in the same order in all rurality classes. Similar changes are happening independent of rurality, although the magnitude of growth is certainly not the same everywhere. Again, the effect of metro-adjacency is evident, with those regions close to large urban centres approaching the rates of the rapidly growing intermediate regions.

Table 4.2. Percent change in employment, Canada, 1981 to 1991

Industry	Agglo-merated	Inter-mediate	Metro-adjacent	Non-adjacent	Northern	Canada
Agriculture	**21**	4	4	3	14	5
Other primary (forestry, fishing, trapping, mining, quarrying and oil extraction)	**-3**	-16	-4	-8	-20	-9
Manufacturing	-16	-8	**-7**	-11	-19	-12
Construction	4	**30**	9	0	5	9
Transportation and communication	2	**19**	14	-0	-4	6
Utilities	4	**44**	16	7	16	15
Trade	9	**29**	21	11	16	16
FIRE (finance, insurance and real estate)	19	**48**	28	19	3	25
Business services	56	**100**	72	44	66	64
Consumer services	31	40	**42**	34	25	35
Education services	23	**27**	26	16	13	23
Health services	40	**50**	44	37	39	42
Defence	24	9	9	6	**33**	14
Government services	14	40	29	21	**44**	23
Total	**14**	**26**	**18**	**10**	**7**	**16**

Source: Statistics Canada, Census of Population, 1981 and 1991.
*Note: The **bold** numbers indicate the highest rate for that sector.*

---

5.   *All industry data in this paper is based on the 1970 Standard Industrial Classification (see Statistics Canada's 1991 Census Dictionary for more details). Note that all statistics shown refer only to those who were employed at the time of the census (June 1), whereas most published census data on employment by industry refers to the experienced labour force, which also includes those not working at census time but who had been employed, if even for a short time, since January of the previous year. An important factor to keep in mind when using data on employment by industry is that the figures are based on the type of business establishment rather than the type of work as such. For example, an accounting job in a manufacturing firm would not be distinguishable from an assembly-line job in the same company.*

Figure 4.9.   The three fastest growing industries: growth was highest in intermediate and metro-adjacent regions

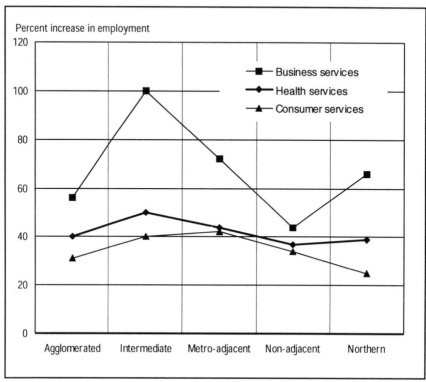

Source: Statistics Canada, Census of Population, 1991.

The fastest growing sector everywhere is the category known as business services[6], sometimes referred to as producer services. This is a very knowledge-intensive sector with great potential for further growth. Though business services have traditionally been tied to urban areas, rural Canada is certainly participating in this growth. While the employment growth for business services nationally is 64 percent, it is almost as high — 61 percent — for all rural regions. "It is intermediate-level business services that provide the real possibilities for expansion in non-metro regions." (Ehrensaft, 1994, p. 146)

In summary, while rural regions had an overall employment growth rate of 14 percent, the national rate was 16.5 percent, i.e. rural job growth was only 14/16.5 = 85 percent of the national rate. Another way of looking at the question

---

6.   *The category of business services includes employment agencies and personnel suppliers, computer and related services, accounting and bookkeeping, advertising, scientific and technical, lawyers and notaries, management consulting, and other services intended primarily for businesses.*

is to consider rural regions' share of all employment. Rural Canada had 30.8 percent of all jobs in 1981; this dropped to 30.2 percent in 1991, a decrease of 0.6 percentage points. By either measure, rural Canada is having some trouble keeping up to the rest of Canada.

Employment structure

For most industries, the share of total employment does not vary significantly with rurality (Table 4.3). However, there are five industries where there is noticeable variation: the shares for agriculture and for other primary industries *increase* with increasing rurality, while the shares for manufacturing, FIRE, and business services *decrease* with increasing rurality.

Table 4.3.   Percent share of employment, Canada, 1991

Industry	Agglo-merated	Inter-mediate	Metro-adjacent	Non-adjacent	Northern	Canada
Agriculture	1	3	9	10	1	4
Other primary	1	1	2	6	13	2
Manufacturing	14	16	13	12	10	14
Construction	5	6	6	6	5	6
Transportation and communication	7	6	6	6	7	6
Utilities	1	1	1	1	2	1
Trade	16	17	16	15	13	16
FIRE	7	6	4	3	3	6
Business services	8	5	3	2	2	6
Consumer services	12	12	11	12	11	12
Education services	7	7	7	7	8	7
Health services	9	9	9	9	8	9
Defence	1	1	1	2	1	1
Government services	7	6	6	6	12	7

Source: Statistics Canada, Census of Population, 1991.

Employment shares for industries in rural versus "urban" (intermediate and agglomerated) regions may be displayed in a different way (Figure 4.10) to give an idea not just of absolute importance but also of the relative importance of each industry in rural regions compared to urban Canada. A point located on the dashed diagonal line would indicate that the particular industry is equally important in rural and urban regions; the greater the distance from that line, the greater the difference between the relative importance in rural and urban. Note that agriculture and "other primary" are clearly rural-intensive industries and that construction, defence, and utilities are marginally rural-intensive sectors.

Figure 4.10.   Share of employment by industry for rural regions versus other regions

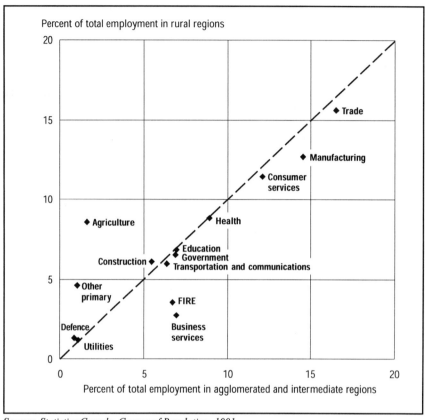

Percent of total employment in rural regions

Source: Statistics Canada, Census of Population, 1991.

Measured in terms of *changes in share* from 1981 to 1991, primary and secondary industries, as well as transportation and communication, utilities, and defence all lost share nationally and in rural regions generally (Table 4.4). Trade (wholesale and retail) lost nationally but not in rural regions generally. Again, a shift away from resource-based industries toward most services is evident.

Table 4.4. Change in share of employment among industries, Canada, 1981–91 (percentage points)

Industry	Agglo-merated	Inter-mediate	Metro-adjacent	Non-adjacent	Northern	Canada
Agriculture	0.1	-0.6	-1.3	-0.7	0.1	-0.4
Other primary	-0.2	-0.6	-0.6	-1.1	-4.5	-0.6
Manufacturing	-4.9	-5.9	-3.7	-3.0	-3.2	-4.6
Construction	-0.5	0.2	-0.6	-0.6	-0.1	-0.4
Transportation and communication	-0.8	-0.3	-0.2	-0.6	-0.8	-0.6
Utilities	-0.1	0.2	0.0	-0.0	0.1	-0.0
Trade	-0.7	0.4	0.3	0.1	0.9	-0.1
FIRE	0.3	0.9	0.3	0.2	-0.1	0.4
Business services	2.1	1.9	1.0	0.5	0.8	1.7
Consumer services	1.6	1.2	1.9	2.1	1.5	1.6
Education services	0.5	0.1	0.4	0.3	0.4	0.4
Health services	1.6	1.5	1.5	1.7	1.8	1.6
Defence	0.1	-0.1	-0.1	-0.1	0.2	-0.0
Government services	0	0.6	0.5	0.5	2.9	0.4

Source: Statistics Canada, Census of Population, 1981 and 1991.

The importance of agriculture varies greatly within Canada (Figure 4.11). Agriculture is obviously most important, as measured by its share of total employment, in the Prairies. In all parts of Canada, the metro-adjacent and non-adjacent regions depend more on agriculture than the other regions.

Figure 4.11. Where is agriculture important?

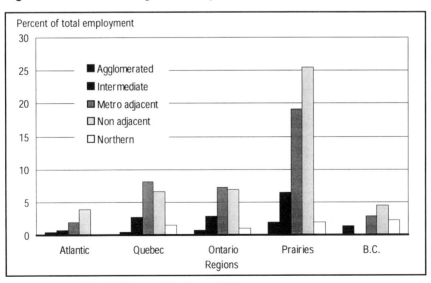

Source: Statistics Canada, Census of Population, 1991.

To summarize the information on employment shares by industry, an *index of dissimilarity* was calculated for the different rurality classes to illustrate the difference in employment structure between each class and Canada as a whole[7]. A minimum value of 0 would indicate an area is completely typical of the country as a whole. The dissimilarity indexes show a decrease for all degrees of rurality during the 1981 to 1991 period (Figure 4.12). This indicates that the areas are becoming more similar to each other in terms of employment structure.

Figure 4.12.   Regions are converging toward similar employment profiles

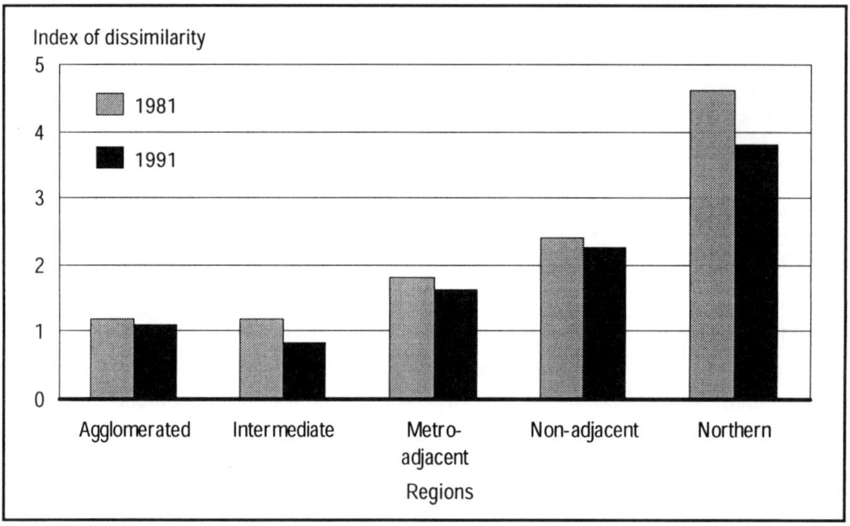

Source: Statistics Canada, Census of Population, 1981 and 1991.

Unemployment

Higher unemployment rates are usually associated with rural areas. In Canada, there is a definite relation between unemployment and rurality (Figure 4.13). Note also that the rate increased in all rurality classes between 1981 and 1991, especially in agglomerated and northern regions. The increases may be due to the fact that the 1981 Census took place during a period of growth preceding the recession of the early 1980s, while at the time of the 1991 Census, Canada was in the middle of a recession. Since urban and rural unemployment rates tended to diverge during the period of growth in the 1980s and to converge during the recession of the early 1990s, one would expect to see the largest proportional increase in the agglomerated regions between 1981 and 1991, which is indeed the case as shown in Figure 4.13.

---

7.   *To derive the index of dissimilarity for a particular rurality class, the difference between the shares for each industry at the regional and national levels is calculated, all the differences are squared and averaged before the square root is taken.*

Figure 4.13. Unemployment grew most in agglomerated and northern regions

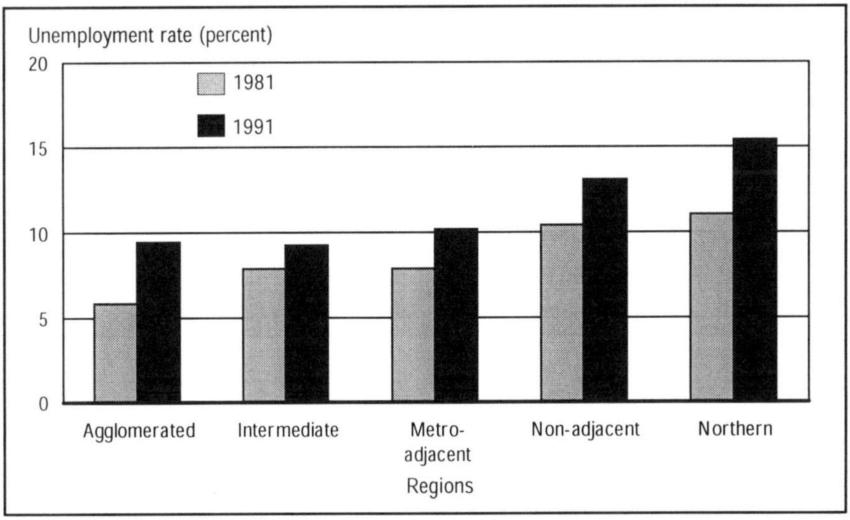

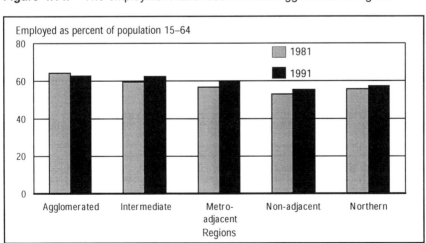

Source: *Statistics Canada, Census of Population, 1981 and 1991.*

However, earlier in this section it was observed that there was significant employment growth during the same period. Between 1981 and 1991, the employment ratio (also known as the employment/population ratio), which is the number of employed as a proportion of the total working age population, grew almost everywhere (Figure 4.14). So even though unemployment increased, the share of the population with jobs went up.

Figure 4.14. The employment ratio rose in all but agglomerated regions

Source: *Statistics Canada, Census of Population, 1981 and 1991.*

Where do we go from here?

Ehrensaft and Beeman (1992) note the dependence of certain areas on certain types of industry — the notion of sectoral dependency. In reference to rural employment, they observed that employment in goods production rises from metropolitan to non-metropolitan areas. Because of this, the general movement toward services leaves non-metropolitan areas more vulnerable. In particular, non-adjacent non-metropolitan areas are the most vulnerable since they rely more on initial manufacturing (manufacturing that is tied more closely to natural resources). Complex manufacturing is very much tied to urban regions while non-complex manufacturing is more evenly distributed (Figure 4.15). Complex manufacturing is associated generally with more technology-intensive and/or knowledge-intensive processing.

Figure 4.15.   Complex manufacturing is concentrated in agglomerated and intermediate regions

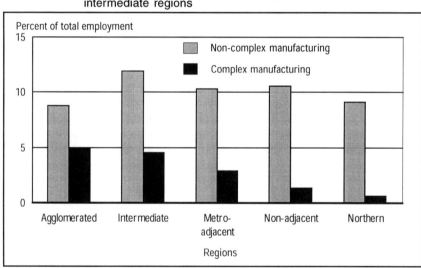

Source: Statistics Canada, Census of Population, 1991.

Another important consideration is that of the interdependency between various sectors. For example, instead of assuming the continuing replacement of manufacturing jobs by service jobs, it is vital to realize that manufacturing will continue to be fundamentally important to the economy but will be increasingly dependent on certain services to support it. Fuller *et al.* (1992) note that "services are provided in order to maintain a system of production and it is around this system of production that social organisation takes place."

Bollman *et al.* (1992) identified three directions that rural Canada needs to follow to have a prosperous future:

1. **Macro-diversification**: rural areas need to become less dependent on traditional rural industries.

2. **Metro-ization**: the market for rural goods and services will become more and more urban. New rural jobs will be based on innovative goods and services of interest to metropolitan residents.

3. **The new economy**: Canada's comparative advantage will be in the "knowledge-intensive" industries[8].

Rural development policy is ordinarily structured by sector (i.e. putting money into industries that are, or are expected to be, fast-growing). But while employment statistics indicate the direction the country has been going, is that necessarily the direction it **should** be going? Should rural development focus on the sectors that are already growing or the ones that have stopped growing?

Or, rather than be sector-specific, should rural analysis/policy be location-specific, i.e. take place at the regional or community level? There is a wide variation in employment growth among the different regions, **independent of their degree of rurality** (Figure 4.16). As the data indicate, there are other factors besides rurality that allow some rural areas to thrive and cause others to struggle. Any rural development policy, to be effective, needs to consider all these elements, recognizing the diversity and potential that make up rural Canada.

Figure 4.16. Many rural regions show high employment growth rates

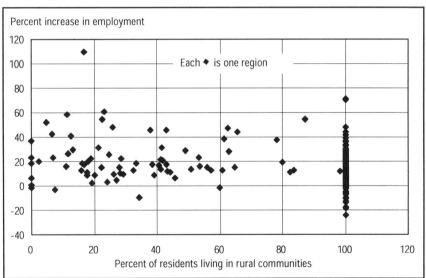

Source: Statistics Canada, Census of Population, 1991.

---

8. *An area for future analysis would be to classify employment data according to Beck's (1992) industrial categories of high, medium, and low knowledge-intensiveness. This would be a labour-intensive exercise, since her scheme cuts across the groupings of Statistics Canada's Standard Industrial Classification. Another approach would be to look at the classification of occupations by skill-intensiveness.*

References and further reading

Armstrong, Robin (1993) *An Accessibility Approach to Defining "Rurals" in Canada.* Paper presented to the "Rural Exchange" Conference, Ottawa, June.

Arundell, Leon (1991) *Rural, Remote and Metropolitan Zones Classification: A classification for Australia as at 30 June 1986 and a methodology for 1991 Census data.* Canberra: Unpublished report, Department of Primary Industries and Energy.

Beck, Nuala (1992) *Shifting Gears: Thriving in the New Economy.* Toronto: HarperCollins.

Bender, Lloyd D. *et al.* (1985) *The Diverse Social and Economic Structure of Nonmetropolitan America.* Washington, D.C.: Rural Development Research Report No. 49, Economic Research Service, US Department of Agriculture.

Bollman, Ray D. (1994) A Preliminary Typology of Rural Canada. In Bryden, John M. (ed.). *Towards Sustainable Rural Communities: The Guelph Seminar Series.* Guelph: University of Guelph, pp. 141-144.

Bollman, Ray D. and Biggs, Brian. (1992) Rural and small town Canada: an overview. In Bollman, Ray D. (ed.). *Rural and Small Town Canada.* Toronto: Thompson Educational Publishing, Inc.

Bollman, Ray D., Fuller, A.M. and Ehrensaft, Philip. (1992) Rural Jobs: Trends and Opportunities. *Canadian Journal of Agricultural Economics* Vol. 40, pp. 605-622.

Ehrensaft, Philip. (1994) Restructuring Rural Institutions. In Bryden, John M. (ed.). *Towards Sustainable Rural Communities: The Guelph Seminar Series.* Guelph: University of Guelph, pp. 145-156.

Ehrensaft, Philip, and Beeman, Jennifer (1992). Distance and diversity in nonmetropolitan economies. In Bollman, Ray D. (ed.). *Rural and Small Town Canada.* Toronto: Thompson Educational Publishing, Inc.

Fuller, A.M., Cook, Derek and Fitzsimons, John. (1992) *Alternative Frameworks for Rural Data.* Ottawa: Agriculture Division Working Paper No.14, Statistics Canada.

Green, Milford B. and Meyer, Stephen P. (1995) *Occupational Stratification of Rural Commuting.* Paper presented at the International Symposium: Perspectives on Rural Employment, Coaticook, Quebec.

Government of Canada. (1995) *Rural Canada: A Profile.* Ottawa: Interdepartmental Committee on Rural and Remote Canada.

Longstaff, G.B. (1993) Rural depopulation. *Journal of the Royal Statistical Society* Vol. LVI.

OECD. (1994) *Creating Rural Indicators for Shaping Territorial Policy.* Paris: OECD.

Statistics Canada. (1995) Custom tabulations.

Statistics Canada. (1992) *1991 Census Dictionary.*

Weiss, Carolyn, Ratcliffe, Michael and Torrieri, Nancy. (1993) *A Comparison of Census Geographic Areas of Canada and the United States.* Ottawa: Geography Series Working Paper 1993-1, Statistics Canada.

Chapter five:

Rural Employment in EU Finland

Kari Gröhn
Ministry of the Interior, Helsinki, Finland

Abstract

Finland is one of the three most rural countries in the OECD. Substantive restructuring is underway in the context of dramatic changes in Finno-Soviet trade, Finland's integration into the EU and the impact of agricultural policy reform. Predominantly rural regions lost jobs in the 1980s, the only OECD country with rural job losses in this period. Rural policy initiatives are being implemented. However, a territorial cross-sectoral approach is severely constrained by rigid sectoral administrative structures.

Introduction

Finnish society is restructuring, driven by changes in Finno-Soviet relations and Finland's joining the EU in 1995. Rural regions in Finland have been the most affected. The purpose of this chapter is to review the employment situation in rural Finland and to review the rural employment policy frameworks presently in place.

Employment in rural Finland

Finland is one of the three most rural countries in the OECD, the other two being Norway and Turkey (OECD, 1994). Almost 57 percent of the Finnish population lives in predominantly rural regions, which account for 98.5 percent of the total area of Finland (Figure 5.1). This observation emphasizes three aspects conspicuous to Finland: a low population density, peripheral location and a harsh climate. Though Finland shares these characteristics with its Scandinavian neighbours, Norway and Sweden, they constitute a significant difference from other European member countries of the OECD.

Figure 5.1.   Population and land area in rural communities

Percent of national land area in rural communities (y-axis)

Percent of national population in rural communities (x-axis)

Iceland, Canada, Sweden, United States, Greece, FINLAND, Australia, Ireland, New Zealand, Norway, Spain, Austria, Japan, Turkey, Turkey, Switzerland, Denmark, United Kingdom, Luxembourg, Italy, France, Portugal, Germany, OECD average, Belgium, Netherlands

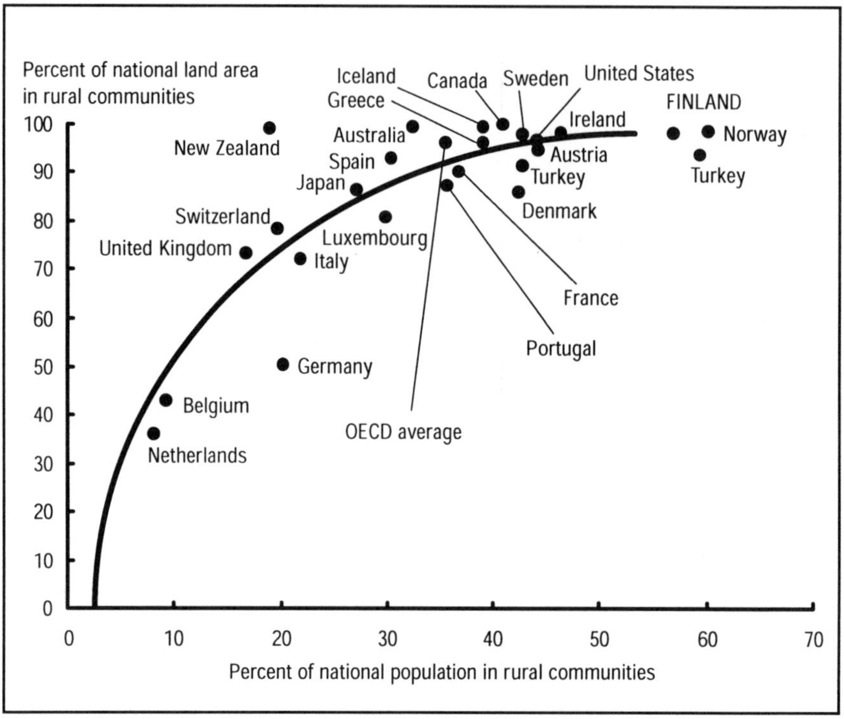

Source: OECD (1994).

Finland's remoteness results in transport costs that account for 15 percent of Finnish export prices. This share is roughly twice that of countries further south in Europe and it is a major handicap for the Finnish economy. In addition, Finland shares a 1,300 km frontier with Russia which has been a dividing line between East and West throughout its history. Keeping the border areas inhabited is not just an issue of rural development policy, but a principle of Finnish security policy. Today, the profound changes in the former Soviet Union pose new challenges. The border underlines the vast economic and income disparities between East and West. Stable development on both sides of it is in the vital interests not only of Finland, but of Europe and OECD countries in general.

Finns are continuing to move from country to town. In 1960, 56 percent of the Finnish population lived in the countryside, compared with 20 percent in 1990. Finland's net migration in predominantly rural areas during the 1980s was -1.7 per thousand per year. This negative migration was exceeded only in Japan (-3.3) and Ireland (-3.0).

Workplaces have become even more concentrated than the population. A third of Finland's inhabited square kilometre squares contain no place of work whatsoever and in 12 percent of them, not a single member of the labour force is to be found. Workplaces are concentrating and becoming differentiated in the whole country. In particular, square kilometre squares containing primary occupation workplaces alone have decreased. Livelihoods have diversified in rural towns and urban-adjacent areas. Areas in which people live and those in which they work are becoming increasingly differentiated in Finland. Rural and sparsely populated municipalities contain 26 percent of the population, 24 percent of persons at work, and 21 percent of the jobs. In certain coastal, lake-shore and island municipalities, the summer population is as much as four times the winter population. The concentration of workplaces and the growth of leisure are increasing the volume of traffic.

Employment decreased by -0.3 percent annually in Finland's predominantly rural areas during the 1980s. In all other countries providing data, employment grew in such areas — the growth was weakest in France (+0.1 percent) and Japan (+0.2 percent). The ratio of persons not at work to those at work is highest (three-to-one) in the most rural municipalities and lowest (one-to-one) in the most urbanized municipalities. This high dependency rate is due to the relatively high proportion of retired persons and children and, more recently, due to high unemployment in rural regions.

Finnish rural policy

Overview

Finland is currently pushing through a fundamental reorientation and restructuring of its territorial policy in general, and of its rural policy in particular. This reorientation must be viewed in the context of changes in the international and national situation. The dramatic changes in the former Soviet Union, Finland's integration with the EU, the ensuing structural adjustment of the economy and the effects of agricultural policy reform are all producing a major impact on the Finnish economy and related structural policies. In addition, Finland is in the midst of a severe economic crisis which is challenging the Scandinavian welfare-state model. Against this background, the creation of a new regional and rural policy is a major task that will have far-reaching consequences for the future territorial equilibrium of Finland and northern Europe.

In the 1950s and 1960s there was no rural policy, as such. Rural problems were treated as sectoral problems of agriculture, forestry and other primary production. They were tackled, as in many countries, mainly via agricultural policy. In the 1970s, rural problems became part of regional policy. The territorial dimension was taken into account more systematically, but sectoral considerations remained strong. During this period the focus shifted to the secondary sector, with an emphasis on industrialization and growth centres. Planning organizations were set up at the regional level, but the planning logic was greatly influenced by a central administration with a top-down perspective.

In the 1980s, village action and the role of municipalities as rural actors rose to prominence in rural policy. Statutory municipal planning was strengthened. At the same time, environmental concerns gained importance. But conflict frequently arose between rural communities striving for economic development and the central administration with its concern for the conservation and management of natural resources.

The Rural Development Project which was initiated by the government in 1988 — the year of the Council of Europe's Living Countryside Campaign — resulted in a National Rural Programme for the whole country in 1991. Up to then, each province had run its own rural programme. The work of the Rural Development Project was continued by a Rural Policy Committee. This committee was the body responsible for planning and implementing rural policy. Its term of office ran from January 1, 1992 to April 30, 1995. Its principal role was to coordinate the various sectors involved in rural development. It was a forum of nine ministries, two interest groups and six individual experts, all concerned with different rural issues. Based on the results of the OECD Review of Finland's Rural Policy (1995), the Finnish government has set up an inter-sectoral Rural Policy Partnership Group to continue the work of the Rural Policy Committee for a term extending from May 1, 1995 to April 30, 1998.

Finnish rural policy can be summarised as:

1. It covers all objectives and measures designed to improve rural conditions; and

2. Its goal is to revitalize the countryside. The objectives are to alleviate structural problems, improve rural livelihoods and services, strengthen the viability of rural communities, make rural areas more competitive and increase their attraction as places to live in and as locations for enterprise.

The Regional Development Act of 1994 marked a new phase of regional and rural policy in Finland. At the national level the new policy signifies a shift from a project approach to a programme-based, integrated territorial policy. Responsibilities are being transferred from the central to the regional level, which up to now has been relatively weak and ill-defined. In essence, a major component of this new policy is decentralization toward regions and municipalities. The new regulations oblige the State's district and regional administration to cooperate with municipalities and, more specifically, with the new regional councils, which represent the municipalities directly. Such cooperation is needed to draft and to implement regional development programmes. Coordination at the central level is the responsibility of the Ministry of the Interior.

Regional development programmes include both national and EU programmes. The national programmes include the Development Area Programme, the Structural Change Programme for industrial areas, the Expertise

Centres Programme to promote high technology, the Border Area Programme, the Rural Area Programme and the Islands Programme. The EU programmes (5b, 6, etc.) support the national programmes and run parallel with them in their main objectives.

The national budget includes regional development funds for programme implementation. These appropriations are used to develop and diversify rural occupations, develop the infrastructure, supply services, and for public investments. Other money, too, is used for implementing the programmes — mostly State funds from other sources and funding from municipalities, joint municipal organizations and the private sector.

The use of budgetary grants for regional development is decided independently by each sector at the national and regional levels. In recent years this decision-making has been delegated increasingly from the central administration to the State's districts and regions. The idea is to use the appropriations more effectively by coordinating their use according to the regions' own programme objectives. In targeting regional development appropriations, the general goals and priorities of national regional policy are taken into account together with the priorities of the regions' own programmes. Projects proposed by regions are given priority provided they do not clash with the overall priorities for national development.

Programme agreements are being used as a tool to ensure the long-term engagement of financing partners in the implementation of the programmes. They are also a good basis for monitoring the use of both national and EU financing. They favour continuity and predictability and they make it easier to coordinate the acquisition and use of resources.

In the autumn of 1995, Finland's new government started a Regional Administration 2000 Project to simplify the State's regional administration and to rationalize the operations of the various State authorities. The objective is to reduce the number of State regional units by combining their operations on a functional basis and to delegate more functions to the regional and local levels.

The challenge of meeting these rural and regional development goals must be understood in the context of the strength of sectoral administrative structures in Finland. Historically, a strong central administration has distributed resources to the State's districts and regions and to the municipalities. There has been little coordination at either the central or the regional level. Sectoral districts and regions are not even coterminous — and this has been an added impediment to cooperation. It has been impossible to coordinate activities within municipalities because budget grants have been strictly earmarked by sector.

A strong sectoral administration is a major obstacle to rural development. To give just one example, in sparsely populated areas it should be possible to combine service supply at multi-service points, but this cannot be done without intersectoral cooperation and coordination. Development of diversification to promote other rural occupations, too, calls for horizontal cooperation and coordination between different sectors.

Development of rural areas calls for specialization to enable them to succeed against the competition. Such specialization is impossible unless it is supported by the decision-making machinery that recognizes local strengths. Mere improvement is inadequate. In the face of massive unemployment (18 percent nationally, and considerably higher in most of the underdeveloped areas), regional development and restructuring are absolute necessities.

Rural policy initiatives arising from EU membership

Finland joined the European Union in January, 1995. Thus, the Objective 5b, 6, and 2 (Converting Regions Seriously Affected by Industrial Decline) programmes have only just been drafted. The 5b, 6 and 2 areas are shown on the map (Figure 5.2). The 5b and 6 regional programmes for the EU's structural funds will continue from 1995 to 1999.

Figure 5.2.   Finland's objective 5b, 6 and 2 areas; other areas in white

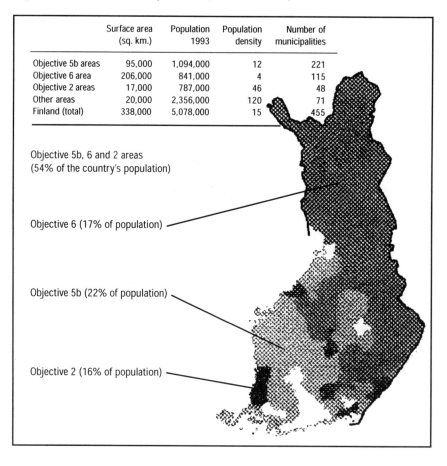

	Surface area (sq. km.)	Population 1993	Population density	Number of municipalities
Objective 5b areas	95,000	1,094,000	12	221
Objective 6 area	206,000	841,000	4	115
Objective 2 areas	17,000	787,000	46	48
Other areas	20,000	2,356,000	120	71
Finland (total)	338,000	5,078,000	15	455

Objective 5b, 6 and 2 areas
(54% of the country's population)

Objective 6 (17% of population)

Objective 5b (22% of population)

Objective 2 (16% of population)

In addition to these regional programmes, EU horizontal objective programmes have been drafted to cover the whole of Finland. EU Objective 3 is to integrate young people into the labour market. Objective 4 concerns vocational training, retraining and guidance, anticipation of changes in labour markets and development of expertise systems. Objective 5a relates to improvement of the efficiency of agriculture, establishment aid for young farmers, compensatory allowances for mountain and hill farming in less favoured areas, development of processing and marketing for agricultural products, establishment of producer groups in agriculture and horticulture and structural development of the fisheries sector. Also to be applied in accordance with the EU's Common Agricultural Policy are environmental support, arable land afforestation and early retirement for farmers.

Most of Finland's 5b areas are predominantly rural and are characterized by traditional rural occupations. Their population density is very low, averaging 11.5 inhabitants/km². The population is even sparser and more scattered in the Objective 6 areas of east and north Finland, where the average density is 4 inhabitants/km². The population density of the whole country is 15 inhabitants/km². Objective 2 areas have 46 inhabitants/km². The areas lying outside 5b, 6 and 2 are the most densely populated in Finland (120 inhabitants/km²).

It is projected that the Objective 5b and 6 programmes will help to create or preserve 40,000 jobs between 1995 and 1999, when they are due to end. The estimated total cost of these two programmes for 1995–99 is US\$ 1,900 million (Fmk 8,400 million) of which 33 percent will be covered by the EU structural funds, 38 percent by the Finnish public sector and 29 percent by the private sector. EU and Finnish public sector funding per inhabitant for the Objective 6 areas will be twice and one-and-a-half times that for the Objective 5b areas, respectively. The total funding per inhabitant will be US\$ 1,500 for the Objective 6 areas and US\$ 880 for the 5b areas.

The 5b and 6 programmes were drafted by a bottom-up method. Their development strategy and objectives were elaborated by the regional councils of the regions in which the areas lie and the analyses of the areas' weaknesses and strengths were based on the councils' assessments. (Regional councils are fairly new. They have borne the main responsibility for regional policy since 1994.)

The priorities advanced by the regional councils were grouped and coordinated to become the priorities for the national 5b and 6 programmes. This work was done by Objective 5b and 6 Programme Working Groups representing the different ministries and sectors involved. At the regional level, collaborators in the drafting also included representatives of the municipalities, local companies, business organizations, universities, training establishments and other interested parties. In the course of the drafting, the central and regional administrations consulted each other on matters regarding strategy and the number and content of the programmes.

The programmes will be implemented cooperatively by regional councils, sectoral districts and regions and the central administration. The regional councils' collaborators mentioned above (business organizations, etc.), committed themselves to their implementation at the drafting stage.

Objective 5b: Development and structural adjustment programme for rural areas

Objective 5b areas are characterized by a steady worsening of future prospects for agriculture, combined with a limited and relatively weak industrial sector. The aim of the 5b programme is to broaden, strengthen and diversify the economic base of these areas.

Most of the 5b areas lie in western, south-western, central and south-eastern Finland. Their total area is 95,000 km^2 — over a quarter of the country total (338,000 km^2). The combined population of the 5b areas is 1.1 million, approximately a fifth of the country total (5.1 million). The 5b areas contain 221 of Finland's 445 municipalities including many municipalities with very small populations.

The 5b areas are distinguished by an aging population and low levels of education and training in the working population. The ratio of persons who have continued education or training after leaving primary school, or who hold university degrees, is lower in the 5b areas than in the rest of the country.

The 5b areas are typified by an abundance of waterways and islands, a unique feature in Europe. They contain 9,600 km^2 of lakes and rivers and 16,400 km^2 of inland salt water. They also include 33,700 islands larger than half a square kilometre, amounting to 45 percent of all islands in the country. Due to this multitude of islands, the 5b areas have an exceptionally long *total* shore line of 60,900 km. This shore line is of paramount importance for construction, recreation and environmental protection. Weekend and holiday residences in the 5b areas number 151,000. Their occupants total 450,000 — 41 percent of all leisure-time residents in Finland. A third of these cottages are habitable in winter. The average time spent in them has lately increased.

According to a national inventory of the built environment (1993), some 700 culturally significant sites are located in 5b areas. Early in 1995 the government issued a policy decision on 156 nationally valued landscape areas and an improvement of landscape management. More than 30 of these sites are located in 5b areas.

From 1980 to 1992 the population of the 5b areas grew by only 1.3 percent. This was far slower than overall growth for the country of 5 percent during the same period. In 1992 the migration into the areas equalled the migration out of the areas. This was due partly to the slump, as a result of which job opportunities were very limited in the whole country. Within the 5b areas, the population of villages and sparsely inhabited areas has been decreasing, while that of municipal and regional centres has been increasing.

The per capita GDP of Finland's 5b areas is very low. In 1992 it was 22 percent below the national average and 33 percent under the EU average. The 5b areas account for 18 percent of Finland's total GDP with a relatively high share from agriculture and forestry (Table 5.1). In 1992 agriculture and forestry occupied 24 percent of the labour force in the 5b areas (and as high as 30 percent in some regions) compared with 9 percent for the country as a whole. In 1994 the unemployment rate averaged 17 percent in the 5b areas (18 percent in the whole country). According to internationally comparable data, Spain was the only EU country with a higher unemployment rate than in Finland.

Table 5.1.   Distribution of value-added among sectors, Finland, 1992

	5b areas (percent)	Whole country (percent)
Agriculture and forestry	18	6
Industry and construction	33	31
Services	30	42
Public sector	19	21
Total	**100**	**100**

Between 1989 and 1993, 90,000 jobs disappeared from the 5b areas. Relatively speaking, the job loss was greatest in industry (-29 percent). It was not so abrupt in services (-14 percent) and primary production (-17 percent). Shrinkage in female-dominant sectors contributed to the trend. These sectors include commerce, textiles, clothing, the shoe industry, and the public sector — mainly health and social welfare and services.

For young people, the job situation is very poor in the whole country. The unemployment rate for persons under 25 was 35 percent in 1994. Since 1991, however, the ratio of young to all unemployed has been decreasing both in the 5b areas and in the whole country. The main reason for this is that young people have been seeking education or training as an alternative to unemployment.

As a share of total unemployment, long-term unemployment has grown tenfold during the 1990s. This applies to the whole country. In the 5b areas, one in four unemployed persons had been jobless for at least a year in 1994. The trend for the unemployed to remain totally excluded from the labour market is becoming a nation-wide problem.

Though economic recovery has begun in certain regions, its impact on employment has been extremely limited. If employment improves, as is hoped, the process will start in the large population centres of southern Finland. It will thus widen regional differences in unemployment and accelerate migration out of both the 5b and the 6 areas, which will be the last to feel the effects of the growth.

The farm structure is extremely problematic in 5b areas. Farms are smaller on the average than they are elsewhere in the country. Almost 80 percent of them have less than 20 hectares and only 1 percent more than 50 hectares of arable land. Forestry is a major source of additional farm income. Nearly a half of all farm forest holdings in Finland lie in 5b areas. The holdings average 34 hectares per farm. The average volume increment is slightly more than 6 m^3 per hectare per year. Subsidiary occupations account for a very low proportion (6 percent) of gross farm income in the 5b areas. The role of off-farm income is much greater. On almost a third of farms, one or both farm spouses also work off the farm. The importance of subsidiary occupations and off-farm jobs depends on local job and other opportunities, and on the type of economic activity that predominates in the area. The share of agriculture and forestry in the total income of farming couples has dropped from 56 percent to 48 percent in ten years (1983–1992). Correspondingly the share of income from pay, real-estate earnings and subsidiary occupations has risen from 32 percent to 37 percent. This has resulted in a proportional growth of part-time farming.

In 1992 the majority of companies in Finland's 5b areas were engaged in commerce (36 percent of the total). Other sectors with large numbers of companies were manufacturing (22 percent) and construction (11 percent). Companies engaged in tourism accounted for 7 percent and those supplying technical or business services for 4 percent. Most companies in the 5b areas are small and employ less than ten persons. Micro-companies (1–9 workers) amounted to 91 percent of all companies in 1992. If companies employing 10–49 are counted, the share of small-scale enterprises in the 5b areas rises to 98.5 percent.

The overall **strategy and objectives for development** may be stated as:

> The employment and income base of Finland's 5b areas will be broadened, and unemployment will be reduced by improving the operating conditions and competitiveness of companies and farms, expanding the use of nature-based resources and improving know-how. The attraction of the countryside will be enhanced by preserving and protecting the rural landscape and environment, and by ensuring access to functional services and opportunities for jobs and commuting. The principles of environmental protection and sustainable development will be incorporated in all modes of development.

The **specific objectives** of the Finnish 5b programme are:

Increasing, strengthening and diversifying the activities of SMEs

Enterprise promotion is the main priority for diversification of the economic structure and for the replacement of jobs lost during recent years in the 5b areas — particularly in the industrial and primary sectors. Promotion of SMEs (small and medium sized enterprises) is especially important because they are the biggest employers in the 5b areas. The viability of these areas will also require a diversification and development of agricultural-based enterprises. Most of the successful rural enterprises will be small, but diversified. Specific measures include:

1. increasing new business activity;
2. investment and development projects for existing companies;
3. improvement of companies' operating environments; and

4. promoting the use of bioenergy and renewable energy sources in non-agricultural sectors.

The target results are 2,200 new enterprises and the creation or preservation of 11,500 jobs.

Diversifying the farm population's sources of livelihood

One key factor in the development of the rural areas will be the successful adaptation of agriculture to the EU's Common Agricultural Policy (CAP). Specific measures include:

1. diversification of rural occupations;
2. promoting the use and value added of forests and the use of wood for energy;
3. small-scale wood-working on farms;
4. development of villages and farm tourism; and
5. technological research and development projects that will benefit activity on farms.

The target results are 7,000 jobs preserved or created, 3,000 new business activities on farms, 60 product development units and 220 research and development projects.

Developing rural services and attractive factors

Services are a prerequisite for the expansion of business activity, for utilizing natural resources, and for increasing the independence of Rural Finland. The quality of rural services will be maintained by modifying their structure and by enhancing and diversifying the know-how of their personnel. Interactions and divisions of labour between rural areas and population centres will be promoted.

Commuting to population centres will become easier. At the same time, teleworking will make it easier for people to work at home in the countryside and for companies to be located in rural areas. The effects will be cumulative: more teleworking, more jobs, more companies, more services and more young people will accelerate the growth of services and job opportunities, and will provide conditions conducive to the improvement of services and country living, and thus enhance the attractive force of the countryside in every respect.

Specific measures to raise the level of know-how include:

1. improving the structure of education and training to enhance the know-how of the labour force;

2. utilizing information generated by research and development units; and

3. promoting business activity by increasing know-how.

The target results are 13,400 trained persons, 2,500 jobs created or preserved and 500 new enterprises.

Specific measures to aid the development of communities include: development of rural transport and international transport connections; development of data-communication services; environmental management; improvement of water and waste management; utilization of unused buildings and landscaping; and reorganization of services. The target results are 1,000 jobs created or preserved and 300 new small enterprises.

The overall 5b targets are:

1. to achieve a clear increase in the 5b areas' per capita GDP and to reduce the difference between it and the mean national GDP by 5 percentage points;

2. to create new jobs and develop existing ones in rural enterprises (totalling 22,000 jobs, 4,400 annually). This presupposes a net increase of 3,000 companies and 3,000 new business activities on farms in the 5b areas;

3. to cut the employment rate in the 5b areas by 1 percentage point annually;

4. to keep the 5b areas' unemployment rate below the national average by preserving existing jobs and creating new ones;

    5. to help limit the decrease of farms, which currently number 62,000, so that there will be 48,000 functioning farms in 1999. 5b measures will enable 4,000 farms to alter their production, mainly in the direction of organic farming, and permit 3,000 farming families to engage in subsidiary occupations on their farms;

6. to bring the ratio of persons who have completed senior-secondary school and/or intermediate-level training up to the national average.

The main objective of the 5b programme is to reduce unemployment by improving the operating environment of farms and companies. The programme stresses the creation of new jobs and preservation of existing ones. The main priority is promotion of business activity; this includes both improvement of operating environments for existing companies and creation of new enterprises.

It is estimated that, during the five years of the programme, the programme measures will lead to the creation or preservation of 22,000 jobs (4,400 annually) and 13,400 persons (2,700 annually) will be involved in measures aimed at increasing know-how.

Objective 6 development programme for very sparsely population areas

Finland's Objective 6 area is the north-eastern frontier zone of the newly expanded EU 15. As can be seen from the map (Figure 5.2), it forms a continuum, so it will mostly be referred to as 'the Objective 6 area' (in the singular). The Objective 6 area totals 206,000 km^2 and covers almost 61 percent of the total area of Finland while its population is only 17 percent of the country total (840,000 inhabitants). Its average population density is 4 inhabitants/km^2. Vast tracts of this area are completely uninhabited. A major problem of the spatial structure is the long distances within the area, and the consequent acute shortage of basic services. Naturally, this applies mainly to its most remote regions.

The total population of the Objective 6 area has decreased clearly in the past 30 years. In 1960 it was 960,000; now it is just over 840,000. This shrinkage has occurred at the same time as the total population of Finland has increased from 4.5 million to over 5 million.

The Objective 6 area has long had the worst unemployment in Finland. In 1993 its unemployment rate was 21 percent; in many parts of the area it was almost 30 percent. Youth unemployment is a particular problem in the Objective 6 area. In many parts, it has climbed above 50 percent of the young labour force.

Sparse population and strong emphasis on agriculture and forestry are the factors that distinguish the Objective 6 area most clearly from the rest of the country. Nearly 30 percent of Finland's farmers live in the area, though it contains only 17 percent of the national population. In several remote parts of the area, over a half of the total labour force gets its income from primary production. The structural change from a predominance of primary production to services in the Objective 6 area has been rapid. In 1960, jobs in primary production and services accounted for 59 percent and 24 percent of the total, respectively. The corresponding figures in 1990 were 18 percent and 58 percent.

The public sector plays a prominent part in the generation of jobs, services and economic activity. Its role is significant in all parts of the Objective 6 area — particularly in Finnish Lapland, where 45 percent of all jobs in the sub-region of Rovaniemi are in public services and only 9 percent in manufacturing. The public sector is a major employer in regional and rural centres as well as in rural districts engaged predominantly in primary production.

The Objective 6 area contains 42 percent of all registered hotels and lodging houses in Finland and 35 percent of the bed capacity. The higher-than-average significance of tourism in certain parts of the area, particularly Lapland and Kainuu, is also evident from the bed capacity and overnight stays in ratio to the population. The proportion of these two factors in the Objective 6 area is roughly double that in the whole country.

Specific measures include:

1. development of business activity and improvement of company competitiveness;

2.   making use of natural conditions (eg. agriculture, forestry, tourism) in the area;

3.   overcoming problems caused by remote location and long distances.

The priorities and measures of the Objective 6 programme are very similar to those of the 5b programme. But there is a greater emphasis on services owing to the extreme sparsity of the population.

The overall Objective 6 targets are:

1.   to ensure that the per capita GDP of the Objective 6 area is not more than 15 percentage points below the Finnish average;

2.   to reduce the number of unemployed persons by 40,000

3.   to ensure that the combined number of jobs in private services and manufacture is 135,000 when the programme ends (total growth compared to 1992: 17,500 jobs);

4.   to achieve a balanced structural change in agriculture. It is estimated that investments in 5,000 farms will be supported during the period of the programme.

Common Agricultural Policy (CAP)

The Objective 5b and 6 programmes are concerned only in part with agricultural policy, but agriculture is a strong background factor. A high proportion of the factors that increase agricultural unit costs in Finland originate in the farm structure. Only a small part of the total agricultural output comes from farms that are efficient in terms of production. Capital and labour costs per unit are therefore high. To make agriculture efficient means that the size of the average production unit should be increased many times over. This is physically impossible because farms and fields are widely scattered.

For such reasons, Finland's integration with the CAP will lead to fundamental changes in the development of the 5b and other rural areas. The adjustment problems are accentuated by the structure of agriculture, financing problems and farm indebtedness. The general growth of competition and the free movement of people, goods and capital will also engender economic changes at the regional level.

Finland will no longer be able to regulate its agricultural production according to self-sufficiency goals. Free exports and imports between EU countries are forcing agriculture and the food industry to operate in market terms. With the abolition of protection against imports, EU membership has led to a market price level that averages 40–45 percent less than earlier. A direct subsidy, calculated in terms of hectares under cultivation and the number of livestock, will compensate for part of the loss of income which this causes to farmers.

Future trends in production will be affected mainly by the farmers' reactions to the level of market prices and supplementary subsidies, and partly by success in reducing the costs of agriculture. According to one estimate, there will be 70,000 functioning farms in 2005 (down from 116,000 in 1993), and the proportion of farms with over 20 hectares will grow. None the less, farming will remain small-scale compared with farming in most European countries.

Natural resources in rural areas, especially forest resources, will be exploited more than earlier. Farms specializing in forestry will be established and low-productivity fields will be afforested. Organic farming will increase. Farming will be supplemented by subsidiary livelihoods that will help alleviate the negative effects of the CAP.

Critical comments

The stated targets for Finnish 5b and 6 programmes in 1995–99 reflect official optimism concerning desired outcomes. In other words they are *envisioned targets* rather than realistic estimates of future changes in rural know-how and competitiveness.

They will be hard to achieve because their implementation still depends on an out-dated *sectoral* administrative machinery. Although the 5b and 6 programmes were drafted by a bottom-up method, they could not include innovative measures to coordinate the rural policies of various ministries and to target measures selectively according to type of rural area.

The reason for this is that both the EU structural funds and the Finnish ministries are so sectoral that a *fully* bottom-up approach was impossible. Every EU structural fund defended its own "territory", and the Finnish ministries followed this example. Such centralization and its built-in "territorial imperatives" is reminiscent of Finno-Soviet trade, when even the distribution of orders between companies was decided on political grounds instead of competitive offers.

OECD advocates flexibility in regional and local policies, especially in these days of tight budgets. It will hardly be possible to reduce the massive unemployment in EU peripheral areas like Finland with the aid of public support programmes which bind the development funds of local companies and organizations to unrealistic expectations.

Owing to the EU emphasis on short-term quantitative targets, it remains impossible to solve Finland's unemployment problem. This can only be done with long-term measures to develop human resources in rural areas. Public measures are ineffective unless they are combined both with local initiative and with commitment.

References and further reading

Ministry of the Interior. (1995) *Objective 5b Programme, Finland.* Helsinki, Finland.
Ministry of the Interior. (1995) *Objective 6 Programme, Finland.* Helsinki, Finland.
OECD. (1994) *Creating Rural Indicators for Shaping Territorial Policy.* Paris: OECD.
OECD. (1995) *OECD Reviews of Rural Policy: Finland.* Paris: OECD.
Statistics Finland (1995) *Tilastollinen Aikakauslehti 2/95* (in Finnish).

Chapter six:

Education and Regional Employment in the 1980s: Comparisons among OECD Member Countries

David A. McGranahan and Kathleen Kassel
United States Department of Agriculture, Washington, D.C., United States

Abstract

*Workforce education is often seen as a key to economic advancement because of its link to productivity. Rural areas able to retain a highly educated workforce may expect a more productive workforce **plus** a more entrepreneurial population. Rural areas appear to be losing their share of the educated workforce. Although growing at less than the national rate, rural areas with a higher educated workforce grew more than rural areas with a lower educated workforce. Growth in rural high education regions was only partly explained by the industrial mix — other factors are also important.*

Introduction

Workforce education, because of its link to productivity, is often seen as key to national economic advancement. This view has strengthened in OECD countries over the past 15 years as the globalization of markets has brought competition from newly industrializing countries and, in conjunction with new technologies, rising unemployment rates among the less well-educated. Many OECD governments are seeking to enhance the level of education and training of the labour force to enable their countries, "to compete — not with low cost/low technology countries, but with countries characterized by high value-added manufacturing and services" (OECD, 1995). This emphasis on workforce skills was highlighted recently in *The OECD Jobs Study.*

Education is also often a cornerstone of rural development policy. Because the more highly educated may leave rural areas for better opportunities in cities, the rationale for improving education in rural regions is more clearly justifiable as a people policy than a place policy. Out-migration may improve the fortunes of those migrating, but impoverish the people left behind. However, to the extent that the more highly educated are retained, benefits are seen to include not only a more productive labour force, but a more entrepreneurial population, with stronger, more effective leadership in both the business and civic arenas (Beaulieu and Mulkey, 1995). If this is true, then economic growth should be greater in regions with more highly educated populations not only because the type of jobs being created are for those with higher education levels, but because the local economies are more likely to be effective in creating jobs. In short, high education rural regions should be more competitive in the global economy.

This study is a preliminary examination of the relationship between education levels and 1980–90 employment trends in rural regions across a range of OECD countries. We first present some basic statistics comparing rural with urban regions in industrial structure, education, and employment growth. Then, we compare high and low education rural regions within countries to identify advantages that regions with highly educated workforce age population may have had during the decade. Our basic findings are:

1. rural regions generally had a small and declining share of their nations' highly educated workforce age population;

2. rural regions with relatively highly educated workforce age populations generally had less unemployment and greater employment growth than rural regions with less educated workforces, but still grew at less than the national rate; and

3. the advantage that rural high education regions had was partly, but only partly, due to their industrial mix.

The analysis presented here depends on data gathered largely for this education and employment project. It is a sign of the importance of the OECD work on rural employment that 11 countries replied to specific requests for education data. Members of the OECD Steering Group on Rural Indicators were extremely helpful in arranging for and answering questions about the data and commenting on earlier drafts. Despite our efforts, the available information was not always complete. This "hands on" experience gave us a much greater appreciation for the work that goes into OECD and other international studies.

Background

Understanding the importance of education for rural economic growth has become a critical issue over the past 15 years because changes in technology and the globalization of markets have undermined the positions of low-skill workers in industrialized countries and rural regions in these countries have tended to specialize in low-skill jobs. Industrialisation has historically been beneficial to rural economic well-being in the US, as elsewhere. From the beginning of this century until the past decade, people on marginal farms were drawn off to the cities by the promise of wages that, if not always good, offered a better standard of living than marginal farming or farm work. Particularly in the four decades up to 1980, movement off the farm was also facilitated by the decentralization of manufacturing out of cities in search of lower cost labour. In the US, rural (non-metropolitan) manufacturing employment grew by nearly a million jobs a decade from the 1940s through the 1970s, absorbing almost as many people as left agriculture. By 1970, the proportion of people working in manufacturing was greater in rural areas than in urban areas and, by 1980, almost three times as many rural people worked in manufacturing as in agriculture, forestry, and fishing combined. Rural incomes rose rapidly in the US during this period, at a faster rate than urban incomes, and regional income disparities shrank significantly.

The legacy of this transformation out of agriculture was a more sparsely settled countryside and a rural economy specializing in agriculture, tourism, and routine manufacturing — all largely low-skill industries. Complex, high-tech manufacturing and financial, legal, accounting, and other producer services — all largely high-skill industries — remained largely confined to urban areas. Although the country histories may be somewhat different, this rural–urban division of labour is evident in all four countries for which we have complete data — Canada, United States, Finland, and Norway.

These countries vary considerably in the share of total national employment that is in (predominantly) rural regions — from about 30 percent in Canada to 50 percent in Norway (Figure 6.1). But, once we take these differences into account, these countries have remarkably similar patterns with respect to the rural shares of different industry group[1]. In all four countries, the rural shares of employment in consumer or household-oriented industries are about the same as the shares of total employment. There is little regional specialization in these industries because households consume most of their services — schools, doctors, retail, transportation, and so forth — locally. However, rural shares of producer services — finance, insurance, consulting, engineering, and so forth — are relatively low. Although present in rural areas, these services are increasingly global in reach and concentrated in the largest urban centres. Rural areas also have relatively low shares of the more complex, high-tech manufacturing industries, which tend to have large research and development components and a need for access to highly skilled labour (although some of the more routine activities in these industries, such as computer assembly, may be located in rural areas or overseas).

---

[1]   *This analysis examines the extent to which industries are located in rural areas. This issue is quite distinct from that of the industrial structure of rural areas. For instance, the rural shares of agricultural employment are about 60 percent in the United States and 77 percent in Finland. However, the proportions of the rural employed who are in agriculture are about 5 percent in the United States and 16 percent in Finland.*

Rural shares of employment in routine manufacturing — activities which tend to involve less research and development and more simple production processes — are relatively high compared with rural shares in both total employment and, especially, complex manufacturing. Rural shares are extremely high in mining and agriculture, as expected. Mining in Norway is an exception, however, largely because the employment reflects oil extraction in the North Sea and the wage and salary employees involved are urban-based.

Figure 6.1. The producer services sector has a low share of its employees in rural regions

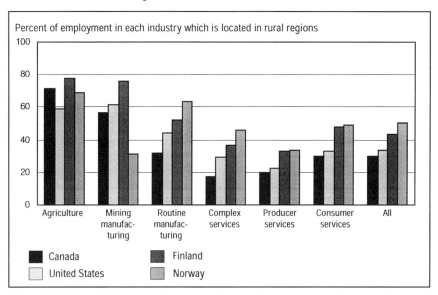

Source: OECD rural data surveys.
For an explanation of industry categories, see Appendix A.

Industrial transformation in the 1980s

The introduction of the microprocessor to manufacturing, communications, and other fields has been heralded as the coming of a new industrial age (Piore and Sabel, 1984; Reich, 1991). The adoption of this new technology in production has been spurred by increasing competition from newly industrializing countries. This combination of technological and market forces engendered an increase in demand for better-educated workers in urban centres and a near collapse of blue-collar production jobs in "industrialized" countries. Manufacturing jobs in the United States declined sharply in urban areas during the 1980s and the historical rural gains of a million manufacturing jobs a year evaporated. The industrial transformation that had allowed at once a substantial exodus from agriculture and rising rural incomes broke down.

In the United States, recent industrial change has been reflected in both a decline in real earnings for young, less-educated male workers of about 20 percent and increasing opportunities for men and women with a university degree. But most of the new high-education jobs have been urban jobs, and this tendency increased over the decade. Rural–urban earnings and income disparities increased (McGranahan and Ghelfi, 1991).

In Europe, the decline in manufacturing employment has been occurring in the more industrialized countries since at least the late 1970s (Chesire, 1991). Because of greater wage rigidities, European industrial change has tended to result less in widening earnings disparities than in growing unemployment, especially for the less well-educated. Unemployment among the less well-educated has gained at a faster rate than among the better-educated in most countries surveyed (Table 6.1).

Should these trends continue, they will have important consequences for agriculture and rural development. Thus far, the new industrial transformation seems to require more highly skilled workers and an urban location. People with fewer skills have consistently seen their opportunities erode. People can no longer leave agriculture for well-paying city jobs, nor have the few jobs moving to rural areas been well-paying.

Table 6.1.   Overall unemployment rates and ratio of unemployment rates of labour force with lower secondary education to rates of those with upper secondary education

Country	National rate of unemployment		Lower secondary unemployment (Upper secondary = 100)		
	1981	1992	1981	1992	92>81
Canada	5.6	10.0	144	155	Yes
United States	5.8	6.6	153	190	Yes
Norway	1.3	4.6	191	145	No
Finland	3.7	11.4	140	123	No
France	5.6	8.8	159	180	Yes
United Kingdom	8.5	8.4	150	176	Yes
Spain	8.2	14.7	110	125	Yes

Source: OECD, 1995.

The industrial transformations of the 1980s make the issue of the importance of education for rural economic change especially relevant for several reasons. First, education has gained salience as a determinant of employment outcomes, both in finding a job and the level of earnings. Rural regions with more highly educated workforces should have an increasing advantage on that account alone. Second, highly educated workforces should be greater attractants of prospective employers than in the past, assuming that more remote areas are suitable for newer industrial activities. Finally, the increasing level of uncertainty brought about by changes in technology and markets makes the ability of local business and civic communities to adapt more critical than in the past, and this adaptability should be greater where education levels are higher.

Rural education levels

The residents of rural regions tend to have considerably lower education levels than residents of urban regions (Table 6. 2)[2]. In all but three of the OECD countries for which we have information, the urban share with high education (college or university graduate, typically) is at least 1.5 times larger than the rural share. Similar results might have been obtained for two of the exceptions, France and Spain, had data been available for the 25–44 age groups. These relatively low rural education levels are consistent with types of industries that tend to locate in rural areas (recall Figure 6.1). Although it is possible that the low rural education levels shape rural industry structure to some extent, the heavy outmigration of the better educated from rural areas, at least in the United States, suggests that the problem has been more that rural industries have historically provided poor opportunities for the better educated.

To examine the importance of workforce education for rural economic growth, we ranked the rural regions in each country according to the proportion who had completed some level of university in 1980–81 (the exact measure varied from country to country according to each's way of measuring education). The top half on the list were classified as high education regions and the bottom half as low education regions. While this procedure generally allowed us to analyse the importance of education in countries with relatively few rural regions, both the United Kingdom and Germany had fewer than 6 rural regions, too few to try to make distinctions among them. For these countries, we combined the predominantly and significantly rural regions into the "rural" category, although this is likely to distort the results. In sum, data were available for 10 OECD countries, but were not always complete or without problems.

We compared rural high education regions with both the nation as a whole and rural low education regions for four measures of regional competitiveness: employment growth 1980–90, level and change in unemployment, and change in share of workforce population with high education. The last measure reflects the ability to maintain a skilled workforce.

---

[2]   *For this study, except where noted, rural regions are those identified in the OECD Rural Indicators Project as "predominantly rural" and urban regions are those identified as "significantly rural" or "predominantly urbanized" (see OECD, 1994).*

Table 6.2.   Rural–urban differences in education, 1990/91

| Country | Age group | Percent of age group with high education level, 1990/91 | | |
		Urban	Rural	U/R Ratio
Austria	25–44	10.4	5.9	1.8✓
Germany	Work force	6.4	3.8	1.7✓
Canada	25–44	19.7	9.4	2.1✓
Finland	25–44	14.1	8.0	1.8✓
Norway	20–39	16.2	10.6	1.5✓
Spain	10 and over	6.2	4.7	1.3
Switzerland	25–44	17.6	11.4	1.5✓
United States	25–44	27.7	18.7	1.5✓
France	16 and over	10.5	7.4	1.4
New Zealand	25–44	13.7	8.6	1.6✓
United Kingdom	30–44	10.9	10.1	1.1

These comparisons suggest that, in general, rural high education regions were more competitive than their low education counterparts. In about half the countries, rural high education regions gained employment at a faster rate than low education regions, although not necessarily as fast as the country as a whole (Table 6.3). Unemployment rates were lower in rural high education regions in almost all the countries included, although the gains in reducing unemployment were not necessarily lower in the high education regions. In most cases, with Finland and Germany the exceptions, rural high education regions did not maintain their share of working age population with high education. Low education regions were generally even less able to hold on to their share of high education population than high education regions. Germany, a very urban country, is the major exception to these generalizations. Both types of rural regions gained in their share of highly educated and the low education regions had the greatest gain[3].

Given that the types of industries that expanded in the 1980s were those that tended to employ more highly educated workers, high education regions may have had an advantage over low education regions because of their industry mix as much as their workforce and entrepreneurial skills. For instance, low education regions may have been disadvantaged by a relatively high concentration of employment in agriculture, which has historically shed employment. To explore the importance of industry mix for employment growth in rural high and low education regions, we calculated what their rates of employment growth would have been if their industries had grown at the national rate for these industries.

[3]   *Because the combination of the predominantly and significantly rural regions in the German analysis could be the explanation for the uniqueness of the German results, we also computed educational shares for the predominantly rural regions only. This more rural set of regions showed an even greater increase in the share of highly educated employees. At least some of this reflects the recent development of universities in these regions.*

The difference between the regional growth rate expected on the basis of industry composition and the national growth rate is the difference due to the region's particular "industrial mix". The rest of the difference between the regional and national growth rates is then ascribable to changes in the shares of industry jobs. (Thus, for instance, if manufacturing declined nationally but grew in a particular region, that region increased its share of manufacturing.) Unfortunately for comparison purposes, industry sector detail was not available for three of the four countries where education was not associated with greater employment gain.

Both low and high education rural regions had unfavourable industry mixes at the beginning of the 1980s. Their tendency to specialize in low-growth or declining industries is reflected in negative signs for industry mix in Table 6.4. Low education regions were considerably more disadvantaged by industry mix than high education regions in all countries except Norway and New Zealand, where the low education region disadvantages were relatively small. In cases where the disadvantages are greatest for low education regions (Finland, Switzerland), specialization in agriculture is a major explanation. Relatively low shares of employment in the finance, insurance and real estate industry group is also an important factor.

Table 6.3.   Measures of economic viability by rural region educational level

High education regions have advantage ✓

Country	Employment as share national total			Unemployment as share of national total				University graduates as share of national total		
	1980	1990	*Ratio 1990/80*	1980	1990	*Ratio to 1990 employment share*	*Ratio 1990/80*	1980	1990	*Ratio 1990/80*
Rural high education regions										
Canada	19.3	19.1	0.99✓	20.6	20.0	1.04✓	0.97	14.0	12.2	0.87✓
United States	19.1	18.6	0.97✓	19.4	17.8	0.95✓	0.92✓	18.1	16.5	0.91✓
Finland	27.6	26.6	0.96✓		30.5	1.15✓		20.4	20.4	1.00✓
Norway	22.7	22.6	1.00✓	27.9	23.4	1.04	0.84✓	19.9	19.7	0.99
Austria	19.0	18.6	0.98	16.4	17.6	0.95	1.07✓			
Spain	6.6	6.5	0.98	4.5	5.6	0.87✓	1.25✓			
Germany	15.1	15.3	1.01	15.2	15.0	0.98✓	0.99	11.4	11.7	1.03
United Kingdom	16.9	18.6	1.10	14.3	14.0	0.75✓	0.98	18.4	18.1	0.99✓
France	14.0	14.1	1.00✓	13.7	14.5	1.03	1.06			
Switzerland	7.3	7.3	1.00✓	5.5	5.9	0.81✓	1.09			
New Zealand	26.3	25.5	0.97					24.4	21.8	0.89
Rural low education regions										
Canada	11.5	10.9	0.95	19.2	15.9	1.45	0.83	6.3	5.4	0.85
United States	15.8	14.9	0.94	18.9	17.7	1.19	0.94	9.9	8.6	0.87
Finland	15.2	13.6	0.89		21.4	1.57		8.0	7.5	0.94
Norway	27.0	26.2	0.97	41.5	27.3	1.04	0.66	20.2	20.1	1.00
Austria	19.9	19.5	0.98	16.3	18.4	0.94	1.13			
Spain	10.8	10.9	1.02	8.8	11.6	1.06	1.32			
Germany	12.4	12.7	1.03	13.9	12.9	1.01	0.93	6.5	7.2	1.11
United Kingdom	7.5	8.2	1.10	7.7	7.1	0.86	0.92	6.7	6.0	0.89
France	16.2	15.2	0.94	15.6	15.2	1.00	0.98			
Switzerland	5.0	4.8	0.96	4.7	4.0	0.83	0.86			
New Zealand	20.4	19.7	0.97					14.0	12.5	0.89

Table 6.4.   Difference in rate of change in employment from national rate, 1980–90, by source of difference

Country	Low education regions			High education regions		
	Industry mix	Change in share	Total difference	Industry mix	Change in share	Total difference
	Percent					
Canada	-3.1	-2.1	-5.3	-1.3	0.6	-0.8
United States	-3.4	-3.9	-7.4	-0.7	-2.3	-3.0
Norway	-2.7	-0.5	-3.2	-2.3	2.0	-0.3
Finland	-10.1	-1.3	-11.4	-4.2	0.1	-4.1
France	-3.9	-2.2	-6.1	-2.4	2.8	0.3
Switzerland	-8.4	4.2	-4.2	-6.7	7.2	0.5
Spain	-4.4	6.1	1.7	-2.6	0.4	-2.2
New Zealand	-1.1	-2.4	-3.5	-0.4	-2.7	-3.1

Except in New Zealand and Spain, high education regions had somewhat greater gains (or, in the US, a lower loss) in employment due to changes in the shares of industry employment relative to the "change in share" component of low education regions. That is, they were better able than low education regions to attract or retain jobs for reasons other than their more advantageous or disadvantageous industry mixes. This is (weak) evidence that greater workforce-age education, because of its link with skilled labour and entrepreneurship, may be an advantage. One disturbing aspect, however, is that manufacturing, a relatively footloose sector (in that its output markets are generally not local), showed a greater tendency to shift to low education regions than to high education regions in six of the eight countries (France and Norway were the exceptions). This suggests that manufacturing shifting to rural areas has tended to seek low-cost labour rather than high-skill labour (see McGranahan (1995) for a fuller analysis of the U.S. case).

Discussion

This brief examination of the importance high regional workforce education levels for rural employment suggests a somewhat limited advantage. Among rural regions, those with relatively high education levels tended to have greater employment growth, lower unemployment, less growth in unemployment, and a better ability to hold onto their share of highly educated workers. The results were by no means uniform across countries, however. Moreover, a substantial part of the employment growth advantage of rural high education regions could be attributed to their favourable industry structures, rather than education *per se*.

One reason that workforce education may be less important than expected for the economic development of rural regions is that the small sizes of their labour markets may limit their ability to develop pools of skilled workers over time. Where local economies are small, workers may have to switch industries or move to get ahead. This is a greater problem among the more highly skilled workers, particularly given the increase in two-career couples. At the same time, employers may be reluctant to shift operations to areas where labour shortages could develop in particular skill areas. This would explain why manufacturers, when they chose rural areas, appear to be looking for low cost labour rather than high skill labour. Household-oriented consumer services, especially those such as health and education which are publicly supported and organized, may be an exception to this locational logic.

Three caveats to the study findings are in order. First, the analysis is confined to the 1980s, which may have been a particularly difficult period for rural areas. For instance, the analysis generally showed an increasing concentration of the more highly educated population in areas with already high proportions of highly educated people. In the United States, this trend was particularly pronounced in the 1980s, but seems to have abated in the 1990s.

Second, it may not be enough to focus on jobs without paying attention to the nature of those jobs — the types of work, job security, and earnings, for instance. In the United States, at least, earnings have been falling even as employment has increased.

Finally, the analysis must be taken as suggestive rather than definitive, even for the 1980s. Differences ascribed here to education may reflect other regional characteristics, such as proximity to expanding urban centres, favourable climate and amenities, and/or the presence of universities and major medical facilities. Also, we have used university completion as our measure of education. The results might have been somewhat different if we had been able to use a lower level of educational attainment as a criterion. And, we have taken only a very rough cut here — in our division of rural regions into high and low education groups, for instance. Hopefully, with a more extensive analysis, further insights will be gained.

Appendix A: Industry categories for Figure 1

Agriculture	Agriculture, forestry, and fishing
Mining	Mining
Routine manufacturing	Food processing; tobacco; lumber and wood products; furniture; textiles; apparel; stone, clay, and glass; rubber and rubber products; transportation equipment except aircraft and missiles; plastic products; leather and leather products; primary metals; fabricated metal products; appliances
Complex manufacturing	Chemicals; electrical and other machinery; computers; refining; pharmaceuticals; printing; scientific instruments; aircraft and missiles
Producer services	Finance, insurance, and real estate; business services; legal, accounting, and engineering services; air transport
Consumer and distributive services	All other services, including personal, social, educational, health, utilities, wholesale/retail, and hotels and eating places

Note: The exact breakdown varied from country to country depending on the categorization available.

References

Beaulieu, L.J. and Mulkey, D. (1995) *Investing in People: The Human Capital Needs of Rural America*. Boulder, CO: The Westview Press.

Chesire, P. (1991) Problems of regional transformation and deindustrialization in the European Community. In Rodwin, L. and Sazanami, H. (eds). *Industrial Change and Regional Economic Transformation: The Experience of Western Europe*. London: HarperCollins Academic, pp. 237-267.

McGranahan, D.A. (1995) *The Importance of Local Workforce Education for Manufacturing Location in the 1980s: A Pessimistic View*. Paper presented to the Annual Meetings of the Rural Sociological Association, Washington, D.C., August.

McGranhan, D.A. and Ghelfi, L.M. (1991) The Education Crisis and Rural Economic Stagnation in the 1980s. In *Education and Rural Economic Development: Strategies for the 1990s*. Washington, D.C.: Economic Research Service, U.S. Department of Agriculture. ERS Staff Report No. AGES 9153, pp. 40-92.

OECD. (1994) *Creating Rural Indicators for Shaping Territorial Policy*. Paris.

OECD. (1995) *Education and Employment*. Paris: CERI.

Piore, M.J. and Sabel, C.F. (1984) *The Second Industrial Divide: Possibilities for Prosperity*. New York: Basic Books.

Reich, R.B. (1991) *The Work of Nations: Preparing Ourselves for the 21st Century*. New York: Knopf.

Chapter seven:

Rural–Urban Differences in Youth Transition to Adulthood

E. Dianne Looker
Acadia University, Wolfville, Nova Scotia, Canada

Abstract

Rural youth have different occupational experiences and expectations compared with urban youth, partially reflecting rural–urban differences in educational expectations and attainments. Education and occupational decisions are linked to rural–urban differences in geographic mobility and in patterns of moving out of the parental home. Gender influences these "pluri-transitions" as well as the way that rural–urban differences are experienced. The data suggest that rurality is not equated with deprivations as much as with difference.

Introduction

Getting a paid job (preferably a full time job) is an important part of the transition to adulthood (Anisef *et al.,* 1980; Ashton and Lowe, 1991; Breton, 1972; Mason, 1985; Pallas, 1993). However, it is not the only criterion for adult status (Wyn and White, 1996). This chapter examines youth transition to adult roles in rural and urban areas. This chapter documents the ways in which decisions about jobs are intertwined with other aspects of the transition out of adolescence.

Data gathering

The data come from a survey of 1,200 youth — 400 from each of three sites: Hamilton, Ontario; Halifax, Nova Scotia; and rural Nova Scotia. For much of the analysis in this chapter, the two urban samples will be combined for comparison with the rural sample. Hamilton is an industrial urban centre, near Toronto. It is more ethnically diverse and is more "blue collar" than

Halifax. Halifax is the capital of the province and is part of one of the two urbanized areas in Nova Scotia. Halifax hosts several universities and is heavily reliant on public sector employment. The rural Nova Scotia sample includes 100 respondents from each of four economic regions outside the Halifax — Dartmouth metropolitan region. For several decades rural Nova Scotia has experienced chronically high levels of unemployment, particularly among youth. There has been heavy reliance on seasonal employment and on government "make work" projects.

The target group for the first stage of the research were those born in 1975[1]. Names and addresses were obtained from schools and school boards; the lists provided included dropouts and graduates as well as those currently enrolled in school (see Looker, 1993 for details). The data gathering involved in-depth face-to-face structured interviews, conducted in 1989, with the youth[2]. The focus of the interview was on the plans and expectations that the youth had for their future. Particular attention was paid to their educational and occupational plans. The interviews contain both precoded, fixed choice items and open ended questions. Responses to the open ended questions, which were recorded verbatim and linked to the numeric data[3], allow for more qualitative analyses. In this phase of the research responses were obtained from twelve hundred youth, comprising a 74 percent response rate.

In 1992 a brief, one page questionnaire was sent out asking for the youths' attainments to that point and their activities since 1989. Addresses were updated, and as many as possible traced[4]. At this stage, information was obtained for about a thousand of the original youth.

A more detailed follow-up was conducted in 1994, with questionnaires sent to all those still in the study for whom we had addresses[5]. Questions at this stage focused on what the youth had been doing since 1989, what they were currently doing, and what their future plans were at this stage in their lives. A brief, one page questionnaire, with key questions was sent to those who did not reply after two reminders. In all, data were obtained from 837 respondents in 1994[6].

---

1. *The choice of birth cohort was made to be comparable to earlier research on 17 year olds in Hamilton (see Looker, 1977; Looker and Pineo, 1983).*
2. *Questionnaires were also distributed to the parents of the youth, but data from these will not be used in this analysis.*
3. *The qualitative and quantitative data were linked using SPSS; see Looker, Denton and Davis, 1989 for details of the procedure.*
4. *As was true at all stages of the research, participation was voluntary. Any who refused at this point were not contacted further.*
5. *In-depth interviews were conducted with 400 of the youth in 1994, but these data were not available for analysis for this chapter.*
6. *While the response rate (70 percent of the original sample) is quite respectable in terms of standards for longitudinal research, it is likely that various sample biases have been introduced with sample attrition. It is beyond the scope of this chapter to go into this issue, but it should, nevertheless be acknowledged.*

Work experiences

The first empirical question that will be addressed is: what are the work experiences and expectations of the youth in rural and urban areas? There are, in fact, few differences in terms of job experiences when the youth are 17. There is a slight tendency for rural youth to have had more unemployment by this stage of their lives. Rural youth also had fewer different jobs than their urban counterparts.

The qualitative data gives us some idea about how rural and urban youth see the two settings. When asked about job prospects in the area, most rural youth make comments like: "there isn't any", "non-existent", "slim", "minimal", "lousy". Urban youth, particularly those in Halifax, are more likely to say: "adequate", "O.K.", "medium". In Hamilton (which had not yet been hit by the recession), one got more comments like: "very good", "excellent", "quite promising", "there are lots."

Table 7.1.   A higher share of rural youth has drawn unemployment insurance, 1994

Youth work experience	Percent of respondents	
	Rural	Urban
Has drawn unemployment insurance (U.I.)	50	23
Prefers seasonal work plus U.I.	18	5
Has accessed a government programme	20	15
Has held a full time job	68	74
Has quit a job	32	46
Has started own business	3	8

By the time of the follow-up in 1994 (when the youth are 23 or 24 years of age), other rural–urban differences emerge. Rural youth are more likely to have drawn unemployment insurance; fully half of the rural youth have been "on UI" compared with only 23 percent of urban youth (Table 7.1). Rural respondents are also more likely to say that they would prefer seasonal work supplemented by unemployment insurance (an option that the government is phasing out). Given the proliferation of government projects that are aimed at rural youth, it is not surprising that rural youth are also more likely than urban youth to have accessed a government programme.

The other side of this picture is that, by 1994, more urban youth (74 percent versus 68 percent of the rural respondents) report having had a full time job, either during the summer months or during the school year. They are also more likely to have quit a job — an act that may be a luxury to hard pressed rural youth. Although only a few (6 percent) in any of the areas have started their own business, there seem to be more budding entrepreneurs in the urban areas (8 percent) than the rural (3 percent).

In terms of the types of jobs youth in the different areas expect, rural youth are more likely to say they see themselves having jobs that they describe as "routine"[7] (data not shown). More of the urban respondents, on the other hand, expect jobs that are "respected", "have good pay", "are rewarding" and "important to the community", even if "tiring", "with long hours", and/or ones with "a lot of power".

These differences are not large[8], but they do point to the fact that rural youth have rather different expectations — and different experiences in the world of work than do youth who live in cities. It is easy, and perhaps tempting, to portray the situation of rural youth in terms of "doom and gloom". Some do: both those who research rural issues (e.g. Lawrence and Williams, 1990; Quixley, 1992) and those who live and work in rural areas often characterize the situation in fairly negative terms.

The youth themselves, when asked to describe the difference between a rural area and living in a city, tend to say that cities are places where there is "more" — more jobs, more opportunities, more options, more excitement. But they also note that there is more noise, more crime, more pollution, more problems. In this view "more" need not mean "better".

Occupational issues are important to these youth. We are dealing with issues relating to access to job markets as well as access to particular jobs, especially jobs "with a future". But jobs are not everything. Looking at the occupational experiences of these youth only gives us part of the picture. Jobs are a means to an end. For youth, part of the "end" goal is the transition to adult status — being treated like an adult. As we will see, there are other ways to attain adult status; not all of them disadvantage rural youth. What is more, many of these other aspects of the transition to adulthood have an impact on occupational decisions as well.

Linked transitions

One of the things that becomes obvious once one starts to examine the paths taken by these young people between the ages of 17 and 23 or 24 is that the various parts of the transition to adulthood are integrally linked (Ashton and Lowe, 1991; Thomas, 1993; Wyn and White, 1996). These youth take part in what could be labelled "pluri-transitions". Occupational and educational decisions are, of course, linked; sociologists have been documenting

---

7.   *The respondents were presented with a list of 16 characteristics and asked how well each described their expected job. Possible responses were "very", "somewhat", "not very", "not at all".*

8.   *The relationships between area of residence and the characteristics of the youths' expected job, noted above, are statistically significant at the 0.05 level or more, but the correlations are modest (from 0.07 to 0.13).*

that for decades (Anisef and Axelrod, 1993; Bellamy, 1993; Boyd *et al.,* 1985; Breton, 1972; Coleman, 1984; Denton *et al.*, 1987; Krahn, 1991; Redpath, 1994). Occupational choice influences educational decisions; educational attainment influences job options, and thereby income and status (Davies *et al.,* 1994; Denton *et al.,* 1987; Grayson and Hall, 1992; Hughes and Lowe, 1993; Little, 1995; Looker and McNutt, 1989). These patterns hold in the current data set as well.

Occupational decisions are also linked to marriage and parenting. These youth are at the stage when many of them are thinking about starting families. Those who do marry and/or have children are simultaneously making decisions that impact on their labour force participation and the type of job they are likely to obtain. Other decisions that influence the youths' occupational experiences are the extent to which they are willing and able to move about geographically and the timing of their leaving of the parental home.

This chapter will examine each of these other transitions, in turn, to help identify some of the key rural–urban differences.

Education

The general pattern is that rural youth tend to aspire to — and attain lower levels of education than their urban counterparts.

Table 7.2.   Rural youth aspire to **and** attain a lower level of education

| | Percent of respondents | | | |
| | | Urban | | |
	Rural	Total	Hamilton	Halifax
1989 Educational expectations				
High school or less	19	11	11	10
Non-university post-secondary	29	25	36	13
University	42	43	38	48
Post-graduate studies	11	22	14	29
1994 Educational attainments				
High school or less	23	17	18	16
Non-university post-secondary	34	23	33	14
University	38	54	43	64
Post-graduate studies	5	6	7	6
1994 Finished all education	55	37	36	38

As of 1989, 19 percent of rural youth, compared with 11 percent of urban youth expect no formal education beyond high school (Table 7.2). At first it appears that more urban youth expect to go to university (65 percent versus 53 percent) but these figures mask a difference between the two urban areas. It is

Halifax that has a high proportion of youth (77 percent) who see themselves as university-bound. Hamilton youth are more likely to plan to go to some non-university postsecondary institution.

By the time the youth have moved into their twenties, the rural–urban difference becomes even more pronounced. Rural youth are more likely (55 percent versus 37 percent) to say they have finished all their education; that is, they plan no further formal education or training (see the bottom row of Table 2). Yet they currently have less education than their urban counterparts. Sixty percent of urban youth (70 percent in Halifax and 49 percent in Hamilton) and 43 percent of rural youth have attended university at the undergraduate or post graduate level. At the other end of the educational hierarchy, a quarter of the rural respondents, but only 17 percent of the urban ones have no formal education beyond high school, as of 1994.

There are two quite different possible explanations for the lower educational aspirations and attainments of rural youth. In some areas, in particular, and for some youth (especially the young men) the traditional patterns of work in primary industries provided solid, regular (if seasonal) employment without the requirement of postsecondary education. Such a situation would encourage a belief that higher education was unnecessary.

However, by the late 1980s and the 1990s, when these surveys were undertaken, many of these primary industries had changed (Krahn and Lowe, 1990; Osberg *et al.,* 1995). Involvement in traditional occupations now tends to require a high degree of technical knowledge to deal with sophisticated chemicals and equipment.

College and university degrees have become more and more a requirement. At the same time, technology was replacing the need for a large number of workers. There have been severe cutbacks, particularly in the fisheries with moratoria on various types of fishing. Fewer jobs are available for those without degrees or diplomas.

The problem is, at the same time as educational credentials were becoming more and more of a necessity, unemployment in general was high in rural Nova Scotia. This pattern was exacerbated by cutbacks in government funding, affecting both regular government employment (a mainstay in many areas of Nova Scotia) and government "make work" projects. Many youth become discouraged. As one respondent put it "I got tired of seeing my friends with their degrees in a drawer." The image seems to be that there are so few jobs available, you are not likely to get one, even if you do have a university degree or college certificate. When asked about factors that influenced their decision about whether or not to pursue any postsecondary education, two of the leading negative influences were the cost of that education and the lack of jobs. On the one hand, there is the increasing expectation that one needs advanced education to get a job. On the other hand, if the perception is that there are no jobs in any case, there seems little point in investing time and money into that education (Denton *et al,* 1980; Denton *et al.,* 1987; Gera, 1993; Quixley, 1992). The two processes are intertwined—

and influence both the educational decisions and the occupational outcomes of rural and urban youth.

So, some of the youth may have picked up the message that postsecondary education is unnecessary — one can get a job without it. Others may well see such an investment of time and money in education as having little pay off, because they feel one won't get a job, regardless. Both these attitudes to education would discourage rural youth from pursuing their formal education.

Other transitions

Occupational decisions are also related to marriage and parenting, and there are some interesting rural–urban differences here as well (Table 7.3). Rural youth are more likely to be married by the time of the follow-up survey in 1994 (when they would be 23 or 24 years of age). Nineteen percent of rural youth and 7 percent of urban youth are married by this point. Similar percentages (18 percent versus 8 percent) of rural and urban respondents have children (but these are not necessarily the same individuals who are married).

The teenage respondents were asked in 1989 at what age they thought they would be married and have a child. At that point half of the rural and 40 percent of the urban youth said they would be married by age 24. Twenty eight percent of rural and 16 percent of urban youth expected to have a child by that age. The results presented above indicate that fewer than expected have, in fact, moved into marriage or parenting by 1994. For some youth it is the demands of pursuing high education that have led to a delay in taking on these roles. For others, the lack of jobs curtails these plans. As one respondent put it "if you don't have a job, you can't do anything — buy a home, get married, have children. You are in limbo!"

Table 7.3.   More rural youth expect **and** attain marriage and parenthood

	Percent of respondents	
Youth transitions	Rural	Urban
1989 – expects marriage by age 24	49	40
1994 – married	19	7
1989 – expects child by age 24	28	16
1994 – has a child	18	8
1989 – expects to leave	72	40
Residence history 1989 to 1994:		
Same community	53	81
Same province	36	10
Different province	11	10
1994 – moved out of parental home	71	54
1994 – lives with parent(s)	40	64

Geographic mobility is particularly an issue for rural youth (see also Sharpe and Spain, 1991). Many of them (and their parents) recognize that the youth "have to leave to get a job". While the urban areas contain several post-secondary institutions within their borders and in nearby areas, most rural youth have to go some distance to pursue higher education. Many of these are also youth with particularly strong ties to their home community. Those who "have to leave" are often those who are most reluctant to (see Looker, 1993 for details).

There is a large difference in the percentage of youth in the rural and urban areas who plan to move out of their home community. Seventy two percent of rural teenagers compared with only 40 percent of urban ones say, in 1989, that they plan to leave. If we look at where the youth are living as of 1994, again we see the higher mobility of rural youth. Only about half (53 percent) of the rural youth are in the community where they lived in 1989. Some of these are individuals who left to attend some post-secondary education (or to look for work) who have returned. This figure contrasts with the 81 percent of urban youth who are living in Hamilton or Halifax in both 1989 and 1994. Many of the rural youth (36 percent) stay in the same province. The tendency is to go from smaller centres to larger ones. So, rural youth move to larger towns, and/or to one of the two urban areas: Sydney, or Halifax/Dartmouth. Hamilton youth often go just down the road to Toronto. Hamilton respondents are least likely to move away from the province; only 4 percent have done so by 1994 (compared with 15 percent of Halifax and 11 percent of rural respondents).

There is also a rural–urban difference in the percentage of youth who are still living with their parents as of 1994. This transition is clearly linked to geographic mobility. Those who feel they "have to" leave their home community are also, in most instances, also leaving their parents and family behind. One of the advantages that many of the urban youth and parents report is that the young person can stay at home while attending university or college. Providing free or reduced rate room and board is one of the assets that urban parents can offer their children. Because of the distance one must travel to attend post-secondary institutions, this is less of an option in rural areas. By 1994, 40 percent of the rural youth and fully 64 percent of the urban youth are living with one or both parents. (About 15 percent have left and "come back".)

Living in the parental home provides some advantages in terms of finances and in terms of access to parental support and guidance. On the other hand, it also represents a prolonged dependence on parents. Adult independence is harder to attain when one is living under the parental roof (Boyd and Pryor, 1989; Cote and Allahar, 1994; Jones, 1995).

In sum, this section shows that there are a number of transitions that the youth undertake as they move from their teenage years to their twenties. The data indicate that not only are these various transitions linked to each other, they also tend to take quite different forms for urban as compared to rural youth.

Gender matters

It quickly becomes evident that one cannot talk about the transition to adulthood or the transition from school to work without recognizing the profound effect of gender (Anisef *et al.,* 1980; Davies *et al.,* 1994; Duffy and Pupo, 1992; Gilbert *et al.,* 1993; Guppy and Pedakur, 1989; Hughes and Lowe, 1993; Mandell and Crysdale, 1993; Porter *et al.,* 1979, 1982). For some issues there are strong and persuasive percentage differences that document the gender differences. For others, the numbers mask differences in experiences. Education, work, marriage, parenting, living at home, leaving home are quite different for young women than for young men — even when and if equal percentages of males and females undertake a particular path.

Young women and men have quite different educational experiences, but not necessarily what one might expect. Girls do better in school: they get higher marks; they are more likely to be in the academic, university stream; they are more likely to say they like school. Girls are more positive than boys about their academic ability, their educational experiences and their educational potential. Of all the subgroups identified in the research, the ones that do least well in school are rural males. They report the lowest marks; they are less likely than other sub groups to like school and they have, as a group the lowest educational aspirations (see Looker, 1993 for details).

In 1989, more women than men expect to attend university (Table 7.4). The young men, especially those in rural areas, are more likely to say they expect to have completed their education once they finish high school.

By 1994 the women and men report similar patterns of educational attainment. That is, similar percentages of women and men attend university, similar percentages attend other, non-university type programmes, similar percentages report no formal education beyond high school. The disappearance of the educational gender gap is not due to the men achieving more than they expected. Rather, it reflects the fact that fewer rural women than expected actually attend university. Other gender differences tend to come through in other areas, including the kinds of jobs one is able to access with a particular level of education.

Men and women certainly differ in terms of the age at which they marry and have children. By age 24 more of the women are married (16 percent versus 5 percent of the men), and similar percentages (16 percent and 7 percent), but not the same individuals, have children. Rural women are particularly likely to have made one or other of these two transitions — to marriage or to parenthood. A quarter of rural women and 10 percent of urban women are married and/or have a child. This compares with 7 percent of rural men and 5 percent or less of urban men.

Table 7.4.   Females have higher expectations than males but similar outcomes

Youth expectations and experiences	Total sample			Rural			Urban		
	Male	Female	Both genders	Male	Female	Both genders	Male	Female	Both genders
1989 educational expectations:			Percent of respondents						
High school or less	17	10	13	26	15	19	14	7	11
Non-university post-secondary	29	24	26	33	25	29	27	23	25
University	36	48	43	33	47	42	38	48	43
Post-graduate studies	18	18	18	8	13	11	22	21	22
1994 educational attainments:									
High school or less	21	18	19	22	24	23	20	14	17
Non-university post-secondary	26	27	27	38	32	34	22	24	23
University	48	50	49	35	40	38	53	55	54
Post-graduate studies	5	6	6	6	4	5	5	7	6
1994 – married	5	16	11	7	23	19	2	10	7
1994 – has a child	7	16	12	6	23	18	5	9	8
1994 – moved out of parental home	52	65	60	60	77	71	52	60	54
1994 – lives with parent(s)	62	51	56	49	35	40	68	61	64

Not only are there differences in the number of women and men married and/or with children, marriage and parenting have quite different impacts on the occupational plans of males and females. Marriage and parenting tend to push young men into the labour force if they are not already there. The attitude seems to be that they "would have to" get a job to support their family.

Marriage tends to constrain the mobility of young women, especially in rural areas. This restriction in mobility has an influence on both educational and occupational options. Motherhood tends to push young women (particularly rural women) out of the labour force.

When asked in 1989, over 80 percent of the men plan to work for pay before and after marriage and child bearing (data not shown). Virtually all of the men prefer and expect to work full time. A similar percentage of women plan to work for pay before and after marriage. The picture changes dramatically when one asks about the women's plans to work with preschool aged children. Only 18 percent say they definitely would work, and less than half (45 percent) would even consider it. Less than a third of the women who say they might or would work with preschool aged children plan to work full time; the majority expect to get part time jobs. Even once their children are in school, a third of the women do not plan to work. The qualitative responses make it clear that the women see caring for young children as their responsibility. Even though many of them think child care *should* be shared by father and mother, few of them seem to expect it to be. Rather they say they would "have to" stay home and look after the baby (see Looker, 1993 for details).

Women were more likely than the young men to have moved out of the parental home at some point by the age of twenty-four. Again there is an urban/rural difference that interacts with gender. Seventy-seven percent of rural women compared with 60 percent of rural men have left home one or more times. The corresponding figures for urban youth are 60 percent of the urban women and 52 percent of the urban men. These figures give the percentage of young adults who report having moved out their parents' home *at some stage*. When questioned in 1994, more urban than rural (64 percent versus 40 percent) and more males than females (62 percent versus 51 percent) are *currently* living with their parents.

Gender interacts with rural–urban differences in other ways that can only be touched on here. Rural youth and their parents are more likely to espouse traditional gender roles. This has an impact on both the young men and young women. The men get the message that "you are the breadwinner". When this message is coupled with the reality of youth unemployment in rural Nova Scotia, it is clear that many will fall short of expectations. Rural women, in particular, are expected to be responsible for child care. While this may relieve them of the responsibility of finding a job, it puts them at a disadvantage should they need to compete for jobs in the future.

Overview

Some of our results, particularly those relating to access to jobs, confirm the image of youth in rural Nova Scotia as disadvantaged. However, as the rest of the analysis shows, this is only part of the picture.

The move into the labour force is only one part of the move into adult roles. Other transitions are involved in this complex process as well. This chapter has emphasized the links between these different transitions and the importance of considering their multiple effects.

Other components of this process include educational attainments, with many youth pursuing formal education beyond the high school level. Rural males maintain relatively low levels of educational aspirations and attainments, but the same cannot be said for young rural women. Many of them aspire to further education, although not all of them were able to realize these plans by the time they were 24.

If one looks at the figures for marriage and parenting, by the time the youth were surveyed in 1994, again there are some pronounced rural–urban differences. Rural youth, especially rural women were more likely to be married and more likely to have children by this stage than was true for their urban counterparts.

Marriage and parenting are themselves part of the shift to adult roles. Young people who have taken responsibility for a spouse and/or a child are often accorded adult status on that basis. Marriage propels young men to look for work, but even if they are unable to find it, or are unable to find the job they'd like, having a wife gives them a level of independence from their parents. Motherhood brings new roles and responsibilities for young women. Some may begrudge these new tasks, but there is no question they are more likely to be able to claim adult status once they have a child.

Moving away from the parental home and from one's home community are also symbols of taking on adult responsibility. Those who move out and/or away are less under the control and supervision of parents and other relatives. As the data suggest, rural youth and their parents often resist this pull away from the community. Nevertheless, this step pushes the young person to take on responsibilities they may well have postponed while still under the parental roof, and/or the parental wing.

In sum, there are three points to be emphasized. The *first* is that the shift from adolescence to adulthood is a complex process, with a number of intertwined transitions. The discussion of one such transition, in isolation from the others, runs the risk of distortion. *Second*, as in many aspects of life, gender matters. The nature, meaning and costs associated with the different components of taking on adult roles are quite different for women and for men. *Finally*, we must be wary of the portrayal of rural youth as simply victims. Rather, as these data show, it is important to recognize the different types of resources available to rural and urban youth and the ways in which these different resources impact on youths' transitions to adulthood.

References

Anisef, Paul, Paasche, G. and Turrittin, A.H. (1980) *Is the Die Cast? Educational Achievements and Work Destinations of Ontario Youth*. Toronto: Ontario Ministry of Colleges and Universities.

Anisef, Paul and Axelrod, Paul. (1993) Universities, graduates, and the marketplace: Canadian patterns and prospects. In Anisef, Paul and Axelrod, Paul (eds). *Transitions: Schooling and Employment in Canada*. Toronto: Thompson Educational Publishing, pp. 103-114.

Ashton, David and Lowe, Graham S. (eds). (1991) *Making Their Way: Education, Training and the Labour Market in Canada and Britain*. Toronto: University of Toronto Press.

Bellamy, Lesley Andres. (1993) Life trajectories, action, and negotiating the transition from high school. In Anisef, Paul and Axelrod, Paul (eds). *Transitions: Schooling and Employment in Canada*. Toronto: Thompson Educational Publishing, pp. 137-157.

Boyd, Monica and Pryor, Edward T. (1989) Young adults living in their parents' home. *Canadian Social Trends* (Summer), pp. 17-20.

Boyd, Monica, Goyder, J., Jones, F., Pineo, P.C., McRoberts, H. and Porter, J. (1985) *Ascription and Achievement: Studies in mobility and status attainment in Canada.* Ottawa: Carleton University Press.

Breton, Raymond. (1972) *Social and Academic Factors in the Career Decisions of Canadian Youth.* Ottawa: Department of Manpower and Immigration.

Coleman, James S. (1984) The transition from school to work. *Research in Social Stratification and Mobility* Vol.3, pp. 27-59.

Cote, James E. and Allahar, Anton L. (1994) *Generation on Hold: Coming of Age in the Late Twentieth Century.* Toronto: Stoddart.

Davies, Scott, Mosher, C. and O'Grady, B. (1994) Trends in labour market outcomes of Canadian post-secondary graduates, 1978-1988. In Erwin, Lorna and MacLennan, David (eds). *Sociology of Education in Canada: Critical Perspectives on Theory, Research and Practice.* Toronto: Copp Clark Longman, pp. 352-369.

Denton, F.T., Robb, A.L. and Spencer, B.G. (1980) *Unemployment and Labour Force Behaviour of Young People: Evidence from Canada and Ontario.* Toronto: University of Toronto Press.

Denton, M.A., Davis, C.K., Hayward, L. and Hunter, A.A. (1987) *Employment Survey of 1985 Graduates of Ontario Universities: Report of Major Findings.* Toronto: Ontario Ministry of Colleges and Universities.

Duffy, Ann and Pupo, Norene. (1992) *Part-time Paradox: Connecting Family, Gender, Work and Family.* Toronto: McClelland & Stewart.

Gera S. (ed.) (1993) *Canadian Unemployment: Lessons From the 80s and Challenges for the 90s.* Ottawa: Economic Council of Canada.

Gilbert, Sid, Barr, L., Clark, W., Blue, M. and Sunter, D. (1993) *Leaving School: Results from a National Survey Comparing School Leavers and High School Graduates 18 to 20 Years of Age.* Ottawa: Minister of Supply and Services.

Grayson, J. Paul and Hall, Michael H. (1992) *Transitions from School: Ontario's Record.* Toronto: Institute for Social Research, York University.

Guppy, Neil and Pendakur, Krishna. (1989) The effects of gender and parental education on participation within post-secondary education in the 1970s and 1980s. *Canadian Journal of Higher Education* Vol. 19, No. 1, pp. 49-62.

Hughes, Karen and Lowe, Graham S. (1993) Unequal returns: gender differences in initial employment among university graduates. *Canadian Journal of Higher Education* Vol. 23, No. 1, pp. 37-55.

Jones, Gill. (1995) *Leaving Home.* Buckingham: Open University Press.

Krahn, Harvey. (1991) The school to work transition in Canada: new risks and uncertainties. In Heinz, W.R. (ed.). *The Life Course and Social Change: Comparative Perspectives.* Weinheim: Deutscher Studien Verlag.

Krahn, Harvey and Lowe, Graham S. (1990) *Young workers in the service economy.* Ottawa: Economic Council of Canada Working Paper No. 14.

Lawrence, Geofrey and Williams, C. (1990) The dynamics of decline. In Cullen, T., Dunn, P. and Lawrence, G. (eds). *Rural Health and Welfare in Australia.* Wagga Wagga: Centre for Rural Social Research.

Little, Don. (1995) Earnings and labour force status of 1990 graduates. *Education Quarterly Review* Vol. 2, No. 3, pp. 10-20.

Looker, E. Dianne. (1977) *The role of value elements in the intergenerational transmission of social status.* Unpublished Ph.D. dissertation, McMaster University.

Looker, E. Dianne. (1993) Interconnected transitions and their costs: gender and urban/ rural differences in the transitions to work. In Anisef, Paul and Axelrod, Paul (eds). *Transitions: Schooling and Employment in Canada.* Toronto: Thompson Educational Publishing.

Looker, E. Dianne, Denton, M. and Davis, C. (1989) Bridging the gap: Incorporating qualitative data into quantitative analyses. *Social Science Research* Vol. 18, No. 4, pp. 313-331.

Looker, E. Dianne and McNutt, K. (1989) The effect of occupational expectations on the educational attainments of males and females. *Canadian Journal of Education* (Spring), pp. 352-367.

Looker, E. Dianne and Pineo, P.C. (1983) Social psychological variables and their relevance to the status attainment of teenagers. *American Journal of Sociology* Vol. 88, No. 6, pp. 1195-1219.

Mandell, Nancy and Crysdale, Stewart. (1993) Gender tracks: male-female perceptions of home-school-work transitions. In Anisef, Paul and Axelrod, Paul (eds). *Transitions: Schooling and Employment in Canada.* Toronto: Thompson Educational Publishing, pp. 21-41.

Mason, Greg (ed.). (1985) *Transitions to Work.* Winnipeg: Institute for Social and Economic Research, University of Manitoba.

Osberg, Lars, Wein, Fred and Grude, Ian. (1995) *Vanishing Jobs: Canada's Changing Workplace.* Toronto: Lorimer.

Pallas, Aaron M. (1993) Schooling in the course of human lives: the social context of education and the transition to adulthood in industrial society. *Review of Educational Research* Vol. 63, No. 4, pp. 409-447.

Porter, Marion R., Porter, J. and Blishen, B.R. (1979) *Does Money Matter? Prospects for Higher Education in Ontario.* Toronto: Macmillan.

Porter, John, Porter, M. and Blishen, B.R. (1982) *Stations and Callings: Making it through the School System.* Toronto: Methuen.

Quixley, Sue. (1992) *Living, Learning and Working: The experiences of young people in rural and remote communities in Australia.* Canberra: National Youth Coalition for Housing.

Redpath, Lindsay. (1994) Education job mismatch among Canadian university graduates: implications for employers and educators. *Canadian Journal of Higher Education* Vol. 24, No. 2, pp. 89-114.

Sharpe, Dennis B. and Spain, William H. (1991) *The Class of '89: Initial Survey of Level III (Grade 12) High School Students.* St. John's: Centre for Educational Research and Development, Memorial University.

Thomas, Alan M. (1993) Transitions: from school to work and back: a new paradigm. In Anisef, Paul and Axelrod, Paul (eds). *Transitions: Schooling and Employment in Canada.* Toronto: Thompson Educational Publishing, pp. 117-127.

Wyn, Johanna and White, Rob. (1996) *Rethinking Youth.* Sydney: Allen and Unwin.

Chapter eight:

Youth in the Periphery: Education, Jobs and a Place to Live

Geir Inge Orderud
Norwegian Institute for Urban and Regional Research, Olso, Norway

Abstract

There is a strong relationship between preferred location of future study and preferred place to live. Potential agricultural students have the strongest preference to settle within their region, followed by medicine students. Social science students show the strongest preference for settling in a big city while tourism, public service and construction students have less specific preferences for a place to settle.

*Plans for future education, the plans for future employment **and** plans for a future place to live are laid down when youth at age 16 make their choice of programme of study in secondary school. It is not generally true that post-secondary education is the factor causing students to educate themselves away from jobs within their region — rather, it appears the programme of study in secondary school plays a crucial role.*

Introduction

Post-war economic development has given rise to fundamental changes in the relationship between town and country, centre and periphery. In general, a *time-space compression* has provided a considerable increase in the mobility of people and likewise an increase in their communication with other people around the world. Looking at the *industrial structure*, agriculture has lost its importance, even in rural areas, and a more mixed industrial structure has emerged, although some individual communities still are strongly dependent on single industries, such as agriculture, manufacturing, tourism or public services. *Educationally*, formal education has grown and almost everyone graduates from secondary school (about 80 percent of youth aged 16 to 19 years) and the willingness to study at colleges and universities has risen sharply in recent years. *Demographically*, decreasing fertility rates in the countryside are contributing to a breakdown in the traditional way to compensate for migration to the city. An ageing population structure is the result in many municipalities in the countryside. We still have a distorted gender balance as more girls migrate than boys. On the other had, the *settlement pattern* has been relatively stable, although the situation is growing more vulnerable in many peripheral communities.

Overall the erosion of the social structure in parts of the countryside has increased and thus the recruitment of younger families has gained greater importance. Obviously, preferences for education, jobs and dwellings play a crucial role in this respect. The type of options available **and** the choices made by youth will be decisive. This paper focuses on youth and their plans for the future. What are the attitudes towards eduction, jobs and a place to live among youth in the countryside? Who most strongly favours a future in one's own district? And who wants to migrate?

To answer these questions, I surveyed youth in the secondary school in Osterdalen, a peripheral region in the interior of southern Norway, north of Oslo (Figure 8.1). The survey was conducted in 1992. In total, 1,100 questionnaires were sent out covering about half the total number of students in the regions and 817 (75 percent) were returned. The sample includes students in the age span of 16 to 50 years, but most of them are 16 to 19 years of age. In this chapter I have selected the 16 to 24 year group. The same survey was conducted in Northern Norway and in Oslo but results from these two areas are not reported in this chapter.

Major findings

Although secondary school attendance is optional, about 80 percent of the youth aged 16 to 19 years graduate and among graduates, about 80 percent want to continue their education. However, there are differences between genders and among students in different programmes of study. The programmes of study are described in Appendix A.

A higher share of girls than boys want to continue their education (84 percent versus 75 percent) (Table 8.1). The highest share wanting more education are presently in the comprehensive and commercial programmes of study (over 90 percent for both and for both girls and boys) (Table 8.1). In the commercial programme of study, the share is highest among the boys. The lowest share wanting more education is found among boys in the household programme, not even reaching the 50 percent mark, while 58 percent of the girls in the same programme of study say they have plans for further studies. The willingness to study beyond secondary school is also at the same level among boys in the manufacturing programme. Generally, the plans for more education are lower in the practical oriented programmes of study than in the more theoretical ones.

Figure 8.1.   The area of study, counties and big cities in Norway

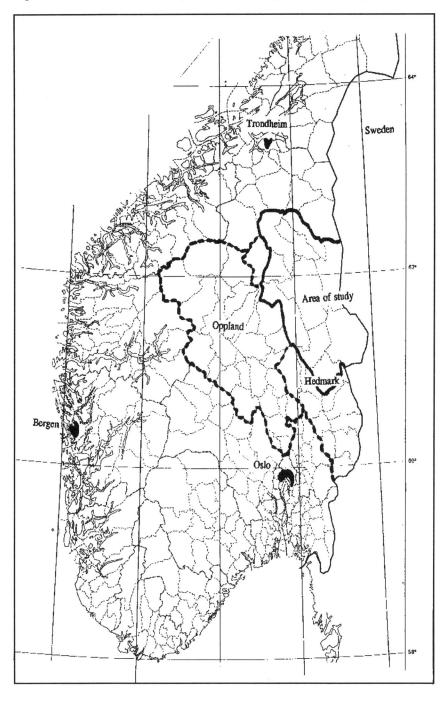

Table 8.1.   Over 90 percent of students in comprehensive and commercial programmes of study prefer further education

	Preferences for further education					
	Girls			Boys		
Programme of study	More	Not more	Total	More	Not more	Total
	Percent distribution					
Comprehensive	97	3	100	94	6	100
Commercial	90	10	100	95	5	100
Manufacturing	--	--	--	56	44	100
Household	59	41	100	48	52	100
Social	74	26	100	--	--	--
Agriculture	--	--	--	69	31	100

Students not wanting more education

The students wanting to leave the school system naturally want to find paid work and in order to describe their preferences we use a fivefold industrial categorization: agriculture; manufacturing/construction; private services; public services; and miscellaneous. As expected, boys and girls make different choices. Nearly half the girls want a job in the public sector, while 35 percent have a job in the private service sector in mind (Table 8.2). Among the boys, 30 percent have agriculture as their first choice, while 34 percent are considering a future in the manufacturing/construction sector. Only 1 percent of the boys want to go into the public sector.

Table 8.2.   Students have a preferred sector of work that highly correlates with their programme of study

	Preferred sector of work (for students not wanting more education)					
Gender	Agriculture	Manu-facturing/construction	Private services	Public services	Miscel-laneous	Total
	Percent distribution					
Girls	5	2	35	45	14	100
Boys	30	34	20	1	14	100
Programme of study						
Comprehensive	--	--	--	--	--	--
Commercial	--	--	--	--	--	--
Manufacturing	12	62	8	--	18	100
Household	--	--	66	10	24	100
Social	--	4	--	93	4	100
Agriculture	94	6	--	--	--	100
Total	**18**	**19**	**27**	**21**	**14**	**100**

Within each programme of study there are students who want to end their education career after secondary school but in the comprehensive and commercial programmes of study, there are not enough students for further analysis. Students in each programme of study are headed for employment in different industrial sectors: two-thirds of the students in the manufacturing programme of study want to get a manufacturing or construction job, while 12 percent of them prefer a job in agriculture; two-thirds of the students in the household programme have a job in the private service sector in mind; nine out of ten students in the social programme want to have a public service job; while nine out of ten in the agricultural programme are heading for the agricultural sector.

In conclusion, the choice of programme of study corresponds well with the industrial sector where the student wants to work after secondary school. Of course, these figures do not tell whether the student really preferred this choice from the beginning or whether they have been socialized into this choice of career during their years in school. Additionally, the biased gender balance of students in different programmes study means there is a corresponding biased gender balance in preference of employment: the boys prefer the agricultural sector and the girls dominate the public sector (e.g. nursing).

To examine preferences for the place to live, I make use of six categories: the local district, within the region (counties of Hedmark and Oppland); a big city (Oslo, Bergen or Trondheim); the rest of Norway; abroad; or anywhere. We find differences between the genders and programmes of study in relation to the question of where the student prefers to live.

Overall, two-thirds of the boys express a desire to stay in their local district while well under half of the girls have this preference (Table 8.3). On the other hand a quarter of the girls tell us they want to stay within the region, while one in ten of the boys have this preference. The difference between boys and girls thus shrinks to ten percentage points when we combine "local district" and "within region". These areas are in the periphery, but, in a Norwegian setting, these areas include some medium sized towns. For both sexes, we find that only about 4 percent are in favour of living in big cities, while more girls than boys prefer to settle abroad, 6 percent and 2 percent respectively.

Especially the boys in the manufacturing programme of study expressed preferences for staying in their local district (three-quarters of them). In the other programmes of study, about half of the students have the same preference. Among the programmes of study, a relatively high share of students in the agricultural programme and the household programme prefer to live within the region (33 percent and 29 percent respectively). This means that nearly nine out of ten in the agricultural programme want to live in or close to the area where they have grown up, compared with seven or eight out of ten in the other programmes of study. Moreover, none of the students in the agricultural programme and the social programme have a big city in Norway as their first choice, and furthermore, nobody in the agricultural programme and the manufacturing programme wants to settle abroad.

Table 8.3.   More boys than girls prefer to live in their local district

| Gender | Preferred location to live (for students not wanting more education) | | | | | | |
	Local district	Within region	Big city	Rest of Norway	Abroad	Anywhere	Total
	Percent distribution						
Girls	43	25	4	9	6	12	100
Boys	67	11	4	1	2	15	100
Programme of study							
Comprehensive	--	--	--	--	--	--	--
Commercial	--	--	--	--	--	--	--
Manufacturing	73	7	2	4	--	13	100
Household	45	29	3	5	5	13	100
Social	54	18	--	7	4	18	100
Agriculture	56	33	--	6	--	6	100
Total	**56**	**17**	**4**	**5**	**4**	**13**	**100**

Table 8.4.   For each preferred sector of employment (except public services), over half prefer to work in their local district

| Preferred sector of employment | Preferred location to live (for students not wanting more education) | | | | | | |
	Local district	Within region	Big city	Rest of Norway	Abroad	Anywhere	Total
	Percent distribution						
Agriculture	62	27	--	4	--	8	100
Manufacturing/ construction	78	11	--	4	--	7	100
Private services	58	21	8	--	8	5	100
Public services	43	20	3	10	3	20	100
Miscellaneous	50	10	5	--	5	30	100
Total	**58**	**18**	**4**	**4**	**4**	**13**	**100**

This pattern is confirmed and strengthened when the preferred industry of employment is cross-tabulated with the preferred place to settle. Nearly two-thirds of the students wanting a job within the agricultural sector also want to live in their local district, while another 27 percent prefer to live within their region (Table 8.4). Thus, nine out of ten prefer to live in or close to the areas where they have grown up. We find the same proportion among students wanting a job in the manufacturing and construction industries, but here the components are 78 percent for the local district and 11 percent for within the region. Nobody wanting a job within these industries prefers living in big cities or abroad. In private services eight out of ten and in public services six out of ten students prefer to live in or close to the areas where they have grown up.

Students wanting more education

For students wanting more education, we need also consider the impact of preferred location of further study **and** the preferred programme for future study upon the preferred location to live. Compared with those not wanting more education, the students planning to continue their education have a lower expressed preference to stay in their local district; a little over half of the students compared with three-quarters of the students not planning further education.

However, there are large differences depending upon the programme of study at secondary school. Only four out of ten in the comprehensive programme want to remain in their local district or within their region, while nine out of ten in the agricultural programme express the same opinion (Table 8.5). The figures for the agricultural programme of study reveal that there is no difference in this respect between students wanting to go out to work after secondary school and the students who want to study agriculture further. Among the other programmes of study, we find that students in commercial programmes have the lowest preference for living in or close to the area where they have grown up (four out of ten) while six out of ten is the proportion for the others. Compared with the students not wanting more education, potential students are more likely to prefer other places to live, but the difference is only about one percentage point for settling abroad. Additionally, we find that students in the comprehensive and commercial programmes are more likely to be planning a future in the big cities in Norway, the rest of Norway or abroad.

To determine the role of planned subjects for further study, we have grouped students into nine categories: agriculture; construction; mathematics/sciences; medicine (doctors and nurses); humanities; social sciences; tourism; public services; and miscellaneous. Not surprisingly, we find differences between the genders: more than a third of the girls want to study medicine (mostly nursing) compared with only 3 percent among the boys (Table 8.6). On the other hand, more boys than girls have mathematics/sciences and agricultural subjects in mind (24 versus 5 and 18 versus 3 percent, respectively).

Table 8.5.   For students wanting to continue their education, the local district is the preferred location to live, regardless of the programme of study

Programme of study	Preferred location to live (for students wanting more education)						
	Local district	Within region	Big city	Rest of Norway	Abroad	Anywhere	Total
	Percent distribution						
Comprehensive	32	11	15	18	7	18	100
Commercial	39	12	10	12	7	20	100
Manufacturing	46	15	8	7	--	24	100
Household	50	9	9	11	2	20	100
Social	40	19	9	6	5	20	100
Agriculture	79	7	--	9	2	2	100
Total	**41**	**12**	**11**	**13**	**5**	**18**	**100**

Table 8.6.   one-thirds of the girls prefer medicine/nursing
a quarter of the boys prefer mathematics/sciences

Gender	Preferred subject for further study (for students wanting more education)									
	Agriculture	Construction	Math./ sciences	Medicine	Humanities	Social sciences	Tourism	Public services	Miscellaneous	Total
	Percent distribution									
Girls	3	6	4	34	15	18	11	4	3	100
Boys	18	8	24	3	16	14	4	8	5	100
Both Genders	**9**	**7**	**13**	**21**	**16**	**16**	**8**	**6**	**4**	**100**

Students in the comprehensive programme want to study medicine, humanities and social sciences (20 percent for each) (Table 8.7). Students in the commercial programme prefer social science and tourism (37 and 22 percent respectively). Mathematics/sciences is the first choice to half of the students in the manufacturing programme, while 28 percent of them are thinking of construction. Three subjects dominate among students in the household programme: medicine with 32 percent; humanities with 23 percent; and tourism with 21 percent. Finally, two-thirds of the students in the social programme of study want to study medicine, while eight of ten in the agricultural programme expect to continue studying agriculture.

Therefore, the main impression is that students as a rule want to continue their educational career on subjects associated with their programme of study at the secondary school. This suggests plans for the future, both regarding type of employment and where they will live, are determined at the age of 16.

Students in the manufacturing, social and agricultural programmes are more likely to want to study within their region. Students in the comprehensive programme, on the other hand, express relatively high preferences for going to a big city or abroad. We also find that boys to a greater degree than girls want to study within their region (44 versus 34 percent) while girls more than boys prefer big cities (28 versus 15 percent) (Table 8.8). The boys, on the other hand, are more willing to study abroad (14 versus 7 percent).

Table 8.7. Most students prefer a subject of future study that is consistent with their present programme of study

	Preferred subject for further study (for students wanting more education)								
Agri-culture	Cons-truction	Math./ sciences	Medi-cine	Huma-nities	Social sciences	Tou-rism	Public services	Miscel-laneous	Total
Programme of study			Percent distribution						
Compre-hensive	4	2	12	21	24	20	5	10	3	100
Commercial	2	2	10	4	14	37	22	5	4	100
Manufactu-ring	9	28	51	2	--	--	--	7	4	100
Household	--	2	--	32	23	7	20	--	16	100
Social	3	20	--	67	6	1	3	--	1	100
Agriculture	84	5	7	--	2	--	--	--	2	100

Table 8.8. Students in the comprehensive programme of study are most likely to prefer to study in a big city

	Preferred location to study (for students wanting more education)					
Gender	Within region	Big city	Rest of Norway	Abroad	Anywhere	Total
	Percent distribution					
Girls	34	28	14	7	17	100
Boys	44	15	12	14	14	100
Programme of study						
Comprehensive	25	34	12	14	15	100
Commercial	35	26	10	11	18	100
Manufacturing	52	11	20	4	13	100
Household	44	4	13	9	30	100
Social	54	10	19	1	15	100
Agriculture	66	5	15	10	5	100
Total	**38**	**23**	**13**	**10**	**16**	**100**

It is the potential agricultural and medicine students who prefer studying within their region (eight and five out of ten, respectively) (Table 8.9). The former is dominated by boys while girls dominate the second. Thus, a segment among the girls also has relatively high preferences for studying in the home region, largely, the nursing segment. Four out of ten of the potential students in the social sciences prefer big cities, but also students in mathematics/sciences, humanities and tourism reveal relatively strong preferences for big cities (a quarter of them). Students in the same four subjects to a greater degree than other subjects also want to study abroad. The students planning for a future in the public services (e.g. defence or police) are the ones who care less about where to study.

Table 8.9.   Only among students preferring future study in agriculture and medicine/nursing do we find over half who prefer to study within their region

Subject of future study	Preferred location to study (for students wanting more education)					
	Within region	Big city	Rest of Norway	Abroad	Anywhere	Total
	Percent distribution					
Agriculture	69	8	14	6	4	100
Construction	38	13	26	8	15	100
Mathematics/sciences	36	25	16	10	13	100
Medicine/nursing	50	17	14	2	16	100
Humanities	33	28	9	15	14	100
Social sciences	25	39	8	16	11	100
Tourism	28	26	13	17	17	100
Public services	21	15	21	6	38	100
Miscellaneous	26	17	9	9	39	100
Total	**39**	**23**	**13**	**10**	**16**	**100**

Knowing the tight relation between the agricultural programme of study and the plan to study agriculture, it is no surprise that students planning to study agriculture have the strongest preference for living in their local district. Eight out of ten of them reveal such preferences, while the same opinion is expressed by three or four out of ten in the other subjects (Table 8.10). When also including those preferring to live within their region, students preferring to study medicine come closest with six out of ten. As noted above, medicine is dominated by girls expressing relatively strong feelings for living within their region. It is the potential students in the social sciences who have the strongest preferences for living in big cities (18 percent). A relatively greater share of the students in the social sciences also want to settle abroad. Another interesting fact is that 30 percent of potential students in tourism, public services and construction say they would settle anywhere they could get a job.

For both girls and boys, those who prefer to study within their region also want to live within their region, those preferring to study in a big city also want to live in a big city and likewise for the rest of Norway, abroad and the willingness to study and to live anywhere (Table 8.11). The relationship between preferred place of study and preferred place to live is stronger for boys than girls for within their region, a big city and the rest of Norway but the relationship is stronger for girls for living abroad or living anywhere. Except for a big city, boys preferring to study in each alternative location reveal a stronger preference for living in their local district than the girls.

Table 8.10. Four areas of future study (social science, tourism, public services, miscellaneous) have more than half of the students preferring to live outside the local district or region

Preferred subject of future study	Local district	Within region	Big city	Rest of Norway	Abroad	Anywhere	Total

Preferred subject of future study	Local district	Within region	Big city	Rest of Norway	Abroad	Anywhere	Total
				Percent distribution			
Agriculture	80	6	--	9	--	6	100
Construction	45	8	10	2	8	28	100
Mathematics/sciences	35	17	12	12	4	19	100
Medicine/nursing	45	18	9	11	2	15	100
Humanities	39	10	12	16	6	17	100
Social sciences	30	13	16	18	10	13	100
Tourism	33	13	7	9	4	33	100
Public services	32	3	12	18	3	32	100
Miscellaneous	17	9	22	17	13	22	100
Total	**41**	**12**	**11**	**13**	**5**	**18**	**100**

Table 8.11. Students preferring to study within their region or in the rest of Norway, prefer to live in their local district

Preferred location to study	Local district	Within region	Big city	Rest of Norway	Abroad	Anywhere	Total
Girls				Percent distribution			
Within region	53	22	1	12	--	12	100
Big city	27	10	28	21	3	11	100
Rest of Norway	32	8	13	23	4	19	100
Abroad	14	9	23	9	41	4	100
Anywhere	30	4	2	4	5	55	100
Boys							
Within region	66	20	3	2	1	8	100
Big city	25	6	42	14	3	11	100
Rest of Norway	45	3	3	38	--	10	100
Abroad	24	9	12	6	27	21	100
Anywhere	33	6	3	3	6	48	100

A job in the public sector is preferred by 44 percent of the potential students, while the other industrial categories are the first choice for 6 to 11 percent of the students (Table 8.12). However, there are significant differences between the girls and the boys. The strong preference for the public sector is to a greater degree due to the girls — 58 percent are planning a job in the public sector, while the same is true for 25 percent among the boys. The boys, on the other hand, more than the girls, want to get a job in the agriculture sector (19 versus 4 percent) and the manufacturing and construction sector (20 versus 1 percent).

Table 8.12.   44 percent of potential students prefer employment in the public sector

Gender	Agri-culture	Manufactu-ring/con-struction	Private services	Banking/consul-tancy	Media	Public services	Miscel-laneous	Total
	Preferred industrial sector of job							
	Percent distribution							
Girls	4	1	11	10	9	58	6	100
Boys	19	20	12	13	6	25	7	100
Both genders	10	9	11	11	8	44	6	100

Students in the social, comprehensive and household programmes contribute most to the high share wanting a job in the public sector (82, 55 and 48 percent, respectively) (Table 8.13). In the commercial programme, 41 percent prefer a job in banking and consultancy while 60 percent in the manufacturing programme have a job in manufacturing and construction in mind. Half the students in the household programme want a job in the public sector and the other half want a job in private services. Finally, nine out of ten in the agricultural programme are planning a job in agriculture.

Table 8.13.   Students in comprehensive, household and social programmes of study prefer public sector employment

Present programme of study	Agri-culture	Manufactu-ring/con-struction	Private services	Banking/consul-tancy	Media	Public services	Miscel-laneous	Total
	Preferred industrial sector of job							
	Percent distribution							
Comprehensive	5	6	4	6	15	54	10	100
Commercial	2	2	22	41	4	24	6	100
Manufacturing	11	60	11	2	--	16	--	100
Household	--	--	52	--	--	48	--	100
Social	1	--	3	4	4	82	7	100
Agriculture	90	5	--	--	--	2	2	100

As we saw of students not planning to continue their education, students who are planning further education have a high association between their preferred subject of study and their preferred industrial sector of employment. Not surprisingly, nine out of ten potential agricultural subjects want a job in agriculture (Table 8.14). A little more than 40 percent of students planning courses in mathematics/sciences are thinking of a job in manufacturing and construction while 15 to 20 percent of them give priority to the public sector. Nearly all potential students in medicine want a job in the public sector, due to the strong public engagement in the health sector. In the humanities, we find that six out of ten are planning for a job in the public sector which includes teaching employment. Half of the potential students in the social sciences look forward to a career in banking and consultancy while 27 and 20 percent are heading for a job in the media and the public sector. Six out of ten potential tourism students have a job in private services in mind while nearly nine out of ten planning an education in public services also want a job in this sector (mostly military defence and police).

Table 8.14. Preferred industrial sector of employment is closely associated with the preferred subject of future study

	Agri-culture	Manufactu-ring/con-struction	Private services	Banking/consul-tancy	Media	Public services	Miscel-laneous	Total
				Preferred industrial sector of job				
Preferred subject of future study				Percent distribution				
Agriculture	92	2	--	--	--	4	2	100
Construction	5	41	10	5	5	15	18	100
Mathematics/sciences	6	45	9	13	2	19	6	100
Medicine/nursing	1	1	--	--	--	98	--	100
Humanities	1	1	13	2	14	59	9	100
Social sciences	--	--	4	49	27	19	--	100
Tourism	2	--	60	9	4	11	13	100
Public services	3	--	--	6	--	88	3	100
Miscellaneous	--	4	48	9	9	4	26	100

For students planning to work in the agricultural sector, eight out of ten plan to settle in their local district and this increases to nine out of ten when those preferring to live within their region is included (Table 8.15). Among the other preferred industrial sectors of employment, the shares vary from three to five out ten preferring to settle in their local district or within their region. Jobs in the media sector would provide the lowest share (three out of ten) of students wanting to settle in or near the area where they grew up — in fact, media students have the strongest preference for settling in a big city (23 percent) or abroad (14 percent).

Table 8.15. The local district is the preferred location to live, regardless of preferred industrial sector

	Local district	Within region	Big city	Rest of Norway	Abroad	Any-where	Total
	Preferred location to live (for students wanting more education)						
Industrial sector of employment				Percent distribution			
Agriculture	81	7	--	9	--	3	100
Manufacturing/construction	32	12	12	14	6	24	100
Private services	39	13	10	8	5	27	100
Banking/consultancy	44	10	16	13	6	11	100
Media	21	12	23	12	14	19	100
Public services	39	14	10	15	3	19	100
Miscellaneous	21	9	12	9	21	27	100

Summary and concluding remarks

More girls than boys want to continue their educational career beyond secondary school. The willingness to continue their studies is high for students in the comprehensive and commercial programmes of study and relatively low in the household and manufacturing programmes of study.

Students in different programmes of study at secondary school have varying subjects in mind for their further educational career but, as a rule, they prefer subjects corresponding with their programme of study at secondary school.

Students in manufacturing, social and household programmes of study reveal the strongest preference for studying within their region while students in the comprehensive and commercial programmes show relatively strong preferences for studying in a big city or abroad. More boys than girls want to study within their region while girls, to a greater degree, are heading to a big city.

Students planning to continue their education in agriculture have the strongest preference for studying within their region, followed by students in medicine (largely nursing). Potential students in the social sciences have the strongest preference for studying in a big city while students planning to enter internal public service education care less about where to study.

There is a strong relationship between preferred location of future study and preferred place to live. Potential agricultural students have the strongest preference to settle within their region, followed by medicine students. Social science students show the strongest preference for settling in a big city while tourism, public service and construction students have less specific preferences for a place to settle.

In summary, it appears that the plans for future education, the plans for future employment **and** plans for a future place to live are laid down when youth at age 16 make their choice of programme of study in secondary school. What about the more or less accepted wisdom that youth are educating themselves away from the periphery or the countryside and ending up in cities? It is not generally true that post-secondary education is the factor causing students to educate themselves away from jobs within their region — rather, it appears the programme of study in secondary school plays a crucial role.

The segment most disposed to continue to live within their region are: boys; those not wanting to continue their education; being a student in the manufacturing and agricultural programme; and preference for a job in agriculture, manufacturing or construction.

However, this analysis is based on preference which may not correspond with actual behaviour. We know that a certain share of youth expressing a wish to find a home within their region will end up in a city. Cohort analyses in regions like Osterdalen indicate that half the boys of age 15 years tend to migrate by age 35 compared with 60 percent of the girls. Higher educational levels increase the tendency to migrate where two-thirds of male university graduates tending to migrate compared with four out of ten individuals who do not continue their education past secondary school. For girls, the proportions are nine out of ten and six out of ten, respectively. Thus, some students are evidently educating themselves away from opportunities in their local district.

Appendix A: Description of programmes of study

The **comprehensive** programme of study comprises students not qualifying for a specific occupation but who are preparing for further study. They may specialize in certain subjects (e.g. mathematics, physics, biology, foreign languages) and this specialization might restrict their choices for further education.

The **commercial** programme of study comprises students qualifying for a lower level job in business plus students preparing for further study in economics and business related subjects.

The **manufacturing** programme of study comprises students qualifying for a job in manufacturing and craft industries such as electronics, building construction, transportation, engine mechanics, etc.

The **household** programme of study comprises students qualifying for a job as a cook, waiter or waitress, household economics, etc.

The **social** programme of study consists of students in artistic subjects and social and health subjects. Many end up in the health sector.

The **agricultural** programme of study prepares students for jobs in farming and forestry.

Chapter nine:

De-mythologizing Rural Youth Exodus

David Hajesz and Shirley P. Dawe
*CoastWood Community and Economic Development, Inc. Ottawa,
Ontario, Canada*

Abstract

*Growing up in a rural community is often perceived as something to be overcome.
Young people tend to base career choices on these perceptions. Each spring
signals the exodus of rural high school graduation classes in search of the brighter
lights of big cities.*

*In rural Newfoundland, there is no exodus. Rural youth love their communities
and want to stay. However, very few state they will "probably never leave".
Rural youth are excited about creating opportunities for entrepreneurship and
they recognize the contribution of entrepreneurship to community development.*

*Youth in remote communities must anticipate large gains from moving to
overcome the high cost of moving and the high cost of return visits. Partly because
of low access or experience in larger communities, remote rural youth also have
a greater fear of living in a larger centre.*

Introduction

Growing up in rural Canada is often perceived as a hardship or something to be
overcome in terms of economic opportunities, social interaction and cultural
exposure. Young people are likely to make career and location decisions based
on these perceptions. As a result, each spring high school graduation in rural
communities across Canada is a precursor to a mass exodus of youth in search of
higher education, better job opportunities and the promise of excitement offered
by the brighter lights of big cities. Sustainable rural community development
must address this exodus and the attitudes or socialization that underlie such
decisions.

This chapter reports the surprising results of some primary research conducted on youth in rural Newfoundland and Labrador in October, 1994. In brief:

1. There is no exodus. Youth are not leaving their communities en masse.
2. Youth love their rural communities. At least for the youth in the small communities in this particular province, home is the place to be and the place to stay.
3. Youth are excited about entrepreneurship; they want to create their own opportunities in their own communities.

These unexpected results have significant policy and programme implications for rural community economic development and the roles for youth.

Research challenge

Rural stay-in-place decisions are often associated with lack of initiative or low achievement. Consequently, rural youth are socialized to seek opportunities elsewhere and are socialized against recognising or developing entrepreneurial skills and local opportunities.

Therefore, the cycle may be described as:

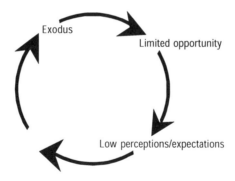

Methodology

This chapter is based on data from a study of 347 youth between the ages of 15 and 24 in ten communities in the fall of 1994. The primary research sites were seven small coastal communities in southern Labrador — Forteau, St. Lewis, Mary's Harbour, Cartwright, Charlottetown, Port Hope Simpson and Black Tickle — and two communities on the island of Newfoundland — Burgeo and Buchans. All the communities are coastal, fishing-dependent except for Buchans which is a former mining community in the interior of the island. The tenth site was Corner Brook, a small city and the second largest community in the province, which was intended to serve as a limited control sample. Corner Brook represents a more urban population and is the community that most of the first two groups are referring to when they talk of "larger places" or "the city". The data have been collated into three subsets: Labrador Sites (Black Tickle, Cartwright, Charlottetown, Forteau, Mary's Harbour, Port Hope Simpson, and St. Lewis); Newfoundland Sites (Buchans and Burgeo); and Corner Brook. A complete description of the methodology is provided in Appendix A.

Research sites: Newfoundland and Labrador

The main reasons for selecting Newfoundland and Labrador for this research were its demographics and geographics. There are few areas in Canada more rural and remote than Newfoundland and Labrador. Outside the seven largest centres, 50 percent of the province's population live in communities with fewer than 1,000 people and 25 percent live in communities of fewer than 500 people. Due to the coastal settlement pattern, communities are insular; many communities are only accessible by sea or by air.

The secondary reason for selecting this province was the increased concerns of youth exodus in the wake of the cod fishery moratorium (Valpy, 1995).

An historically economic dependent peripheral region, this predominantly rural province has been further challenged by the recent collapse of the cod fish industry which has directly resulted in more than 30,000 displaced workers. While this environmental collapse has already had drastic economic, social and cultural effects, the full extent of the devastation for the people of Newfoundland and Labrador is yet to be realized.

This crisis will have significant impacts on the young people of Newfoundland and Labrador. Attitudes, perceptions and reactions are most greatly influenced by a person's "microsystem"; the everyday roles, activities and face-to-face interactions in which a person is involved in (Bronfbrenner, 1979). Rural youth within Newfoundland and Labrador are now shaping their attitudes and perceptions of community and work in a milieu that has lost a primary economic justification for existence.

Literature review

Out-migration

Throughout the world, particularly since the Second World War, young people have moved from more traditional, less modern rural areas to the industrialized and more populous urban centres (UNESCO, 1981; Lichter *et al.*, 1993b). This out-migration of youth has occurred within countries, within regions and across continents. In general, macroeconomic models indicate that migration is a result of the natural tendency of people to leave areas of decline in response to the pull of more prosperous areas (DaVanzo, 1981). Poor rural youth are forced to leave declining rural areas out of economic necessity and youth from more affluent families "escape" to urban areas for better opportunities (Wenk and Hardesty, 1993; O'Hare, 1989). In developing countries, the implications of the migration of educated rural youth, referred to as the "rural brain drain", have been well-documented.

Within Canada, and North America as a whole, the exodus of rural youth has become a virtual epidemic. A recent front page story in the *New York Times* (September 5, 1994) entitled "It's Not Hip to Stay" tells of entire graduating classes leaving rural communities on the Great Plains with no intention of returning. This article reports that the imperative for these kids to leave exceeds employment opportunities or big city excitement. The real motivation lies in the valuation that these youth place on rural areas — "you're a loser if you don't leave". The article illustrates this attitude with the story of a graduation dinner in a small mid-west town in which the 13 graduates were asked to stand and announce their plans for the future. Twelve graduates proudly described their plans to leave and attend college. One young man stared at the floor and apologized that he would "just be staying here to farm with (his) Dad".

Exodus for success

Some rural experts have attributed the growing distaste for rural life among young people with the cynicism portrayed through the media *(New York Times*, September 5, 1994). The traditional values of small communities seem "square" compared with the "hip" urban culture popularized in music videos, T.V. sitcoms and movies. Often the image of the "country cousin" is used as a comedic foil. The strong influence of media image on young people discourages them from dressing, talking or acting like they are from "the country" and encourages them to make career and locational decisions away from rural areas.

Traditional sociological thought has also devalued the experiences of growing up or living in rural areas (Kuvelsky, 1973; Carlson, Lassey and Lassey, 1980). Rural youth were seen as having limited access to the variety of experiences and events that could broaden their perspectives and increase their capacity for achievement. Despite the inherent cultural richness and natural recreational opportunities of rural areas, lack of access to the arts and state-of-the-art facilities were seen as limitations to the range of activities available to rural youth.

The formal education system in rural areas might contribute to the exodus of young people. One of the ongoing dilemmas in rural education is the possibility that rural schools are educating youth to leave rural areas through urban-biased curriculum (Knight, 1993; Haas, 1991). To a large extent, curriculum within Canada is "urbanized"; it is standardized in terms of content and programme delivery within Canadian provinces to primarily meet the educational needs of larger cities. Consequently, rural educators provide their students with the knowledge, skills and attitudes to compete in an urbanized context in the global economy.

The results are counter-productive to the desirability and viability of rural life. This suggests that improvements in rural education, a typical ingredient in any rural development scheme, may only accelerate the rural brain drain.

Economic backwater

Job creation and wealth generation are the main concerns for Canada's current economic agenda. Nowhere is the need for these concerns more apparent than in Canada's rural and remote areas where traditional reliance on primary and resource-based industries is being compromised by technological advancements, environmental pressures, changing world trade patterns and increasing global competition. As a result, rural and remote Canada has higher unemployment rates, lower incomes, and a higher level of dependence on transfer payments in comparison to urban areas (Bollman and Biggs, 1992).

The economic decline of rural areas must be seen as a contributing factor to rural youth's negative perceptions of their communities (Broomhall and Johnson, 1994). Young people are particularly hard hit by the difficult economic conditions in rural areas; unemployment rates for rural youth are extremely high and income levels for rural youth are low in comparison to both national averages and averages for other age cohorts in rural areas (Wenk, 1993; O'Hare, 1989). In response, youth are leaving Canada's rural and remote areas and taking with them many of the valuable resources and human capital required for the rejuvenation of rural employment. As youth leave these areas, their perceptions of limited opportunities become self-fulfilling.

The cycle can be described as: limited opportunity causes low perceptions/ expectations; low perceptions causes exodus; and, exodus causes limited opportunity.

Results

Exodus

There is no exodus. Most of the assumptions and expectations on which this research was based were not confirmed. Instead of hearing that the youth were displeased with the opportunities that existed in their communities and that they were determined to leave for larger centres, we heard that the youth wanted to stay in their communities despite economic hardship. They spoke of wanting to stay close to their families and they would like to try to do more with the resources they had at hand. Therefore, the most striking feature of our results was the absence of an "exodus". We found that the youth are staying in their remote communities and that they have no desire to leave.

The 1991 population data from Statistics Canada shows that youth as a share of the total population in the research sites was much higher than the provincial or national averages. As well, the share was highest in the smallest and most remote Labrador communities.

Table 9.1. Each Newfoundland community has a higher share of youth than the Canadian average

Community	Total population	15–24 year olds (as percent of total population)
Labrador Sites		
Black Tickle	238	23
Cartwright	611	18
Charlottetown	292	26
Forteau*	781	19
Mary's Harbour	470	22
Port Hope Simpson	614	26
St. Lewis	339	24
Newfoundland Sites		
Buchans	1,164	15
Burgeo	2,400	21
Corner Brook	22,410	17
Newfoundland and Labrador (total)	568,474	18
Canada (total)	27,296,859	14

Source: Statistics Canada. 1994 a and b. Catalogues No. 95-301 and 95-337
*   *Forteau numbers include the neighbouring community of Lance aux Clair.*

The youth in these communities are either not leaving or leaving and returning. Traditionally, young people in Newfoundland and Labrador have left the province for employment reasons. However, unlike most rural areas, this youth exodus tends to be temporary, i.e. youth who leave Newfoundland and Labrador often maintain their permanent residence status and return when they have made an adequate amount of money or have satisfied their requirements for unemployment insurance.

Perceptions of communities

The youth "love" their communities. They spoke of their communities as good places for both adults and youth to live and would prefer to not leave if "there was something to do".

Advantages of the rural and remote communities

In the survey, youth were asked to describe what they liked about their communities. Respondents identified traditional, rural quality-of-life characteristics as positive attributes of their communities. This idea was expressed by such expressions as "small town feeling", "not too busy", "quiet", "close to everything", "nice people", "friendly". These were the most frequent responses in both the Labrador sites (81 percent) and the Newfoundland sites (72 percent). Each site also had a considerable share of respondents who refer to "natural recreational opportunities" as a positive attribute, although these responses were less frequent. Thus, the positive attributes seem to be more social than aesthetic.

Table 9.2.   Positive attributes appear more social than aesthetic

	Labrador sites	Newfoundland sites	Corner brook
	Percent reporting positive attributes (likes and advantages) of the community		
Quality of life	81	72	59
Safety/low crime rate	50	67	67
Natural recreational opportunities	28	23	26
Work and job opportunities	-	-	-
Clean and healthy environment	-	-	26

Note: *The response categories marked with a dash indicate that there were no responses given for this category at this particular research site.*

Disadvantages of rural and remote communities

Negative attributes of the communities were listed as "lack of excitement", "lack of jobs" and "lack of facilities". Youth spoke of "nothing to do", "boring" and "nothing for young people to do". The youth also indicated that there was a "lack of recreational facilities/infrastructure", or more specifically, "arenas", "pool halls", "somewhere to skateboard" and "arcades". It should be noted that these negative attributes are all described as a "lack of ."... rather than an inherently negative attribute. This could be more a function of the age group that we studied rather than the location or size of the research communities. Perhaps the phenomenon of having "nothing to do" has more to do with the age group than the locations, i.e. youth everywhere, regardless of community size, may claim that there is a lack of excitement and things to do.

Table 9.3.   Negative attributes appear more social than job related

	Labrador sites	Newfoundland sites	Corner Brook
		Percent reporting negative attributes (dislikes and disadvantages) of the community	
Lack of excitement	62	68	78
Lack of jobs	23	38	33
Lack of recreational Facilities/infrastructure	23	20	-
Too small	-	-	18

Note: The response categories marked with a dash indicate that there were no responses given for this category at this particular research site.

Respondents in each of the research sites identified "lack of jobs" as a negative attribute. This was often qualified with phrases such as "no opportunities" and "no future". It is interesting to note that the Labrador sites, which are the most economically challenged of the research sites, had the smallest percentage (23 percent) of respondents identify lack of jobs as a negative attribute. This may be because the enormity of the employment challenge in these communities goes beyond a mere lack of jobs. The fact the employment levels have historically been lower in these communities may also contribute to the lower share of responses in this category.

Advantages of larger communities

Each of the research sites identified "variety of activities" as an advantage of larger communities. Respondents used expressions such as "lots to do" and "excitement". This reinforces the fact that a large proportion of respondents, in all of the research sites, identified "lack of excitement" as a negative attribute of their own communities. Still, the share of respondents who have identified variety of activities as an advantage in larger communities are significantly smaller (31 percent to 44 percent) than the proportion who listed lack of excitement as a negative attribute (32 percent to 78 percent).

Disadvantages of living in a larger community

According to the respondents, the biggest disadvantage of larger communities, by far, is "too much crime". Respondents described larger communities as "dangerous" and identified "gangs" as a prevalent problem. "Too much alcohol/ drugs" was also identified as a disadvantage of larger communities. In fact, a very high share of respondents identified either too much crime or too much alcohol/drugs or both as a disadvantage. It is interesting to note the high proportion of Corner Brook respondents who identified too much crime and drugs as a disadvantage of larger communities because Corner Brook is the urban area that most of the other respondents are referring to when they speak about "larger communities".

Table 9.4.   Advantages of living in a larger community are both social and job related

	Labrador sites	Newfoundland sites	Corner Brook
		Percent reporting advantages of living in a larger community	
Variety of activities	35	31	44
Employment opportunities	22	25	44
Good/better schools	32	16	15
More people/anonymous	20	15	11
Recreational opportunities	11	16	-
None	13	18	11

Note: The response categories marked with a dash indicate that there were no responses given for this category at this particular research site.

Table 9.5.   Disadvantages of living in a larger community are largely perceptions of safety

	Labrador sites	Newfoundland sites	Corner Brook
		Percent reporting disadvantages of living in a larger community	
Too much crime	55	60	67
Too much development	19	19	11
Too much alcohol/drugs	17	7	11

Although respondents identified a wide variety of advantages and disadvantages for living in a larger community the overwhelmingly consistent response was the disadvantage of "crime" and "drugs". This was reinforced during the discussion groups and interviews. This ties into the earlier section in which 50 percent or more of the respondents in each site identified "safety/low crime rate" as one of their communities' positive attributes.

Perceptions of mobility

Plans to leave

A Likert scale was used to ask respondents if they planned to "never leave", "probably never leave", "undecided", "probably leave" or "definitely leave". In the Newfoundland sites, 94 percent of the respondents indicated that they would "probably" or "definitely" leave. The Labrador sites, the most remote communities surveyed, were the only communities to yield "never leave" responses.

Table 9.6. Almost no youth state they will "probably never leave" their community

Research sites	Never leave	Probably never leave	Undecided	Probably leave	Definitely leave
			Percent distribution of respondents		
Labrador	2	4	27	28	37
Newfoundland	0	1	5	26	68
Corner Brook	0	7	37	37	18

Reasons for leaving

Despite the fact that most of the youth would prefer to stay, the results indicate that the youth see leaving as a good idea, particularly in the eyes of their peers and the adults in the community (leaving is perceived as a good idea and leavers are considered smart while staying is seen as a bad idea and stayers are losers). Yet, positive reactions to stayers were more prevalent than negative reactions to leavers. It seems that leaving is considered to be the best option, but there is not an absolute aversion to stayers. As well, during the community visits and group interviews, youth in the smaller communities consistently claimed that they would prefer to stay in their communities if they could.

Leaving is seen as a necessity as opposed to a preference; they plan to leave for "something to do", i.e. jobs or education. Some respondents also indicated that they would leave for "a change" and a small percentage in each of the sites, except Corner Brook, indicated that they "preferred urban lifestyles".

Reasons to return

In order to augment the reasons given for leaving their communities, the youth were also asked what it would take for them to return to their communities if they left. The highest proportion of respondents indicated that either "family/ roots" or a "family crisis/event" such as a wedding, funeral or graduation would bring them back. This seems to indicate that the youth equate their communities with family and place a high value on their family structures. As well, many youth stated that their parents would be happy if they stayed and that they felt some pressure to stay close to the family.

Attitudes toward entrepreneurship

The youth are very interested in entrepreneurship. Many had considered or would consider starting their own businesses ("opportunities") in order to stay in their communities. The youth were not naive and did not have a romantic vision of "being their own boss" and "making lots of money"; they appeared to have specific and realistic attitudes toward entrepreneurship. They spoke of "hard work", "honesty", and "creativity" as necessary ingredients for self-employment.

High degree of interest

Of particular interest, youth are highly motivated to have access to, and participate in entrepreneurship education both within and outside the high school. Many of the youth would take an entrepreneurship course offered outside of the regular high school curriculum.

Table 9.7.   Strong interest in entrepreneurship education

	Labrador sites	Newfoundland sites	Corner Brook
		Percent responding "Yes"	
Should entrepreneurship be taught in school?	85	88	93
Would you take an entrepreneurship class?	67	85	85
Should entrepreneurship be taught to youth outside of high school?	71	71	85
Would you take an entrepreneurship class outside of high school?	52	50	48

Entrepreneurship for "community development"

When asked where they would start their business, a surprising number of youth identified their own community and a significant share indicated that their motivation was community development. In fact, this was the most common response. Of course, the youth did not use the term "community development" but rather used phrases such as: "it would be good for the town", "I want to help out" and "we need more jobs here".

Resources, skills and assistance

The respondents had definite opinions on the resources that are available and needed for the development of youth entrepreneurship. They believe that there is a need for youth-specific programmes and facilities and that they are anxious to become involved in such activity. They appear to be poised for action but are waiting for assistance with the first steps.

When asked, *where or to whom would you go for advice or assistance*, the youth indicated a wide variety of sources including: business people, teachers, family, Atlantic Canada Opportunities Agency (ACOA), Enterprise Newfoundland and Labrador (i.e. the provincial Department of Industry, Trade and Tehnology), Community Futures and the development associations. In discussions, the youth indicated that they believe that the government agencies, such as ACOA and the provincial development associations have the most likely jurisdiction for delivering entrepreneurship training in the community.

Table 9.8.   Youth in smaller communities recognized the potential community impact if they started a business

	Labrador sites	Newfoundland sites	Corner Brook
	Percent reporting reasons for starting a business in own community		
Community development	34	31	-
"Where I'd prefer to live"	33	17	15
Know people/have a network	25	23	54
Recognized need for product or service	-	-	38

Interpretations and conclusions

Conflicting pressures — conflicting results

The youth with whom we spoke are wrestling with several conflicting pressures. Simultaneously, they want to stay in their "home" community, they hear that they should seek opportunities in larger centres, they hear of mass layoffs and high unemployment in other areas, they sense the anxiety that their parents feel over their leaving, they are curious for adventure, and they likely feel a slight inferiority complex for having grown up with limited exposure and experiences.

The results reflected these conflicting pressures. There were inconsistencies in responses and attitudes. However, there were a number of identifiable themes which we attempt to interpret and raise for discussion and conclusions.

Retention — pride or fear?

In the majority of our participating communities, especially the more remote areas, population statistics show that youth are remaining in their communities. At first, this appeared to be a positive statement about their communities and about valuing the quality of life in rural Canada, however, this is more likely a response that is based on fear than on pride.

The youth expressed a great deal of fear with respect to larger communities. They talked about "gangs" and "drug problems". During discussions with the youth, many spoke of their experiences in larger centres and related stories of feeling lost and out of place. The youth of Black Tickle (population 238) who had been on a field trip to Cambridge, Ontario said that they enjoyed the luxuries such as the mall and McDonald's but would not want to live there because "the people were not friendly — they were too busy". The more remote and insular the community the more pronounced these attitudes appeared.

There appears to be a large discrepancy between the youths' claims that they are going to leave and the population statistics which show that they do not actually leave. When the youth say that they are going to leave perhaps they are simply resisting the stigmas that are attached to those who stay. If there is, in fact, a fear of larger communities, perhaps the youth do not want to admit these fears. If they are torn between feeling these fears and admitting them, they are most likely to express only indecision.

Is leaving a realistic option?

A high proportion of respondents will likely remain in their communities, despite the poor employment opportunities. Perhaps the reason for the high youth cohort percentages is that the safest response to a difficult situation is to do nothing and remain among family, friends and familiar surroundings.

Newfoundland and Labrador has a history of economic hardship, low levels of formal education and dependency on transfer payments. There is also a history of retaining its people; while Newfoundlanders and Labradorians are often attracted by the promises in the "bright lights" of the cities, they will generally adopt a pattern of "leaving and returning" rather than completely severing their ties with the province.

In recent years, these conditions have received more media attention, but they did not begin with the closure of the cod fishery in 1992. Economic hardship has become a way of life in these communities and it seems the youth are not as concerned with or panicked by their current circumstances as is the rest of Canada; it is what they are used to and they just accept it.

Perhaps leaving is only a pipe dream for the youth in these communities. Going off to the city is a big move and is only feasible if it will yield big results. With the pervasiveness of the high unemployment, perhaps the value of this move is questioned.

Rural versus remote? The importance of context

A recent *Globe and Mail* article (Valpy, 1995) argues against these ideas. It claims that things are changing in Newfoundland and Labrador: youth are motivated by the economic crisis in the province to leave their communities and even the province in search of better prospects. However, the youth referred to in the *Globe and Mail* article are in St. John's, the capital city, and Trespassey, a community less than a two hour drive from St. John's.

Similarly, 94 percent of the respondents in the Newfoundland sites, Burgeo and Buchans, said that they would leave their communities. Neither Burgeo nor Buchans is particularly remote — Corner Brook is approximately a two hour drive from either community — consequently, moving to Corner Brook is neither difficult nor intimidating for these youth. Conversely, the youth in the Labrador sites have less exposure to larger communities and, therefore, leaving is a more ominous option. It seems that rural youth are attracted to the excitement and opportunities of larger centres and more remote youth are intimidated by it.

There is a danger in extrapolating urban and peri-urban findings to suggest that this will also hold true for more remote communities.

Perhaps communities which are reasonably accessible to larger centres and feel some influence due to this proximity, are more likely to be drawn toward that larger centre; and, communities that are more remote and have little direct contact with significantly larger communities develop an isolation mentality and strongly resist contact with larger centres.

The decision to stay — a theory

Indubitably, there are several factors contributing to the complex explanation for the restricted perception or willingness of mobility among the residents of remote communities. However, this chapter suggests that there is one factor which underlies all other factors when considering a change in location: people are equipped to take only one step in community size and, the size of the step is directly related to the insularity of the community. In other words, the residents of the most insular communities might not be comfortable going to any other community even if it is not significantly larger than the "home" community.

Due to the settlement patterns of Newfoundland and Labrador, the majority of the communities are consistently small, coastal, and traditionally fishing-dependent. Therefore, when people move from one community to the next, for business or pleasure, they are going to communities with similar population sizes and lifestyles. This style of mobility is perceived as very different from mobility between rural fringe and urban.

Among the other factors is the physical distance component of mobility range. Virtually all the youth surveyed made reference to the need to being able to come back to the community for family events, and that some places were "too far away" or "too difficult/expensive to get back". This is a very practical concern because many of the communities have only air or sea links to other communities, and these links truly are expensive.

Another component of the decision not to move away may be the low expectation of getting a job, even in a larger centre. The youth spoke of seeing news reports of layoffs and high unemployment in "the cities" so there is little optimism to motivate a job-seeking move. If there is a high likelihood of living on social assistance, staying to live with the family is a more effective use of this limited income. The majority of respondents in all of the research sites indicated that they would leave for "more/better job opportunities". This supports the basic assumptions of this research that youth in rural areas do not see reasonable career opportunities in their communities and this is the primary motivator for leaving. Perhaps the reason that they are not leaving is the low expectation that "more or better job opportunities" actually exist elsewhere. In the absence of the primary motivator, the youth are not leaving.

Inferiority of education is a perception held by the rural and remote communities. This will contribute to concerns over preparedness for post-secondary education and unemployment. Respondents in all of the research sites also described "good/better schools" as an advantage of larger communities. In the Labrador sites, a particularly high share (32 percent) noted this advantage. This unprompted positive valuation of education and educational opportunities is a surprising result from an area with historically low levels of formal education and high levels of illiteracy. This perception will lead to more general feelings of inferiority. There is little attraction to moving to a new place where one is likely to feel like a second-class citizen.

Youth and entrepreneurship: an opportunity for rural employment

Most of the assumptions and expectations on which this research was based were not confirmed. Instead of hearing that the youth were displeased with the opportunities that existed in their communities and that they were determined to leave for larger centres, we heard that the youth wanted to stay in their communities despite economic hardship. They spoke of wanting to stay close to their families and they would like to try to do more with the resources they had at hand.

We described the cycle of limited opportunity as: limited opportunity causes low perceptions/expectations; low perceptions causes exodus; and, exodus causes limited opportunity. Since this research has found that there are no low perceptions/expectations and that there is no youth exodus, the issue of limited opportunities must be dealt with. The cod moratorium has precipitated a lot of effort in the area of increasing employment opportunities. Perhaps one area for greater focus is youth entrepreneurship.

The youth in rural and remote Newfoundland and Labrador are not leaving their communities, by choice or external factors, and are a human resource waiting to be harnessed.

As communities struggle for economic development, and search for sources of innovation, determination and enthusiasm, youth entrepreneurship may provide a source that, traditionally, is undervalued or ignored completely.

Recommendations

Due to the fact that this research produced results that were diametrically opposed to the basic premise of the research proposal and design, it would be premature to make concrete policy and programme recommendations The unpredicted results of this research make it imperative that further research on several topics be undertaken. Specific issues that require further research are as follows:

Demographic profile of youth in rural communities

This research has shown that the youth in the small and remote communities in coastal Labrador account for 18 percent to 26 percent of the total population of the communities. This is much higher than the national or provincial averages. Research is required to determine if this phenomenon exists in other rural communities in Canada and if it is more pronounced in the more remote communities. As well, research should be undertaken to determine if the statistics are accurate. Are there a higher percentage of youth remaining in these communities or are they merely there as a statistical artefact? Typically, Newfoundlanders who leave the province retain a temporary resident mentality. That is, they never really consider their new location to be home and continue to consider Newfoundland as their permanent residence. Often this is reinforced by maintaining a paper trail of Newfoundland residency: voting by proxy, appearing on the local jurors lists or being "counted in" by Statistics Canada as a Newfoundlander. This leads to the question as to whether or not such a high proportion of the youth are actually residing in these communities or are they merely residents on paper (i.e. the parents recorded the "home" as the permanent resident on the census questionnaire but the youth were in fact "temporarily" somewhere else)?

The relationship between education and employment

The relationship between education and rural employment is a popular research topic. Hypotheses include, increased levels of education are required in rural areas in order to stimulate rural employment and increased levels of education contribute to rural exodus. However, this research has indicated that there is an inverse relationship between participation in education and the workforce or, more simply, that education is viewed as an alternative to employment.

Historically, the formal education levels in Newfoundland and Labrador have been comparatively low. This was due to the structure of the economy. There has been a high dependency on the fishery and other primary resource industries which do not require a highly formally educated workforce. Often, the most prosperous fishing communities in the province have had the highest levels of illiteracy due to people leaving school early to work in the fishery.

Now, however, the situation is reversing. The high school drop out rate has fallen and is zero in some areas of the province (Valpy, 1995). As well, this research indicated that the youth are placing a high value on education and they identified better schools as an advantage of larger communities. However, there are few jobs in these communities and if, in fact, the youth are not leaving, education may have merely become an alternative to employment; i.e., if there is nothing else to do you can always stay in school.

Research is required to determine if education has become an alternative to employment in these areas and to investigate the possible implications of this attitude and behaviour for employment generation and community sustainability.

The role of entrepreneurship

In the context section of this chapter the cycle of limited opportunity is described: limited opportunity causes low perceptions/expectations; low perceptions causes exodus; and, exodus causes limited opportunity.

Since this research has found that there are no low perceptions/expectations and that there is no youth exodus, future work must be done on the issue of limited opportunities. The cod moratorium has precipitated a lot of effort in the area of increasing employment opportunities. However, it must be ensured that the efforts are appropriate to the areas and to youth. One area for consideration is entrepreneurship.

Entrepreneurship is in vogue as an educational or career planning tool and as a focus for local economic development or rural community revitalization (Allen, 1989; Rosenfeld, 1983; Rounds, 1991). In April 1994, the province of Manitoba and the Chamber of Commerce brought 250 high school students together to discuss entrepreneurship and the future of rural communities *(Rural Developments,* Summer 1994). The students talked of "making jobs" in rural communities and stressed the importance of acquiring appropriate skills. The province of Manitoba now identifies "Developing Young Entrepreneurs" as part of its strategy for sustainable economic renewal for rural areas.

A wide variety of tools, facilities and programmes are springing up across Canada to facilitate youth entrepreneurship: entrepreneurship education classes through the high school curriculum, the "I Want to Be a Millionaire" Program, Junior Achievement, and youth entrepreneurship centres at various locations. As well, business start-up assistance is available to youth through several provincial programmes and the Federal Business Development Bank.

Research is required to determine if this new emphasis on youth entrepreneurship is appropriate and effective. More specifically:

1. An inventory of entrepreneurship programmes and tools for youth should be compiled and used to develop screening mechanisms. These mechanisms could then be used to assess both policies and programmes, concerning youth entrepreneurship, in terms of appropriateness and effectiveness for Canada's most remote rural communities.

2. Entrepreneurship training and education should be given more focus within the high school curriculum. A more appropriate body of case studies, which reflect the scope and nature of businesses that are relevant to rural and remote communities, should be developed. Also, because the teachers that are delivering entrepreneurship education have limited time and resources, a more user-ready workbook should be available for each student. In some schools each teacher has one hour per week to prepare for each course, and resources such as photocopying are grossly inadequate.

3. Entrepreneurship training and education should be provided in the community by agencies and bodies such as ACOA, the development associations, Community Futures, or Enterprise Newfoundland and Labrador. Efforts to deliver such programmes to the community in general should have youth-specific components.

4. Any agency or office which services entrepreneurial activity should have a special officer or programme designated for youth entrepreneurship. Although it is not recommended that youth be segregated out of mainstream "business", special efforts must be made to encourage youth in this field and to reduce the intimidating nature of bureaucracy.

Appendix A: Methodology

This chapter is based on data from a study of 347 youth between the ages of 15 and 24 in ten communities in the fall of 1994. The primary research sites were seven small coastal communities in southern Labrador — Forteau, St. Lewis, Mary's Harbour, Cartwright, Charlottetown, Port Hope Simpson and Black Tickle — and two communities on the island of Newfoundland — Burgeo and Buchans. All the communities are coastal, fishing-dependent except for Buchans which is a former mining community in the interior of the island. The tenth site was Corner Brook, a small city and the second largest community in the province, which was intended to serve as a limited control sample. Corner Brook represents a more urban population and is the community that most of the first two groups are referring to when they talk of "larger places" or "the city".

Sample selection and size

The research sample was limited to youth between the ages of 15 and 24. This age cohort was chosen to correspond to the Statistics Canada definition of youth. As well, while the focus of the research was on the perceptions and attitudes of high-school aged youth who are beginning to make career and location decisions, the research attempted to include the views of youth who have finished secondary school. One limitation to the research is that it only surveyed those post-secondary youth who have remained in or returned to the community. Nonetheless, the sample is primarily composed of youth between the ages of 15 and 19.

The research is not designed to be statistically significant. Rather, it is a descriptive work using statistical, anecdotal, and personal observation evidence. Consequently, the study sample size varied among communities for a variety of reasons including research time constraints, community interest and community size.

The Labrador sites comprise very small communities ranging in population from 781 to 238 and the Newfoundland sites, Burgeo and Buchans, have populations of 2,400 and 1,164, respectively (Statistics Canada, 1994a).

In Corner Brook, a single high school class was surveyed and interviewed. This was intended as a random sample for control comparison only and, as such, is limited in size.

Data collection/survey design

Three research tools were used to inform this work: a survey questionnaire, group interviews and personal observations.

Survey questionnaire

A self-administered, written questionnaire was used to survey the perceptions and attitudes of the youth. When possible, the questionnaire was forwarded to the high schools to be completed by the youth prior to the scheduled community visits of the researchers. Due to adverse weather conditions that resulted in delayed mail service, the survey administration in several Labrador communities coincided with the community visit.

The questionnaire contained several pre-coded questions that dealt with the youths' plans to stay in or leave their communities and their perceptions of leavers and stayers. However, for the most part, the questionnaire contained open ended questions designed to elicit their perceptions and attitudes towards their communities and/or larger communities. Despite a recognition of the difficulties of coding and analysing open-ended questions, this questionnaire design was deemed the most appropriate to the topic area; in order to ascertain most effectively the youths' perceptions and attitudes it was imperative that they use their own words and not be "lead" or directed by suggested responses and categories. As well, open ended questions allow for multiple responses. The categories that are presented in these results represent interpretive coding of the youths' own responses.

Group interviews

Whenever possible in terms of timing and the ability of the schools to accommodate the flexible schedule of the research, the community visits included group interviews with the youth. The interviews served to augment the survey results. They were unstructured and were used to elicit candid reactions of the youth to the research topic and design. The interviews also allowed the youth an opportunity to question the researchers and, occasionally, lead the discussion in a direction they preferred. Often, teachers attended the group interviews and either participated in or facilitated the discussion.

Personal observation

The researchers have incorporated personal observations into the research design and results. Personal journals were kept during the community visits to keep an accurate record of observations and responses. This information was used to interpret the data and inform the conclusions.

Sample profile

The data have been collated into three subsets: Labrador sites (Black Tickle, Cartwright, Charlottetown, Forteau, Mary's Harbour, Port Hope Simpson, and St. Lewis); Newfoundland sites (Buchans and Burgeo); and Corner Brook.

References and further reading

Allen, Lagneia (1989) Survey of students on entrepreneurship and small business. *Small Business Report No. 31.* Toronto: Small Business Branch, Ontario Ministry of Industry, Trade and Technology.

Beaulieu, Lionel J., Israel, Glenn D. and Smith, Mark H. (1990) Community as social capital: the case of public high school dropouts. *Rural Sociology.*

Blake, Judith (1986) Number of siblings, family background, and the process of educational attainment. *Social Biology* Vol. 33, pp. 5-21.

Bollman, Ray D. and Biggs, Brian (1992) Rural and small town Canada: an overview. In Bollman, Ray D. (ed.). *Rural and Small Town Canada.* Toronto: Thompson Educational Publishing, Inc.

Broomhall, David E. and Johnson, Thomas G. (1994) Economic factors that influence educational performance in rural schools. *American Journal of Agricultural Economics* Vol. 76 (August), pp. 557-567.

Broomhall, David E. (1993) *Educational Performance in Virginia's Rural Schools.* Blacksburg: Rural Economic Analysis Program, Department of Agricultural Economics, Virginia Polytechnic Institute and State University.

Bronfbrenner, U. (1979) *The Ecology of Human Development: Experiments by Nature or Design.* Cambridge, MA: Harvard University Press.

Canadian Youth Foundation. (1988) *Canada's Youth "Ready for Today": A Comprehensive Survey of 15-24 Year Olds.* Ottawa.

Carlson, John E., Lassey, Marie L. and Lassey, William R. (1980) *Rural Society and Environment in America.* New York: McGraw-Hill, Inc.

DaVanzo, Julie S. (1981) Microeconomic approaches to studying migration decisions. In DeJong, G. and Gardner, R. (eds). *Migration Decision Making: Multidisciplinary Approaches to Microlevel Studies in Developed and Developing Countries.* New York: Pergamon Press.

Dornbusch, Sanford M., Ritter, Philip, I. and Steinberg, Laurence. (1991) Community influences on the relation of family statuses to adolescent school performance: differences between African Americans and non-Hispanic whites. *American Journal of Education*, Vol. 99, pp. 543-567.

Fitchen, Janet M. (1991) *Endangered Spaces, Enduring Places.* Boulder, CO: Westview Press.

Fitchen, Janet M. (1986) *Poverty in Rural America: A Case Study.* Boulder, CO: Westview Press.

Fuguitt, Glenn V., Brown, David L. and Beale, Calvin L. (1989) *Rural and Small Town America.* New York: Russell Sage Foundation.

Gorham, Lucy. (1992) The growing problem of low earnings in rural America. In Duncan, C. (ed.). *Rural Poverty in America.* Westport, Connecticut: Auburn House.

Haas, Toni. (1991) Why reform doesn't apply: Creating a new story about education in rural America. In DeYoung, A.J. (ed.). *Rural Education: Issues and Practice.* New York: Garland Publishing.

Jensen, Leif and McLaughlin, Diane K. (1993) Human capital and non-metropolitan poverty. In Beaulieu, L. and Mulkey, D. (eds). *Investing in People: The Human Capital Needs of Rural America.* Boulder, CO: Westview Press.

Killian, M.S. and Parker, T.S. (1991) Education and local employment growth in a changing economy. In Long, Richard (ed.). *Education and Rural Economic Development.* Washington, D.C.: ERS, U.S. Department of Agriculture.

Knight, Doug (1993) Understanding change in education in rural and remote regions of Canada. In Newton, Eric and Knight, Doug (eds). *Understanding Change in Education: Rural and Remote Regions of Canada.* Calgary: Detselig Enterprises Ltd.

Kuvelsky, William P. (1973) Rural youth — current status and prognosis. In Gottlieb, David (ed.). *Youth in Contemporary Society.* Beverly Hills: Sage Publications.

Lichter, Daniel and Eggebeen, David J. (1992) Child poverty and changing rural family. *Rural Sociology*, Vol. 57, pp. 151-172.

Lichter, Daniel, Cornwell, Gretchen T. and Eggebeen, David J. (1993a) Harvesting human capital: family structure and education among rural youth. *Rural Sociology*, Vol. 58, No. 1, pp. 53-75.

Lichter, Daniel, McLaughlin, Diane K. and Cornwell, Gretchen T. (1993b) Migration and the loss of human resources in rural America. In Beaulieu, L. and Mulkey, D. (eds). *Investing in People: The Human Capital Needs of Rural America.* Boulder, CO: Westview Press.

Looker, Dianne E. (1993) Interconnected transition and their costs: gender and urban-rural differences in the transitions to work. In Anisef, Paul and Axelrod, Paul (eds). *Transitions: Schooling and Employment in Canada.* Toronto: Thompson Educational Publishing, Inc.

McGranahan, D.A. and Ghelfi, L.M. (1991) The rural education crisis and rural stagnation in the 1980s. In Long, Richard (ed.). *Education and Rural Economic Development.* Washington, D.C.: ERS, U.S. Department of Agriculture.

New York Times. (1994) It's not hip to stay. September 5, p.1.

O'Hare, William. (1989) *Poverty in America: Trends and New Patterns.* Washington, D.C.: Population Reference Bureau, Population Bulletin 40:3.

Rosenfeld, S. (1983) Something old, something new: the wedding of rural education and rural development. *Phi Delta Kappan.* December. pp. 270-273.

Rounds, Richard (1991) *A Preliminary Analysis of Selected Educational Issues in Rural Manitoba.* Brandon: RDI Report Series 1991-4. The Rural Development Institute, Brandon University.

Rural Developments. Summer 1994. Vol. 1, No. 2. Winnipeg, Manitoba.

Sherman, Arloc (1992) *Falling by the Wayside: Children in Rural America.* Washington, D.C.: Children's Defence Fund.

Statistics Canada. (1994a) *Profile of Census Divisions and Subdivisions in Newfoundland and Labrador — Part A.* Ottawa: Statistics Canada, Catalogue No. 95-301.

Statistics Canada. (1994b) *Profile of Census Divisions and Subdivisions in Ontario — Part A.* Ottawa: Statistics Canada, Catalogue No. 95-337.

UNESCO. (1981) *Youth in the 1980s.* Switzerland.

Valpy, Michael (1995) The kids are alright. *Globe and Mail.* February 25.

Wenk, DeeAnn and Hardesty, Constance (1993) The effects of rural-to-urban migration on the poverty status of youth in the 1980s. *Rural Sociology* Vol. 58, No. 1, pp.76-92.

Chapter ten:

Two Contexts, One Outcome: The Importance of Lifestyle Choice in Creating Rural Jobs in Canada and Sweden

Lars Olof Persson
The Royal Institute of Technology, Stockholm, Sweden

Erik Westholm
Dalarna Research Institute, Falun, Sweden

Tony Fuller
University of Guelph, Guelph, Ontario, Canada

Abstract

Job accessibility is having less influence on the decisions of individuals to move to rural residences. The ability of the rural locale to provide social interactions and other dimensions of personal self-fulfilment are new and important factors to consider in rural labour market analysis. Two conceptual frameworks are offered to sort the clutter of observations. An "Arena Society" concept is advanced wherein a new "Open Society" with few boundaries is overlaid on features of the recent "Industrial Society" and the former "Short-Distance Society" to understand how rural residents are now functioning in a society with an industrial mentality and a short-distance settlement pattern. The concept of "reach" is advanced to understand the distance over which individuals and households operate in varying social, economic and spatial dimensions. Public policy should pay as much attention to the micro-regional character of rural communities as is paid to expensive job creation programmes.

Introduction

New spatial arrangements are emerging in many rural areas which reflect not only a change in economic structure but a shift in values and lifestyles (Marsden, Lowe and Whatmore, 1990; Reid and Mazie, 1994; Bryden, 1994). The observation that lifestyle choices may be important in creating rural employment opportunities is the focus of this chapter.

In Dalarna County in central Sweden, a survey of in-migrants to rural areas showed that, for the majority, employment was not the main reason for their move (Kåks and Westholm, 1994). In the Saugeen Valley in southern Ontario, Canada, survey results show that more than 47 percent of farm families have diversified their income streams, reportedly to maintain their chosen lifestyle (Frouté, 1990; Gordon, 1991). Lifestyle choices are an integral part of contemporary rural conditions. We employ the concepts of the **Arena Society** and **reach** to describe and analyse complex patterns of activity, mobility, and awareness.

Rural areas in Canada and in Sweden are very different despite the similarity of latitude, physiography, and climate. The common historical dependence on primary production creates some economic similarities (for example, an export-based economy), but the scale and cultural history of the two nations create more differences than similarities. Because of its small scale, Sweden has greater socio-political coherence, with a fairly homogeneous and tightly knit rural population (Persson and Westholm, 1993); in Canada there are great differences between rural populations and places (Bollman, 1992). Despite their differences, all rural regions are facing the same global forces of change. How their history, contemporary structures, and outlook will enable them to adjust to global forces is a crucial question for this chapter. We trace the policy options in rural and economic development as a reaction to global and rural restructuring. This discussion is balanced by reference to rural community development and two brief case studies: Dalarna County in Sweden and the Saugeen Valley, Canada. This will illustrate the policy issues arising from this period of rapid adjustment, the new rural conditions that have emerged, and the rise of lifestyle choices as a strong option in the job-creation process in specific rural communities.

From a Swedish point of view, this bilateral comparison may reveal changes that may emerge as rural Sweden faces reduced public involvement to a level that has been the norm in Canada for some time. From a Canadian point of view, the broad Swedish experience of affirmative rural policy may provide insights into the options and limitations of such programmes.

Global restructuring and the labour market

Trade liberalization has become the main logic in this advanced form of capitalism, and competitiveness is the key rationale for economic restructuring. Describing global restructuring in this way is useful as it enables us to divide the processes of economic restructuring into two stages: the **enabling** activities and the **responses** (Figure 10.1). Three selected responses to global restructuring — **Labour Market Adjustment, Declining Role of the State**, and the **Rise of Community** — collectively contribute to the central argument of this chapter.

Figure 10.1.   Schema of global restructuring

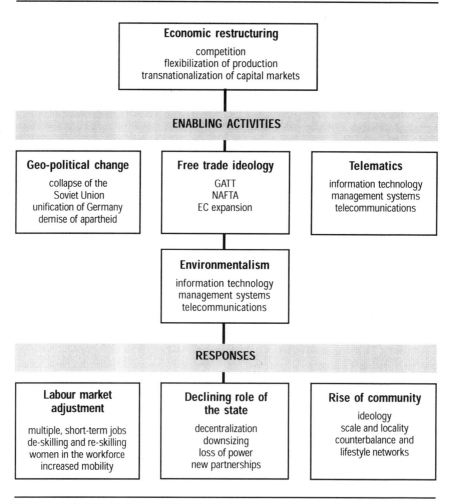

| Economic restructuring |
| competition |
| flexibilization of production |
| transnationalization of capital markets |

ENABLING ACTIVITIES

Geo-political change	Free trade ideology	Telematics
collapse of the Soviet Union unification of Germany demise of apartheid	GATT NAFTA EC expansion	information technology management systems telecommunications

| Environmentalism |
| information technology management systems telecommunications |

RESPONSES

Labour market adjustment	Declining role of the state	Rise of community
multiple, short-term jobs de-skilling and re-skilling women in the workforce increased mobility	decentralization downsizing loss of power new partnerships	ideology scale and locality counterbalance and lifestyle networks

Source: van den Bor, Bryden and Fuller (1996).

The role of the state in a liberalizing economy is to facilitate competitiveness of production and services by adjusting the labour force, dealing with the fallout of restructuring (the social safety net), maintaining international relations, and controlling the main costs of environmentalism. Stringent fiscal policy to reduce national debts in nations with a fiscal imbalance and the downsizing of government programmes are universal prerequisites for the restructuring process to have effects. Modifying the regional redistribution mechanisms, downsizing programmes, and privatizing others all have implications for rural areas, whether in Sweden or in Canada.

Reich (1991) argues that "the key to attracting the best jobs is to have the best educated and best trained workforce and the best up-to-date infrastructure". The policy implications of these new conditions are evident, but difficult to achieve in rural areas. In addition, there are other forces at play which challenge these precepts and which add to the complexity and range of conditions in rural areas. To provide a context for policy discussion applicable to this diversity, we provide a Canadian and a Swedish section, each with a case study. The concepts of the **Arena Society** and **reach** are then introduced as potential ways to assess the significance of the new conditions. The outcome is a comparative discussion of some new rural conditions with a focus on lifestyle choice as a building block in rural job creation policy.

Juxtaposed to globalization is the rise of community, which is both an effect and a reaction to restructuring. Decentralization has produced community programming on the one hand and, on the other, a genuine search for community: people looking for place and new roots. **Community has become important again.**

Canada: New rural conditions

Rural policy

Canadian rural policy in the period since the Second World War has been inconsistent (Phidd, 1994). The major initiatives for promoting rural development have come from the federal government, which has inaugurated a series of national and regional programmes on a cost-sharing basis with the provinces (Lapping and Fuller, 1985). With the conclusion of the settlement and nation-building phases that occupied the state in the nineteenth century and with the establishment of a staples economy (Innis, 1956), most rural areas were served by the sector policies that generally met economic and social goals (Martin and MacRae, 1991). Thus a rural policy *per se* was not required and any shortcomings in the sector policy applications were ameliorated by short-term area or population-based special programmes. In the post Second World War period, the first national initiative was the ARDA (Agricultural Rehabilitation and Development Act) programme, which was designed in 1965 to eliminate rural poverty, indicators of which were found to be most prevalent among Canada's remote rural populations. This quickly became transformed in 1969 into regional economic development with the creation of the Department of Regional Economic Expansion (DREE).

> *The notion of balanced regional development has been — implicitly or explicitly — a key objective of national policy since Confederation. (Coffey and McRae, 1989)*

The adoption of growth-pole principles of economic development and the subsequent application of funds to infrastructural upgrading in towns and cities became the norm for twenty years. It did very little for rural development, especially if one defines rural development as community development in which the participation of local people is required. Regional economic development was part of the national redistribution policy undertaken via General Development Agreements with the provinces, which sought to adjust access and opportunity across Canada via equalization payments to the provinces. It succeeded in developing regional urban centres in Canada's rural areas into which migrants were attracted from the countryside (Matthews, 1977). This raises the ornery question of the extent to which regional development policy is an effective approach to rural development. As argued by Lapping and Fuller (1985), the Canadian approach to rural development, such as it is, has a distinct urban bias. In 1969, a national watch committee called the Canadian Council on Rural Development (CCRD) was formed, and for more than a decade it counselled governments on rural development issues. A wide range of topics was examined by the CCRD, recognizing a broader conception of rural issues other than agriculture. Overall, delivering "people to jobs" was the development orientation rather than a strict rural development policy of delivering "jobs to people".

The main initiatives in the realm of human resource development were the labour market adjustment approaches undertaken by the federal Department of Employment and Immigration Canada, which pursued policies of community, household, and individual adjustments in areas facing severe economic decline and structural unemployment. However, with globalization, such declines largely derived from de-industrialization and were urban-based as opposed to the more subtle but equally damaging problems in the primary sectors of rural areas. The bureaucratization of economic development inevitably produced an urban bias and a technocratic tendency to rationalize rural systems. Centralizing schools is a prime example (Fortin, 1966). Rural policy in Canada in this period was largely a token gesture.

In the current period (the 1990s), a new set of conditions and associated dilemmas for rural development have occurred. Rural areas have been recognized as vulnerable by both federal and some provincial governments and new branches for rural development have been created, mainly within ministries of agriculture. An Interdepartmental Committee on Rural and Remote Canada consisting of more than a dozen federal agencies has been in operation since 1988 and has achieved considerable success at raising awareness of rural issues among bureaucrats (Donnelly, 1994). In 1994, a new Rural Secretariat for Canada was located in Agriculture and Agri-Food Canada (Stevens, 1994). An informal group of academics and rural leaders called the Agricultural and Rural Restructuring Group (ARRG) has created a discourse on rural restructuring and has filled part of the role left by the CCRD. In 1990, Ehrensaft, Fuller, and Gertler noted that with the decline of the portfolio, no rural policy was forthcoming. As of 1995, no new national agency has been created to develop, coordinate, or deliver rural policy in Canada. In reality, rural areas face a period of decline, in the traditional economy and in social services, a decentralization of responsibility to local municipalities without matching fiscal resources, a growth in the third sector (volunteerism), and continued environmental restrictions. These are the universal problems being generated by globalization which are producing new conditions in rural Canada.

Perhaps the most significant indicator of policy reaction to globalization has been the federal Community Futures Programme (CFP), designed to stimulate community-based economic development. The CFP can be seen as an extension of the special areas approach by the state as it is targeted at rural areas that have high unemployment rates, low incomes, and slow economic growth. It is visionary in recognizing that several fiscal benefits derive when local municipalities work together. The programme is predicated on the collaboration of key community agencies to form a Community Futures Committee (CFC), which is charged with stimulating local economic growth (Freshwater, Thurston, and Ehrensaft, 1993). Most importantly, the CFC, after development of a strategic plan, can resource some of its approved economic development proposals through the Business Development Bank, a lender of last resort (Douglas, 1994). Of the 228 CFCs in Canada, almost all of them are in rural areas and many have had a good deal of success. The programme reflects the three responses to global and economic restructuring: the rise in importance of community, the changing nature of rural labour markets, and the need to stimulate more local autonomy in the face of the declining role of the state (see Figure10.1) (Bryant, 1992; Broadhead, 1990).

Rural community

At the local level, rural community development has also been a mixed experience, with periods of invention and progress and periods of inactivity, at least with regard to the role of the state. After a period of activity in the 1960s, characterized by the use of "animation sociale" techniques for community development in Quebec, there followed a bleak period where nothing concerted was undertaken (Draper, 1971). We can best understand this period of experience through syntheses of case studies offered by Douglas (1989), Broadhead (1990), ICURR (1990), and O'Neill (1990). Since 1990, the growth in the state's role (both federal and provincial) in encouraging local economic development has been more visible and more positive (Douglas, 1994).

In terms of the local labour market development, there have been fewer studies and initiatives. The attention given to local economic development is recognition that growth in employment and economic activity can be successfully generated by small businesses and entrepreneurial activity at the local level. "Chasing smokestacks" has slowly given way to forms of small investment (e.g., community bonds), training programmes, and local business development (Fuller and Rounds, 1993). This also reflects changes in the rural labour market towards greater emphasis on short-term, contractual service jobs in a highly segmented market. Contingent labour, multiple-income households, commuting, and teleworking have become common elements in the Canadian rural labour market, although the promise of the service sector as a means of stimulating regional growth has been challenged by Coffey and McRae (1989).

Canadian studies of local labour market changes are few and far between. The multiple job-holding structure of farm households has been examined by Bollman and Smith (1987), Fuller (1991), and Fuller and Bollman (1992) and related to rural job patterns by Bollman, Fuller and Ehrensaft (1992). How jobs and economic activity have been created to form and adjust local labour markets has not been examined systematically, although there is much talk of the advantages and vitality of small business enterprises and the need for entrepreneurship. Government training programmes for labour adjustment (TABs) are the main attempts to manage the effects of globalization and little direct impact is visible yet at the local or rural level.

It is in this light that the economic diversity, job mix, and new forms of social service activity in rural areas become of interest.

Case study: the Saugeen Valley

The Saugeen Valley area, situated in southwestern Ontario about 120 km northwest of Toronto, provides an example of household diversity in economic activity which illustrates the general theme of this paper. The information is drawn from two separate farm household surveys undertaken by Frouté (1990). The Saugeen Valley, comprising six rural and two urban municipalities (towns) is a mixed farming area largely devoted to livestock production. In terms of labour market conditions it is beyond the "regular" commuting distance (one-hour drive) to Toronto, Kitchener, and Guelph and because it is relatively close to recreational centres along Lake Huron and Georgian Bay it has a highly mixed employment structure for both males and females.

The measure of lifestyle choice is taken from the strong presence of farm household diversification in the area, which is attributed, by the farm household members themselves, to the need for supplementing farm income (on average, less than 50 percent of total income) and to contribute to disposable income. Frouté discovered that on-farm diversification was undertaken "to improve the quality of family life" on the majority of the eighteen households interviewed in depth. Gordon (1991) reports that there is very little gender difference in the motivation for taking off-farm work. Off-farm incomes were used to sustain family consumption patterns, to take holidays, and to benefit children. Although the conventional thesis of non-farm income being required for farm family survival was tested, it is evident that a greater number of cases are based on various lifestyle choices. Although not conclusive, evidence suggests that for those who have resided in rural areas for many years, behavioural and employment changes are driven as much by lifestyle motives as by strictly economic considerations. It is also possible to conclude from the Saugeen case study that many of the entrepreneurs with above-average education and income are the most likely to diversify their income streams for lifestyle purposes. For example, the Frouté study reveals that three farm-based diversifications subsequently employed 14, 17, and 20 people respectively and that these jobs, although not all regular and highly paid, have provided opportunities for the under- and unemployed in the area. In this way, such farm-based entrepreneurs become job-makers rather than job-takers.

Consumption of the countryside is also evident in the Saugeen Valley. In one township all the farms sold since 1990 have been to non-farm people (artists, television producers, airline pilots) who have moved there to enjoy the perceived benefits of countryside and community. Note that these "consumers" can access Toronto within two hours. Thus, residential choice based on lifestyle is still, at least in part, based on access to metropolitan employment. Nevertheless, comprehending the mixture of patterns and motives and what people do or consume as part of their lifestyle choice has yet to be thoroughly studied and evaluated.

Sweden: New socio-economic conditions in micro-regions

Rural policy

The original Swedish policy towards rural regions was a universal social policy, focusing on the low-income farm households. The Swedish Social Democracy, which was in power for 44 years until the mid-1970s, was based largely on the power and lifestyle of the urban and small town industrial worker, typically employed by a large corporate firm. For most, the guiding vision of the spatial structure of Sweden was probably a network of modern urban centres. In the transition process, the remaining, less mobile, rural population should be supported within the framework of a broad welfare policy. Hence, the effective rural policy instruments — at least after 1947 — were largely farm product price support and measures for structural change. The implementation of welfare policy depended on municipal reforms, the first in 1952, the second in 1972. These reforms aimed at creating viable local labour market areas surrounding a local service centre. Rural areas were expected to be integrated into this functional unit, inspired by the ideas of central place theory (Hägerstrand, 1970).

An explicit regional policy was introduced in 1965 targeted to the sparsely populated northwest. The regional policy was also aimed at industrializing the lagging rural areas, but it became evident that investments were largely concentrated on the medium sized central places in the vast interior of Norrland (Aldskogius, 1992).

In retrospect, there is little doubt that the urbanization process, including both migration of labour to expanding metropolitan regions and concentration of population in small towns in rural regions was largely accepted and even stimulated by other and more powerful policy measures.

Active rural development policy, bringing investment support to small businesses, was not introduced until the 1970s. Since then, rural policy has been a forerunner to local planning with a bottom-up perspective. Rural development projects are now supported in all relevant parts of the country. The policy includes financial state support delivered by County Administrative Boards and often involves local agents (rural development advisors). The range of projects supported has eventually been widened. Rural policy has been successful in diversifying the rural economy in many places and in promoting rural entrepreneurship. However, it should be noted that jobs created are generally at a qualitatively low level.

In 1996, after entry into the European Union, the Structural Policy for the Swedish 5b-regions (rural regions) was determined by the European Commission. The programmes are largely based on the previous experiences of the national rural policy and involve a substantial increase in financial resources to these regions. At the same time, there is an increasing awareness of the much stronger impact of what is now recognized as the "large regional policy" (Prop, 1993-94). The large policy consists of the spatial implications of all state policy programmes, i.e. within the educational, defence, social and environmental sectors. This means that there is also an increasing awareness of the vulnerability of rural regions as a consequence of restructuring of all these state sector policies and of globalization.

Crisis in the welfare state

A recent national study (Socialstyrelsen, 1994; also quoted in Persson and Wiberg, 1995) provides a general overview of changing living conditions in Sweden.

The economic crisis of the early nineties caused an extremely high unemployment rate, severely hurting both men and women. Demand for labour decreased in most sectors and unemployment increased. Unemployment is highest among young people and immigrants and is also prevalent among single parents. In households with two adults, it is once again becoming less common that both are economically active. Long-term unemployment is increasing and chances of finding a regular job decrease as the unemployment period increases. In addition to open unemployment, there are increasing numbers of persons with weak links to the labour market — under-employed and those in labour market programmes. Low incomes are numerous among young people, but also among the very oldest with many close to the poverty level. Disposable incomes below the poverty level are more common among blue collar workers and although more men than women are below the poverty level, larger numbers of women are closer to the border of being classified as poor than men. Poverty is more common among foreign citizens. Income transfers reduce the impact of poverty, first of all among the elderly but to some extent also among the young. As many as 80 per cent of single parent families are moved out of poverty by social transfers (i.e. regular programmes, not social benefits).

The present social problems in Sweden are more obvious in metropolitan than in non-metropolitan and rural regions. Sparsely populated regions in northern Sweden share the characteristics of an aging population and depend on the public sector both for service provision and supply of jobs. These areas are threatened by the eventual cutback of the welfare state. The rural districts at the fringes of urban regions in the southern and central parts are strongly influenced by the economic and social processes in urban regions. Starting in the 1980s, middle-class households increasingly chose rural areas for the quality of life offered. At the same time, less affluent rural households chose to stay in these rural areas because of the low housing costs. However, as we will show later, there is an increasing variation within each of these two stereotypes of rural Sweden.

More room for local priorities

Most social services in Sweden are delivered by municipalities and counties. Previously, central government had a strong influence on the allocation of resources in each municipality. There is a trend toward stronger independence, reinforced by the way resources are now transferred to local authorities, i.e. largely in a lump sum. This leaves more room for local priorities. Local priorities are also decisive for the local income tax rate. There is a tendency for high-income municipalities to keep local taxes low, while low-income municipalities usually have to finance expensive social programmes by increasing the tax level.

In principle, reorganization of social services has followed three steps: first, there has been a tendency to stimulate efficiency within the existing organization; secondly, service producers have been allowed or forced to compete; and thirdly, privatization has been introduced. Private entrepreneurs are allowed to compete in the fields of technical services, childcare, homes for elderly and health services. Private schools — still very few — are operating with 85 per cent of their costs covered by the government. As long as they follow the core of the national curriculum they are free to choose a profile. In 1994, 20 per cent of the services financed by local governments were produced by private firms. Only a few years ago the corresponding figure was a few percent. The principle of free access to all social services is abandoned and fees have been introduced in many services.

Altogether, we anticipate increasing differences between the municipalities due to local policies concerning service subsidies and accessibility. Still, however, the general principle is that there should be public control of the quality of services and regulation of fees.

It is essential to understand the importance of changes of the labour market in different regions in this process. The Swedish labour market policy was known to be aggressive, i.e. active in training and rehabilitating everybody wanting to enter or re-enter the labour market. After 1990, with persisting high unemployment, the labour market policy has had to spend more resources just to support the unemployed economically.

Increasing differentiation

We identify three factors leading to increasing differentiation in Sweden, between and within regions:

1. internationalization and organization of economic activity;
2. diversity of lifestyles and mobility patterns among people; and
3. policy formation and practices (Persson and Wiberg, 1995).

It should be clear that all of these changes have to be studied against the background of the transition of the Swedish welfare state into a more market-oriented system.

Internationalization implies, among other things, that private enterprises are becoming dependent on exploiting and developing markets, and creating joint ventures with partners located at long distances from headquarters. Production sites are chosen with less concern for national borders but rather according to local cost structures and accessibility to relevant infrastructure. New organizational modes, including less hierarchical and more network based management principles, are becoming essential in this development. This kind of organization is appropriate to achieve flexibility and speed. At the same time, the micro-regional locality remains and evolves as an important base for production. The quality of the environment and cultural diversity play important roles in attracting and keeping competent labour in general. Hence, local growth can be promoted successfully by efforts to develop specific local infrastructure. But local development does not mean isolation. It is crucial that the local community is provided with effective links for transportation of people and goods as well as for information through telecommunications to other regions. However, a large number of firms will not be able to liberate themselves from their "home base" even if it has poor qualities in terms of business services and professional labour. Their only way to stay in business will be through price competition, meaning that the wage level has to remain low. At the micro-regional level, this will contribute to the survival of a number of small industrial districts with a generally low income level.

The second category of factors leading to increased regional fragmentation is the tendency towards diversified individualistic lifestyles. Throughout the long period of industrialization and the rise of the public sector, the lifestyle of the wage earner was developed and became dominant. The local community, with its cultural traditions and social networks, was providing an important coherence.

The nationwide equalization of living standards in terms of real income, housing, and education was a commonly held value. Among the young generations, we now observe the development of a new lifestyle with more pluralistic characteristics and influenced by global trends, with all their variations. Together with an increasing level of general education and the emergence of knowledge and information based small production units with flexible working conditions for labour, individualistic lifestyles are fostered. For a growing share of the population, it will become possible, and preferred, to make one's own decisions about where to live and work and make these arrangements rather flexible in time and space. The individual search for quality of life will have greater impact on the whole settlement pattern in the post-industrial society. Where demand for housing and services will grow is becoming less predictable, whether at the micro-level as well as the macro-regional level. We anticipate an increasing socioeconomic housing segregation in Sweden with micro-regional implications.

The third differentiating factor is policy formation and practices. We now face a situation where Swedish policy-making is considering more market aspects and adjusting to supranational policy-making. This leads Swedish policy and planning towards a model with less public intervention and with much greater awareness and dependence on processes outside the borders of the national state.

In general, top-down sectoral planning and implementation systems have dominated for many centuries in Sweden. However, changes have occurred. The general effect of increased responsibilities of local government in Sweden will be to intensify competition, putting further stress not only on the comparative advantage of different municipalities, but also on management, competence, and creativity in local government. This stress is reinforced by the increasing financial problems generated by deficits in the national budget and constraints on the maximum level of local taxes.

Privatization is one response to the changes. In some cases private enterprises have taken over the provision of social services. Cooperative enterprises are one new way of producing certain services. Finally, municipalities are transferring operational responsibility to voluntary associations. It is likely that this development will lead to a quantitatively and qualitatively more diversified and locally adjusted service provision than before. Simultaneously, however, many municipalities / local governments will experience economic and social problems which will force them to call for more state resources and regulations.

Persson and Wiberg (1995) question if the strong and growing fragmentation tendencies may be neutralized by new regional policy measures. One specific issue is the way to handle differences among regions. An aspect lacking in the new regional policy is how the important interplay between various types of regions should be handled. Fragmentation and widened regional gaps in living standards is expected from growing competition between regions plus strategic alliances among the stronger regions. The critical transfers of resources between regions — the cornerstone in the welfare model — will be more problematic when unemployment hits all types of regions harder. The present regional policy, largely oriented to specific zones, must be replaced by a flexible system for stimulation of economic growth and distribution of welfare in any kind of micro-region.

Case study: Dalarna County

Job creation in small and medium sized enterprises has been a main task for planning at the local (municipal) level in Sweden. Recent research indicates that both the business climate and the actual location advantages can be important for small firms. We have already identified the tendency towards more individualistic lifestyles as an important regional differentiating factor. A qualitative study of 50 households moving to the county of Dalarna between 1985 and 1990 reveals some of the phenomena discussed (Kåks and Westholm, 1994).

Dalarna is situated some 300 km northwest of Stockholm. The landscape is mainly forested and relatively sparsely populated. The area is regarded as very "traditional" with houses and villages steeped in historical and cultural heritage. Some parts of the county are traditionally touristic, with large lakes and attractive landscapes. Folk music, local crafts, and other such activities complete the image.

The study is built up from interviews penetrating two interrelated fields of reported behaviour. The first concerns the motives for moving to the area: what kind of an individual or household situation or process underlies the decision to move to Dalarna from another part of the country. The second is the life pattern of the household some years after the move. Different spheres of communication are examined: work, social relations, consumption, education, leisure, and holiday activities. The interviews indicate that although a change of workplace may be involved in household migration it is rarely a main driving force. A variegated and complex mix of social, environmental, cultural, and economic aims was identified. Some of the most prominent themes were:

1. **Back to the roots**

   Urbanization in Sweden was compared with other European countries. Urban dwellers often retain links with their rural origins in the form of a village, a cottage or a farm and then may avail themselves of geographical mobility in order to move back "home" permanently to areas within physical reach of cities. Sometimes the search for roots is more symbolic — individuals settle where the natural and infrastructural landscape resembles their childhood surroundings.

2. **In search of community**

   Individuals and households move to be near people, groups, or organizations with lifestyles and values similar to their own. People inspired by the New Age movement have assembled in the Stjernsund area and they have attracted a constant stream of new migrants. The local authority has facilitated this process by investing in a school, a nursery school, shops etc. In Leksand, a religious group started a school which caused substantial immigration. Obviously, in some cases we can identify distinct subcultures whereas in others the degree of community may be less distinct but still present — interest groups or even looser aggregations presenting an image corresponding to the preferences of certain households. A possible explanation of the strength of "search for community" migration is that the emerging flexible structures of production and related demands cannot fulfil the human need for community. In the Industrial Society, community for most households was an integral aspect of work relations and local institutions in everyday life.

3. Non-metropolitan lifestyle

A general striving to live a more rural life is paramount for another group. Landscape, buildings, and social life in various combinations are main determinants. Some places have a middle-class rural image and attract the traditional highly educated and often mobile migrants. Other places in the same area offer cheap houses and a rural lifestyle to people who can raise their standard of living substantially by leaving metropolitan areas.

One conclusion from the interviews is that the determinants for individual and household choices are very subtle. At first, for a single household, most places are out of the question as they cannot offer a reasonable compromise between household history, roots, landscape preferences and social demand, job possibilities, access to services, etc. The places that are feasible are rather limited in number and they are individualized, varying from person to person. The individual (or the household) sometimes looks for a place in a way similar to that in which marriage partners are found: the criteria are fairly fixed, not many can be of interest, in the end it is not possible to single out any obvious factors. Obviously, no discussion on rural development can ignore the post-materialistic values increasingly influencing migration.

Any place has its own set of qualifications to offer and appeal to people with differing motives for considering a rural locale — subcultures, housing, sceneries, social differentiation, land accessibility or communications. Hence geographical space is increasingly used for its varying possibilities for self-fulfilment and thus the relation between humans and places is more sophisticated than single place-relations like "place-of-work" can explain. The choice of place to settle has become a function of self-expression.

Altogether the analysis indicates that important social change resulting from a transformation of the labour market is taking place giving job accessibility less influence over migration patterns. Interpretation of the private situation, including social interactions and self-fulfilment processes, seems to be a necessary complement to labour market analysis.

New ways to examine the new conditions

The effects of globalization are difficult to trace at the local level in Canada and Sweden, because the responses by local areas are diverse and seemingly without pattern. Increased differentiation at the micro-regional level is apparent in Sweden and broad regional differences are being re-enforced in Canada. The new values identified broadly in Section One — labour market adjustments, the declining role of the state, and the rise of community — combine to confuse rather than to clarify the process of change (see Figure 10.1). Complexity, diversity and fragmentation are increasingly common characteristics of local economies and the result, especially for many of those involved at the local level, is one of confusion. It is in this light that new concepts and analytical constructs are required to examine critically the impact of global forces on local economies and social systems. Two new constructs will be introduced here that allow us to look more critically into local processes of change. The Arena Society is a three-tier theoretical construct that provides an historical perspective on present conditions. It accounts for complexity as a layered amalgam of old and new labour market features. The key element is the dislocation over time of the spatial and functional aspects of local labour markets. The second concept, that of "reach", is a way of conceiving and measuring physical or mental awareness. It provides a measure of the range of individual and collective activity. Utilizing these two concepts sequentially, one can review the rural experience of both Canada and Sweden and draw some tentative conclusions for understanding rural labour market outcomes. Ultimately it will be critical to test these concepts on the ground.

The *Arena Society* and the changing dynamics of rural labour markets

One way to capture the nature of the rural community labour market changes and to account for its current complexity is to take an historical approach and use the Arena Society concept devised by Johansson and Persson (1993) and developed by Persson and Westholm (1993) and Fuller (1994). What this enables us to do is to trace those elements in contemporary rural labour markets that derive from past market and community conditions. Although much has changed, much has also remained the same and it is useful to be able to identify residual as well as contemporary features in the present and unfolding community labour market system.

The **Arena Society** consists of three stages of development in rural society:

1. The **Short-Distance Society** was largely a product of agrarian conditions which laid out farms and farming communities at regular intervals. In Canada this was designed deliberately to extract food resources and to support the staples economy. The distance between communities was governed by what was considered feasible for horse-drawn conveyance. The labour market was

confined to the farm and to service centres where basic food processing and distribution jobs prevailed.

In diagrammatic form, the Short-Distance Society can be visualized as closely overlapping circles, implying that most social, economic, and political activities took place more or less within the same local area (Figure 10.2). The concentration of activity in one central place points to an inward-looking labour market, with relatively high cohesion and simplicity in its activity patterns.

Figure 10.2a. The short-distance society

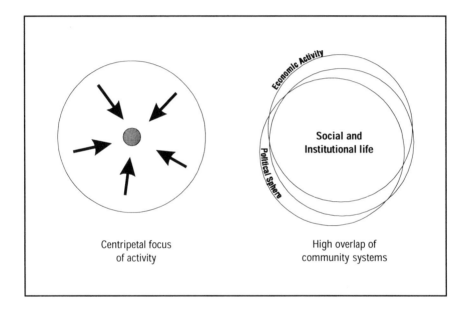

Centripetal focus
of activity

High overlap of
community systems

Figure 10.2b. The industrial society

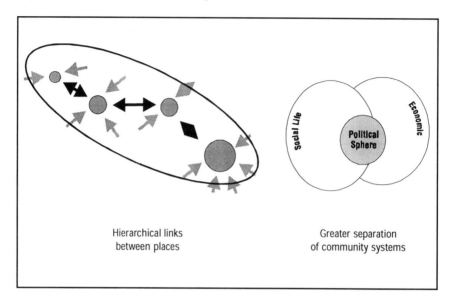

Hierarchical links between places	Greater separation of community systems

Figure 10.2c. The open society

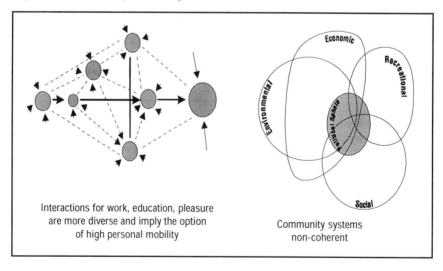

Interactions for work, education, pleasure are more diverse and imply the option of high personal mobility	Community systems non-coherent

2. The **Industrial Society** in both Canada and Sweden entrenched the nodal focus of the Short-Distance Society as various phases of industrialization took place in small-towns in the nineteenth and early twentieth centuries.

    In terms of the labour market, the Industrial Society brought wage labour and the factory system to many rural areas, as well as the social relations of a proletarianized society. People were introduced to the "workplace" and learned to work "only" from 8 until 6, six days a week. Industrial processes such as Fordism (assembly-line production) changed not only the means of production but the very way of thinking about production. Industrialism took different forms in different areas, with primary processing dominant in the forestry areas, manufacturing the main form in southern and central regions, and storage and processing of foodstuffs, mainly grains and oilseeds, in southern Sweden and western Canada.

The increased geographic scope of activities in the Industrial Society depicts greater dissonance between the spheres of human activity (Figure 10.2b). The Industrial Society, which began by entrenching the proximity of residence and work, later contributed to the separation of the two as people moved to jobs rather than jobs to people. This is especially the case in Canada.

3. The **Open Society** implies a more wide-open development of rural society where fewer boundaries exist and more choices prevail. It is not an absolute state, but relative, suggesting that contemporary society is more open than previous ones. For example, differences between rural and urban society are diminishing as we become increasingly subject to the same information, standards, and values.

    Mobility of people and information is an important feature which brings a new dynamic to the Open Society. There is a new propensity of people to move over increasingly larger spaces to fulfil the standard needs of contemporary life while information technology makes it possible for some people to stay at home and work with central agencies. Both forms of mobility suggest new linkages and a gradual reorientation of the use of space from the Short-Distance and Industrial Society. Access to personal transportation and the increasing private and business use of new communications technology both have distance-shrinking effects in the Open Society.

In the Open Society, more choices are based on lifestyle preferences than on Industrial Society imperatives. Many farm families, like people in rural communities generally, do not look simply to their local town for all their needs, nor do they see everything in terms of a hierarchical system of progress. It is no longer deemed necessary or even possible to join an institution for life and work up through the ranks. We still have a Short-Distance settlement pattern and an Industrial Society mode of thinking about the work ethic and full employment, the organization of production and the division of labour. Onto this is being grafted the Open Society, where more potential economic and social choices, personal mobility and inundation by information produce a less structured lifestyle. It is not that these societies change from one to the other, but that they accumulate one on top of the other. This largely explains the confusions we are witnessing as restructuring changes occur in contemporary rural life.

The Arena Society is an amalgam of all three societies and helps to explain the new rural conditions, the diversity of labour markets, and the increasing importance of lifestyles in rural Canada today. In the Arena Society, the situation is one of overlap. From the Short-Distance Society to the Arena Society, the rural labour market has become increasingly more complex, often causing confusion among the labour force and dilemmas for policy makers. From the predominance of self-employment in the Short-Distance Society on farms and in small businesses, we have moved to a wage economy (Industrial Society) and are now returning to more self-employment and fragmented work cycles. Even the concept of work is being challenged (Reid, 1995). At the household level it means that different members may have different activity patterns depending mainly on their age, skills, and access to transportation. Many people still lead a Short-Distance Society lifestyle. Many are still geared to the Industrial wage economy. Open Society lifestyles add a further layer of activity which is motivated by new values associated with ecological sustainability, new age beliefs, and the search for community. In the labour market, there is a new generation of entrepreneurs who can work at home, supply business services and attendant education and health counselling. Rural areas that can maintain old systems and attract new ones become diversified in very different ways. The implications for community control, conflict, and empowerment are many in the Arena Society.

"Reach" differences

During the last decade, the population patterns in Sweden and Canada have taken new directions. A more complex spatial differentiation has replaced both the steady urbanization and the labour migrations, from north to south in Sweden and from east to west in Canada. Examples of growth and decline can now be found in all kinds of regions, in places of different size, in cities as well as in rural areas. In Sweden it is a mosaic pattern rather than one of concentration. A similar transformation is taking place in most of Europe (Illeris, 1994). One explanation is the increased priority given to non-job factors by individuals and households. The choice of living in a rural area has often more to do with perceived quality of life than with quantity and quality of local labour demand. Increased commuting, new communication technology, increased dependence on transfers and more flexible organization of jobs are some common explanations. Another rationale for the mosaic pattern is that local conditions are getting more important in economic decision-making. A flexible economy, based more on knowledge than on raw materials, provides and gives room for local/regional activity. It seems as if locality matters. Education, housing/environment, and the cultural context are some elements that can be acted on and improved locally and they are all becoming more relevant as human resources become equally important in the new era of economic competition.

The new differentiation is not only creating inter-regional imbalances; it also alters the social and economic relations within a single area. The internal homogeneity which characterized both the agrarian (Short-Distance) and the Industrial Society is broken. In places and areas with increasing population, the new mix of households is especially complex. Some household members may be constantly travelling and take only a minor part in local social life while others have all their different spheres of communication gathered locally. An increasing share of the households seem to be able to produce their own mix of rural and urban components of life (Ennefors, 1991). Hence, physical accessibility, or **reach**, is an important variable by which to examine social life.

The **reach** concept has many dimensions and can be fruitful when the capacity and orientation of individuals and households is to be analysed. It has been used by phenomenologist geographers (Buttimer, 1978) and is also used by Hägerstrand for discussing the lack of ability of the welfare state to use human capacity (Hägerstrand, 1978). **Reach** could be defined as "the capacity to comprise the surrounding world in one's sphere of interest". We can identify many dimensions of reach: **social reach** (the individual's ties to other individuals); **time reach** (the span of time that the individual's consciousness enhances); **knowledge reach** (the ability to take in and work over information); and **economic reach** (a "wild card" which can be used to extend reach in other dimensions: physical, knowledge, technological, etc.).

The reach for a single person is determined by personal resources and by the possibilities offered in the environment. As it is restricted by time and capability as well as by external factors, it cannot grow without limits. When it stretches out in one dimension it tends to contract in another. Hence, when physical mobility increases, for example by commuting or travelling for studies, social life will diminish — a brake in the social dimension of reach. Physical reach in terms of communications to population centres and bigger cities is commonly held to be an important factor for rural development. An analysis of migration gives some support to this thesis on a regional level. Growth in rural areas is more common near to Toronto, Montreal, and Stockholm. At a more detailed level, the necessity of good communications seems to be more uncertain. The pattern of growth and decline is more like a mosaic pattern which cannot be explained in terms of accessibility only. Increasing quality of roads and cars extends physical reach, which people then use to produce their own mix of rural and urban components of life.

Introducing the reach concept into research on social and economic change in rural areas opens up our understanding of the increasing differences between households. For example, there are important differences between "traditional" households characterized by roots and close social networks, "immigrant or ex-urban" households with their extended physical spheres of communication, and "educated households" with their potential ability to adapt to changes in the labour market.

New technology is often anticipated to extend the reach of individuals. Communication technologies are shortening and sometimes even eliminating distances (Bryden and Fuller, 1986). The networks of individuals and organizations are growing, the media bring instantaneous long-distance information.

Technological progress, however, also causes exclusive reach; workplaces that have been very accessible locally are changing their technology and become out-of-reach for those who cannot meet the rising educational requirements. Technology in this sense is exclusive.

Education is obviously an important aspect of reach. It is related to mobility because the highly educated tend to be more mobile than others. In general, education is a way of stretching reach to meet the hastily growing demands from the labour market. Some 70 per cent of the fastest growing occupations in Sweden demand a solid education after secondary high school (Florman, 1994). It is forecast that a continuing intra-regional differentiation is taking place in which the periphery is increasingly lagging in terms of formal education and is having greater difficulties adapting to demands from the labour market (Axelsson *et al.*, 1994). This differentiation is obvious on a regional level where the centre of the region can supply higher education and is constantly increasing the level of education among the citizens, while the peripheral communes increasingly lose the young, who leave to access further education (Westholm, 1994). Correspondingly, the skill-demanding jobs in the growing service sector do not occur in the periphery.

Social reach is another aspect of human life with relevance to the future of rural areas. The traditional view of rurality is one of cohesion and belonging. Research on contemporary rural life, however, reveals that loneliness and the lack of community can be present in rural areas as well as in cities. We also recognize from Swedish studies of farming (Westholm, 1992) and of life expectations among young Swedes (Andersson and Fürth, 1993) that "search for community" stands out as ever more important in the Swedish welfare state.

Household differentiation sometimes occurs as differences in reach. While some households have long distance social networks, others have theirs locally. While some travel, others stay in the village. While some take part in local activities, others use the locality more as a natural landscape and residential asset. The spheres of communication are increasingly separated in a way that can only partly be explained by social class. Changing modes of production, which is a different kind of social organization, is also a factor. The agrarian society had its short-distance networks; the industrial society was also built mainly on local social life. The flexible post-modern (Open) society is breaking up the structure and creates turbulence. In a rural place all of the different modes of production that had their dominance during different periods are still present. Together they form a complex social and economic structure. The demands of social life and the possibilities to fulfil demands vary greatly among households and among household members. Some are living in a community that has grown over generations while some have no connections to the landscape they live in. For policy and planning it may become an important task to heal the fragmentation of everyday life that is taking place.

As a theoretical concept, "reach" is problematic and needs to be defined more precisely. Nevertheless, measuring differences in terms of "reach" raises the issue of preferences made by individuals and households which are vital when assessing the rural labour market. Small firms and industry rarely move to a rural areas, rather they develop from the initiative of someone who lives there, someone whose values and preferences may be crucial to the future of the village or community. In the study of migration to rural areas in Dalarna (Kåks and Westholm, 1994), it was also evident that "job-creators" were over-represented among the immigrants. Many of them started a business within a few years of moving to the rural place or they bought a small firm to develop in the rural environment. Overall, moving was not usually instigated by employment opportunities; the aim of moving was more personal.

Conceptualizing new rural conditions

Synthesis

Comparing the policy and rural development experiences of Canada and Sweden highlights some important similarities and differences in the new rural conditions that emerge. The measures are not strictly compatible, yet it is evident that despite facing similar globalization effects, the two countries have made different responses at the macro level. In Canada, rural regions appear to be increasingly differentiated by the standard indicators of economic well-being and development. In vulnerable areas (those still dependent on primary sector economies) where people tend to stay (e.g. Eastern Canada), the economic indicators are the poorest, and where people tend to leave (e.g. the central Prairies), the indicators are average (Hawkins, 1995). The best overall conditions are in central Canada (southern Ontario and Quebec) and on the west coast. In Sweden, differentiation is occurring at the level of the micro-regions where privatization and withdrawal of government programmes has left many communities and people vulnerable to new competitive forces and predations. Such differentiation reflects the comparative success of the former Swedish model in flattening the differentials between communities and areas. Much more research needs to be done about which areas and people are directly affected by the knock-on effects of globalization and especially the economic and social impact of Sweden and Canada joining mega-trading blocks such as the European Union and the North American Free Trade Agreement respectively.

During the search for understanding the new rural conditions in northern nations, two innovative concepts have been employed which are worthy of further development as they assist the process of isolating key relationships for further examination in an evolving milieu of complexity and diversity. The two concepts are the Arena Society and the idea of "reach". Both need testing in the field.

The Arena Society enables us to appreciate the increasing complexity of rural conditions as landscape elements of the Short-Distance Society and structures from the Industrial Society combine to shape the options and constraints of the

Open Society. In the Short-Distance Society, community and place are the same, occupying the same space and symbolizing spatial and functional unity. In the Industrial Society, community and place become more individually distinct, as place of residence and place of work become increasingly separated in terms of location. Transportation and mobility improve substantially in the Industrial Society. In the Open Society, people and information can move even more freely, which enables a wider sphere of acquaintance and knowledge to develop for many people and organizations. The prospects for extended reach are increased.

In essence, this suggests that the Arena Society contains at least three levels of experience of community: **community of place, community of acquaintance** and **community of awareness**. These contain three spatial contexts of "reach" (Figure 10.3).

Figure 10.3.   Three spatial components of the increasingly global community and three spheres of "reach"

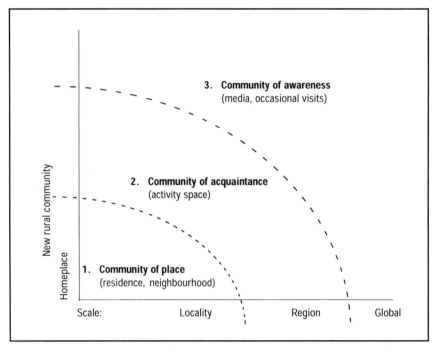

Given these three types of community experience, it is not surprising that the composition and function of rural society is changing. On the one hand it has become increasingly diffused with urban values and standards and on the other shows tendencies to differentiate spatially. People have knowledge of rural areas either because they migrated from a rural area in the first place, or can visit rural areas frequently, even if sometimes from far away. It is this acquaintance and awareness of rural life that, together with lifestyle expectations, contributes to the selective re-evaluation of rural areas. It raises lifestyle as an increasingly important incentive for urban to rural relocation.

The concept of "reach" adds further to this discussion as it provides a more exact set of measures of the spatial activities, mental and physical, of people and groups. Social, time, knowledge, and economic forms of "reach" acknowledge the multi-dimensionality of thought and activity and the complexity behind patterns of human behaviour. Importantly, the concept connects the resource fields of the individual to the opportunities perceived in the environment such that the sum of activities undertaken may reflect the values of the decision-making process. Clearly, empirical studies of the "reach" concept are required to help examine the new rural lifestyles of contemporary society.

Implications for policy and planning

Two main changes in the local planning system seem to be appropriate. First, the kind of planning that made towns and villages in Sweden and Canada similar to each other will be less appropriate in the future. As place-specific images are becoming more important, towns, villages, and districts must develop their own advantages — go their own way. Thus, the differences between places may increase rather than diminish. There will be fewer universal visions, as the only appropriate planning level is the local one. Rural planning will need many templates to assist the individuation of rural communities and a main instrument will be that of partnerships with central agencies (OECD, 1995). Secondly, the importance given to the labour market in local planning must be questioned. In Sweden, job creation in small and medium-sized enterprises has been a main task for municipal planning. In an "Arena" perspective it would be necessary to widen the scope of such planning. While place-hunting firms have been in focus, place-hunting individuals have to be given similar importance. The environment must have increasing priority as the landscape, the image, and the physical resources that places offer become more important. Towns and villages within the same area must also be involved in new partnerships and image-building projects. Instead of drawing on the national vision, the starting point must be local, penetrating place specific conditions, local culture, and heritage. Conventional planning will be inhibited by the patterned structures from the past if new arrangements are not quickly forthcoming. Flexibility and creativity will be needed to combat complexity and confusion.

The development programme for the objective 5b area in Western Sweden was largely developed by means of a partnership procedure, securing strong participation by local actors. When it comes to priorities in the actual projects, however, the traditional importance given to job-creating activities remain. Almost two-thirds of the financial resources are allocated to "Development of small businesses" and "Development and diversification of agriculture and forestry". The policy question remains, whether to develop the strengths or resolve the weaknesses.

Globalization has demonstrated the low level of understanding between the state and rural economies. As new rural conditions emerge they will not all be distributed equally, nor will they be of a quality sometimes obtained in the past.

Two contexts, one outcome

Canada and Sweden start from very different positions despite their similar locational and bio-physical conditions. The sheer size and recent history of Canada makes the regional pattern of development very different from that of Sweden, which has followed a strong equalizing and homogenizing set of policies. Canada's regional differences are on a larger scale than Sweden's and the nature of Canada's short economic history has also differed. The Swedish model produced a relatively stable state in rural areas by the early 1980s and only in recent years has the price been considered too high. Perhaps most importantly, Sweden has had a local level of government with considerable powers, both to raise and select the expenditure of taxes and to influence land-use planning. In Canada, although local governments have been effective, they do not have the power or resources to deal with health and education, for example, and consequently are less accomplished in these areas. Although regional policy in the form of transfer payments has existed in Canada for thirty years, it has not affected local people very much as provincial governments and regional development agencies have directed most of the payments to large-scale infrastructure and business enterprises in urban locations. Maintaining small rural communities has been an issue in Swedish rural policy, although at the same time, the urbanization process has largely been favoured in most other policy programmes. In Canada the "people to jobs" approach has prevailed to the detriment of many rural and remote areas. The adaptation to the free market was much earlier in Canada and the result has been greater differences in the quality of conditions in Canada's rural regions which are larger and less homogeneous than those in Sweden.

Against this broad structural differential has come into play the effects of global restructuring on governments, labour markets and public perceptions. Diminishing government services, the restructuring of rural labour markets and the rise of the concept of "community" are leading to a profound re-evaluation of rural assets in many areas. Some regions/micro-regions are well placed to do well, while others are destined to lag further behind, unless local initiatives are successful and can prevail. There is no conventional wisdom on this matter. Responses to global restructuring are likely to be as individual as the communities themselves and much greater differentiation will occur both within the Canadian regions and between micro-regions in Sweden. Thus, we are seeing one general outcome — increasing differentiation among rural areas arising from two separate starting points.

Micro-regions will attract newcomers as much for lifestyle reasons as for employment reasons. Not all areas will be equally attractive, either because of location or natural conditions and patterns and flows of people and job-making activity should be tracked and examined at the micro-regional level to further understand this general hypothesis. If valid, public policy should pay as much attention to micro-regional character as is paid to expensive job-creation programmes.

References and further reading

Aldskogius, G. (1992) *Svensk regionalpolitik: Utreckling och framtid.* Stockholm: Allmänna förlaget.

Andersson, Å. Fürth, T. and Homberg, I. (1993) *70-talister. Om värderingar förr, nu och i framtiden.* Stockholm: Sekretariatet för framtidsstudier.

Axelsson, S., Berglund, S. and Persson L.O. (1994) *Det tudelade kunskapssamhallet.* Stockholm: ERU-rapport 81.

Bergström, V. (ed.). (1993) *Varför överge den svenska modellen?* Tiden: Eskilstuna.

Bollman, Ray D. (ed.). (1992) *Rural and Small Town Canada.* Toronto: Thompson Educational Publishing, Inc.

Bollman, Ray D. and Smith, P. (1987) The changing role of off-farm income in Canada. *Proceedings of the Canadian Agriculture Outlook Conference.* Ottawa: Agriculture Canada, pp. 155-166.

Bollman, Ray D., Fuller, A.M. and Ehrensaft, Philip. (1992) Rural jobs: trends and opportunities. *Canadian Journal of Agricultural Economics* Vol. 40, pp. 605-622

van den Bor, W., Bryden, J.M. and Fuller, T. (1996) *The Implications of Rural Restructuring for Higher Education and Training.* London: Wiley.

Bröadhead, P. Dal. (1990) Lessons from Canadian case studies of community self-sustaining growth. In *Sustainable Rural Communities in Canada.* Saskatoon: Agricultural and Rural Restructuring Group, Proceedings of Rural Policy Seminar 1.

Bryant, C. (1992) Community development and changing rural employment in Canada. In Bowler, I.R., Bryant, C.R. and Nellis, M.D. (eds) *Contemporary Rural Systems in Transition. Volume II: Economy and Society.* Wallingford: CAB International.

Bryden, J.M. (ed.). (1994) *Towards Sustainable Rural Communities: The Guelph Seminar Series.* Guelph: University School of Rural Planning and Development.

Bryden, J.M. and Fuller, Tony. (1986) *New Technology and Rural Development.* Enstone, U.K.: Seminar Report, Arkleton Trust.

Buttimer, A. (1978) Home, Reach and the Sense of Place. In Regional identitet och förändring i den regionala samverkans samhälle. Uppsala: University of Uppsala, Department of Geography.

Castells, M. (1989) *The Informational City.* London: Basil Blackwell.

Coffey, W. and McRae, J. (1989) *Service Industries in Regional Development.* Halifax: The Institute for Research on Public Policy.

Donnelly, K. (1994) Interdepartmental Committee on Rural and Remote Canada. In Bryden, J. M. (ed.). *Towards Sustainable Rural Communities: The Guelph Seminar Series.* Guelph: University School of Rural Planning and Development.

Douglas, D. (1989) Community economic development in rural Canada: a critical review. *Plan Canada* Vol. 29, No. 2, March.

Douglas, D. (1994) *Community Economic Development in Canada.* Toronto: McGraw-Hill Ryerson. Vols. 1 and 2.

Draper, J. (ed.). (1971) *Citizen Participation: Canada.* Toronto: New Press.

Ennefors, K. (1991) Att leva mellan stad och land — livskvalitet i den urbaniserade landsbygden. Arbetsrapport fran Cerum, *CWP*, 15.

Florman, C. (1994) *Yrkesstrukturens utveckling i Sverige* (The Occupational Structure in Sweden). Stockholm: AMS.

Fortin, G. (1966) The challenge of a new rural world. In *Rural Canada in Transition*. Ottawa: Agricultural Economics Research Council of Canada.

Fournier, S. and Persson, L.O. (1995) The fall and revival of the Swedish welfare model: spatial implications. In Eskelinen, H. and Snickers. F. (eds). *Competitive European Peripheries*. Berlin: Springer.

Freshwater, D., Thurston, L. and Ehrensaft, P. (1993) Characteristics of successful community development partnership strategies. In Rounds, R. (ed.). *The Structure, Theory, and Practice of Partnerships in Rural Development.* Selected Papers from the ARRG National Rural Economics Seminar, Merrickville, Ontario, ARRG Working Papers Series Number 5.

Frouté, J. (1990) *Study of On-Farm Diversification in the Saugeen Area, Ontario.* Guelph: Technical Report, University School of Rural Planning and Development, University of Guelph.

Fuller, Anthony M. (1991) Multiple job-holding among farm families in Canada. In Hallberg, M.C., Findeis, Jill L. and Lass, Daniel A. (eds). *Multiple Job–holding among Farm Families*. Ames: Iowa State University Press, pp. 31–44.

Fuller, Anthony M. and Bollman, Ray D. (1992) Farm family linkages to the non–farm sector: the role of off–farm income of farm families. In Bollman, Ray D. (ed.). *Rural and Small Town Canada*. Toronto: Thompson Educational Publishing, Inc., pp. 245–268.

Fuller, T. (1994) Sustainable rural communities in the arena society. In Bryden, J.M. (ed.). *Towards Sustainable Rural Communities*. Guelph: The Guelph Seminar Series, University School of Rural Planning and Development, University of Guelph.

Fuller, T. and Rounds, R. (ed.). (1993) *Stimulating Rural Economies for the 2000s: The Challenge for Rural Manufacturing and Tradeable Services.* Proceedings of the 4th Annual ARRG Conference, October 1992, Goderich (ARRG Working Papers Series Number 4).

Fuller, T., Ehrensaft, P., and Gertler, M. (1990) Sustainable rural communities in Canada: issues and prospects. In Baker, H. and Gertler, M. (eds). *Sustainable Rural Communities in Canada.* Saskatoon: Agriculture and Rural Restructuring Group, Proceedings of Rural Policy Seminar 1.

Gordon, S. (1991) *Farm and Non-Farm Income and the Family Farm in the Saugeen Area, Ontario.* Guelph: Master of Science Thesis, Department of Geography, University of Guelph.

Hägerstrand, T. (1970) Tidsanuändning och omgiuningsstruktur. *SOU*, 14, bilaga 4, pp. 4:7–4:37.

Hägerstrand, T. (1978) Att skapa sammanhang i en människas värld - problemet. *In Att forma regional framtid*. Stockholm: Publica, Expert Group on Regional Research, pp. 183-197.

Hawkins, Liz (1995) *Mapping the Diversity of Rural Economies: A Preliminary Typology of Rural Canada.* Ottawa: Statistics Canada, Agriculture Division Working Paper No. 29.

Illeris, S. (1994) *Essays on Regional Development in Europe*. Roskilde: Department of Geography and International Studies.

Innis, H.A. (1956) *Essays in Canadian Economic History.* Toronto: University of Toronto Press.

ICURR (Intergovernmental Committee on Urban and Regional Research). (1990) *Community Development: An Interprovincial Forum.* Toronto: Ontario Ministry of Municipal Affairs.

Johansson, M. and Persson, L.O. (1993) *Sekelskiftets arbetemarknad i Stockholms län.* Mimeo FORA/ERU.

Kåks, H. and Westholm, E. (1994) *En plats i tillvaron.* (A Place in Life). Falun: Dalarna Research Institute, 8.

Lapping, M.B. and Fuller, A.M. (1985) Rural development policy in Canada: an interpretation. *Community Development Journal: An International Forum* Vol. 20, No. 2., Oxford University Press.

Marsden, T., Lowe, P. and Whatmore, S. (eds). (1990) *Rural Restructuring: Global Processes and their Responses.* Critical Perspectives on Rural Change Series. London: David Fulton Publishers.

Martin, J. and MacRae, D. (1991) The impact of trade liberalization and federal regional development programs on rural Canada. In *Trade Liberalization and Rural Restructuring in Canada.* ARRG Working Papers Series, Number 1.

Matthews, R. (1977) Canadian regional development strategy: a dependency theory perspective. *Plan Canada* Vol.17, No. 2, June.

OECD. (1995) *Local Economies and Globalization.* Paris: LEED Notebooks, 20.

O'Neill, T. (1990) *From the Bottom Up: The Community Economic Development Approach.* Ottawa: Economic Council of Canada.

Persson, L.O. and Westholm, E. (1993) Turmoil in the welfare system reshapes rural Sweden. *Journal of Rural Studies* Vol. 9, No. 4.

Persson, L.O. and Wiberg, U. (1995) *Microregional Fragmentation. Contrasts between a Welfare State and a Market Economy.* Heidelberg: Physica-Verlag.

Phidd, R.W. (1994) The state and rural development in Canada. In Bryden, J.M. (ed.). *Towards Sustainable Rural Communities: The Guelph Seminar Series.* Guelph: University School of Rural Planning and Development, University of Guelph.

Prop. (1993/94) 140. (White Paper) *Bygder och regioner i utveckling.* Stockholm: Government of Sweden.

Reich, R.B. (1991) *The Work of Nations.* New York: Vintage Books.

Reid, J.N. and Mazie, S.M. (eds). (1994) *Conceptual Frameworks for Understanding Rural Development: An International Dialogue.* The Aspen Institute.

Reid, L. (1995) Flexibilisation: Past, present and future?. *Scottish Geographical Magazine* Volume III, pp. 58-64.

Social Rapport (1994) *Socialstyrelsen.* Stockholm.

Söderström, L. (1988) *Inkomsffördelning och fördelningspolitik.* Stockholm: SNS förlag.

Stevens, D. (1994) The Rural Renewal Secretariat in Agriculture and Agri-food Canada. In Bryden, J.M. (ed.). *Towards Sustainable Rural Communities: The Guelph Seminar Series.* Guelph: University School for Rural Planning and Development

Westholm, E. (1992) *Mark, människor och moderna jordreformer i Dalarna.* (Modern Land Reforms in Dalarna). Uppsala: Geografiska regionstudier nr 25, Uppsala University.

Westholm, E. (1994) *Vägen till högre utbildning — sa ser den ut i Dalarna.* Falun: Dalarna Research Institute.

Chapter eleven:

Commuting: Its Importance for Rural Employment Analysis

Friedrich Schindegger and Cornelia Krajasits
Austrian Institute for Regional Studies and Spatial Planning
Vienna, Austria

Abstract

There are more workers than jobs in predominantly rural regions. In other words, there is net out-commuting from predominantly rural regions. This implies a spatial concentration of jobs into non-rural regions. However, inter-regional labour market linkages are significant. Interestingly, for some countries (e.g. Finland and Austria), predominantly rural regions were also a major destination for commuters. These interdependencies appear to be increasing. Commuting increased during the 1980s in the countries able to provide these data. It is important to take the functional division of space into account — the analysis of rural employment should not be limited to rural regions.

Introduction:
International comparative analysis at the regional level

The distribution of employment opportunities and development trends vary among rural areas. Shifts in economic structure — for example, the decreasing significance of agriculture on the one hand and the increase of services on the other hand — leads to new regional distributions of employment opportunities. Increased mobility is the reaction to geographic concentration of the demand for workers. The response on the supply side is increased mobility which takes on two forms: migration movements (i.e. change of residence) and more commuting between place of residence and place of work. Mobility plays a significant role as a regional balancing mechanism for the labour market and thus mobility is a major factor to understand the structure and trends of employment in rural areas.

The intensification of mobility in the form of commuting leads to consequences not only for labour market and social policy but also the additional traffic poses new challenges for transportation infrastructure policy.

This chapter compares the role of commuting for rural workers among six OECD member countries. It presents the first results of a cooperative project within the OECD Rural Development Programme and uses the regional typology of the OECD Steering Group on Rural Indicators rural indicators project (OECD, 1994) which has been developed for international comparative analysis at a regional (i.e. subnational) level. This subnational analysis organized by OECD's Steering Group on Rural Indicators represents an innovation for the OECD's analytical work.

Assumptions, objectives and implications of the study

The starting hypotheses may be summarized as follows:

1. Labour market regions are expanding in size and commuting is on the rise. The distances between place of residence and place of work are becoming longer and the time spent commuting is increasing.
2. The concentration of jobs in urbanized areas and the increasingly dynamic changes in employment are leading to increased linkages between urban and rural areas where rural areas may become more dependent on the economic trends that occur in economic centres.

An analysis of regional trends requires a more detailed analysis of the available data than can be provided by an analysis of national data. When analysing regional labour markets, the fact whether a set of data has been gathered at the place of residence or the place of work is significant for interpretation as well as for regional and labour market policy implications. A comparison of these two concepts provides explanations of:

1. the available labour force potential of a region;
2. the actual availability of jobs in a region;
3. the ratios between available workers and available jobs in a region; and
4. the structural factors, as far as the available data permits.

These two different concepts underlying the way data is gathered allow us to gain a more detailed knowledge of the distribution of jobs on the one hand, and on the other hand, the characteristics of workers according to where they reside. Moreover, the analysis of commuting provides information on regional labour market relationships and interdependencies by showing the numbers and characteristics of workers flowing among regions.

With this is mind, the aim of this study on commuting was twofold. Firstly, to illustrate the results of these different concepts (place of residence and place of work) for the individual countries by three types of regions (according to the regional typology of the Steering Group on Rural Indictors), and on the other hand, to describe the role of interregional commuting as a balancing mechanism.

Based on the census data of the years 1980 and 1990 (1981 and 1991 for some countries), a country comparison was made based on the data for Austria, Canada, Finland, Germany, United Kingdom and Switzerland. The evaluation of the data shows — depending on the size of the region as well as on the distribution of the population between the types of regions — very different settlement structures. A glance at the fundamental data clearly illustrates the differences among the countries. Two blocks of countries emerge, one whose population is more or less evenly distributed across the three types of regions, namely Austria, Canada and Finland, and those countries where the population is relatively concentrated in urbanised regions, namely Germany, the United Kingdom and Switzerland.

Table 11.1.   Country comparison — basic data

	Population ('000,000)	Area ('000 km²)	Number of regions	Average population of regions ('000)	Predominantly rural	Significantly rural	Predominantly urban	Total
Population is evenly distributed								
Austria	7.7	83.9	77	100.2	40	39	22	100
Canada	26.6	9,976.1	266	100.1	33	23	44	100
Finland	5.0	338.0	82	60.8	47	32	21	100
Two-thirds of population is urban								
Germany	79.6	356.9	47	1,692.9	8	26	66	100
United Kingdom	57.4	244.8	65	883.2	15	17	68	100
Switzerland	6.8	41.3	106	64.1	14	25	61	100

Source: OECD (1994).

The two concepts of surveying employment

Similar to the differences in population distribution, the distribution of regional employment opportunities by the three types of regions show very different patterns across the individual countries (Figure 11.1). While in Austria and Finland the predominantly and significantly rural regions have the largest share of employment, in Canada, Germany, Switzerland and the United Kingdom the predominantly urbanized regions are the ones with the highest share of employment opportunities.

Figure 11.1. Comparison of distribution of employment by place of residence and by place of work, 1990

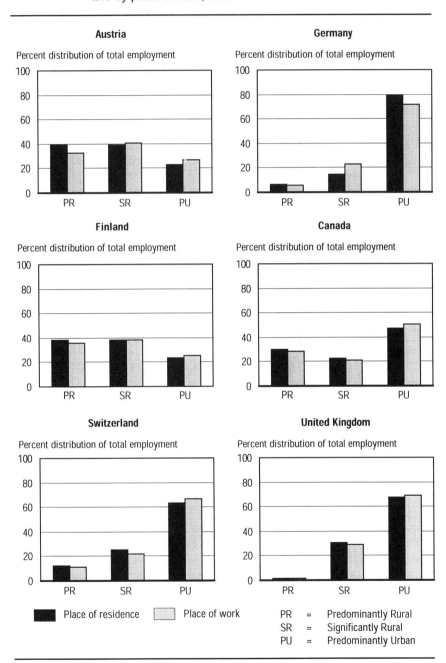

Employment has increased in these countries over the past 10 years, although Austria reports comparatively low growth rates (Figure 11.2). When one differentiates between place of residence and place of work, we see that with the exception of Austria and Switzerland, the number of employed persons counted at place of work in all countries has increased much stronger than those counted at place of residence. This points to a rise in the spatial concentration of jobs.
A comparison of the two enumeration concepts shows that, with the exception of Finland and Switzerland, the highest growth rates of both employed persons at place of residence and at place of work are in the significantly rural regions. Labour market growth lagged in the predominantly rural regions in Austria and Finland. Note the high growth rates of employed persons in the significantly rural regions in Canada, whether enumerated on the basis of place of residence or place of work. In contrast, the predominantly urbanized regions grew faster in Finland.

The ratio of jobs (employed persons at place of work) to employed persons (at place of residence) illustrates the availability of jobs in a region. Values below 100 indicate a relative lack of jobs whereas values over a 100 indicate a higher supply of jobs relative to the number of employed persons residing in the region.

The situation in the predominantly rural regions is very uniform (Table 11.2). The ratio is below 100 in all countries which means there is an insufficient number of jobs relative to the supply of resident workers. The situation is most pronounced in Austria. During the 1980s, the ratio of available jobs to resident employed persons has declined everywhere except in Finland.

Table 11.2.   Predominantly rural regions have a lack of jobs relative to available workers

	Ratio of jobs (employed persons at place of work) to employed persons (at place of residence) (percent)					
	Predominantly rural regions		Significantly rural regions		Predominantly urbanized regions	
	1980	1990	1980	1990	1980	1990
Austria	84	82	103	104	116	117
Canada	95	93	92	91	105	107
Finland	92	94	100	101	115	108
Germany	..	89	..	94	..	103
Switzerland	94	88	92	85	104	102
United Kingdom	..	97	70	89	81	98

Source: OECD rural data surveys.

Figure 11.2. Change in employment at place of residence and at place of work, 1980 to 1990

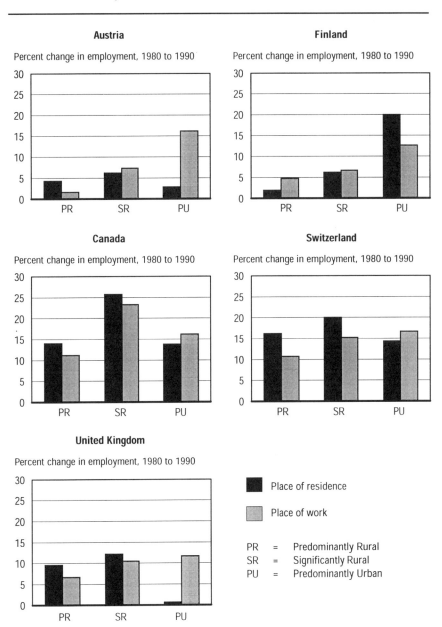

Source: OECD rural data.

Differences among the countries is especially clear in the significantly rural regions. In Austria, a surplus of jobs exists. In Finland the situation has changed from a relative deficit to a relative surplus in significantly rural regions. A different pattern is seen in Canada and Switzerland where the relative lack of jobs has worsened.

Clear job surpluses relative to the supply of resident workers exist in the predominantly urbanized regions in all countries. Austria shows the highest concentration of jobs relative to the resident workforce. The job surpluses in predominantly urbanized regions increased in Austria, Canada and Finland.

Commuting as a balancing mechanism

The hypothesis has been advanced that labour market regions are becoming larger as a consequence of concentration tendencies which make commuting necessary and causes it to increase over time. The comparison above of the number of employed persons at their place of residence and at their place of work shows clear labour market imbalances among the regions. The predominantly urbanized regions are emerging as labour market centres.

The commuting data may now be integrated into the analysis to provide information on the extent to which commuting works as a balancing mechanism. Commuters are persons who cross a regional (i.e. predominantly rural, significantly rural, predominantly urbanized) boundary to get to his/her place of work. The results thus depend on the size and the classification of the regions.

If one compares the countries of Austria, Germany, Finland, Canada and the UK according to the distribution of commuters across the different types of regions, two main patterns can be identified. In Austria and Finland, more than half of all commuters come from predominantly rural regions (Figure 11.3). Predominantly urbanized regions account for a very low share of cross-regional commuting. The situation is different in Germany, Canada, and the United Kingdom. Here the highest percentage of commuters is found in the predominantly urbanized regions. These differences in the distribution of the share of commuters may be ascribed to several factors which cannot be analysed within this study. Such factors include the distribution of population, the structure and trends of settlement and the economic and infrastructural performance.

Figure 11.3. In Austria and Finland, over one-half of all commuters reside in predominantly rural regions

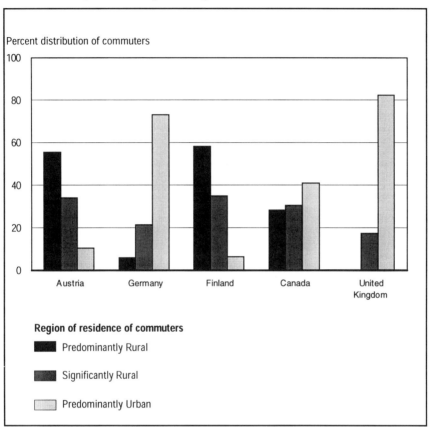

Source: OECD rural data surveys.

The ratio of commuters to resident employed persons indicates the regional significance of commuting. Here a comparison of countries also reveals very different patterns. Commuting as a balancing mechanism for labour market imbalances is the strongest in Austria, the predominantly rural regions having the highest share of out-commuters (Figure 11.4). Also in Finland, the share of commuters in this type of region is proportionately high. In Germany and Canada, the significantly rural regions are those with the highest (out)commuting intensity while in the UK, it is the predominantly urbanized regions with the highest (out)commuting intensity.

Figure 11.4.   Over 25 percent of the Austrian rural workforce are
commuters

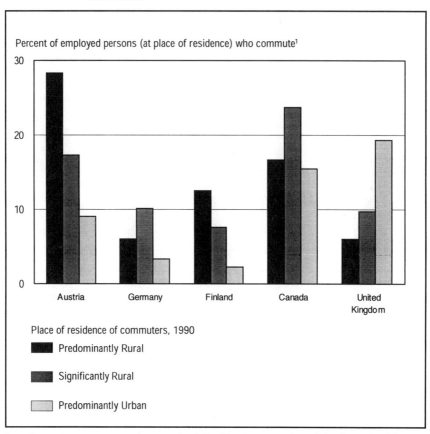

Percent of employed persons (at place of residence) who commute[1]

Place of residence of commuters, 1990
■ Predominantly Rural
■ Significantly Rural
□ Predominantly Urban

1.   *Commuters are persons who cross the defined borders to get from their place of residence to
their place of work.*
Source: OECD rural data surveys.

For analysing trends that took place between the beginning of the 1980s and
the beginning of the 1990s, we only have data for three countries (Austria, Canada,
UK). The clearest rise in number of commuters occurred in Canada (+40 percent)
and also in Austria (+27 percent) (Figure 11.5). No uniform trend is discernible
by type of region. In Austria — starting at a low share of commuters — the
strongest increases have been recorded in predominantly urbanized regions. In
Canada and in the UK on the other hand, the strongest increases were in the
significantly rural regions.

Figure 11.5.   In Canada during the 1980s, commuting in the significantly rural
workforce increased by over 50 percent

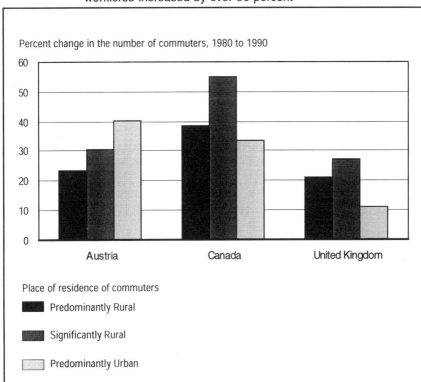

Percent change in the number of commuters, 1980 to 1990

Place of residence of commuters

■ Predominantly Rural

■ Significantly Rural

□ Predominantly Urban

1.   *Commuters are persons who cross the defined borders to get from their place of residence to
their place of work.*
Source: OECD rural data survey.

Austria: A case study

In addition to the trends described above, there are concrete economic, settlement
and infrastructure differences unique to each country. We present a detailed
assessment of Austria to illustrate the options open for further analysis of the
available data within some countries.

Total employment in Austria grew 6 percent from 1981 to 1991. The strongest
growth rates for employment, measured at the place of work, were in significantly
rural regions (7 percent). The lowest growth rates were in predominantly rural
regions (2 percent).

Another picture emerges when employees are counted at their place of
residence. Again the significantly rural regions show the strongest increase
(6 percent, clearly slower than in the 1970s) and lowest growth rates (3 percent)
are predominantly urbanized regions.

The ratio of employed persons enumerated at their place of residence to available jobs (measured by the number of employees at their place of work) indicates the availability of jobs or employment performance in a region. Over time, this indicator shows that jobs are concentrating in regional centres and provincial capitals. In 1991, predominantly rural regions had the worst ratio (18 percent out-commuting) and predominantly urbanized regions had the highest ratio (17 percent in-commuting).

In Austria, there is a remarkable difference in the changes in employment among regions of the same type. Within the group of predominantly rural regions, one can identify both very dynamic regions and less dynamic regions (Figure 11.6). The largest decline in employment (jobs or employed persons at place of work) was recorded by regions in northern, eastern and southern Austria. Many of these regions are border regions to the central and eastern European countries in transition. These changes are in contrast to the high growth rates of employment in the western Austrian regions, as well as in areas with small and medium-sized towns of eastern Austria and in some districts near Vienna. The expansion of the services sector (especially for tourism) as well as a process of displacement toward the urban hinterlands have contributed to this development.

Figure 11.6.   Wide variability in regional growth rates across degrees of rurality, Austria, 1981 to 1991

Specific characteristics also explain changes for significantly rural regions. Remarkable are the declines in the regions of southern and eastern Austria. This is a consequence of a structural crises in the dominant iron and metal working industries. On the other hand, a clear rise in jobs took place during the period of observation in the regions surrounding the provincial capitals as well as in the districts to the south of Vienna.

Among the predominantly urban regions, the higher growth rates occurred in the urbanized districts in the far west of Austria along the border to Switzerland.

Based on the background of a traditionally very low residential mobility of households, commuting in Austria is the main mechanism to balance the concentration tendencies of the labour market. Developments over the past decades have shown that the tendency of economic activities to concentrate has continued and is becoming stronger. This spatial redistribution occurs both from the periphery to the urbanized areas as well as within them. The concentration of jobs in the central areas is being confronted with migration from the city to urban hinterlands. This serves to intensify the functional division of regions.

This tendency also leads to a further increase in the number of employed persons that commute daily between place of residence and place of work. The districts with the worst ratios of employed persons (at place of residence) and available jobs are those along the Austrian–Hungarian border, as well as the strongly agrarian districts in the catchment areas of Linz and Vienna, some of which are also border regions to the Czech and Slovakian frontiers.

As can be deduced already from the relation between jobs and resident population, the provincial capitals and their urban hinterlands are the centres of commuting. The significance of Vienna as the centre of the labour market in eastern Austria and the larger regional catchment area is made very clear by the percent of commuters in the affected districts. The regions with the highest percent of commuters in relation to employed persons (at place of residence) are the northern and southern hinterland districts of Vienna as well as those in southeastern Austria for which Vienna is the job centre. High commuting rates are also recorded in the catchment areas of the employment centres in mid Austria.

On the other hand, the regions with the lowest share of commuters among employed persons at place of residence are mainly regions with a strong industrial base and/or an intensive tourism base in the central and western parts of Austria.

High shares of long distance commuters (more than 60 minutes travel time) are found in the regions of the border areas in the southeast and northeast of the country and in the Alpine regions of southern Austria. Most of these regions are still oriented to agriculture (up to 25 percent of the total employment in agriculture) with few jobs in industry and in the service sector. They have a low potential for tourism and they are located out of the catchment areas of the provincial capitals.

The changes in the ratio of commuters to resident employed persons point to a very interesting development that occurred during the period of between 1981 and 1991. The strongest increase took place in the predominantly rural regions to the north and to the west of Vienna, as well as in most of the regions along the Austrian–Hungarian border, all regions that may be considered within the greater catchment area of Vienna. Also, in the industrialized regions of the east and south of Austria as well as in the border regions to Switzerland and Germany, (cross-border) commuting has strongly increased to above average rates as a consequence of structural crises and declining employment opportunities.

Conclusion

In all countries included in this case study, there are more workers than jobs in predominantly rural regions. In other words, there is net out-commuting from predominantly rural regions. This implies a spatial concentration of jobs into non-rural regions.

However, inter-regional labour market linkages are significant. Interestingly, for some countries (e.g. Finland and Austria), predominantly rural regions were also a major destination for commuters.

Finally, these interdependencies appear to be increasing. Commuting increased during the 1980s in the countries able to provide these data.

It was not possible to analyse the trends in commuting distances although this is possible from some national sources.

There are strong interregional dependencies and linkages that are especially significant for trends in employment and the labour market. Thus, it is important to take the functional division of space into account. Any analysis of rural employment should not be limited only to rural regions.

References

OECD. (1994) *Creating Rural Indicators for Shaping Territorial Policy.* Paris: OECD.

Chapter twelve:

The Relationships between Occupational and Residential Urban-to-Rural Migration

Michel Blanc and Gabriel Tahar
Institut national de la recherche agronomique, centre de Toulouse, Toulouse, France

Abstract

In the literature on urban-to-rural migration, it is usually assumed that occupational migration implies a change in residence. This chapter shows that such an assumption is not supported by empirical evidence. By distinguishing between urban, periurban and deep rural areas, we will argue that the two types of migration must be kept separate and that occupational change is job-related while residential migration is typically a family matter. However, occupational change affects residents' migration, but a change in residence does not imply a change in occupation, as shown by a two-equation simultaneous probit model.

Introduction

In the 1970s, a reversal of the long-term "rural exodus" occurred in developed countries. In the late 1980s, a second reversal — a return to the long-term trend — emerged in some of these countries (Serrow, 1991), but not in most of them. In France, for example (Cavailhès *et al.,* 1994), there are still more people moving from the city to the country than vice versa. Many analysts are trying to explain this migration pattern and to find reasons for the urban-to-rural population shift.

On the basis of census data on **net** urban-to-rural migration in a number of industrialized countries, Serow (1991) concluded that it was a life-cycle phenomenon. The reasons for migration appeared to be occupational in nature for working-age people, whereas mobility among older people was attributable to an interest in the specific amenities of rural living, a desire to be closer to family or a need for access to better health care and treatment.

On the basis of their survey of recent in-migrants to North Devon in the United Kingdom, Bolton and Chalkey (1990) found the same difference between lifestyle and career motives. They took their analysis further than Serow in that they distinguished between the factors that drove people to leave their urban habitat and the factors that attracted them to their new location. This led Bolton and Chalkey to define three groups of migrants:

1. people who want a certain lifestyle but are not willing to sacrifice their careers: these people decided to settle in North Devon not only for environmental and social reasons but also because of the employment and business opportunities available in the area;

2. people who move exclusively for occupational reasons;

3. people interested primarily in the social interaction and pleasant environment of rural living; this group naturally includes retired people.

Williams and Jobes (1990) adopted a similar approach to that of Bolton and Chalkey. For their study, they conducted a series of interviews with in-migrants to the Gallatin Valley in Montana asking them why they were attracted to the area and the role played in the decision to move by the desire for a certain quality of life as opposed to economic considerations. Unlike Bolton and Chalkey, Williams and Jobes observed a strong association between respondents' reasons for relocating and their reasons for choosing their new surroundings.

Halfacree (1994) demonstrated the need to differentiate between migration to periurban rural areas and migration to deep rural areas. Through a review of the literature, he showed very clearly that long-distance migration is connected with employment-related concerns, while short-distance migration has to do with housing needs. Thus, he associates migration distance with the two types of mobility, occupational and residential.

Though diverse, all these studies have two major features in common, one analytical, the other methodological:

1. there are essentially two types of migration, job-related migration and lifestyle-related migration, and they are not mutually exclusive;

2. only residential migration is investigated, since occupational mobility is assumed necessarily to lead to residential mobility.

Unfortunately, the latter assumption is contradicted by empirical observations — in France, for example, between 1980 and 1985 only 47 percent of occupational migration to deep rural areas (and a mere 25 percent to periurban locations) was accompanied by residential migration.

The argument put forward in this chapter distinguishes between occupational mobility and residential mobility. It is based on two main hypotheses:

1. each type of mobility is governed by a unique set of factors: a review of the literature suggests that occupational mobility has job-related motivations and residential mobility has lifestyle-related motivations;

2. with regard to the interaction of the two types of mobility, occupational mobility influences residential mobility, but the reverse is not true. Since rural areas typically have low population density, there are fewer job openings and less available housing in any given location, and therefore it is difficult for people moving into a new residence to find work and for people starting a new job to find a place to live. However, the labour market and the housing market are very different for three reasons:

● building one's own house is easier than creating a job for oneself;

● vacant houses are not uncommon in the countryside after the long period of rural exodus; and

● a person's skills are more specific than housing preferences, and finding a match when there is a shortage is easier on the real estate market than on the job market.

In view of all these obstacles to finding employment, it is safe to assume that residential mobility depends on occupational mobility. Conversely, there is no *a priori* reason why occupational mobility should depend on residential mobility, which has fewer restrictions.

The analytical method used here will nevertheless be quite different from the one employed in the sociological studies cited above, which laid the groundwork for this research. The sociological approach is founded primarily on interviews with migrants, where a meticulous analysis is intended to reveal the objective motives for their mobility behaviour. As Halfacree (1994) points out, the results depend heavily on how the interviews are conducted, on how leading the questions are, and the implicit logic they contain. Yet the subjective aspect of the information gathered in this way is present in all research into social issues, even where highly "quantitative" questionnaires take on the appearance of complete objectivity! Surveys of actual participants are valuable to those attempting to understand the differential behaviour of individuals who share a specific set of statistically measurable characteristics, provided they are based on *a priori* knowledge of the major behavioural tendencies, in this case the propensity to relocate.

Our aim in this chapter is to analyse the effect of a number of individual characteristics on the migration behaviour of city-dwellers. We will compare urban people who have migrated to rural areas with other urban people and not with rural people. The latter comparison would shed no light on the reasons for moving. A comparison with the rural people would, of course, be essential in order to study the impact that urban in-migration has on social life in the countryside and on the rural labour market. However, that is not our purpose here.

The database we used is described briefly in section 2. Section 3 deals with the econometric model we decided to estimate and the lessons to be learned are discussed in section 4.

Data

We drew our data from INSEE's 1985 survey on vocational training and skills (INSEE, 1988). As its name suggests, this periodic survey is designed primarily to gather information about initial and continuous training, type of employment, and mobility. In the 1985 survey, just over 39,000 respondents were asked about their social and occupational background and their situation at the time of the survey and five years earlier (1980). From this database we pulled the records of all 1980 city-dwellers who were in the labour force (employed or unemployed, whether they had ever worked or not, which excludes students, members of the armed forces, retired people and others not in the labour force) and all persons in the labour force in 1985, regardless of their place of work or place of residence. This left a survey population of 18,570.

In fact, most of the sample consists of non-movers. After eliminating 360 questionnaires because of missing data, we found that 16,896 respondents out of 18,210 reported no occupational or residential migration, at least not in relation to the three types of areas we defined.

When one studies migration between urban and rural areas, many things depend on how these areas are defined. Almost every country has its own administrative definition of "rural", and this heterogeneity simply reflects the various territorial divisions and the effects of each society's history and city/country differences. As Mormont (1987) clearly shows, "rural" is more a subjective social representation than an objective geographic entity. For this reason, the lack of consensus among nations on what "rural" means does not matter very much; it should not stand in the way of international comparisons since the factors governing individual behaviours stem as much from representations of reality as from reality itself!

In France, the traditional official definition states that any agglomeration with a population of less than 2,000 is rural. In the late 1960s, there arose a need to distinguish between rural areas under urban influence (referred to as periurban areas) and deep rural areas. As a result, urban industrial settlement areas (UISAs) were created. Each UISA corresponds roughly to the gravitational sphere of an urban centre, and when the urban centre is large, the associated UISA has a large population and may contain a number of towns, with intervening spaces. For official censuses, rural *communes* that belong to a UISA are deemed to be periurban, while those which do not are considered to be in deep rural areas.

In our study, it is important to define two types of rural areas for an additional reason, the effect of variables related to occupational and residential migration probably depends on the distance over which the migration takes place and relocation from an urban to a deep rural area is likely to be over a longer distance than a move to a periurban area. In any case, our definitions are somewhat different from the administrative boundaries:

1. we consider isolated small towns to be rural, even if their population is slightly above the 2,000 threshold;

2. we regard rural *communes* that are part of small UISAs as belonging to deep rural areas because urban influence on them is likely to be limited.

Accordingly, we define the two rural areas as follows:

Deep rural: agglomerations with a population of less than 2,000 located in a UISA with a population of less than 50,000, and *communes* with a population of under 5,000 situated in a UISA with a population of less than 5,000.

Periurban: all other rural *communes*.

As noted above, less than 8 percent of the survey population had moved in one way or another. This percentage shrinks further when we define two rural areas and two types of mobility: 177 and 379 people made occupational and residential moves, respectively, to deep rural areas, and 278 and 647 respectively, moved to periurban areas. In qualitative-response models such as the model of mobility we intend to estimate, excessively disproportionate sampling of the various possible values of the non-explanatory variable can be overcome by decreasing the size of the over represented group through random sampling. This alteration of the relative sizes of the two groups improves the significance of the econometric model without changing the marginal effects of the explanatory variables (Maddala, 1983, p. 90). Only the model's constant is biased since the average probability of being a mover increases as the relative size of the non-mover group declines[1].

We compared the means of the exogenous variables for the entire survey population with those for a 10 percent random sample of non-movers[2]. The means of all variables remain unchanged at the 10 percent level (Table 12.1). Hence the two populations (survey and sample) can be considered to have come from the same reference population. All of our econometric results will be based on this sample population of 1,690 urban non-movers, to which are added all urban movers.

The definitions of the exogenous variables are presented in Table 1. The endogenous variables are indicators of the type of migration:

RESDEEP equals 1 in the case of residential migration to deep rural, 0 otherwise;

---

1.   *For a 10% sample with a probit specification, the estimate must be decreased by approximately $0.625log(0.1) = 1.44$ to obtain the true value of the model's constant.*

2.   *If we let x_1, x_2, v_1, v_2, n_1 and n_2 be the means, variances and values, respectively, of two distributions assumed to be normal, testing the homogeneity of the two populations is simply a matter of examining the reduced normal variable $d = (x_1 - x_2)/(v_1/n_1 + v_2/n_2)^{1/2}$. Using normal distribution tables, the equation $P(d>\lambda) = p$ can be solved, where p is the significance level and λ is the tabulated value of the distribution.*

RESPERI equals 1 in the case of residential migration to periurban, 0 otherwise;

OCCDEEP equals 1 in the case of occupational migration to deep rural, 0 otherwise;

OCCPERI equals 1 in the case of occupational migration to periurban, 0 otherwise.

Table 12.1.   Definition of exogenous variables and means for non-movers

Symbol	Definition	Survey mean (n_1=16,896)	10% sample mean (n_2=1,690)	Equality test
YREXPER	Labour market experience in years since started first job	21.886 (11.30)	22.244 (11.20)	1.29
YRSENIOR	Seniority in job held in 1980, in years	9.0167 (8.38)	8.9875 (8.01)	0.14
UNSTABLE	Dummy variable= 1 if 1980 job unstable, =0 otherwise	0.03385 (0.1809)	0.03846 (0.1924)	1.04
FIRM500	Dummy variable= 1 if 1980 job was in establishment with over 500 employees, =0 otherwise	0.20597 (0.4044)	0.20639 (0.4048)	0.04
PUBLIC	Dummy variable= 1 if 1980 job was in public sector, =0 otherwise	0.07588 (0.2648)	0.08613 (0.2806)	1.58
UNEMP	Dummy variable= 1 if unemployed in 1980, =0 otherwise	0.02847 (0.1663)	0.02871 (0.1670)	0.06
GENDER	Dummy variable= 1 if female, =0 if male	0.38482 (0.4866)	0.38787 (0.4874)	0.26
PARDEEP	Dummy variable= 1 if person's parents lived in deep rural when person finished education, =0 otherwise	0.10494 (0.3065)	0.11268 (0.3163)	1.03
PARPERI	Same as above except periurban	0.06096 (0.2393)	0.05471 (0.2275)	1.07
MARRIED	Dummy variable= 1 if person was in spousal relationship in 1985	0.79356 (0.4048)	0.78927 (0.4079)	0.43
CHILD<16	Dummy variable= 1 if person had more than one child under 16 in 1985, =0 otherwise	0.28918 (0.4534)	0.28386 (0.4510)	0.48

Standard deviation in parentheses.
Significance at 10% level: 1.645.

The urban-to-rural migration model

As mentioned earlier, the model has three underlying hypotheses:

1. occupational migration is based on job-market factors, residential migration is determined by personal reasons;
2. occupational migration influences residential migration;
3. residential migration does not influence occupational migration.

The model, which is supposed to describe the migration behaviour of city-dwellers, is composed of two submodels that must be tested using the data described above and then compared. One model concerns relocation to deep rural areas, the other concerns relocation to periurban areas. It is assumed that these two submodels are formally identical, having the same structure, as discussed in this paragraph. This means we consider that the choice to migrate to a given area or not to migrate is not affected by the fact that one can migrate or not migrate to the other area. This assumption, known as independence from irrelevant alternatives (Maddala, 1983, p. 61), was used implicitly by Blanc (1994) in a study of the same data; the model estimated was a multinomial logit model for which the assumption was known to be satisfied.

The structure of the proposed model consists of two equations, one for occupational migration (E_1), the other for residential migration (E_2). Let y_1 and y_2 be the dependent variables, corresponding to the dichotomous variables OCC... and RES... defined above (the ellipsis points stand for the area of destination, deep rural or periurban, in each submodel). Let X_1 and X_2 be the exogenous variable vectors for the two equations. Hence we have the following system of two equations:

$$(E_1) y_1 = f_1(X_1)$$

$$(E_2) y_2 = f_2(y_1, X_2)$$

Since one of our aims is to test the reciprocal effects of variables y_1 and y_2, we will consider the following system instead:

$$(EE_1)\ y_1 = f_1(y_2, X_1)$$

$$(E_2)\ y_2 = f_2(y_1, X_2)$$

with special attention to the significance of y_2 in (EE_1), which is expected to be weak, and of y_1 in (E_2), which is expected to be strong.

The choice of the exogenous variables X_1 and X_2 is, of course, limited by the available data source. Furthermore, in order to obtain genuinely exogenous variables that are unchanged by any mobility decisions made between 1980 and 1985, we selected only those which described the situations of individuals in 1980 (see Table 12.1 for details).

The employment-related variables (vector X_1) describe:

1. whether the person was employed or unemployed in 1980, whether the job was unstable or stable, seniority in the job, overall employment experience, gender (which reveals any discrimination against women and the constraints imposed by the male partner's career (Barrère-Maurisson, 1992));

2. characteristics of the business size and industry;

3. accessibility of information about the local job market: the geographic origin of the person's parents is used as an indicator; if it is the same as the person's area of destination, the person may hear about potential jobs.

Lifestyle-related variables (vector X_2) describe marital status, the presence of children and, once again, the parents' geographic origin, this time used as a proxy for a degree of familiarity with rural life.

There are two econometric problems in estimating a two-equation model $\{(EE_1),(E_2)\}$: simultaneity, which is a standard problem; and the qualitative nature of the dependent variable, a more delicate problem. With two separate equations for the residential and occupational models, there is no doubt that the relationship between the two types of migration will be bidirectional or non-existent, since the same partial correlation will apply in the two equations taken separately. We know that the estimate of a regression is biased if there is a correlation between the residual and an explanatory variable; this is the case where the explanatory variable becomes an explained variable in another equation. The simultaneous nature of the equations would be dealt with by the usual method of two-stage least squares if variables y_1 and y_2 were quantitative. Then we would apply the reduced-form method, followed by estimation of structural equations, where the explanatory endogenous variable is replaced by its estimated value from the corresponding reduced form. However, care must be taken when using this technique on non-linear models, which is what qualitative-response models are. This is known as the "forbidden regression" (Hausman, 1983, p. 440) because it usually results in inconsistent estimates[3]. To overcome this difficulty, we opted to estimate a probit model in two simultaneous equations, in which we use two-stage least squares, with a variance–covariance matrix adjusted as suggested by Maddala (1983) (see Appendix A for details).

---

3.   *An estimator is said to be consistent if the probability of its being close to the parameter's actual value increases with the number of observations considered.*

Results

The relationship between residential and occupational migration

The main difference between the estimates using separate and simultaneous equations has to do with the migration variables. The results are consistent with our expectations: while the separate probit model yields an artificial two-way effect, the rigorous simultaneous two-stage probit model produces a unidirectional correlation, whereby occupational migration affects residential migration and not vice versa. This "one-way" correlation does not, however, imply a causal relationship, which would have to be established first at the theoretical level, as outlined above.

Table 12.2.   Summary of results for the models

	OCCDEEP		RESDEEP		OCCPERI		RESPERI	
	Separate probit	Two-stage probit	Separate probit	Two-stage probit	Separate probit	Two-stage probit	Separate probit	Two-stage probit
Constant	-1.2	-0.55	-1.6	-1.8	-0.95	-0.73	-1.4	-1.7
RESDEEP	0.96	ns						
RESPERI					0.14	ns		
OCCDEEP			1.2	4.0				
OCCPERI							0.25	3.8
YREXPER	-0.018	-0.030			ns	-0.011		
YRSENIOR	ns	ns			-0.026	-0.027		
UNSTABLE	ns	ns			0.24	ns		
FIRM500	-0.48	-0.44			ns	ns		
PUBLIC	-0.41	-0.52			-0.34	-0.34		
UNEMP	0.51	0.44			0.50	0.51		
GENDER	-0.36	-0.38			-0.27	-0.27		
MARRIED			0.22	ns			0.43	0.46
CHILD<16			0.48	0.43			0.38	0.38
PARDEEP	0.30	0.73	0.59	ns	ns	ns	0.27	ns
PARPERI	ns	ns	ns	ns	0.31	0.47	0.79	0.53
Number of movers	177		379		278		647	

The variables RESDEEP, RESPERI, OCCDEEP and OCCPERI, when explanatory, correspond to the observed values in the separate probits and to the reduced-form probability estimates for the two-stage probit model.
ns: coefficient not significant at the 10 percent level.
In each case, the 1,690 non-movers are added to the number of movers.
For detailed information about the estimation methods, especially the size of the adjustment made in the variance–covariance matrix, see Appendices B and C.

The effects of occupational migration on residential migration appear to be of a comparable intensity level regardless of the relocation area. Two opposing influences may be offsetting each other here: the distance of the deep rural areas makes the decision to move a more difficult one, and conversely, transportation facilities between cities and periurban areas may make permanent residential relocation unnecessary (there is now a sharply rising trend toward commuting migration).

In the residential migration model, the large values of the coefficients of the OCC... variables (4.0 for deep rural and 3.8 for periurban) stem from the 10 percent sampling of the non-mover population. As we have seen (note 1 above), the value of the constant should be reduced in this case. As a result, a single native city-dweller with no dependent children will have a probability of about 0.58 of moving to a deep-rural residence if he/she is already switching to a job in a deep-rural area. The probability is 0.44 for moves to periurban areas, because alternating migration is much easier in the case of periurban areas.

Occupational migration

One might assume that city-dwellers' job-search strategies depend on how well integrated they are in their jobs. The least integrated people would have a greater tendency to look for a better position elsewhere: in another company, in another town, perhaps in the country. Although our models are not directly based on a knowledge of individual strategies but rather on their results, they are consistent with this view of job-seeking behaviour.

Unemployed people in 1980 (UNEMP) showed a greater propensity to migrate, with similar numbers moving to all destinations. Unstable urban employment (UNSTABLE) does not show up as a factor, probably because the official definition of instability is related to contract status; indeterminate contracts, of course, do not necessarily guarantee stable, lasting employment, and conversely, an apprenticeship contract or an initial term contract may lead to a permanent job.

Seniority (YRSENIOR) is a stabilizing factor, mitigating moves to periurban areas, but not to deep rural areas: the size of the job-search area shrinks with length of employment, but occupational migration to a deep rural area, because it involves a greater distance, is another matter. Employment experience (YREXPER) weighs against migration to both areas, though it must be borne in mind that this variable is strongly correlated with age and may serve as an indicator of what is known as return migration, much of it toward deep rural areas.

Women (GENDER) seem less inclined to move than men do. It is generally believed that this is due to constraints placed on their careers by the requirements of their husbands' careers and by their children's need for stability. To push this analysis any further would require statistics for families instead of individuals.

Internal labour markets (Doeringer and Piore, 1985) are more common in urban areas than in the country. Paid workers in these internal markets are assumed to be sufficiently attached to their employers that they do not want to migrate. Public-sector firms (PUBLIC) are the archetype of this way of organizing work, offering both stability and career opportunities. Their employees are less likely to migrate, even less so to deep rural areas than to periurban locations. Being part of a large production unit (FIRM500), a special internal market place, also reduces one's chances of moving, albeit, oddly enough, only to deep rural areas. This tendency may be due to the fact that it is more appealing to switch from one large firm to another large firm rather than to a small company, and since there are very few establishments with over 500 employees in deep rural areas, migrating there means having to give up a prized position. In 1985, only 27 percent of those who had worked for a large business and made an occupational move to a deep rural area had a new job in a large establishment. The corresponding figure for occupational migration to periurban areas, to which urban internal markets undoubtedly extend, is 64 percent.

As expected, those who have relatives in their new location (PARDEEP, PARPERI) are more likely to move for occupational reasons. We saw earlier the effect that information about local opportunities had on occupational migration, especially to deep rural locations (a coefficient of 0.73, compared with 0.47 for periurban areas). It may be that networks of friends and relatives are more active there than in periurban regions, which were populated much more recently, and where information about labour demand circulates more through formal institutions than through personal relationships.

Residential migration

This type of migration appears to be closely associated with family life. We omitted the GENDER variable from the estimation process because it was never significant, probably because it is usually couples who migrate.

Having a dependent child (CHILD<16) encourages people to move to a rural setting because the natural and social environment is more congenial and housing is more spacious and less expensive. Like having parents living in the area, having a spouse (MARRIED) increases one's propensity to move to a periurban location, but does not affect migration to deep rural areas. If we regard this variable as a proxy for the parents' "current" place of residence, we may conclude that moving close to one's parents' home has advantages (such as easier access to child care), but it also has a price — it entails a change in lifestyle, all the more indeed that the new location is more remote. Our results suggest that urban people without rural roots tend to be more attracted by such settings than people who have had prior experience of living in this kind of place. The cost, which depends on the distance of the move, is higher for migration to deep rural areas, which is therefore less strongly correlated with the parents' place of residence.

The model for deep rural areas appears to be less helpful, with few significant variables, while the model for periurban areas seems clearer. As Goffette-Nagot (1994) has demonstrated, the periurban area offers easy reconciliation of career and family considerations, and the tradeoffs, being more rational, are perhaps more easily modelled!

Conclusion

In the literature on urban-to-rural migration, it is usually assumed that occupational change implies a change in residence. This chapter shows that such an assumption is not supported by empirical evidence. By distinguishing between urban, periurban and deep rural areas, we found that the two types of migration must be kept separate, and that they are based on different factors.

Occupational migration is job-related and appears to be informed by a particular segmentation of the labour market — rural space is characterized by a limited primary sector and a secondary sector where working relationships are probably of a "paternalistic" kind (Doeringer, 1984). Residential migration, on the other hand, is typically a family matter.

By estimating a probit model in two simultaneous equations, we were able to show that occupational migration fostered residential migration but, contrary to usual assumption, the reverse was not true. We also saw the usefulness of dividing rural space into two areas, as it enabled us to detect whether certain city-to-country gradients existed for the various determining variables.

Using statistics for individuals before migration, our analysis focused on the factors that "push" people to migrate. The factors that "pull" people (i.e. what attracts them to their new location), whether they have to do with labour demand or the various kinds of amenities in the new area of residence, remain to be investigated. This suggests some ways of improving the econometric model, though increasing the number of explanatory variables heightens the risk of multicollinearity and may hinder the identification of major influences.

Appendix A: A two-equation simultaneous probit model

The description here is based on Maddala's work (1983, p. 246).

Suppose the structural model is composed of the following two probit equations:

(EE_1) $y_1 = f_1(y_2, X_1)$

(E_2) $y_2 = f_2(y_1, X_2)$

Letting $X = X_1 \cup X_2$ be the vector of all exogenous variables in the system, we begin by estimating the following probit reduced form equations using maximum likelihood:

(R_1) $y_1 = g_1(X)$

(R_2) $y_2 = g_2(X)$

From these equations we obtain the estimates y_{1r} and y_{2r}, which we will use in estimating the structural model, again using maximum likelihood. We obtain:

$$y_1 = \alpha_1 y_{2r} + \beta_1 X_1$$
$$y_2 = \alpha_2 y_{1r} + \beta_2 X_2$$

The coefficients are unbiased, but the variance–covariance matrix must be recomputed because the one produced by the standard method is incorrect. The principle behind this method (Maddala, 1983, p. 243) is to consider an expression computed from the first and second derivatives of the likelihood with the same asymptotic distribution as the difference $(\hat{e}_1 - e_{01})$, where e_{01} is the true value of the coefficient vector and $\hat{e}_1$ is its two-stage least squares estimate.

Let Z be the vector (y_{2r}, X_1) of the structural form's regressors and let φ_1 and ϕ_2 be the estimated distribution functions of y_1 and y_2 respectively, and φ_1 and ϕ_2 their respective density functions.

Letting

$a_1 = \varphi_1 / (\varphi_1 (1-\varphi_1))$ $a_2 = \phi_2 (1-\phi_2))$ $A_1 = a_1 . \varphi_1$ $A_2 = a_2 . \phi_2$

$M = \Sigma A_1 . Z . Z' / n$

$N = \Sigma A_2 . X . X' / n$

$P = \Sigma A_1 . \alpha_1 . Z . X' / n$

$Q = \Sigma a_1 . a_2 . (y_1 - \phi_1) . (y_2 - \phi_2) . X . Z' / n$

Then the variance–covariance matrix V_1 of $n^{1/2} (\hat{e}_1 - e_{01})$ is given by the expression

$$V_1 = M^{-1} . [M - P . N^{-1} . Q - Q' . N^{-1} . P' + P . N^{-1} . P'] . M^{-1}$$

The matrix V_2 of $\hat{e}_2$ is a similar expression, with the appropriate changes in the definitions of Z, M, N, P and Q.

Appendix B: Occupational migration model

	OCCDEEP		OCCPERI	
	Separate probit	Two-stage probit	Separate probit	Two-stage probit
Constant	-1.224 (11.4)	-0.5543 (2.58) (2.17)	-0.9549 (11.0)	-0.7263 (3.74) (3.06)
RESDEEP	0.9559 (10.4)	-1.094 (1.60) (1.36)		
RESPERI			0.1444 (1.86)	-0.4289 (0.96) (0.80)
YREXPER	-0.01830 (3.25)	-0.03046 (4.55) (3.93)	-0.006080 (1.48)	-0.01123 (1.99) (1.65)
YRSENIOR	-0.002731 (0.33	-0.009949 (1.20) (1.04)	-0.02597 (3.96)	-0.02675 (4.05) (3.44)
UNSTABLE	-0.05097 (0.23)	-0.1743 (0.81) (0.67)	0.2426 (1.68)	0.1779 (1.17) (1.03)
FIRM500	-0.4772 (3.54)	-0.4361 (3.42) (3.00)	-0.05976 (0.58)	-0.03216 (0.36) (0.31)
PUBLIC	-0.4077 (1.66)	-0.5160 (2.17) (1.92)	0.3396 (2.00)	0.3361 (1.98) (1.80)
UNEMP	0.5070 (2.79)	0.4383 (2.45) (2.15)	0.4952 (3.30)	0.5074 (3.37) (2.83)
GENDER	-0.3650 (3.91)	-0.3817 (4.24) (3.57)	-0.2715 (3.71)	-0.2747 (3.75) (3.16)
PARDEEP	0.2958 (2.76)	0.7325 (4.17) (3.46)	-0.08581 (0.76)	-0.02440 (0.20) (0.17)
PARPERI	-0.04435 (0.24)	0.08139 (0.44) (0.38)	0.3149 (2.88)	0.4733 (2.93) (2.42)
Number of movers	177	177	278	278
Likelihood ratio	216.9	112.6	97.7	95.2

Appendix C: **Residential migration model**

	RESDEEP		RESPERI	
	Separate probit	Two-stage probit	Separate probit	Two-stage probit
Constant	-1.622 (18.1)	-1.812 (17.3) (6.37)	-1.360 (17.5)	-1.745 (17.8) (7.52)
OCCDEEP	1.213 (11.7)	4.030 (6.66) (2.44)		
OCCPERI			0.2531 (2.96)	3.781 (7.31) (2.96)
MARRIED	0.2230 (2.35)	0.2938 (3.08) (1.22)	0.4349 (5.30)	0.4622 (5.58) (2.53)
CHILD<16	0.4808 (6.97)	0.4296 (6.33) (2.26)	0.3833 (6.70)	0.3837 (6.66) (2.69)
PARDEEP	0.5870 (7.02)	0.3314 (3.45) (1.33)	0.2651 (3.25)	0.3419 (4.13) (1.53)
PARPERI	0.2121 (1.58)	0.2082 (1.59) (0.55)	0.7872 (8.77)	0.5304 (5.40) (2.34)
Number of movers	379	379	647	647
Likelihood ratio	270.4	176.9	187.1	231.9

The variables OCCDEEP, OCCPERI, RESDEEP and RESPERI, when explanatory, correspond to the observed values in the separate probits and to the reduced-form probability estimates for the two-stage simultaneous probit model.

Student's t-test in parentheses: for the two-stage probit models, the value on the left relates to the unadjusted model

Levels of significance for t: 1.645 (10%)
1.960 (5%)
2.576 (1%)
3.291 (0.1%)

Levels of significance for the likelihood ratio: always less than 0.1%

References and further reading

Amemiya, T. (1978) The estimation of a simultaneous equation generalized probit model. *Econometrica*, No. 5, September.

Barrère-Maurisson, M.A. (1992) *La Division Familiale du Travail*. Paris: PUF.

Blanc, M. (1994) Urban to rural migrations: which relationships between occupational and residential migrations? In Copus, A.K. and Marr, P.J. (eds). *Rural Realities, Trends and Choices*. Aberdeen: University of Aberdeen, June.

Bolton, N. and Chalkey, B. (1990) The rural population turnaround: a case study of North Devon. *Journal of Rural Studies*, No. 1.

Cavailhès, J., Dessendre, C., Goffette-Nagot, F. and Schmitt, B. (1994) Change in French countryside: some analytical propositions. *European Review of Agricultural Economics*, No. 3-4.

Doeringer, P.B. (1984) Internal labor markets and paternalism in rural areas. In Osternam, P. (ed.). *Internal Labor Markets*. MIT Press.

Doeringer, P.B. and Piore, M.J. (1985) *Internal Labor Markets and Manpower Analysis*. Armoek: M.E. Sharpe.

Goffette-Nagot, F. (1994) *Analyse microéconomique de la périurbanisation: un modèle de localisation résidentielle*. Thèse, Dijon, University de Bourgogne.

Halfacree, K.H. (1994) The importance of "the rural" in the constitution of counterurbanization: evidence from England in the 1980s. *Sociologia Ruralis*, No. 2-3.

Hausman, J.A. (1983) Specification and estimation of simultaneous equation models. In Griliches, Z. and Intriligator, M.D. (eds). *Handbook of Econometrics*, Vol. I. North-Holland.

INSEE (1988) Enquête formation-qualification professionnelle. *Collections de l'INSEE*, série D, No. 121, pp. 126 and 129.

Maddala, G. (1983) *Limited-dependent and Qualitative Variables in Econometrics*. Cambridge: Cambridge University Press.

Mormont, M. (1987) Rural nature and urban nature. *Sociologia Ruralis*, No. 1.

Nelson, F. and Olson, L. (1978) Specification and estimation of a simultaneous equation model with limited dependent variables. *International Economic Review*, No. 3, October.

Serow, W.J. (1991) Recent trends and future prospects for urban-rural migration in Europe. *Sociologia Ruralis*, No. 4.

Tahar, G. (1994) Migrations ville-campagne et chômage: un test d'interdépendance. *Cahiers d'Economie et Sociologie Rurales*, No. 36, 3ème trimestre.

Williams, A.S. and Jobes, P.C. (1990) Economic and quality of life considerations in urban-rural migrations. *Journal of Rural Studies*, No. 2.

Chapter thirteen:

Commuting and Rural Employment on the Canadian Prairies

Jack Stabler
University of Saskatchewan, Saskatoon, Saskatchewan, Canada

Richard C. Rounds
Brandon University, Brandon, Manitoba, Canada

Abstract

Declining labour requirements in Prairie agriculture are causing population declines in agricultural-dependent communities. However, some of these communities are able to maintain their population base if workers are able to commute to larger centres. Resident workers who commute do contribute to small community viability but only via their personal consumption expenditure (and volunteer community participation, etc.). The jobs and related spinoffs are urban-based. The local community multiplier of these urban-based earnings is small — about 20 percent of the value of multipliers in larger centres. More jobs will be created in larger centres per dollar spent. Present trends are therefore expected to continue.

Introduction

The continuing decline in labour requirements for Prairie agriculture is causing a population decline in agriculturally-dependent communities. Communities within commuting distance of a major centre are able, however, to maintain a population base. The purpose of this chapter is to document these patterns among Prairie communities and to indicate expected future patterns.

Background

Rural economies have experienced significant change during the last few decades and the restructuring process may be accelerating rather than stabilizing. Modern telecommunications, growth in service industries and technological advances in the predominantly rural industries threaten to marginalize rural economies. Rural depopulation is testimony to outmigration as one major method of adjustment to changing economies and this process continues in most rural areas located beyond the shadow of major metropolitan areas. Hall (1990) reports that restructuring has aggravated regional disparities in the United Kingdom and similar patterns are documented in the United States (Bernat and Frederick, 1992; Deavers, 1991; Hady and Ross, 1990; Porterfield, 1990).

Rural restructuring has been characterized by loss of jobs in agriculture, energy, forestry, and mining. Growth in employment, therefore, has occurred almost exclusively in the service sectors in rural as in urban areas. Rural service sector employment, however, is both concentrated in the lower-order industries and increasing less rapidly than in urban areas (Stabler and Olfert, 1994). In rural Manitoba, the number of jobs in service industries increased rapidly between 1985 and 1990, but stabilized in 1991 and decreased in 1992 (Bollman and Rounds, 1993).

Other than relocation, one major response within farming families to changing economic circumstances has been an increase in off-farm non-agricultural employment. Although long-established as a diversification strategy, permanent, planned pluriactivité has increased in many regions. Farm women in particular have joined the rural non-farm workforce, with their participation rates now virtually identical to urban women in the workforce. In Manitoba, 36 percent of main farm operators (primarily men) and 55 percent of spouses worked off-farm in 1992 (Bessant *et al.*, 1993).

Most studies of commuting behaviour indicate that women generally commute shorter distances to work than do men (Deseran, 1989; Hanson and Johnston, 1985; Madden, 1981). This does not hold unequivocally in either Saskatchewan or Manitoba, however. In Manitoba, rural men commuted an average distance of 35 km and women an average of 45 km (Bessant *et al.*, 1993). In Saskatchewan, Olfert and Stabler (1994b) report overall commuting distances of 24 km for both farm males and females, and 23 km for both male and female non-farm rural workers. Off-farm earnings now represent a larger share of household income than farm income (Stabler and Olfert, 1994). Since job growth is occurring almost solely in larger centres and since public services are concentrating in larger centres, rural and farming families outside these commuting zones must travel further for both possible jobs and to access public services.

Commuting patterns have been used to assess the various aspects of the influence of metropolitan areas on adjacent rural areas. Mitchelson and Fisher (1987b) constructed percentage commuter isolines around Georgia's cities in

1960, 1970 and 1980. Most rural growth in Georgia occurred as intensification within metropolitan commuting fields. Larger centres typically have larger commuting fields (e.g. Atlanta, Georgia). In New York state, the largest commuting fields are 80–100 km (50–60 miles) (Mitchelson and Fisher, 1987b). Berry (1970) states that a community must have a population of 40,000 to 50,000 before a significant commuting field develops and Parr (1987) argues that commuting is less likely between major centres owing to greater distance. Parr claims that larger centres usually experience net in-commuting while smaller centres experience net out-commuting (Parr, 1987).

Data and methods

Labour market areas (LMAs) are defined by commuting patterns. Statistics Canada data on place of residence and place of work are available at the census subdivision (CSD) level, which allows identification of commuters by city, town, village, township or rural municipality. For the provinces of Saskatchewan and Manitoba, in Canada's prairie region, the smallest government units are numerous, small and identified individually as CSDs in the Census of Population, allowing delineation of micro-level commuter patterns. A commuter is defined as a person who lives in a CSD that is different than the CSD where that same person works. For Saskatchewan, more than 900 CSDs were aggregated into 298 RMs (Rural Municipalities) first, and commuting was then calculated among RMs.

A labour market area (LMA) is defined as an area that is large enough to contain the work places of most of the people who reside within it and the residences of most of the people who work within it (Heilbrun, 1987). LMAs may contain one or more communities. Most residents likely will be employed within larger communities while some residents will commute to rural areas for primary production or other employment. Conversely, rural residents usually will commute to jobs in the communities. The LMA, therefore, is an integrated, functional unit, the boundaries of which may be defined by the strength of flow of commuters at any predetermined level.

Studies of Saskatchewan's central place hierarchy (Stabler, Olfert and Fulton, 1992; Stabler and Olfert, 1992) recognized 62 centres as viable communities over a 30-year period. These centres occupy the top four functional categories in central place analysis (primary and secondary wholesale/retail centres and full and partial shopping centres), and were selected as focal points for defining LMAs in Saskatchewan. Place of work and place of residence data were obtained by special tabulations for 1981 and 1991 from Statistics Canada's CSD census data.

Rounds and Shamanski (1993) completed central place analysis for 41 of Manitoba's largest centres in 1966 and 1986, and for 279 centres in 1991. The 28 largest communities were selected as centres for LMA definition. Place of work and place of residence data were used to define LMAs for 1991 in Manitoba. A review of the statistical methods used to define LMAs is available in Tolbert and Killian (1987) and Stabler *et al.* (1996).

Commuting patterns in Saskatchewan and Manitoba

Labour market areas in Saskatchewan were defined for 1981 and 1991 and were analysed in light of related research on the role of communities in regional economic development (Stabler *et al.*, 1992; Stabler and Olfert, 1992; Stabler *et al.,* 1996). Skotheim and Olfert, 1996). There were 38 LMAs identified in 1981 and 37 in 1991 (Figure 13.1). Three patterns are apparent in the analyses. First, the 15 largest LMAs (including two metro LMAs) increased in population and commuter activity, while the 23 smaller centres declined during the decade (Table 13.1). Second, commuting from urban to rural areas decreased, while that from rural to urban increased. Third, commuting patterns are intensifying.

Table 13.1.   Rural-to-urban commuting increased and urban-to-rural commuting decreased, Saskatchewan, 1981 to 1991

	Males		Females		Total	
LMA Type	1991	1981 to 91 Change	1991	1981 to 91 Change	1991	1981 to 91 Change
Metro LMAs						
To focal points from rural	7,555	+1,215	5,995	+2,260	13,550	+3,475
From focal points to rural	2,910	+105	1,315	+445	4,225	+550
Total	**10,465**	**+1,320**	**7,310**	**+2,705**	**17,775**	**+4,025**
Mid-sized 13 LMAs						
To focal points from rural	9,465	+935	9,425	+2,825	18,890	+3,760
From focal points to rural	1,955	-1,200	1,065	-210	3,020	-1,410
Total	**11,420**	**-265**	**10,490**	**+2,615**	**21,910**	**+2,350**
Smallest 23 LMAs						
To focal points from rural	1,865	-340	3,005	+810	4,870	+470
From focal points to rural	245	-480	35	-115	280	-595
Total	**2,110**	**-820**	**3,040**	**+695**	**5,150**	**-125**
Total						
To focal points from rural	18,885	+1,810	18,425	+5,895	37,310	+7,705
From focal points to rural	5,110	-1,575	2,415	+120	7,525	-1,455
Total	**23,995**	**+235**	**20,840**	**+6,015**	**44,805**	**+6,250**

Source: Statistics Canada. Censuses of Population, unpublished tabulations.

In 1981, 16 percent of the labour force was commuting and this increased to 18 percent in 1991. The total number of jobs increased throughout the Province, but those for non-commuters increased by 9 percent while those for commuters increased by 21 percent. The two primary wholesale/retail centres (Regina and Saskatoon) accounted for 56 percent of the increase in commuters and 93 percent of the net job gains. Mid-size to small LMAs actually lost 4,000 jobs during the decade.

Distances travelled by commuters is increasing everywhere, but larger centres are extending their labour fields faster than are smaller centres. Using weighted average commuting distances, average distances travelled (radius of the LMAs) in core areas near major centres in Saskatoon increased from 25 to 26 km (15.5 miles to 16.2 miles) between 1981 and 1991, while average distances for commuters from outlying rural areas (radius of the LMAs) increased from 48 to 51 km (30.2 miles to 32.1 miles). Commuting distances increase with an increase in the size and central place function of the centre. Maximum average straight-line distances travelled from peripheral areas to major centres average 62 km (38.7 miles), which equates to approximately 88 km (55 miles) on an actual road system. The commuter fields generated by all centres other than Regina and Saskatoon are considerably smaller than those for these primary wholesale/retail centres.

Figure 13.1.   Major labour market area centres in Saskatchewan and Manitoba

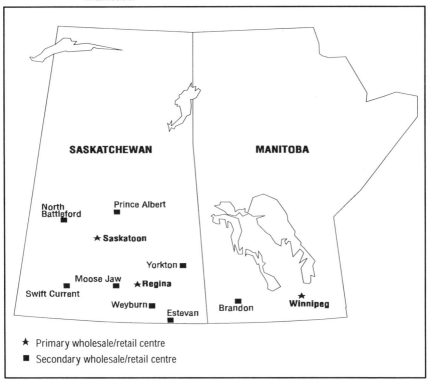

Note: *The complete and partial shopping centres are not shown: Dauphin, Selkirk, Portage la Prairie, Steinbach, Winkler/Morden, Humboldt, Kindersley, Meadow Lake, Melfort, Nipawin, Tisdale and Melville.*

Four sub-patterns evolve from the Saskatchewan analyses:

1. Commuting to town for work is a viable option for rural people who live near big cities, but is becoming less common but still possible for those near smaller centres;

2. Restructuring and loss of employment in primary industries coupled with concentrations of high-order service jobs in cities changes the distribution of employment, and rural residents can access jobs only by relocation or commuting;

3. The fact that off-farm earnings in Canada now make a greater contribution to farm family income than does net farm income reflects the change of employment patterns on income sources, and will have far-reaching effects on farm structure; and

4. Declines in urban to rural movement and increases in rural to urban commuting are making the pattern a one-way street.

Within the above patterns there also appears to be intense competition for employment in mid-sized centres. Between 1981 and 1991, 2,330 new jobs in mid-sized towns went to urban residents, while 4,835 new jobs went to rural-based commuters. Employment in rural areas from which these commuters came decreased by 6,736. Rural residents, therefore, depend increasingly on mid-sized rural towns for their livelihood.

The patterns of employment in Manitoba relate closely to the unusual urban hierarchy in the province (Rounds and Shamanski, 1993). The only primary wholesale/retail centre (Winnipeg) had 302,905 persons in the experienced labour force in 1991 (Table 13.2). The only secondary wholesale/retail centre (Brandon) provided 18,505 jobs. The five complete shopping centres had a total of 20,205 jobs, and the 21 partial shopping centres had a combined total of 19,805 jobs. Winnipeg, therefore, totally dominates provincial employment, and is 15 times larger than Brandon. Brandon (population of 38,000), in turn, provides approximately the same level of employment opportunities as the five regional centres combined (populations 5,000–10,000). The fourth-level partial shopping centres provide average employment for about 1,000 persons each.

The total dominance of Winnipeg in providing employment has several significant ramifications. Because commuting is limited by time and distance, rural residents who live within 100 km (60 miles) or about one hour driving time have the only viable possibilities for work in the city. Accordingly, Manitoba has one of the lowest percentages of commuters in Canada (14 percent of the work force). Winnipeg has 9 percent of its workforce as commuters, with 6 percent in-commuting. This 6 percent, however, represents 20,000 jobs for rural or nearby small urban centre residents. This is approximately equivalent to all employment in Brandon, all employment in the five complete shopping centres (regional centres, three of which lie within one-hour of Winnipeg), or all employment in the 21 partial shopping centres (five of which lie within one hour of Winnipeg).

Table 13.2.   Labour force statistics for Manitoba's main employment centres

Class/Centre	Total labour force	Percent commuters in labour force	Percent resident labour force that out-commutes
Primary wholesale/retail: Winnipeg	302,905	9	3
Secondary wholesale/retail: Brandon	18,505	15	8
Complete Shopping			
Dauphin	3,555	33	18
Portage	5,930	29	30
Selkirk	4,255	51	30
Steinbach	3,760	49	17
Winkler	2,705	44	16
Total	**20,205**	**42**	**24**
Partial Shopping			
Altona	1,345	42	16
Arborg	490	60	21
Ashern/Siglunes	765	17	10
Beausejour	1,115	56	35
Boissevain	655	37	10
Carman	1,020	51	25
Gimli	1,190	58	60
Killarney	965	28	15
Melita	415	34	10
Morden	2,455	26	22
Morris	720	30	38
Neepawa	1,260	39	11
Roblin	660	42	44
Russell	685	24	25
Shoal Lake	330	37	38
Souris	685	34	15
Ste. Rose	410	42	26
Stonewall	1,365	49	55
Swan River	1,550	33	15
Teulon	460	67	45
Virden	1,265	39	13
Total	**19,805**	**40**	**26**

Source: Statistics Canada. Census of Population, 1991, unpublished tabulations.

One important aspect of employment opportunities in regional and smaller centres, however, is not reflected in total numbers of jobs. Within the four highest levels of the central place hierarchy, the percentage of commuters in the workforce of a community increases as the size of community decreases (Figure 13.2). Winnipeg has 3 percent out-commuters and 9 percent in-commuters in its experienced labour force. The percentages for Brandon increase to 8 percent out-going and 15 percent in-coming. A major contrast, however, occurs in third and fourth level communities. Complete and partial shopping centres have 24 percent out-commuters and 42 percent in-commuters. Although the actual number of jobs is lower, the smaller centres create a disproportionate number of employment opportunities for rural residents. The pattern for Saskatchewan is virtually identical. The fact that the smaller centres have more incoming than outgoing commuters is the reverse of the patterns hypothesized by Parr (1987). The incoming–outgoing commuter ratios are not known for the lowest two tiers of communities (convenience centres). Small communities, however, do not function as LMAs.

Figure 13.2.   In-commuting is much larger than out-commuting in small centres, Manitoba, 1991

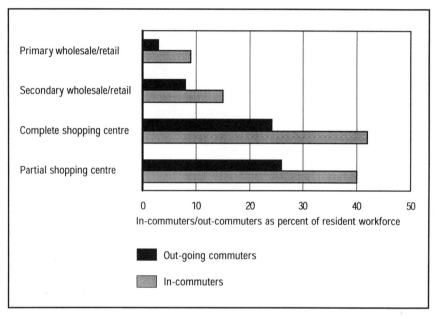

A distinct sub-pattern of commuting occurs in smaller centres (partial shopping centres) near Winnipeg. Gimli lies approximately one hour north of Winnipeg and has 60 percent of its residents out-commuting for work, but a compensatory 58 percent of in-commuting workers for employment in the town (Table 13.2). Teulon (approximately 1/2 hour from Winnipeg) has 45 percent out-commuters and 67 percent in-commuters. It appears that these communities have many residents who prefer to work, or find better jobs in Winnipeg. In turn, by vacating jobs in these towns, or by simply creating jobs by being residents, the out-commuters who prefer to live in small towns and work in the city create opportunities for rural residents to work in town. Although not verified by analysis, the pattern may suggest that the more mobile exurbanite, or small-urban to large-urban commuter, may be creating local opportunities for the less mobile farm family members, or rural to small urban commuter. Near the outer limits of a major urban field (e.g. Gimli), this relationship may effectively extend the influence of a major metropolitan area.

In the rural areas immediately adjacent to Winnipeg the impact of the city on rural employment is dominant. In the Rural Municipality of Springfield, which lies adjacent to Winnipeg, 75 percent of the residents work in Winnipeg. In total, however, they constitute only 0.5 percent of Winnipeg's workforce, clearly illustrating the difference in influence between urban and rural employment fields.

A perspective on commuting and employment

Canada's Prairie Region is vast and productive, but is limited climatically in the variety of crops that can be grown. This has led to specialized agriculture, with cereal grains, oilseeds and cattle as the major commodities. The lack of diversification in rural areas owing to the dominance of focused primary production creates few job opportunities, especially as technologies progressively reduce the need for farm labour. The need for added income in rural areas, coupled with the lack of employment opportunities drives the need to commute to urban centres for work. The pattern is so well-established that one must understand commuting patterns to understand employment of rural residents.

Variation in off-farm opportunities for employment are reflected in the structure of agriculture itself. Many small farms occur near major centres because of off-farm employment opportunities. Also, farms near large cities are more specialized than those in remote areas, either serving urban markets with special commodities or utilizing spare time afforded by specialization for off-farm, off-season work. The result is a concentration of off-farm work and pluriactive farm families near urban centres, with commuting as a way of life.

Patterns in commuting

Evidence suggests that the smaller the urban centre, the higher the likelihood of commuting. Green and Meyer (1995) report commuting by 24 percent of the labour force in towns with populations of less than 2,500, 16 percent for towns with between 2,500 and 9,999 residents and 11 percent for centres with populations between 10,000 and 49,999. Our Prairie data are congruent with this pattern — the percentage of commuting workers in the experienced labour force increases as the resident population of the community decreases.

These patterns, however, are not consistent for all areas, suggesting a complex relationship between employment, residence and commuting. The near-urban employment fields of major metropolitan areas are different than those surrounding smaller remote communities because larger centres are growing and smaller centres are not. For example the two major LMAs in Saskatchewan accounted for 56 percent of the increase in commuting and 93 percent of the net job gain between 1981 and 1991. Although comparative data are not available over time for Manitoba, the role of Winnipeg in overall rural employment, and the commuter activity in its employment field in 1991 suggest a similar relationship.

Within a Canadian context, the Prairies are most divergent in regional rural employment patterns. Agricultural employment is relatively higher, urban and rural skill levels are similar, age distributions do not vary greatly, and average urban income is higher than rural income. The fact that the lowest percentage of commuting workers of all Canadian regions occurs on the Prairies (Green and Meyer, 1995) reflects the fact that the few large cities are widely scattered in the region and many rural residents live too far from the major centres to take advantage of the employment opportunities created. Although the myriad of smaller centres is important for rural residents for off-farm employment and although they actually support a disproportionate number of commuters, the fact remains that they generate fewer job opportunities. Thus, the low population density and devolving community system on the Prairies (Stabler *et al.*, 1992; Rounds and Shamanski, 1993) are not conducive to the extensive inter-urban movements recognized in Ontario (Dahms, 1980; Troughton, 1981). Although commuting between smaller urban centres is common on the Prairies, the small size and greater distances between these centres restricts both the number of employment opportunities and the viability of commuting to find work.

Observed patterns of employment in rural Saskatchewan and Manitoba have both positive and negative connotations. First, commuting does bring the earnings of workers back to the local community. Second, some families may continue farming if one or more family member commutes to obtain off-farm earnings. Third, the concentration of employment growth in regional centres may encourage rural development efforts to focus on a regional strategy, rather than attempting to deal with each community separately.

On the negative side, however, rural employment continues to decline making commuting essential. Commuting is a "tax" and an investment of both the time and income of rural residents. At the same time, rural labour is becoming more dependent on urban centres for employment. Because the viability of commuting is limited by distance, rural residents who reside more than 100 km from major centres have limited employment options. If commuting is not an alternative, relocation may be the only option, thus continuing the trends toward rural depopulation in areas away from major cities.

A final problem concerns the diminishing of the impact of external money through "leakage" because the jobs are not rural-based. With no locally-generated value-added from wages, salaries and interest, the multiplier for incomes is low in rural areas. In Saskatchewan, for example, rural multipliers are as low as 1.1 in small communities. This is only 20 percent of the value of multipliers in larger centres and means that progressively more jobs will be created per dollar spent in larger centres and fewer in smaller centres. The present patterns and trends of employment, therefore, will continue.

References and further reading

Bernat, A. and Frederick, M. (1992) Goods-producing industries added more rural than urban jobs in 1989. *Rural Conditions and Trends*, Vol. 3, USDA Economic Research Service, Rockville, Maryland.

Berry, B.J.L. *et al.* (1988) *Market Centres and Retail Location: Theory and Applications.* Englewood Cliffs, New Jersey: Prentice-Hall.

Berry, Brian J.L. (1970) Labor market participation and regional potential. *Growth and Change* Vol.1, pp. 3-10.

Bessant, K., Rounds, R.C. and Monu, E. (1993) *Off-farm Employment in Agro-Manitoba.* Brandon, Manitoba: RDI Report Series 1993-5, The Rural Development Institute, Brandon University.

Bollman, R.D. and Rounds, R.C. (1993) *Employment Trends in Rural Manitoba — The Role of Manufacturing.* Brandon, Manitoba: RDI Report Series 1993-6, The Rural Development Institute, Brandon University.

Dahms, F.A. (1980) The evolving spatial organization of small settlements in the countryside — an Ontario example. *Tijdschrift voor Economische en Sociale Geografie*, Vol, 71, No. 5, pp. 295-306.

Deavers, K.L. (1991) 1980's, a decade of broad rural stress. *Rural Development Perspectives*, Vol. 7, USDA Economic Research Service, Rockville, Maryland.

Deseran, F.A. (1989) Part-time farming and commuting: Determinants of distance to off-farm work for Louisiana farm couples. In Falk, W.W. and Lyson, T.A. (eds). *Research in Rural Sociology and Development: Rural Labour Markets.* Greenwich, Connecticut: JAI Press Inc.

Green, M.B. and Meyer, S.P. (1995) *The Employment Characteristics of Commuters in Canada: With Special References to Rural Employment Analysis.* Paper presented to the Annual Conference of the Agricultural and Rural Restructuring Group. Coaticook, Quebec, October 1995.

Hady, T.F. and Ross, P.J. (1990). *An Update: the Diverse Social and Economic Structure of Non-metropolitan America.* Washington, D.C.: USDA Economic Research Service.

Hall, P. (1990) *Structural Transformation of the Regions of the United Kingdom.* Berkeley, California: Working Paper 507, Institute of Urban and Regional Development, University of California — Berkeley.

Hanson, S. and Johnston, I. (1985) Gender differences in work-trip length: Explorations and Implications. *Urban Geography* Vol 6, pp. 193-219.

Heilbrun, J. (1987) *Urban economics and public policy.* New York: St. Martins Press.

Madden, J.F. (1981) Why women work closer to home. *Urban Studies* Vol. 18, pp. 181-194.

Mitchelson, R.L. and Fisher, J.S. (1987a) Long distance commuting and population change in Georgia, 1960-80. *Growth and Change* Vol. 18, pp. 44-65.

Mitchelson, R.L. and Fisher, J.S. (1987b) Long distance commuting and income change in the towns of upstate New York. *Economic Geography* Vol. 63, pp. 48-65.

Olfert, M.R. and Stabler, J.C. (1994a) Industrial restructuring of the Prairie labour force: spatial and gender impacts. *Canadian Journal of Regional Science* Vol. 17, No. 2, pp. 133-152.

Olfert, M.R. and Stabler, J.C. (1994b) Commuting level multipliers for rural development initiatives. *Growth and Change* Vol. 25, No. 4, pp. 467-486.

Parr, J.B. (1987) Interaction in an urban system: aspects of trade and commuting. *Economic Geography* Vol. 63, pp. 223-239.

Porterfield, S. (1990) Service sector offers more jobs, lower pay. *Rural Development Perspectives* Vol. 6, USDA Economic Research Service, Rockville, Maryland.

Rounds, R.C. and Shamanski, K. (1993) *The Internal and Functional Restructuring of Rural Communities in Agro-Manitoba*. Brandon, Manitoba: RDI Report Series 1993-3, The Rural Development Institute, Brandon University.

Stabler, J.C. (1987) Trade centre evolution in the Great Plains. *Journal of Regional Science* Vol. 27, pp. 225-244.

Stabler, J.C. and Howe, E.C. (1993) Services, trade and regional structural change in Canada, 1974-84. *Review of Urban and Regional Development Studies* Vol 5. pp. 29-50.

Stabler, J.C. and Olfert, M.R. (1992) *Restructuring rural Saskatchewan: the challenge of the 1990s*. Regina, Saskatchewan: Canadian Plains Research Centre.

Stabler, J.C. and Olfert, M.R. (1994) Farm structure and community viability in the northern Great Plains. *The Review of Regional Studies*, pp. 265-286.

Stabler, J.C., Olfert, M.R. and Fulton, M. (1992) *The Changing Role of Rural Communities in an Urbanizing World, Saskatchewan: 1961-1990*. Regina, Saskatchewan: Canadian Plains Research Centre.

Stabler, J.C., Olfert, M.R. and Greuel, J.B. (1996) Spatial labour markets and the rural labour force. *Growth and Change* Vol. 27, pp. 206-230.

Tolbert, Charles M. and Killian, Molly (1987). *Labor Market Areas in the United States*. Washington, DC: USDA, Economic Research Service.

Troughton, Michael J. (1981) Aspects of employment and commuting in the fringe zone of London, Ontario. In Beesley, Ken B. and Russwurm, Lorne H. *The Rural-Urban Fringe: Canadian Perspectives*. Toronto: Geograhical Monographs No. 10, York University, Atkinson College, pp. 144-178.

Chapter fourteen:

Rural Employment Issues in the Periurban Fringe[1]

Andrew Errington
*The University of Plymouth, Seale Hayne Campus, Newton Abbot,
United Kingdom*

Abstract

*Rural issues in general and rural employment in particular appear to be
commanding increased attention among policy-makers. In the periurban fringe,
the case for rural employment rests largely on the desire to reduce the
environmental and social costs of daily commuting and to secure more-balanced
and hence sustainable rural communities.*

Introduction

While rural employment issues have occupied centre stage in Development
Economics, they have been relatively neglected in Market Industrialized Countries
(Errington, 1990a, 1990b). However, rural issues in general and rural employment
in particular have begun to rise nearer to the top of the policy-making agenda in
recent years. This change was exemplified by publication in 1988 of *The Future
of Rural Society* (EC, 1988) and more recently by the publication of a "Rural
White Paper" jointly by the United Kingdom Ministry of Agriculture and
Department of the Environment (DoE/MAFF, 1995).

There are a number of reasons which might explain the increased attention
given to rural employment issues. In the first place, as the "Strategic Reserve"
and "Balance of Payments" rationale for agricultural support came under increased

---

1. *I am very grateful to Mr Carlos Barahona of the Rural Research Group who has collaborated in
    the analysis of data from the recently-completed* Lambourn Valley Baseline Study, *upon which
    much of the latter part of this chapter draws. However, the author remains responsible for any
    errors or omissions in the chapter.*

pressure (see, for example, Bowers and Cheshire, 1983; Buckwell *et al.*, 1982) at a time of high national unemployment in the United Kingdom, agriculture's employment-providing role (on farms, in the ancillary industries and elsewhere in rural areas) assumed greater importance in the policy debate (see, for example, Craig *et al.*, 1986). Second, the counterurbanization debate has focused attention on rural areas. Some have argued that technological change has freed firms in both manufacturing and service sectors from the need to locate in the major urban centres. The newer, more "footloose" industries such as microelectronics and software design are attracted to rural areas since they not only offer a lower ground rent and a more attractive living and working environment but also a more flexible workforce, without the same level of unionization found in many traditional industrial areas (Newby, 1985; Fothergill *et al.*, 1985; Errington, 1987). Finally, a variety of organizations — both public and private — have raised the level of awareness of rural issues among policy-makers and the general public. The activities of pressure groups concerned specifically with rural areas as well as the higher profile of public organizations such as the Rural Development Commission have done much to increase public awareness of these issues. Meanwhile, a growing rural middle class, as articulate as it is affluent, is focusing attention on the perceived conflict between employment-generating development and the conservation of an attractive residential environment. Indeed, the prospect for increased employment generation through the further development of "greenfield" sites in the periurban areas of South-East England now appears to command more public attention than the continuing problems of depressed peripheral rural areas facing economic decline. More recently still, the changing party-political complexion of District Councils in the more rural areas (especially of southern England) has done much to stimulate the interest of Ministers concerned to reverse recent trends.

But while such factors might provide an explanation of the growing interest in rural employment among policy-makers, the issues exercising the mind of the applied economist are rather different. As Hodge and Whitby (1981) reminded us in their own review of rural employment trends and policy options, where public resources are devoted to interventions designed to stimulate employment, allocation decisions should be based on the *ex ante* estimation of net social benefits and the *ex post* evaluation of resulting welfare gains. A brief review of what might be termed "the case for rural employment" may help to identify some of the issues which the economics profession needs to address when helping to evaluate the net social benefit of various policy measures, and thus determine the place of rural employment issues in our own research agenda.

The case for rural employment

The general case for state interventions to maintain or develop employment opportunities in rural areas rests on the usual thesis of market failure, and in particular the failure of individuals and entrepreneurs to take into account a variety of externalities in their decision-making. Historically, the prime concern of government (arising from the major population movements from village to town and from economic periphery to industrial core) has been the perceived problem of depopulation. Indeed, at a European level, such considerations still appear to be the main driving force behind regional and structural policies. However, the reversal of some of these population flows and the discovery of "counterurbanization" in the United Kingdom in the 1970s and 1980s (Champion, 1981; Robert and Randolph, 1983) have made it necessary to modify this argument if the case for rural employment is to be sustained. Increased human longevity and the growth of both private and state pension schemes mean that rural employment opportunities are no longer the necessary prerequisite for an area to remain, or indeed become, populated. The retirement village in England or even the retirement State in the United States (Long, 1994) are both striking testimony to this fact.

There are perhaps seven more or less tenable lines of argument in favour of public support for rural employment, each of which has potential interest for the economist since it concerns the allocation of scarce resources and necessitates the measurement of social costs and benefits.

1. The maintenance of cultural diversity

This argument stresses the need to maintain the level of population in remoter rural areas in order to conserve society's cultural diversity. Implicit values are assigned to the continued existence of particular cultures and the distinctive features which they embody (such as language, music, dance or cuisine). These are analogous to the particular landscapes, flora and fauna whose value some of our colleagues are currently seeking to measure (Brown *et al.*, 1994; Hutchinson *et al.*, 1995). In the context of rural employment policies, the central issue here is not only the value to society of continuing cultural diversity, but the extent to which this diversity is dependent on particular forms of employment in occupations such as fishing, farming or mining. In this context, Hughes and Midmore (1990) have provided some interesting evidence on the relationship between the prosperity of farming and the persistence of the Welsh Language.

2. The strategic argument

The need to keep remoter frontier areas populated for defensive purposes provides another strand of the case for rural employment in some regions. It has, for example, been suggested that one of the prime objectives of state support to the settlement of some of the remoter areas of Northern Australia was to secure national borders against possible incursions from southern Asia. Within Europe, it seems possible that the maintenance of population in the mountainous areas along the Franco-German border might have had a similar objective earlier this century. Clearly, the net social benefit of investment in rural employment in pursuit of these objectives is likely to be influenced substantially by geopolitical change and changes in military technology.

3.   Making use of existing infrastructure

Where resources have previously been invested by society in local infrastructure, there may be an argument that the maintenance of a population sufficient to make adequate use of that infrastructure ensures that such investments achieve an adequate return and are not "wasted". Clearly, this argument is strongest where fixed investments such as those in land improvements, roads, railways, mains services, schools and public-sector housing are concerned. However, it will be recognized that not all of these resources require an employed population to make use of them — the existence of a resident population (which may be retired or commuting to work elsewhere) may be quite sufficient. Moreover, there are supplementary questions to be addressed about the level of current maintenance costs where most of these investments are concerned.

4.   Reducing the congestion costs of "over-development"

While the 19th century impetus towards urban development came from the economies of agglomeration achieved by manufacturing firms heavily reliant on new roads, canals and railways for the transport of their bulky raw materials, intermediate goods and finished products, by the late 20th century these factors are much less important to economic development. The infrastructure outside the main urban centres has greatly improved and an increasing proportion of producer and consumer services can now be obtained through the national (and indeed international) telecommunications network. At the same time, significant costs arise from urban congestion, such as declining air quality, rising levels of noise pollution and the lengthening travel times faced by commuters stuck in traffic jams. Since these are borne by individuals rather than firms, the location decisions of economically rational entrepreneurs can lead to significant welfare losses among the rest of the population. In these circumstances it is quite conceivable that the induced relocation of some forms of economic activity to rural areas might lead to a net increase in welfare both in the congested urban areas and at their new rural location.

5.   Maintaining an attractive rural environment

The rural environment in the more densely populated Market Industrialized countries is largely man-made — the product of generations of economic activity, particularly in farming and forestry. The population at large, urban as well as rural, derives some benefit from the appearance of the countryside, particularly (but not exclusively) to the extent they are able to use it for recreational purposes. The impact of the conservation lobby in the United Kingdom during the 1980s is striking testament to the perceived importance of the countryside's appearance to at least one articulate and influential segment of society. Though there is debate over the extent to which particular agricultural practices have a beneficial rather than a detrimental effect on the appearance of the countryside, all protagonists share the view that its appearance is an important by-product of those economic activities which are extensive users of land. With appropriate safeguards, certain types of rural economic activity can thus generate significant external economies in the form of an attractive countryside. A maintained or improved appearance of the countryside is thus one of the benefits which must be weighed when measuring the social benefits of rural employment creation. However, in this case, it is likely that such benefits accrue only to certain forms of employment, most notably in agriculture, forestry and conservation.

6. Removing social inequalities

In a period when rural depopulation was regarded as the central problem facing rural areas, the maintenance or expansion of rural employment was seen as a vital measure to stem the depopulation tide by providing jobs for the rural poor and thus reducing income disparities between urban and rural areas. By the 1980s the disparity in average incomes between rural and urban areas in many Market Industrialized countries has narrowed and may even have been reversed. However, as McLaughlin (1985) and Cloke *et al.* (1994) have pointed out there are still significant pockets of deprivation in rural areas. Indeed, the growing disparity of incomes **within** rural areas is regarded by some as their most pressing social problem (Errington, 1994b). The provision of suitable employment opportunities in rural areas can certainly contribute to the solution of this problem, but the employment opportunities must be of a type which suit the needs and abilities of those rural residents who are currently unemployed. Once again, the social benefit accruing to employment generation is a function not so much of the number as of the type of jobs provided.

7. Maintaining "balanced" rural communities

The maintenance of "balanced rural communities" is another theme central to the arguments for generating employment in the rural areas of Market Industrialized countries. In part this appears to be based on a deeply-ingrained view that rural communities are in some respects fundamentally different from urban communities (and is thus a facet of the "cultural diversity" argument referred to earlier). Not only do rural communities provide a reservoir of alternative cultures, characteristics and values that make a vital contribution to the richness of the nation's social fabric and economic life but the resulting diversity might even contribute to our ability to survive as a species in the face of evolutionary pressures (Allanson *et al.*, 1994).

This belief has sometimes been translated into the policy objective of maintaining "balanced rural communities", containing inhabitants varied in age, economic and social status. In order to obtain this balance, some inhabitants must be in employment — a rural area populated exclusively by retired people or by commuters would not be "balanced" in this sense.

However, if this line of argument is to be used in support of the case for rural employment it is necessary to identify whence the distinctive characteristics of the inhabitants of rural communities derive. Certainly, the spread of mass culture, facilitated by the mass media has eliminated many of the historic differences in life-style between rural and urban areas in the United Kingdom. It may be that the distinctions which do remain rest on particular types of occupations. For example, the resourcefulness, independence, resilience and physical toughness most closely associated in the popular imagination with outdoor work (in farm, forestry plantation or conservation area) may be particularly important. Indeed, it is conceivable that these characteristics of the rural population were regarded as particularly important to those countries (such as the United States and United Kingdom) with no large regular standing army. In times of war, the strong and healthy farm-hands would prove better conscripts than the debilitated factory worker ground down through years of urban toil. Government reports on the comparative health of the rural and urban working class at the time of the Boer War and First World War give some support to this hypothesis. But if this type of argument still underlies the case for rural employment, it must again be recognized again that it is not rural employment *per se* but particular forms of rural employment that are being valued in this way.

More recently, the case for achieving more balanced rural communities has been supported by the group preparing a *Rural Community Strategy* for the English county of Berkshire (CCB,1994) but using a rather different line of argument. The strategy document explains (CCB, 1994, p.15) that the concept of balanced communities "implies both a diverse social and economic mix in rural settlements (in terms of age, incomes, occupations, etc.) and a range of activities within them (villages which contain services and appropriate employment opportunities for local people, as well as housing)". It goes on to argue that the encouragement of more balanced rural communities is a desirable goal because:

> *it can contribute much to the intrinsic character and vitality of rural life;*
>
> *an appropriate range of homes, workplaces and services in rural areas enhances the ability of local people to continue living in the countryside, and is therefore important for the retention of community ties;*
>
> *the presence of various social groups and of rural employment (*sic*) can provide valuable patronage for local services (which are themselves an important lifeline for the less mobile who live in rural settlements);*
>
> *a "balanced community" provides opportunities for communal self-help in the provision of both services and social care;*
>
> *the existence of appropriate employment opportunities within rural areas generates wealth to help maintain the countryside and can help reduce commuting to jobs elsewhere (and the energy consumption, pollution and social costs which that entails);*

> *a range of jobs within rural areas can also help reduce the*
> *vulnerability of the rural economy to structural decline within*
> *particular industries (such as falling employment within agriculture*
> *and related businesses).*

While some of these points merely reflect those strands in the case for rural employment already covered in this chapter (e.g. "cultural diversity", "attractive rural environment" and "urban congestion"), others add important new points to the argument. For example, the authors of the *Rural Community Strategy for Berkshire* assume that the presence of rural employment increases the patronage of local services and increases the opportunity for communal self-help. As the state withdraws from some areas of welfare provision and emphasizes programmes such as "Care in the Community", an adequately balanced population becomes even more essential to provide support to the elderly and disabled in rural areas.

These, then, appear to be the main strands in the case for rural employment. Each rests on assumptions that need to be tested and each suggests a range of different criteria against which policy instruments designed to maintain or promote rural employment should be assessed. However, in view of the heterogeneity of rural areas, we should recognize that some strands of the argument will have more relevance than others in any particular rural area.

The periurban fringe

Much recent work has emphasized the heterogeneity of rural areas, particularly in terms of their social and economic structure. For example, our own study of *Rural Employment and Training* for the Rural Development Commission (Errington *et al.*, 1990a) used the Special Workplace Statistics of the 1981 Census of Population to compare the employment structure of the rural and urban wards in five English counties (Northumberland, Shropshire, Berkshire, Northamptonshire and Dorset). It concluded:

> *In short, what impresses most is the heterogeneity of the rural areas*
> *of the five counties — rurality was not a good predictor of industrial*
> *structure. Indeed, it may be that the rural areas of these five counties*
> *have more in common with their neighbouring towns than they do*
> *with rural areas in another part of the country.*

There are many different ways of classifying different types of rural areas (see Hodge and Monk, 1991) and the value of each approach will depend on the purpose of the classification. One category appearing in some classifications refers to the *periurban fringe*. In terms of the land-use definition of rurality used by Office of Population Censuses and Surveys (Craig, 1987), it encompasses those *wholly* or *mainly rural* wards that lie on the fringes of the major metropolitan areas. Situated within relatively easy commuting distance of major urban centres, the periurban areas have proved particularly attractive to the more affluent commuters, particularly with the expansion and improvement of the motorway network in the last 30 years. The high price of residential properties in many of these areas (including farm-houses and converted farm buildings) is testimony to this fact.

The European Commission emphasized that its own analysis of the three "standard problems" of rural areas in *The Future of Rural Society* (EC, 1988) had no direct spatial connotation and that in any given area "the fact that a particular standard problem dominates does not mean that it excludes all others" (EC, 1988, p.32). Nevertheless, the impression remains that some rural areas, and particularly those periurban areas surrounding London are equated with the first type of rural problem ("the pressure of modern development"). They present a problem to society because of the high social costs associated with excessive development and resultant "overheating". The Commission document argues that solutions to this first problem will lie in the field of local planning, which has the responsibility to arbitrate in cases of conflict over different potential uses of land and to gather the necessary information so that such decisions are made "with full knowledge of the facts" (EC, 1988 p. 32). In this way, such periurban areas will be able to play their proper role in relation to the neighbouring city:

> *The crux of this problem is to keep the countryside intact from an environmental point of view, not only so that it can fulfil its function as an ecological buffer and source of natural reproduction, but also to provide it with new and lasting scope for development as an area providing recreation and leisure for the city-dwellers (EC, 1988, p. 32)*

Such a view is founded in the same "Green Belt" philosophy that has so influenced periurban areas in the United Kingdom and elsewhere since the Second World War (Elson *et al.,* 1993; DoE, 1994) and sees such areas primarily in terms of servicing the recreational and leisure needs of visitors from the city. However, it is not an uncontested view of the function of these rural areas. For example, the *Rural Community Strategy for Berkshire* (CCB, 1994) presents a rather different vision for rural Berkshire, speaking of:

> *a multi-purpose countryside which addresses the requirements of those who live in, work in and visit rural areas, and which is "sustainable" both in terms of the use of resources and maintenance of balanced local communities.*

While the EC's vision of the periurban fringe stresses its role as "environmental reservoir" and emphasizes the needs of those who visit the countryside, seeking relief from the pressures of urban life, the Rural Community Strategy places greater emphasis on the needs of those who live and work in the rural areas of the county. Nevertheless, the Strategy document itself stresses the enormous variation to be found even within the rural areas of Berkshire, arguing that "most readily-available sources of information fail to reflect fully the characteristics of small areas" and concludes: "Where appropriate, it is desirable that further studies should be carried out to investigate in more detail the distribution of particular needs and opportunities". The first research project to flow from this recommendation was a baseline study of the Lambourn Valley in west Berkshire which was completed in the autumn of 1994. This study provides the opportunity to explore some strands in the case for rural employment in the periurban fringe.

The Lambourn Valley

Focusing on Lambourn itself (a large village with a population over 3,000) but including smaller villages along the valley such as Eastbury (pop. 530), East Garston (pop. 680) and Great Shefford (pop. 1,300), the study gathered information on aspects of employment, unemployment, transport and the use of various shops and facilities in order to inform and guide the initiatives planned by its sponsors — Thames Valley Enterprise, Newbury District Council, Berkshire County Council and the Community Council for Berkshire. Primary data was collected through field interviews at 98 businesses and in 239 households. A recently-compiled trade directory, together with local Yellow Pages provided the sampling frame for the business survey (which covered about half of the businesses in the valley) while for the household survey every third household was selected from a random sample of grid squares drawn on village plans and OS maps. It was estimated that the household survey covered about 10 per cent of all households in the study area. Response rates were very high (86 per cent among businesses and 76 per cent among households) reflecting the strong support of the Parish Council and the extent of pre-publicity in the local press.

Information was gathered through personal interviews with the managers of the businesses and all members of the selected households aged 16 or above (428 in all). The household respondents were also asked to complete a daily travel-log for one week following the interview. The log was used to record the total number of journeys out of the village and for up to three individual journeys, the destination, mode of transport and main purpose (classified as work, shopping, education, medical, leisure, bank visit, other).

Lambourn village has several features which distinguish it from many other villages in Berkshire. Located within the Berkshire Downs it is relatively remote, though surrounded by several substantial towns — Newbury (12 miles), Wantage (8 miles) and Swindon (8 miles). It lies very close to the route of the M4 motorway though the nearest junction giving access is five miles from the village. From the late 19th century the local economy was dominated by the racehorse training industry and Lambourn is today second only to Newmarket in the number of horses under training. Because of its location and relatively large local population, Lambourn has for the time-being retained a much wider range of shops than are found in most villages of comparable size. However, it has recently lost its only full-time bank and this has caused considerable concern among local businesses and the local community.

Table 14.1.   Labour force participation of inhabitants (aged 16 and over)

Village	Full-time employment	Part-time employment	Full-time education	Unemployed	Retired	Other	Total
			Percent distribution				
Lambourn	50.5	11.6	5.1	5.6	22.2	5.1	100.0
Eastbury	36.4	18.2	6.8	0.0	27.3	11.4	100.0
East Garston	48.9	6.4	8.5	2.1	19.1	14.9	100.0
Great Shefford	56.8	14.7	7.4	0.0	16.8	4.2	100.0
Hamlets	60.5	10.1	15.3	2.8	11.3	0.0	100.0
Scattered*	48.3	20.0	16.7	0.0	6.7	8.3	100.0
Total	50.9	12.7	7.4	3.1	19.5	6.4	100.0

*   *Individual residences and farmhouses scattered throughout the area.*

In analysing the employment patterns of the valley, the study highlighted some differences between Lambourn itself and Great Shefford, which lies further down the valley towards Newbury. The occupational structure of the two villages is broadly similar with about two-thirds of the population aged 16+ in employment (Table 14.1). However, the employment patterns of the two villages are strikingly different in one important respect. While 21 per cent of the jobs held by Great Shefford residents were located in the village, among Lambourn residents the proportion was more than half (51 per cent). With 40 per cent of its population having lived in the village for less than 5 years (Table 14.2), Great Shefford has some of the hall-marks of the commuter village so common in the periurban fringe, but Lambourn is markedly different. In its age and occupational structure, this village comes much closer to the "more balanced community" described in the *Rural Community Strategy for Berkshire*. It is therefore of particular interest to examine the employment patterns of the village in more detail and to explore the relationship between these patterns and factors such as car-use and the use of local shops and facilities. In this way we can test some of the assumptions underlying the case for encouraging "more balanced rural communities".

Our findings suggest that of the 1,500 people living in Lambourn who were in employment at the time of the survey, 770 worked in the village, 250 worked elsewhere in the study area (mainly at two industrial estates, at Lambourn Woodlands and Membury) and 480 worked outside the study area. At the same time, there was some reverse commuting, with about 190 people commuting into Lambourn village each day, 35 from the study area and 155 from outside.

Table 14.2. Number of years having lived in present village

Village	All my life	Less than 5 years	5 to 9 years	10 to 19 years	20 or more	Total
			Percent distribution			
Lambourn	30.7	11.2	12.3	24.6	21.2	100.0
Eastbury	2.6	38.5	7.7	25.6	25.6	100.0
East Garston	17.5	20.0	10.0	15.0	37.5	100.0
Great Shefford	7.9	39.5	22.4	23.7	6.6	100.0
Hamlets	25.0	25.3	11.4	13.2	25.2	100.0
Scattered*	10.5	28.9	18.4	28.9	13.2	100.0
Total	20.8	21.9	14.1	23.2	20.0	100.0

* *Individual residences and farmhouses scattered throughout the area.*

A description of rural employment using even a very disaggregated Standard Industrial Classification tends to miss the richness of the nature of local employment. The listing in Appendix A therefore contains the job titles given by the respondents working within Lambourn and Great Shefford, and those working outside. An attempt has been made to distinguish those jobs related directly or indirectly to the racehorse training industry. The analysis suggests that one-third of the respondents both living and working in Lambourn itself are in this sense dependent on racehorse training. However, equally striking is the number and variety of other jobs reported by our respondents, many of which have no direct or indirect link with this primary industry. This echoes the point made in the *Rural Community Strategy for Berkshire* that the sustainability of rural communities depends on a mixture of employment opportunities rather than reliance on a single industrial sector.

The list also underlines the importance of the service sector with a number of employees working in firms providing **producer** services, some to the racehorse sector, e.g. the veterinary practice and bloodstock agents, but many others unconnected with racing. Others provide **consumer** services, some of which will again be explained by the presence of the racehorse industry and its employees. It is important to recognize that the primary land-using industry in this area is particularly labour-intensive — we estimate that in the valley there are four times as many jobs in racehorse training as there are in farming. Compared with other periurban areas where farming rather than racehorse training predominates as the major land-user, the proportion of jobs associated with the primary land-using sectors in the Lambourn Valley is therefore unusually large.

The "case for rural employment" in the Lambourn Valley

Only some facets of the general case for rural employment outlined earlier in this chapter are relevant to the Lambourn Valley. The strategic argument has no relevance to this area. Far from facing underutilization of their infrastructure, some Lambourn residents currently complain of its inability to support the growing number of people seeking to live in the village, but other strands of the argument may be important. In relation to the arguments for "cultural diversity" and "maintaining an attractive rural environment", it may be that it is employment in racehorse training rather than rural employment *per se* that is most important in this locality; where the argument regarding social inequalities is concerned, there is certainly some evidence of pockets of deprivation, particularly among those such as the unemployed and elderly with little access to a private car (Errington, 1994a). However, it is probably the arguments concerning congestion costs (particularly those associated with commuting) and the argument for encouraging more-balanced (and hence sustainable) rural communities that are most relevant in this part of the periurban fringe. The household surveys in Lambourn and the daily travel-logs completed by the residents provide some useful data with which to test some of the assumptions underlying these two strands of the case for rural employment. In the first place, the travel logs provide the basis for a crude quantification of the effect of job relocation on car-use. Secondly, the shopping patterns and use of village facilities by those who work in the village can be compared with those commuting out in order to assess the validity of the argument that the existence of local employment opportunities can help sustain the viability of existing shops and facilities.

Commuting

English rural life in the late 20th century is founded on the private car. Car ownership is now the prime determinant of the quality of life of those who live in rural areas (Errington, 1994). At the same time, the car-based lifestyle has substantial costs to society in terms of the environmental damage with which it is associated. The presence of more jobs in the village would not alter this fact — Lambourn residents would continue to use their cars for a variety of different purposes. Indeed, we found that levels of car-ownership were virtually identical between those commuting out of the village to work and those working in the village itself. However, the survey data does give some indication of the extent to which more local employment opportunities for those who live in Lambourn might reduce the environmental and social costs of commuting. Table 14.3 summarizes the travel-logs completed by 23 Lambourn residents who worked in the village and 31 residents whose jobs were based elsewhere. Covering a single seven-day period in the summer of 1994, this analysis underlines the fact that even those working in Lambourn are very dependent on the car and cover a substantial distance each week. Indeed, nearly half reported that they regularly take their car to work in the village even though this may be close at hand. However, the distance travelled in the week by those working outside the village is two and half times greater than the distance travelled by those working in the village. Clearly, there would be a substantial reduction in travelling if all residents worked in the village[2].

Table 14.3. Average distance travelled over a seven-day period: Employed Lambourn residents

Main purpose	People working in Lambourn (*n*=23)		People working elsewhere (*n*=31)	
	Miles	Percent	Miles	Percent
Work	19.6	32.7	56.4	38.8
Shopping	13.0	21.7	19.0	13.1
Medical	1.5	2.5	4.6	3.2
Bank	2.5	4.2	2.2	1.5
Leisure	21.6	36.1	51.3	35.3
Other	1.7	2.8	12.0	8.2
Total*	57.3		143.4	

* *Not equal to sum of columns because some journeys accomplished more than one main purpose.*

The second point to note is that those who travel out of the village for work also cover more miles for other activities such as leisure or shopping, hinting at a generally more mobile life-style. Inasfar as commuting to work encourages travel out of the village for other activities the reduction in travelling would be even greater if all residents worked in the village[3]. Since virtually all the journeys recorded were by private car, these figures suggest a potential reduction in car-use among commuters of the order of 25–50 percent. Clearly such calculations are very crude indeed and make many untested assumptions, but the orders of magnitude do underline the potential gains to society of increased rural employment in the periurban fringe.

2. *If those presently commuting out of the village adopted the travel-to-work patterns of those working in the village, the reduction would be 56.4 - 19.6 = 36.8 miles, or 26 percent of their present weekly travel.*

3. *If those presently commuting out of the village adopted the travel patterns of those currently working in the village, the reduction would be 143.4 - 57.3 = 86.1 miles, or 60 percent of their present weekly travel.*

Table 14.4.   Use of Lambourn service and retail establishments: Proportion of total visits per year to stores or facilities in Lambourn

	People working in Lambourn (n=55)	People working elsewhere (n=55)	Total number of visits per year	Probability for χ^2 test $H_0: p^1 = p^2$
Bank	0.88	0.12	1,377	0.000
Post office	0.64	0.36	5,240	0.000
Newsagent	0.58	0.42	14,340	0.000
Betting shop	0.77	0.23	1,626	0.000
Bakers	0.63	0.37	3,579	0.000
Chemist	0.67	0.33	2,619	0.000
Hairdresser	0.56	0.44	264	0.065
Launderette	0.50	0.50	105	0.922
Grocers	0.64	0.36	9,699	0.000
Hardware store	0.71	0.29	4,948	0.000
Delicatessen	0.79	0.21	1,289	0.000
Clothes shop	0.66	0.34	352	0.000
Lambourn market	0.67	0.33	1,822	0.000
Nippy Chippy	0.55	0.45	1,190	0.000
Chinese take-away	0.60	0.40	1,468	0.000
Pub	0.53	0.47	4,064	0.000
British Legion Club	0.60	0.40	1,127	0.000
Library	0.60	0.40	758	0.000
Church	0.46	0.54	491	0.078
Doctor	0.46	0.54	299	0.183
Vet	0.59	0.41	218	0.010
Lambourn Centre	0.91	0.09	516	0.000

The sustainable community

The case for rural employment in the periurban fringe is also based on the assumption (made explicit in the *Rural Community Strategy for Berkshire*) that the existence of jobs in rural areas increases the "sustainability" of rural communities. While there are, as we have seen, several facets to this argument, the Lambourn study provides the opportunity to test one of them. The *Community Strategy* claims that those who work in a village are more likely to use its shops and other local facilities. Information was gathered on the frequency of use of a number of shops and facilities in Lambourn village and elsewhere.

Virtually all Lambourn residents travel out of their village to a local superstore for their main food shopping and there was no statistically significant difference in this respect (at the 5 percent level) between those who worked in the village and those who commuted elsewhere. However, there was a statistically significant and in many cases substantial difference in the use of other shops and facilities. In virtually all cases those working locally were more likely to use local shops and facilities and less likely to use leisure and social facilities outside the village (Table 14.4 for the use of Lambourn shops and facilities by the two groups; Table 14.5 for the use of facilities outside the village, where "visits per year" was calculated from a question which asked respondents to indicate frequency of use in six discrete categories (from "daily" to "annually").)

Table 14.5.   Use of facilities outside Lambourn: Proportion of total visits per year to facilities

	People working in Lambourn (n=55)	People working elsewhere (n=55)	Total number of visits per year	Probability for χ^2 test H_o: $p^1 = p^2$
Sports	0.31	0.69	2,195	0.000
Cinema	0.33	0.67	477	0.000
Social club	0.32	0.68	426	0.000
Pub	0.46	0.54	2,890	0.000
Restaurant	0.49	0.51	1,116	0.472

There are many factors that might explain these differences — the rational evaluation of the trade-off between price differentials and the marginal costs of shopping in town, the lack of opportunity to use facilities that are only open during normal working hours, the fact that newcomers to the village are more likely to be commuters and to bring urban-based shopping habits with them, and so on. The data allows us to explore some of these hypotheses a little further. Our preliminary analysis has focused on the use made of the grocers shops in the village, because their opening hours are "Eight-till-late" seven days a week and thus make them accessible to villagers involved in daily commuting. A logistic regression model was fitted to the data with frequency of use of the grocers as the dependent variable.

Table 14.6.   Use of Lambourn grocers shops: Logistic regression model

Terms in the model	Degrees of freedom	Deviance	Prob χ^2 for deviance
Works in the village	1	4.79	0.029
+ Number of cars in household	6	13.65	0.034
+ Length of time lived in the village	4	1.43	0.838
+ Age category	7	40.47	0.000
+ Gender	2	4.66	0.097
+ Full-time or part-time employment	2	8.68	0.013
+ Education	3	0.83	0.843

The results show that those residents aged less than 19 were markedly less likely to use Lambourn grocers, as were those in full-time employment (Table 14.6). The number of cars in the household seems to have some relationship with frequency of use of the local grocers but it is neither simple nor linear. Contrary to our initial expectations, those with no car appear **less** likely to use the local grocers than those with one car. Those with two or three cars in the household are also less likely to make use of this facility.

One point of particular interest among these results is the fact that the length of time they have lived in the village does not appear to be significantly associated with the frequency with which Lambourn residents use of these shops. This is contrary to our initial assumption that newcomers would tend to bring their established shopping habits with them and thus make less use of village facilities.

Perhaps most important of all, the results of the logistic regression confirm the influence of location of employment upon the use of local shops and facilities, supporting the contention that the maintenance of rural employment promotes the sustainability of the community by securing the continued use of local shops and facilities.

Conclusion

A preliminary outline of the general case for government intervention in support of rural employment has been presented. The role of the professional economist in the development and implementation of policies in support of rural employment lies primarily in the *ex ante* and *ex post* assessment of the social costs and benefits of such policies. In conducting this analysis, the assumptions underlying the various strands in the case for rural employment need to be tested more rigorously than have been in the past.

The case for government intervention to maintain or increase rural employment will vary from one type of rural area to another and in the periurban fringe of cities and towns in South-East England, the concern to retain more balanced rural communities and to reduce dependence on daily commuting to work are likely to be particularly important. Evidence from the Lambourn case study suggests that the relocation of more jobs to rural areas within the periurban fringe may lead to a substantial reduction in car use and increase the use of shops and facilities within the village thereby improving the sustainability of this rural community.

Appendix A: Jobs held by survey respondents

Those living and working in Lambourn

Primary land-using industries (11) = 20 percent
secretary, racehorse industry; stable lad; stable lass; gallop man; travelling head lad; stable girl; gallop man; racehorse trainer; farm assistant; farmer; farm worker

Producer services for above (7) = 13 percent
secretary (veterinary practice, predominantly equine); bloodstock agent (race horses); bloodstock agent (race horses); box driver; managing director of horse transport company; sales office manager, horse transport; secretary, veterinary practice

Other sectors (23) =42 percent
stock controller/vdu operator (import/distribution of christmas decorations); warehouse assistant (manufacturer of christmas decorations); machinist (clothing manufacture); seamstress (machinist); care assistant for those with learning disabilities; driver's mate, confidential waste company; kitchen manager, educational establishment; promotion of business and administration courses; warden (sheltered accommodation); company director, graphic design and promotional services; company director, graphic design and promotional services; chemical supervisor; qualified machinist (sewing and textiles); home care, social services; forklift driver, wholesaling/distribution; structural engineer consultancy; broadcaster/journalist; artist and paintwork restorer; teacher/art and design; property developer; machinist, tie factory; packer, children's books; make soft furnishings, curtains etc.

Consumer services for local population (14) = 26 percent
catering assistant; cleaner; cleaner (private households); joint proprietor of taxi business; cleaner; mechanic, motor repair; motor industry mechanic (garage); domestic help, private households; painter/decorator (private households); own building business; carpenter, painter/decorator, private households; assistant manager, newsagents; shop manager, newsagents; shop assistant, chip shop

---

Those living in Lambourn, but working elsewhere

Primary land-using industries (8) = 16 percent
stable lad; yard man; stable lad; groom, horse racing; racing trainer's secretary; secretary and caterer, racing industry; foreman sprayer; harvest worker

Producer services for above (1) = 2 percent
HGV driver, race horses

Other sectors (39) = 77 percent
dispatch supervisor, medical equipment; computer systems operator trainer; plant operator/ashphalter; art teacher; management accountant; pensions manager, building supplies industry; factory labourer; nurse (cancer patients) general health service; credit control administrator (electrical retailer); database manager; carpenter, light engineering firm; production supervisor, chemical industry; sales assistant, Motorway Service area; HGV driver, transportation/haulage; sales assistant, Motorway Service area; temp controller for a recruitment agency, personnel recruitment; systems tester (computing); international technical support engineer; security (catering industry); training officer (catering/retail); car valeter (private/ trade cars. Motor industry); mechanical fitter/driver (Chemicals industry); senior assistant (packaging/distribution); handfitter (roof tiles); production manager, defence industry; rehabilitation officer for the visually impaired; hairdressing salon owner/hairdresser; packer, mailorder firm; plumbers mate; engineer for a manufacturer of vehicles for the disabled; finance officer/secretary and lecturer in hairdressing; catering assistant, local government; technology

director, packaging for soft drink cans; lecturer in further education; partner in two businesses, motor trade; colour matcher (printing); secretary to the chief geologist (mining and exploration company); storewoman, Motorway Service area; Plant driver/ashphalter;

Consumer services for local population (3) = 6 percent
gardener/caretaker, private homes; gardener; cleaner, private households

---

Those living and working in Great Shefford

Primary land-using industries
None

Producer services for above
None

Other sectors (10) = 77 percent
playgroup general assistant; paper shredder; proprietor (manufacturer), design greeting cards; secretary/treasurer, social club; school cleaner; receptionist, computing firm; personnel projects manager, water industry; writer, children's books; potter (small retail business not operating from a shop); marketing consultant (medical equipment)

Consumer services for local population (2) = 6 percent
forecourt cashier, filling station; proprietor of Post Office/newsagents

---

Those living in Great Shefford but working elsewhere

Primary land-using industries
None

Producer services for above (3) = 8 percent
technical advisor, agriculture; manager European regulatory affairs, animal health; assistant marketing manager, agricultural merchants

Other sectors (34) = 90 percent
supervising surveyor, local government; MLSO (pathology), National Health Service; sales assistant, retailing; housing officer, housing association; accountant, housing association; acting assistant senior director, strategy and quality assurance, Social Services Dept., local government; social worker, care manager; solicitor, construction industry; managing director computer software; corporate pensions consultant; regional manager, construction industry; General Medical Practice, practice manager; accountant in food distribution industry; motorway maintenance; driver's mate, collection/ distribution environmental waste; control shop peering, engineering/helicopters/aircraft; engineer, construction industry; seamstress (cravats) and Saturday job in Newbury fabric shop; assistant accountant, catering industry; teaching; kitchen porter, pub/hotel; fireman; production manager, electronics; bar person/receptionist, snooker club; deployment assistant; general foreman, construction industry; company chairman

and shareholder, motor industry and commercial stationary; fitness consultant; fitness consultant; marketing assistant, finance company; accountant; flight engineer;

Consumer services for local population (1) = 2 percent
cashier, petrol station

References

Allanson, P., Murdoch, J., Lowe, P. and Garrod, G. (1994) *An Evolutionary Perspective on the Changing Rural Economy*. Paper presented to the 35th EAAE Seminar, "Rural Realities", Aberdeen, June 27-29.

Bowers, J.K. and Cheshire, P. (1983) *Agriculture, the Countryside and Land Use*. London: Methuen.

Brown, G., Layton, D. and Lazo, J. (1994) *Valuing habitat and endangered species*. University of Washington: Discussion paper series (No. 94-1), Institute for Economic Research.

Buckwell, A. *et al.* (1982) *The Costs of the Common Agricultural Policy*. London: Croom Helm.

CCB. (1994) *Berkshire Rural Community Strategy*. Reading, U.K.; Community Council for Berkshire.

Champion, A.G. (1981) Population trends in rural Britain. *Population Trends* Vol. 26, pp. 20-24.

Cloke, P., Milbourne, P. and Thomas, C. (1994) *Lifestyles in Rural England*. Salisbury: Rural Development Commission.

Craig, J. (1987) An urban-rural categorisation for wards and local authorities. *Population Trends* Vol. 47, pp. 6-11.

Craig, G.M., Jollans, J.L. and Korbey, A. (1986) *The Case for Agriculture: An Independent Assessment*. Reading, U.K.: University of Reading, Centre for Agricultural Strategy Report No. 10.

DoE. (1994) *Planning Policy Guidance: Green Belts Consultation Draft* (PPG2 revised). London: Department of the Environment.

DoE/MAFF. (1995) *Rural England: A Nation Committed to a Living Countryside*, Cm 3016. London: HMSO.

Elson, M., Walker, S., MacDonald, R. and Edge, J. (1993) *The Effectiveness of Green Belts, Report for the Department of the Environment*. London: HMSO.

EC. (1988) *The Future of Rural Society*. Luxembourg: Bulletin of the European Communities Supplement 4/88, Office for Official Publications of the European Community.

Errington, A.J. (1987) *Rural Employment Trends and Issues in Market Industrialised Countries*. Geneva: World Employment Programme Research Working Paper WEP 10-6/WP90, International Labour Office.

Errington, A.J. (1990a) Rural employment in England: some data sources and their use. *Journal of Agricultural Economics* Vol. 41, pp. 47-61.

Errington, A.J. (1990b) Investigating rural employment in England. *Journal of Rural Studies* Vol. 6, pp. 67-84.

Errington, A.J. (1994a) *The Lambourn Valley Baseline Survey: Report to Sponsors.* Reading, U.K.: Rural Research Group, Department of Agricultural Economics and Management, The University of Reading.

Errington, A.J. (1994b) The periurban fringe: Europe's forgotten rural areas. *Journal of Rural Studies*, Vol. 10, pp. 367-375.

Fothergill, S., Kitson, M. and Monk, S. (1985) *Urban industrial decline: The causes of the urban-rural contrast in manufacturing employment change.* London: HMSO.

Hodge, I. and Whitby, M. (1981) *Rural Employment: Trends, Options, Choices.* London and New York: Methuen.

Hodge, I and Monk, K. (1991) *In Search of a Rural Economy.* Cambridge: University of Cambridge, Department of Land Economy Monograph 20.

Hughes, G.O. and Midmore, P. (1990) *Agrarian change and rural society: a regional Case-study Approach.* Paper presented to the 14th Congress of the European Society for Rural Sociology, Giessen, July 16-20.

Hutchinson, W.G., Chilton, S.M. and Davis, J. (1995) Measuring non-use value of environmental goods using the contingent valuation method: Problems of information and cognition and the application of cognitive questionnaire design methods. *Journal of Agricultural Economics.* Vol. 46, pp. 97-112.

Long, R. (1994) Rural Experiences in the USA. In Copus, A.K. and Mann, P.J. (eds). *Rural Realities: Trends and Choices.* Aderdeen: Aberdeen School of Agriculture, Economics Division, pp. 195-18.

McLaughlin, B.P. (1985) Assessing the extent of rural deprivation. *Journal of Agricultural Economics* Vol. 36, pp. 77-80.

Newby, H. (1985) *Rural Communities and New Technology.* Langholm, Dumfriesshire: The Arkleton Trust.

Robert, S. and Randolph, W.G. (1983) Beyond decentralisation: The evolution of population distribution in England and Wales 1961-1981. *Geoforum* Vol. 14, pp. 75-102.

Chapter fifteen:

Occupational Stratification of Rural Commuting

Milford B. Green and Stephen P. Meyer
The University of Western Ontario, London, Ontario, Canada

Abstract

A review of the factors creating the modern urban/rural environment indicated the importance of commuting for employment reasons. In 1991, 7 percent of the workforce commuted across regional (rural, intermediate, agglomerated) boundaries. An additional 2 to 11 percent commute across census division (CD) boundaries within each type of region. Finally, another approximately 30 percent commute from one census sub-division (CSD) to another CSD with their CD of residence. The occupational skill group most likely to commute from one type of region to another is the management group (9 percent). Skilled and technical workers have a slightly higher propensity to commute from a rural region to an agglomerated region.

Introduction

Due in large part to the low level of manufacturing and service activity in many rural areas, non-agricultural employment opportunities within the rural environment are often limited. To overcome this lack of employment opportunity, many inhabitants commute to other (often urban) areas. Thus, if one is to gain a better understanding of the present status of rural employment in Canada, it is necessary to fully realize the patterns and characteristics inherent in commuting. The Canadian research has not extended its scale of assessment beyond the "boundaries" of urban influence (typically denoted as the urban shadow within the urban–rural fringe) and/or has only considered the commuting patterns surrounding only the largest Canadian urban centres. We present a more comprehensive view of rural commuting and its employment structure that includes not only urban–rural commuting flows, but also includes all types of commuting for all areas of Canada.

A selected literature review

Rural employment: contemporary developments

Overall, the historical trend of increasing urbanization has levelled off in Canada and the share of people living in rural areas has remained constant or, in some areas, has shown some increase (Government of Canada, 1995, p. 78; Parenteau, 1981; Bowles and Beesley, 1991). That is not to say that the activity structure of rural populations has remained unaltered. The number employed in farming has steadily declined but this trend has been offset by the movement of urban populations to the urban–rural fringe and beyond (Dahms, 1988, pp. 26–7; Statistics Canada, 1991, p. 53). Rural employment has been drastically affected by two important trends. First, the increasing size of farm lots with the related decline in the number of farm-owners and, second, the movement of industry into the rural setting. We expand upon these points before more fully addressing the characteristics of rural employment.

As has been the case with most forms of economic activity, technological innovations have encouraged the formation of larger more efficient business structures. In the case of farming in Canada, "technological developments in machinery, fertilizers, chemicals and other farm outputs" have encouraged both a decline in farm numbers and an increase in farm size (Hay, 1992, p. 26). As also reported by Hay, in 1941 the number of farms in Canada totalled 732,832 but by 1986 this number had declined by approximately 60 percent. Also during this time frame, the mechanization of farming created a 141 percent increase in the average acreage of farms in Canada. Regionally, the largest increases were realized within the Maritimes and the Prairie provinces (Hay, 1992, p. 27).

Thus, as one farmer is able to produce for a larger proportion of the demand, the need for farm-related labour has diminished over time. Both federal and provincial governments in Canada have consistently made rural employment an issue of priority within the realm of rural development policy (Cummings, 1988, p. 48). Previous government agencies such as ARDA (Agricultural Rehabilitation and Development Act) and the Department of Manpower and Immigration have provided some assistance to farmers in marginal areas. By either providing training so that farmers can find alternative employment, or by financing technical improvements in farm operations, some success has been realized in reducing rural poverty (McDonald, 1972, p. 232).

Clearly, commuting to the area of alternative employment activity has become an important consideration to the off-farm worker. And, in turn, the spatial distribution of small farms has become, in part, dependent upon the relative locations of off-farm employment opportunities (MacDougall, 1970, p. 127). As well, the commuting patterns of non-farm rural residents (which as a group are almost six times larger than their farming counterparts in Canada) are no less important (Hay, 1992, p. 23). There is evidence from US-based studies (Carroll and Wheeler, 1966) and from Canadian studies (Robinson, 1991; Henshall-Momsen, 1984) that recent arrivals into the rural environment still retain many of their "urban" characteristics. As a result, many of the non-farming rural residents exhibit strong social and economic ties with the urban environment; a trait not often shared with the more traditional farming residents.

Thus, one may expect that the commuting patterns of the non-farming population may exhibit a strong urban bias, but can the same be said for farming residents? With more industry locating in the rural setting, can more urban to rural or rural to rural commuting be expected? The studies that have considered the link between commuting and rural employment will be detailed in the next section.

Commuting studies

Byrant and Russwurm (1978, p. 16) lamented that a number of gaps existed in the "journey to work" literature with respect to, especially, information on economic activity. It was reasoned that this was a symptom of data restrictions. As will be discussed, this problem has been somewhat overcome as the Canadian census of population began in 1971 to include place of residence and place of employment categories on the questionnaire (Ricour-Singh, 1981, p. 11) and the data have improved in comprehensiveness in subsequent years (Bryant and Russwurm, 1978, p. 90). This has somewhat lessened what was a serious problem for rural researchers intent on noting the spatial interactions between farm and non-farm economies (MacDougall, 1970, p. 131). Despite these improvements in data collection, exceedingly few studies have made use of this information (Ricour-Singh, 1979; Dahms, 1980; Troughton, 1981a,b) and none have as of yet considered all directional flows of rural commuting for all regions of Canada.

It has been known for some time that as cities have continued to extend beyond their original political boundaries, commuting (for both economic/ employment and social reasons) has become a major aspect of modern life (Goldstein and Mayer, 1964, p. 472). It has been estimated that about 50 miles around one's home would be a common area of interaction for most urban residents (Hodge, 1972, p. 239) and that the average trip length has been estimated to be slightly higher for rural residents (9.8 versus 8.4 miles for urban residents) (Hoch, 1981, p. 300). As well, it has also been long established that movements to the fringe areas of the city was a two-directional phenomenon. As the fringe attracted more economic activity, increasingly more urban residents have moved out of, and rural people into, this area of transition (Rodehaver, 1947, p. 50).

Evidence suggests that the smaller is the non-metropolitan area, the higher the likelihood of commuting. Saltzman and Newlin (1981, p. 26) reported that commuting from very small towns was the most pronounced (24 percent), when compared with larger centres with populations of 2,500 to 9,999 (16 percent) and 10,000 to 49,999 (11 percent). In addition, it is important to distinguish the commuting patterns of smaller settlement agglomerations from those exhibited by urban centres for reasons other than just differences in actual volume of interaction. Smaller towns exhibit different geographical patterns of housing, employment and economic opportunity from those found in near-metropolitan and metropolitan cities and, as such, migration and commuting patterns will be affected accordingly (Meyer, 1981, p. 65; Maraffa and Brooker-Gross, 1988, pp. 14–15).

Also, the size of the centre can have an affect on a person's necessity for commuting (as less employment opportunities may be available locally) and also on the overall "price" that must be paid on these movements. Essentially, the cost of commuting can be considered a "tax on daily earnings" (Bollman, 1979b, p. 49), and some have argued that those situated in smaller and more remote non-metropolitan centres may be comparatively disadvantaged in gaining access to adequate employment, public assistance and various social transfers (Seninger and Smeeding, 1981, p. 396). This of course has rural poverty ramifications. Interestingly, this conclusion has been used as a criticism of government incentives aimed at improving the efficiency of agriculture in marginal areas. In that, by encouraging farmers to remain on marginal lands; out-migration has been discouraged, off-farm work stimulated, and the problems associated with financing local services worsened (Bollman, 1979b, p. 37).

Therefore, the factors affecting commuting are both socioeconomic and spatial (Taaffe *et al.*, 1980, p. 314) and need to be considered at the various levels of centre size within the "rural–urban hierarchy". Three Canadian studies (Ricour-Singh, 1979; Dahms, 1980; Troughton, 1981a, b) used the 1971 census to, at least partially, fulfil data requirements.

Ricour-Singh's 1979 assessment of commuting was the only one that provided a Canada-wide view. By aggregating work-residence relations for 235 municipalities ("poles of attraction"), she was able to demonstrate the influence that urban centres have on their surrounding peripheries. Specifically, these poles of attractions were defined as municipalities that were net importers of workers (in which the ratio of the employed labour force within a municipality divided by the its resident labour force was greater than one). These 235 urban-based poles, represented only 5 percent of all the municipalities in Canada but contained 70 percent of the nation's population.

The study was by and large a collection of maps that illustrated these poles across Canada. Ricour-Singh's research also include a correlation analysis that attempted to uncover any association between the poles and various population, economic and social variables. But like so many other studies that have attempted a similar procedure, it was determined that: "the attractive power of a centre (as measured by the job ratio) is not significantly related to its characteristics" (Ricour-Singh, p. 15).

With the use of a Wellington County case study, Dahms was able to address "the changing spatial organization of society beyond the urban field" (Dahms,

1980, p. 295). Although this county has one small urban centre (Guelph) and is situated about midway between Toronto and London, the author was able to show that most intercounty interaction was free of Toronto's influence.

Dahms considered commuting, shopping patterns and business linkages for places within the county and relied on many sources for information (census data, business publications and questionnaires). His findings tend to down-play the importance of urban poles of attraction.

Finally, Troughton's research of London's "fringe zone" provided yet another view of the complexities of human interaction (as measured through commuting and employment) that exist within competing rural–urban space. The area of study included communities of various settlement size: the major city of London, 28 other urban municipalities, three small cities, seven towns, 18 villages and a remaining 41 rural municipalities. With the use of 1971 census sub-division flow data that includes place of residence and place of employment specifications, Troughton was able to consider both in-commuting and out-commuting throughout the London fringe area.

His findings add more evidence to what would seem to be a growing trend of rural "self-sufficiency" that is coupled with a declining "urban shadow" influence from major metropolitan cities. He established that the city of London remained the main focus for employment and commuter destination in absolute terms, but in relative terms more movements were detectible to and from smaller cities and other municipalities in the region. Thus, in- and out-commuting was not just prevalent for London and other larger centres (like St. Thomas and Woodstock) but "includes significant foci somewhat randomly distributed in the outer fringe zone" (Troughton, 1981a, p. 176).

Commuting and employment characteristics in Canada

Income and employment structure

The OECD geographic classification defines an intermediate region between predominantly rural and predominantly urban region types (OECD, 1994; Government of Canada, 1995). The utility in adding this third category to the study of rural/urban trends is to see if these "semi-rural/semi-urban" areas confirm a spatial continuum (from rural to urban) with regard to employment and commuting criteria or if these intermediate regions tend to be a more unique subset of the Canadian socioeconomic landscape.

With regards to average income from employment, the intermediate census divisions (CDs) in Canada collectively ranked behind both the rural and the urban CDs (Table 15.1). Thus, at least with regard to income, a gradual increase from rural-based activities towards urban is not suggested; it would appear that on average the lowest paying jobs in Canada were situated in these intermediate areas. The provincial trends generally reinforced the national picture where urban incomes are greater than rural incomes, but some exceptions are notable. For instance, in Québec, Manitoba and British Columbia, those earning the most tended to be employed in rural-based activities.

Table 15.1.   Rural incomes are higher in Québec, Manitoba and British Columbia

| Province | Average income from all sources for individuals with some income | | | |
	Rural	Intermediate	Agglomerated	All regions
Newfoundland	24,405	24,500	..	24,475
Prince Edward Island	21,012	..	..	21,012
Nova Scotia	23,871	22,816	..	23,747
New Brunswick	20,839	..	24,160	23,191
Québec	26,404	23,834	25,862	26,154
Ontario	27,652	27,061	29,890	28,917
Manitoba	23,648	..	22,485	23,575
Saskatchewan	22,263	23,210	..	22,900
Alberta	21,834	..	27,151	26,199
British Columbia	27,753	27,753	25,456	27,254
Yukon	29,535	..	..	29,535
Northwest Territories	35,667	..	..	35,667
Canada	**26,186**	**25,681**	**28,509**	**27,049**

Source: Statistics Canada. Census of Population, 1991.

Interestingly, the intermediate CDs are "intermediate" between rural and urban landscapes when the skill level of occupations is considered (Figure 15.1). The rural and urban groups, however, did dominate specific occupations. Generally, occupations requiring the most expertise (management, professions and technical) were likely to be found in urban CDs and (with the exception of the "lower skills" category) most of the occupations with more ubiquitous employment requirements were most apparent in rural areas.

Commuting

The most striking conclusion is the low level of commuting from one type of region to another (i.e. among rural, intermediate and agglomerated regions (Table 15.2)). The largest inter-regional commuting is from intermediate to agglomerated commuting (3.2 percent of all workers). These movements likely occur around larger metropolitan cities with a labour shed that extends well into adjacent census divisions.

Figure 15.1. Rural regions have higher share of skilled, intermediate and labourer occupations, Canada, 1991

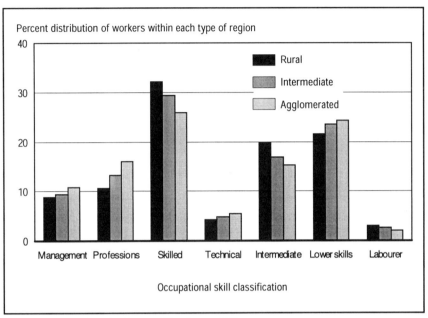

Source: Statistics Canada. Census of Population, 1991.

Table 15.2. Distribution of workers by place of residence and place of work, Canada, 1991

Place of residence	Place of work			All work locations
	Rural	Intermediate	Agglomerated	
	Percent of total workers			
Rural	24.2	0.6	1.4	26.2
Intermediate	0.3	18.1	3.2	21.6
Agglomerated	0.3	1.3	50.6	52.2
All residence locations	24.8	20.0	55.2	100.0

Source: Statistics Canada. Census of Population, 1991.

Overall, only 7 percent of Canadian workers reside in one type of region and work in another (Table 15.3). Note that agglomerated regions received more workers from commuting (4.6 percent of all workers) than they lost due to commuting (1.6 percent of all workers).

Table 15.3.   Distribution of commuters by place of residence and place of work, Canada, 1991

Place of residence	Place of work			All work locations
	Rural	Intermediate	Agglomerated	
	Commuters as percent of total workers			
Rural		0.6	1.4	2.0
Intermediate	0.3		3.2	3.5
Agglomerated	0.3	1.3		1.6
All residence locations	0.6	1.9	4.6	7.1

Source: Statistics Canada. Census of Population, 1991.
Note: A "commuter" is an individual who lives in one type of region and works in a different type of region.

Both rural areas and intermediate regions were net contributors to the agglomerated regions. In 1991, 70 percent of rural (cross-regional) commuters and 91 percent of intermediate (cross-regional) commuters worked in agglomerated regions (Table 15.4).

Table 15.4.   Destination of commuters for each type of place of residence, Canada, 1991

Place of residence	Place of work			All work locations
	Rural	Intermediate	Agglomerated	
	Percent of workers at each type of residence location			
Rural		31.2	68.8	100.0
Intermediate	7.7		92.3	100.0
Agglomerated	18.9	81.2		100.0
All residence locations	8.1	27.8	64.1	100.0

Source: Statistics Canada. Census of Population, 1991.

However, within each type of region, there is considerable commuting across CD boundaries. Within agglomerated regions, 11 percent of all workers commute across CD boundaries (Table 15.5). Another 32 percent of agglomerated workers commute from their census sub-division (CSD) (i.e. town, municipality, township) of residence to another CSD within their agglomerated CD. The degree of commuting among CSDs is similar within each of rural, intermediate and agglomerated regions. Within rural regions, 29 percent commute to another CSD (possibly a town or small city).

Table 15.5.   Commuting within and among types of regions, Canada, 1991

Percent of all workers	Place of residence	Place of work	Percent of workers not commuting across types of region	
50.6	Agglomerated	Agglomerated	100.0	Total
			57.3	No commuting to a different CSD
			31.5	Commutes to different CSD within CD
			11.2	Commutes to different agglomerated CD
1.3	Agglomerated	Intermediate		
0.3	Agglomerated	Rural		
3.2	Intermediate	Urban		
18.1	Intermediate	Intermediate	100.0	Total
			67.1	No commuting to a different CSD
			30.9	Commutes to different CSD within CD
			2.0	Commutes to different intermediate CD
0.3	Intermediate	Rural		
1.4	Rural	Agglomerated		
0.6	Rural	Intermediate		
24.2	Rural	Rural	100.0	Total
			68.1	No commuting to a different CSD
			28.6	Commutes to different CSD within CD
			3.3	Commutes to different rural CD
100.0	Total			

Source: Statistics Canada. Census of Population, 1991.
Note: CD=Census Division, CSD=Census Sub-division.

Occupational skills of commuters

The occupational skill group most likely to commute from one type of region to another is the management group (9 percent) (Table 15.6). Only 6 percent of intermediate and lower skilled workers are (cross-regional) commuters. Most management (cross-regional) commuters live in intermediate regions and work in agglomerated regions. Skilled and technical workers have a slightly higher propensity to commute from a rural region to an agglomerated region.

Table 15.6.   Commuting by occupational skill classification, Canada, 1991

Place of residence	Place of work	Occupational skill classification							
		Manage-ment	Profes-sions	Skilled	Tech-nical	Inter-mediate skilled	Lower skilled	Labourer	All occu-pations
Commuters as a percent of workers in each occupational skill classification									
Agglomerated	Intermediate	1.6	1.2	1.6	1.5	1.1	1.1	2.1	1.3
Agglomerated	Rural	0.3	0.3	0.3	0.3	0.3	0.2	0.5	0.3
Intermediate	Agglomerated	5.0	3.8	3.2	3.7	2.3	2.5	2.0	3.2
Intermediate	Rural	0.3	0 .3	0.3	0.3	0.2	0.2	0.4	0.3
Rural	Agglomerated	1.4	1.4	1.6	1.7	1.3	1.3	1.2	1.4
Rural	Intermediate	0.5	0.5	0.8	0.7	0.6	0.6	0.7	0.6
TOTAL commuters		9.1	7.5	7.8	8.2	5.8	5.9	6.9	7.1
Agglomerated	Agglomerated	53.6	57.3	46.2	53.4	46.4	53.9	41.0	50.6
Intermediate	Intermediate	16.6	17.0	18.7	17.9	18.7	18.1	19.9	18.1
Rural	Rural	20.6	18.2	27.3	20.5	29.0	22.1	32.3	24.2
TOTAL non-commuters		90.8	92.5	92.2	91.8	94.1	94.1	93.2	92.9
Total workers		100.0	100.0	100.0	100.0	100.0	100.0	100.0	100.0

Source: Statistics Canada. Census of Population, 1991.

Summary

A review of the factors creating the modern urban/rural environment indicated the importance of commuting for employment reasons. However, due in large part to data restrictions, commuting research in Canada has been less than complete. In 1991, 7 percent of the workforce commuted across regional (rural, intermediate, agglomerated) boundaries. An additional 2 to 11 percent commuted across census division (CD) boundaries within each type of region. Finally, another approximately 30 percent commuted from one census sub-division (CSD) to another CSD with their CD of residence.

References and further reading

Beale, Calvin L. (1980) The changing nature of rural employment. In Brown, David L. and Wardwell, John M. (eds). *New Directions in Urban-Rural Migration*. New York: Academic Press, pp. 37-49.

Beesley, Kenneth B. (1993) *The Rural-Urban Fringe: A Bibliography*. Peterborough, Ontario: Department of Geography, Trent University.

Beesley, Kenneth B. (1994) *Sustainable Development and the Rural-Urban Fringe: A Review of the Literature*. Winnipeg, Manitoba: Institute of Urban Studies, The University of Winnipeg.

Benson, Richard C. (1975) Part-time farming in a physically marginal area of Northern Ontario. In Fuller, Anthony M. and Mage, Julius A. (eds). *Part-Time Farming: Problem or Resource in Rural Development,* Guelph, Ontario: Proceedings of the First Rural Geography Symposium, Department of Geography, University of Guelph, pp. 114-125.

Bollman, Ray D. (1979a) *Selected Annotated Bibliography of Research on Part-Time Farming in Canada*. Monticello, Ill: Vance Bibliographies.

Bollman, Ray D, (1979b) Off-farm work by farmers: an application of the kinked demand curve for labour. *Canadian Journal of Agricultural Economics* Vol. 27, No. 1, pp. 37-60.

Bowles, Roy T. and Beesley, Kenneth B. (1991) Quality of life, migration to the countryside and rural community growth. In Beesley, Kenneth B. (ed.). *Rural and Urban Fringe Studies in Canada*. Toronto: Geographical Monographs No. 21, York University, Atkinson College, pp. 45-66.

Bryant, Christopher R. (1976) Some new perspectives on agricultural land use in the rural–urban fringe. *Ontario Geography* No.10, pp. 64-78.

Bryant, Christopher R. (1980) Manufacturing in rural development. In *Planning Industrial Development*. New York: John Wiley and Sons, pp. 99-128.

Bryant, Christopher R. and Russwurm, Lorne H. (1978) *A Report and Synthesis of the Workshop on a Rural Information System for Canada*. Ottawa: The Canadian Council on Rural Development.

Carroll, Robert L. and Wheeler, Raymond H. (1966) Metropolitan influence on the rural nonfarm population. *Rural Sociology* Vol. 31, No. 1, pp. 64-73.

Clemente, Frank and Summers, Gene F. (1975) The journey to work of rural industrial employees. *Social Forces* Vol. 54, pp. 212-219.

Crewson, Daryl M. and Reeds, Lloyd G. (1982) Loss of farmland in south-central Ontario from 1951-1971. *The Canadian Geographer* Vol. 26, No. 4, pp. 355-360.

Cummings, F. Harry, 1988, Canadian rural development policy: federal and provincial considerations. In Dykeman, Floyd W. (ed.). *Integrated Rural Planning and Development*. Sackville, New Brunswick: Rural and Small Town Research and Studies Programme: Department of Geography, Mount Allison University, pp. 45-60.

Dahms, Fredic A. (1980) The evolving spatial organization of small settlements in the countryside — an Ontario example. *Tijdschrift voor Econ. en Soc. Geografie* Vol. 71, No. 5, pp. 295-306.

Dahms, Fredic A. (1988) *The Heart of the Country*. Toronto: Deneau Publishers and Company.

Dahms, Fredic A. and Hallman, Barry. (1991) Population change, economic activity and amenity landscapes at the outer edge of the urban fringe. In Beesley, Kenneth B. (ed.). *Rural and Urban Fringe Studies in Canada*. Toronto: Geographical Monographs No. 21, York University, Atkinson College, pp. 67-90.

Driedger, Leo. (1991) *The Urban Factor: Sociology of Canadian Cities*. Toronto: Oxford University Press.

Fuguitt, Glenn V. (1991) Commuting and the rural-urban hierarchy. *Journal of Rural Studies* Vol. 7, No. 4, pp. 459-466.

Goldstein, Sidney and Mayer, Kurt (1964) Migration and the journey to work. *Social Forces* Vol. 42, pp. 472-481.

Government of Canada. (1995) *Rural Canada: A Profile*. Ottawa: Interdepartmental Committee on Rural and Remote Canada.

Hay, David A. (1992) Rural Canada in transition: trends and developments. In *Rural Sociology in Canada*. Toronto: Oxford University Press, pp. 16-32.

Henshall-Momsen, Janet. (1984) Urbanization of the countryside in Alberta. In Bunce, Michael F. and Troughton, Michael J. (eds). *The Pressures of Change in Rural Canada*. Toronto: Geographical Monographs No. 14, York University.

Hoch, Irving. (1981) Energy and location. In Hawley, Amos H. and Mazie, Sara Mills. (eds). *Nonmetropolitan America in Transition*. Chapel Hill: The University of North Carolina Press.

Hodge, G. (1972) The emergence of the urban field. In Bourne, L.S. and MacKinnon, R.D. (eds) *Urban Systems Development in Central Canada: Selected Papers*. Toronto: University of Toronto Press, pp. 234-243.

Krout, John A. (1983) Intercounty commuting in nonmetropolitan America in 1960 and 1970. *Growth and Change* Vol. 14, No. 1, pp. 9-19.

Krueger, Ralph R. (1980) The geographer and rural Southern Ontario. *Ontario Geography* No. 16, pp. 7-18.

Larson, Olaf F. (1981) Agriculture and the community. In Hawley, Amos H. and Mazie, Sara Mills. (eds). *Nonmetropolitan America in Transition*. Chapel Hill: The University of North Carolina Press, pp. 169-193.

MacDougall, E. Bruce. (1970) An analysis of recent changes in the number of farms in the north part of central Ontario. *The Canadian Geographer* Vol. 14, No.2, pp. 125-138.

Mage, J.A. (1982) The geography of part-time farming — a new vista for agricultural geographers. *GeoJournal* Vol. 6, No. 4, pp. 301-312.

Maguire, Garth. (1979) The urban fringe: perspectives on land use in the North Okanagan. *The Urban Fringe in the Western Provinces*. Toronto: Intergovernmental Committee on Urban and Regional Research, pp. 11-20.

Maraffa, Thomas A. and Brooker-Gross, Susan R. (1988) Residential relocation and commuting in a nonmetropolitan laborshed. *Geographical Perspectives* No. 62 pp. 14-23.

McDonald, G.T. (1972) Ontario agriculture in an urbanizing economy 1951-1966. In Bourne, L.S. and MacKinnon, R.D. (eds). *Urban Systems Development in Central Canada: Selected Papers*. Toronto: University of Toronto Press, pp. 222-233.

Meyer, Judith. (1981) Migration to near-metropolitan areas: characteristics and motives. *Urban Geography* Vol. 2, No. 1, pp. 64-79.

Network Data Library Service (NDLS). (1995) Social Science Computing Laboratory, University of Western Ontario, London, Ontario.

OECD. (1994) *Creating Rural Indicators for Shaping Territorial Policy*. Paris: OECD.

Parenteau, R. (1981) Is Canada going back to the Land? In Beesley, Ken B. and Russwurm, Lorne H. (eds). *The Rural-Urban Fringe: Canadian Perspectives*. Toronto: Geographical Monographs No. 10., York University, Atkinson College, pp. 53-70.

Parson, Helen E. (1979) An analysis of farmland abandonment trends: a study of central Ontario. *Ontario Geography* No. 14, pp. 41-57.

Pryor, Robin J. (1968) Defining the rural-urban fringe. *Social Forces* Vol. 47, No. 2, pp. 202-215.

Reimer, Bill. (1992) Modernization: technology and rural industries and populations. In *Rural Sociology in Canada*. Toronto: Oxford University Press, pp. 51-62.

Ricour-Singh, Françoise. (1979) *Poles and Zones of Attraction*. Ottawa: Statistics Canada.

Ricour-Singh, Françoise. (1981) The Montreal labour shed. In Beesley, Ken B. and Russwurm, Lorne H. (eds). *The Rural-Urban Fringe: Canadian Perspectives*. Toronto: Geographical Monographs No. 10, York University, Atkinson College, pp. 136-143.

Robinson, Guy M. (1991) The city beyond the city. In Robinson, Guy M. (ed.). *A Social Geography of Canada*. Toronto: Dundurn Press.

Rodehaver, Myles W. (1947) Fringe settlement as a two-directional movement. *Rural Sociology* Vol.12, No. 1, pp. 49-57.

Russwurm, Lorne H. (1971) Urban fringe and urban shadow. In Krueger, Ralph R. and Bryfogle, R. Charles. (eds). *Urban Problems: A Canadian Reader*. Toronto: Holt, Rinehart and Winston of Canada, pp. 104-122.

Saltzman, Arthur and Newlin, Lawrence W. (1981) The availability of passenger transportation. In Hawley, Amos H. and Mazie, Sara Mills. (eds). *Nonmetropolitan America in Transition*. Chapel Hill: The University of North Carolina Press, pp. 255-284.

Seninger, Stephen F. and Smeeding, Timothy M. (1981) Poverty: a human resource-income maintenance perspective. In Hawley, Amos H. and Mazie, Sara Mills (eds). *Nonmetropolitan America in Transition*. Chapel Hill: The University of North Carolina Press, pp. 396-436.

Sim, R. Alex. (1988) *Land and Community*. Guelph: University of Guelph Press.

Smit, Barry. (1979) Regional employment changes in Canadian agriculture. *The Canadian Geographer* Vol. 23, No.1, pp. 1-17.

Statistics Canada. (1991) *Population and Dwelling Counts*. Ottawa: Statistics Canada, Catalogue No. 93-301.

Statistics Canada. (1993) *Trends and Highlights of Canadian Agriculture and Its People*. Ottawa: Statistics Canada, Catalogue No. 96-303E.

Stock, George E. (1975) Off-farm work by small scale farmers in Ontario. In Fuller, Anthony M. and Mage, Julius A. (eds). *Part-Time Farming: Problem or Resource in Rural Development.* Guelph: Proceedings of the First Rural Geography Symposium, Department of Geography, University of Guelph, pp. 68-82.

Taaffe, Edward J., Gauthier, Howard L. and Maraffa, Thomas A. (1980) Extended commuting and the intermetropolitan periphery. *Annals of the Association of American Geographers* Vol. 70, No. 3, pp. 313-329.

Troughton, Michael J. (1981a) Aspects of employment and commuting in the fringe zone of London, Ontario. In Beesley, Ken B. and Russwurm, Lorne H. (eds). *The Rural-Urban Fringe: Canadian Perspectives*. Toronto: Geographical Monographs No. 10. York University, Atkinson College, pp. 144-178.

Troughton, Michael J. (1981b) The rural-urban fringe: a challenge to resource management. In Beesley, Ken B. and Russwurm, Lorne H. *The Rural-Urban Fringe: Canadian Perspectives*. Toronto: Geographical Monographs No. 10. York University, Atkinson College, pp. 218-243.

Troughton, Michael J. (1988) Rural Canada: what future? In Dykeman, Floyd W. (ed.). *Integrated Rural Planning and Development.* Sackville, New Brunswick: Rural and Small Town Research and Studies Programme, Department of Geography, Mount Allison University, pp. 3-20.

Walker, Gerald. (1979) Farmers in Southern Simcoe County, Ontario: part-time full-time comparisons. *Ontario Geography* No. 14, pp. 59-67.

Wehrwein, George S. (1942) The rural-urban fringe. *Economic Geography* Vol. 18, No. 3, pp. 217-228.

Chapter sixteen:

Establishment Structure, Job Flows and Rural Employment

Olaf Foss
Norwegian Institute for Urban and Regional Research, Oslo, Norway

Abstract

The gross flow of jobs into and out of regional labour markets numerically exceeds by many times the net employment change in the same period. There are systematically different regional patterns of change based on variation in establishment structure and behaviour. The average size of establishments differs among types of regions as well as among countries. Small establishments are prevalent in all types of regions, with only a slight relative predominance in rural regions. This is in contrast to the more complex picture of differential growth rates by size of enterprise, region type and country. The predominance of very small establishments does not, however, indicate a corresponding importance for total employment. A significant share of rural employment is with the small number of larger enterprises.

Introduction

Economic development is usually characterized by considerable replacement and renewal of establishments and jobs. The *gross flows* of jobs into and out of the economy in a given period numerically exceeds by many times the *net changes* in the number of jobs. Even in periods of employment decline a large number of new establishments are created and many establishments experience substantial growth.

In Norway during the period 1976–1983, a gross growth of more than 70,000 person-years were recorded in manufacturing industries in spite of a net loss of more than 50,000 person-years in the sector in the same period. Several studies from different countries indicate that on average large establishments experienced net job losses in the period whereas small establishments recorded net gains. Births of new establishments seemed to account for a substantial share of the total gross job creation (usually 50 percent or more). A high establishment birth rate in its turn increases the share of young and, presumably, potentially expansive establishments in the economy (Isaksen, 1988).

In France between 1981 and 1991, a net gain of more than 160,000 establishments was the result of a vast increase in firm births and a slightly smaller increase in firm deaths. The total number of firm births between 1981 and 1991 corresponded to 97 percent of the initial stock of firms in 1981. This led to a redistribution in favour of small and medium size establishments, a sectoral restructuring and changes in the spatial distribution (Guesnier, 1994). Considerable variation exists in new establishment formation rates between as well as within EU countries from the middle to the late 1980s. Similar variation is assumed to exist in establishment death rates and in rates of expansion and contraction in existing establishments (Reynolds *et al.,* 1994).

The general message is that the development of employment in a region reflects changes in the balance of gross movements in the number of jobs as establishments experience expansions, contractions and closures and new establishments are created. Closures (or out-migrations) and contractions of establishments cause *outflows* of jobs from the region's stock of jobs. New establishments (or in-migrations) and expansions cause *inflows* of jobs. These are the *gross components* — or the "demographic" explanatory factors at the establishment level — of the change in the number of jobs available in a region.

Impacts of economic forces on establishment demography in a region are contingent on as well as causal to *compositional characteristics* of the regional economy. These characteristics include the relative representation of different industries, the distribution of establishments across different size classes and stages in the establishment "life-cycle", different types of ownership, enterprise attachment, etc. Economic development forces such as sectoral shifts, shifts in the functional and regional division of labour and the subsequent recomposing of regional economies influence the gross components of establishment demography. The impact of these forces differs according to the economic sector and according to the particular location.

In order to promote rural employment opportunities, purposeful public policies should understand the structural basis of rural employment and employment change at the establishment level. Policies should be targeted to influence the processes which actually determine net change in the size and composition of the stock of jobs in rural regions. These structural characteristics and processes vary among countries and types of regions.

The first steps in establishing a purposeful knowledge base is to investigate the status and variation in structural conditions and their relations to employment and employment change. The next step is to determine the relative influence of gross flows of jobs on the observed net change and further to decompose these flows into their relevant gross components of change at the establishment level (as discussed above). Important keys to rural employment policy are found in the absolute and relative influence of the respective components of change.

This chapter is an initial attempt to present some basic but simple background information related to this kind of approach for research and policy considerations, with an emphasis on the *territorial* (i.e. rural/urban) dimension. This document intends to shed light on four sets of basic questions:

1. What are the basic structural characteristics of the organization of economic activity in different types of regions (rural/urban) in OECD countries? What differences and similarities seem to exist between countries in this respect? What relevant features of recent change are indicated?

2. What relationship exists between structural conditions, structural development and employment change in different types of regions and in similar types of regions in different countries?

3. What is the relative importance of small and medium sized establishments to employment and employment change in different types of regions and in similar types of regions in different countries?

4. What is the relative importance of gross job flows and their gross components of change at the establishment level to the development of rural employment? Is it possible to compile a data set which will enable cross-national comparison of gross flow dynamics at a sub-national level for OECD countries?

Structural characteristics of rural and urban economic organization

The composition of a region's stock of establishments according to size (number of employed persons in the establishment) and industry class are used as rough indicators of structural characteristics of the regional economy and labour market. Regional employment change is due to spatially differential impacts of sectoral shifts, favouring and disfavouring sectors characterized by small and large establishments respectively. Change in the size structure of establishments is also assumed to be the outcome of intrasectoral and regional reorganization of the economy due to changes in technology, economic integration and other conditions influencing the terms of market competition. Either way, such structural characteristics of the population of establishments are a basic quality of the foundation of a region's employment and potentially important determinants of prospective employment change.

Average size of establishments

Data available for this study allow comparison of average establishment size among five countries (Finland, Norway, Switzerland, United Kingdom and the United States)[1] at the beginning of the 1990s. Considerable differences exist among countries and regions. In all countries the smallest establishments on average are to be found in predominantly rural regions (see OECD (1994) for a description of the territorial scheme) and the differences among classes of regions according to degree of rurality in most countries are significant. In the two Scandinavian countries rural establishments are remarkably small. In Norway the average size of establishments is very low even in semi-rural and urban regions (Figure 16.1). Some of the differences between the Scandinavian and the other countries are due to different data coverage. Finnish and Norwegian data do not in principle exclude firms with no employees (e.g. self-employed people with no employees), although coverage may vary somewhat. Data for the other countries include firms with at least one employee only. Similarly, data on change in firm size (Figure 16.2) may be influenced by an increase in self-employed persons without employees in Norway and Finland.

Figure 16.1.   Norway has the smallest firm size for each type of region

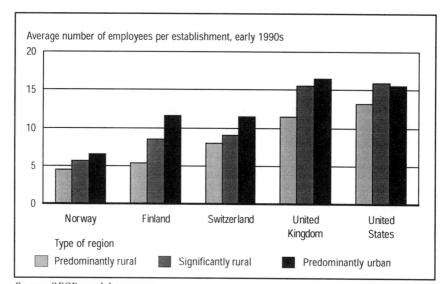

Source: OECD rural data surveys.

1.   *Data sources, concepts and coverage differ among the countries, reducing comparability. For instance, the Swiss data include ISIC sectors 2 and 3 only. In the Norwegian data, the primary sector and "electricity, gas and water supply" are excluded along with small groups of services under sector 7, 8 and 9. In all classifications by size group, most of the public sector is excluded along with "finance and insurance". In the Norwegian data, person-years are used instead of employed persons. Other important limitations are reflected in the figures or are explained in the text.*

Figure 16.2.   Firm size decreased in all regions in Norway and Finland

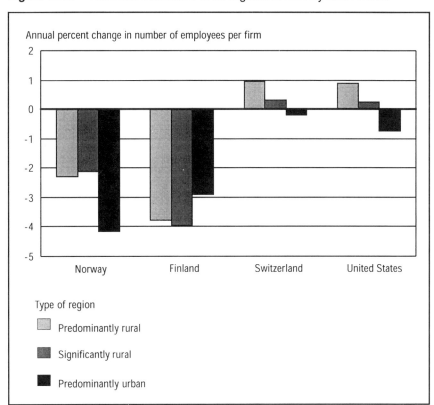

Source: OECD rural data surveys.
*   *Norway, 1987 to 1992; Finland 1986 to 1990; Switzerland, 1985 to 1991; USA, 1987 to 1992.*

According to Norwegian and United States data, differences in average size of establishments between rural and urban regions are due to regional size variation within economic sectors as well as regional differences in sectoral composition. In the United States this is primarily a service-sector phenomenon, whereas traditional sectors ("extraction, making and moving"[2]) show very little regional variation in average establishment size (Figure 16.3). In Norway regional variation exists within all sectors (Figure 16.4).

---

2.   *A crude intuitive classification of industries into three classes is used: "extraction, making and moving" (agriculture, other primary, mining, construction, manufacturing, transportation, communications); "finance, insurance and business services"; and "other services".*

Figure 16.3.   United States shows rural/urban firm size differences in the service sectors

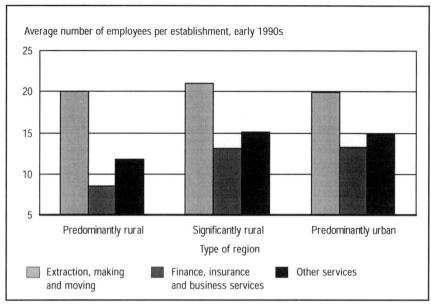

Source: OECD rural data surveys.

Figure 16.4.   Norway shows rural/urban size differences in all industry groups

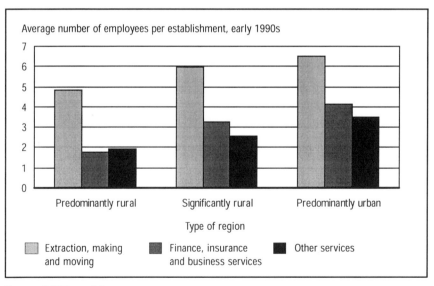

Source: OECD rural data surveys.

In all countries except Switzerland (mid 1980s data for United Kingdom are not available) the average size of establishments dropped in predominantly urban regions from mid 1980s to early 1990s, while in the two rural categories this was the case in the Scandinavian countries only (the Swiss data comprise extractive and goods-producing industries only, i.e. ISIC-sectors 2 and 3). Data indicate that differences in average size of establishments between the three types of regions were slightly reduced during this period. Data for Norway and the United States further indicate that this could correspond to a parallel process of equalization of the industrial structure between rural and urban regions (see also Spilling and Isaksen (1994)).

Size structure of establishments

The distribution of establishments according to size class (number of employees) confirms the dominance of very small establishments (fewer than 10 persons employed) in all types of regions in every country which is represented. Generally well above 70 percent of the establishments employ fewer than 10 persons; in the Scandinavian countries around 90 percent are in this size category in predominantly rural regions (Table 16.1). Remarkably small differences exist across the three types of regions in the countries included in this study. Establishments with 50 persons or more employed constitute a very small portion of the population of establishments in the regions.

Table 16.1.   Over three-quarters of rural establishments have less than 10 employees, early 1990s

	Number of employees per establishment					
	1–9 employees	10–19 employees	20–49 employees	50–99 employees	100+ employees	Total
	Percent distribution of establishments					
Norway						
Predominantly rural	92	4	2	1	0	100
Significantly rural	91	5	3	1	1	100
Predominantly rural	89	6	3	1	1	100
Finland						
Predominantly rural	89	6	4	1	1	100
Significantly rural	85	8	5	2	1	100
Predominantly rural	80	9	6	2	2	100
Switzerland						
Predominantly rural	83	10	5	1	1	100
Significantly rural	82	10	5	2	1	100
Predominantly rural	80	10	6	2	2	100
United Kingdon						
Predominantly rural	75	16	6	2	1	100
Significantly rural	75	15	6	3	2	100
Predominantly rural	73	15	6	3	3	100
United States						
Predominantly rural	76	12	7	2	2	100
Significantly rural	73	13	9	3	2	100
Predominantly rural	74	12	8	3	2	100

Source: OECD rural data surveys.

From the United States data we learn that the size distribution of establishments are rather similar across broad classes of industries, although the lowest size category seem to be a little less dominant in traditional extractive and goods-producing industries and in service industries other than finance, insurance and business services.

Internationally no fixed definition of "small and medium sized establishments" (SMEs) exists. Thresholds vary according to purpose and national states of affairs, usually within the span of 20 to 500 persons employed. The above documentation confirms the well known fact that in all countries with a market economy the large majority of establishments tend to be very small, usually with fewer than 20 or 10 persons employed, which emphasizes that considerable attention should be paid to this segment.

In the United Kingdom and the United States the average size of establishments in predominantly and significantly rural regions is about 12–13 and 16 respectively (Figure 16.1), mostly due to a considerable share of small establishments (less than 10 persons employed) among the regions' establishments (73–76 percent)

(Table 16.1). In Norway the figures are about 4–6 (average) and 90-92 (share of small establishments).

The United States data for the period 1987–1992 indicate considerable differences in growth rates for establishments of different size according to industry class and type of region. Traditional industries excepted, especially in other than predominantly rural regions, no clear picture of small establishment prominence appears. In predominantly and significantly rural regions in the United States, substantial growth was recorded even in the number of establishments with 100 persons or more employed. Once again the situation in Finland and Norway seems to differ significantly from the other countries, the largest growth rates being recorded for the class of very small establishments in all region types.

Establishment size and employment

Our emphasis here is primarily on the relationship of establishment size structure to *employment*. We have data for four countries (Finland, Norway, Switzerland, United Kingdom) showing the distribution of employment by establishment size class in the three region types. Employment data show an altogether different picture of the importance of establishment size than the mere distribution of establishments by size class (Table 16.2).

Table 16.2. Over one-fifth of rural employees work in establishments with 100+ employees, early 1990s

	Number of employees per establishment					
	1–9 employees	10–19 employees	20–49 employees	50–99 employees	100+ employees	Total
	Percent distribution of employees					
Norway						
Predominantly rural	40	13	15	11	21	100
Significantly rural	31	12	15	10	32	100
Predominantly urban	27	12	15	12	34	100
Finland						
Predominantly rural	39	14	17	8	22	100
Significantly rural	25	12	16	12	36	100
Predominantly urban	18	11	16	12	43	100
Switzerland						
Predominantly rural	34	16	19	12	18	100
Significantly rural	29	14	18	13	26	100
Predominantly urban	22	12	16	12	38	100
United Kingdom						
Predominantly rural	25	20	17	12	27	100
Significantly rural	18	16	14	13	40	100
Predominantly urban	17	14	13	13	44	100

Source: OECD rural data surveys.

Firstly, there are no regions in the countries represented where very small establishments account for more than two fifths of the employment. In all region types (and countries) establishments with more than 50, and between 20 and 50, persons employed play a numerically substantial role in total employment. *Secondly*, the importance to employment of establishments of different size classes varies significantly between region types and countries; in all countries very small establishments are most important in predominantly rural regions (from about 25 to 40 percent of the employment) and least important in predominantly urban regions (from about 15 to around 25 percent).

The figures clearly demonstrate the relative importance of very small establishments to employment in rural regions compared with urban regions, the substantial differences that exist between and within countries with regard to the relative importance of small establishments, *and* the considerable discrepancy that exists between the numerical dominance of small establishments in the population of establishments in all regions on the one hand and their somewhat more modest role as an employment base on the other hand.

Rural employment change: the importance of establishment structure

The important question concerning the interplay of regional industrial restructuring and employment change is whether certain classes of establishments, specifically very small establishments, are *increasing* or *decreasing* their contribution to the development of employment, especially in rural regions. Is industrial activity more and more being organized into small establishments with the implication that the contribution of small establishments to the overall development of employment increases as well? Available data so far allow only a superficial treatment of this question, without any specification of the complex underlying dynamics of spatial intersectoral and intrasectoral restructuring.

Structure of establishment and employment change

Figure 16.5 shows simultaneous change in the number of establishments and employment in four OECD countries from the middle of the 1980s to the early 1990s. The Finnish experience may be characterized as "jobless" establishment growth; a considerable growth in the number of establishments along with zero or rather moderate growth of employment in each region type. In Switzerland and the United States, establishment and employment growth rates correspond more closely, while in Norway a substantial net job loss occurred without a corresponding net loss of establishments.

Figure 16.5.   Finland shows virtually no job growth but relatively high growth in the number of establishments, mid 1980s to early 1990s

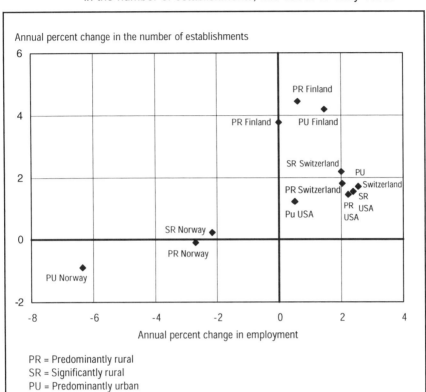

Source: OECD rural data survey.

International differences seem larger than variation among types of regions within countries indicating that varying *national* economic forces are at work in the period, affecting different regions in generally similar ways. Data clearly indicate that there are no simple relationships between net changes in the number of establishments and net changes in the number of jobs. Differences between countries are (surprisingly) larger than differences within countries.

Data for three countries allow specification by establishment size class. Both establishment and employment shares in small establishments increased visibly in rural and semi-rural regions in Finland and Norway (in Norway this was the case even in urban regions). Switzerland recorded no structural change in urban regions by this measure, but a slightly opposite pattern compared with the Scandinavian countries appeared in the rural regions. Especially in Finland larger establishments lost ground as a location for employment in all types of regions. It is important to remember that Swiss data include ISIC sector 2 and 3 only.

In traditional sectors ("extraction, making and moving") in Norway and the United States employment either fell more rapidly than the number of establishments (Norway), or grew more slowly than the number of establishments (United States). In Switzerland employment increased more than the number of establishments in this sector. The two service sector groups displayed a rather different rural development in Norway and the United States. Especially among "other service" industries (i.e. excluding "finance, insurance and business services"), employment and establishment change showed little correspondence; either employment fell almost as much as the number of establishments grew (Norway), or employment grew much faster than the number of establishments (United States).

Structural determinants of employment change

During the late 1980s and early 1990s Norway experienced a substantial net loss of jobs in the predominantly rural regions in the industries included here (Table 16.3). Similar regions in Finland recorded no change in employment, while rural employment in Switzerland (ISIC sectors 2 and 3) increased substantially. In Norway relative employment *decline* in the period was strongest in predominantly urban regions, while these regions in Finland recorded the strongest *increase* in employment. Switzerland recorded a regionally more evenly distributed change along with an overall rise in employment.

Table 16.3.   Employment increased in rural small business, mid 1980s to early 1990s

	Number of employees per establishment					
	1–9 employees	10–19 employees	20–49 employees	50–99 employees	100+ employees	All establishments
	Percent change in the number of employees in each establishment size class					
Norway						
Predominantly rural	4	-12	-20	-17	-26	-12
Significantly rural	2	-13	-18	-21	-10	-10
Predominantly urban	-4	-15	-23	-16	-39	-24
Finland						
Predominantly rural	17	3	6	-12	-21	0
Significantly rural	20	7	15	11	-14	2
Predominantly urban	22	13	25	8	-6	6
Switzerland						
Predominantly rural	11	21	18	20	20	17
Significantly rural	15	20	22	29	12	18
Predominantly urban	12	15	17	15	12	14

Source: OECD rural data surveys.

In the two Nordic countries, and especially in Finland, very small establishments (fewer than 10 employed persons) *contributed positively* to the development in the number of jobs in both types of rural regions, while larger establishments (100 or more employed persons) (in Norway even medium sized establishments) *contributed negatively*. The negative contribution to employment by larger establishments in Finland's predominantly rural regions corresponded exactly to the positive contribution to employment of very small establishments. It is important to notice that data for Table 16.3 represent overall employment growth in each size category in the period. Hence employment in a small size category may increase due to shrinkage of larger establishments as well as the growth or birth of small establishments.

Rural employment change: the importance of establishment demography

As indicated in the introduction, changes in the distribution of jobs and employment by the size class of establishments reflect alterations in the size distribution of establishments due to the combined effects of several different types of processes — expansions and contractions of existing establishments, births (and in-migrations) and deaths (and out-migrations) of establishments and reorganization of production (e.g. mergers).

The *quantitative* knowledge foundation for rural industrial and employment policy evaluation is presently limited in accuracy and information value. The general information base is better developed in some countries than in others, but a common experience is that transferability of information and insights among nations and regions is poor due to a number of factors. One important reason is the lack of attention paid to territoriality in an international context. There is a need to adopt a standard territorial scheme which will enable a regional classification suited to fruitful comparisons at a subnational level.

A focus on business demographics invites a consideration of numerous hypotheses for subsequent research:

1. In the general process of decline in manufacturing industries, large establishments are most affected by contractions and closures, while small establishments adjust and survive for a longer time. Decline in manufacturing industries therefore tends to increase the share of small establishments.

2. Small establishments are generally more competitive than larger establishments in all industries. Increasing international market integration and competition therefore tends to favour the growth of small establishments at the expense of larger establishments.

3. Small establishments are functioning better than larger establishments in rural regions. Changes in the regional division of labour leading to relative decline in manufacturing in central urban regions and relative expansion in non-urban regions tend to increase the share of small establishments.

4. Intrasectoral restructuring of manufacturing industries favours industries characterized by small-scale production at the expense of industries characterized by large-scale production.

5. Long-term sectoral shifts are favouring sectors characterized by low average establishment size (e.g. service industries) and disfavouring sectors with high average establishment size (e.g. manufacturing).

6. Shifts in the principles of production organization (i.e. horizontal and vertical integration and disintegration) presently bring about enterprise fragmentation and externalization of functions, leading to growth in small establishments.

7. Increasing competition generally leads to faster turnover and shorter duration of establishments, increasing the share of "young" establishments in the economy. Young establishments tend to be small.

The implications of these hypotheses for rural employment are mediated through the sectoral and intrasectoral territorial distribution and division of labour, through regional differences in qualities of labour markets, industrial traditions and environments, and other conditions favouring and disfavouring different modes of production; and through "spatial affinities" of different types of production and establishments (location requirements).

Norwegian data indicate that regionally uneven net employment growth in the private non-primary sector from the late 1970s to the early 1980s to a large extent was due to systematic spatial variation in gross job *inflows*, while gross *outflows* of jobs were more evenly distributed among regions. Especially at the end of the 1970s rural regions seemed to produce relatively larger numbers of *new jobs* than centrally located urban regions, a tendency that started to turn at the beginning of the 1980s. The majority of new private sector jobs in rural areas appeared in small, independent establishments in traditional sectors like labour-intensive manufacturing and retail trade. In urban regions the replacement processes in the 1970s and 1980s to a larger degree seemed to reflect industrial restructuring and renewal of the private economic sector, while rural areas experienced a consolidation of the existing industrial base.

Conclusions

The gross flows of jobs into and out of regional labour markets numerically exceed by many times net employment change in the same period. There are systematically different regional patterns of change based on variation in establishment structure and behaviour. This study initially intended to compile a data set which would enable an initial comparison of aspects of the relationship between "demographic" movements of the "population" of establishments in a region, and changes in the size of the regions stock of jobs, based on a "gross components" approach and the OECD territorial scheme (OECD, 1994).

The establishment of such a data set may be possible for a few OECD countries from the middle of the 1980s, enabling comparisons of gross flows of establishments and jobs traced to the four components of change (establishment births, expansions, contractions and deaths) at a sub-national level. Several countries seem to be in the process of developing such possibilities. There are obstacles, however, related to differences in definitions, methods of measurement and data coverage. We have not been able to utilize this kind of data for this report.

The empirical emphasis in this report considers establishment structure and employment change in different types of regions. Comparisons focus on employment by establishment size class, defined according to the number of employed persons in the establishments. Generalizations are limited by the relatively small number of countries represented and by data differences. Main findings cited below are to be considered *indications of relevance*, as the degree of generality cannot be determined:

1. Average size of establishments differ considerably and systematically among types of regions, as well as among countries, the smallest establishments on average are to be found in predominantly rural regions. Regional variation may be traced to variation in intra-sectoral size differences as well as to variation in sectoral composition. Regional size differences tend to shrink during the period around 1990, possibly due to decreasing sectoral variation.

2. The general numerical importance of very small establishments in all types of regions are confirmed, with only a slight relative predominance of rural regions. This is in contrast to the more complex picture of differential growth rates by size class, region type and country. The numerical predominance of very small establishments do not, however, indicate a corresponding importance to employment, although their importance to employment is more pronounced in rural than in urban regions.

3. The relationship between relative change in the number of establishments and jobs varies in strength with industry class, type of region and country, indicating structural as well as business cycle and other differences in the

respective national processes of economic change. Data (especially for the two Scandinavian countries) indicate that very small establishments contributed positively to employment change in rural regions in the period studied, while larger establishments contributed negatively. Changes in the relationship of establishment size structure to employment seem to display varying patterns by region type and country.

Our data confirm the relevance of establishment level analysis in the study of regional and rural employment creation and development and the necessity to take the territorial dimension explicitly into consideration in this respect. Data also indicate that the regional dimension may have varying types of relevance according to structural and other economic features of different countries, but are too limited to display any distinct patterns. There is a need to expand the databases, as well as looking behind the net figures, in order to detect systematic patterns of regional and cross-national variation in causal dynamics of employment change at the establishment level.

References

Guesnier, Bernard. (1994) Regional variations in new firm formation in France. *Regional Studies,* Vol. 28, No. 4, pp. 347-358.

Isaksen, Arne. (1988) *Noeringsutvikling i sentrum og periferi. Bedrifts- og sysselsettingsutvilingen i norske regioner pa 1970- og 1980-tallet* (Industrial development in centre and periphery. Development of establishments and employment in Norwegian regions in the 1970s and 1980s). Ostlandsforskning, Rapport 5/88, Lillehammer.

OECD. (1994) *Creating Rural Indicators for Shaping Territorial Policy.* Paris: OECD.

Reynolds, Paul, Storey, David J. and Westhead, Paul. (1994) Cross-national comparisons of the variation in new firm formation rates. *Regional Studies,* Vol. 28, No. 4, pp. 443-456.

Spilling, Olav R. and Isaksen, Arne. (1994) *Regional utviking og sma bedrifter i Norge. En analyse av utviklingen 1950-90. Del 1* (Regional development and small establishments in Norway. An analysis of the period 1950-90. Part 1). Ostlandsforskning/Agderforskning, Lillehammer/Kristiansand.

Chapter seventeen:

The Vitality of Small and Medium Enterprises (SMEs) in Rural Québec[1]

André Joyal
Université du Québec à Trois-Rivières, Trois-Rivières, Québec, Canada

Abstract

The purpose of this research is to determine the influence that a given milieu exerts on the propensity of a small business to export. The concept of "milieu" is a support space for small exporters which may be geographic but also includes dimensions of history, tradition, culture and social behaviour.

Businesses tend to act alone. Although networking to exchange information among businesses is promoted as an appropriate strategy, such networking is not really occurring. Contacts with local and regional development officers are very limited. Many company executives feel that government programmes are not worth the effort to qualify for them. The presence of the elements of an information network do not imply that a network will operate. Although distance is a rural factor limiting the successful operation of networks, urban researchers have noted that even the existence of a critical (urban) mass does not necessarily ensure the existence of information exchanges among firms.

> We set up shop in this town seven years ago, and we're very happy we did. Even though we export 80 percent of our products to the United States, we don't suffer because of our location. On the contrary, we benefit because our employees have a work ethic typical of rural communities, which doesn't exist in large cities. *(Manager of a business in Champlain County, Québec)*

---

1. This chapter is based on research funded by the Social Sciences and Humanities Research Council of Canada.

Introduction

Dynamic, innovative, successful, forward-looking — these are the terms used to identify businesses whose managers are not afraid to take the lead and carve out a niche for themselves in this increasingly competitive world. They make their mark not only with their production methods and the products they offer but also with the way in which they market them. Even today, rural businesses are often characterized by traditional products (agri-food, furniture, other primary sector products), unskilled labour, underfinancing, distance from information sources, outdated manufacturing techniques and so on. Although this stereotype has not disappeared from the map — far from it — there are, fortunately, a good number of rural firms that present a different picture. We examine small and medium-size enterprises (SMEs) that have established themselves in the export market.

Innovations in the manufacturing process and the type of products produced explain the export focus of innovative firms. Not surprisingly, many of these companies have already earned their ISO 9002 certification or are well on the way to getting it. This is particularly true of companies that sell their products to large firms rather than directly on the consumer market. The confidence of business people in the superior quality of their products indicates they are ready to meet the challenges of a globalized economy.

Obviously, it is important to keep a level head and not to expand too quickly. In Québec in 1990, only 12 percent of SMEs, all industries combined, were successful in penetrating a foreign market (only the United States market in most cases). While the total value of manufacturing exports that year was $17 billion, the small business share was no more than $1.4 billion (8 percent) (Québec, 1994). Much remains to be done before SMEs, particularly those in rural areas, will achieve significant results. Nevertheless, our research shows there are some spectacular success stories in rural Québec. There are opportunities to learn from those who did not wait for free trade with our neighbours to launch their business ventures (Joyal, 1996).

The first objective in our research is to describe the roles of the various players in rural areas[2] who may have a favourable impact on SMEs that export. We consider the extent to which businesses use both formal and informal networks. In other words, we explore to what degree the "network paradigm" (Cooke and Morgan, 1993) applies in rural central Québec. Our approach is based largely on the work of the *Groupe de recherche européen sur les milieux innovateurs* [European research group on innovative milieux] (GREMI) (Maillat, 1995) and on what is known in Europe as local or territorial production systems.

Once we have developed the concept of a "milieu" as it is applied in this research project, we will use some general findings to provide an overview of

---

2.   *For the purposes of this study, municipalities with a population of less than 3,000 are considered rural areas, while those with a population of 3,000 to 6,000 are considered semi-rural.*

our sample of 23 SMEs, paying particular attention to their innovativeness. Four case studies will make these findings easier to understand and provide a concrete illustration of the various approaches taken by business executives who, relying essentially on their own resources, have demonstrated that industrial diversification in rural areas is not a utopian dream.

The concept of "milieu"

> *We know about the various agencies that can supply us with information, and we are aware of other small exporters operating in the same field as we are, but we prefer not to contact them. Deep down, we are individualists. (Manager of a business in Maskinongé County, Québec)*

When we talk about the milieu of a business, we envision the various players operating in its environment. The environment is a space that is distinct in its geography, history, traditions, heritage and, in some cases, social behaviour. Socio-economic agents that exist in a particular space necessarily interact with the businesses located there. The milieu corresponds to their sphere of influence or action. By definition or necessity, an exporting company must deal with some organizations and businesses that are far away, and therefore its milieu possesses an extraterritorial dimension. Nevertheless, the local or domestic territorial connotation of a business's milieu is important. It may be a city and its satellite municipalities or a group of towns in a well-defined space, sometimes containing a number of administrative divisions. At this level, there may be strategic plans devised by actors whose specific mandate is to drive a process that may lead to the consolidation or diversification of productive activity. As may be imagined, however, the concept of milieu cannot be purged of a certain degree of fuzziness in view of the interpretations to which it lends itself, depending on the observer and the context which inevitably vary from country to country. The GREMI's work is of critical importance here.

Established in 1984, the GREMI looks at the local milieux and attempts to assess the role of the milieu in making, developing and disseminating technological innovations. The objective is to study the external prerequisites for the creation and consolidation of innovative firms. It is assumed that these businesses do not already exist in the local milieu as they arise from the milieu. Thus, an association is suggested between the microregion, or territory, and the milieu since, according to Maillat (1994), the milieu is based on the role played by the territorial context and its capacity to exploit the proximity of its actors. In the same vein, however, Maillat makes it clear that the geographic area involved has no predefined borders and does not correspond to a specific region in the usual sense of the word. Consequently, the terms milieu and territory should not be linked. Understandably, though, the three main components revealed by the GREMI's research strongly point to a relationship with a specific, limited sphere of action, commonly referred to as the territory in which the business is located:

1. a microanalytic approach to the milieu where the milieu manifests itself as an efficient structure of the marketplace by helping to reduce transaction costs;

2. a cognitive approach to the milieu which involves the notions of learning, know-how and technical training; and

3. an organizational approach to the milieu, focusing in particular on the existence of an interdependence among the actors in exploiting available resources.

There is some degree of overlap here with the characteristics used to identify a milieu (Maillat and Perrin, 1992). Milieu is, first of all, a **local framework** in which there is a certain homogeneity in behaviour and outlook in dealing with problems. Secondly, it is an **organisational logic** that helps actors to work together toward innovation. As noted above, our research shows that this characteristic is not found in rural Québec. Lastly, the milieu contains a collective drive to learn that fosters behaviour modification as the environment in which businesses exist evolves.

Despite the warning to avoid confusing milieu and territory, the existence of the three components makes it very tempting to link these observations with a regional or microregional sphere of action. Milieu is often regarded as a system consisting of all components that can supply the innovative business with the various inputs it needs. This suggests the potential for "local synergies" or "territorial synergies". Hence a milieu may exert a varying degree of influence on the innovative process in SMEs. This in turn leads to the concept of "innovative milieu".

Innovative milieu is defined as a territorial whole in which the interactions among economic agents develop as they learn from the multilateral transactions that generate externalities specific to innovation and as their learning experiences converge toward increasingly effective forms of the common management of resources. That said, we must question the relevance of the idea that business is not an isolated innovator. For the GREMI's researchers, a business is part of a milieu that acts as an incubator of innovation. Thus, territories are, in their view, active milieux in which innovation takes place. According to them, innovation results from the exploitation of know-how and technical training using the internal dynamic of a particular place. To what extent do these apparently relevant statements apply to rural or semi-rural Québec?

The answer to this question, as previously noted, comes from a study of 23 SMEs that manufacture and export their products. These businesses are considered highly innovative and may be described as "complex manufacturers" as opposed to traditional manufacturers. In this case, complexity embraces a number of considerations: the use of computer-assisted manufacturing techniques, the importance of managerial staff, research and development activity aimed at marketing new or improved products, the presence of skilled workers, and so on. Using the same methodology as GREMI's researchers, we attempted to determine the extent to which business executives use resources in their milieu to develop their **export** strategy. In so doing, of course, we were also able to determine if any of the business functions we investigated require input from various economic agents in the milieu.

Thus, we are concerned with the concept of milieu as a support space for small exporters. We are assuming that like innovation, exporting is not an isolated activity. Hence our goal was to determine how much influence a given milieu exerts on the commitment of a small business to export to a foreign market.

Methodology

Twenty-three SMEs were visited in rural central Québec (roughly encompassing a broad corridor from Montréal to Québec City) and a 90 to 120 minute interview was conducted, in most cases with the business's owner/manager or an assistant responsible for exports. The interview included questions on the business's history, the main phases in its development, employee training, methods used to keep abreast of new technology, use of government assistance programmes, research and development, the initial export strategy and how it evolved and the influence of the business's milieu through the various phases of its development with particular attention to export-related activities. In addition, a small number of development officers working for business support organizations were interviewed. See Table 17.1 for an overview of the sample. One business was just about to make its debut in the export market at the time of the interview, while 13 others had started exporting only ten years earlier. In fact, a high percentage of SMEs in Québec got into exporting a few years before the 1989 Canada–United States Trade Agreement. The average annual sales of the businesses studied was nearly $9 million and close to one-third of those sales (32 percent) came from exports. The average number of employees was 66.

The reasons for establishing the business in a rural area were of a personal nature, in the majority of cases (65 percent) (Figure 17.1). Most of these businesses were started by local entrepreneurs whose principal motivation was a desire to work in the community where they were born. Other factors were the availability of suitable sites or premises (13 percent) and the fact that labour costs were lower than in urban areas.

Table 17.1.　Businesses included in this study

Year started exporting	Annual sales ($ millions)	Percent of sales from exports	Number of employees	Industry
1981	3.3	1	21	Machinery
1992	1.5	15	20	Chemicals
1992	15	13	150	Furniture
1985	5	60	57	Machinery
1946	15	25	112	Wood
1989	3	75	75	Machinery
1985	3	33	49	Furniture
1987	12	35	70	Transportation
1987	5	60	13	Clothing
1978	3	30	40	Metal products
1970	3	1	50	Minerals
1972	30	1	62	Paper
1991	2.5	85	40	Furniture
1992	0.2	5	3	Machinery
1988	18	14	185	Metal processing
1980	15	5	85	Metal products
1988	6	18	65	Machinery
1976	20	40	150	Transportation
1970	9	55	60	Furniture
1990	3	7	50	Printing
1940	15	5	50	Plastics
1990	15	80	90	Other
Not available	1.5	80	10	Wood

Average for rural businesses

Year founded	before 1980	
Year started exporting	13	years after being founded
Annual sales	$8.9	million
Percent of sales from exports	32.3	
Number of employees	66	

Figure 17.1.　Two-thirds of the entrepreneurs stated "personal preference" as the reason for locating in a rural area

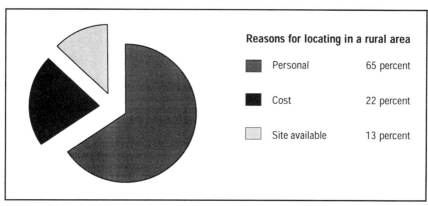

Reasons for locating in a rural area

▨	Personal	65 percent
■	Cost	22 percent
▧	Site available	13 percent

We asked the extent of contacts between the businesses and their environments at start-up and at the time of the survey. This covers contacts of all types, including support during start-up from organizations that help people open their own businesses, and input by local players in the companies' functions.

Figure 17.2. Only 18 percent of respondents reported regular contacts within their milieu at the time of business start-up

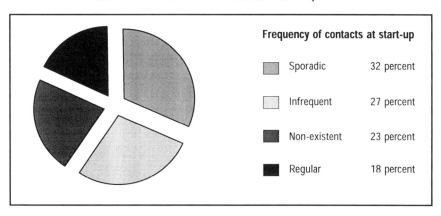

It may seem surprising that a total lack of contacts is more common in the early years (23 percent) (Figure 17.2) than at the time of the survey (14 percent) (Figure 17.3). This may be due to the fact that a majority of the businesses were started at a time when there were fewer support organizations than there are now.

Figure 17.3. At the time of the survey, 33 percent of the respondents reported regular contacts within their milieu

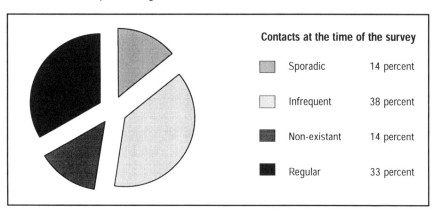

The fact that on-third of the businesses reported regular contact with other players in their milieu could be misleading. In most cases, the managers attend the monthly meetings of a business association to learn from the experience of

others. Sporadic contacts (14 percent) may represent exchanges of information between representatives of businesses in the same industry. This demonstrates that competition does not completely eliminate cooperation when it comes to gathering information about specific kinds of equipment, suppliers of raw materials, and useful contacts abroad. In general, however, businesses tend to act alone.

"By and large, we prefer to rely on our own information." This statement would probably be echoed by the managers of most of the businesses studied in this part of the research project. For the majority of businesses, ties with other players are confined to occasional contact with an employment development officer of a local business assistance organization, or with the relevant business association, whose head office is located elsewhere. Yet networking — the exchange of information between businesses — is very much the "in" thing today. There was every reason to believe that for purposes such as consolidating their export activities, businesses were becoming more involved in formal or informal territorial networking. However, this is not really occurring.

Small exporters occasionally take advantage of a government programme (more often than not to participate in an international exhibition), but the individual approach is characteristic of our entire sample. Various initiatives by managers led to initial contacts in a foreign market, contacts that were subsequently cultivated and diversified. Many entrepreneurs won their stripes as exporters in the mid-1980s essentially by fending for themselves.

Case studies

Neigobeq

Founded in 1976 in a small town in the St. Lawrence Valley, *Neigobeq* was owned by United States interests until 1992 when a small group of Québec shareholders purchased it. Through the first part of its history, the company manufactured a variety of products associated with transportation equipment, but when the new owners took over, they soon realized that the business would do better by specializing in snow-clearing equipment. In only a few years, it became a leader in the Canadian market through its sales to the various levels of government.

In 1985, the company's annual sales were $7 million and 10 percent of this amount was from exports to the United States. Nine years later, despite the recession in the early 1990s, the company was producing goods worth $12 million and 35 percent of its products were being shipped across the border. According to the manager we interviewed, this growth is expected to continue over the next few years.

Neigobeq recently bought some computer-assisted equipment and, at the time of the interview, it had embarked on the difficult, costly process of acquiring ISO 9002 certification. Its 70 employees, though not highly skilled, receive on-going training in the use of new manufacturing techniques.

Neigobeq, unlike many companies in the sample, networks with other businesses, including some suppliers. The exchange of information relates mostly to market opportunities in the United States. For example, the company's supplier of hydraulic jacks, which is also part of the sample, helped it make inroads in a number of western US states. One of *Neigobeq*'s executives always attends the monthly meetings of the *Groupe des chefs d'entreprise du Québec*. The information he receives at those meetings apparently helps in making decisions about the company's operations. On the other hand, contacts with local and regional development officers are very limited.

Meubloteq

Meubloteq, founded in the late 1960s, is the only business in a charming village in the Lanaudière area. It is a perfect example of a rural business that successfully restructured. Operating in what could be described as a "soft" sector at a time when many Québec companies in the sector were closing their doors, the business was given a complete facelift by its energetic management. In the company's early years, the owner/manager did not take advantage of the various resources available in the milieu. After producing business furniture for some years, *Meubloteq*'s managers felt it would be better to switch to the consumer market (living-room, dining-room and bedroom furniture). The business made a name for itself in the Montréal market and then extended its sales network across much of Canada.

Meubloteq began exporting to the United States in 1985 after taking part in a Toronto exhibition attended by many American buyers. Anxious to market a quality product made under optimum conditions, the management completely modernized the manufacturing process. The company kept its employees, many of whom had been there for over 15 years, and provided them with training programmes. At the time of the interview, *Meubloteq* had committed itself to the demanding process of obtaining ISO 9002 certification. This change will oblige management to regularly provide information and feedback to the company's 35 employees, who were trained with government assistance.

The owner travels frequently to Europe and the United States looking for ideas for new product lines. He also attends the meetings of the *Groupe des chefs d'entreprise du Québec*, which provides him an opportunity to benefit from other entrepreneurs' ideas on how to improve the company's operations.

Agriteq

Founded in 1988 with support from an economic expansion committee in a town of 600 people, *Agriteq* immediately made its mark in the farm machinery market. The development of a machine that wraps hay bales has provided the company with an advantage that the owner must retain if he wants to stay ahead of the competition. A typical rural entrepreneur, the owner designs the equipment that the company manufactures. His ideas are tested by a few of his 25 employees and, depending on the results, they may lead to innovations that end up as products on the market. Computer-assisted design and metal-cutting have been in use since shortly after the company was established.

After three years of operation, *Agriteq*'s sales totalled $1.2 million a year. By the end of 1994, the value of goods produced had more than doubled, as a result of the product's reputation, which was spread, in part, by agronomists on both sides of the border. The company entered the export market only one year after opening its doors; exports now account for 22 percent of total production. A lucky break put *Agriteq* in touch with a French buyer, and after giving an on-site demonstration of its product's effectiveness, the company received an order that exceeds its current production capacity.

With regard to local resources, a municipal councillor, himself a former business owner, provides assistance by doing promotional work on a voluntary basis. Although *Agriteq* has received government support for the development of new products, the owner, like many other business people, hardly has anything good to say about governments. He complains that government programmes are inefficient and poorly designed to meet the needs of small business. Consequently, he intends to consolidate the company's position by relying chiefly on its own resources.

Plastiteq

Unlike the rest of the businesses, *Plastiteq* has been in its present location, a town on the south shore of the St. Lawrence, since the turn of the century. Yet the company's past is visible only in some old photographs and a few old walls, as the plant contains nothing but computer-assisted compression-moulding equipment. Like others, the company is in the process of obtaining ISO 9002 status. It began exporting in the early 1940s and, as you can well imagine, there have been changes since then in both the range of products and the way in which they are manufactured. Although the manager we interviewed was nearing 60, he claimed to be very comfortable with the computer world and had only good things to say about the recent introduction of an EDI (electronic data interchange) accounting system.

Over the last eight years, *Plastiteq*'s sales have doubled to $15 million with exports accounting for 5 percent of sales. While most businesses in the sample planned to increase production without hiring any new employees, *Plastiteq* expects to start recruiting in the near future.

Echoing the opinion of almost every other manager, the company's executives feel that government programmes are not worth the effort required to qualify for them. Something else they have in common with other managers is the fact that they very rarely have contact with local development officers. If an executive belongs to a local association, it is more likely to be connected with charity work than with a business information network. The company obtains the information it needs at exhibitions and through contacts with clients and distributors.

Conclusion

As M.-U. Proulx (1995) has shown, the mere presence of the elements needed for an information network do not guarantee that it will operate effectively. Even if the components that facilitate such exchanges are present, the businesses for which they are intended may not use them for one reason or another. Three kinds of factors may help explain such an outcome:

1. Factors related to the business: The importance that the business attaches to exports may lessen the relevance of the connections or contacts that played a role in establishing or consolidating the business, for example. The company's executives may get into the habit of dealing with intermediaries outside their immediate environment. This "extended milieu", or milieu that is disconnected from the territory in which the company is situated, provides the information required to manage the company. This applies to both business and technology information.

2. Factors related to the environment: The absence of a critical mass of population or productive activity undermines the solidity of the connections between a network's components. Even informal meetings between business executives seem unlikely to occur if the businesses are many kilometres apart, as is usually the case in rural areas. Distance also constitutes an obstacle when an executive considers whether to travel to meet with a development officer or a government representative, or to attend a function sponsored by a professional association (e.g. a luncheon).

3. Factors related to the manager: A majority of the business people interviewed stated that they were used to getting by without local services. The same behaviour has been observed among executives of businesses situated in urban areas even though the various economic players clearly form a sufficient critical mass and are close enough to ensure that the information network operates effectively. As E.J. Malecki (1994) notes, the existence of a critical mass does not necessarily ensure the existence of information exchanges among firms. This indifference to potential support from elements in the milieu is sometimes due to unpleasant experiences; more often, though, it has to do with the individualistic temperament of the executives. Since they feel that have nothing to gain by approaching governments or economic development corporations (similar to France's economic expansion committees), they refrain from asking for their services.

As mentioned above, it remains to be seen whether such behaviour is also found among executives of younger businesses. Since there is now a wider variety of support mechanisms than ever before established both in response to current economic conditions and out of a desire to help regions to help themselves, the milieu may exert greater influence on new entrepreneurs. In conducting our research, therefore, we should pay particular attention to so-called occasional exporters and exporters in transition (Joyal *et al.*, 1997), provided they are new businesses. Executives of young companies who want to acquire the resources they need for the export market (new technologies, employee training) and to find out what possibilities foreign markets offer may deem it necessary to travel in order to take advantage of networking opportunities. Like executives of older businesses, however, they may regard the milieu as less important once they have made their mark as professional exporters.

References

Cooke, P. and Morgan, K. (1993) The network paradigm: new departures in corporate and regional development. *Environment and Planning Society and Space* 11.

Joyal, A. (1996) *Les PME face au défi de la mondialisation.* Québec: Presses Inter Universitaires.

Joyal, A. *et al.* (1997) A typology of strategic behaviour among small and medium - sized exporting businesses. *International Small Business Journal,* Vol. 15, No. 2.

Maillat, D. (1994) Comportements spatiaux et milieux innovateurs. In Auray, J.P., Bailly, A., Derycke, J.-P. and Huriot, J.-M. (eds). *Encyclopédie d'économie spatiale : concepts, comportements, organisations.* Paris: Economica.

Maillat, D. (1995) Territorial dynamic, innovative milieus and regional policy. *Entrepreneurship and Regional Development* 7.

Maillat, D. and Perrin, J.-C. (eds). (1992) *Entreprises innovatrices et développement territorial.* GREMI, EDES, Neuchatel.

Malecki, E.J. (1994) Entrepreneurship in regional and local development. *International Regional Science Review.* 16.

Proulx, Marc-Urbain. (1995) *Réseaux d'information et dynamique locale.* Chicoutimi: GRIR.

Québec. (1994) *Les PME au Québec : état de la situation 1994.* Québec: Ministère de l'Industrie, du Commerce, de la Technologie et de la Science.

Chapter eighteen:

Entrepreneurial Dynamism in Québec: Strong but Unevenly Distributed Across the Province

Marc-Urbain Proulx and Nathalie Riverin
Université du Québec à Chicoutimi, Chicoutimi, Québec, Canada

Abstract

There has been a strong net growth in the number of businesses in Québec in recent years. A detailed geographic analysis of this growth identified many fertile business areas but they were unevenly distributed across Québec. Many fertile business areas are aligned along an east–west axis generally from Sherbrooke to Hull including the area north of the Montréal metropolitan area. The strongest entrepreneurship is located on the fringes of the major centres, in many cases the remote fringes. However, neither the primary poles (Montréal or Québec City) nor the secondary ones (Trois-Rivières, Sherbrooke, Hull, Chicoutimi, Rimouski) appear to contribute to the entrepreneurial dynamic, except, paradoxically, through depolarization. Thus, there are places in Québec that, from the perspective of entrepreneurship, should be dynamic but are not. The spatial reality of entrepreneurship in Québec suggests government measures to promote industrial development should be linked to local and economic development measures.

Introduction

There are 200,500 operating businesses in Québec in 1995. Specifically, these are businesses registered with the *Commission de la santé et de la sécurité au travail* (CSST). This record number was reached due to a net gain of 8,600 businesses in the previous three years. During the 1992 to 1994 period, 84,600 new businesses were launched in the province of Québec, while 76,000 closed their doors. With the number of businesses growing by 3,000 a year, entrepreneurship is strong in Québec. This dynamism clearly helps create both jobs and wealth.

Using this specific measure of economic activity, it would be instructive to examine the distribution of this entrepreneurial dynamism across Québec. Our inquiry will focus specifically on determining where entrepreneurship is located.

The concept of fertile business areas

Most countries in the world have a number of highly dynamic areas that are clearly different from neighbouring areas. During the last decade, an abundant literature has developed on this subject. Various terms are used to denote these successful areas: dynamic districts, innovative milieux, pockets of activity, start-up areas, cradles of growth, growth areas, fertile locations, and so on. It almost seems as if it is the place that innovates or starts new businesses by virtue of its own inherent qualities.

Some places have advantageous positions in the so-called new economy because of their intrinsic economic dynamism. Such places are scattered, sometimes around large urban centres, but sometimes in more remote peripheral areas. Is this a ground swell or a number of small, isolated waves? (Joyal, 1995). The question remains unresolved. Some local and regional areas with no distinguishing features show a very high level of net new business creation.

In many cases, the fertile areas identified in the literature coincide with formal administrative units. Examples include the Canton of Jura in Switzerland, Orange County in California, some departments in the south of France, and many other science, technology and industrial parks around the world. Closer to home, various municipalities and a few MRCs (Municipalité Régionale de Comté [regional municipal county]) have risen above the rest because of their entrepreneurship. However, a number of locations where the entrepreneurial spirit is strong have paid no attention to administrative boundaries drawn by governments. This is the case for the industrial districts of what is commonly known as the third Italy, for a number of francophone countries, for the growth areas of southern Britain, and for many places in the United States. Although governments currently provide businesses with a great many valuable services, it appears that "fertile business areas" do not necessarily conform to officially sanctioned administrative divisions such as regions, counties, townships, and departments. For this reason, we decided that in order to capture the spatial aspect of entrepreneurship in Québec, we would have to use a highly disaggregated index.

Efforts to develop an explanatory model

How can we explain the phenomenon of innovative, fertile or start-up areas? Numerous monographs have cited a wide range of success factors. The many different terms and concepts in this extensive literature certainly hamper any effort at synthesis, though any attempts would be welcome.

Many descriptive studies are built around one or two specific explanatory factors such as skilled labour, a favourable natural environment, research and development, economic leadership, venture capital, business start-up services and innovation networks. These models are usually based on broad empirical studies whose data are rigorously compiled and processed, then synthesized and formalized into theories; but their weakness is their strength, in that they do a very thorough job of describing one or two aspects of a complex reality. For interested readers, we recommend Planque (1983), Aydalot (1986), Guesnier (1986), Coffey and Runte (1986), Cooke (1989), Benko and Lipietz (1992), Gagnon and Klein (1992), Maillat *et al.* (1992), Proulx (1994a), Côté *et al.* (1995), *Revue internationale PME* (1989), *Entrepreneurship and Regional Development* (1989), *Revue d'économie régionale et urbaine* (1991), and the *Canadian Journal of Regional Science* (1992). All of these collections are valuable for their contribution to local development theory and for the courses of action they propose regarding specific factors.

Other models offer detailed recommendations for organizing (planning) the local environment as a whole to stimulate endogenous development. The salient feature of these theoretical approaches is the therapeutic and operational aspect of local development. Each model adds its own nuances to the local planning process, which is supposed to be carried out in a number of stages. There are a number of excellent books on the subject, especially Blakely (1989), which we recommend highly. With regard to Québec, the procedure suggested by Prévost (1993) is a "must" for practitioners looking for methods and tools.

There are also more general models based on a set of considerations implicit in the accumulated regional science theory. Though imperfect because they are general and require a substantial amount of work to adapt them to individual circumstances, these models have the important quality of providing a comprehensive overview of the many factors in local development, as well as unifying concepts and a standard vocabulary. They include some older models mentioned earlier in this chapter, and some more recent models, such as the ones proposed by Becattini (1992), Perrin (1992), Friedmann (1992), Nijkamp *et al.* (1993), Crevoisier (1994) and Maillat (1995). These theorists rely on extended, generally multidimensional, definitions of local development. Despite the generality of their principles, they nevertheless attempt to circumscribe the major analytical components to the extent possible and to present a closed model. If one considers the fact that local development theory is still incomplete, the conceptual framework they provide, though inadequate, is none the less encouraging. In other words, the main components are being drawn with increasing precision in the great fresco of local development theory. It is clear, however, that there is no single model. Each local area has to keep looking for the right combination of factors.

In our own model, described elsewhere (Proulx, 1994a), we made a serious attempt at a synthesis, proposing eight general components[1] that embrace a majority of the variables (factors) the scientific literature considers relevant to transforming a local, supra-local or regional space into a fertile business area. The process of weighting all of these factors in different parts of Québec quickly made it clear that the qualitative or optimal combination of factors is much more important than the quantity of factors. Each area has to find the correct recipe by examining the many players that act on the various factors. In connection with the search for the right recipe, we believe that local autonomy and decentralization (Proulx, 1995) are inevitable steps for positive action on the components of development.

Entrepreneurial dynamism in Québec

Our data, drawn from the CSST's central file, concern the number of establishments that opened and closed in each municipality in 1992, 1993 and 1994, but do not include self-employed workers or intentions to start a business. The data provide a reasonably good picture of the number of businesses operating in each municipality, since most new businesses that hire employees must register with the CSST when they open their doors. We also assume that businesses that are closing notify the Commission right away so that they will no longer be charged its levies.

Hence we use relative net business creation as a measure of entrepreneurial dynamism in Québec municipalities. Specifically, we define our index as:

$$\text{Relative net business creation} = \frac{(\text{Net business creation})_{nT}}{(\text{Actual number of businesses})_{nt}}$$

n = territory (region, MRC, municipality)
T = period covered
t = start of period covered

This provides an easy gauge of the entrepreneurial dynamism of a given area in relation to the initial number of businesses there. The measure is simple, reliable, comparable and easy to update in the future.

Uneven distribution of entrepreneurial dynamism

The first thing our index reveals is that entrepreneurial dynamism varies considerably from place to place. For example, between 1992 and 1994 the number of businesses increased by 350 percent in Blanc-Sablon, while it declined by 13 percent in Beaconsfield.

---

1.   *Satisfaction of people's basic needs, availability of environmental amenities, presence of land development equipment and infrastructure, education and training, access to information, socioeconomic leadership, entrepreneurship and venture financing.*

Over the same period, the most dynamic MRC had an entrepreneurial index of 24 percent, whereas the least dynamic had an index of -1 percent. Differences between towns are generally quite large within most of the 96 MRCs. For instance, the Domaine-du-Roy MRC ranks tenth out of 96 with an entrepreneurial index of 11 percent; within it, there is a 36 percentage point gap between St-André (33 percent) and St-Prime (-3 percent). Within the Étang-du-Nord MRC, the difference between Grosse-Île (97 percent) and Cap-aux-Meules (2 percent) is even larger (95 percentage points).

At the regional level, our index shows that the Gaspé-Magdalen Islands is the most dynamic region, as the number of businesses there rose by 11 percent in the three-year period. The Lower St. Lawrence and North Shore regions were close behind with an index of 8 percent. In view of the large area included in each region, it is worth noting that the interregional differences in our index are substantial: the least dynamic region has an index of -0.5 percent, 11 percentage points lower than the most dynamic.

It is also interesting that entrepreneurship is very common in outlying areas. Except for Northern Québec, all of the province's outlying regions have entrepreneurial indexes greater than 7 percent. In other words, regions located far from Québec's major urban centres increased their net number of businesses by at least 7 percent between 1992 and 1994.

Identification of highly fertile business areas

On the basis of our classification of the 1,441 municipalities in Québec, we selected 520 that have above-average entrepreneurial dynamism, i.e. whose entrepreneurial indexes are greater than 9 percent. Scattered over the length and breadth of Québec, these municipalities clearly form groups or clusters that make up small, medium or large fertile business areas.

In fact, there are 146 such dynamic areas in the populated parts of Québec. Each area encompasses between one and 20 municipalities. For convenience, we have plotted the areas that contain four or more municipalities (Figure 18.1); 96 very small areas are not included. Thus, the map shows the pattern of medium and large fertile business areas in Québec.

Of the 50 fertile business areas located in Québec, only five (M1, M2, M3, M4 and M5) embrace 12 or more municipalities. There are nine medium-sized areas containing between 8 and 12 municipalities. The remaining 36 areas shown on the map are somewhat smaller, with 4 to 8 municipalities. As the map illustrates, entrepreneurial dynamism clearly forms fertile areas in various locations.

Figure 18.1.   Fertile business areas in Québec by number of municipalities per area, 1992–1995

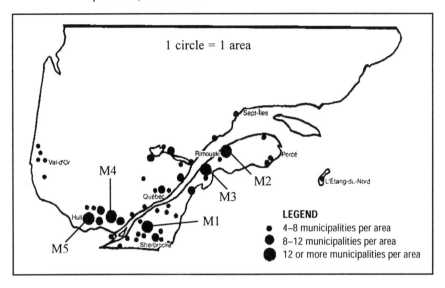

We observe that northern Montréal and the Montréal–Hull corridor have a number of fertile business areas, and that the Sherbrooke–Drummondville–Montréal triangle also has quite a few. We can therefore conclude that entrepreneurial dynamism is aligned on an east–west axis generally from Sherbrooke to Hull including the area north of the Montréal metropolitan area (M1, M4 and M5). With this observation, we can further refine the conclusion of various recent economic studies regarding the depolarization of Montréal.

Our map of entrepreneurial dynamism reveals some surprising facts about the geographic locations of fertile business areas. First, two large areas (M2 and M3) are situated in the Lower St. Lawrence region, which is not generally known for its economic vitality. Second, several other fertile areas are, curiously, scattered across the outlying parts of Québec. Abitibi–Témiscamingue (to the far west) has five small fertile business areas, and there is a modest concentration of four fertile areas in the Saguenay–Lac-St-Jean region.

In addition, the Gaspé region exhibits substantial entrepreneurship (with an index of 11 percent), though it is fairly uniformly distributed since there are no large fertile business areas. The same analysis applies to the North Shore, St. Maurice and Beauce regions, all of which clearly have considerable entrepreneurial dynamism, even though it is not concentrated into fertile areas.

Interpretation of the results

Using the five largest fertile business areas, we will now try to interpret the phenomenon of entrepreneurial dynamism in Québec. This interpretation is very delicate because very little quantitative and qualitative information is available about those areas. In fact, demographic statistics are just about the only readily accessible data we have. Nevertheless, on the basis of factors drawn from regional development theories, we will attempt an initial interpretation, however incomplete, of the kind of entrepreneurship present in Québec's five largest fertile areas.

First, the areas are located in administrative regions whose economies fared well from the perspective of employment during the period in question. This period saw the end of a recession (1992) and the beginning of an economic recovery (1993–1994).

St. Maurice–Bois-Francs

This area (M1) comprises 20 municipalities in the southern part of the Bois-Francs region and a few others in the Montérégie region. The municipalities are all roughly the same size in both population and number of businesses. There has been a small amount of population growth in the area since 1991.

This area does not benefit much from the depolarization of Montréal since it is not part of the region lying just outside of that city, as Laval, Bromont and Boucherville are. However, its geographic location (in the Sherbrooke–Drummondville–Montréal triangle) places it close to large markets, while preserving rural and environmental characteristics that are appealing in many respects today. Interregional mobility is very high in central Québec, and this area clearly has many features that would attract entrepreneurs from elsewhere. Moreover, the same features provide local entrepreneurs with the incentives they need to start their own businesses in the area.

We also learned that a number of large investments were made in M1 municipalities. Two of the largest ventures were in the pulp-and-paper industry: $100 million in Kingsey Falls and $25 million in Warwick. We estimate that a total of over $200 million was invested in this area between 1992 and 1994. Such investment unquestionably fosters economic activity and, by extension, business creation.

In concluding this tentative interpretation of entrepreneurial dynamism in this large area in southern Bois-Francs, we should point out that farming and tourism in the region have recovered somewhat in recent years. Finally, it is clear, in our view, that this fertile area warrants much closer attention and study so that its qualitative and quantitative attributes can be measured more precisely.

The two fertile areas in the Lower St. Lawrence

Of the five largest fertile areas identified in this study, the two in the Lower St. Lawrence region (M2 and M3) are undoubtedly the most surprising, and the most difficult to explain. Neither one is close enough to the major regional centre, Rimouski, to consider attributing its presence to the effects of a development pole. In fact, depolarization seems to be a more plausible explanation.

Most of the 37 municipalities that make up these two areas are small localities that had few operating businesses in 1992. A burst of entrepreneurial dynamism between 1992 and 1994 boosted their index appreciably. For example, the municipality of Amqui posted an excellent index of 13 percent during the period. Yet the net number of businesses created was only 39, since Amqui started with a mere 310.

Economic and employment trends indicate that this region was pretty much spared by the last recession; it has very few manufacturing industries, which are generally hard hit by economic slumps. The key primary industries, on the other hand, remained the basis of the region's economy. We can probably attribute its high level of entrepreneurship to the fact that it has a much higher unemployment rate than the average for Québec and the lowest labour force participation rate in the province. In the same vein, the 1991 closure of the Donohue paper mill (500 workers) probably gave some impetus to local entrepreneurship. Since demographic factors are not favourable in the region, they did not play a role in business creation.

In addition, a number of large investments, especially in the region's forest industry, were made during the period being studied. They undoubtedly had considerable impact on entrepreneurship, particularly in the construction trade and industries upstream from the forestry sector.

Finally, the seasonal nature of many industries in this region is probably responsible, to some degree, for the proliferation of businesses. Some experienced employees who end up unemployed for a season may decide to establish their own businesses

The Laurentians

We identified several fertile business areas in the Laurentians region. The largest (M4), clearly visible on the map, includes 17 very dynamic neighbouring municipalities. Two of those municipalities, the towns of St-Sauveur and Bellefeuille, have high rates of population growth, which partly account for their high business creation indexes between 1992 and 1994 (29 percent and 25 percent respectively). The region had no difficulty in absorbing the in-migrants while keeping its unemployment rate below the provincial average. The labour force participation rate remained at about 60 percent during the three years.

The depolarization of Montréal would appear to be a reasonable, perhaps even verifiable, explanation for the sharp increase in population. We note, also, that there are nearly 14,000 self-employed workers in the Laurentians region.

The strength of the M4 area is its geographic location. Tourism and tertiary industry are the hallmarks of economic activity in the area. There were major investments in the tourist industry between 1992 and 1994, especially in St-Sauveur. The creativity of business people in developing innovative, all-year-round tourist attractions helped boost the business fertility of this important region.

The Outaouais

This area (M5) embraces 13 neighbouring municipalities that exhibited substantial dynamism in the three years being studied. There was net population growth during the period.

A number of investments were made in the area, chiefly in the towns of Buckingham and Aylmer. Most of the investments were municipal government projects or residential developments.

There is every indication that the depolarization or decentralization of the Ottawa-Hull agglomeration is largely responsible for the existence of this large fertile business area in the Outaouais.

Conclusion

The entrepreneurial dynamism of Québec, as measured by our index of relative net business creation, is clearly unevenly distributed across the province. Some municipalities, some MRCs and some regions are very dynamic, while others are much less so. The strongest entrepreneurship is located on the fringes of the major centres, in many cases the remote fringes. Neither the primary poles (Montréal and Québec City) nor the secondary ones (Trois-Rivières, Sherbrooke, Hull, Chicoutimi, Rimouski) appear to contribute to the entrepreneurial dynamic, except, paradoxically, through depolarization. Thus, there are places in Québec that, from the perspective of entrepreneurship, should be dynamic but are not.

Furthermore, the data described in this chapter clearly illustrate the existence of fertile business areas in this huge province. Start-up areas, innovative milieux, booming districts, dynamic regions — no matter what they are called, entrepreneurship in Québec is concentrated in specific places that we have named fertile areas.

This suggests that by virtue of its qualitative and quantitative features, space apparently influences entrepreneurship, one way or the other.

These findings will be of great interest to Québec's economic policy makers. For instance, our industrial policy has been largely focused on sectoral development in recent years. Analysis of the foregoing map of entrepreneurial dynamism in Québec suggests that the argument for an industrial policy (at least its entrepreneurship and small-business component) that takes the spatial dimension into account should surely be reconsidered. We submit that concrete implementation of mechanisms for coordinating industrial and regional policy should be envisaged. In other words, the spatial reality of entrepreneurship in Québec is telling us that certain government measures designed to promote industrial development ought to be linked with other measures aimed at local and regional development.

References

Aydalot, P. (ed.). (1986) *Milieux innovateurs en Europe.* Paris: Groupe de recherche européen sur les milieux innovateurs.

Becattini, G. (1992) Le district marshallien : une notion socio-économique. In Benko, G. and Lipietz, A. (eds). *Les régions qui gagnent.* Paris: P.U.F.

Benko, G. and Lipietz, A. (eds). (1992) *Les régions qui gagnent.* Paris: P.U.F.

Blakely, E.J. (1989) *Planning Local Economic Development.* London: Sage Publications.

Canadian Journal of Regional Science (1992), Special issue on the creation of innovative milieux, Vol. XV, No. 2.

Coffey, W. and Runte, R. (eds). (1986) *Le développement local.* Nova Scotia: Presses de l'Université Sainte-Anne.

Cooke, P. (ed.). (1989) *Localities.* London: Unwin Hyman.

Coté, S., Klein, J.L. and Proulx, M.U. (eds). (1995) *Et les régions qui perdent ...?* Rimouski: GRIR — GRIDEQ - UQAM, 402 pages.

Crevoisier, O. (1994) Dynamique industrielle et dynamique régionale : l'articulation par les milieux innovateurs. *Revue d'économie industrielle* No. 70, 4th quarter, pp. 33-48.

Entrepreneurship and Regional Development (1989). Special Issue, Vol. 1, No. 2.

Friedmann, J. (1992) *Empowerment.* Cambridge, MA.: Blackwell Publishers.

Gagnon, C. and Klein, J.L. (eds). (1992) *Les partenaires du développement face aux défis du local.* Chicoutimi: GRIR - UQAC.

Guesnier, B. (ed.). (1986) *Développement local et décentralisation.* Paris: Éditions régionales européennes, Anthropos.

Joyal, A. (1995) *Le développement économique local : vague de fond ou vaguelettes isolées?* Paper presented at the annual meeting of ACFAS for the symposium entitled "Avenir du Québec des régions".

Maillat, D. (1995) Territorial dynamic, innovative milieus and regional policy. *Entrepreneurship and Regional Development.*

Maillat, D. *et al.* (eds). (1992) *Entreprises innovatrices et développement territorial.* Neuchâtel: GREMI, EDES.

Nijkamp, P. *et al.* (1993) *Regional development and engineering creativity: an international comparison of science parks in a knowledge society,* Paper presented at the thirty-second annual meeting of the Western Regional Science Association, Maui, Hawaii.

Perrin, J.C. (1992) Pour une révision de la science régionale : l'approche par les milieux. *Canadian Journal of Regional Science* Vol. XV, No. 2.

Planque, B. (ed.). (1983) *Le développement décentralisé.* Paris: GRAL, LITEC.

Prévost, P. (1993) *Entrepreneurship et développement local.* Montréal: Éd. Transcontinentales.

Proulx, M.U. (ed.). (1994a) Milieux innovateurs : concept et application. *Revue international PME.*

Proulx, M.U. (ed.). (1994b) *Développement économique : clé de l'autonomie locale.* Montréal: Publications Transcontinentales, 362 pages.

Proulx, M.U. (ed.). (1995) *Regards sur la décentralisation gouvernementale au Québec.* Chicoutimi: GRIR, UQAC, 422 pages.

Revue d'économie régionale et urbaine (1991), Special issue on innovative milieux, No. 3-4.

Revue internationale PME (1989), Special issue on Italian industrial districts, vol. 2, No. 2-3.

Chapter nineteen:

Rural Employment Alternatives: Wage Work Versus Self-Employment Among Rural Households

Jill L. Findeis, Leif Jensen and Gretchen Cornwell[1]
The Pennsylvania State University, University Park, Pennsylvania, United States

Abstract

Self-employment is an alternative income-generating strategy for rural households. The likelihood of participation in market wage work is influenced principally by the individual's characteristics, and for women, is constrained by children. Self-employment is found to be sensitive to local unemployment rates and is associated with vocational and technical training, access to land, and the extent to which the local economy can be considered "rural". However, participation in self-employment activity is less constrained by the factors included in this study, relative to participation in wage work. This suggests that self-employment deserves attention within a rural employment policy framework.

Introduction

Rural areas in many developed countries have witnessed high rates of unemployment and underemployment in recent years (Findeis, 1993). The lack of adequate employment opportunities and the difficulties that rural communities have attracting new employers or even maintaining existing employers has focused increased attention on self-employment and local entrepreneurial activity as means of providing jobs (Mangum and Tansky, 1993; Rees and Shah, 1986; Fuchs, 1982). Given this interest, this chapter:

---

1.   *The research reported here, including the Livelihood Strategies Survey, was funded through the College Research Initiative Grants Program of the College of Agricultural Sciences at The Pennsylvania State University. The authors gratefully acknowledge this support. The authors also gratefully acknowledge the financial support received from NICHD through the P-30 Population Center Grant Program.*

1. examines the determinants of the likelihood that rural labour will participate in different "formal" income-generating work activities, specifically wage work **versus** self-employment; and

2. assesses the constraints to participation in "formal" market work — either wage work or self-employment.

The paper is based on the Rural Livelihood Strategies Survey (RLSS) conducted by the authors in 1990–91. The survey sample includes 505 households sampled from selected rural areas of Pennsylvania.

The RLSS provides useful data for understanding the prevalence of different forms of economic activity, and the characteristics of those rural households more likely to depend, at least in part, on self-employment. The chapter first presents descriptive data on rural households participating in different forms of work that generate earned income for the household. In addition, following Hill (1989), trichotomous labour participation models are estimated for the survey respondent and the second primary adult in the household, differentiating between three potential labour states: wage or salary market work (only); self-employment; and no formal market work or self-employment. Of particular interest to this study are the influences of individual worker and household characteristics versus characteristics of the local labour market, including the extent of rurality, on decisions to participate in different forms of employment.

Data

The Rural Livelihood Strategies Survey (RLSS) used face-to-face interviewing to obtain information on household economic coping strategies. Survey questions related to the demographic composition of the household, employment (past and present), education, migration, child care, welfare receipt and other issues relevant to generating a sufficient level of income to support a household.

The household sample was disproportionately poor. To ensure that poor households were represented in the sample, a multistage cluster design was used, which allowed for oversampling in geographic areas of Pennsylvania with high poverty rates. A detailed description of the survey methodology is available in Jensen, Cornwell and Findeis (1995). Respondents were first contacted by mail, and then by phone or in person to schedule interviews in the respondent's home. All respondents to the survey were women, either female householders with children or women with an adult cohabitant, typically a spouse. The women surveyed for the study were asked questions about the households in which they lived and about their own employment history. They were also asked questions about the employment history of the second principal adult in the household (i.e., the "cohabitant"), if present. In many cases the cohabitant was a spouse, but in other cases the other principal adult was a parent or other adult cohabitant. In some households, there were no other adults, beyond the respondent, present in the household. Each face-to-face interview took an average of 75 minutes to complete.

The RLSS surveys provide both the individual-level and household-level data needed for the study. The RLSS data were supplemented with local labour market area (LMA) data were from the Regional Economic Information System developed by the US Bureau of Economic Analysis (REIS/BEA). All LMA data used in the study were derived to be consistent with the local labour market areas delineated by Tolbert and Killian (1987). It is reasonable to expect that local labour market characteristics as well as individual and household characteristics will influence participation in alternative forms of employment.

Employment status

Survey respondents were asked questions regarding their current participation in a set of work alternatives, and the current participation of the other principal adult of the household in similar activities. Of the female respondents, 167 responded that they worked at a paid job **away from home** and 13 responded that they worked at a paid job **at home**. Further, 21 respondents reported that they had a job but were not currently working. In total, 56 of the respondents reported being self-employed. Some of the respondents were engaged in multiple job-holding, and some combined both self-employment and market wage work. Among the cohabitants, 238 worked at a paid job, with 229 working away from home and nine working at home. A total of 36 cohabitants were with a job but not at work. Fifty-eight (58) cohabitants were self-employed.

The work status of an individual may be influenced by the individual's characteristics, the characteristics of the household, and by local economic structure and conditions. It is anticipated that there will be observable differences in the characteristics of those individuals who are not working for earned income and those individuals employed in market wage work (solely) or who are self-employed. Human capital is expected to be an important determinant of work status. Individuals with more human capital are expected to be more likely to engage in market wage work and may be more likely to engage in self-employment if the (marginal) returns to time allocated to self-employment is enhanced by more human capital. Further, the individual's age also likely influences the likelihood of allocating time to any form of work. The empirical literature on labour supply generally has supported the observation that a curvilinear relationship exists between age and the likelihood of participation in work (i.e., work participation is lower for younger and older workers relative to "middle-aged" workers).

Household and location-related characteristics may also affect work decisions. Participation in wage work may be constrained by the presence of children, particularly pre-school age children, in the household. This is particularly likely if child care options do not exist locally or are not affordable. Additionally, the presence of other adults in the household may affect the individual's own work decisions. Location-related characteristics may also be important, for example, by influencing the demand for labour. Local labour market economic structure reflects the types of employment opportunities available locally, whereas local labour market conditions such as the unemployment rate reflect the availability of opportunities for wage and salary work. Both the economic structure of the local economy and local economic conditions are anticipated to affect the likelihood that potential workers find jobs that match their training and abilities.

Table 19.1 includes selected demographic characteristics of the surveyed households, by employment status of the survey respondent and the second principal adult in the household. Table 19.1 also includes the average values of a derived "rurality index" that reflects the extent of rurality of the household's residential location. To determine those factors most likely to influence the patterns of work, multivariate models are estimated in this chapter, focusing on the roles of individual, household, and local labour market characteristics. Of particular interest, are the determinants of participation in self-employment.

Table 19.1.   Mean characteristics of RLSS respondents and cohabitants, by employment status, 1990–91

	Current employment status[1]		
Characteristics	Wage employment (only)	Self-employment	No work for pay
Respondent (*n*=434):			
Average age (years)	38.12	38.44	42.66
Average education (years)	12.72	12.69	11.68
Percent attended vocational or technical school	26.62	35.42	19.84
Percent attended job training or placement programme	12.95	8.33	15.79
Percent with adult cohabitant in household	83.45	85.42	73.68
Average number of children:			
Less than 1 year	0.04	0.08	0.11
1–5 years	0.37	0.33	0.44
6–18 years	0.59	0.77	0.59
Average rurality index[2]	2.03	2.42	1.88
Cohabitant (*n*=310):			
Average age (years)	40.67	45.41	49.49
Average education (years)	12.36	12.14	11.43
Percent attended vocational or technical school	32.08	28.36	28.43
Percent attended job training or placement programme	7.55	4.08	11.77
Average number of children:			
Less than 1 year	0.08	0.04	0.05
1–5 years	0.40	0.31	0.33
6–18 years	0.64	0.59	0.37
Average rurality index[2]	2.13	2.47	1.95

1. *The mean statistics presented in this table are for the data used in the empirical analyses. A total of 434 observations for respondents and 310 observations for the second principal adult (i.e., the cohabitant) were included. These observations include full information on the set of exogenous and endogenous variables used in the study. The observations that were deleted included missing values for at least some of the relevant variables.*
2. *A larger value of the rurality index indicates a more rural location of the household's residence.*

Empirical methodology

Most labour supply studies in the late 1970s and early 1980s estimated labour supply as a two-stage process: a dichotomous "work — no work" participation decision model in the first stage, followed by estimation of a second-stage hours of work model (Killingsworth, 1983; Heckman, 1974). Labour supply models with this basic formulation are common in the literature, and have been applied in many contexts. In recent years these models have been expanded to consider joint household decisions (e.g., Lass and Gempesaw, 1992; Lass, Findeis, and Hallberg, 1989; Huffman and Lange, 1989). Models of work decisions have also been expanded to include consideration of more than two labour states (i.e., more than the "work — no work" alternatives). Specifically, Hill (1989) extended the basic two-stage Heckman model to examine three time allocation alternatives facing women in Japan: work as an employee, work as a family worker, and nonparticipation in either form of work.

In this study, three alternative labour states are also analysed. The three alternative decisions ($j = w, s, n$) include work for wages and salaries ($j = w$), work in self-employment ($j = s$), and not working the labour market ($j = n$). Those individuals who are *both* employed in wage work and self-employed are included in the self-employed category. These categories are defined as follows for the survey respondent (r):

$$D^r_{iw} = \begin{cases} 1 & \textit{if (only) employed for wage} \\ 0 & \textit{if otherwise} \end{cases}$$

$$D^r_{is} = \begin{cases} 1 & \textit{if self-employed} \\ 0 & \textit{if otherwise} \end{cases}$$

$$D^r_{in} = \begin{cases} 1 & \textit{if not working in the labour market} \\ 0 & \textit{if otherwise} \end{cases}$$

and for the second primary adult in the household, i.e., the cohabitant (c):

$$D^c_{iw} = \begin{cases} 1 & \textit{if (only) employed for wage} \\ 0 & \textit{if otherwise} \end{cases}$$

$$D^c_{is} = \begin{cases} 1 & \textit{if self-employed} \\ 0 & \textit{if otherwise} \end{cases}$$

$$D^c_{in} = \begin{cases} 1 & \textit{if not working in the labour market} \\ 0 & \textit{if otherwise} \end{cases}$$

Following Hill (1989) and others (e.g., Cogan, 1980; Heckman, 1974), the probabilities that the k adults in rural households choose a particular jth labour state can be written as follows for the survey respondents (r):

$$P_{ij}^r = \Pr\left[D_{ij}^r = 1\right]$$
$$= \Pr\left[U_{ij}^r - U_{ik}^r \; for \; j \neq k; j, k = w, s, n\right]$$

and for the principal adult cohabitants (c):

$$P_{ij}^c = \Pr\left[D_{ij}^c = 1\right]$$
$$= \Pr\left[U_{ij}^c - U_{ik}^c \; for \; j \neq k; j, k = w, s, n\right]$$

where U_{ij}^r and U_{ij}^c are the maximum utilities associated with the individual's work decisions. As shown in Hill (1989), the indirect utility functions can then be decomposed into the non-stochastic and stochastic components, i.e.:

$$U_{ij}^r = S_{ij}^r + u_{ij}^r, \; and$$
$$U_{ij}^c = S_{ij}^c + u_{ij}^c$$

Therefore, by substitution:

$$P_{ij}^r = \Pr\left[S_{ij}^r - S_{ik}^r > u_{ik}^r - u_{ij}^r\right]$$
$$P_{ij}^c = \Pr\left[S_{ij}^c - S_{ik}^c > u_{ik}^c - u_{ij}^c\right]$$

Multinomial logit estimation techniques can then be used, if the U_{ij} are independently and identically distributed in a Weibull distribution. Given this condition, the difference $(U_{ik} - U_{ij})$ follows a logistic distribution (McFadden, 1974). In this chapter, multinomial logit models are estimated for the survey respondents as a group and for those adults in each household designated by the survey respondent as the second principal adult (cohabitant) in the household. The nonparticipation category is used as the reference group for comparisons.

Results

The influence of individual characteristics

The results of the multinomial logit model estimations for (female) respondents are presented in Table 19.2 and the results for cohabitants are presented in Table 19.3. Participation in market wage work, to the exclusion of self-employment, is affected by the respondent's age. For the female respondents, the likelihood of participation in market wage work increases with age, but at a decreasing rate up to a maximum age where the likelihood of participation begins to decline. For rural women, this occurs at about 34 years of age. As shown in Table 19.3, the likelihood of market work by the second principal adult (cohabitant) also has a curvilinear relationship with age. Further, the estimated coefficients for the years of formal education variable are positive and statistically significant in the wage work participation equations for both the survey respondents and the cohabitants. Increases in years of formal education improve the likelihood of market wage work. However, neither attendance at vocational or technical school nor participation in a job training or job placement programme are found to influence the likelihood of working in a wage or salary job.

The similarities in the **direction** and **statistical significance** of the estimated coefficients for age, age-squared, and education in the wage work participation models for (female) respondents (Table 19.2) and for cohabitants (Table 19.3) are noteworthy. Since the majority of the cohabitants in the study were male, the results in Tables 19.2 and 19.3 suggest similarities in the individual-level determinants of participation in market work, regardless of gender. Similar comparisons can be made across models with respect to the estimated coefficients for the self-employment participation equations. Unlike the results found for the wage work models, the age, age-squared, and years of formal education variables are not significant determinants of self-employment, with the exception of years of formal education for the female respondents. In addition, for the female respondents, attendance at a vocational or technical school has a positive effect on self-employment. Women who are self-employed are more likely to have participated in such programmes.

Individual characteristics strongly differentiate those that work for wages and salaries from those that do not work. However, the results for the age and education variables for the cohabitants show that neither age nor education serve to differentiate those cohabitants that are self-employed from those that do not work. For the survey respondents, age is also not an important determinant of self-employment. What does have an important positive influence on self-employment among women is education, either in the form of years of formal schooling or years of technical or vocational education. The education variables serve to differentiate the women that are self-employed from those that do not participate in work for income. At least for women, vocational and technical training programmes may serve as a gateway to facilitate the development of entrepreneurial activity through self-employment.

Table 19.2.   Multinomial logit models of participation in market work or self-employment by Pennsylvania RLSS (female) **respondents**, 1990–91

Variables	Estimated coefficients	
	Wage employment (only)	Self-employment
Intercept	-14.388 (-3.742)[3]	-6.908 (-1.447)
Individual characteristics		
Age (years)	0.169 (2.316)[2]	0.052 (0.502)
Age-squared	-0.0025 (-2.991)[3]	-0.0011 (-0.970)
Education (years)	0.304 (4.021)[3]	0.229 (2.241)[2]
Vocational or technical school (1=yes, 0=no)	0.158 (0.567)	0.867 (2.311)[2]
Job training or job placement program participant (1=yes, 0=no)	-0.072 (-0.199)	-0.552 (-0.903)
Household characteristics		
Presence of cohabitant in household (1=yes, 0=no)	0.391 (1.203)	0.103 (0.206)
Number of children:		
Less than 1 year	-1.421 (-2.605)[3]	-0.384 (-0.609)
1–5 years	-0.420 (-2.139)[2]	-0.564 (-1.861)[1]
6–18 years	-0.257 (-1.807)[1]	-0.0081 (-0.043)
Local labour market area (LMA) characteristics		
Rurality index	0.120 (0.762)	0.872 (3.581)[3]
Percent of LMA employment in manufacturing	0.099 (2.077)[2]	0.055 (0.889)
Percent of LMA employment in high-wage services	1.025 (2.557)[2]	0.053 (0.101)
Unemployment rate % in local labour market area	-0.069 (-0.689)	-0.225 (-1.477)
Log-likelihood	-344.30[3]	
Percent correct predictions	61.29%	
Number of observations	434	

Asymptotic t-statistics are presented in parentheses.
1.   *Significant at 0.10 level;*
2.   *significant at 0.05 level;*
3.   *significant at 0.01 level.*

Table 19.3. Multinomial logit models of participation in market work or self-employment by Pennsylvania RLSS **cohabitants**, 1990–91

| Variables | Estimated coefficients | |
	Wage employment (only)	Self-employment
Intercept	-11.758 (-2.822)[3]	-12.367 (-2.352)[2]
Individual characteristics		
Age (years)	0.136 (1.724)[1]	0.135 (1.287)
Age-squared	-0.0020 (-2.401)[2]	-0.0016 (-1.498)
Education (years)	0.173 (2.254)[2]	0.149 (1.615)
Vocational or technical school (1=yes, 0=no)	0.023 (0.073)	-0.549 (-1.178)
Job training or job placement program participant (1=yes, 0=no)	-0.540 (-1.036)	-0.652 (-0.741)
Household characteristics Number of children:		
Less than 1 year	-0.033 (-0.056)	-0.224 (-0.246)
1–5 years	-0.057 (-0.248)	-0.017 (-0.050)
6–18 years	0.556 (0.290)	0.114 (0.452)
Local labour market area (LMA) characteristics		
Rurality index	0.407 (2.105)[2]	0.960 (3.546)[3]
Percent of LMA employment in manufacturing	0.124 (2.251)[2]	0.085 (1.245)
Percent of LMA employment in high-wage services	1.172 (2.624)[3]	1.015 (1.759)[1]
Unemployment rate (%) in local labour market area	-0.281 (-2.371)[2]	-0.323 (-1.857)[1]
Log-likelihood	-269.93[3]	
Percent correct predictions	62.90%	
Number of observations	310	

Asymptotic **t**-*statistics are presented in parentheses.*
1. Significant at 0.10 level;
2. Significant at 0.05 level;
3. Significant at 0.01 level.

The effects of household characteristics

The influence of household characteristics are likely to be gender-specific. **None** of the estimated coefficients for the household-level variables (i.e., number of children less than one year, number of children 1–5 years, and number of children 6–18 years of age) are statistically significant for the cohabitants (Table 19.3). These results are consistent across the cohabitant models, regardless of type of work. In contrast, the estimated coefficients for the number of children variables in the market wage work participation equation are statistically significant and negative for the female respondents. Work in the market appears to be constrained, at least for women, by children, regardless of the child's age. As anticipated, as children get older, they pose less of a constraint to market work. Also as anticipated, children are less likely to constrain self-employment activity, since much of this activity takes place in or near the home. Whether or not the female respondent participates in self-employment may be affected by children of preschool age, with higher numbers of preschool children making self-employment more difficult and therefore less likely. The number of children less than one year or greater than five years old do not differentiate those women that are self-employed from those that do not work for income.

The influence of location and local labour markets

Estimates of the effects of location-related characteristics and local labour market variables on work participation are also provided in Tables 19.2 and 19.3. The local labour market characteristics incorporated into the models were found to have important effects on the likelihood of market wage work, for both the respondents and cohabitants. The greater the concentration of local employment in manufacturing or in the high-wage service industries, the greater the likelihood of wage work. These effects are likely due to the higher average wages paid in these industries, which lead to greater participation rates. When wages are low, it is less likely that the wage paid in the market will exceed the individual's reservation wage. In addition, the participation of the cohabitants in wage work is greater when local unemployment rates are lower, and in more rural areas. Among the respondents, neither the local unemployment rate nor the extent of rurality affected participation in wage work.

In contrast, neither variation in the concentration of employment in manufacturing nor the prevalence of high-wage service employment affected participation in self-employment by the RLSS respondents. Instead, the rurality of the respondent's residence was an important determinant of self-employment; respondents in more rural locations were more likely to be self-employed. This observation probably is the result of proximity of more rural resources and may reflect the lack of certain services in rural areas that are likely more prevalent as population concentrations increase. Rural residents may provide such services to each other through self-employment or even through more informal economic activities involving under-the-table work for cash or barter.

Self-employment activity among the cohabitants is also higher in more rural areas (highly significant), where the unemployment rate is lower (weakly significant), and in those areas where high-wage services are more prevalent (also weakly significant). The extent of rurality generally tends to enhance participation in self-employment. Among the cohabitants, both wage work and self-employment are also more likely when local unemployment rates are lower. This differs from the results for the female respondents, whose work participation was not influenced by variations in the local unemployment rate.

Table 19.4. Reasons given for not working for pay by (female) **respondents** to the rural livelihood strategies survey, Pennsylvania, 1990–91

Reasons	Very important	Somewhat important	Not important
Lack of adequate employment		Percent	
There are too few available jobs	43.7	22.2	34.1
The jobs I could get don't pay enough	29.1	21.6	49.3
Lack of education/skills			
I don't have the "degrees" employers want	23.3	21.8	54.9
I don't have enough education for the jobs that are available	20.4	19.4	60.2
I'm not sure if my skills are useful to employers	10.1	20.9	69.0
Lack of job search skills			
I don't feel confident enough to look for a job	7.9	14.6	77.5
I don't know how to look for a job	4.0	9.7	86.3
Constraints associated with infrastructure/policy			
Lack of transportation	21.1	10.7	68.2
Lack of available child care services	18.3	13.6	68.1
Loss of social programme benefits	5.4	5.0	89.6
Family constraints			
I want to be at home with children	44.3	12.9	42.9
Other family responsibilities	26.3	14.0	59.7
I do not want to work outside the home	23.3	17.2	59.5
My spouse doesn't want me to work	16.5	10.4	73.1
My friends and relatives don't think I should work	5.0	3.9	91.1
Physical constraints			
I am older	18.1	10.1	71.8
Physical disability or poor health	19.1	5.4	75.5

The percentages in each row of this table may not sum to exactly 100 percent due to rounding.

Table 19.5.   Reasons given for not working for pay for co-habitants in the
Pennsylvania rural livelihood strategies survey, 1990–91

Reasons	Very important	Somewhat important	Not important
Lack of adequate employment		Percent	
There are too few available jobs	43.7	8.7	47.6
The jobs co-habitant could get don't pay enough	20.2	14.4	65.4
Lack of education/skills			
Co-habitant doesn't have "degrees" employers want	15.5	14.6	69.9
Co-habitant doesn't have enough education for the jobs that are available	10.6	17.3	72.1
Co-habitant's skills are not useful to employers	5.8	9.6	84.6
Lack of job search skills			
Co-habitant doesn't feel confident enough to look for a job	1.9	7.7	90.4
Co-habitant doesn't know how to look for a job	3.8	4.8	91.3
Constraints associated with infrastructure/policy			
Lack of transportation	7.7	5.8	86.5
Lack of available child care services	1.0	4.8	94.3
Loss of social programme benefits	6.8	2.9	90.3
Family constraints			
Co-habitant wants to be at home with children	1.9	6.6	91.5
Other family responsibilities	1.0	5.9	93.1
Co-habitant does not want to work outside the home	15.9	7.5	76.6
Respondent doesn't want co-habitant to work	4.8	5.7	89.5
Friends and relatives don't think co-habitant should work	4.8	4.8	90.5
Physical constraints			
Co-habitant is older	29.0	5.6	65.4
Physical disability or poor health	40.8	9.7	49.5

The percentages in each row of this table may not sum to exactly 100 percent due to rounding.

Concluding observations

When the respondents to the Rural Livelihood Strategies Survey were asked why
they or the adult cohabitant were not currently working for pay, the principal reason
given in both cases was that there were "too few jobs available" (Tables 19.4 and
19.5). The reasons most frequently given for lack of work by respondents included
reasons related to: lack of adequate employment opportunities ("too few available
jobs," "jobs don't pay enough"); lack of education ("lack of 'degrees' employers
want," "lack of education for available jobs"); lack of local infrastructure, including
lack of transportation and child care services; and the constraints of family

responsibilities, particularly the presence of children. Reasons less frequently cited as important or even somewhat important included lack of job search skills and physical constraints such as advancing age or poor health. Loss of social programme (welfare) benefits was only given as a constraint to work by a very few respondents.

The constraints to work believed to be facing the cohabitant group were less diverse but were clearly no less important. Specifically, lack of jobs as well as, to a lesser extent, lack of jobs that "pay enough" and lack of "degrees" employers want were viewed as constraints to work among the cohabitants. Compared with the respondents, the cohabitants were believed to be less constrained by their education but were constrained by lack of jobs in the local area. The cohabitant group was also constrained by age, physical disability and/or poor health. Approximately 50 percent of the cohabitants that were not working were reported to be either disabled or in poor health.

These responses reflect the endemic problems that exist in rural areas in many developed countries in terms of providing adequate employment for rural residents. Those individuals employed for wages or salaries in the market are those less likely to be constrained by age, education, children, disability or illness, infrastructure, or lack of self-confidence or job search skills. In areas where it is difficult to attract and retain employers such as in the rural United States, the potential for additional self-employment deserves more attention. This conclusion is supported by this study that shows that the self-employed are less likely to be differentiated from those that do not work for income on the basis of at least some of the constraints discussed above. That is, some of the constraints to work shown to limit participation in market wage work, appear to be less important, if not important, to participation in self-employment.

References and further reading

Cogan, J. (1980) Married women's labor supply: a comparison of alternative estimation procedures. In Smith, J. (ed.). *Female Labor Supply: Theory and Estimation.* Princeton: Princeton University Press, pp. 90-118.

Ferman, L., Henry, S. and Hoyman, M. (1987) Issues and prospects for the study of informal economies: concepts, research strategies, and policy. *The Annals* Vol. 493 (September), pp. 154-172.

Findeis, J. (1993) Utilization of rural labor resources. In Barkley, D. (ed.). *Economic Adaptation: Alternatives for Nonmetropolitan Areas.* Boulder, Co: Westview, pp. 49-68.

Fitchen, J. (1981) *Poverty in Rural America: A Case Study.* Boulder, Co: Westview.

Fuchs, V. (1982) Self employment and labor force participation of older males. *The Journal of Human Resources* Vol. 17, No. 2, pp. 339-357.

Heckman, J. (1974) Shadow prices, market wages, and labor supply. *Econometrica* Vol. 42, pp. 679-94.

Hemmer, H. and Mannel, C. (1989) On the economic analysis of the urban informal sector. *World Development* Vol. 17, No. 10, pp. 1543-1552.

Hill, M.A. (1989) Female labor supply in Japan: implications of the informal sector for labor force participation and hours of work. *The Journal of Human Resources* Vol. 24, No. 1, pp. 143-161.

Huffman, W. and Lange, M. (1989) Off-farm work decisions of husbands and wives: joint decision-making. *The Review of Economics and Statistics* Vol. 71, pp. 471-480.

Jensen, L., Cornwell, G. and Findeis, J. (1995) Informal work in nonmetropolitan Pennsylvania. *Rural Sociology* Vol. 60, No. 1, pp. 91-107.

Killingsworth, M. (1983) *Labor Supply*. Cambridge: Cambridge University Press.

Lass, D. and Gempesaw, II. C., (1992) The supply of off-farm labor: a random coefficients approach. *American Journal of Agricultural Economics* Vol. 74, pp. 400-411.

Lass, D., Findeis, J. and Hallberg, M. (1989) Off-farm employment decisions of Massachusetts farm households. *Northeastern Journal of Agricultural and Resource Economics* Vol. 18, No. 2, pp. 149-159.

Mangum, S. and Tansky, J. (1993) Displaced workers turned small business operators: a viable economic development or reemployment strategy? *Economic Development Quarterly* Vol. 7, No. 3, pp. 243-254.

McFadden, D. (1974) Analysis of qualitative choice behavior. In Zarembka, P. (ed.). *Frontiers in Econometrics*. New York: Academic Press.

Rauch, J. (1991) Modelling the informal sector formally. *Journal of Development Economics* Vol. 35, pp. 33-47.

Rees, H. and Shah, A. (1986) An empirical analysis of self employment in the U.K. *Journal of Applied Econometrics* Vol. 1, No. 1, pp. 95-108.

Tolbert, C., II and Killian, M. (1987) *Labor Market Areas for the United States*. Washington, D.C.: Staff Report AGES870721, Economic Research Service, U.S. Department of Agriculture.

Chapter twenty:

Self-employment in Rural Virginia

Judith I. Stallmann
Texas A&M University, College Station, Texas, United States

Bageshwari Sherchand
Development Alternatives, Inc., Bethesda, Maryland, United States

Abstract

Encouraging small businesses and self-employment has been proposed as a way to create rural employment. Education, previous self-employment, parental self-employment, and having other sources of income increase the probability of being self-employed. The equation explaining the probability of being self-employed has poor predictive power, suggesting self-employment programmes cannot be easily targeted.

Introduction

Increasing rural poverty and a slow recovery from the recessions of the early 1980s have lead many policy makers to re-examine traditional approaches to rural economic development. Among the new approaches considered are incubation of small business and fostering self-employment. The interest in self-employment and small businesses is due to a growing awareness of the large number of jobs created by small businesses (Birch, 1979; Fisher, 1989; White and Osterman, 1991; Harrison, 1994) and the increasing numbers of self-employed (SBA, 1988). A further impetus to look at small business was the suggestion that self-employment might be an alternative to unemployment (Mangum and Tansky, 1993). Research in the United States suggests that the unemployed are twice as likely to start their own business as are the wage employed (Lichtenstein, 1990). Several European countries have begun programmes to help the unemployed make the transition to self-employment (Rees and Shah, 1986).

Studies of small firms have been national in scope or concentrated on urban firms. There are very few studies of rural firms (Miller, 1987; Lin, Buss and Popovitch, 1990). The available studies of self-employment use data from the period before self-employment began to rise in the 1970s. In addition, most of these studies use only correlation analysis, rather than multivariate techniques, to examine which individual characteristics are associated with self-employment. Thus, policy makers need more information about small firms and self-employment in rural areas before designing policy to revitalize rural areas based on small firms and self-employment. Because most small businesses start with self-employment, an accurate understanding of who is self-employed is vital.

This study concentrates on one aspect of small business in rural areas — the owner of the small business. A model with two probit equations is used to determine the factors that influence the probability of being self-employed. The data are from a random telephone survey of 600 rural Virginia households for 1989. The self-employed are defined as those who own their own firm, whether or not incorporated, and whether or not they have employees.

Literature review and model

People decide to seek employment if the marginal revenue product (MRP) of their labour is higher than their returns to leisure, which is their reservation wage (r) (Pencavel, 1986). Once they decide to seek employment they choose the type of employment that offers the highest marginal return to labour. The individual will choose to be self-employed if the marginal revenue product of self-employment (MRP_{self}) is higher than the marginal revenue product for wage employment (w) (Lee, 1965).

When economic decisions are non-marginal, requiring discrete choices, such as being employed or not, the decision can be modelled as a binary choice model. The choice made depends on the individual's reservation wage, which is determined by the characteristics of the individual, of the household, and of the local labour market. If the reservation wage is lower than the marginal returns to labour, the individual chooses to work. If the reservation wage is higher than the marginal returns to labour, the individual chooses not to work.

The choice to be self-employed will be made if the return to self-employment is higher than to wage employment. If the wage is higher than the marginal return to self-employment, the individual chooses to be wage-employed. This second decision is not independent of the first. Because people self-select into employment, those who are most likely to command a higher income through employment than through unearned income (including welfare) will self-select into employment. In other words, based on comparative advantage, people self-select into one group or another and they are not randomly distributed. Thus, they do not have the same probability of being self-employed. The equation for the probability of employment provides a selection factor which will be used in a second equation to determine the probability of self-employment (Heckman, 1979).

Probability of employment equation

Factors that affect the probability of being employed include human capital variables, household variables that affect labour supply and labour market conditions that affect demand. To avoid an unduly lengthy chapter, the justification of variables will be brief to allow for discussion of the model results. The employment equation is similar to others found in the literature (Tokle and Huffman 1991, Heckman, 1979).

Human capital

Age and age squared are used as proxies for the accumulation and deterioration of job skills over a lifetime and are expected to be positively and negatively associated with the probability of employment (Lass *et al.*, 1989; Reddy and Findeis, 1988; Bowen and Finegan, 1969).

Education, measured as years of formal schooling, is expected to be positively associated with the probability of employment because it provides access to higher paying occupations and higher wages within a given occupation (Becker, 1984; Rungeling, 1977; Mincer, 1974; Hill, 1973). The impact of education is expected to be higher for men than for women because of the documented wage gap between men and women with the same education (Tokle and Huffman, 1991; Hersch, 1991; Scott, 1977).

Vocational training increases productivity and, consequently, the wage rate (Mincer, 1974). Non-farm vocational training is defined as a binary variable (1=has; 0=does not have) and is expected to increase the probability of employment.

Labour market experience increases the individual's stock of productivity-augmenting skills and the individual's seniority, both of which increase wages (Medoff and Abraham, 1980). Increasing years of wage-job experience are expected to increase the probability of employment.

Health problems impair one's ability to work, leading to lower productivity, which discourages employers from hiring the individual. In addition, poor health may undermine satisfaction in one's job performance and lead to early retirement (Hill, 1973; Sumner, 1982). Health is defined as a binary variable (1=good health; 0=poor health), and is expected to increase the probability of employment.

Given the same set of characteristics, men receive higher wages than women (Hersch, 1991; Holzer, 1990; Scott *et al.*, 1977). In addition, women are more likely to be employed in jobs that pay lower wages (Deseran *et al.*,1984; Cautley and Slesinger, 1988). Sex is defined as a binary variable (1=man; 0=woman) where men are expected to have a higher probability of employment than women.

Household characteristics

Marriage affects employment decisions and the literature suggests that it affects men and women differently. For men, marriage implies more financial responsibility, so that married men are more likely to work than single men (Scott *et al.*, 1977; Bowen and Finegan, 1969). Married women are expected to be less likely to work than single women (Holzer, 1990; Lundberg, 1988; Shackett and Slottje, 1986; Mincer, 1962).

Children increase the amount of work needed in the home while at the same time increasing the need for income. Given the division of labour in the family, the presence of children has different effects on males and females. The presence of children under six (1=yes; 0=no) is expected to decrease female employment and increase male employment (Deseran *et al.*, 1984; Tokle and Huffman, 1991; Scott *et al.* 1977). While older children (6 to 18) need less supervision, they increase the need for income (Bowen and Finegan, 1969; Scott *et al.*, 1977). Their impact on the probability of employment is expected to be similar to that of younger children.

Other sources of income for the household are expected to decrease the probability of employment (Lass *et al.*, 1989; Sumner, 1982). Unearned income is expected to decrease the probability of employment for both men and women. An employed spouse is expected to decrease the probability of employment for women (Shackett and Slottje, 1986; Lundberg, 1988; Mincer, 1962). For men, however, an employed spouse does not appear to negatively affect employment (Lundberg, 1988). Thus, the impact for men, in comparison to women, is expected to be positive. The presence of other employed members of the household is expected to decrease the probability of employment for both men and women.

Labour demand factors

The unemployment rate of the county is used to reflect employment opportunities and conditions that affect the local wage rates (Tokle and Huffman, 1991; Lass *et al.*, 1989). The unemployment rate is expected to negatively affect the probability of employment for both men and women (Holzer, 1990; Bowen and Finegan, 1969; Mancer and Brown, 1979).

Rural areas generally have fewer job opportunities than do urban areas. A binary variable reflecting location (1=rural; 0=urban) is expected to be negatively associated with the probability of employment. Counties with a Beale Code of 6, 7,8,or 9 are defined as rural (Butler, 1990).

Probability of self-employment equation

Once an individual has made the decision to work, the next decision is the type of employment — self or wage. Thus, the second decision is not independent of the first. To control for the selection bias that results, the Inverse Mills Ratio, calculated from the first equation, is included as a variable in the second equation (Heckman, 1976 and 1979). Similar variables affect the probability of both employment and self-employment, but often in different ways.

Human capital

The self-employed are older than the wage-employed (SBA, 1986). The rate of entry into self-employment increases with age and at the same time the rate of exit decreases as people near the traditional retirement age (Evans and Leighton, 1989; Fuchs, 1982; Quinn, 1980). The log of age is used to reflect the low probability of self-employment among young workers and the more rapidly increasing probability with age.

The probability of being self-employed increases with education because education provides the managerial, organizational and technical skills to successfully operate a business (Evans and Leighton, 1989; Rees and Shah, 1986; Borjas, 1986; SBA, 1986). The SBA (1986) reports that this association is not as strong for men as for women. Vocational training tends to emphasize production not management skills. Thus, non-farm vocational training (1=has, 0=does not have) is expected to decrease the probability of self-employment.

Two variables are defined to reflect labour market experience. A binary variable indicates whether the individual has previous self-employment experience (1=yes, 0=no) and is expected to increase the probability of self-employment (Evans and Leighton, 1989; Fuchs, 1982). The SBA (1988) also reports that people with more wage experience are likely to be self-employed because they have acquired the assets and skills necessary to run a firm. Fuchs (1982) found that above average years of work experience increased the likelihood of being self-employed. Wage-experience is expected to be negatively related to self-employment, and wage experience squared is expected to be positively associated with self-employment.

Among the employed, those with health problems are more likely to be self-employed because they may have been forced out of the wage market and/or because self-employment allows them to set their own bounds for their capacity (Evans and Leighton, 1989; Fuchs, 1982). A variable reflecting health (1=good health, 0=poor health) is expected to negatively affect the probability of being self-employed.

The self-employment rate is much higher among men than among women (Balkin, 1989; SBA, 1986; Becker, 1984; Fain, 1980). The variable sex (1=male, 0=female) is expected to increase the probability of self-employment.

The parent's occupation tends to influence the occupational choice of their children. Individuals whose parents were managers or self-employed are more likely to be self-employed (Evans and Leighton, 1989). A binary variable if either parent was (farm or non-farm) self-employed (1=yes; 0=no) is expected to have a positive impact on the probability of being self-employed.

A high proportion of newcomers to rural areas start their own business (Bradshaw and Blakely, 1983). A variable, residence, was defined as =1 if the person or their spouse grew up in the county in which they currently live (=0, otherwise) and is expected to be negatively associated with the probability of self-employment.

Factors affecting labour supply

Married persons are more likely to be self-employed than are single persons (SBA, 1986; Rees and Shah, 1986; Borjas, 1986). This association is stronger for men than for women. Marriage (1=married, 0=not married) is expected to increase the probability of self-employment.

The literature on farm self-employment indicates that men are more likely to seek wage employment (a more stable source of income) with children under six in the family, while women are more likely to be self-employed on the farm (Lass *et al.*, 1989; Deseran *et al.*, 1984). Self-employment allows the woman to combine income-earning with caring for young children (Lichtenstein, 1990). Children under six are expected to decrease the probability that a man will be self-employed and increase the probability for women. While older children (6–18) require less care than younger ones, their impact on the probability of self-employment is expected to be similar to that of younger children. Both variables are binary variables with one indicating the presence of children in that age group, and zero indicating that no children in that age group are present.

Other income sources decrease the family's risk of self-employment and also may provide the capital needed for self-employment (Evans and Jovanovic, 1989; Evans and Leighton, 1989). Unearned income, an employed spouse (Balkin, 1989), and the presence of other employed household members are expected to increase the probability of self-employment. The latter two variables are binary variables (1=yes, 0=no).

Labour demand factors

In areas with low wages or high unemployment, more people enter self-employment (Lichtenstein, 1990; Evans and Leighton, 1989). These findings are the basis for programmes targeted to the unemployed to start their own businesses. An increase in the county's unemployment rate is expected to increase the probability of self-employment.

Self-employment, including farming, is nearly twice as common in rural as in urban areas (Block *et al.*, 1983; Bradshaw and Blakely, 1983; Shapira, 1983). Even when farming is excluded, non-farm self-employment remains an important source of both primary and secondary income in rural areas (Block *et al.*, 1983; Bryant *et al.*, 1980). A binary variable reflecting location (1=rural; 0=urban) is expected to be positively associated with the probability of employment. Counties with a Beale Code of 6, 7, 8 or 9 are defined as rural (Butler, 1990).

Results

The probability of being employed

Eleven of 20 coefficients in the equation estimating the probability of employment are significantly different from zero, and were of the predicted sign (Table 20.1).

Table 20.1.   Probability of employment equation

Independent variable	Expected sign	MLE coefficient	t-ratio	Marginal probability
Intercept		-0.90610	-0.950	-0.28354
Age	+	+0.05507	+1.685[2]	+0.01723
Age-squared	-	-0.00125	-3.789[2]	-0.00039
Good health	+	+0.43423	+2.472[2]	+0.13587
Education	+	+0.08922	+2.830[2]	+0.02791
Male and education	+	+0.00903	+0.199	+0.00283
Training	+	+0.28992	+2.192[2]	+0.09072
Wage-job experience	+	+0.04468	+6.887[2]	+0.01398
Male	+	-0.07202	-0.117	-0.02254
Married	-	+0.14751	+0.563	+0.04609
Male and married	+	-0.31087	-0.074	-0.09727
Children < 6	-	-0.62092	-2.639[2]	-0.19429
Male with children < 6	+	+0.62645	+1.611[1]	+0.19601
Children 6 to 18	+	-0.01910	-0.108	-0.00598
Male with children 6 to 18	+	-0.02201	-0.075	-0.00689
Unearned income	-	-0.03000	-4.049[2]	-0.01000
Employed spouse	-	-0.19518	-0.800	-0.06107
Male with employed spouse	+	+0.80708	+2.529[2]	+0.25253
Employed household members other than the spouse	-	+0.19981	+1.069	+0.62520
Unemployment rate	-	-0.07044	-2.188[2]	-0.02204
Rural	-	+0.14650	+0.829	+0.04584

Log-likelihood ratio = -267.57; Chi-squared (20) = 517.27
McFadden's Pseudo R^2 = 0.491; *Number of observations = 851*
1.   1-tail t-test statistically significant at the 10 percent level (>1.28)
2.   1-tail t-test statistically significant at the 5 percent level (>1.64)
A 1-tail t-test is used because the direction of impact of each variable has been hypothesized.

Several of the human capital variables significantly affect the probability of being employed. As expected the probability of being employed increases and then decreases with age. Wage-job experience increases the probability of being employed, as does good health. Education significantly increases the probability of being employed. For men, the coefficient was of the expected sign, but not significantly different from zero, indicating the affect for men is no different than that for women. Vocational training also significantly increases the probability of employment.

In contrast to previous studies, after accounting for other variables, men did not have a higher probability of being employed than did women. Marital status also did not affect the probability of being employed.

Children under six years of age significantly decrease the probability that a woman is employed. For men the relationship was positive as expected and significant. Children between 6 and 18 do not significantly affect the probability of either men or women being employed.

In general, other sources of income for the family are expected to reduce the probability that an individual will be employed. Unearned income reduced the probability of being employed. Women with an employed spouse were expected to be less likely to be employed. Instead, an employed spouse did not significantly affect the probability of a woman being employed. In comparison to women, the predicted impact of an employed spouse on the probability that a man would be employed was positive. Having additional employed members of the household did not affect the probability of employment.

The equation provided a relatively good fit to the data. The log-likelihood ratio is statistically significant. Eighty-eight percent of the cases were correctly predicted (Table 20.2). The equation, however, more accurately predicted the employed than the not-employed.

Table 20.2.   Prediction success for the employment equation

	Actual total	Predicted		Prediction success rate (%)
		Employed	Not-employed	
Total	851	629	222	88
Employed	588	556	32	94
Not-employed	263	73	190	72

The probability of being self-employed (given that one is employed)

Eight of the 24 variables are significantly different from zero (Table 20.3). Others have the hypothesized sign, but are not significantly different from zero.

Several of the human capital variables significantly affect the probability of self-employment. Education positively influences the probability of self-employment. Its impact on men is not significantly different than for women. Previous self-employment experience increases the probability of being self-employed. In addition, individuals whose parents were self-employed are more likely to be self-employed. As expected increasing wage experience beyond some threshold (33 years), increases the probability of self-employment.

Other human capital variables: age, health, non-farm vocational training, sex, and residence, had no impact on the probability of being self-employed. Age, health and residence were of the expected sign.

Married males have a higher probability of being self-employed than married females. The presence of children did not significantly affect the probability of being self-employed for either males or females.

Table 20.3. Probability of self-employment equation

Independent variable	Expected sign	MLE coefficient	t-ratio	Marginal probability
Intercept		-2.95400	-1.790[2]	-0.70589
Log (age)	+	+0.59632	+1.175	+0.14249
Good health	-	-0.21004	-0.858	-0.05019
Education	+	+0.06706	+1.641[1]	+0.01602
Male and education	+	-0.02413	-0.451	-0.00512
Training	-	+0.01991	+0.143	+0.00476
Wage-job experience	-	-0.08109	-3.099[2]	-0.01938
Wage-job experience squared	+	+0.00122	+2.672[2]	+0.00029
Male	+	+0.12853	+0.175	+0.03071
Previous self-employment	+	+0.60375	+3.251[2]	+0.14427
Parents' self-employment background	+	+0.18529	+1.381[2]	+0.04428
Residence	-	-0.09185	-0.619	-0.02195
Married	+	-0.46229	-1.144	-0.11047
Male and married	+	+0.90018	+1.709[2]	+0.21511
Children < 6	+	-0.13366	-0.433	-0.03194
Male and children < 6	-	+0.20959	+0.564	+0.05008
Children 6–18	+	+0.10505	+0.508	+0.02510
Male and children 6–18	-	-0.12287	-0.446	-0.02936
Unearned income	+	+0.02000	+1.534[1]	+0.01000
Employed spouse	+	+0.07002	+0.196	+0.01673
Male with employed spouse	+	-0.35588	-0.841	-0.08504
Employed household members other than the spouse	+	+0.36102	+2.029[2]	-0.02195
Unemployment rate	+	-0.04179	-1.155	-0.00999
Rural	+	+0.20656	+1.139	+0.04936
SELF-SELECTION TERM (λ)		+0.30306	+0.720	+0.07242

Log-likelihood ratio = -240.42; Chi-squared (24) = 70.964
McFadden's Pseudo R^2 = 0.13; Number of observations = 588
1. = 1-tail t-test statistically significant at the 10 percent level (> 1.28)
2. = 1-tail t-test statistically significant at the 5 percent level (> 1.64)
A 1-tail t-test is used because the direction of impact of each variable has been hypothesized.

An employed spouse did not affect the probability of self-employment for either males or females. But employment of another member of the household significantly increased the probability of self-employment. Increasing unearned income also increased the probability of being self-employed. Other sources of incomes can both provide capital for the business and reduce the risk of self-employment by diversifying family income.

The unemployment rate and a rural location did not significantly affect the probability of being self-employed. The insignificance of the unemployment rate suggests that, while the unemployed become self-employed at a higher rate than the employed (Lichtenstein, 1990), they do not remain self-employed.

The Inverse Mills Ratio estimated from the employment equation was included to correct for potential sample selection bias. It functions as an omitted variable to test whether there are unobserved differences between the employed and the not-employed. The variable is not statistically significant, suggesting that any differences between the two groups are adequately captured by the variables in the equation.

The McFadden pseudo R^2 statistic of 0.13 indicates a weak fit. The χ^2 value for the model, however, is significant. The overall prediction success rate of 84 percent, indicates a reasonably good model (Table 20.4). The overall rate, however, is misleading. The model correctly predicts 98 percent of the not-self-employed, but correctly predicts only 19 percent of the self-employed. The low prediction success may indicate a growing similarity between the self- and wage-employed. A poor fit also suggests that the readily available demographic and socio-economic variables, cited in the literature as being associated with self-employment, do not actually determine who is or is not self-employed. Results from similar research have reached a similar conclusion. Rees and Shah (1986) found only age and previous self-employment experience to be significantly related to the probability of self-employment in Great Britain.

Table 20.4.   Prediction success for the self-employment equation

	Actual total	Predicted		Prediction success rate (%)
		Self-employed	Not-self	
Total	588	27	561	84
Self-employed	105	20	85	19
Not self-employed	483	7	476	98

Model testing

The model reported here included a male slope variable for those cases where previous research had suggested that a difference between men and women could be expected. Specifically, a new variable is created where the binary variable =1 if male is interacted with, or multiplied by, a variable where differential impacts are expected between men and women. Examples are education and being male, marital status and being male, having children and being male and having a spouse and being male. A restricted model, which assumed no differences between males and females was also estimated. A log-likelihood ratio test suggested that there were significant differences between the two equations indicating that the male response to the selected variables was different than the female response. A third model, which included male slope interaction variables for all variables, was also estimated. That model was not significantly different in explanatory power from the reported model.

Conclusions

This research is the only known study to date that examines the probability of being self-employed in rural areas. Education, previous self-employment experience, parental self-employment experience, above average wage experience, and access to other sources of income positively influence the probability of being self-employed. For men, being married also increases the probability of being self-employed.

The unemployment rate had no influence on the probability of being self-employed, suggesting that even if the unemployed enter self-employment, they do not remain there for long. Programmes that aim to increase employment by helping the unemployed to start their own business, may not be feasible.

The poor predictive power of the equation suggests that the self-employed do not differ significantly from the wage employed on the basis of the variables in the equation. In other words, the self-employed are not identifiable using the readily available demographic and socioeconomic factors suggested by the literature as being associated with self-employment. In general this research suggests the need for more information about the self-employed before programmes to increase employment can be built around them.

This research assumed a two-step employment-decision process. It is possible that the decisions are made simultaneously rather than sequentially. Further research using a bivariate probit model to test whether the employment decisions are made simultaneously is warranted.

References

Balkin, Steven. (1989) *Self-Employment for Low-Income People.* New York: Praeger Publishers.

Becker, Eugene H. (1984) Self-employed workers: an update to 1983. *Monthly Labor Review* Vol. 107, No. 7, pp. 14-18.

Birch, David L. (1979) *The Job Generation Process.* Cambridge, Massachusetts: The MIT Center for Policy Alternatives.

Block, John R., Naylor Jr, Frank W. and Phillips Jr, Willard. (1983) *Better Country: A Strategy for Rural Development in the 1980s.* Washington, D.C.: Office of Rural Development Policy, United States Department of Agriculture, April.

Borjas, George J. (1986) The self-employment experience of immigrants. *The Journal of Human Resources* Vol. 21, No. 4, pp. 486-506.

Bowen, William G. and Finegan, T.A. (1969) *The Economics of Labor Force Participation.* Princeton, New Jersey: Princeton University Press.

Bradshaw, T.K. and Blakely, E. (1983) The changing nature of rural America. In Blakely, Edward D., Bradshaw, T.K., Shapira, Phil and Leigh-Preston, Nancey (eds). *New Challenges for Rural Economic Development.* Berkeley, California: Working Paper No. 400, Rural Development Policy Project, Institute of Urban and Regional Development, University of California, January.

Bryant, Clifton D., Dudley, C.J. and Shoemaker, Donald J. (1980) *Occupational Diversity of Rural Residents in Virginia: A Research Study of Multiple Job Holding and Labor Exchange*. Blacksburg, Virginia: Department of Sociology, Virginia Tech.

Butler, Margaret A. (1990) *Rural-Urban Continuum Codes for Metro and Nonmetro Counties*. Washington, D.C.: Staff Report No. 9028. Agriculture and Rural Economy Division, Economic Research Service, United States Department of Agriculture, April.

Cautley, Eleanor and Slesinger, Doris P. (1988) Labor force participation and poverty status among rural and urban women who head families. *Policy Studies Review* Vol. 7, No. 4, pp. 795-809.

Deseran, Forrest, Falk, William W. and Jenkins, Pamela. (1984) Determinants of earnings of farm families. *Rural Sociology* Vol. 49, No. 3, pp. 210-229.

Evans, D.S. and Leighton, L.S. (1989) Some empirical aspects of entrepreneurship. *American Economic Review* Vol. 79, No. 3, June, pp. 519-533.

Evans, D.S. and Jovanovic, Boyan. (1989) An estimated model of entrepreneurial choice under liquidity constraints. *Journal of Political Economy* Vol. 97, No. 4, pp. 808-827.

Fain, T. Scott. (1980) Self-employed Americans: their number has increased. *Monthly Labor Review* Vol. 103, No. 11, pp. 3-8.

Fisher, Peter S. (1989) Risk capital and rural development. In *Towards Rural Development Policy for the 1990s: Enhancing Income and Employment Opportunities*. Washington, D.C.: Joint Economic Committee, Congress of the United States. S. Rpt. 101-50. 101st Congress, 1st Session, United States Government Printing Office, pp. 130-148.

Fuchs, Victor R. (1982) Self employment and labor force participation of older males. *Journal of Human Resources* Vol. 17, No. 2, pp. 339-357.

Harrison, Bennett. (1994) The myth of small firms as the predominant job generators. *Economic Development Quarterly* Vol. 8, No. 1, pp. 1-18.

Heckman, James. (1976) The common structure of statistical models of truncation, sample selection and limited dependent variables and a sample estimator for such models. *Annals of Economic and Social Measurement* Vol. 5, No. 4, pp. 475-492.

Heckman, James. (1979) Sample selection bias as a specification error. *Econometrica* Vol. 47, No. 1, pp. 153-161.

Hersch, Joni. (1991) The impact of nonmarket work on market wages. *American Economic Review* Vol. 81, No. 2, pp. 157-160.

Hill, C. Russell. (1973) Determinants of labor supply for the working urban poor. In Cain, G.G. and Watts, H.W (eds). *Income Maintenance and Labor Supply*. New York: Academic Press, pp. 182-204.

Holzer, Harry J. (1990) Labor force participation and employment among white men: trends, causes, and policy implications. *Research in Labor Economics* Vol. 11, pp. 115-136.

Lass, Daniel A., Findeis, Jill L. and Hallberg, Milton C. (1989) Off-farm employment decisions of Massachusetts farm households. *Northeastern Journal of Agricultural and Resource Economics* Vol. 18, No. 2, pp. 149-159.

Lee, John E., Jr. (1965) Allocating farm resources between farm and nonfarm uses. *Journal of Farm Economics* Vol 47, No. 1, pp. 83-92.

Lichtenstein, Jules H. (1990) *Helping the Unemployed Start Businesses: Strategies and Results*. Paper presented to the 29th Annual Meetings of the Southern Regional Science Association, Washington, D.C., March 23.

Lin, Xiannuan, Buss, Terry, F. and Popovitch, Mark. (1990) Entrepreneurship is alive and well in rural America: a four-state study. *Economic Development Quarterly*

Vol. 4, No. 3, pp. 254-259.

Lundberg, Shelly. (1988) Labor supply of husbands and wives: a simultaneous equations approach. *Review of Economics and Statistics.* Vol. 70, No. 2, pp. 224-235.

Mancer, Marilyn and Brown, Murray. (1979) Bargaining analyses of household decisions. In Lloyd, C.B., Andrews, E.S., and Gilroy, C.L (eds). *Women in the Labor Market.* New York: Columbia University Press, pp. 3-26.

Mangum, Stephen L. and Tansky, Judith, W. (1993) Displaced workers turned small business operators: a viable economic development or reemployment strategy? *Economic Development Quarterly* Vol. 7, No. 3, pp. 243-254.

Medoff, James L. and Abraham, Katharine G. (1980) Experience, performance, and earnings. *The Quarterly Journal of Economics* Vol. 95, No. 4, pp. 703-736.

Miller, James P. (1987) *Recent Contributions of Small Businesses and Corporations to Rural Job Creation.* Washington, D.C.: Staff Report AGE861212, Economic Research Service, United States Department of Agriculture.

Mincer, Jacob. (1962) Labor Force Participation of Married Women: A Study of Labor Supply. *Aspects of Labor Economics.* National Bureau of Economic Research. Princeton: Princeton University Press for the National Bureau of Economic Research.

Mincer, Jacob. (1974) *Schooling, Experience, and Earnings.* New York: Columbia Press for the National Bureau of Economic Research.

Pencavel, John. (1986) Labor Supply of Men: A Survey. In Ashenfelter, Orley and Layard, Richard (eds). *Handbook of Labor Economics, Vol. I.* New York: North Holland.

Quinn, Joseph F. (1980) Labor-force participation patterns of older self-employed workers. *Social Security Bulletin* Vol. 43, No. 4, pp. 17-28.

Reddy, Venkateshwar K. and Findeis, Jill L. (1988) Determinants of off-farm labor force participation: implications for low income farm families. *North Central Journal of Agricultural Economics* Vol. 10, No. 1, pp. 91-101.

Rees, Hedley and Shah, Anup. (1986) An empirical analysis of self employment in the U.K. *Journal of Applied Econometrics* Vol. 1, No. 1, pp. 95-108.

Rungeling, Brian, Smith, Lewis H., Briggs, Vernon M. Jr. and Adams, John F. (1977) *Employment, Income, and Welfare in the Rural South.* Praeger Special Studies. New York: Praeger Publishers.

Scott, Loren C., Smith, Lewis H. and Brian Rungeling. (1977) Labor force participants in southern rural labor markets. *American Journal of Agricultural Economics* Vol. 59, No. 2, pp. 266-274.

Shackett, Joyce R. and Slottje, D.J. (1986) Labor supply decisions, human capital attributes, and inequality in the size distribution of earnings in the U.S., 1951-1981. *The Journal of Human Resources* Vol. 22, No. 1, pp. 83-99.

Shapira, Phil. (1983) A summary of employment trends affecting nonmetropolitan areas of the United States. In Blakely, Edward D., Bradshaw, T.K., Shapira, Phil and Leigh-Preston, Nancey (eds). *New Challenges for Rural Economic Development.* Berkeley, California: Working Paper No. 400, Rural Development Policy Project, Institute of Urban and Regional Development, University of California, January.

Small Business Administration (SBA), Office of Advocacy. (1986) *The State of Small Business: A Report to the President.* Washington, D.C.: U.S. Government Printing Office.

Small Business Administration (SBA), Office of Advocacy. (1988) *Handbook of Small Business Data: 1988.* Washington, D.C.: U.S. Government Printing Office,

November.

Sumner, Daniel A. (1982) The off-farm labor supply of farmers. *American Journal of Agricultural Economics* Vol. 64, No. 3, pp. 499-508.

Tokle, J.G. and Huffman, Wallace E. (1991) Local economic conditions and wage labor decisions of farm and rural nonfarm couples. *American Journal of Agricultural Economics* Vol. 73, No. 3, pp. 652-670.

White, Sammis B. and Osterman, Jeffrey D. (1991) Is employment growth really coming from small establishments? *Economic Development Quarterly* Vol. 5, No. 3, pp. 241-257.

Chapter twenty-one:

The Changing Role of Agriculture in Rural Employment

Jaap Post and Ida Terluin
Agricultural Economics Research Institute LEI-DLO
The Hague, The Netherlands

Abstract

In the "most rural" regions, the share of agriculture employment in regional employment is higher than in the intermediate and the most urbanized regions. However, in the 1980s the agricultural labour force declined at the most rapid rate in the most rural regions. On the other hand, growth rates of non-agricultural employment in the intermediate and most rural regions were relatively high indicating diversification of the local economy. Various kinds of policies affect agricultural income. Differences in the intensity of these policies among regions results in different patterns of decline of the agricultural labour force and in a redistribution of agricultural labour opportunities among regions or countries. Among countries the share of part-time and pluriactive farmers in the labour force varies considerably, but within countries differences among the three categories of regions are quite small. A large number of part-time farm holders do not have other gainful activities, which can partly be explained by the large number of 65+ farmers. Since a further decline of agricultural employment can be expected in the near future, labour opportunities in the industry and services sector and new types of agricultural employment have to be created. This objective would benefit from an integrated, region specific approach of local private initiatives and local, regional and national policy measures.

1. Introduction

Traditionally, rural areas in many OECD countries are associated with agricultural activities and urban areas with other economic activities like industry and services. In the course of the process of economic development labour migrated from the agricultural sector in rural areas to the industry and services sectors in urban areas. However, since the 1970s a reversal of this traditional labour migration movement can be observed in most developed countries. Rural areas transformed into local economic units with a diversification of agricultural, industrial and service activities and a supply of rural amenities for urban people. These "local economies" now need to be assessed in relationship to the global market rather than as a source of raw products for the urban area. As a consequence the conceptualization of rural — a spatial category with agricultural activities — and urban — a complementary spatial category with industrial activities and services — has lost its validity. The old sectoral approach of rural–urban differences has to be replaced by a spatial one (Saraceno, 1994).

The extent to which regions are affected by the transformation process into local economies widely varies, depending on, among other things, regional endowments and infrastructure. Thus, in some regions agriculture is still a major actor, both in terms of employment and in land use while in other regions agriculture plays a minor role compared with other economic activities. The objective of this chapter is to analyse the structure and trends in agricultural employment across regions to understand the role of agriculture in rural employment.

This chapter starts with some introductionary remarks on the classification of regions. In section three the focus is on the share of agriculture in total employment and the development of the agricultural labour force in the three groups of distinguished regions. In section four the impact of various types of policies on agricultural mobility is discussed. A large number of farm labourers do not work full-time on the farm, but are part-time employed and sometimes engaged in other gainful activities. In section five attention is paid to this group of part-time and pluriactive farmers. Perspectives on the future development of the agricultural labour force, on alternative opportunities for the agricultural labour surplus and on rural employment policies are discussed in section six. In the last section some concluding remarks are made.

2. Regional classification

Within the OECD Steering Group on Rural Indicators, a territorial classification of regions into predominantly rural, significantly rural and predominantly urban regions has been developed (OECD, 1994 and von Meyer, Chapter 2 in this volume).

In this chapter, we follow the basic idea of the OECD approach of three types of regions. However, since we define our EU regions at a higher level of aggregation, we use different labels for the three types of regions to prevent confusion with the official OECD classification. We identify regions with more than 50 percent of the population living in rural communities as "most rural"; regions with 15–50 percent of the population living in rural communities as "intermediate"; and regions with less than 15 percent of the population living in rural communities as "most urbanized". Differences in the grid of regions occur in the EU Member States. In this analysis

87 EU regions are distinguished[1] while the OECD classification identifies 446 regions. Small EU Member States (Belgium, Denmark, Ireland, Luxembourg and the Netherlands) are not divided into rural and urbanized regions. Data for these countries are only specified at the national level.

Table 21.1.   Number of regions by rural category and average area per region

Country	Most urbanized Number	Most urbanized Percent	Intermediate Number	Intermediate Percent	Most rural Number	Most rural Percent	Total Number	Average area of region ('000 km²)
Japan	8	17	22	47	17	36	47	8.0
United States	18	2	69	9	678	89	765	12.3
Canada	19	8	38	16	186	77	243	37.5
Finland	1	1	20	23	67	76	88	4.1
Switzerland	35	33	32	30	39	37	106	0.4
Austria	3	4	21	27	53	69	77	1.1
Spain	8	15	25	48	19	37	52	9.7
EU-12	16	19	55	64	15	17	86	27.0
Belgium							1	30.6
Denmark							1	43.1
Germany	3	33	6	67			9	27.1
Greece			1	25	3	75	4	33.0
Spain	3	18	11	65	3	18	17	29.6
France	2	9	17	77	3	14	22	29.0
Ireland							1	68.9
Italy	4	20	11	55	5	25	20	15.1
Luxembourg							1	2.6
Netherlands							1	41.6
Portugal			2	67	1	33	3	30.7
United Kingdom	2	33	4	67			6	40.7

Source: OECD AGRI-REMI data source; OECD (1994); Commission of the European Commnunities: The regions in the 1990s (1991); adaptation LEI-DLO.

This analysis covers 18 OECD countries: Austria, Canada, Finland, Japan, Switzerland, the USA and the 12 EU Member States. The average area of regions varies from less than 400 km² in Switzerland to about 40,000 km² in Canada and the UK (Table 21.1). Obviously, the differences in grid affect the distribution of regions over the three categories. Data for the non-EU countries and for Spain have been derived from the OECD rural indicators (AGRI-REMI) data source. For the EU Member States, data from the Eurostat Farm Structure Survey and REGIO have been used. Spain presents a unique position, as data are available from both the OECD AGRI-REMI data source and the other two data sources. As our level of regional disaggregation of Austria, Canada, Finland, Japan, Spain, Switzerland and the United States corresponds to that of the OECD, our

---

1. *This specific level of disaggregation has been chosen since it enables an easy combination from three main data sources of EU regions: Farm Accountancy Data Network (FADN), Farm Structure Survey (FSS) and REGIO.*

classification of regions for these seven countries coincides with the OECD classification. As two different levels of regional disaggregation have been used for Spain (one into 52 regions and one into 17 regions), differences in indicators due to differences in disaggregation can be assessed.

3. Agriculture as a source of rural employment

The importance of the agricultural sector goes beyond its share in regional employment and regional income. Due to its considerable land use, the agricultural sector determines the attractiveness of the rural landscape. The agricultural sector affects economic and social relationships in many rural areas. It is a source of both direct and indirect employment. Indirect employment is generated in industries supplying inputs for agriculture, in processing industries of agricultural outputs, in trade and other agricultural services. These activities are often located in or near the main agricultural production areas. As a source of purchasing power, agriculture and related business create non-agricultural employment for services like shops and as a source of population it contributes to the maintenance of schools, clubs, etc. These links show that the agricultural sector is an important contributor to the viability of the countryside.

Table 21.2.   Agriculture employment in rural regions varies from 10 to 35 percent, 1990

Country	Most urbanized	Intermediate	Most rural	National average
	Agriculture employment as a percent of total employment			
Japan	3.1	9.6	14.8	7.1
United States	1.9	2.0	9.5	2.5
Canada	1.3	3.5	11.0	3.8
Finland	0.7	6.4	20.1	8.5
Switzerland	2.7	6.5	9.9	4.1
Austria	1.2	5.7	14.2	6.2
Spain	3.2	13.7	23.3	11.1
EU-12	3.0	8.0	18.0	6.0
Belgium				2.5
Denmark				5.7
Germany	1.3	4.6		3.7
Greece				22.8
Spain	2.7	12.7	20.1	11.0
France	2.3	8.3	12.1	6.1
Ireland				14.8
Italy	7.8	11.8	14.8	9.6
Luxembourg				3.2
Netherlands				4.5
Portugal		17.7	34.5	20.3
United Kingdom	1.8	4.8		2.4

Source: OECD AGRI-REMI data source and Eurostat REGIO; adaptation LEI-DLO.
Note: "Agriculture" includes primary agriculture, fishing and forestry for the non-EU countries.

The share of agriculture in total employment rather varies among countries due to different stages in economic development and country specific characteristics of agricultural production. In our group of OECD countries this share varies from about 2.5 percent in the United States, Belgium and the UK to over 20 percent in Portugal and Greece (Table 21.2). These figures refer to the primary agricultural sector — if the other links of the agricultural sector were taken into account, these figures would be larger. For example, in the EU, employment in the supplying and processing industries varies from 1.6 percent in Italy to about 3.5 percent in Denmark, Spain and Ireland (Bruchem *et al.*, 1995, p.105). It can be seen that within each country the share of agriculture in total employment is lower in the most urbanized regions. The high share of agriculture in the most rural regions reveals the relative importance of agriculture as a source of rural employment.

Although on average agriculture is relatively important in the most rural regions, the importance of agriculture in rural employment is rather hetergeneous. Within countries like the United States, Canada and Switzerland, agriculture's share of employment across the most rural regions varies from less than 5 percent to over 20 percent. High rates of agricultural employment do not exclusively occur in less developed countries like Spain and Portugal.

In the course of the process of economic development, labour is pushed from the agricultural sector and pulled into the other economic sectors. The strength of the push sector depends on income in agriculture which is related to the scale of agricultural activities and the ability to sell agricultural products above production costs whereas the strength of the pull factor is determined by employment opportunities outside agriculture in the local labour market and the income which can be earned outside the agricultural sector. Strong pull factors are more likely to occur in urban areas, since these are centers of economic activities, and strong push factors are likely to be present in rural areas, especially in those with less developed agricultural structures. However, it can not be argued *a priori* which type of region would have the highest rate of out-migration from the agricultural sector due to the presence of counteracting factors. In urban regions, the push factor of labour from the agricultural sector is weakened by the relatively well-developed market structure, due to the concentration of population. However, in rural regions, the push factor of agricultural labour towards the other economic sectors can be reduced by moderate employment opportunities.

The annual rate of decrease in the agricultural labour force in the 1980s varied from -1 to -4 percent in most countries (Table 21.3). However, the United States, Canada and the Netherlands showed an annual increase of about 0.5 percent. Within each country the decline of the agricultural labour force in the intermediate and the most rural regions was larger than in the most urbanized regions. In countries where an increase in the agricultural labour force occurred in the 1980s, the growth rate of the agricultural labour force was highest in the most urbanized regions. Thus, rural regions are in a weaker position than urban regions in keeping labour in the agricultural sector or creating new agricultural employment.

Table 21.3.   Agricultural employment is declining in almost all countries, 1980 to 1990

Country	Most urbanized	Intermediate	Most rural	National average
	Annual percent change in agricultural employment			
Japan	-3.1	-3.5	-3.3	-3.3
United States	3.6	2.2	-0.5	0.7
Canada	2.1	0.7	0.7	0.5
Finland	-0.8	-3.4	-3.4	-3.4
Switzerland	-2.1	-3.1	-4.0	-2.7
Austria	-0.8	-2.5	-3.6	-3.1
Spain	-1.4	-3.7	-3.6	-2.1
EU-12	-1.8	-3.2	-3.6	-3.0
Belgium				-1.7
Denmark				-2.7
Germany	-2.7	-4.1		-3.3
Greece				-1.5
Spain	-4.3	-5.1	-3.9	-3.9
France	-4.0	-3.1	-2.2	-3.2
Ireland				-2.5
Italy	-2.3	-2.9	-2.9	-2.9
Luxembourg				-4.0
Netherlands				0.4
Portugal		-2.7	-4.6	-3.2
United Kingdom	-1.4	-1.3		-1.3

Source: OECD AGRI-REMI data source and Eurostat REGIO; adaptation LEI-DLO.
Note: "Agriculture" includes primary agriculture, fishing and forestry for the non-EU countries.

Within each category of regions and within each country, the dispersion of the rate of decline of the agricultural labour force in the individual regions around the mean is relatively small, except for a few United States regions. A bimodal distribution does not occur. The largest differences in the growth rates of the agricultural labour force among countries are among the most urbanized regions, where the growth rate varied from 3.6 percent in the United States to -4 percent in France. In the group of intermediate regions the growth rate varied from over 2 percent in the USA to -4 percent in Germany and Luxembourg, and in the group of most rural regions it ranged from 0.7 percent in Canada to -4.6 percent in Portugal.

Table 21.4.   Total employment increased in rural regions in almost all countries, 1980 to 1990

Country	Most urbanized	Intermediate	Most rural	National average
	Annual percent change in total employment, 1980 to 1990			
Japan	1.7	0.7	0.1	1.0
United States	2.4	2.0	0.7	1.7
Canada	2.0	1.9	1.2	1.5
Finland	1.9	0.2	-0.4	0.5
Switzerland	1.8	2.0	1.3	1.6
Austria	0.7	0.3	0.0	0.4
Spain	1.7	-1.5	-0.2	0.7
EU-12	0.5	0.2	0.3	0.3
Belgium				0.2
Denmark				0.6
Germany	-0.1	0.3		0.2
Greece				0.8
Spain	1.1	0.9	0.6	1.0
France	-0.3	-0.2	-0.5	0.0
Ireland				-0.4
Italy	0.6	0.5	0.5	0.5
Luxembourg				1.8
Netherlands				2.8
Portugal		-0.2	-2.4	-0.4
United Kingdom	-0.2	-0.5		-0.1

Source: OECD AGRI-REMI data source and Eurostat REGIO; adaptation LEI-DLO.

A relatively high growth rate of total regional employment may be an indication for a strong pull factor. The annual growth rate of total employment in the 1980s varied from just below zero in Ireland, the United Kingdom and Portugal to almost 3 percent in the Netherlands (Table 21.4). Within most countries annual growth rates of the total regional employment in the 1980s are highest in the most urbanized regions, except for Switzerland, France and Germany. The most urbanized regions tend to be the centres of economic activities. Growth rates of total regional employment in the intermediate areas usually exceed those in the most rural areas. Growth rates in the intermediate and most rural regions tend to lag because of the larger share of agriculture in total employment. Thus, the growth rate of non-agricultural employment may be a better indicator of the relative strength of the pull factor in a region. Within each country, differences in the growth rates of non-agricultural employment among the three types of regions tend to be smaller than those of total employment, and especially in the EU countries, the relatively high growth rates in the most rural regions are striking (Table 21.5). As in the case of agricultural employment, within each group of regions the dispersion of the annual growth rates of total and non-agricultural employment of the individual regions around the mean is small. The relatively high growth rates of non-agricultural employment in the intermediate and most rural regions are an indication for the diversification of the local economy.

Table 21.5.   Non-agricultural employment increased in rural regions in all countries (except Portugal), 1980 to 1990

Country	Most urbanized	Intermediate	Most rural	National average
	Annual percent change in non-agricultural employment, 1980 to 1990			
Japan	2.0	1.2	0.8	1.4
United States	2.4	2.0	0.9	1.7
Canada	2.0	2.0	1.3	1.6
Finland	1.9	0.5	0.6	1.0
Switzerland	1.9	2.5	2.0	1.8
Austria	0.7	0.5	0.8	0.7
Spain	1.9	-1.1	0.6	1.1
EU-12	0.6	0.6	1.4	0.6
Belgium				0.2
Denmark				0.9
Germany	-0.0	0.7		0.5
Greece				
Spain	1.5	2.1	2.1	1.9
France	0.0	0.3	0.9	0.2
Ireland				0.0
Italy	1.0	0.9	1.5	1.0
Luxembourg				2.1
Netherlands				3.0
Portugal		0.6	-1.0	0.5
United Kingdom	0.0	-0.4		-0.1

Source: AGRI-REMI data source and Eurostat REGIO; adaptation LEI-DLO.
Note: Non-agriculture includes total employment minus primary agriculture, fishing and forestry for the non-EU countries.

Table 21.6.   The greater the share of agriculture in total employment, the more likely a "most rural" region reports modest (0 to 2 percent) growth in total employment

	Annual growth rate of total employment, 1981 to 1991 (percent)									
	less than -2		-2 to 0		0 to 2		2 and over		Total	
	Number of regions	Percent	Number of regions	Percent	Number of regions	Percent	Number of regions	Percent	Number of regions	Percent
	Percent distribution of Canada's "most rural" regions									
under 5	2	3	11	15	43	57	19	25	75	100
5 to 10	--	--	2	5	27	64	13	31	42	100
10 to 25	--	--	1	2	34	81	7	17	42	100
25 and over	--	--	3	11	23	85	1	4	27	100
Total	**2**	**1**	**17**	**9**	**127**	**68**	**40**	**22**	**186**	**100**

Source: OECD AGRI-REMI database; adaptation LEI-DLO.
Note: "Agriculture" includes primary agriculture, fishing and forestry.

For the most rural areas in Canada we show the number of regions in terms of growth rates of total employment and the share of agriculture in total employment (Table 21.6). The share of regions showing modest growth (0 to 2 percent) is higher for regions with higher shares of employment in agriculture. For regions with over 25 percent of employment in agriculture, declining employment is more likely (11 percent of regions) than if growth is greater than 2 percent per year (4 percent of regions).

We turn now to some characteristics of farm structure in order to gain more insight in the push factor of labour out of the agricultural sector. The economic farm size is used here as an indicator of agricultural constraints. Our hypothesis is that a higher economic farm size implies a lower push factor and the decline of agricultural employment is expected to be lower. Lacking comparable data for the whole group of OECD countries, we focus here on EU regions.

In this chapter the economic farm size is given in standard gross margins (SGM). A SGM is defined as the value of output from one hectare or from one animal less the costs of variable inputs required to produce that output. By multiplying the number of livestock and the number of hectares with the related SGM, the total SGM for each farm can be determined. In the Farm Structure Survey, farm size is expressed in European Size Units (ESU). A farm has an economic size of 1 ESU when its total SGM equals 1,200 ECU (SGM of 1984).

Table 21.7. Average farm size in ESU and in hectares in the EU regions, 1987

Country	Most urbanized		Intermediate		Most rural		National average	
	ESU	ha	ESU	ha	ESU	ha	ESU	ha
Belgium	24	15					24	15
Denmark			35	32			35	32
Germany	21	18	16	17			17	17
Greece			3	4	5	4	4	4
Spain	9	11	5	9	6	25	5	14
France	37	38	22	28	19	32	22	29
Ireland			9	23			9	23
Italy	8	4	8	5	6	10	7	6
Luxembourg			20	30			20	30
Netherlands	45	15					45	15
Portugal			4	4	8	21	4	5
United Kingdom	61	65	57	69			58	67
EUR 12							11	13

Source: Farm Structure Survey 1987; adaptation LEI-DLO.

The economic size of farms varies due to differences in production circumstances, farming type, inputs, output per hectare and per animal, costs structure, labour productivity, management skills, economies of scale, etc. The average economic farm size is highest in the United Kingdom and the Netherlands. In these countries farm size is about ten times as large as in the countries with the smallest farm size: Spain, Portugal and Greece (Table 21.7). In Germany, Spain, France and the United Kingdom the economic farm size is largest in the most urbanized regions. Differences in economic farm size among the most rural and the intermediate regions are more diffuse: in France and Italy farm size in intermediate regions exceeds that in most rural regions while the opposite applies in Greece, Spain and Portugal.

The average number of hectares per farm in the EU is about 13 hectares. Among countries it varies from 4 hectares in Greece to 67 hectares in the United Kingdom. Within most countries, the number of hectares per farm is highest in the most rural regions and in the intermediate and most urban regions, farm size is about the same. The intensity of farming — measured as ESU per hectare — is lowest in the most rural regions and highest in the most urbanized regions. These differences in farm size and intensity reveal a difference in farm characteristics among regions. The relatively large number of hectares per farm and the more extensive production in rural areas compared with urban regions may be due to a less severe pressure of competing functions, like housing, infrastructure and non-agricultural activities that claim space.

It has to be noted that we focus here on the "average farm", which in reality is composed of different farming types. In the case of the Netherlands, in the most urban regions in the western and southern part of the country, there is an overrepresentation of intensive farming types like horticulture under glass and pig farming. In the more rural parts of the Netherlands, dairy and arable farming are more common. Agricultural employment has especially increased in the greenhouse sector.

Based on the comparison of the economic farm size among regions, it appears that the push factor is weakest in the most urban regions. In these regions, we found the decline of the agricultural labour force to be slower, or the increase to be higher, than in the intermediate and most rural regions. For those EU countries in which agricultural employment in the most rural regions declined at a slower rate relatively to the intermediate regions, it can be observed that farm size in these regions exceeds that in the intermediate regions.

4. Impact of policies on employment in the agricultural sector

The demand for agricultural products and agricultural productivity largely determines the volume of agricultural employment. Various kinds of policies are directed towards the agricultural sector. Some policies even have a direct impact on demand and/or productivity and thus on agricultural employment. In this section the impact of these policies on agricultural labour mobility is discussed, in which a distinction between volume and location of agricultural employment is made.

Market and price policies

Market and price policies exist in OECD countries with differences in forms and intensity. After the Second World War countries like Japan, the Scandinavian countries and the EU developed policies with a high degree of protection for agriculture. These policies boosted agricultural production and prevented a bigger exodus of agricultural workers. On the other hand the rate of protection was low in countries like New Zealand and Australia. As a result of the relative low prices, agricultural production increased less and agricultural employment decreased more. It can be argued that agricultural employment opportunities were transferred by these differences in policies from the second group to the first group of countries. In the course of time this aspect became less important as more quantitative restrictions were introduced in the market and price policies in the first group of countries[2]. Trade liberalization may result in a further reduction of the global redistribution of agricultural employment.

Market and price policies do not only affect the distribution of agricultural employment among countries, but they can also affect the distribution of agricultural employment within a country because of differences in market and price policies between agricultural products. An example of this is the inequity of price policies for the raw materials of animal feed in the EU: cereals are protected by high prices (in particular before 1993) and substitutes for cereals can be imported almost freely. As a consequence it was attractive to expand pig production in the neighbourhood of the big harbours. So agricultural employment was boosted in these areas at the cost of agricultural employment in more distant areas.

Structural policies

Generally speaking structural policies aim to increase productivity and thus contribute to a decrease in agricultural employment. To the extent structural policies strengthen the competitiveness of a given region, re-allocation of production and employment among regions may be expected.

Environmental policies

Environmental policies usually aim to decrease chemical inputs such as fertilisers and pesticides and the use of manure. The effects of these policies on agricultural employment may be both positive and negative. In general terms it can be said that policies of this kind will have negative effects on agricultural employment in regions with intensive agricultural production methods, and in particular when rotation schemes are affected. These negative effects will be only partly compensated by a substitution of labour for chemical inputs.

---

2. *For the Netherlands the negative short term effect of the introduction of the milk quota in 1984 was estimated between 5,000 and 7,000 person years in agribusiness as a whole (Breedveld and Van Bruchem, 1985; Giessen and Post, 1985).*

The policies aiming at a reduction of organic manure are more important with respect to agricultural employment. In a number of regions in the EU, but in regions of other countries as well, the density of animals per hectare has reached such a high level that animal waste is creating environmental problems such as eutrophication and pollution of drinking water. In a number of European countries environmental measures are taken or will be taken in the years to come to reduce phosphate and nitrogen surpluses. Recently, the EU implemented the so-called Nitrate Directive which will limit application rates of manuare to 185 kg of nitrogen per hectare of agricultural land. The result of these policies may be a considerable decrease in the number of livestock units in regions with a high concentration of animals and consequently a decrease in agricultural employment. Leuck (1994) concluded that the implementation of the Nitrate Directive would decrease EU production of beef by 5 percent, poultry by 10 percent and pork by 12 percent, which creates export opportunities for other countries like the United States. In other words, this policy could result in an important transfer of agricultural employment from rural areas in Europe to rural areas in other countries. However, the most important impact of the Nitrate Directive may be an increase in animal production in areas of the EU with a relatively low animal density. In any case, the result will be a geographical redistribution of agricultural employment[3].

Policies for nature, landscape and forestry

The impact of policies to protect nature may have positive as well as negative effects on agricultural employment. The objectives of the EU policy for Less Favoured Areas (LFA) are the continuation of farming in LFA and thus to maintain a minimum level of population or to conserve the countryside. Without subsidization of farmers in the framework of the LFA policy, agriculture might disappear from some of these areas. At the moment, more than 50 percent of the agricultural area of the EU is selected as LFA (Terluin *et al.*, 1995).

However there are also nature conservation policies with negative impacts on agricultural employment. In the EU, some policies exist which aim to restore or create natural values by extensification of agricultural land use. Agricultural production and agricultural employment is reduced by these policies. However, some farmers may be compensated for producing a "natural" environment. In the scope of the agri-environmental regulation of the EU (2078/92) farmers can request compensation for about 3 percent of the agricultural area in use in the Netherlands and up to 15 to 25 percent of agricultural area in Spain, Portugal, Ireland, Germany and France (Bruchem *et al.*, 1995).

---

3.   *In the 1980s a political discussion about the introduction of a phosphate norm for the application of manure started in the Netherlands. Depending on the level of the norm, the decrease in employment in agribusiness was estimated at some ten thousand person years (Post et al., 1985).*

Forestry policies also affect agricultural employment. In the EU the self-sufficiency rate for forestry products is rather low relative to agricultural products. Thus, the EU stimulates the afforestation of agricultural land. However, labour needed per hectare of forestry is considerably lower than per hectare of agriculture. Thus, forestry policies in the EU contribute generally to a decrease in rural employment.

Most of the policies discussed above affect the rate of decline of agricultural employment. Employment in upstream and downstream industries will be affected too. In the design of rural policies, all these impacts should be taken into account.

5. Part-time and pluriactive farmers

A large number of farm workers do not work full-time on the farm. Often the farm requires less than a full-time worker. Many farm workers are engaged in other gainful activities. In this section territorial differences in part-time farm labour and pluriactivity are discussed. Full-time labourers in agriculture are those workers who spend one annual work unit on agricultural activities[4]. When a person spends less than one annual work unit on agricultural activities, he or she is classified as a part-time farm labourer. Broadly spoken there are three reasons for being part-time employed:

1. a person has other gainful activities;
2. employment on the farm is insufficient to offer a full-time job; or
3. a person chooses voluntarily for working part-time.

These reasons are not mutually exclusive: some labourers are part-time employed for more than one of these reasons. Pluriactive farm labourers are those part-timers who are engaged in other gainful activities in addition to their agricultural activities. These gainful activities consist of:

1. para-agricultural activities (e.g. cheese making, wine production, production and sale of regional products);
2. non-agricultural activities on the farm (e.g. tourism on the farm, farmers as producers of landscape and nature);
3. employment on other farms (hired labour); and
4. off-farm activities.

Para-agricultural activities and non-agricultural activities are farm based and can be considered as forms of self-employment, whereas the two latter kinds of activities are generally wage employment (Fuller, 1990).

---

4. *An annual work unit (AWU) is defined as being equivalent to the annual labour input (in terms of working hours) of a person employed full- time for agricultural work on the holding. Full-time labour input is measured as the minimum amount of working hours according to national labour contracts. When that amount is not determined in a country, an AWU is equivalent to 2,200 working hours. Full-time includes persons who spend more than one annual work unit on the farm.*

In this analysis we focus on individual labourers and farm holders and disregard the interrelationships with other household members in determining the labour allocation for the farm labourer or farm holder. The farm household is a unit of production, consumption and reproduction, with resources of land, labour, capital, management and other skills, cultural and demographic characteristics (Bryden *et al.*, 1992). These resources are deployed to maximise household goals. When for instance within a farm household, labour is allocated in such a way that the male farm holder works part-time on the farm and his wife works full- or part-time on the farm, the male farm holder is registered as a pluriactive part-time farmer in the labour statistics. However, when that household decides that the male farm holder works full-time on the farm and that the wife is employed outside the farm, the male farm holder is registered as a full-time farm holder. Due to the lack of data on the labour allocation of farm households for the OECD area, we opt for the second best solution of individual workers.

The choice of being part-time employed in the agricultural sector and being engaged in other gainful activities can be considered as a possible alternative of migration, since it involves a transfer of labour from agricultural to non-agricultural employment (Efstratoglou-Todoulou, 1990). Hence these choices are affected by a push and pull process in which the same factors are at work as in the case of the decision to leave the agricultural sector, as discussed above. Among countries the share of part-time farm labourers in the total agricultural labour force varies considerably: the share amounts to about 30 percent in the United States and to about 90 percent in Greece and Italy (Table 21.8). In the case of farm holders, the share of part-timers more or less fluctuates in the same range. In a comparison of the share of part-time farm labourers and part-time farm holders among the three categories of regions within countries, we see that in countries like Japan and Finland this share is highest in the most urbanized regions (Tables 21.8 and 21.9). On the other hand, in the EU Member States the highest share of part-time labour in the total agricultural labour force is found in intermediate and most rural regions. Nevertheless, differences in the share of part-time labour in the total agricultural labour force among the three categories within each country are quite small, and for countries like Austria, Greece and Italy differences are more or less absent.

The variation in the share of farm holders with other gainful activities among countries is smaller than that of part-time farmers — it varies from less than 20 percent in Finland, Austria and Luxembourg to over 40 percent in Canada and Germany. One could expect that the share of farmers with other gainful activities tends to be higher in urban areas, because of the larger concentration of economic activities in these areas. However, it appears that within countries the share of farm holders with other gainful activities in the intermediate areas exceeds that of most urbanized areas, except for Finland and the United Kingdom (Table 21.9). For countries like Canada, Finland, Austria and Portugal the share of farmers with other gainful activities in most rural areas is higher than that in the intermediate areas, but in other countries the opposite applies.

Table 21.8. From 37 to 94 percent of rural farm labourers are part-time, 1990/91

Country	Most urbanized	Intermediate	Most rural	National average
	Percent of farm labourers who are part-time, 1990/91			
United States	34	30	37	33
Canada	76	66	60	58
Finland				
Switzerland	53	55	60	56
Austria	46	44	45	44
EU-12				76
Belgium				48
Denmark				56
Germany	66	71		70
Greece		93	94	94
Spain	67	77	75	76
France	41	56	58	55
Ireland				64
Italy	86	89	86	88
Luxembourg				57
Netherlands				48
Portugal		72	71	73
United Kingdom	45	48		47

Source: OECD AGRI-REMI data source and Farm Structure Survey 1987; adaptation LEI-DLO.
Note: The data are for 1987 for the EU countries. See Appendix A for definitions.

Table 21.9. From 19 to 43 percent of rural farm holders are pluriactive, 1990/91

Country	Most urbanized Part-time	Most urbanized Pluri-active	Intermediate Part-time	Intermediate Pluri-active	Most rural Part-time	Most rural Pluri-active	National average Part-time	National average Pluri-active
	Percent of farm holders who are part-time or pluriactive, 1990/91							
Japan	85		85		82		84	
Unted Stated								
Canada	46	36	56	38	56	43	62	42
Finland	59	24	55	21	53	22	53	19
Switzerland	44		41		40		42	
Austria	69	15	68	18	68	19	68	19
Spain	83	37	86	33	86	32	88	37
EU-12	69	27	74	33	82	28	75	31
Belgium							41	34
Denmark							66	34
Germany	55	38	60	45			59	44
Greece			85	31	84	24	84	26
Spain	70	32	81	35	81	32	80	34
France	36	16	51	24	48	23	50	24
Ireland							31	26
Italy	88	29	89	31	89	29	89	30
Luxembourg							39	19
Netherlands							32	24
Portugal			77	35	83	37	78	36
United Kingdom	43	31	45	29			44	30

Source: OECD AGRI-REMI data source and Farm Structure Survey 1989; adaptation LEI-DLO.
Note: The data are for 1989 for the EU countries. See Appendix A for definitions.

One of the explaining factors for the relatively high rate of pluriactivity in intermediate regions may be a lagging farm income. From data for the EU, it can be seen that in countries with an income above the EU average, family farm income per family work unit is highest in the most urbanised regions, whereas in countries with relatively low incomes, differences in farm income among the three types of regions are relatively small (Table 21.10). At least for Germany and France the relatively low incomes in intermediate regions compared with the most urbanized regions are an incentive for farmers to be engaged in other gainful activities.

Table 21.10.   Farm income per family work unit in the most urbanized regions does not always exceed that in rural regions in "1989"

Country	Most urbanized	Intermediate	Most rural	National average
	Farm income per family work unit relative to EU average = 100			
Belgium				273
Denmark				103
Germany	164	126		131
Greece		60	53	55
Spain	66	75	96	79
France	173	145	142	146
Ireland				111
Italy	88	94	90	92
Luxembourg				203
Netherlands				313
Portugal		27	38	28
United Kingdom	220	148		176
EUR 12	149	95	71	100

Source: Farm Accountancy Data Network (FADN); adaptation LEI-DLO.
Note: "1989" = (1988+1989+1990)/3.

In a comparison of the shares of part-time farm holders and farmers with other gainful activities, it can easily be seen that a large number of part-time farm holders do not have other gainful activities. The difference between the share of part-time farm holders and the share of pluriactive farm holders — corrected for those farmers, who voluntarily choose to work part-time and for unregistered gainful activities in the scope of an informal economy — can be interpreted as an indication for hidden unemployment (Terluin *et al.*, 1994). In most countries, except for Canada, Belgium, Ireland, the Netherlands and the UK, more than half of part-time farm holders are not engaged in other gainful activities. Within countries no large differences in the share of part-time farm holders without other gainful activities exist among the most urbanized, intermediate and most rural regions. In some less-developed countries of the EU — Italy, Greece and Portugal — about 30 percent of the farm holders are over 65 years old. Undoubtedly, a lot of part-time farm holders without other gainful activities in these countries are these elder farmers.

In a comparison among countries there seems to be a tendency that when the share of agriculture in total employment is relatively high, the share of part-time labour in the total agricultural labour force is also high (Table 21.11). However, within each country differences in the share of agriculture in total employment varies among the three categories of regions, whereas the share of part-time farm labourers in the total labour force does not. Obviously, within countries the regional level of part-time farming is not strongly affected by the share of agriculture in regional employment. In addition, there is also no close relationship between the share of agriculture in total regional employment and the share of pluriactive farm holders.

Table 21.11.   Incidence of part-time and pluriactive status, 1990/91

Country	Agriculture employment as percent of total employment	Farm labourers who are part-time	Farm holders who are part-time	Farm holders who are pluriactive	Holders who are hidden unemployed
			Percent		
United Kingdom	2.4	47	44	30	14
United States	2.5	33			
Belgium	2.5	48	41	34	7
Luxembourg	3.2	57	39	19	20
Germany	3.7	70	59	44	15
Canada	3.8	58	62	42	20
Switzerland	4.1	56	42		
Netherlands	4.5	48	32	24	8
Denmark	5.7	56	66	34	32
EU-12	6.0	76	75	31	44
France	6.1	55	50	24	26
Austria	6.2	44	68	19	49
Japan	7.1		84		
Finland	8.5		53	19	34
Italy	9.6	88	89	30	59
Spain-EU	11.0	76	80	34	46
Spain-OECD	11.1		88	37	51
Ireland	14.8	64	31	26	5
Portugal	20.3	73	78	36	42
Greece	22.8	94	84	26	58

Source: OECD AGRI - REMI data source and Farm Structure Survey 1987 and 1989; adaptation LEI-DLO.

Note: *1987 for part-time labourers in the EU; 1989 for part-time farm holders and pluriactive farm holders in the EU. Hidden unemployment is indicated by the percentage point difference between the share of holders who are part-time and the share of holders who are pluriactive. See Appendix A for definitions.*

In a study on farm household adjustment in 24 EU regions, it appeared that pluriactivity is not a temporary but a permanent phenomen and that it takes different forms and performs different functions under different circumstances (Bryden *et al.*, 1992). Key functions of pluriactivity are:

1.   optimization of labour allocation within households in order to improve income;

2. an individual career choice of household members (especially women) on larger farms in richer rural areas;

3. survival of farm households at low income levels on small farms;

4. assisting with the transition of farms through generations, especially on farms which can not provide work to more than one full-time farmer; and

5. assisting in the process of disengagement and exit from farming.

With regard to the kind of jobs which were performed by pluriactive farm labourers, Bryden *et al.* (1992) found that in regions with poor agricultural structures and poor local labour markets, male farm holders were often engaged in low status and seasonal jobs, whereas in regions with better agricultural structures and local labour markets, female household members usually are involved in professional jobs.

6. Perspectives

Employment in agriculture in OECD countries declined sharply after the Second World War and a further decrease may be expected. The extent of this decline is uncertain. Stagnating demand, increasing labour productivity and trade liberalization will result in a continued decline of the agricultural working population. By using a general equilibrium model, a group of Dutch researchers estimated the change of agricultural employment in the EU for a number of policy scenarios (Folmer *et al.*, 1995). Without further changes of the agricultural policies after the MacSharry reform (1993), agricultural population will decrease by 2.6 percent per year, which implies a reduction of 50 percent in 25 years. This is a bit more than under a continuation of the pre-MacSharry policies. Trade liberalization would even accelerate the decrease of agricultural employment further. The decrease in related employment in upstream and downstream industries have still to be added to this figure. This kind of calculation makes clear that the importance of agriculture and related industries in rural regions will decline further in the next decades. In the EU this will partly be due to changes in agricultural and trade policies. The extra decrease in EU agricultural employment by more liberalized policies can be seen as a transfer of agricultural employment from the EU to other parts of the world.

The continuing decline of the agricultural employment reveals the need for other employment opportunities outside the sphere of traditional agriculture in rural areas in order to maintain economic viability. There are opportunities to develop or transfer industries from urban to rural areas. However, in our post-industrial society, industrial employment is also declining. On the other hand, employment in the services sector is increasing and this trend can be expected to continue in the future. This sector offers new opportunities for rural areas in part due to continuing growth of disposable personal income and the increase in leisure time. A relative strong point for rural areas is the availability of space, for recreation, landscape and nature. An analysis of rural strengths and weaknesses can be seen as a pre-condition for the development of plans to "commercialize products of space".

Quite a number of pluriactive farmers are already working in this sphere. However, it is not sufficient if only individuals and individual farmers develop initiatives. To attract people and purchasing power from urban areas, a number of conditions have to be fulfilled and a package of facilities has to be offered. This can vary from an improvement of roads to the building of swimming pools and investments in the strengthening of the quality of the landscape. In other words, the success of individual initiatives depends, in part, on an integrated rural development approach. A multiplier of effects can be attained if there is a clear cohesion in the initiatives of different agents.

7. Concluding remarks

The share of agriculture in total employment varies from about 2.5 percent in the United States, Belgium and the UK to over 20 percent in Portugal and Greece. Within each country the share of agriculture in total employment in the most rural areas exceeds that in the most urbanized regions. However, the group of most rural regions incorporates regions in which the share of agriculture in regional employment is less than 5 percent, but also regions in which this share is over 25 percent. The importance of the agricultural sector as a source of rural employment in rural regions is heterogeneous.

Various policies are directed towards the agricultural sector. These policies affect — directly or indirectly — costs and farmers prices and hence agricultural income. Differences in the intensity of these policies among regions results in different patterns of decline of the agricultural labour force and in a redistribution of agricultural labour opportunities among regions or countries.

Within each country the decline of the agricultural labour force in the intermediate and the most rural regions in the 1980s was greater than in the most urbanized regions. In countries, where an increase in the agricultural labour force occurred, the growth rate of the agricultural labour force was highest in the most urbanized regions. Thus, rural regions are in a weaker position than urban regions in keeping labour in the agricultural sector or creating new agricultural employment. Within each country, differences in the growth rates of non-agricultural employment among the three types of regions tend to be relatively small. The relatively high growth rates of non-agricultural employment in the intermediate and most rural regions are an indication of the diversification of the local economy.

A large number of farm labourers do not work full-time on the farm, but are part-time employed and are sometimes engaged in other gainful activities. Among countries the share of part-time labour in the total agricultural labour force varies considerably, but within countries differences in the share of part-time labour among the three categories of regions are quite small. Among countries there seems to be a tendency that when the share of agriculture in total employment is relatively high, the share of part-time labour is also high. In some countries the share of part-time labour in the total agricultural labour force is highest in the most urbanized regions, but in other countries the highest share is found in rural regions.

Among countries, differences in the share of pluriactive farm holders are smaller than in the share of part-time farm holders. Within most countries the share of farm holders with other gainful activities in the intermediate areas exceeds that in most urbanized areas. A large number of part-time farm holders do not have other gainful activities. Within countries no large differences in the share of part-time farm holders without other gainful activities exist among the most urbanized, intermediate and most rural regions. A lot of part-time farm holders without other gainful activities are farmers of over 65 years of age.

A further decline of agricultural employment can be expected in the future. In order to absorb the surplus of agricultural workers, labour opportunities in the industry and services sector and new types of agricultural employment have to be created. These new types refer to the production of goods demanded by society such as landscape, nature, recreation and regional products. The development of these labour opportunities would benefit from an integrated, region specific, development framework and a close cooperation among farmers, local business agents, and local, regional and national authorities.

Appendix A: Definitions of part-time and pluriactive status

Conceptually, full-time labourers or holders are workers who spend one annual work unit in agricultural activities.

Initially, the concept of a part-time farmer referred to a farm holder with an off-farm job. However, this concept appeared misleading since the farms of the part-time farmers were not necessarily different from those in the surrounding area. Also, the labour allocation decisions within the farm household were not considered. In the 1980s, the concept of multiple job holding was emphasized to make the connection between the patterns of household behaviour and circumstances in the external environment. At the end of the 1980s, the concept of pluriactivity was adopted which includes activities remunerated in cash, activities with payment in kind, mutual labour exchange and other informal arrangements (Fuller, 1990).

EU, Austria, Japan, Finland
An annual work unit (AWU) is defined as being equivalent to the annual labour input (in terms of working hours) of a person employed full-time for agricultural work on the holding. Full-time labour input is measured as the minimum number of working hours according to national labour contracts. When that time is not determined in a country, an AWU is equivalent to 2,200 working hours. Full-time includes persons who spend more than one annual work unit on the farm.

Definitions of part-time holders and labourers used in this study:

EU, Austria, Japan, Finland: individuals who work less than 1 AWU.

United States: individuals who work less than 200 days on the farm.

Canada: part-time labourers are individuals 15 years of age or older whose major occupation is "farming" and who work less than 2,200 hours at all jobs (where hours is calculated by multplying "hours worked last week" times "weeks worked last year").

part-time holders are self-employed individuals 15 years of age or older whose major occupation is "farming" and who work less than 2,200 hours at all jobs (where hours is calculated by multiplying "hours worked last week" times "weeks worked last year").

Switzerland: part-time labourers are calculated as part-time workers as a percent of the sum of part-time plus full-time workers.

part-time farm holders are calculated as "other farmers" as a percent of the sum of main-time farmers plus "other farmers".

Definitions of pluriactive holders and labourers used in this study:

EU, Austria, Finland: individuals with other gainful activities.

Canada: percent of farm operators less than 65 years of age who report some days of off-farm work.

References

Breedveld, J. and Bruchem, C. van. (1985) *Gevolgen van een Lagere Melkproductie voor de Economie* (Consequences of a decrease in milk production for the economy). The Hague: LEI mededeling 323.

Bruchem, C. van, Terluin, I.J. and Silvis, H.J. (ed.). (1995) *Landbouw-Economisch Bericht 1995* (Agricultural Economic Report 1995). The Hague: Agricultural Economics Research Institute LEI-DLO; Periodieke Rapportage 1-95.

Bryden, J.M., Bell, C., Gilliatt, J., Hawkins, E. and MacKinnon, N. (1992) *Farm Household Adjustment in Western Europe 1987-1991* (Final report on the research programme on farm structures and pluriactivity). Oxford: Arkleton Trust.

Efstratoglou-Todoulou, S. (1990) Pluriactivity in different socio-economic contexts. *Journal of Rural Studies,* Vol. 6, No. 4, pp. 407-413.

Folmer, C., Keyzer, M.A., Merbis, M.D., Stolwijk, H.J.J. and Veenendaal, P.J.J. (1995) *The Common Agricultural Policy beyond the MacSharry Reform.* Amsterdam: Elsevier.

Fuller, A.M. (1990) From part-time farming to pluriactivity: a decade of change in rural Europe. *Journal of Rural Studies,* Vol. 6, No. 4, pp. 361-373.

Giessen, L.B. van der and Post, J.H. (1985) Macro and micro effects of the superlevy in The Netherlands. *European Review of Agricultural Economics,* Vol.12, No. 4, pp. 449-460.

Leuck, D. (1994) The EC Nitrate Directive and its potential effects on EC livestock production and exports of livestock products. In USDA. *Environmental policies: Implications for agricultural trade.* Washington: Foreign Agricultural Economic Report no. 252.

OECD. (1994) *Creating Rural Indicators for Shaping Territorial Policy.* Paris.

Post, J.H., Wijnands, J., Luesink, H.H., Breedveld, J. and Strijker, D. (1985) *Mestnormen: Enkele Nationaal Economische Gevolgen* (Norms for the application of manure: some consequences for the national economy). The Hague: LEI publication 1.20.

Saraceno, E. (1994) Recent trends in rural development and their conceptualisation. *Journal of Rural Studies,* Vol. 10, No. 4, pp. 321-330.

Terluin, I.J., Godeschalk, F.E., von Meyer, H., Strijker, D. and Post, J.H. (1994) *The Agricultural Income Situation in Less Favoured Areas of the EC.* Luxembourg/ Brussels.

Terluin, I.J., Godeschalk, F.E., von Meyer, H., Post, J.H. and Strijker, D. (1995) Agricultural income in less favoured areas of the EC: a regional approach. *Journal of Rural Studies,* Vol. 11, No. 2, pp. 217-228.

Chapter twenty-two:

Employment in Agriculture and Closely Related Industries in Rural Areas: Structure and Change, 1981–1991

Sylvain Cloutier
Statistics Canada, Ottawa, Ontario, Canada

Abstract

Rural regions account for 47 percent of the jobs in agriculture and closely related industries and 31 percent of the experienced labour force. Between 1981 and 1991, the increase in employment in agriculture and closely related industries was half the increase registered by the experienced labour force. The largest increases in the number of jobs took place in the retail and wholesale trade of agricultural and food products. If employment in trade is excluded, the remaining sectors show job losses between 1981 and 1991. Overall, females showed increases in the number of jobs, whereas males posted losses. The food and fibre processing industry fared relatively better in rural areas than in urban areas.

Introduction

In Canada, persons working in agriculture and closely related industries represent a major share of the experienced labour force. In 1991, for every 11 persons in the experienced labour force, one person was working in agriculture and closely related industries. A number of changes occurred in this industry during the period 1981–1991. What was the impact of these changes on agriculture and closely related industries during that period? Did the number of workers in this industry increase? In this industry, was there a movement of workers from rural areas toward the large urban centres? What has happened in rural areas? What was the place of women in this industry? Which sectors were advancing and which were losing ground? This analysis will answer these questions but will probably raise a great many more!

To conduct this analysis, industries are grouped into four major categories: "agriculture", "closely related to agriculture", "other resources" and "others". "Agriculture" includes employment on farms plus services incidental to agriculture. The "closely related to agriculture" group includes food and fibre processing, industries supplying farm inputs, and wholesale and retail trade of farm inputs and food products (for details, see Cloutier, 1996). According to this industry-based approach, all persons working for a company are counted as belonging to the group in which the company is classified. For example, the food and fibre processing industry includes employees engaged in food processing but also all administrative personnel in this industry.

Five geographic area designations were used for this analysis: "urban", "intermediate", "rural area adjacent to a metropolitan area," "rural area not adjacent to a metropolitan area," and the "rural north" (Government of Canada, 1995). The data from 1981 and 1991 were tabulated on the basis of the 1986 boundaries. Use of the 1986 boundaries made it possible to minimize the influence that boundary changes during the period 1981–1991 might have had on the number of jobs in areas classified as rural. The data are drawn from the Census of Population for 1981, 1986 and 1991.

Experienced labour force and agriculture and closely related industries

How did the experienced labour force and the number of persons employed in agriculture and closely related industries evolve during the period 1981–1991?

From 1981 to 1991, the increase in the number of persons in the experienced labour force was two times greater than in agriculture and closely related industries. The total number of persons in the experienced labour force increased by nearly 20 percent, whereas for agriculture and closely related industries, the increase registered was just over 10 percent (Figure 22.1). Another noteworthy difference has to do with the period during which the greatest increases occurred. The experienced labour force grew twice as fast from 1986 to 1991 as from 1981 to 1986. By contrast, the increase in the number of persons in agriculture and closely related industries was only slightly greater from 1981 to 1986 than from 1986 to 1991. It is also worth noting that during this ten-year period, the greatest increase registered by agriculture and closely related industries (1981–1986) was still less than the lowest increase registered by the experienced labour force during the same period.

Figure 22.1. The increase in employment in agriculture and closely related industries is half that of the experienced labour force, Canada, 1981–1991

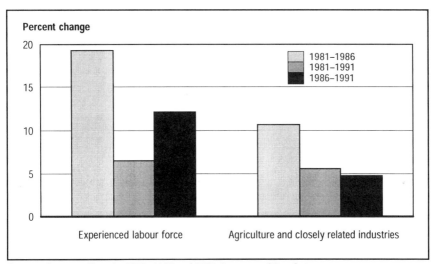

Source: Statistics Canada, 1981, 1986 and 1991 Censuses of Population.

Since agriculture and closely related industries are made up of two groups, namely the "agriculture" group and the "closely related to agriculture" group, it was possible to determine which of the two had contributed the most to the increase in the number of persons in this industry. Most of the increase was in the "closely related to agriculture" group. The number of persons in that group increased by 14 percent during the period 1981–1991, as compared to a 6 percent increase for the "agriculture" group (Figure 22.2). In the latter group, the increase was concentrated almost entirely in the period 1981–1986. The "closely related to agriculture" group registered its greatest advance between 1986 and 1991. As in the case of the experienced labour force and agriculture and closely related industries, the lowest increase for the "closely related to agriculture" group (between 1981 and 1986) was nevertheless greater than the increase for the "agriculture" group during its best period, namely between 1981 and 1986.

Figure 22.2.   The increase in employment in industries related to agriculture
was twice as great as in agriculture, Canada, 1981-1991

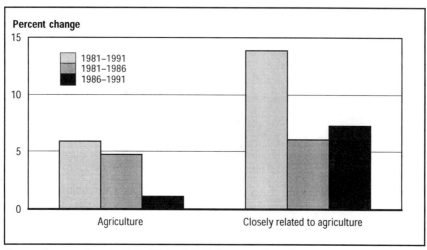

Source: Statistics Canada, 1981, 1986 and 1991 Censuses of Population.

Where were those persons working?

Between 1981 and 1991, the changes observed for all geographic areas studied,
whether upward or downward, were not major. As might be expected, the
experienced labour force was largely concentrated in urban areas. In 1991, those
areas accounted for 47 percent of the experienced labour force, the same
proportion as in 1981 (Table 22.1).

Table 22.1.   47 percent of jobs in agriculture and closely related industries
are located in rural areas, Canada, 1981–1991

	Total	Urban	Interme-diate	Rural metro adjacent	Rural non-metro adjacent	Rural north
Experienced labour force			Percent distribution			
1981	12,005,320	47	21	15	14	3
1986	12,783,505	47	22	15	13	3
1991	14,329,095	47	23	15	13	3
Agriculture and closely related industries						
1981	1,187,190	32	21	24	22	1
1986	1,253,280	31	21	24	22	1
1991	1,313,365	32	22	24	22	1
					47	

Source: Statistics Canada, 1981, 1986 and 1991 Censuses of Population.

Intermediate areas are the only areas that registered an increase in their share of the experienced labour force between 1981 and 1991. Rural areas not adjacent to a metropolitan area (hereafter 'rural non-adjacent') are the only ones to show a decrease.

The three types of rural areas — rural areas adjacent to a metropolitan area (hereafter 'rural adjacent areas'), rural non-adjacent areas and rural north areas — account for 47 percent of jobs, a share that did not change during the period 1981–1991. Nearly one-third of the jobs in agriculture and closely related industries were located in urban areas.

The number of persons employed in agriculture and closely related industries increased in all types of areas, including the three rural areas. However, urban areas and intermediate areas received more than 60 percent of the new jobs in agriculture and closely related industries during the ten years studied.

Do jobs in agriculture and jobs in industries closely related to agriculture have a similar geographic distribution?

We expected that the distribution of jobs in the "agriculture" and "closely related to agriculture" groups would be similar in each type of area. In other words, we expected that for an area with a sizable number of persons working in the "agriculture" group, there would also be a sizable number of persons working in the "closely related to agriculture" group. But this was not the case.

The three types of rural areas accounted for 69 percent of jobs in agriculture but only 32 percent of jobs in industries closely related to agriculture (Table 22.2). Rural adjacent areas and rural non-adjacent areas registered slight decreases in their share during the period 1981–1991. It was urban areas that increased their share during the period studied. In 1991, they accounted for 13 percent of all jobs in agriculture.

Regarding industries closely related to agriculture, no change in their employment share in the rural areas was registered between 1981 and 1991. The greatest number of jobs closely related to agriculture are in urban areas, more than 40 percent. However, there was some shifting of jobs from urban areas to intermediate areas during the 1980s.

Two trends may be identified. Between 1981 and 1991, urban areas increased their share of the "agriculture" group at the expense of two types of rural areas. By contrast, the "closely related to agriculture" group tended to "distance" itself from urban areas in favour of intermediate areas. In rural areas, the "closely related to agriculture" group showed no change.

Table 22.2.   Rural areas represent 69 percent of employment in agriculture and 32 percent of employment in industries closely related to agriculture, Canada, 1981–1991

	Total	Urban	Interme- diate	Rural metro adjacent	Rural non-metro adjacent	Rural north
Agriculture group				Percent distribution		
1981	481,280	11	18	36	34	1
1986	504,240	12	18	35	34	1
1991	509,775	13	18	35	33	1
					69	
Closely related to agriculture group						
1981	705,910	46	22	16	14	2
1986	749,040	45	23	16	14	2
1991	803,590	44	24	16	14	2
					32	

Source: Statistics Canada, 1981, 1986 and 1991 Censuses of Population.

What were the changes in the "agriculture" and "closely related to agriculture" groups?

From the analysis of these two groups, two major trends emerge. The first trend has to do with the industries closely related to agriculture group, which is divided into three components. The food and fibre processing industry and the inputs supplier industry are mainly concerned with the production aspect. The wholesale and retail trade of agricultural and food products, for its part, is more concerned with the purchase and sale of goods than with their production. It is hard to ignore the performance of the trade sectors. In trade alone, there were 125,000 jobs more in 1991 than in 1981 (Table 22.3). Without its contribution, industries closely related to agriculture would have shown a decrease of 27,000 persons. The retail component accounts for more than 90 percent of the new jobs in agricultural and food trade. It is also retail agricultural and food trade that shows the strongest increases in the number of jobs among both males and females. The inputs supplier industry and the food and fibre processing industry, for their part, each show losses of more than 10,000 jobs.

A second trend is that females show increases in terms of the number of workers, whereas males show decreases. Thus, there appears to be a shift of jobs from males to females. This trend is quite clearly illustrated by the "agriculture" group. Overall, the "agriculture" group increased by 28,000 persons, with an increase of 53,000 jobs among females and a decrease of 25,000 jobs among males. The change is mainly attributable to the "agriculture" sector, one of the two components of the "agriculture" group.

Table 22.3.   The retail trade of agricultural and food products exhibited the strongest increase among industries closely related to agriculture, Canada, 1981–1991

	Total	Women	Men
	Change between 1981 and 1991		
Agriculture group	**28,495**	**53,450**	**-24,955**
Agriculture	16,930	46,025	-29,085
Services incidental to agriculture	11,565	7,435	4,135
Closely related to agriculture group*	**97,680**	**84920**	**12,755**
Food and fibre processing industry	-11,385	5,295	-16,680
Inputs supplier industry	-12,840	-680	-12,165
Trade of agricultural and food products	124,565	80,210	44,365
Wholesale trade	10,175	5,730	4,440
Retail trade	114,395	74,475	39,920

Source: Statistics Canada, 1981, 1986 and 1991 Censuses of Population
*   *Includes the grain handling sector which is not reported separately.*

The two types of rural areas: rural areas adjacent to a metropolitan area and rural areas not adjacent to a metropolitan area

What happened in these two types of rural areas?

Between 1981 and 1991, rural adjacent areas showed a greater increase in the number of jobs in agriculture and closely related industries than did rural non-adjacent areas. The most striking difference appears in industries closely related to agriculture. In comparison with rural non-adjacent areas, 5,000 more jobs were created in rural adjacent areas (Table 22.4). The two types of rural areas exhibited similar gains for jobs in agriculture, although the increases were slightly higher in rural adjacent areas. Industries closely related to agriculture provided three times more new jobs than the "agriculture" group between 1981 and 1991.

Table 22.4.   Three times more jobs came in industries closely related to agriculture than in agriculture, Canada, 1981–1991

	Total	Women	Men
	Change between 1981 and 1991		
Rural metro adjacent areas	**25,085**	**33,070**	**-7,965**
Agriculture group	6,570	17,445	-10,865
Closely related to agriculture group	18,515	15,625	2,900
Rural non-metro adjacent areas	**19,035**	**31,920**	**-12,890**
Agriculture group	5,360	17,780	-12,420
Closely related to agriculture group	13,675	14,140	-470

Source: Statistics Canada, 1981, 1986 and 1991 Censuses of Population.

For these two types of rural areas, the "agriculture" sector generated the most jobs in the "agriculture" group (Figure 22.3). As was seen earlier, females showed gains in terms of the number of jobs, while males posted losses. In these two types of rural areas taken together, there were 17,000 more females employed in the "agriculture" group in 1991 than in 1981. By contrast, there were 11,000 fewer males in rural adjacent areas and 12,000 fewer males in rural non-adjacent areas. These two types of rural areas accounted for just over 80 percent of the decrease in the total number of males in the "agriculture" group.

Figure 22.3.   More jobs in agriculture were created in rural metro adjacent areas than in rural non-metro adjacent areas, Canada, 1981–1991

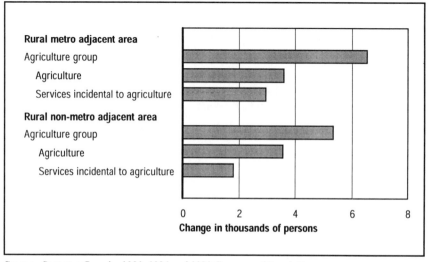

Source: Statistics Canada, 1981, 1986 and 1991 Censuses of Population.

As noted at the national level, trade in agricultural and food products drives the increase in the number of persons in the "closely related to agriculture" group and hence in agriculture and closely related industries. This is also the case in rural areas (Figure 22.4). Without agricultural trade, these two types of rural areas would show job losses for the "closely related to agriculture" group as a whole.

Unlike what was seen at the national level, where the food and fibre processing industry exhibits job losses, the situation is different in rural areas. The three types of rural areas registered slight increases in the number of jobs in food and fibre processing. The food and fibre processing industry maintained its job numbers in rural areas, unlike what happened in urban areas, where sizable losses were registered. The inputs supplier industry posted job losses between 1981 and 1991. For females, the largest increases in the number of jobs took place in the "agriculture" sector, whereas for males they occurred in retail trade.

Figure 22.4. The agricultural and food products trade accounts for almost all the increase in the number of jobs in closely related industries, Canada, 1981–1991

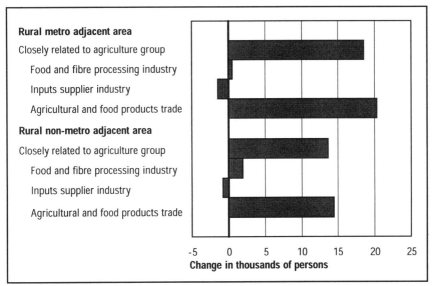

Source: Statistics Canada, 1981, 1986 and 1991 Censuses of Population.

The "other resources" group in rural areas

Did the "mines, petroleum and gas", "forestry" and "fishing and trapping" sectors participate in the rise in employment in rural areas adjacent to a metropolitan area and in rural areas not adjacent to a metropolitan area?

The number of persons employed in the "other resources" group changed little between 1981 and 1991 (Cloutier, 1996). In rural adjacent areas, employment increased in this group between 1981 and 1991, whereas in rural non-adjacent areas there were job losses. For rural adjacent areas, the "forestry" and "fishing and trapping" sectors together offset the losses in the "mines, petroleum and gas" sector. In non-rural adjacent areas, the "fishing and trapping" sector posted a good performance, but it was not sufficient to offset the losses registered in the "mines, petroleum and gas" and "forestry" sectors.

Employment in "other" sectors

How significant is the "other" group?

This group includes the majority of persons employed in rural adjacent and rural non-adjacent areas. In 1991, this group accounted for 1.8 million persons in rural adjacent areas and 1.5 million persons in rural non-adjacent areas. For these two types of rural areas, it was community services that showed the most jobs (Cloutier, 1996). Included under community services are persons employed in schools, restaurants, hotels and motels. Community services account for approximately 35 percent of the jobs in the "other" group. Non-agricultural trade ranks second for rural adjacent areas and third for rural non-adjacent areas. It is the non-agricultural manufacturing industry that ranks third in rural adjacent areas but second in rural non-adjacent areas. In both types of areas, more females than males are employed in finance and community services.

Which sectors showed the greatest change during the 1981 to 1991 period?

In the two types of rural areas, all subgroups of the "other" group posted increases in the number of persons employed in them between 1981 and 1991, except for the non-agricultural manufacturing industry (Cloutier, 1996). The increases in jobs were greater in rural adjacent areas than in rural non-adjacent areas. In both these types of areas, community services largely dominated the other subgroups. Nearly four times more jobs were created in this subgroup than in the one ranking second.

In general, females registered greater increases than males. In rural adjacent areas, the most notable increases in the number of females were observed in community services (139,000) and non-agricultural trade (23,000). Among males, the greatest increases were in community services (53,000) and non-agricultural trade (22,000). As in the case of rural adjacent areas, it was females who posted the greatest increases in rural non-adjacent areas. In the latter areas, jobs held by females increased the most in community services (100,000) and public administration (15,000). Among males, community services (30,000) and public administration (7,800) exhibited the greatest job increases.

The only decrease registered among females was in the non-agricultural manufacturing industry in rural adjacent areas. Males also registered decreases in this industry, but the decreases were observed in both types of rural areas.

Conclusion

The three types of rural areas — rural areas adjacent to a metropolitan area, rural areas not adjacent to a metropolitan area and rural north areas — account for 47 percent of the jobs related to agriculture and closely related industries and 31 percent of the experienced labour force. Between 1981 and 1991, the increase in employment in agriculture and closely related industries was half the increase registered by the experienced labour force.

The largest increases in the number of jobs took place in the retail and wholesale trade of agricultural and food products. Excluding agricultural trade from the industries closely related to agriculture, these industries exhibit job losses between 1981 and 1991. It may also be observed that overall, females scored increases in the number of jobs, whereas males posted losses. The food and fibre processing industry fared relatively better in rural areas than in urban areas. A final point worthy of note is the sizable increase in the number of persons working in community services during the period 1981–1991.

Numerous new questions emerge. For example, why did the number of females rise significantly, whereas the number of males mainly fell? How did the jobs held by females compare with those held by males? Did females hold primarily part-time positions? Were their wages lower than men's? What explains the performance of the food and fibre processing industry in rural areas? What are the provincial and regional differences? What factors explain the rise in the number of persons working in "community services"? These many questions could be answered by a more detailed analysis.

References and further reading

Cloutier, Sylvain (1996) *Employment in Agriculture and Closely Related Industries in Rural Areas: Structure and Change, 1981-1991*. Ottawa: Statistics Canada, Agriculture Division, Working Paper.

Dominion Bureau of Statistics. (1971) *Standard Industrial Classification Manual*. Ottawa: Dominion Bureau of Statistics, Cat. No. 12-501E, 309 pp.

Ehrensaft, P. and Beeman, J. (1992) Distance and diversity in nonmetropolitan economies. In Bollman, Ray D. (ed.). *Rural and Small Town Canada*. Toronto: Thompson Educational Publishing.

Government of Canada. (1995) *Rural Canada: A Profile*. Ottawa: Interdepartmental Committee on Rural and Remote Canada.

Statistics Canada. (1992) *1991 Census Dictionary*. Ottawa: Statistics Canada, Cat. No. 92-310E, 362 pp.

Chapter twenty-three:

Trends in Rural Policy: The Employment Issue

Christian Huillet
Deputy Head, Rural Development Programme, Organization for Economic Cooperation and Development (OECD), Paris, France

Abstract

The aspiration of each individual to make his or her way in society and of each generation to live better than the preceding one has become one of the characteristics of developed countries. The OECD Rural Development Programme is striving to forge a new rural policy involving a territorial dimension that recognizes the diversity among regions and it is not limited to a specific sector. Such a policy seeks to strengthen the competitiveness of rural areas while ensuring the standard of living of rural residents and protecting the environmental or amenity value of rural areas. Four types of policy instruments are discussed: direct aid; indirect aid; human resource development; and infrastructure policies. The impacts on rural employment differ depending upon whether we consider rural populations in predominantly rural, significantly rural or predominantly urban regions.

Context

Unemployment problems and job creation difficulties are some of the most serious economic and social phenomena of our day. In the OECD countries, there are more than 35 million unemployed. This represents 7.4 percent of the labour force (March, 1995). More worrisome yet, more than 18 percent of young people are unemployed.

Employment in primary sectors, especially agriculture, continues to decline. This has relatively larger impacts in regions with a sizable proportion of their employment in agriculture. The decline in farm employment is largely due to improved efficiency in agriculture and increased productivity among farmers. Farm employment will continue to decline in most OECD countries. In the past, urban economies could absorb the many rural inhabitants who migrated from the countryside, but it is becoming increasingly difficult to find work in the cities. Often where such work exists, it comes at a high social cost, not only for the communities that are left behind but also for the cities that must accommodate the newcomers.

Fortunately, current economic growth is accompanied by the creation of new jobs in occupations or sectors with higher value-added. This growth has prevented or slowed the depopulation of rural areas following the decline of employment in farming and other primary sectors. Some of these new opportunities have permitted pluriactivité of farming families.

Lastly, and perhaps even more importantly, unemployment and job creation do not occur in the same manner across the territory of any given country. Just as there are differences across countries (in February 1995, unemployment stood at 14.3 percent in Ireland, 9.6 percent in Canada and 5.4 percent in the United States), there are considerable differences in unemployment and job creation among rural regions within a country.

With this quick overview, one may conclude that the future viability and vitality of rural economies in terms of jobs depends on two factors: the speed of the structural adjustment process in the primary sector, especially in agriculture; and the rate at which jobs are created in other sectors.

Not surprisingly, during the past three years the OECD has made the employment issue one of its highest priorities. It is a small step from employment in general to employment in rural areas; accordingly, the issue of job creation in rural areas has been made one of the highest priorities of the OECD Rural Development Programme.

What exactly does "rural" mean?

It is essential to review how the concept of "rural area" is understood in the OECD. "Rural" — or better yet "the rural sphere" — should be understood as encompassing the population, territory, resources and small population centres in areas located outside the sphere of direct economic influence of urban centres. Hence, rural development is a concern for more than 36 percent of the population of the member countries, 40 percent of Canada's population and 44 percent of the US population (Table 23.1). Canada is one of eight of the 25 member countries of the OECD in which more than two-fifths of the population lives in "rural" communities.

But rural areas, in Canada as elsewhere, are not identical. For purposes of analysis and international comparison, the OECD member countries have agreed to speak of three types of regions: predominantly rural regions, significantly rural regions and predominantly urban regions.

Predominantly rural regions are those in which both population density and incomes are the lowest. Significantly rural regions are those in which the economy is based on a mix of activities in the primary and secondary sectors. Predominantly urban regions, for their part, have experienced population growth, and within these areas, employment is supported by one or more activities in the secondary or tertiary sector.

Table 23.1.   Rural population in OECD member countries, 1990

| | Population in rural communities[1] | Population by type of region[2] | | |
		Predominantly rural	Significantly rural	Predominantly urban
		Percent of national population		
Turkey	59	58	30	12
Norway	59	51	38	11
Sweden	43	49	32	19
Finland	55	43	37	20
Denmark	42	40	38	22
Austria	42	40	39	22
Mexico	..	..	..	..
United States	44	36	34	30
Canada	40	33	23	44
Australia	30	23	22	55
New Zealand	49	47	25	28.
Iceland	39	35	8	57
Ireland	43	47	16	38
Greece	39	47	19	34
Portugal	36	35	22	43
France	37	30	41	29
Spain	30	17	46	37
Italy	22	9	44	47
Japan	27	22	35	43
Switzerland	19	13	25	62
Germany	21	8	26	66
United Kingdom	13	1	27	72
Luxembourg	30	-	100	-
Belgium	9	2	18	80
Netherlands	8	-	15	85

Notes:

-    *Not applicable*

..   *Not available*

[1]   *Local communities with a population density of fewer than 150 inhabitants/km² (500 habitants/ km² in the case of Japan)*

[2]   *Regions are classified according to the proportion of the population living in rural communities: "Predominantly Rural" (PR), more than 50 percent; "Significantly Rural" (SR), between 15 and 50 percent; "Predominantly Urban" (PU), less than 15 percent.*

Source: OECD. (1994) Creating rural indicators for shaping territorial policy. Paris: OECD.

Under these conditions, it is not surprising that a rural development policy requires a territorial focus that recognizes the diversity among regions and is not limited to a specific sector of the economy. It is an economic policy with social and environmental dimensions. It primarily seeks to strengthen the competitiveness of rural areas, while not only ensuring that rural residents enjoy a standard of living comparable to that of the rest of society, but also protecting the key elements of the natural and built heritage (amenities) that are present in these areas.

Employment problems specific to rural areas

Quite obviously, the problems of job creation in rural areas are directly affected by overall job creation trends, but they also have specific consequences. There is now unanimous agreement that agricultural jobs will continue to decline in both relative and absolute terms. More than 60 percent of farmers no longer farm as their only activity on a full-time basis. Rural youth, especially in isolated areas, continue to emigrate in large numbers. Furthermore, the creation of jobs in the service sectors is not offsetting job losses in the goods-producing sectors. OECD studies in this area only confirm that no turnaround in the situation can be expected in the next decade.

Many, but not all, rural communities lie within regions that are marginalized with respect to new locations for industrial investment and services. A closer analysis of rural communities is required because the situation differs greatly depending on whether the focus is on predominantly rural regions or significantly rural regions or predominantly urban regions (Table 23.2). OECD studies on employment indicators reveal that a third of unemployed persons — in 1990, nearly 7.5 million persons out of the 25 million unemployed in the OECD countries — live in predominantly rural areas. And as paradoxical as it may seem, some rural regions have been much better than the national average at generating new job opportunities.

Job creation in rural areas

The OECD studies in this field were conducted in two stages. The first consisted of trying to assess, on the basis of case studies, the effects of job creation measures and policies in rural areas. The second consisted of looking more generally at the most promising measures for job creation in rural areas.

A first stage: assessing the effects of government measures by means of case studies

The study assessing the effects of government job creation measures in rural areas on the basis of case studies showed that it was extremely difficult to draw

Table 23.2.   Change in employment in OECD member countries, 1980–1990

	Growth of national employment	Employment growth by type of region[2]		
		Predominantly rural	Significantly rural	Predominantly urban
		Index 1980=100		
Turkey	117	..	..	..
Norway	104	102	108	100
Sweden	112	111	112	114
Finland	105	98	104	121
Denmark	107	..	..	..
Austria	107	105	109	107
Mexico	109	..	..	..
United States	118	113	122	121
Canada	116	114	126	114
Australia	120	..	..	..
New Zealand	102	98	99	110
Iceland	119	..	..	..
Ireland	98	..	..	..
Greece	111	..	..	..
Portugal	118	..	..	..
France	104	101	106	104
Spain	107	107	97	118
Italy	104	..	..	..
Japan[1]	111	102	108	118
Switzerland	117	115	121	115
Germany	107	114	107	106
United Kingdom	104	109	112	99
Luxembourg	120	-	120	-
Belgium	102	104	97	103
Netherlands	183	-	150	166

Notes:

\-   *Not applicable*

..   *Not available*

[1]   *Local communities with a population density of fewer than 150 inhabitants/km² (500 habitants/ km² in the case of Japan)*

[2]   *Regions are classified according to the proportion of the population living in rural communities: "Predominantly Rural" (PR), more than 50 percent; "Significantly Rural" (SR), between 15 and 50 percent; "Predominantly Urban" (PU), less than 15 percent.*

Source: OECD. (1994) Creating rural indicators for shaping territorial policy. Paris: OECD.

conclusions. However, the following points were noted:

1. by this method the cost per job created cannot really be determined, at this stage it may merely be stated that the cost appears to be relatively low;
2. measures designed to provide premises and equipment as a means to promote job creation in rural areas have only limited influence on job creation;
3. measures to assist companies through direct grants do not appear to be very conducive to job creation.

A second stage: after an inventory of measures, an assessment of their effectiveness

This second stage consisted of first making an inventory of the measures that governments can take to promote employment in rural areas as part of a broader development strategy. From this it was possible to identify four action areas and then analyse the usefulness of each in an integrated approach to job creation. These four action areas were as follows: direct aid, indirect aid, human resources development, and infrastructure.

Types of policy instruments for job creation in rural areas

Direct aid: Such aid focuses directly on a specific enterprise rather than on overall economic activity in a given rural area. The various forms of public aid and involvement target the firm's internal activity and they include financial aid and direct grants to companies, as well as aid for technological innovation, in-house training or job creation.

Indirect aid: Such aid is intended to strengthen an area's overall economic environment. It deals with the various economic activities in an area and seeks to improve the competitiveness of all the companies within it. Such aid includes the creation of services to facilitate technology transfer and aid for the marketing of local products or for the improvement of local information or telecommunications systems. An example of indirect aid is the creation of business services centres responsible for providing commercial and technological assistance to all companies in an area.

Human resources development: This category encompasses all measures and programmes designed to develop the human capital of rural areas. Programmes may target the labour force or persons who are not included in official labour markets. Among the main policies promoting human resource development are those oriented toward general education or worker training and development, as well as programmes to encourage entrepreneurship. Another facet of such programmes is the development of a range of social services designed to improve the quality of life of the rural population (housing, health, cultural activities, etc).

Infrastructure policies: Infrastructure programmes are generally understood to consist of public works programmes such as the construction of roads, sewers, telephone lines or public buildings for use by the population of a rural area as a whole. It is preferable to measure the infrastructure level according to the amount and quality of the services provided by the infrastructure, rather than by the quantity of infrastructure itself. It may be, for example, that two areas will be equally equipped with water treatment plants, but that the services provided by the plants in one of the two areas are markedly superior in terms of unit cost, regularity of water supply and general level of maintenance of facilities.

On the basis of the four action areas identified, the analysis focused on two types of principles: what should be the guiding principles for developing new policies on job creation in rural areas, and what should be the basic principles for implementing these job creation policies? These principles were chosen because they apply to all types of rural regions.

It should first be noted that in the OECD countries, the problem of job creation in rural areas is inextricably linked with the general problem of employment. This being the case, a policy on job creation in rural areas should give priority to the following two objectives:

1. to increase the capacity of rural economies to innovate and develop human resources;

2. to open up rural economies to the global economy and to regional, national and international trade.

The implementation of job creation instruments should be integrated into an overall approach that encompasses direct and indirect aid, a human resources development policy and infrastructure development. As each of these instruments contributes differently to the creation of lasting jobs, they should be applied within the framework of multi-year integrated programmes if they are to be truly effective.

It should be kept in mind that these different instruments do not all produce effects at the same time. Human resources development policies show results only in the medium term, which means that they should be implemented without delay. Direct aid measures will yield results in the short term.

There is an order of priority for implementing job creation measures in rural areas, and it corresponds to the order of enumeration of the elements of the job creation strategy. This order should be respected in order for the policies to be truly effective. Priority should be given to human resources development and indirect aid programmes. Efforts to develop entrepreneurship should be matched with programmes to improve manpower qualifications. Direct aid and the infrastructure policy can foster employment only if the necessary foundations for development are already in place.

Education and training are the two key elements of human resources development policies. Priority should be given to the training of young unemployed persons, who are especially numerous in rural areas, and in particular to the creation of ongoing training programmes in conjunction with local businesses. These policies should be based on the principle of equity, since the whole community can derive lasting benefit from the investment in human capital.

Indirect aid measures should be the key element of rural development policies, since they strengthen the economic environment of local companies and contribute to the expansion of the rural production system as a whole. Priority should be given to the development of business services, particularly in the fields of information, management and marketing, since such services are especially lacking in rural areas.

Direct aid measures should first and foremost enable local businesses to carve a place for themselves on external markets, and they should primarily benefit companies that launch new products, since when all is said and done, these are the only ones that create jobs. Such aid should be provided more selectively and should give preference to local businesses that have a strategic vision and the capacity for innovation. Economic efficiency should be the main criterion for granting direct aid.

This being said, a policy on job creation in rural areas should give priority to increasing the capacity of the rural economy to innovate and to develop human resources, so that it can open itself to the global economy and to regional, national and international trade.

Job creation initiatives should respect the balance between economic efficiency and social equity. The economic efficiency criterion should prevail when choosing and implementing strategies for improving the economic prospects of rural populations. In the short term, programmes tending to develop the potential of rural areas must also be guided by equity considerations. Equity and efficiency are thus important criteria in matters of public aid, for all types of regions.

One final point — in order to be really effective, job creation policies must take account of the diversity of production systems across the types of rural regions. It is in the rural regions intermediate between remote regions and metropolitan regions that job creation policies will have the most significant impact and achieve the greatest economies of scale.

Conclusion

Obviously, work on the employment issue will continue. In our largely employment-based societies, it is unacceptable that the effort should falter. It should continue so that rural inhabitants have an occupation and a stable job with good prospects for advancement. These are indispensable to social status, the consideration that everyone wants to receive, and access to housing, bank loans, education, etc. The aspiration of each individual to make his or her way in society and of each generation to live better than the preceding one has become one of the characteristics of developed countries.

The OECD Rural Development Programme will strive to forge new solutions in the coming years. There has been strong interest in having efforts focus in particular on the dissemination of technology, flexible hours of work, upgrading of manpower qualifications, and so on — a vast agenda. It is no exaggeration to say that unless solutions are found to the problem of employment in general and employment in rural areas in particular, a basic feature of our societies would be seriously threatened if not driven into decline.

Chapter twenty-four:

Policy Alternatives for Stimulating Rural Employment[1]

David Freshwater
University of Kentucky, Lexington, Kentucky, United States

Abstract

Employment is the primary measure by which the economic performance of both individuals and society is judged. In most countries, current policies are designed to deal with cyclical unemployment, not structural adjustment. The costs of continuing to use counter-cyclical policies to address structural problems are so great as to be beyond the fiscal capacity of most nations. Nations should focus on improving the functioning of labour markets by improving information flows about jobs, supporting employer based skill development programmes, increasing the capacity of the educational system to foster life-long learning skills, and trying to ensure that those with limited skills have an opportunity to earn an income.

Introduction

Employment is the primary measure by which the economic performance of both individuals and society is judged. Governments in nations with low unemployment rates typically face fewer political pressures than those with high ones and they are seen as doing a better job of managing the economy. At the

---

1. *The ideas discussed in the chapter reflect my understanding of rural labour markets in the United States and Canada. The relative importance of the problems and even their basic nature may be very different in other countries. In the hope of covering topics that are relevant to most countries I have tried to make the arguments as general as possible, but I recognize that certain of the ideas are specific to Canada and the United States. I would like to thank Stephan Goetz for his comments on an earlier draft. I would also like to acknowledge financial support from the Social Science and Humanities Research Council of Canada through Grant 90493009 and from the United States Department of Agriculture National Research Initiative Grant 93-37401-8974.*

sub-national level, economic development efforts are judged primarily in terms of jobs created. For an individual, status in society typically hinges upon the nature of one's job, but more importantly, on whether one has a job (McLarin, 1995). Employment plays this dominant role, in part because it is a measure that is not seen as being subjective, but primarily because in a market economy the exchange of labour for income is the basic means by which wealth is created and people gain access to goods and services.

The member nations of the OECD now recognize that employment opportunities in their countries are evolving rapidly in response to changing technology, greater integration of markets within the developed world and increased trade with the developing world (OECD, 1994a). In addition, the demographic structure of the labour force of some OECD countries is changing as the effects of the Second World War, in the form of a compressed generation formed by those of military age in the 1930s and 1940s, and the subsequent "baby boom" of the 1950s and 1960s, move through the population structure. These factors have led to a growing concern with the effects of structural change, particularly growth in the numbers of long-term unemployed.

Once the main employment problem is seen in terms of structural adjustment, the search for appropriate policies must take a different approach than when the concern is buffering cyclical variability (Woodford, 1994). Much of current employment policy still presumes that the main task is providing temporary assistance to bridge periods of recession until demand recovers and workers resume their current occupation. A secondary role for policy is to improve the market intermediation process that matches workers with jobs. Finally, while some adjustment assistance might have been required in the past to take into account the evolution of the job market, this has typically been a relatively minor concern in terms of financial resource commitments. However, "adjustment assistance" is now moving to the forefront of the discussion of reform of employment policy.

As economies evolve the sources of employment change. There is a growing premium on adaptability and a broad range of skills both for enterprises and workers. Shifting from mass production to flexible production is widely seen as the best development strategy for the OECD. Employment policy should be designed to facilitate this change in both firms and the workforce so that firms may be competitive and workers may be fully employed. The OECD Jobs Study makes a series of policy recommendations for member countries to help address the significant increase in unemployment and underemployment that has characterized national labour markets. The study notes that structural unemployment is a problem in virtually all countries, but the nature of the problem varies significantly among countries. What is not indicated in the Jobs Study discussion is that the nature of the unemployment problem can vary within a country as well. Thus, the Jobs Study ignores a potentially critical component of structural adjustment, shifts in the demand for labour among various portions of a nation's territory.

Rural areas face particular challenges in adapting to the structural change in labour markets. In many ways they are the point where the forces of change are exerting their greatest influence. In rural areas, new technologies are reducing employment opportunities as firms replace workers with capital or move off-shore. Similarly, increased pressures for agglomeration of industry associated with increases in the minimum efficient scale of production and reorganization of production to emphasize "just-in-time" process and proximity to markets make rural places less desirable production sites. Because rural places are engaged primarily in the production of tradeable goods they face immediate pressures from changes in relative prices, including exchange rate effects. Because rural places have traditionally specialized in the production of low-technology, low-skill products they face the greatest competition from the industrialization of developing countries. They also face greater challenges in improving the quality of the labour force, in part because labour-force skills have seldom been a priority in rural places, and in part because the unit costs of skill improvement programmes are higher in rural areas. Finally, those rural areas that depend upon a natural resource base face the inevitable question of how to deal with the effects of depletion and the resulting loss of community viability.

Defining a territorially sensitive employment strategy adds a spatial dimension of complexity to an already challenging task. Employment policy must already cope with significant differences in conditions within the labour-force in terms of existing skills and opportunities both for jobs and skill development. However, evidence suggests that territorial policy is essential in those countries where spatially distinct labour markets exist. The simple neo-classical assumption of equalization of wages and employment levels due to the movement of jobs and labour does not appear to hold in practice. If the chronic employment problems of many rural and urban places are to be resolved, policies that explicitly recognize that people are rooted in a particular place will be required — if only to provide the incentive and the means for some to leave those places where employment prospects are slim.

Structural change

After several decades of relatively robust job creation following the Second World War, the mid-1970s saw a rapid increase in unemployment in the OECD region (Figure 24.1). For over a decade this increase was rationalized as being cyclical in nature, and expectations were that the return of past trend rates of economic growth would restore employment. However not only was growth disturbingly slow over the subsequent decades, but employment levels did not rebound. It is now widely acknowledged that the nature of the economies in the OECD countries has significantly changed and that a consequence of this change is labour market turmoil as skills that were once valued become irrelevant (Phelps, 1994). One result of this change in most countries has been higher rates of unemployment for women and youths. In most countries low skilled workers also have higher rates of unemployment (Table 24.1). In addition, between 1983 and 1993 there has been a steady increase in the incidence of long-term unemployed in most countries, excepting the United States, the United Kingdom and Canada (Figure 24.2 and Table 24.2).

Figure 24.1 Over 30 million are unemployed in OECD countries

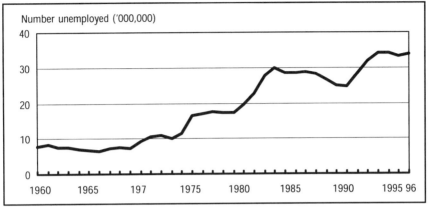

Source: OECD.(1994a) The OECD Jobs Study: Facts, Analysis, Strategies. Paris: OECD.

Table 24.1. The profile of OECD unemployment, 1994

	Unemployment rate (percent)			
	All persons	Women	Youth	Low skilled(1992)
North America	5.8	6.0	10.4	13.8
Canada	10.3	9.9	16.5	15.2
United States	6.0	6.0	12.5	13.5
Mexico	2.5	3.2	4.4	N/A
Japan	2.9	3.0	5.1	N/A
EU	11.1	12.6	18.6	10.0
Austria	4.3	4.5	4.8	5.6
Belgium	10.3	14.4	20.0	13.0
Denmark	10.1	11.2	10.6	14.1
Finland	18.2	16.7	30.5	14.9
France	12.5	13.6	23.4	12.1
Germany	6.9	6.7	5.2	8.9
Greece	9.6	15.3	28.8	6.1
Ireland	14.7	19.7	26.4	19.8
Italy	12.0	17.8	31.1	7.3
Luxembourg	3.3	4.4	7.1	2.0
Netherlands	7.2	11.7	7.8	8.0
Portugal	6.8	7.3	11.4	3.9
Spain	23.8	30.9	38.3	16.0
Sweden	8.0	6.7	16.6	4.6
United Kingdom	9.5	7.4	14.9	12.6
EFTA	4.4	4.5	8.2	5.0
Iceland	5.3	5.7	9.9	7.8
Norway	5.4	4.7	12.6	7.1
Switzerland	3.8	4.3	5.7	3.5
Turkey	8.3	6.7	15.3	5.1
Oceania	9.4	9.1	16.4	11.2
Australia	9.7	9.4	16.3	11.2
New Zealand	8.1	7.8	17.4	11.2

Source: OECD.

Figure 24.2.   Total and long-term unemployment

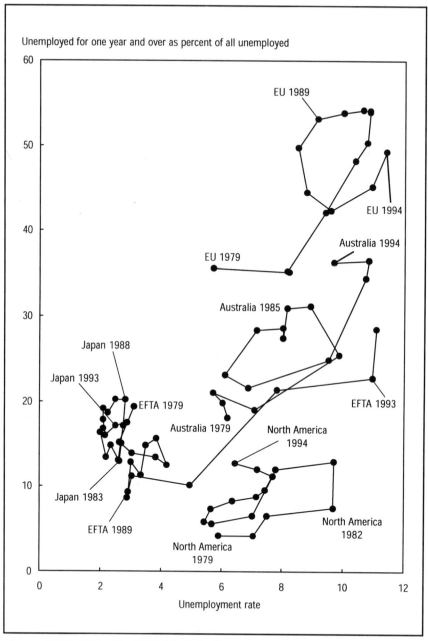

Unemployed for one year and over as percent of all unemployed

EU 1989

EU 1994

Australia 1994

EU 1979

Australia 1985

Japan 1988

Japan 1993

EFTA 1979

EFTA 1993

Australia 1979

North America
1994

Japan 1983

EFTA 1989

North America
1982

North America
1979

Unemployment rate

Source: OECD. (1994a) The OECD Jobs Study: Facts, Analysis, Strategies.

Table 24.2.   Incidence of long-term unemployment in selected OECD countries

| | Long-term unemployment as percent of total unemployment | | | | | |
| | 1983 | | 1990 | | 1993 | |
	6 months and over	12 months and over	6 months and over	12 months and over	6 months and over	12 months and over
Australia	51.3	25.4	40.9	21.6	57.1	36.5
Austria			25.2	13.1	30.2	17.2
Belgium	82.6	64.8	81.4	68.7	70.4	52.9
Canada	28.8	9.9	18.9	5.7	31.4	14.3
Denmark	67.2	44.3	53.3	30.0	45.5	25.2
Finland	30.0	19.2	32.6	9.2	52.2	30.3
France	67.0	42.2	55.5	38.0	58.2	34.2
Germany	65.8	41.6	64.7	46.8	60.1	40.3
Greece	58.4	33.2	71.9	49.8	1.0*	50.9
Ireland	64.0	36.7	81.0	66.0	7.4*	58.9
Italy	82.5	58.2	85.2	69.8	6.5*	57.7
Japan	31.5	12.9	39.0	19.1	34.4	17.2
Luxembourg	56.3*	35.4*	66.7*	42.9*	62.2*	-32.4
Netherlands	70.7	48.8	63.6	49.3	9.1*	52.3
New Zealand			38.0	18.7	52.5	33.2
Norway	20.3	6.3	40.4	19.2	45.6	27.2
Portugal			62.4	44.8	45.2	43.4
Spain	72.8	52.4	70.2	54.0	69.6	50.5
Sweden	24.9	10.3	16.0	4.0	32.0	10.9
United Kingdom	66.4	45.6	50.3	34.4	62.9	42.5
United States	23.9	13.3	10.2	5.6	20.4	11.7

Source: OECD. Employment outlook, July, 1995, p. 219.
*   *Based on small sample sizes and therefore must be treated with care.*

The underlying causes of structural change are many and include technological advance, improved flows of capital, reduced trade barriers, macroeconomic policies of national governments and an increase in the sophistication of production of a number of developing countries (Federal Reserve Bank of Kansas City). In rural areas of the OECD, the major consequences of the change have been:

1.   a reduced demand for primary products, as other nations increase their supply capability and raw materials play a smaller part in the aggregate production of member countries;

2.   the shedding of jobs in primary production as capital is used to replace labour;

3.   a loss of manufacturing jobs as within the OECD production is concentrated in a smaller number of larger more-efficient plants, and outside the OECD, developing nations take over or compete for low-wage, low-skill jobs; and

4. a limited ability to develop jobs in producer services, which has been one of the faster growing components of the job market, because of the difficulty in reaching efficient minimum scale sizes and in developing agglomerative linkages to other related services.

Over time these forces have resulted in a growing mismatch between available workforce skills and the skills that are necessary to now find employment, either as a worker or as a business operator (Commission of the European Communities, 1993; Narisetti, 1995). The critical question for government in framing a new employment policy is the role it should play in trying to facilitate a better match between employment opportunities and the capacities of the labour-force, for both rural and urban participants.

In the past when the focus of employment policy was mediating cyclical effects, simple income transfer programmes were sufficient. But, when structural adjustment is the primary cause of unemployment the task for policy is much harder (Human Resources Development Canada, 1994). Workers now require income support while they develop new skills to make a transition from careers with little opportunity to ones where a shortage of workers exists[2]. In providing skill development programmes the government must not only have a good idea of where job opportunities currently exist, but where they will exist in the future. These opportunities have to be defined both in the terms of types of employment and in terms of geographical location.

At the same time that the nature of job opportunities and markets is changing, there is also a growing belief in the limitations of the ability of government to direct the economy (OECD, 1994b). Proponents of market forces suggest that price signals will do a better job of allocating resources to meet social needs. This might be interpreted as an argument for a greatly reduced role for employment policy. However, as the OECD Jobs Study recognizes, employment policy must be concerned with social equity as well as with economic efficiency.

> *Governments are faced with designing and redesigning a range of policies across the economy and society in order to foster — or in some cases, stop hindering — adaptation to evolving ways of production and trade. But governments cannot meet the challenge alone. A high degree of social consensus will be needed to move forward with the necessary changes. Businesses, trade unions and workers need to be innovative to develop the new products, processes, and ways of working that will create new jobs, and help to shape skills to fit with the jobs of the future.*

> *Some people, however, will have particular difficulty in making the needed adaptation. The most successful economies and societies will be those which plough back some of the gains from change into accelerating the process by helping them to adapt.*

---

2. *In this environment the importance of the education system preparing workers for a lifetime of continual learning cannot be overemphasized. The years of formal education are the foundation for subsequent skill development programmes.*

Even so, some in society will find it impossible to adapt to the
requirements of advancing economies. Yet they, too, must benefit from
the progress. Their exclusion from the mainstream of society risks
creating social tensions that could carry high human and economic
costs. (OECD, 1994a, p. 7)

Employment problems in rural places

If national governments are to develop effective employment policies for rural
areas they will first have to develop a clearer understanding of the opportunities
and problems that rural places face. Rural areas are characterized by a number
of features that make them a particular challenge in designing employment policy
(Pankratz, 1989). Rural places are by definition remote and sparsely populated.
People do not live in significant concentrations so it is hard to achieve a critical mass
of resources or support a wide range of activities. At the same time, distance from
urban centres makes it difficult to gain access to the broader variety of goods and
services in larger places for those needs that cannot be met locally. As a result, rural
areas have truncated economies with only a limited ability to capture value-adding
activities before commodities are shipped out. Another consequence of truncated
economies is limited employment opportunity, both in terms of the total number of
positions and in the variety of careers.

The nature of the rural labour force provides one starting point in developing
the framework for considering employment policy. Rural areas are typically
characterized by a workforce that has less formal education, relatively limited
opportunities for formal skill development and there is often a significant
component of the labour force that is only loosely attached to the labour market.
Many rural workers are reluctant to accept change in the form of either relocation
to areas where jobs may be available, or in terms of investing in new skills that
could provide them with employment opportunities closer to home.

Certain rural areas also have longstanding dependency relations that reduce
their internal ability to adapt to change. These can stem from the dominance of
a large company, cultural or ethnic barriers, or reliance on government policy
and programmes. Patterns of dependency lower incentives to participate in the
labour force, and in particular have limited the development of indigenous
entrepreneurial capacity.

Single industry communities can face difficulty in attracting other types of
enterprise. The dominant firm may actively oppose new firms that could dilute
its position, or its wage structure may be too high for other industries. For example,
single industry communities are often unable to diversify their economic base
because the dominant employer is able to pay high wages in good times and
other potential employers recognize that while they may be able to attract workers
in weak periods from the dominant firm, they will lose their best workers when
conditions for the dominant firm improve.

In some rural areas a significant proportion of the population may be excluded
from full participation in the economy. People of the wrong race, religion or

ethnic background may have a hard time gaining access to capital or in making the contacts that are necessary to get a job or start a business. In other areas, governments may control the resource base and manage it to meet objectives that do not give much weight to the needs of the local populace. Governments can also foster dependency by providing long-term subsidies to prop up non-economic enterprises in rural areas, thereby providing the illusion of economic stability.

Rural labour market reform

Employment policy can be thought of as altering either the supply of labour, the demand for labour, or altering the environment in which labour markets operate (Eberts and Montgomery, 1994; Wren, 1994). While labour market policies are developed in a national context, actual labour markets operate locally (van der Laan, 1991). However, our knowledge of the workings and boundaries of rural labour markets is incomplete. Economic models of labour markets are now based on search theories that try to explain how an individual locates employment that matches his or her capabilities (Devine and Kieffer). However, while the theories incorporate the effects of time on the search process, they do not worry about distance. In an urban setting where a wide range of employment opportunities can be found in a compact area this is not a major shortcoming. In a rural area distance may be the critical factor in explaining individual job search decisions.

We lack a good understanding of what determines how far rural people commute between residence and job. For some people with advanced skills the choice of residential location is increasingly unconnected to their job because they rely on advanced telecommunications rather than actual travel. For others, limitations in transportation systems may make a job more than a short distance from the home impossible.

Similarly, we have a weak understanding of how skill requirements can segment labour markets. It appears that the labour force is being divided into two distinct groups — those with advanced skills and the ability to deal with modern technology, and those without (Gittleman and Howell, 1995). In any particular labour market there may be excess demand for one of these groups and an excess supply of the other. Given the segmented nature of the market there is little reason to expect strong equilibrating forces. If policy does not recognize the segmented nature of the market, and provide the opportunity for workers to move from the unskilled to the skilled category, then a permanent underclass may result at the cost of increased social tension. While it may be tempting for political leaders to assume that a rural underclass will be confined to remote areas and not cause significant trouble this is a high risk strategy.

In developing a territorially sensitive employment policy member countries will have to tailor specific policies to their particular conditions. The following three lists of factors that operate on the supply and demand sides, and factors that can improve the workings of labour markets, identifies a number of general principles that should be included to improve employment prospects in rural areas.

Critical issues for the labour supply side are:

1. fostering a strong learning ethic in the school systems so children are prepared with the basic tools to adapt to changing job requirements;

2. finding a way to provide employment opportunities for that portion of the labour force that has limited skills and is beyond the age where retraining programmes can provide much benefit;

3. providing innovative ways for highly skilled workers to obtain employment in rural areas even though no single firm may be able to offer them full-time permanent employment (coordinated part-time work, perhaps through employment services);

4. finding ways to facilitate worker movement among jobs when labour markets are thin and physical distances among jobs are great;

5. weakening the rigidities caused by strong unions that wish to preserve obsolete working conditions;

6. finding ways to increase attachment to the labour force as a means to offset the inevitable reduction in need-based transfer payments.

Critical issues on the labour demand side include:

1. increasing the demand for workers of all skill levels, but most importantly those with limited skills so there is an opportunity for the economically disadvantaged to offset the loss of transfer income with earned income;

2. encouraging the development of small and medium size firms that are attached to the particular community;

3. developing an appropriate role for industrial recruitment activity;

4. finding ways to mitigate the risk associated with having a specialized economic base (recognizing that significant diversification is not possible in small communities);

5. finding ways to ensure that dominant industries do not abuse their monopoly power over workers; and

6. increasing the survival rate of local entrepreneurial activity which can form a base over the longer term for higher levels of employment.

Critical issues for facilitating labour market mechanisms include:

1. finding ways to improve the linkages among local labour markets so excess supply or demand levels in one market are recognized in other markets and equilibrating flows take place;

2. improving knowledge of existing job opportunities, and existing worker capabilities over an extended physical area (in rural areas a local labour market may extend several hundred miles);

3. developing rural employment services that can act as brokers between workers and employers and allow both workers and employers the opportunity of full time or part time work; and

4. ensuring that other critical factors, such as access to capital and infrastructure are available in quantity and quality to support rural businesses.

The OECD Policy Framework

The nine planks of the Jobs Study (OECD, 1994a) provide an integrated approach for addressing employment problems and can serve as a basis for suggesting policy change in the member countries. This makes it vital that those interested in improving rural employment opportunity consider how implementing these planks will alter the workings of labour markets and the creation of establishments at a sub-national level.

The nine planks

1. **Set macroeconomic policy so it encourages sustainable growth**
    While macroeconomic reform is a critical issue, there is little scope for developing a rural component for this plank. By definition macroeconomic policy can apply only at the national level. However, it should be noted that there are territorially distinct effects of specific policy choices. For example, a policy that favours high interest rates and a high exchange rate may make it harder for rural areas to exhibit steady growth if they produce goods for export with capital-intensive technology.

    Because rural areas are a relatively small part of national economies they are often not considered when macro policy is set. It may not be possible to develop macro policies that favour rural areas, but if policies are adopted that impede their development then other policy planks may have to be particularly sensitive to the needs of rural places.

2. **Enhance the creation and diffusion of technology**
    There are numerous theories of technological diffusion and adoption processes. All of them suggest that smaller and more remote places are typically laggards in adopting new technologies. The first phase of the employment policy research noted the importance of indirect policy as a means to enhance the modernization of rural business. Industrial extension services and the fostering of networks were suggested as two important steps that could be taken to stimulate the growth of rural business.

    In addition, there are examples of small firms that have innovative ideas but lack the means and knowledge to bring these ideas into production. Not only is it important to increase the flow of ideas from urban places to more remote areas, but attention must be given to improving the chance for innovations that are developed by rural residents, to reach their market potential. Finally, rural areas may be more dependent on publicly sponsored research and development than are urban places. A higher dependence on small firms and branch plants means that little research capacity is available in the area and that cutbacks in public research may have important consequences.

3. Increase flexibility of working time

Increasing the flexibility of working time is not a promising area for defining a territorially sensitive policy. Increased flexibility may be of interest to workers and employers in rural areas, but their interests are not likely to differ systematically from those in urban locations.

Perhaps the most important issue in rural areas has to do with the functioning of local labour markets. In rural areas where the number of employers is limited there is considerable potential for labour standards to provide the only protection for workers from abusive employer actions. In these places compulsory overtime or other practices may be forced upon workers who have no other employment opportunities.

4. Nurture an entrepreneurial climate

There is widespread agreement that stimulating indigenous enterprise is the best hope for the development of rural areas. Various studies by the OECD including those on niche markets, farm employment, the role of women's work and others point to the importance of entrepreneurial behaviour. In some rural areas there is a long-standing tradition of entrepreneurship while in other areas very little entrepreneurial activity can be detected.

The obvious issues for examining entrepreneurship include studies to determine why certain rural areas are or are not entrepreneurial, to determine how one enhances entrepreneurial behaviour in different types of rural settings, and to examine the potential for self-employment as a vehicle for economic growth in different rural milieus.

5. Increase wage and labour cost flexibility

While levels of the minimum wage are important in rural areas because a large proportion of rural workers earn minimum, or near minimum, wage there are few rural-specific elements to focus on in considering wage flexibility. In those countries where the minimum wage is set at a very high level it may be contributing to high levels of unemployment. Conversely in many countries with high levels of rural unemployment, reductions in the minimum wage would not lead to a significant decrease in unemployment because the labour supply greatly exceeds the feasible demand.

6. Reform employment security provisions

Employment security provisions do not appear to offer opportunity for developing a major thrust for rural employment policy. As noted above, rural areas differ from urban places in terms of the size and efficiency of local labour markets with implications for unfair bargaining power between employers and employees. However the general issues involved in setting minimal standards of employee security transcend location.

7. **Increase the emphasis on active labour market policies**
Improving the functioning of local labour markets through active labour market policies is a plank that has considerable potential for rural employment policy. The small size and large geographic area of rural labour markets introduces problems in policy design that are fundamentally different from those in urban areas. Studies under this plank provide a way of addressing concerns about the functioning of rural labour markets noted in comments on planks 3, 5 and 6. Because the demand for rural labour is thin, conditions of monopsony often apply. Conversely, in some places, the thin nature of local labour markets may lead to shortages of workers with particular skills.

8. **Improve labour force skills**
This will be a critical issue for rural areas if they are to modernize their economic base. It may be possible to design policies that help to address problems of inadequate demand or supply of skills. Part of the process will certainly involve finding ways to increase labour force mobility so that workers can move to areas where opportunities are greater. Another critical element will involve designing cost-effective skill development and training programmes that can provide small numbers of people with necessary skills. In a period where national governments are trying to reduce their expenses, it will be important to examine how access to skill development programmes can be maintained. Innovative ways to use telecommunications are prime candidates for skill development in rural areas.

9. **Reform unemployment and related benefit systems**
This topic is one of considerable importance to rural areas because these benefits have been used extensively by some governments as a way to stabilize rural communities. Extended benefits have been used to allow people to remain in rural areas when they might otherwise have moved. In some cases this has allowed people to wait while cyclical industries recovered, but in other cases where employment decline reflects structural change the payments have resulted in people dissipating their assets and losing attachment to the labour force.

In some rural areas where a large portion of the local economy is outside the formal market structure, government benefits provide a cash infusion to the local economy that allows the import and purchase of goods that cannot be locally produced. Removing or reducing benefits in these circumstances could have a far greater impact on the welfare of the population than the size of the transfers would suggest.

The set of policy prescriptions implicit in these nine planks suggest a direction for major reform of how national governments conduct employment policy. For rural areas a critical factor will be whether policy reform takes into account territorial differences. The first phase of the rural employment work conducted by the OECD suggested that there were significant differences in conditions among rural areas. In particular, the three-part rural typology adopted for the work suggested that both problems and opportunities (and thus policy impacts) vary among integrated, intermediate and remote areas. In developing a territorially sensitive policy there may be more in common between, say, remote areas in two different countries, than between those areas and the integrated areas within each country.

Of the nine planks the most critical ones for defining a specific territorial focus to address rural employment appear to be 2, 4, 7, 8 and 9. While the other planks have a significant effect upon rural residents the nature of the reform is less amenable to defining a spatially differentiated policy. Among the planks that have a territorial dimension there are variations in importance depending upon the type of rural area. The table below suggests how the relative significance can be examined for the three types of rural area defined by the OECD. Following the table is a stylized discussion of the circumstances in each of the three zones (drawn primarily from OECD (1995b)).

Table 24.3.   Rural areas and their sensitivity to policy reform

	Integrated areas	Intermediate areas	Remote areas
Diffusion of technology	- close to urban places so faster diffusion, but more pressure to adopt new technology	- in between	- furthest away from most innovations, but less likely to be in direct competition with early adopters
Nurture entrepreneurs	- most exposed to existing forces - best access to existing support structure	- potential for in-migrants to bring skills - some existing support system	- most dependent on indigenous entrepreneurs, but little capacity to support them
Active labour market policy	- most likely to have flows across local labour market boundaries	- labour market closed, but large enough to support competition and diversity	- very small local labour market that will require new approaches for active policy to work
Improve work force skills	- greatest access to programmes and greatest availability of existing work force skills	- common skills available but limited supply and demand for specialized skills	- fairly limited set of skills needed, but the range of skills is most limited
Reform benefits to workers	- least likely to experience adverse effects from change due to strong worker attachment to labour force	- in between	- high degree of dependency on current benefit levels, but benefits act as a barrier to change in occupation and location

Integrated places

Because these rural areas are physically near urban areas and their economies are closely linked, they face immediate pressure to adapt to new conditions. However, integrated areas have smaller scale local markets and have somewhat slower access to new technologies. As a result they may run the risk of becoming dependent on urban areas. While they may not need large amounts of assistance in gaining access to new information, the information they do need is vital. They typically have good entrepreneurial capacity and have a diverse employment structure in terms of a wide range of sizes of enterprise. Because they have relatively large work-forces and diversified economies they have a wide variety of skills available. These can often be supplemented by workers from urban places. Because there is a strong attachment to the labour-force and relatively high levels of employment, the current set of benefits is unlikely to provide a strong incentive not to work.

Employment policy for integrated areas should focus on improving the skills of workers and finding ways to tap into urban areas for skills that cannot be provided locally. Broader use of consultant services and temporary labour service companies are two possible ways to add specialized skills. Because these areas have a potentially large local market if neighbouring urban places are included, it may be possible to add entrepreneurial activities that provide specialized niche services.

Intermediate places

These areas are somewhat further from major sources of innovation but the nature of their economy may make it less critical that they rapidly adopt innovations. These places may be more dependent on formal transmission mechanisms rather than word of mouth. Indigenous entrepreneurial capacity is less likely to be as well developed, but entrepreneurs may be willing to locate in these areas if opportunities exist. Typically the mix of skills in the labour-force is more limited and there may be inadequate opportunity to develop sufficient demand for particular skills. Branch plants are common in these areas so there is some alternative to indigenous entrepreneurship as a source of employment growth.

Employment policy in these areas should begin to focus on improving the matching of employment opportunity with skills, because in these areas the spatial density of jobs and the work-force makes it likely that simple search processes may not be doing a good job. While these areas may not need a wide variety of specialized highly skilled workers, they are likely to experience critical gaps that can impede employment creation. Training programmes that are geared to employers needs could be very important. In intermediate areas there may be a significant number of low-skilled workers who face the loss of jobs due to restructuring, and it is important to find ways to keep these people engaged in the labour-force. Programmes that supplement wages may be an option for those who have limited potential for retraining.

Remote areas

Remote areas are almost by definition at the end of the diffusion cycle. However, the often rudimentary nature of the local economy may make early adoption less critical. They are often characterized by a population that is only weakly attached to market forces and this has considerable implications for entrepreneurial activity, skill development and dependence on transfer payments like unemployment. Opportunities for employment are often constrained to a narrow range of skills and labour markets are often dominated by a single employer.

In many remote areas there are far more people than there are currently jobs. Expanding employment opportunities, particularly for individuals with limited skills is a critical issue. To the extent that social assistance programmes are curtailed this becomes an even more critical concern. Because the labour market is limited in scope, there is a significant role for government in facilitating the development of a market-based exchange of labour. Entrepreneurial activity in these areas should focus on expanding the supply of basic goods and services. It may also be possible to work with existing employers to find ways to make greater use of local labour. Finally, considerable attention should be paid to finding ways to facilitate relocation to places where employment prospects are greater.

Conclusion

In each country the appropriate set of employment policies will have to be defined so that the goals of improving efficiency and preserving social equity can be met. By and large the OECD countries will have to make adjustments in their employment policies. In most countries current policies are designed to deal with cyclical unemployment, not structural adjustment, and the costs of continuing to use these policies to address problems that they are not designed for are so great as to be beyond the fiscal capacity of the nation.

One set of criteria for assessing ideas to reform employment policies has been put forward by Duane Leigh.

> *Program services should facilitate the transition of displaced workers to jobs in expanding industries and growing sectors within existing industries.*
>
> *Program activities must meet the needs of displaced workers — that is, programs should be flexible, job-oriented, and low cost to participants.*
>
> *Programs must serve the entire spectrum of displaced workers, not just those easiest to place.*
>
> *Training programs must supply marketable skills to program graduates.*
>
> *Programs should effectively utilize existing education and training institutions.*
>
> *A broadening of the concept of job skills should be encouraged — that is, restructured employers require workers who are retrainable and adaptable to new technologies and work organizations. (Leigh, 1995, pp. 172–173)*

The key challenges in designing employment policy for rural areas are to develop programmes that deal effectively with small numbers of people that seek employment in a labour market that is both thin and geographically large. As one moves from integrated to remote areas this problem becomes larger. The search for policies must focus on ways to overcome this challenge. In this environment increasing the flexibility of both the labour-force and of employment opportunities would seem to be a critical concern.

In an ever-evolving global economy governments are not likely to be able to identify specific growth poles, growth industries or skill gaps at a fine enough geographic scale to play an active role in managing labour markets. Instead they may want to focus on improving the functioning of labour markets by: improving information flows about jobs, supporting employer-based skill development programmes, increasing the capacity of the educational system to foster life-long learning skills, and trying to ensure that those with limited skills have an opportunity to earn an income. This will be particularly important if current trends in social welfare policy continue to distinguish between the deserving poor — those who have a job — and the undeserving poor. For many rural areas this type of segmentation could be particularly brutal, given current limited opportunities available to much of the populace.

References and further reading

Bartik, Timothy. (1995) Economic development incentive wars. *Employment Research* Vol 2, No. 1 Spring.

Commission of the European Communities. (1993) *White Paper on Growth, Competitiveness and Employment*, COM(93) 700 final, mimeo. Brussels, Dec.

Cunningham, Thomas. (1995) Development incentives: good or bad? *Regional Update: Federal Reserve Bank of Atlanta* Vol 8, No. 1, Jan.

Devine, Theresa and Kieffer, Nicholas. (1991) *Empirical Labor Economics*. New York: Oxford University Press.

Eberts, Randall and Montgomery, Edward. (1994) Employment creation and destruction. *Economic Review: Cleveland Federal Reserve Bank* Vol. 30, No. 2.

Federal Reserve Bank of Kansas City. (undated) *Reducing Unemployment: Current Issues and Policy Options, Symposium Proceedings*. Kansas City MO. Federal Reserve Bank of Kansas City.

Gittleman, Maury and Howell, David (1995). Changes in the structure and quality of jobs in the United States: effects by race and gender, 1973-1990. *Industrial and Labor Relations Review* Vol 48, No. 3, April.

Human Resources Development Canada. (1994) *Improving Social Security In Canada: Discussion Paper Summary*. Ottawa: Human Resources Development Canada, October.

Leigh, Duane. (1995) *Assisting Workers Displaced by Structural Change*. Kalamazoo MI: W.E. Upjohn Institute.

McLarin, Kimberley. (1995) For the poor, defining who deserves what. *New York Times*. Sunday, September 17.

Narisetti, Raju. (1995) Manufacturers decry a shortage of workers while rejecting many. *Wall Street Journal*. September 8.

OECD. (1993) *What Future for Our Countryside?* Paris: OECD.

OECD. (1994a) *The Jobs Study: Facts Analysis Strategies*. Paris: OECD.

OECD. (1994b) *The Jobs Study: Evidence and Explanations*. Paris: OECD.

OECD. (1995a) *The Jobs Study: Implementing the Strategy*. Paris: OECD.

OECD. (1995b) *Creating Employment For Rural Development — New Policy Approaches*. Paris: OECD.

Pankratz, John. (1989) *Job Creation In Rural Areas: A select annotated bibliography*. Corvallis OR: WRDC 37, Western Rural Development Center, Oregon State University.

Phelps, Edmund. (1994) *Structural Slumps*. Cambridge MA: Harvard University Press.

Segal, Lewis and Sullivan, Daniel. (1995) The temporary labor force. *Economic Perspectives: Federal Reserve Bank of Chicago* Vol. XIX, No. 2, March.

van der Laan, Lambert. (1991) *Spatial Labour Markets In The Netherlands*. Delft: Eburon.

Woodford, Michael. (1994) Structural slumps. *Journal of Economic Literature* Vol. XXXII No. 4.

Wren, C. (1994) Some anatomy of job creation. *Environment and Planning* Vol. 26 No. 4.

Chapter twenty-five:

Designing Employment Policy: The Importance of Recognizing Territory

Kirsten Agerup
Ministry of Local Government and Labour, Oslo, Norway

Abstract

Designing a differentiated employment policy which recognizes the territory to its full extent is an important, albeit difficult, task. Today's employment policies must be territorially differentiated, but not along the traditional centre–periphery dimension which has characterized the traditional approach in Norway. It is also a challenge to design an employment policy for the urban areas which is more than just a blueprint of the rural policy and which avoids the zero-sum problem where employment solutions in one region cause employment problems in another region.

Introduction

The importance of recognizing territory in designing employment policy may be summarized with three main observations:

1. priority has traditionally been given to employment problems in the periphery;

2. co-ordination of sectoral policies with implications for employment can best be achieved within limited territorial units; and

3. today's employment policies must be territorially differentiated, but not along the traditional centre–periphery dimension.

Priority has traditionally been given to employment problems in the periphery

In Norway, as in many western countries, we recognize that certain regions have more substantial needs for a broadly designed employment policy than other regions, as indicated by labour market measures and measures of industrial development.

The traditional regional policy approach implies that peripheral areas are given priority within sectoral policies, due to the special needs of these areas. The traditional regional policy in Norway has thus mainly been a policy for the periphery, involving special initiatives, transfers, etc. The aim of this special periphery policy is to compensate for certain peripheral disadvantages. The remote parts of the country have more substantial needs for public support due to long distances and a small population spread over a large area. These special demographic and topographic features affect the basis for development of trade and industries and employment. The problems of unemployment have thus been most dominant in these parts of the country.

Norway is a sparsely populated country (Figure 25.1). Substantial parts of the country have fewer than 5 persons/km^2. The population density in predominantly rural regions in Norway is 8 persons/km^2. However, Canada has a lower population density (3 persons/km^2) with 1 person/km^2 in predominantly rural regions.

As in most industrialized countries, the internal migration from the countryside to the cities has been an ongoing process. The remote areas have experienced a decrease in population, especially among young people and women (Figure 25.2). The remote parts of the country, especially those areas outside commuting distance to a bigger city, have lost more than 5 percent of their population in this period.

Sparse population and long distances to big cities and markets affects the basis for the development of the private sector. It means higher transportation costs for companies competing on national and international markets, limited industrial and commercial environments for business development and limited access to (local) skilled labour.

The main industrial base in rural Norway is the extraction of natural resources, such as fisheries, agriculture, mining and energy-intensive manufacturing. Thus, many firms located in the periphery are heavily dependent on raw materials and they are labour intensive. Like the primary sector industries, these sectors are being forced to rationalize which has lead to a severe decline in employment (Figure 25.3). Municipalities with low centrality and municipalities with medium centrality have both had a larger decrease in employment in the primary and secondary sectors during the 1980s, compared with central areas. As far as the tertiary sector is concerned, the small variations among the different centrality levels masks an important difference — in the periphery, a substantial share of tertiary employment is in the public sector.

Figure 25.1.   Population density in Norwegian municipalities, 1990

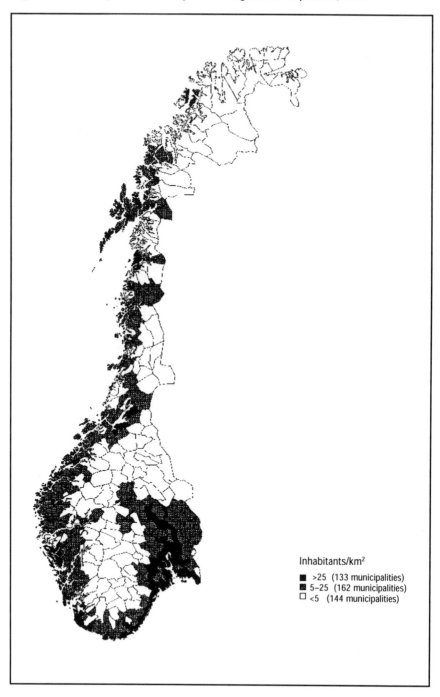

Inhabitants/km²

■ >25 (133 municipalities)
▣ 5–25 (162 municipalities)
□ <5   (144 municipalities)

Figure 25.2.   Population change in Norwegian municipalities, 1980 to 1990

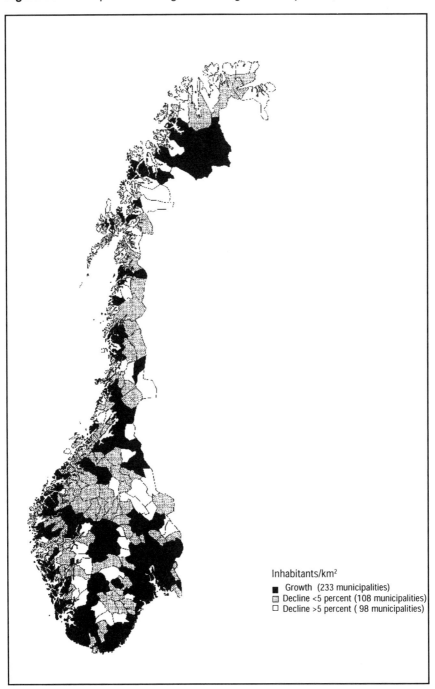

Inhabitants/km²

■ Growth (233 municipalities)
▦ Decline <5 percent (108 municipalities)
□ Decline >5 percent (98 municipalities)

Figure 25.3.   Within each industrial sector, job change was similar, regardless of degree of centrality of the municipality

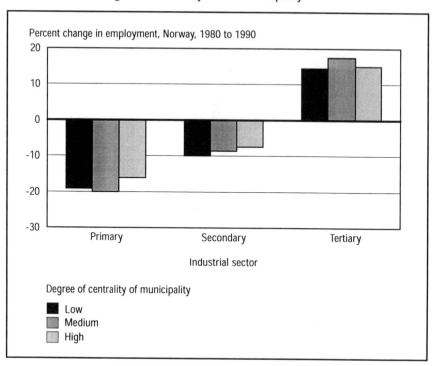

The aim of the special peripheral policy in Norway has thus been to compensate for these disadvantages and to make sure that jobs are distributed so that it is possible to find a means of income in all parts of the country. Most efforts within this rural policy can be understood to be part of a broadly defined employment policy. Particular measures and programmes have been applied in order to stimulate economic activity and employment in general. The most important measures are investment and business development grants, risk capital, special trade programmes and programmes aiming to increase the competence in small and medium-sized enterprises (SMEs).

In addition, special policies have been developed for industries with a significant impact in rural areas. Such policies are applied via government transfers to various industries, mainly agriculture, fisheries and certain manufacturing industries dependent on government support for survival. Such policies are also applied via the geographical distribution pattern of the general state grants to municipalities and counties, the labour market policy and through government investments and operating expenses.

The rural dimension in the agriculture and fishery policy is based on higher levels of fishery quotas and agricultural subsidies to those parts of the country where these industries are of crucial importance for maintaining employment. Labour market measures are much more extensive in rural areas due to higher unemployment. The general state grants to municipalities and counties are higher due to higher expenditures in developing and maintaining public services and administration.

The establishment of state-owned production units has also made a significant contribution to employment development in rural areas. The primarily goal of these units is "production" — they have as a rule not been regarded as part of a rural employment policy. However, the scope of the effort and the arguments for establishing the production units have often taken into account that fact that the units also served peripheral policy objectives. In recent years, state-owned production has been created more to solve local crises in the labour market, implying a more direct peripheral connection.

In general, this broadly defined employment policy has been successful in the sense that both employment and income levels in the remote parts of the country have to a large extent been equal to the rest of the country. The introduction of the state transfer-system to regional and local levels in the 1970s has however had the greatest effects on the employment development in remote areas. Public services expanded at high growth rates and ensured a strong growth in public employment. The share of employment in public sector accounts for more than 36 percent of total employment in the remote municipalities, compared with 32 percent in the central areas.

Co-ordination of sectoral policies with implications for employment can best be achieved within limited territorial units

The other approach to recognizing territory is to recognize the importance of regional and local levels when it comes to designing employment policy. The regions have different advantages and when more decisions are co-ordinated within limited territorial units, it will be easier to adapt the measures to the different regional conditions. Since increased interregional and international competition encourages regional specialization, decentralized systems may, in fortunate circumstances, lead to a more flexible adjustment to escalating competition.

During the 1980s, increasing national problems connected to stronger competition from abroad, serious structural problems in production and increasing unemployment posed new challenges to the special peripheral employment policy. In this situation, it was convenient for the central authorities to delegate more responsibility to lower regional levels. An altered orientation, with less attention to redistribution and more to local entrepreneurship and economic growth, also emphasized the importance of local co-ordination of labour market measures and measures promoting industrial development.

These factors accelerated the process of decentralization of responsibility and authority to local levels. This process was partly pushed by local bodies and partly encouraged by the central authorities. The political climate throughout the 1970s made legitimate a grass-roots based philosophy which encouraged the idea of greater local responsibility. Moreover it was easy to point to problems resulting from specific national decisions, often made on a narrow sectoral basis, and very often lacking a territorial approach. The favourable development in the periphery during this period also gave rise to increasing local self-confidence.

To improve the ability of local authorities to develop a comprehensive employment policy, regional and local levels were given a greater degree of control over funds and general public budgets. It became the responsibility of regional authorities to design suitable measures for the development of employment. In addition special experiments have been initiated to improve coordination of different employment measures at the regional level and to improve the cooperation among different local authorities.

These different initiatives have proved that a coordination of measures and a more tailor-made employment policy can best be obtained within limited territorial units. Several evaluations have emphasized the positive effects of a comprehensive local policy for the development of local labour markets.

Today's employment policies must be territorially differentiatcd, but not along the traditional centre–periphery dimension

The last approach to recognizing territory is that today's employment policies must be territorially differentiated, but not only along the traditional centre–periphery line. A broadly defined policy to increase employment must encompass the different roles and problems of the various regions. Different regions play different but equally important roles in the national economy and the state efforts to promote economic growth must be correspondingly differentiated.

This perspective is controversial in Norway. The Norwegian employment policy has not recognized or encountered the special features or problems in the cities, or in the more central parts of the country. In designing an employment policy, the focus has been, as I have outlined above, directed to a large extent to development problems and possibilities in the remote areas. In this way one might say that the scope has been geographically limited. The recognition of territory has been limited to the peripheral areas and special measures to compensate peripheral disadvantages have been implemented at the cost of urban areas and bigger cities.

This perspective is however changing. The increasing unemployment in central areas has to some extent altered the traditional focus and lead to a redefinition of the territorial profile of employment policy. This implies that the attention has been extended and the problems of unemployment in the central areas are placed on the agenda. In addition, increased internationalization has lead to a redirection of the political focus towards Norway's ability to compete on the international market. With this new basis, it has become important to stimulate the growth of the centres, as many of the firms best equipped to compete internationally are located there. The result of this new approach is a steady attempt to develop an urban policy that gives the large centres better opportunities to meet stronger international competition.

A first step is just being taken to encompass the cities within the regionally differentiated employment policy. This has not however lead to a special policy towards these areas. The discussion so far has focused on welfare problems in the cities and less on how to stimulate economic growth and employment possibilities. The discussion has also focused on the unequal distribution of state transfers among the different parts of the country.

The general challenge concerning a employment policy tailor-made for each region is thus to avoid a zero-sum situation, where solving employment problems in one region causes unemployment in other areas. It is also a challenge to design an employment policy for the urban areas which is more than just a blueprint of the rural policy.

Designing a differentiated employment policy which recognizes the territory to its full extent is thus an important and a rather difficult task. And we are yet to begin to develop a policy along this line.

Chapter twenty-six:

Employment Policies and Economic Restructuring in the Canadian North: Roots of a Paradox

Scott McLean
University of Saskatchewan, Saskatoon, Saskatchewan, Canada

Abstract

There are few economically viable activities upon which wage employment can be based in remote regions of northern Canada. nevertheless, federal policies locate training and jobs as central to northern development. Public policies supporting wage employment in the North resulted from peculiar historical circumstances rather than strategic initiatives to manage economic restructuring. Prior to 1945, Canadian policies discouraged Inuit employment and endeavoured to maintain traditional Inuit self-sufficiency. It was only with the collapse of the fur trade, and the increased pressure to assert Canadian sovereignty over the North during the Cold War, that federal governments began promoting Inuit employment. Within a few years, the official policy of tolerating Inuit wage employment had developed into a policy actively celebrating wage employment as a means to promote northern development and Inuit welfare. There is a need for creative alternatives to contemporary economic policy for remote areas.

Introduction

Wage employment in northern Canada involves a paradoxical combination of public policies and economic structures. On the one hand, wage employment is widely accepted as central to northern development and diversification. On the other hand, there are few economically viable activities upon which wage employment can exist in the North without government support. Northern communities typically have high rates of unemployment and welfare dependency and where substantial numbers of jobs do exist, they depend on government spending or non-renewable resource extraction. Official policies encouraging wage employment in regions where such employment is not tenable without government subsidies are clearly not sustainable and would even seem irrational if viewed in isolation from their historical and political context.

This chapter investigates the evolution of economic structures and employment policies in the Canadian North. It seeks to understand the roots of paradoxical policies of promoting employment where employment cannot be sustained. It demonstrates that public policies supporting wage employment in the North resulted from peculiar historical circumstances rather than strategic initiatives to manage economic restructuring. To accomplish these tasks, this chapter examines the history of economic activities and federal employment policies in the Kitikmeot region of the Northwest Territories. By focusing on a particular region, one can recognize how public policies concerning employment and economic restructuring in the North have shifted dramatically. Current policies promoting Inuit wage employment are directly opposed to earlier policies promoting a self-sufficient, domestic northern economy. While this chapter deals exclusively with the Canadian North, its observations concerning wage employment policies and economic restructuring are relevant to the experiences of other countries with remote rural populations.

The Kitikmeot: contemporary economic structures

The Kitikmeot is one of three administrative regions in Nunavut, which is the eastern political and administrative territory currently being created through the division of the Northwest Territories. About 4,500 people now live in the region's seven communities, four of which are on the central Arctic mainland and three of which are on Victoria and King William Islands. There are no roads or railways into the region. Roughly 90 percent of the people in the Kitikmeot are Inuit, and most of the remaining people are Euro-Canadians whose residence in the region is typically not permanent. Wage employment is central to the region's economy. Labour force participation is low and unemployment is high (Table 26.1).

Table 26.1. High variability in labour force attachment among communities in Kitikmeot, 1989

Community	Persons over 15	Participation rate (percent)	Unemployment rate (percent)
Bathurst/Bay Chimo	51	10	20
Cambridge Bay	671	71	18
Coppermine	598	47	37
Gjoa Haven	394	54	52
Holman	214	59	13
Pelly Bay	200	58	45
Spence Bay	329	46	32
KITIKMEOT:	**2,457**	**56**	**31**

Source: N.W.T. Bureau of Statistics, 1989, p. 16.

Kitikmeot patterns of economic activity are common across northern Canada. Wage labour participation is fairly widespread and unemployment rates are very high. Government jobs provide nearly half of all cash income in the region and over half of that income is earned in the administrative centre of Cambridge Bay (Table 26.2). Direct transfer payments are substantial sources of income in most communities, and hunting and trapping account for between one-third and one-half of gross income outside of Cambridge Bay. Income per capita is low, especially when one considers that food and consumer goods typically cost more than twice what they would in Edmonton.

Table 26.2.   Private sector wage income represents only 39 percent of Kitikmeot cash income, 1984

	Part I: Sources of cash income ($,000)					
Community	Private wages	Gov't wages	Trapping transfers	Federal transfers	N.W.T. cash	Total
Bathurst/Bay Chimo	43.5	nil	12.0	nil	5.5	61.0
	71%	20%	9%	100%		
Cambridge Bay	3967.8	6947.2	54.1	279.4	150.0	11398.5
	35%	61%	0.5%	2.5%	1%	100%
Coppermine	603.1	1002.2	112.5	355.0	164.4	2237.2
	27%	45%	5%	16%	7%	100%
Gjoa Haven	1135.4	846.7	32.9	179.9	206.1	2401.0
	47%	35%	1%	7%	9%	100%
Holman	892.0	274.4	63.2	159.8	36.4	1425.8
	63%	19%	4%	11%	3%	100%
Pelly Bay	775.0	358.8	24.5	116.0	50.4	1324.7
	59%	27%	2%	9%	4%	100%
Spence Bay	768.6	804.3	43.9	159.3	217.9	1994.0
	39%	40%	2%	8%	11%	100%
KITIKMEOT	**8185.4**	**10233.6**	**343.1**	**1249.4**	**830.7**	**20842.2**
	39%	**49%**	**2%**	**6%**	**4%**	**100%**

	Part II: Non-Cash and Total Incomes ($,000)			
Community	Estimated value of country foods	Total income	Trapping and country foods as percent of total	Income per capita
Bathurst/Bay Chimo	271.2	332.2	85	4.0
Cambridge Bay	1,383.3	12,781.8	11	14.2
Coppermine	1,556.5	3,793.7	44	4.2
Gjoa Haven	1,639.2	4,040.2	41	6.6
Holman	1,189.5	2,615.3	48	7.6
Pelly Bay	558.2	1,882.9	31	6.6
Spence Bay	1141.4	3,135.4	38	6.7
KITIKMEOT	**7,739.3**	**28,581.5**	**28**	**8.0**

Source: N.W.T., D.E.D.T., 1985, p. 116 and p. 147).

Wage employment in the Kitikmeot is divided among a number of sectors: government services (25 percent); wholesale and retail sales (16 percent); education (12 percent); other services (12 percent); transportation and communications (9 percent); resources (9 percent); construction and manufacturing (6 percent); food and accommodation (2 percent); and miscellaneous (4 percent) (N.W.T., D.E.D.T., 1989, p.13). Certain jobs are common throughout the Kitikmeot, including: government jobs with schools, nursing stations, and administrative offices; municipal services such as trucking water, sewerage, or garbage, and maintaining houses; retail services in the Co-op or Northern stores, small convenience stores, or restaurants; transport jobs such as taxi driver or airline agent; summer labour building houses or maintaining roads; and tourism work with hunting outfitters, fishing lodges or the Co-op hotel. Two important aspects of employment in the Kitikmeot must be noted. First, there are substantial ethnic and gender differences in economic activities. Second, governments either directly employ, contract, subsidize, or fund almost all wage workers in the region. The importance of government spending to the economy is even greater when one considers the role of statutory income transfers, welfare payments, and food, fuel and shelter subsidies.

A labour force survey conducted in 1989 (N.W.T. Bureau of Statistics, 1990b) found a total of 2,136 Inuit and 322 Euro-Canadians over the age of 15 years in the Kitikmeot. Of these totals, 60 percent of Inuit and 95 percent of Euro-Canadians participated in the wage labour market. However, while 85 percent of Euro-Canadians were employed for more than half of 1988, only one-quarter of Inuit were employed for such a duration. Euro-Canadians were not significantly engaged in non-wage economic activities. Non-wage activities were very important for Kitikmeot Inuit. Hunting, fishing and trapping were very common for Inuit men. Roughly 76 percent hunted or fished during 1988 and 22 percent trapped. For Inuit women, traditional crafts were a significant area of economic activity, with 44 percent of them involved. These numbers suggest different patterns of subsistence for Inuit and Euro-Canadians in the Kitikmeot. Euro-Canadians worked for wages in offices, schools, stores and other institutions. Most Inuit had less regular employment patterns and mixed a variety of activities in order to subsist. Hunting, fishing, trapping, and handicraft production were combined with periods of employment or dependence upon government transfer payments. Wage and non-wage economic activities were interdependent. Cash income was needed to buy equipment for non-wage activities, while hunting and fishing provided subsistence goods which reduced the need to labour.

There is substantial income inequality between different communities in the Kitikmeot (Tables 26.1 and 26.2). Such inequality also existed between individuals, as indicated by income tax returns. In 1986, there were 2,340 people over the age of 15 years in the Kitikmeot. Of these: 24 percent filed no personal income tax return; 41 percent claimed incomes between $1 and $10,000; 10 percent earned between $10,001 and $20,000; 9 percent earned between $20,001 and $30,000; 5 percent earned between $30,001 and $40,000; and 11 percent earned more than $40,000 (N.W.T., D.E.D.T., 1989, p. 16). Substantial income inequality reflects differential access to high paying, stable jobs. Most Euro-Canadians and some Inuit hold such jobs, while a majority of Inuit do not.

Government wages and transfers are the cornerstones of the contemporary Kitikmeot economy. Without such wages and transfers, neither private employment nor hunting could continue at their present levels. The region lacks internally generated economic activities that could sustain its population. Currently, this lack of self-sufficiency is offset by maintaining a regional trade deficit. There is a substantial commodity flow deficit (Tables 26.3 and 26.4).

Table 26.3.   Arts and crafts account for 63 percent of Kitikmeot commodity exports, 1984

Community	Commodity exports ($,000)			
	Arts/crafts	Fish	Fur	Total exports
Bathurst/Bay Chimo	nil	nil	12.4	12.4
Cambridge Bay	160.4	180.2	21.0	361.6
Coppermine	134.3	nil	67.7	202.0
Gjoa Haven	85.1	nil	21.1	106.2
Holman	182.2	nil	33.9	216.1
Pelly Bay	13.3	nil	4.2	17.5
Spence Bay	45.1	nil	19.0	64.1
KITIKMEOT	620.4	180.2	179.3	979.9

Table 26.4.   Kitikmeot had a regional trade deficit of $5,400 per capita in 1984

Community	Net commodity imports ($,000)			
	Total imports	Total exports	Net imports	Net imports per capita
Bathurst/Bay Chimo	386.8	12.4	374.4	4.7
Cambridge Bay	6,559.5	361.6	6,197.9	7.3
Coppermine	3,184.6	202.0	2,982.6	3.7
Gjoa Haven	2,438.4	106.2	2332.2	4.4
Holman	1,507.9	216.1	1,291.8	4.4
Pelly Bay	1,104.5	17.5	1,087.0	4.2
Spence Bay	3,204.9	64.1	3,140.8	7.2
KITIKMEOT	18,386.6	979.9	17,406.7	5.4

Source: N.W.T., D.E.D.T., 1985, p. 73 and p. 116.

Arts and crafts accounted for 63 percent of all exports, while fur trapping and the Cambridge Bay commercial fishery each accounted for slightly less than 19 percent. Wage employment was involved in very little export generating activity. For the region as a whole, imports were distributed in the following general categories: fuel (48 percent); food (16 percent); vehicles and equipment

(16 percent); building supplies (15 percent); and general merchandise (5 percent). A very large regional trade deficit existed, with net imports of $5,400 worth of goods per capita. These figures do not include the value of services, such as transportation and tourism. However, if data were available for the flow of services in and out of the Kitikmeot, the quoted trade deficit would expand greatly.

Clearly, the Kitikmeot economy is dependent upon external sources of goods, services, and income. A huge trade deficit exists and two forms of income transfers are important. Government to government transfers provide wages, services, and subsidies for the region. Government to individual transfers are a significant source of income in most communities. In both cases, the government providing the transferred income receives the overwhelming majority of its resources from outside the Kitikmeot. Thus, the Kitikmeot economy depends upon the continued willingness of governments to collect resources from elsewhere in Canada, and redistribute them into the Kitikmeot. Despite such dependence, and despite the lack of internally sustainable economic activities upon which to base wage employment, official policies place wage employment at the centre of northern development initiatives (D.I.A.N.D., 1989; N.W.T. Department of Education, 1990; N.W.T. Legislative Assembly, 1989). To understand the paradox of promoting employment where employment does not appear sustainable, one needs to investigate the history of northern policies and economic structures.

Protecting them from civilization: economic restructuring and employment policies in the fur trade era

Kitikmeot Inuit experienced two massive economic restructuring processes in the past 80 years. In the first half of this century, aboriginal patterns of subsistence activity were transformed through fur trade practices and increasing dependence on Euro-Canadian products. In the second half of this century, the world market for white fox furs collapsed and Kitikmeot Inuit became dependent on wage employment and government transfer payments. Canadian policies concerning Inuit employment changed dramatically between these two periods. In the fur trade, government policies opposed northern development and sought to maintain the self-sufficiency of traditional Inuit subsistence practices. With the collapse of fur prices in the Cold War however, government policies began to promote Inuit modernization and sought to transform the northern economy through education, employment and the construction of permanent settlements.

For centuries prior to the twentieth, Kitikmeot Inuit lived in flexible, semi-nomadic collectivities and met their subsistence needs through annual cycles of economic activities (Balikci, 1989; Damas, 1984, 1988; Freeman, 1976). In the winter, Kitikmeot Inuit lived on the sea ice and hunted seals. In some areas, additional food was procured by hunting polar bears and using supplies of caribou and fish which had been killed the previous summer. In the spring, the main activities were hunting seals and caribou and fishing through the ice on lakes and rivers near the coast. In the summer Kitikmeot Inuit moved inland, fishing and hunting caribou. Additional food was obtained in various areas by: hunting musk-oxen, birds, and small game; picking berries; and collecting eggs from birds' nests. In the fall, Kitikmeot Inuit prepared for their return to the sea ice and survived on cached food and freshwater ice fishing. While life expectancy, food security and material comforts would have been unacceptable by contemporary standards, Kitikmeot Inuit had community-based economic structures that were both ecologically and economically sustainable.

Euro-Canadian exploration in the Kitikmeot began in the late eighteenth century, but sustained Euro-Canadian activities did not begin until the second and third decades of this century. These activities were structured by the rise and fall of white fox fur trading, which began just prior to 1910, boomed in the 1920s, and virtually collapsed by the late 1940s. The number of active fur trade locations expanded rapidly in the 1920s, declined steadily from 1930 to 1950, and then levelled off at ten or less (Table 26.5). During the peak of the fur trade, virtually every inhabited area of the Kitikmeot became an active site of white fox trapping and trading. Fur trade posts were scattered along the coastline throughout the region.

Table 26.5.   The number of Kitikmeot fur trade posts peaked in the 1925–29 period

Years	Number of active locations			Number of active posts		
	Regional total	Western Kitikmeot	Eastern Kitikmeot	Regional total	Western Kitikmeot	Eastern Kitikmeot
1916–1919	5	5	0	6	6	0
1920–1924	9	7	2	9	7	2
1925–1929	25	18	7	35	25	10
1930–1934	21	17	4	34	28	6
1935–1939	19	16	3	28	21	7
1940–1944	14	10	4	17	11	6
1945–1949	12	6	6	13	7	6
1950–1954	9	4	5	9	4	5
1955–1959	10	4	6	11	4	7
1960–1964	10	5	5	10	5	5
1965–1969	8	3	5	9	4	5
1970–present	6	2	4	6	2	4
Grand total	**39**	**28**	**11**	**67**	**48**	**19**

Source: Usher, 1971.

The fur trade brought substantial changes to Kitikmeot Inuit subsistence practices (Balikci, 1989; Damas, 1984, 1988; Freeman, 1976). White fox trapping and trading began gradually and there was much local variation in the speed and intensity with which trapping was adopted. Initially, "floating" posts supplied Inuit with steel traps, iron tools and a few guns. During the trading boom of the

1920s, Inuit acquired fairly regular supplies of ammunition, rifles, steel traps, fish nets and boats. The introduction of trapping into annual cycles of subsistence activities, combined with the technological changes introduced through trading with Euro-Canadians, eventually transformed Kitikmeot Inuit subsistence practices. Even in areas where trapping never became a primary activity, the introduction of rifles and fish nets was a substantial technological change.

The cumulative impact of these basic changes was **a significant disorganization of aboriginal subsistence practices.** By the end of the fur trade era, economic production and consumption had been significantly individualized and Kitikmeot Inuit had become dependent upon Euro-Canadian trade goods. For centuries, Inuit had depended for survival upon the resources of land and sea and upon the social cooperation of larger collectivities of Inuit. With the entrenchment of fur trading, they gradually depended upon Euro-Canadian equipment and consumer goods and upon fluctuations in white fox prices. Over time, Kitikmeot Inuit became dependent upon trade for the very means with which they produced their subsistence. Earnings from trapping were converted into productive equipment. Such equipment needed regular income for its maintenance and use, so Kitikmeot Inuit entered a cycle of dependence upon commercial exchange. Dependency intensified as changes in technology, skills, and social organization prohibited Inuit from relying upon traditional subsistence practices. Unfortunately, the fur trade was characterized by both cyclical variations in fox catches and an overall decline in the terms of trade for trappers (Public Archives of Canada: RG 85, v. 1389, f. 405-6, pt. 1 and 2; RG 85, v. 1497, f. 405-6, pt. 3; RG 85, v. 1215, f. 405-6, pt. 5). During the 1920s, the average price per white fox pelt in Canada was $39.79; this figure declined to $18.36 for the 1930s, $20.59 for the 1940s, and $9.92 for the first five years of the 1950s. During the same period, the prices charged for trade goods, and the dependence of Kitikmeot Inuit on such trade goods, increased substantially.

Although Kitikmeot Inuit were still living on the land in 1950, their subsistence practices had changed substantially since 1910. Fur trading was the most obvious change. Fox trapping had become a significant activity by the 1940s; fox catches at each locale varied widely from year to year; and mean family incomes from fur were substantial, but extremely variable (Table 26.6).

Economic restructuring during the fur trade had an important impact on life in the Kitikmeot. By 1950 Kitikmeot Inuit subsistence practices had been altered considerably through: inclusion of white fox trapping as a significant economic activity; technological changes in hunting, especially the use of guns, fish nets and boats; consumption of foreign goods, such as food, tobacco, clothing, and canvas; and access to statutory transfer payments and government relief.

Table 26.6.   Family earnings from fur varied from $99 to $2,079

	Community				
	Holman	Read Island	Coppermine	Bathurst Inlet	Cambridge Bay, Gjoa Haven, Perry River
	Gross number of white foxes trapped per post (mean family income in parentheses)				
1942	1,277 ($762)	1,937 ($597)	554 ($166)	2,045 ($687)	6,929 ($599)
1943	3,006 ($2,079)	5,716 ($2,026)	423 ($141)	2,171 ($836)	12,025 ($1,249)
1944	462 ($418)	792 ($362)	208 ($116)	993 ($503)	3,242 ($407)
1945	494 ($406)	702 ($299)	198 ($99)	867 ($354)	2,910 ($291)
1946	1,763 ($1,226)	3,740 ($1,357)	638 ($311)	1,459 ($583)	10,706 ($1,021)
1947	3,744 ($1,978)	3,272 ($329)	661 ($152)	1,483 ($457)	10,635 ($751)
Number of families	23	46	55	43	175

Source: H.B.C. statement of Inuit fur earnings, from RG 85, v. 98, f. 252-1-2, pt. 1; Letter from R.H. Chesshire to R.A. Gibson.

Wage employment never became a significant economic activity during the fur trade era. Within the mercantile exchange relations of the fur trade, Inuit were simple commodity producers, and only engaged in wage labour during special circumstances, such as annual unloading of supplies from trading company ships. Government policy concerning Inuit employment was clear — Inuit were to be encouraged to follow their traditional means of earning a livelihood and those traditions did not involve wage labour. In an effort to minimize expenditures on Inuit affairs, federal governments prior to the Second World War explicitly opposed Inuit education and employment. The goal of maintaining traditional economic activities even led federal governments to restrict the activities of fur traders in the Kitikmeot. Throughout the fur trade era, Canadian governments were relatively inactive in the Kitikmeot. State organized interventions were generally limited to: using R.C.M.P. patrols to enforce laws, collect vital statistics, survey health and welfare conditions, and symbolize Canadian sovereignty; creating regulations to govern hunting, trapping, and trading practices; and providing medical supplies to missions for distribution to sick Inuit. All three of these projects explicitly tried to keep Kitikmeot Inuit living on the land and to "protect" them from the impact of civilization.

While it may seem surprising to those familiar with contemporary government policies in the North, federal policies in the fur trade era actually opposed northern development. Several examples illustrate the opposition of federal officials to any activities that had the potential to interfere with Inuit self-sufficiency and thus increase government expenditures in the North. By 1923, game preserves prevented non-natives from hunting or trapping in much of the Kitikmeot (RG 85, v. 1069, f. 251-1, pt. 1). These restrictions did not apply to the operation of trading posts. By 1924, R.C.M.P. officers were reporting an "unprecedented scarcity" of caribou in the Coronation Gulf and attributing that scarcity to the presence of fur trade posts. Reports of caribou scarcity were taken quite seriously by bureaucrats in Ottawa. On October 16, 1924, W.W. Cory (Commissioner of the Northwest Territory (N.W.T.)) wrote letters to two representatives of the Hudson's Bay Company:

> *From time to time reports are received in this office advising us of the disappearance of caribou and other game in the western Arctic, and the privation of the natives and their want through lack of food and clothing.*
>
> *It is reported that, to a large extent, these conditions are brought about by reason of the establishment of trading posts of your company and others and I thought it advisable to inform you of these reports, in order that you might have an opportunity of replying....*
>
> *There are trading posts established at Bernard Harbour, Coppermine River, Kugaruk River, Tree River, Kent Peninsula, and Cambridge Bay. They are not all your posts but they are established at strategic points and seem to have been the means of preventing the caribou from making their usual migration to and from Victoria Island. The smell of the coal smoke also seems to have been a factor in driving them away. It is estimated that eight hundred Copper Eskimo will be affected by the shortage in caribou this year, while the entire dependence of all natives on this animal for food, clothing, bedding, and summer shelter, lends a very serious aspect to the situation....*
>
> *I wish also to refer to the alleged exorbitant prices charged in many cases for supplies to the natives...The consequence is, in the native villages there seems to be a great many instances of actual want and privation and in some places they are actually boiling old deer skins from which the hair has been scraped, for food. This is naturally very severe on the children and is the result, in some cases, of infanticide and the destruction of the old and infirm. As evidence of the lack of food it is stated your Tree River detachment ordered frozen Reindeer to be shipped in this summer from Point Barrow. No doubt the introduction of modern firearms by traders has much to do with this deplorable condition.*
>
> *It is possible that the Department may consider setting apart an area on the Arctic coast, including the Arctic Islands, on which trading posts would not be allowed (85, v. 1069, f. 251-1, pt. 1).*

Concern over game scarcity led to: the 1925 establishment of permit requirements for establishing or maintaining trading posts within the N.W.T. (85, v. 1069, f. 251-1, pt. 1); the 1926 expansion of existing game preserves to include all of the Arctic Islands, and most of mainland eastern Kitikmeot (85, v. 1069, f. 251-1, pt. 1); the 1927 closure of three Hudson's Bay Company (H.B.C.) posts in the Kitikmeot; and the prohibition of exporting caribou skins from the N.W.T. (Jenness, 1964, p. 34).

Despite efforts to regulate fur traders and maintain traditional patterns of Inuit economic activity, Canadian governments were faced with pressures for increased expenditures on Inuit affairs during the fur trade. In a May 23, 1933 memorandum to H.H. Rowatt (Deputy Minister of the Interior), H.E. Hume (Department of the Interior) made the following assessment of government relief expenditures in the Coppermine area:

> *The gathering of destitute natives and widows at this post since the establishment of the Missions and Government Services indicates that certain of the natives are becoming indolent, which, experience has shown, often is the case, when our institutions become established in native settlements. The natives are attracted to such points and it is difficult to persuade them to return to their hunting grounds. Prior to the establishment of trading posts in Coronation Gulf, which took place about ten years ago, the Department was not called upon to provide relief for the natives of that district. Congregation of the natives at such points is detrimental to their health and it is apparent that it will become necessary to increase our appropriation for relief purposes in the Coppermine area. In light of experience it seems desirable that the policy of the Department which restricts trading to three points in the Arctic Islands Preserve, be rigidly adhered to. This will prevent the traders extending their activities to the east of the Coppermine area (85, v. 1129, f. 253-1, pt. 1).*

Through the 1920s and 1930s, Canadian governments minimized expenditures by preventing Inuit from congregating at fur trade posts and by requiring fur traders to pay relief costs for Inuit with whom they traded. O.S. Finnie summarized this policy in a June 22, 1928 letter to C.H. French of the H.B.C. Finnie stated that the company, rather than the government, was responsible for the maintenance of fur trading Inuit during "periods of stress". He stated that the H.B.C. and Government had a common interest:

> *to keep the native strong and healthy and to make him a self-reliant and independent citizen and I am satisfied that if we work together wholeheartedly along these lines, the amount of relief which will be necessary to grant will be reduced to a minimum and the condition of the native greatly improved (85, v. 1130, f. 253-1, pt. 2).*

Through the 1930s, Canadian governments used systems of permits and game preserves to control the number of posts in the Kitikmeot and to force trading companies to pay the costs of relieving destitution.

Government correspondence from the 1930s reveals a consistent effort to minimize expenditures on relief. On July 13, 1933, the N.W.T. Commissioner wrote to all active fur trade companies:

> *As a matter of Departmental Policy very little, if any, relief will be advanced in cases where there seems to be no reason why the half-breed or native should not be able to maintain himself and family ... It is not desired that any steps should be taken that would lessen in any way the sense of responsibility on the part of the natives towards their aged and helpless brethren, and we do not wish to encourage these natives to congregate in settlements away from hunting and trapping areas.*

> *The necessary relief will be distributed sparingly and in such fashion*
> *that those capable of earning sustenance otherwise (for themselves and*
> *their dependants) will not be encouraged to settle down comfortably*
> *under relief conditions and continue to live on charity (85, v. 1129, f.*
> *253-1, pt. 1).*

In order to enforce this parsimonious relief policy, the Department of the Interior endeavoured to maintain Inuit aboriginal subsistence practices. On Jan. 13, 1934, J. Lorne Turner (Director, Dominion Lands Branch) received a memorandum which summarized government strategies for minimizing Inuit relief costs. The memo suggested:

> *The large game preserves already created in the N.W.T. for the sole*
> *benefit of the Indian and Eskimo, and the increased license fees and*
> *similar restrictions placed upon white trappers and traders, have*
> *already shown beneficial results and the native is following his*
> *traditional means of earning a livelihood. Both traders and*
> *missionaries are co-operating with the Department to prevent the*
> *Eskimo becoming a public charge and are using their best endeavours*
> *to keep him a respectable and responsible citizen (85, v. 1129, f.*
> *253-1, pt. 1).*

In the 1930s, Canadian governments endeavoured to spend as little as possible on Inuit affairs, with the apparent belief that hunting and trapping economies would continue indefinitely.

In the 1940s, Canadian governments became increasingly active in providing relief to Kitikmeot Inuit. In 1940–41, the entire federal outlay for direct relief in the region was $307.76. In addition to the remarkable expansion of direct relief costs in the late 1940s (Table 26.7), the federal government also began paying Family Allowances and Old Age Pensions to Kitikmeot Inuit. Family Allowances quickly became an important source of credit at fur trade posts. Although Family Allowances were initiated in 1945, Kitikmeot Inuit did not begin to receive them until 1948. These transfer payments were paid in kind; Inuit received credit at fur trade posts, for which they could obtain articles from an "authorized list of food, clothing, and equipment" (85, v. 1130, f. 253-1, pt. 2). Increases in government relief expenditures can be attributed to three main factors: declining terms of trade for white fox trappers; increasing reliance of Kitikmeot Inuit subsistence practices upon Euro-Canadian equipment; and an overall increase in Canadian government interventionism after 1945.

Table 26.7.   Federal relief expenditures in Kitikmeot increased by 60 times from 1945 to 1955

Year	Spence Bay	Cambridge Bay	Coppermine	Total
1945–46	-	32.50	388.74	421.24
1946–47	-	140.36	869.13	1,009.49
1947–48	-	145.93	684.21	830.14
1948–49	-	1,790.68	1,580.23	3,370.91
1949–50	2,009.00	3,191.65	4,393.44	9,594.09
1950–51	2,360.57	1,175.85	4,590.58	8,127.00
1951–52	3,214.71	1,407.70	2,880.89	7,503.30
1952–53	2,863.78	2,609.61	5,616.01	11,089.40
1953–54	6,561.98	15.75	5,604.94	12,182.67
1954–55	5,913.81	10,330.71	9,161.09	25,405.61

Sources: 85, v. 1130, f. 253-1, pt. 2, pt. 4; 85, v. 1475, f. 253-1, pt. 6).

In 1948 and 1949, both the H.B.C. and the federal government expressed concerns "about the welfare of the Eskimos and the effect on them of the virtual collapse of the White Fox market" (85, v. 1130, f. 253-1, pt. 3; Letter from Chesshire to Gibson, May 13, 1949). The basic presumptions of correspondence from these years were that: fur prices would recover; Inuit would still obtain their subsistence from hunting and trapping; during periods of low fur prices, the H.B.C. would continue to support efficient trappers and the government would provide subsistence relief to inefficient trappers, and Inuit unable to provide for themselves. A circular letter of October 24, 1949 summarized official policy:

> *The Eskimos have always been independent and characteristically dependent upon each other. There is no reason for this custom to be discontinued. Every encouragement should be given these people to live upon the resources of the land and sea, and relief should not be issued unless it is definitely established that it is necessary to do so. Particular care should be given when considering issuing assistance to able-bodied, inefficient trappers - they should be encouraged as much as possible to rely on their own efforts rather than upon Government assistance (85, v. 1130, f. 253-1, pt. 3).*

This policy statement was consistent with the overall policy of Canadian governments toward Inuit in the 1910–1950 era. In the words of one Canadian bureaucrat, this policy amounted to "keeping the native native" (Diubaldo, 1989).

Preparing them for the modern world: employment policies and economic restructuring during the Cold War era

Prior to the Second World War, Canadian policies consistently endeavoured to restrict the modernization of the Kitikmeot economy. The Department of Mines and Resources (1943, p. 18) suggested that the federal government wanted to preserve Inuit self-reliance:

For generations the Eskimos of Canada have wrested a living, mated, and reared a family in a country where only a hardy and intelligent race could survive. They are slowly assimilating a certain amount of civilization while still retaining their independence, pride, and ability to care for themselves. Most of them now appreciate the value of conserving the natural resources of the country in which they live and co-operate in that work to a marked degree. Even though they may not always quite understand the meaning and purpose of the law, the natural tendency of the Eskimos is to obey it. Their communal life has taught them that the wishes of the individual must be subordinated to the good of the majority and this has made them especially easy to deal with. For a number of years the Government of Canada has been paying special attention to its Arctic citizens, in order to keep them independent, self-reliant, and self-supporting, and with this object in view has put forth continuous and unremitting efforts to preserve the natural resources of the country so that the Eskimos may continue to be the admirable race of people they now are.

During the Cold War era however, the romantic policy of maintaining Inuit traditions was gradually replaced with a concerted effort to modernize the Inuit and restructure the Kitikmeot economy. From 1945 to 1955, government policy concerning Inuit employment was reversed; rather than being seen as a dangerous threat to Inuit self-sufficiency, wage employment became seen as an essential path to prosperity, economic growth and northern development.

Canadian governments dramatically increased their activities in the Kitikmeot after 1950. Diubaldo (1985, p. 163), commenting on the lack of government activity in the Arctic prior to 1945, states that administrative "parsimony and the relative inaccessibility of the North were determining factors, but just as important were the prevailing laissez-faire philosophies regarding government intervention, and the view that Inuit should rely almost exclusively on the land and its resources". In the decade after the Second World War, several factors combined to end this laissez-faire orientation toward Inuit and the North (Diubaldo, 1985, 1989; Morrison, 1986; Nixon, 1990; Zaslow, 1988). First, there was a growing perception that the fur trade economy had collapsed and that Inuit were suffering as a result. Second, concern for asserting Canadian sovereignty in the Arctic was heightened by American military presence during and after the Second World War. Third, changing technologies gave the Arctic greater strategic significance during the Cold War. Fourth, government intervention increased throughout Canadian society. Fifth, a popular notion emerged that northern resources would be the engine of Canada's future economic growth. Finally, improvements in communication and transportation made Arctic regions more accessible.

These factors did not lead to an immediate shift in Canadian policies concerning Inuit wage employment. In the early 1950s, government activities were still aimed at preserving hunting and trapping lifestyles. Official correspondence from this period frequently lamented the tendency for Inuit to congregate near posts, where Family Allowances and relief could be obtained (85, v. 1069, f. 251-1, pt. 1a). For example, in a January 16, 1952 memorandum for the N.W.T. Commissioner, F. Cunningham (N.W.T. Deputy Commissioner) wrote that a "major problem" in "Eskimo affairs" was the reaction of

> *Eskimo to relief and family allowances. In particular, it appeared that the knowledge that relief and family allowances were available results in many cases in decreased effort by Eskimo to make a living by hunting and trapping, and that an attempt was being made to overcome this difficulty by refusing relief where the Eskimo was not doing all that he could to support himself and his family, and by restricting as far as possible the benefits of family allowances to the children for whose benefit they are intended.*

Cunningham went on to suggest that all sources and uses of Inuit income should be regulated by either the N.W.T. Council, or the H.B.C. Frustration with the impact of Family Allowance payments and low fur prices was widespread. On November 23, 1951, J.G. Wright (Chief, Arctic Division) wrote:

> *Apart from the rising cost of relief there is the even more important problem of stopping the drift of Eskimos towards general indigence. If they feel they can be fed without working, why trap foxes at present low prices? ... Practically every informed person who has come in contact with the Eskimos in recent years agrees that the present situation is unsatisfactory and that the Eskimo economy should be controlled in some way (85, v. 1069, f. 251-1, pt. 1a).*

The sense that something needed to be done about Inuit economic activities created a series of studies and projects that began in the 1950s and never relented (85, 251-1-4 series).

On October 27, 1949, the N.W.T. Council discussed "the depressed state of the long-haired fur trade," and recommended that a complete investigation analyse the feasibility of five specific government interventions to improve the Inuit economy: opening government stores or co-operatives at points where fur trade posts had closed; introducing new industries or handicrafts for Inuit; subsidizing fur prices; "taking over all trading in Eskimo territory"; and supervizing H.B.C. operations more closely (85, v. 1069, f. 251-1, pt. 1a). In 1950, J. Cantley investigated economic conditions in the Mackenzie and Kitikmeot regions. He concluded:

> *The economic problems of the North arise mainly from a lack of diversification of the means by which the native populations can earn a cash income. On the Arctic coast, the economy is based almost entirely on the white fox and in the Delta on the muskrat. Wide fluctuations in the numbers of these animals, or in the market prices from year to year, create cycles of "booms and busts" which do not make for a stable economy. With an improvident population living from hand to mouth, a failure in either of these two resources, or a marked decline in the prices of skins, can and does lead to widespread distress. This has been particularly evident during the past few years among the coastal Eskimos throughout the Arctic as a result of a collapse of the market for white foxes (85, v. 1234, f. 251-1, pt. 2).*

Official dissatisfaction with Inuit dependence upon fur trading led to economic diversification initiatives in the 1950s and 1960s. Initially, such initiatives combined "old" policies of protecting Inuit traditions with "new" policies of promoting modernization. In 1951, an anonymous federal official wrote:

> *The real problem facing the Northwest Territories Administration in connection with the transition of the native peoples from their nomadic, hunting and especially Neolithic existence to a modern life consonant in most of its forms with that of the more settled parts of Canada is the necessity of controlling the change in such a way that the native peoples will not lose their natural virtues in acquiring the forms and advantages of modern life (85, v. 1506, f. 600-1-1, pt. 3).*

Through the 1950s, promoting modernity became a much more salient objective of federal policies and protecting traditional "virtues" disappeared as an official priority.

Government initiatives to stimulate northern economic development in the 1950s combined old programmes aimed at the improvement of hunting and trapping practices with new programmes aimed at promoting Inuit wage employment. On May 19 and 20, 1952, a major meeting on "Eskimo Affairs" was held in Ottawa, with representatives from five federal departments, the N.W.T. Council, the H.B.C., the Anglican missions and the Roman Catholic missions (85, v. 1234, f. 251-1, pt. 2; 85, v. 1072, f. 254-1, pt. 2). This meeting signalled a departure from previous policies of minimizing government intervention and keeping Inuit out on the land. The summary of the proceedings from the May, 1952 meeting indicates four key discussions. First, "recent changes in Eskimo economy" were discussed, including: local declines in game availability; low white fox prices; increased prices of trade goods; increased relief costs; and advent of statutory transfer payments. The participants stated:

> *Although there are reported declines in some food resources in certain areas, most Eskimo groups can still obtain a large part of their living within their own country. All, however, have now passed the primitive stage when they were wholly self-sufficient and they could not survive without much of the supplies and equipment they obtain from the trade stores. The drastic decline in white fox prices during recent years, accompanied by greatly increased prices of store goods, has therefore had a very adverse effect on the economy of most groups. The least affected have been the more remote settlements where hunting has remained the principle occupation.*

Thus, by 1952 there was an official perception that Inuit could no longer subsist on their own, without some form of cash income.

The second theme discussed in the proceedings was the "cumulative effects of government aid". The perceived impact of such aid included a tendency for Inuit to congregate around posts, a decline in Inuit "morale and independence", and an Inuit awareness of alternative sources of income. Participants asserted:

> *The decline in fur revenue has been off-set in part since 1945 by issue of family allowances and direct relief, amounting in all to some $1,687,000. While these issues have done much to assist the Eskimos*

> *over this difficult period, the effect on morale has not been all that could be desired. It has now become apparent that in many instances the natives are coming to depend on such issues rather than on their own efforts for a living. There has been a decided tendency, particularly among the poorer groups, to forsake their former hunting way of life and to congregate in larger groups near the settlements where they can obtain this assistance more regularly. This trend raises the question as to whether present policy and arrangements for issuing family allowances and relief should not be carefully revised.*

This passage echoed widespread frustration about the unintended impact of transfer payments upon Inuit subsistence practices.

Third, "suggestions for improving the situation" were discussed, including: subsidizing fur prices; appointing "Eskimo agents"; forming a government trading organization; "closer co-operation with the H.B.C."; managing Inuit income and spending; and establishing a "trust fund" for Inuit economic development. The participants came to "no definite conclusions" for improving the Inuit economy, but education and diversification were seen as requirements. Fourth, "policy on employment of Eskimos" was discussed, including: the need to formulate a long-term policy, given Inuit population growth; the debate over whether Inuit should be encouraged to remain as hunters and trappers, or be encouraged to enter wage employment; and various possibilities for Inuit employment, including military service, handicraft production, fisheries, reindeer herding, building and maintaining Arctic settlements, airports, and radio and weather stations. The participants asserted that employment opportunities in the Arctic were extremely limited, and therefore "the immediate need was to assist the natives to continue to follow their traditional way of life as hunters." Assistance was to be provided through programmes to relocate hunters to better hunting areas and provide them with sufficient equipment. However, the emphasis placed upon hunting

> *did not mean the Eskimos should be discouraged from accepting any suitable employment that may be offered so long as they could be assured that it would be reasonably permanent or that by following it they would not become wholly incapable of returning to their native way of life if it should fail.*

The participants concluded that Inuit employees should be rotated and given ample time off for hunting, in order to help them maintain their ability to live off the land. **Within a few years, the official policy of tolerating Inuit wage employment had developed into a policy which actively encouraged such employment.** This policy change reflected factors such as: the persistence of low prices for white fox furs; the rising costs of Inuit relief payments; the perception that Inuit would not return to hunting-trapping once they became accustomed to receiving transfer payments; the need for labourers at government military, transport, and communication facilities in the North; and the desire to establish effective levels of administration and sovereignty over the Arctic.

New policies with respect to social welfare, settlement patterns, wage employment and economic diversification were all designed to contribute to a renewal of Inuit self-sufficiency. Together, these new policies amounted to a major reversal; from policies of discouraging Inuit wage employment, sedentarization and welfare payments, the Canadian government began encouraging education, employment, and the creation of permanent settlements where health and welfare could be supervised. Federal policies of promoting Inuit wage employment were firmly established by 1955. The Annual Report of the Department of Northern Affairs and National Resources (D.N.A.N.R.) in that year clearly expressed the rationale of such policies:

> *In future years the Eskimo will be brought ever more under the influence of our civilization. There is no purpose in arguing whether this is good or bad. It is inevitable. As our civilization encroaches on the Eskimo culture these people must be helped to adjust their lives and thoughts to the changes involved ...*
>
> *Integration into our industrial society will take time but for many Eskimos it is unavoidable in the long run, unavoidable both because of the attraction of the possibilities presented by our way of life and also because a growing population cannot continue long to secure a livelihood by hunting and trapping (D.N.A.N.R., 1955, p. 12).*

Given the inescapable reality of modernization, the Canadian government had to assist Inuit adapt to their destiny. The D.N.A.N.R. (1955, p. 12) gave both moral and practical justifications for government intervention into Inuit life:

> *geography and history have made the Eskimos of northern Canada part of the population of our country. The nation as a whole therefore has a moral responsibility to assist the solution of the problems of the changing Eskimo society. Because of special circumstances — the remote geographical location and the obstacles of language and culture — a measure of special assistance is necessary. The self-sufficient primitive Eskimo is passing. To leave the Eskimo alone would involve his segregation and isolation from the increasing activity in the north. It would involve denial of the humane services modern society can provide. At the same time, to fail to protect him, during his period of change, from contacts and influences which might be injurious to him would be to invite chaos.*

In addition to moral imperatives, practical considerations made expensive interventions for "Eskimo development" an economically prudent step. The D.N.A.N.R. (1955, p. 20) suggested that careful planning would "transform Canada's Eskimos from a financial liability to a national asset", and that eventually Inuit would "be able to develop their abilities and make their full contribution to the nation's growth and to their own welfare".

Given the problems facing Inuit, and the government's responsibility to intervene, the D.N.A.N.R. (1955, p. 12) prescribed certain long-term solutions, within which education and employment had central places:

> *The Canadian Eskimos are today in an in-between state; their mode of life is in transition. They have received a few of the benefits of our civilization. For their white fox furs they obtain some of our foods, tools, and clothing. With the nation as a whole they share family*

> *allowances, old age security pensions, old age assistance allowances,*
> *blind persons allowances and disabled persons allowances, and when*
> *they are indigent, they are provided with relief. But these measures*
> *do not meet the much broader needs — and they are immediate*
> *needs — of health, education and a sound economy. These are not*
> *separate problems. Each is related to the other. It is not enough to*
> *cure disease, the cause of disease must be removed; this is largely a*
> *matter of education, and the improvement of economic conditions.*
> *Education must be provided, but this depends on good health and*
> *opportunities of the economy. A sound economy means a diversified*
> *economy based not on white fox trapping alone; new occupations*
> *are needed, but if Eskimos are to undertake these occupations*
> *satisfactorily they require better health and more education.*

The solution of Inuit problems required substantial cultural change on their part.
The D.N.A.N.R. (1955, p. 19) asserted that Inuit,

> *because of their temperament, face difficult problems in their*
> *adaptation to the economic and social life of our modern society.*
>
> *The developing economic activities of northern Canada create basic*
> *problems of adjustment to new ways of life and necessitate marked*
> *departures from traditional native customs and attitudes. Some of*
> *these problems involve such matters as acquiring and living in a*
> *permanent house and learning how to keep it clean, working regular*
> *hours for wages, working every day for long periods of time, making*
> *the best use of time available for leisure, and changing traditional*
> *attitudes.*

The D.N.A.N.R. Annual Report in 1955 provided a foundation for new policies
concerning Inuit employment and economic restructuring. Rather than protecting
Inuit from civilization, federal governments became committed to actively
promoting wage employment, education and economic modernisation in the
North.

During the Cold War era, economic restructuring in the Kitikmeot was driven
by government intervention and by a prolonged crisis in the white fox fur trade.
In the early 1950s, Kitikmeot Inuit still lived in dozens of dispersed hunting-
trapping camps, and still obtained most of their food from caribou, fish, and seal
(85, v. 1127, f. 201-1-8, pt. 2 and 2a). However, in order to procure such food,
Kitikmeot Inuit now needed cash income to maintain equipment such as rifles,
fish nets and outboard motors. Such cash income was derived from a mixture of
activities (Table 26.8).

Table 26.8.   Cash income was obtained from Euro-Canadians and most was held in trade accounts by the H.B.C., Kitikmeot, 1950–1952

	1950–1951		1951–1952	
	Gross	Per capita	Gross	Per capita
Earned income				
Furs	231,909	167.08	74,897	53.96
Other income				
on H.B.C. account	4,759	3.43	50,625	36.47
on other accounts	10,796	7.78	18,802	13.54
in cash	6,886	4.96	4,742	3.42
Total earned income	**254,350**	**183.25**	**149,066**	**107.39**
Unearned income				
Family allowances	49,656	35.77	47,399	34.15
Old age allowances	206	0.15	185	0.13
Government relief	5,204	3.75	7,246	5.22
H.B.C. relief	405	0.29	827	0.60
H.B.C. unpaid debts	531	0.38	5,513	3.97
Total unearned income	**56,002**	**40.34**	**61,170**	**44.07**
Total cash income	**310,352**	**223.59**	**210,236**	**151.46**

Source: 85, v. 1234, f. 251-1, pt. 2.

Three aspects should be emphasized. First, fur trading was the most important source of cash income (59 percent of two year total), while Family Allowance payments were also quite significant (17 percent of two year total). Second, income from furs dropped radically from one year to the next, largely because the white fox price fell substantially; the national average price in 1950–51 was $13.02, while the mean price in 1951–52 was only $8.16. Third, all cash income was obtained from Euro-Canadians and the vast majority of it was held in trade accounts by the H.B.C.

After 1950, Kitikmeot Inuit slowly began to abandon their hunting-trapping camps and to settle into permanent communities. There were significant local variations in the timing of sedentarization. Some groups, particularly around Cambridge Bay and Coppermine, moved off the land in the 1950s. Most groups moved into one of the six administered settlements in the 1960s, when low-cost housing units were built. Four major factors structured the movement of Kitikmeot Inuit into settlements: persistent health problems and the increasing availability of medical services in the settlements; recurring food shortages and the increasing availability of welfare assistance in the settlements; closure of fur trading posts and the persistence of low white fox prices; and increased availability, in settlements, of wage employment, heated housing, and facilities for health, welfare, recreation, and education.

In the 1950s and 1960s, wage labour and transfer payments began to eclipse fox trapping as the main source of Kitikmeot Inuit cash income. In 1950, ten trading posts were open in the region. By 1970, there was only one post open at each of the six main settlements (Usher, 1971, pp.110–117). For the 231 Kitikmeot Inuit "households" outside of Cambridge Bay in the early 1960s, 41 percent received most of their cash income from transfer payments, 38 percent from wages, and only 22 percent from furs and handicraft production (Abrahamson, 1963, Villiers, 1968). By the 1960s, a "fur trade economy" no longer dominated the Kitikmeot. Only one in five Inuit households relied on trapping and handicraft production as its main source of income — such activities accounted for only 21 percent of gross income in the west and only 14 percent of gross income in the east. Wages and transfer payments were the main source of cash income for nearly 80 percent of households. Hunting and fishing still accounted for most of the food consumed by Kitikmeot Inuit, but cash incomes were becoming increasingly important to supply and maintain equipment needed to hunt and fish, and to purchase food, clothing, and merchandise needed for life in permanent houses. Kitikmeot Inuit received a substantial amount of cash income in the 1960s. To recall from Table 26.8, Kitikmeot Inuit gross income in 1951–52 was $210,236, of which 37 percent came from furs. By 1962 (west) and 1968 (east), gross annual income had risen to $721,803, of which only 14 percent came from furs (Table 26.9). Using 1951 and 1961 census figures, these figures correspond to an increase in per capita cash income from $152.23 to $477.70.

Table 26.9a. 50 percent of cash income comes from wages, Western Kitikmeot, 1962–63

	Coppermine	Cambridge Bay	Holman	Bathurst Inlet	Perry River	Total Western
Casual wages	31,439 (23%)	19,175 (11%)	2,626 (6%)	2,134 (12%)	648 (4%)	56,022 (15%)
Permanent wages	29,523 (22%)	104,200 (61%)	– (0%)	– (0%)	1,200 (7%)	134,923 (35%)
Social legislation	25,363 (19%)	16,800 (10%)	6,441 (15%)	5,040 (28%)	6,048 (36%)	59,692 (16%)
Relief (assistance)	23,416 (17%)	12,500 (7%)	10,019 (24%)	3,248 (18%)	3,779 (22%)	52,962 (14%)
Furs traded	17,458 (13%)	17,650 (10%)	19,369 (46%)	5,247 (30%)	5,262 (31%)	64,986 (17%)
Handicrafts produced	9,329 (7%)	– (0%)	4,106 (10%)	2,060 (12%)	– (0%)	15,495 (4%)
Grand total	136,528 (100%)	170,325 (100%)	42,561 (100%)	17,729 (100%)	16,937 (100%)	384,080 (100%)

Table 26.9b.   59 percent of cash income comes from wages, Eastern Kitikmeot, 1967

	Gjoa Haven	Spence Bay	Pelly Bay	Thom Bay	Total
Wages	61,559	84,890	44,597	7,357	198,403
	(58%)	(58%)	(68%)	(35%)	(59%)
Social legislation	14,364	22,251	11,190	3,202	51,007
	(14%)	(15%)	(17%)	(15%)	(15%)
Relief (assistance)	15,178	21,302	4,989	1,124	42,593
	(14%)	(15%)	(8%)	(5%)	(13%)
Furs traded	10,595	16,483	2,454	9,244	38,766
	(10%)	(11%)	(4%)	(44%)	(12%)
Handicrafts produced	4,026	863	1,940	· 115	6,944
	(4%)	(1%)	(3%)	(1%)	(2%)
Grand total	**105,722**	**145,789**	**65,170**	**21,042**	**337,723**
	(100%)	**(100%)**	**(100%)**	**(100%)**	**(100%)**

Sources: Abrahamson, 1963; Villiers, 1968.

If wage employment had become an important form of subsistence practice for Kitikmeot Inuit, then what kinds of jobs did they have? First, a few Inuit in each settlement were employed by government agencies, in positions such as janitor, cook, clerk, teaching assistant, special constable, and community health worker. Second, many Inuit were employed at Distant Early Warning (D.E.W.) Line stations located across the region. Third, the H.B.C. or the Co-operative store in each community generally employed several Inuit as clerks, cashiers, and stock keepers. Fourth, many Kitikmeot Inuit were employed as seasonal labourers for projects such as handling freight and building roads, houses, and government buildings. While hunting and fishing remained central subsistence activities, casual and permanent employment became significant methods of financing these activities, and of directly purchasing food, clothing, and merchandise.

Obviously, both federal employment policies and Kitikmeot economic structures changed substantially in the Cold War era. These changes were fundamentally linked, since opportunities for wage employment in the Kitikmeot depended upon government spending. The construction, in the 1950s, of the D.E.W. Line created the first significant demand for Inuit wage labour in the Kitikmeot. Ongoing wage labour opportunities grew along with government interventions in northern health, social services, education, administration, transportation, communication and defence. The growth of such direct intervention was connected to the numbers of Euro-Canadian employees working in the Kitikmeot. In addition to transient D.E.W. Line workers, there were 47 Euro-Canadians working in the Kitikmeot in 1956 (85, 630 series; 85, v. 1072, f. 254-1, pt. 2). By 1967 there were over 100 Euro-Canadians working in the region, and by 1976, there were more than 200 (Abrahamson, 1963; Villiers, 1968).

Conclusions

In the contemporary Kitikmeot economy, wage employment in the region is completely dependent upon transfer payments from outside the region. In spite of the apparent lack of viable economic activities upon which to sustain jobs, Canadian policies locate wage employment as the fundamental relationship through which economic diversification and development will occur in the North. To understand this paradoxical policy, I narrated the history of employment policies and economic restructuring in the Kitikmeot since the early part of this century. Far from being a timeless policy, government support for northern development and Inuit employment was reluctantly and slowly adopted in the Cold War era. Prior to 1945, Canadian policies discouraged Inuit employment and endeavoured to maintain traditional Inuit self-sufficiency. It was only with the collapse of the fur trade, and the increased pressure to assert Canadian sovereignty over the North during the Cold War, that federal governments began promoting Inuit employment. Initially, wage employment was seen as a temporary response to short-term fur price declines and non-sustainable opportunities presented by defence activities in the North. It was not until the middle of the 1950s that official policies began actively celebrating wage employment as a means to promote northern development and Inuit welfare.

If wage employment does not appear tenable without massive government subsidies in regions such as the Kitikmeot, and if current policies which promote wage employment in such regions are themselves the product of peculiar historical circumstances, then perhaps there is a need for creative alternatives to contemporary economic policy for remote areas. Rather than presuming to have answers to this dilemma, I conclude with a set of questions for social scientists and policy makers active in other remote rural and northern regions. What alternatives exist to wage employment as the basis for economic life in rural and northern areas? Could government support for domestic economies and producer cooperatives more effectively promote self-sufficiency in such regions? What could Canadian policy makers learn from the experiences of other countries with remote rural and northern regions? To what extent are the issues raised in this chapter relevant to other, less remote areas, where wage employment depends upon external subsidies?

Through responding to questions such as these, social scientists and policy makers may reorient employment and economic development policies toward more realistic paths of sustainable development for remote regions.

References and further reading

Abrahamson, G. *et al.* (1963) *The Copper Eskimos: An Area Economic Survey.* Ottawa: Department of Northern Affairs and Natural Resources (D.N.A.N.R.).

Balikci, Asen. (1989) *The Netsilik Eskimo.* Prospect Heights: Waveland Press.

Canada. Department of Indian Affairs and Northern Development. (1989) *Looking North: Canada's Arctic Commitment.* Ottawa: Department of Indian Affairs and Northern Development (D.I.A.N.D.).

Canada. Department of Mines and Resources. (1943) *The Northwest Territories: Administration, Resources, Development.* Ottawa: D.M.R.

Canada Department of Northen Affairs and National Resources. (1955) *Annual Report of the D.N.A.N.R. 1954-1955.* Ottawa: D.N.A.N.R.

Damas, David. (1984) Copper Eskimo. *The Handbook of North American Indians* Vol. 5. Washington: Smithsonian, pp. 397-414.

Damas, David. (1988) The contact-traditional horizon of the central Arctic. *Arctic Anthropology* Vol. 25, No. 2, pp. 101-138.

Diubaldo, Richard. (1985) *The Government of Canada and the Inuit.* Ottawa: D.I.A.N.D.

Diubaldo, Richard. (1989) You can't keep the native native. In Coates, K. and Morrison, W. (eds). *For Purposes of Dominion.* North York: Captus, pp. 171-188.

Freeman, Milton (ed.). (1976) *Inuit Land Use and Occupancy Project.* Ottawa: Department of Indian and Northern Affairs (D.I.N.A.).

Jenness, Diamond. (1994) *Eskimo Administration: Volume II, Canada.* Montreal: Arctic Institute of North America.

Morrison, William. (1986) Canadian sovereignty and the Inuit of the Central and Eastern Arctic. *Inuit Studies* Vol. 10, No. 1-2, pp. 245-259.

Nixon, P.G. (1990) The welfare state north: early developments in Inuit income security. *Journal of Canadian Studies* Vol. 25, No. 2, pp. 144-154.

Northwest Territories. Bureau of Statistics. (1989) *1989 N.W.T. Labour Force Survey: Overall Results and Community Detail.* Yellowknife: G.N.W.T.

Northwest Territories. Bureau of Statistics. (1990a) *1989 Labour Force Survey: Labour Force Activity, Education, and Language.* Yellowknife, G.N.W.T.

Northwest Territories. Bureau of Statistics. (1990b) *1989 Labour Force Survey: Wage Employment and Traditional Activities.* Yellowknife: G.N.W.T.

Northwest Territories. Department of Economic Development and Tourism. (1985) *Kitikmeot Region Economic Base Study.* Yellowknife: G.N.W.T.

Northwest Territories. Department of Economic Development and Tourism. (1989) *Kitikmeot Region Economic Facts.* Yellowknife: G.N.W.T.

Northwest Territories. Department of Education. (1990) *Preparing People for Employment in the 1990s.* Yellowknife: G.N.W.T.

Northwest Territories. Legislative Assembly. (1989) *The SCONE Report: Building Our Economic Future.* Yellowknife: G.N.W.T.

Public Archives of Canada. (various dates) References to materials from the Public Archives of Canada are fully cited within the text. Citations are organized according to Record Group (R.G.). Volume (V.), File (F.) and Part (Pt.).

Usher, Peter. (1971) *Fur Trade Posts of the Northwest Territories.* Ottawa: D.I.A.N.D.

Villiers, D. (1968) *The Central Arctic: An Area Economic Survey.* Ottawa: D.I.A.N.D.

Zaslow, Morris (1988) *The Northward Expansion of Canada, 1914-1967.* Toronto: McClelland and Stewart.

Chapter twenty-seven:

Informal Rural Networks: Their Contribution to "Making a Living" and Creating Rural Employment

Bill Reimer
Concordia University, Montréal, Québec, Canada

Abstract

Informal social networks are important for understanding employment in general and rural employment in particular. Characteristics of social relations which enhance "social capital" are connectedness, trustworthiness, social support, norms and sanctions, and openness to goal substitution. Their relationship to four structural elements of groups are discussed (the frequency of contact, extent of closure, multiplicity of relations, and mobility).

Access to employment, socialization and training, new business opportunities, labour, opportunities for collective action, and a climate for economic activity are all dependent on the development and utilization of informal networks. This means that changes in the relative importance of kin and friendship relations, the division of gender roles, the family structure, social cohesion and political impact are all crucial to consider when dealing with rural employment issues.

Several policy issues arise, namely the importance of social infrastructure, the maximization of community-level involvement, the provision of social support institutions, and the enhancement of inter-organizational communication.

Introduction

The economic model of job creation usually focuses on the individual entrepreneur. The story told is one of the imaginative person who sees a product that others do not, or the one who finds an unexploited market. The woman in Prince Edward Island (PEI), for example, who discovered that many of the waitresses and nurses "who wore uniforms on the job were dissatisfied with their design, comfort, and availability" (AEI, 1993, p.4). So she established a small business to create more comfortable, less formal uniforms. Or the owner of a castings factory in Québec who had the energy and foresight to look to the USA for his markets — eventually shipping to locations all over North America.

On the basis of such stories, training programmes are constructed to teach entrepreneurial skills, programmes are established to free up capital for small business people, and the unemployed are reprimanded for lacking the motivation and initiative which will find them a job.

Most of these stories fail to mention the social context making it possible for the individual entrepreneur to act. For example, the woman in PEI was able to consider the production of uniforms because she had a sister with a background in fashion design. This sister was the first person she turned to for help. The castings factory owner had family members who settled in the USA. He frequently travelled to visit them over a number of years, thus facilitating expansion of his business.

In these cases, as in most, there exists an informal network of family, friends, and acquaintances that is essential to the initiation of the project — most likely even to the emergence of the idea itself. If we focus only on the skills, motivation, and characteristics of the individual, we fail to understand and develop the informal social context which is essential for the creation of employment and the search for jobs. We also fail to see the important role this context plays when people are unable to find employment or they lose their job.

This chapter is a first step to rectify such neglect. I will outline a framework for understanding the role of informal social networks and follow this with an examination of the relationship between these networks and employment related issues. I will then turn to a brief discussion of some of the major trends affecting the structure of informal networks in non-metropolitan societies before outlining some general implications of my analysis. Although the general approach is equally relevant to metro regions, our focus will on non-metropolitan regions.

Social capital and informal social networks

Social capital

James Coleman (1988) has used the concept "social capital" to highlight the importance of social relations for getting things done in an economic sense. Social capital refers to "the structure of relations between actors and among actors" that facilitate productive activity (Coleman, 1988, p.98). Production requires materials (physical capital) and skilled persons (human capital), but it also requires the social organization to make it possible. This includes a structure in which others may be contacted, obligations and expectations can be safely formed, information can be shared and sanctions can be applied. To the extent that a particular social organization makes these activities possible, the social capital of that organization is enhanced.

The characteristics of social capital will vary to some extent depending on the dominant organization of production in a society. However, we are able to identify several which are sufficiently basic to our form of capitalism to warrant special attention. We have modified to some extent the three forms of social capital identified by Coleman (1988): trustworthiness, information channels, and norms and sanctions.

First of all, social capital will be enhanced to the extent that social relations provide **connectedness** to other people. Those networks which include many people increase the production potential by providing access to new people or networks and by providing access to information. Within these networks, the uncertainty of relating to others can be mediated through familiar and trusted people. Such trust serves as a conduit to new contacts by way of introduction. New jobs, new business opportunities, or new markets are more likely to be found with larger networks (Granovetter, 1974). In addition, the costs of acquiring information can be significantly reduced by relying on others in one's network.

Social capital is also enhanced by the **trustworthiness** of the social environment. Without some assurance that expectations will be met and obligations fulfilled, there can be no coordination of activities to reach goals and to satisfy the interests of individuals or of groups. In formal organizations the limits of obligations are specified by contract which are protected by law, within less formal groups, they are achieved through norms and convention.

Closely related to the trustworthiness is the extent to which **social support** is provided by the social organization or network. Such support can vary both in terms of the amount and the type of support provided. It may include financial resources in the form of gifts, loans, or guarantees, or it may include non-financial aspects such as goods, services, and emotional support.

A fourth aspect of social capital is the extent and type of **norms and sanctions** of a group. They may vary from those which place the group interests above those of the individual, to those which sanction or reinforce deviant behaviour. Norms supporting friendly relations with strangers are a valuable resource for tourist ventures; those holding scholastic achievement in high regard help to build human capital.

Finally, the extent to which a social network can be **appropriated** for a variety of goals will generally increase its social capital. In most cases, formal organizations are established for particular objectives. To the extent that the resources and structure of the organization can be used for other objectives, its social capital is increased. Informal organizations and networks tend to be more flexible in this respect since the objectives are usually less rigid or broader in scope. Thus we find that voluntary associations are more frequently the source of contacts, information, and experience for new social movements than more formal institutions.

Both the amount and type of social capital vary from one social group to another. Family groups may be high in trust yet relatively low in the extent to which a variety of information is accessed. On the other hand, a large corporation may require an elaborate system of contracts to establish trustworthy expectations and obligations on the part of its members, yet have access to a wide variety of information to further its goals.

The level of social capital available in a social group or network can be significantly affected by its structural characteristics. We will outline several of them before focusing on informal networks.

The **frequency of contact** between the members of the group or network is an important aspect for virtually all of the characteristics of social capital. More frequent contact increases the connectedness of the group, builds trust, increases support, maximizes social control and increases the chance of new objectives being generated.

The **extent of closure** within the network is also important. It reflects the extent to which each of the members of the network know and can sanction the others. Closure increases the possibility of coalitions to sanction others and thereby reinforces the trustworthiness of the members. On the other hand, closure limits access to information and can thus decrease the level of social capital. As Granovetter argues (1973) it is most often the low key or "weak ties" which are crucial for evaluating jobs, employees, potential partners, or business opportunities.

Groups in which people are linked to the others through many different contexts are more likely to be appropriable than those in which the members meet only in one or two situations. The former have been identified by Gluckman as forming "**multiplex**" relations as opposed to "simplex" ones (1967). Those networks with a high level of multiplex relations constitute greater social capital than those with simplex relations, at least for most objectives.

The **mobility** of group members is likely to affect the extent to which social capital can be formed. High mobility makes both frequency of contact and closure difficult, thus undermining the level of trustworthiness and social control possible. To some extent this can be overcome through the use of communication technology and improved transportation, but the long-term effects of mobility and distance on social capital are very difficult to eliminate.

In summary, the concept of social capital provides a useful framework for viewing social networks. Social capital reflects a number of characteristics: connectedness, trustworthiness, social support, social control and appropriability. Each of them provides a resource for action by individuals or groups. They are also significantly affected by several social structural features: the frequency of contact, closure, complexity of relations and mobility.

Informal social networks

Informal social networks are composed of the wide variety of relationships we have with kin, friends, acquaintances and neighbours. They are loosely distinguished from formal relations by their non-legal character. Informal relationships are not limited and proscribed by explicit objectives and policies, but they tend to have diverse objectives which are freely open to modification. They are usually characterized by familiarity, relatively long-term occurrence, and interaction which occurs within a multiplicity of contexts. As with most social relations, they are not limited to face-to-face interaction, yet spatial proximity facilitates their establishment and maintenance.

Informal networks are not independent from more formal relations. As a result of working in a formal enterprise, for example, informal relations may develop and begin to play an important part in the objectives of the organization, for better or worse. Similarly, there are many formal organizations which owe their existence to the operation of informal networks. A rigid definition of the two types of relations would detract from the fluid nature of these networks.

Informal networks contribute all aspects of social capital identified above. First, they serve as a means of connectedness to new people. Within these networks, the uncertainty of relating to others can be mediated through familiar and trusted people. Such trust serves as a conduit to new contacts by way of introduction. The informal contacts also serve as a source of information regarding a wide range of employment-related issues.

Second, informal networks serve to increase the level of trust which people have in one another. Since they tend to be discretional relationships of a long-term nature, they provide considerable opportunity to develop and confirm the confidence of those involved.

A third aspect of informal networks is the support which they provide. At an individual level, most people turn first to family and friends for emotional support during times of stress. They also provide the elements of familiarity and trust which are necessary for sharing good news. Support may also come in the form of services. Most people will count on family and friends to help with housecleaning, transportation, or maintenance if the circumstances make it possible. Even in a commercial society such as ours, informal networks are an important source of financial support. This is clearly the case within a marriage relationship where the force of law can be used to enforce financial support and one can find many arrangements involving financial exchanges among friends.

Fourth, informal networks are an important source of social control. They are a primary basis for the values and beliefs which people hold, they often are the social space in which new ideas and perspectives are explored, and they act to dispense sanctions and rewards in a wide variety of ways.

Finally, informal networks include some of the most appropriable social groups available because of their loose structure and broad-based goals. For example, the organizational skills built around a baseball team or a church bazaar can be utilized for conference or tourist activities.

Each of these elements contribute to the overall social capital available to the network members. As such they become resources which can be drawn upon for the benefit of individuals or of the group. We will turn to explore the ways in which this might relate to the issue of employment in general before looking more specifically at the rural context.

Implications for employment

Access to employment

Informal social networks contribute to employment in a number of ways. One of the most direct is through the provision of employment to those in the network. In spite of the rationalization of employment procedures, the use of friends and kin for identifying prospective employees is pervasive throughout the world (Salaff and Lun, 1994). Even in corporate North America, the pattern is widespread (Granovetter, 1974).

In Canada, where job mobility is official policy, the role of informal networks becomes crucial. One of the most consistent findings in migration research is that people move where their kin and friends live. As demographers point out, both migration and immigration are guided by the channels of information and support afforded by informal networks (MacDonald and MacDonald, 1964). Official policy and programmes by and large act only to inhibit or enhance the flows established and maintained by informal networks.

Not only do informal networks act to encourage migration, they also serve to inhibit it. Strong kin and friendship bonds can make migration difficult, especially where a high degree of social closure is found. Under such circumstances information regarding employment opportunities in other locations may be hard to find, and the risks of migration become large. Even if conditions "at home" are difficult, the prospects of moving to an unknown location appear even worse.

Socialization and training for employment

In our society, the responsibility for primary socialization has been given to immediate kin and family. The complex network of mutual obligations and interpersonal relations between parents and their offspring become the basic social capital for the production of human capital and employment training (Lichter *et al.,* 1993). Not only do family and kin provide a context for the physical survival of the next generation, but the culture, values, and skills which are passed to children lay the basis for the particular interests, desires, and requirements for employment training and motivation. Even though much of the training has been taken over by formal institutions of learning, the legacy of informal kin and friendship networks is felt throughout these institutions in ways which directly and indirectly affect the level and type of employment-related skills which are produced by these institutions.

Kinship networks show many of the variations in organization which we have identified as important for the assessment of social capital. They vary with respect to the frequency of contact, degree of closure, complexity of the relations, and extent of mobility. Since they are likely to be long-term relationships, they tend to be more cohesive than other relations, however, and thus play a more central role as structures of socialization and training.

Partnerships and new business opportunities

Analysis of personal networks in a corporate context (the securities industry) shows that "the more different kinds of people you know, the more information you come into contact with, and the wider your information base becomes" (Erickson, 1993). This personal network diversity increases within the hierarchy of the enterprise as well. Supervisors had more diverse networks than their employees, managers' networks were more diverse than supervisors, and the owners of the companies had the most diverse networks of all. These translate directly into business opportunities since the wider the network, the more likely one is to discover new markets, new partners and new techniques.

Access to labour

The search for competent, motivated, and trustworthy labour is not easy. It not only requires access to a labour supply, but also the use of screening techniques to select appropriate employees. Informal networks are frequently employed to facilitate this task (Granovetter, 1974). Using networks to solicit information via informal contacts, one is often able to assess potential candidates without forming any commitment or expectations on their part. These contacts also increase the chance that potential candidates come to the negotiations with a more complete assessment of the job requirements since they are likely to have discussed some of the details with network members.

Informal networks also serve to ensure trustworthiness on the part of potential employees. Network members who refer potential candidates are likely to feel somewhat responsible for the performance of those they refer and this will usually increase the chance that they can be trusted. In addition, the new person will be more quickly integrated into the organizational culture as those in the network provide information and support relevant to their new tasks. Under such circumstances the usual informal mechanisms of social control operate to reduce the risk to the employer and provide a constraint against high turnover.

Opportunities for collective action

Informal networks do not always operate to the advantage of employers. The same characteristics which make them useful to corporate objectives, make them effective in the organization and influence of labour. The ease of communication, potential for closure, and cohesion afforded by informal networks increase the chance of grievances to be formulated and collective action to be taken. The long history for improved labour conditions is first of all a history of the impact of informal networks. Bringing labour together within large enterprises was one of the most important ingredients in the process. This increased the possibility of communication and created the conditions of cohesion which made collective action probable.

Climate for economic activity

Finally, informal networks help to create a climate which makes economic activity possible. Often referred to as the culture of a corporation, it is a central ingredient in the way in which work gets done. The many assumptions and interpretations of activities which are necessary for coordinated work to occur are established and nurtured by the informal exchanges that occur within the workplace. Many formal organizations recognize the importance of this social feature and attempt to enhance it through the encouragement of clubs, leisure activities, retreats, and informal groups among their employees. It can be influenced to some extent through formal means, but there are important limitations imposed by the obligations and reciprocity of the social relations. Economic organization and planning must take these limitations into account.

Changing conditions for rural networks

Changes in rural Canada are altering the character and role of informal networks. Several of these have important connotations for employment. I will outline them briefly before turning to some policy implications.

The importance of kin and friendship networks in rural areas

Traditionally, informal kin and friendship networks have been more important in rural areas than in urban areas (Straus, 1969; Wellman, 1992). This is most likely a result of three aspects of rural areas. First, the geographical proximity imposed by small towns increases the frequency of contact, closure and multiplex nature of social interaction. All of these features operate to increase cohesion.

Second, the isolation of many rural communities meant that closure was imposed at the same time that people were dependent on one another, often for the basic necessities of life (Mirande, 1970). Under such circumstances informal networks serve to impose rather strong moral limitations on peoples' behaviour by way of ensuring a high level of trustworthiness and social support.

Third, the low levels of mobility imposed by the level of technology simply reinforced the features above. It was therefore more difficult to hear of activities in the world outside the local community, let alone to travel to these areas on a regular basis.

All three of these aspects have undergone radical change over the past 50 years, largely as the result of technological changes relating to communication and transportation. Geographical proximity still increases the chance of interaction, but the consistency of this generalization is severely limited by the ease with which people can travel or communicate with others over a long distance (Wellman and Tindall, 1992).

In a similar manner, individuals and households are no longer as dependent on those who live close by. A variety of commercial and public services are often found within easy travelling distance in rural areas, making options for support services both more varied and less local. In addition, as the state has taken over much of the education, health and social control functions traditionally handled by local communities, the networks of interdependence have become more diffuse.

These trends mean that the relationship between informal networks and employment in rural areas has become more like that found in urban areas: more connected, more open, more multiplex and more mobile. However, the similarity is not complete. Our data shows that the relationship between the use of employment and kinship networks for support remains strongest in rural and small town Canada, as do the general extent of involvement in voluntary associations and kinship networks (Norris and Joyal, 1992; Reimer, 1993)[1]. In both these cases the general role which informal networks play in the establishment and maintenance of employment is amplified.

Division of gender roles

Gender roles are more sharply divided in rural as opposed to urban regions. This has included a tendency for networks to be gender specific. Women's networks have supported many of the social, religious, economic, and family activities of rural areas through such organizations as church auxiliaries, l'AFEAS, the Cercle des Fermiers, the Women's Institute, and the many local bazaars, fund-raising events and political campaigns which take place in rural areas. Men have tended to specialize more in business, sports and service club networks (Reimer, 1993) As a result there is more closure within gender groups in rural as compared to urban networks. This means on the one hand, complementarity of activities, and on the other a specialisation of information.

Changes in family structure

As family structures undergo change they are likely to significantly affect the structure of informal networks. The requirement for seasonal employment in rural areas has produced a wide variety of family arrangements in Canada: from periodic migration of one spouse, the short-term movement of smaller nuclear families, to the repeated movement of larger family units. We now find that families are getting smaller in rural areas as they have in urban regions, that there are more female-headed families, there are a higher proportion of older families, and a greater frequency of divorced and remarried adults. These patterns

---

1.   *We would like to thank the Housing, Family and Social Statistics Division of Statistics Canada for making this data available.*

are more consistent with the high level of labour mobility required by official labour policy, but at the same time, they tend to undermine the extent of trustworthiness which can be expected of the social unit, create special problems of social support for the individuals involved, produce a greater variety in socialization, and thus increase the variety of norms and sanctions which are to be found in the population. In effect, we are likely to find a more mobile labour force, but one which is less committed to a strong work ethic, and less trained to those skills which require a long period of apprenticeship.

Speed of change

The speed with which these social changes have occurred introduces additional problems for rural communities. As Seydlitz demonstrates, the faster the social change, the greater the extent of social disorganization (Seydlitz *et al.*, 1993). Within rapidly changing communities, many of the characteristics which contribute to social capital are undermined. When those changes are fast, it becomes difficult if not impossible to develop modes of relating which are more conducive to the new conditions. Until that occurs to the extent that people can anticipate the future and prepare for it, trustworthiness, the operation of clear norms and sanctions, and the provision of social support are all likely to decline. This is a general problem for rural communities and one which affects their ability to establish and maintain a basis for employment and a strong economic base.

Declining power base

Finally, the increased mobility and changes in family and community structure that are found in rural areas have decreased the capacity for collective action. This makes it more difficult for communities and labour groups to organize to protect their interests. We can therefore expect that the relative power of these two groups will decline, a situation which places them in a more vulnerable position vis-à-vis urban and corporate interests.

Implications for rural policy

Given these changing conditions, what suggestions can be made for rural policy? First, I have made the case that non-economic relations are crucial to understanding and responding to economic problems. Rather than treat them as non-rational behaviour of the sort that impedes market processes, we must see them as an integral part of economic behaviour. Informal relations with friends, kin, neighbours, workmates, and even lovers all play an important part in the creation and loss of economic opportunities and they often provide the normative context which will encourage or discourage economic initiatives.

Current economic policy encourages labour mobility and retraining to deal with the current crisis in rural regions. Both of these policies support the relatively narrow view of the problem by emphasizing the human capital of individuals. Mobility undermines social cohesion, and retraining assumes that a major part of the problem lies with the skills and motivation of individuals. Neither of them recognize the important role which informal relations play in the creation and maintenance of employment.

Searching for and maintaining employment in rural regions places considerable demand on family structures. As two income earners become essential for a reasonable quality of life, the energy and time left for child raising becomes smaller. This means that children are more likely to be left on their own, rely more on urban-oriented mechanisms of socialization, and find fewer local resources to challenge and interest them. If the parents are finding it more difficult to provide them, then the local community can help if it has sufficient support. My first proposal is therefore to:

> *provide adequate support for recreational, educational, day care,*
> *transportation, and communication infrastructure in rural areas.*

This infrastructure includes both the facilities for meeting as well as the training and support for personnel to maintain and develop programmes. Community halls, hockey rinks, libraries, school buildings, hiking trails are examples of the type of facilities which make networks possible, and so are the child care centres, vehicles, computers and the personnel to operate them.

This infrastructure will also help to minimize the community disintegration which is associated with increased mobility. As new people move into rural communities they must be quickly integrated and potential sources of conflict must be addressed before they create significant social divisions. In order for rural community members to cope with these changes, they must become aware of the potential problems and develop the social resources to respond to them. One of the most effective ways to do this is to:

> *provide communities with the authority and resources for a wide*
> *range of local and regional projects — not just economic ones.*

This brings people together, develops their organizational skills, and creates an opportunity for trust-building which is necessary for social cohesion.

If social cohesion declines, the demands on the state for social control will increase. The usual increase in crime, alcoholism and suicide which are associated with rapid social change are now found in most rural areas. Not only are preventive measures necessary to avoid these problems, but policies regarding a response to them must be developed. This means that:

> *health, welfare, and justice facilities must be improved, not left to*
> *deteriorate. In doing so, significant community involvement should*
> *be a central feature of those programmes.*

Such a policy should include considerable experimentation with various forms of community involvement. Projects such as mobile clinics, community-based policing and healing circles should be supported and evaluated. This approach also has the advantage of reinforcing the local community network. It increases the extent to which local people feel they have a stake in their community and will add to the speed with which newcomers can be integrated into the local organization. In this way, it is a more socially constructive organization for a mobile society.

As mobility increases, so do the threats to the natural environment in rural areas. This is due, not only to the short-term interests of the corporations and enterprises which provide the employment, but it is likely to be the result of a short-term view among rural employees as well. In order for people to protect and maintain the environment, they must see its relevance to their future, as it affects them and their children. Social and labour instability undermine this long term view. Strong local communities can counter this trend, but additional mechanisms are necessary under conditions of social mobility. Therefore, we propose that:

> *policies to protect the rural environment be formulated and implemented with the full participation of local people.*

Local participation is crucial for a number of reasons. First, they will be most likely to know of the local issues related to environmental quality. Second, their cooperation will be necessary to make the policies work. Third, their participation will have the effect of increasing control over their lives and the level of social cohesion within the region. Finally, the process of negotiation will allow them to learn and hone their social skills. All of these aspects will contribute to the creation and maintenance of a strong local community.

A final policy proposal arises out of the declining influence of rural areas at an economic and political level. As the proportion of rural population and the cohesion of rural communities declines, they will find it more difficult to make their concerns heard and to affect the political process. This problem is exasperated because of the departmental fragmentation which is built into the current political structure. Issues common to rural areas are difficult to deal with since the relevant agencies are spread across agriculture, mining, fishing, health, employment, and other institutions. We propose therefore that:

> *organizations at all levels be developed which focus on an integrated approach to rural issues. These should have sufficient resources to develop rural policies and to have them adequately represented within the political structure.*

Since we are at a crucial point in the evolution of rural social systems, it is extremely important that we are able to conduct the research and explore the various responses made to the changing conditions. Only in this way can we avoid the problems which are sure to arise and support those features of rural regions which are crucial to the quality of life of all citizens.

In general, people in rural Canada have become more open, more connected, and more mobile over the last 50 years. Although this has served the short-term problems of labour mobility, it has undermined several important ingredients of social capital and the quality of life in rural areas. The trustworthiness of social relations, the level of informal support and the strength of social norms have all declined as people have become more mobile.

We must act to reduce the negative effects of these changes. It means first of all providing alternative ways for rural citizens to find the social support which has been lost. It also means that we must identify the new forms of social capital which are emerging and discover ways to enhance trust, learning and social cohesion. These objectives are crucial for employment, but they are also essential for a reasonable quality of life. Both are dependent on strong informal networks.

References

AEI (Atlantic Entrepreneurial Institute). (1993) *Entrepreneurship in Atlantic Canada: Women in Business Case Studies*. St. John's: Atlantic Entrepreneurial Institute, Memorial University.

Coleman, James S. (1988) Social capital in the creation of human capital. *American Journal of Sociology*, Vol. 94, Supplement S95-S120.

Erickson, Bonnie. (1993) *Class, Work and Social Support in the Service Industry*. Paper presented to the annual meeting of the Canadian Sociology and Anthropology Association, Ottawa, June.

Gluckman, Max. (1967) *The Judicial Process among the Baroise of Northern Rhodesia*. 2nd edn. Manchester: Manchester University Press.

Granovetter, Mark. (1973) The strength of weak ties. *American Journal of Sociology*, Vol. 78, pp. 1360-1380.

Granovetter, Mark. (1974) *Getting a Job: A Study of Contacts and Careers*. Cambridge: Harvard University Press.

Lichter, Daniel T., Cornwell, Gretchen T. and Eggebeen, David J. (1993) Harvesting human capital: family structure and education among rural youth. *Rural Sociology* Vol. 58, No. 1.

MacDonald, J.S. and MacDonald, L.D. (1964) Chain migration, ethnic neighbourhood formation, and social networks. *Milbank Memorial Fund Quarterly*, Vol. 62, No. 1, January.

Mirande, Alfred M. (1970) Extended kinship ties, friendship relations and community size: an exploratory inquiry. *Rural Sociology*, Vol. 35, pp. 261-266.

Norris, Douglas A. and Joyal, Kubir. (1992) Social indicators from the General Social Survey: some urban-rural differences. In Bollman, Ray D. (ed.). *Rural and Small Town Canada*. Toronto: Thompson Educational Publishing, Inc., pp. 357-367.

Reimer, Bill. (1993) *Social Networks in Rural and Small Town Communities: Implications for Development Partnerships*. Presented at the ARRG National Seminar, Merrickville, Ontario.

Saliff, Janet and Lun, Wong Siu. (1994) Exiting Hong Kong: Social class experiences and the adjustment to 1997. In Lun, Wong Siu, Kwan, Lee Ming and Kai, Lau Siu (eds). *Inequalities and Development: Social Stratification in Chinese Societies.* Hong Kong: The Chinese University of Hong Kong and the Hong Kong Institute of Asia-Pacific Studies.

Seydlitz, Ruth, Laska, Shirley, Spain, Daphne, Triche, Elizabeth, W. and Bishop, Karen L. (1993) Development and social problems: the impact of the offshore oil industry on suicide and homicide rates. *Rural Sociology,* Vol. 58, No. 1, pp. 93-110.

Straus, Murray A. (1969) Social class and farm–city differences in interaction with kin in relation to societal modernisation. *Rural Sociology*, Vol 34, pp. 476-495.

Wellman, Barry. (1992) Which types of ties and networks provide what kinds of social support? *Advances in Group Processes*, Vol. 9, pp. 207-235.

Wellman, Barry and Tindall, D. (1992) Reach out and touch some bodies: how social networks connect telephone networks. In Barnett, G. and Richards, W. Jr. (eds). *Advances in Communication Networks.* Norwood, N.J.: Abex.

Chapter twenty-eight:

Niche Markets, Niche Marketing and Rural Employment

Heather A. Clemenson
Agriculture and Agri-Food Canada, Ottawa, Ontario, Canada

Bernard Lane
University of Bristol, Bristol, United Kingdom

Abstract

The market for rural products and services is urban-based and increasingly comprises numerous segmented markets (or "niches") of specialty goods and services. Rural entrepreneurs need to develop a "culture" of market research to identify market niches, rather than the traditional rural culture of the efficient production of undifferentiated primary goods. This change may be facilitated with training or, sometimes, it may occur via the in-migration of individuals with an interest in niche market entrepreneurship. The unique characteristic of the territory may be captured by "certificates of area of origin", generally requiring regulatory enforcement.

A series of case studies illustrate the range of niche products and services produced in contrasting rural areas and exemplify the role of entrepreneurship and management skills required. Private enterprise actions need support from the public sector. Six areas of policy response are identified.

Introduction

Traditional rural development interventions have been problem-based and have relied heavily on state intervention as the motor for change (Cloke, 1988; Robinson, 1990). Niche marketing, on the other hand, is opportunity-based (OECD, 1995a, 1995b) and begins to explore private sector/market sector intervention as a motor for change. The objective of this chapter is to review the opportunities of niche marketing for rural communities, enterprises and governments at all levels. It draws on a research and review study into niche market potential for rural areas carried out between 1993 and 1995 by the OECD Rural Development Programme, in which the authors were part of the enquiry team[1].

What is a niche market?

The concept of the niche market relies heavily on the ideas of product differentiation and market segmentation. Schnaars (1991) explains product differentiation as follows: "A strategy of differentiation ... is concerned with making the tangible and intangible aspects of a product different from those offered by other sellers ... Product differentiation takes a competitor orientation, but it also provides consumer benefits. On the supply side, it allows firms to minimize competition and earn higher profits. On the demand side, it provides consumers with a greater variety of goods and services." Product superiority is established by differentiating quality, function, design, service support or image.

Schnaars goes on to describe market segmentation as a system relying on specialization. "It does not seek to satisfy all customers. Instead it provides something special to a small but defensible part of the market." Market segmentation may be achieved by price, by product or both. Both technological development and skilled marketing may be key factors in segmenting a market.

Niche markets can be obvious or they can be latent, awaiting the arrival of a product — or a marketing policy — which can tap that latent demand. Niche markets may be defensible, or eventually, if too successful, succumb to mass market attack. And niche markets can also be heavily dependent on fashion and changing consumer behaviour: repositioning and rethinking of niche market products may be necessary from time to time (Dickson and Ginter, 1987).

Niche markets and the rural economy

For the rural world, economic performance has traditionally been dominated by the production of primary goods. The perceived function of the countryside was to provide the growing cities and towns of the industrial world with food and raw materials, commodities which were generally in short supply. The concept of the niche market was almost unknown.

Seven factors can be identified over the last thirty years as fostering market segmentation or niche markets:

1. the increase in spending on consumer goods due to the rapid rise in disposable incomes;

---

1.   *The authors would like to thank the many collaborators involved in the niche market project in the OECD Rural Development Programme. We especially thank Mr Kenji Yoshinaga and Mr Christian Huillet without whose assistance and support, this chapter could not have been written.*

2. education, the media and trends in fashion have combined to create a new type of consumer demanding speciality goods and services;

3. new techniques in manufacturing, in marketing and in retailing have facilitated the production of speciality products and services;

4. improvements in transport and communications services have reduced problems of distance for rural areas;

5. there is now an over-supply of many rural primary products and rural entrepreneurs have been forced to examine new business opportunities;

6. the rising interest in rural recreation and tourism has increased the value of formerly valueless rural scenic, heritage and cultural amenities; and

7. the value of rurality itself has changed — rising urban crime and congestion have increased the attractiveness of rural life styles.

Rural areas now have the possibility and the incentive to produce niche goods and services for urban markets. Rural niche products are more likely to succeed if they have a comparative advantage. Specific examples are: goods requiring high quality water or other locally produced raw materials; food and related products with special qualities and/or regional attributes; craft goods related to specific raw materials, rural skills or heritage; and tourism and recreation services which rely on scenery, wildlife, cultural heritage of all kinds and rural qualities such as scale, space and ambience.

The example of rural tourism services illustrates the market for many rural niche products and services. Plog (1991) divided the market into enquiring, active and demanding allocentrics and less adventurous, more passive and conservative psychocentric personalities. Lane (1995a) also considered a range of life-style analyses (including Shih, 1986) which indicated that a growing proportion of the North American and UK population (up to 40 percent) were trying to develop life-styles which expressed independent, yet heritage and quality conscious purchasing modes. This group was most likely to purchase niche market holidays and goods. The basic characteristics of the market for rural niche products were assessed to be:

1. largely middle class, well educated and with above average incomes;

2. mildly adventurous and keen to try new products, but only within certain parameters;

3. environmentally aware, culturally aware and extremely health conscious;

4. conscious of the perceived values of country life and traditions;

5. territorially aware and perceiving certain regions to be fashionable;

6. a multi-faceted market, varying from country to country in its interests and requirements;

7. requiring high quality in several senses: a quality reputation, quality in performance, and a civic and environmental quality;

8. a very mobile and fickle market and demanding in terms of service and value;

9. typically comprising about 20 percent of the total market;

10. a growing market, largely urban based, and global in outlook.

There are several implications for successful niche market promotion in the above findings. Although only 20 percent of total market may be interested in niche products, because that market thinks globally, potential market size is enormous. However, care must be taken in interpreting the figure of 20 percent. The rural tourism research showed that the overall niche market is made up of numerous tiny niche markets within the whole: thus in socioeconomic terms, eco-tourists may be similar to those taking guided cycle tours, but in other respects the two groups are very discrete.

The quality demands of the niche market means that quality control, image control and attention to detail in service provision must be very carefully considered. Equally, while price level may not be as such a deciding factor as in mass markets, perceived value is a critical feature. These factors point to the need for skilled training and, where necessary, appropriate technology.

Perhaps the most important finding is the way to reach and influence the purchasing decisions of the niche market. The target market is influenced by very specific sections of the media. Many are members of clubs, societies and organizations. Therefore knowledge of the quality media, its editorial staff, circulation levels, readership types and typical appropriate advertising is essential. Direct mail using carefully assessed databases is also an effective promotion technique.

Finally, the power of regional images and the "green" image of the countryside is considerable, but equally a power that must not be misused. Bad publicity over environmental issues could be disastrous in a market which enjoys critical media coverage.

The overall implication of the tourism market study was that local people would need considerable and sympathetic assistance to develop niche market/ marketing opportunities. That assistance could be provided by public or private sectors, but financial support would most likely come from the public sector in the early years.

Case studies of rural niche markets

Examples of rural niche products and services were reviewed by the OECD (1995a). In Amagase in the rural part of Japan's Oita Prefecture, floriculture using water from local hot springs is a successful niche activity. Beginning in 1983, the area now ships 3.4 million boxes of roses to market annually, resulting in increased local employment and prosperity. The hot springs enable year-round energy savings for heating glasshouses; energy saving is coupled with skilled marketing and cooperative organization. This illustrates the importance of re-assessing local resources, in this case the hitherto unused hot springs.

Speciality food production, specifically foie gras production, is a rural niche activity in Magnoac in the Hautes Pyrénées of France. An area of ageing population with poor agricultural structures was persuaded by a local politician to develop production of foie gras and related products. Between 1985 and 1992, the number of ducks and geese slaughtered rose from 4,500 to 25,000 annually. A local processing plant has been set up. The new prosperity has helped population levels to stabilise and average age levels have fallen. Key factors in success were noted to be growing consumer demand, regional brand promotion and partnerships among producers.

In Norway in 1990, a government backed but private trust, Norway Crafts, was charged with the renaissance of the craft industries in rural Norway. Measures taken included establishing a data base of enterprises and associated trades, development of training courses, quality labelling and better marketing strategies. Norway Crafts aims to create 2,000 new rural jobs by the year 2000.

A speciality niche rarely considered, that of retirement living, is being pursued in Elliot Lake, a community 600 km north of Toronto, Canada. The mining town of Elliot Lake reached a peak population of 18,000 in 1986. Mine closures then began which predicated the loss of 3,000 jobs over the period 1991–6. Massive economic decline seemed inevitable. Elliot Lake is, however, situated in a very scenic area providing a healthy environment and opportunities for recreational activities. A private sector/public sector local partnership was formed to take over the surplus housing stock, resulting from the out migration of unemployed miners, and to promote the concept of the community as a first class retirement living area. Its rural attributes — good scenery, small town friendliness, low crime levels, low property costs — were key features of a carefully targeted marketing campaign. Since the beginning of the Retirement Living programme over 3,000 retirees have moved to Elliot Lake. This influx created 765 direct and indirect jobs. Many of the in-migrants were in the early retirement category, aged from 55 to 65; these still energetic people have been important in a rapid rise in voluntary activities in the town. While there are problems which remain to be overcome in Elliot Lake, a well founded partnership approach is one key to marketing niche services in rural locations.

At Litschau in Austria, a series of measures aimed at the niche market seeking health and activity holidays in rural but not mountainous environments successfully expanded bed nights spent in the Litschau area from 22,600 in 1988 to 72,263 in 1992. Fifty-five new jobs came from the establishment of a new holiday village and golf course and other businesses took on 80 new employees, while building activities accounted for 350 temporary jobs. Key factors here were a long-term partnership between outside experts (bringing "know-how", contacts and coordinating skills), the local and regional public sector, and private sector initiatives at both the local and national scale. Considerable public sector infrastructure investment was also necessary, guided and controlled by a broad regional policy plan for the entire area.

Although there has been great interest in the Amvrakikos Gulf in Greece in establishing a niche market activity based on natural heritage — especially eco-tourism based on birds and other wetland features — economic success has not yet been achieved. Although the Gulf is one of only 11 wetland complexes in the world protected under the Convention of Ramsar because of their wildfowl species, the development step from concept to reality, from natural environment to tourism product, has not been completed. But important pre-requisites in setting and attaining conservation goals, obtaining local support and enlisting outside technical and legal assistance are in place. The complex and often slow nature of the niche market development process has been recognized. The next steps are to create private/public sector partnerships, complete the infrastructure, animate and develop local expertise in tourism skills, and undertake the sophisticated task of contacting niche eco-tourism markets in foreign countries.

Among these case studies, there was a basic requirement for success: the re-assessment of local resources with a careful mix of local knowledge and outside expertise. Eight supporting elements were identified as important for niche market exploitation:

1. **Local initiative and entrepreneurship**. Enterprise training may be necessary.

2. **Partnership and organizational structure**. Partnerships among businesses, residents, farmers, experts and public sector officials and organizations will smooth the complex paths to development, offset the small scale nature of many rural businesses and offer support. A range of organizational structures were identified as working well.

3. **Territorial linkages**. The image of a rural region and its associations can be a powerful one for consumers. Successful rural niche marketing campaigns typically draw on rural landscapes, traditions or the perception of the intrinsic qualities of the countryside.

4. **Advertising**. Modern techniques for marketing and advertising are not traditional to rural life but are critical to success. The markets for rural niche products are usually in distant cities, sometimes in foreign countries. The niche product has to compete for its share of the consumers' disposable income with a range of other goods and services. Effective marketing depends on local awareness of the market combined with the use of special expertise from the region and often beyond.

5. **Information, communications and transport networks**. Without effective links to the outside world, niche market activity becomes extremely difficult. There are still many problems of cost and time created by distance and remoteness.

6. **Technical and financial assistance**. While the private sector is key to success, public sector assistance also plays a key role. Assistance was delivered in many different ways. The dilemma of long-term help causing dependency and discouraging innovation is problematic.

7. **Regulatory measures**. The role of the public sector in regulation is important in two senses. There is a need for regional strategies and environmental conservation regulations to coordinate activities and to maintain the quality of the rural environment. Also, certificates of area of origin and quality charters are important issues for the regulators.

8. **Re-evaluation**. Changes in niche market behaviour and new competition within niches are frequent. To remain successful and to retain competitive advantage, regular reviews and re-assessment of activities are essential.

How can rural amenities lead to niche employment and enterprise creation?

The concept of amenity is interpreted to include not just scenic values but also values of heritage and rural lifestyles (OECD, 1994). Rural amenity can lead to employment and enterprise creation through tourism, through linking amenity values to locally produced food, and also through recreation, retirement to rural areas, and the attraction of enterprises to rural areas because of perceived amenity benefits. One must also recognize the value of "rural sentiment", a "perception and interpretation of the environment in terms of attributes such as rural ambience, wholesomeness, peace and quiet, historical nature and quaintness..." (Coppack *et al.*, 1990).

An analysis of Canadian examples (Clemenson, 1995a; Canadian Economic Advisory Council, 1992; Heritage Canada, 1991, 1992) identified five issues to consider:

1. The need to **seek niche markets on a global basis** to take full advantage of amenity. The remote town of Yellowknife in Canada's Northwest Territories (population 15,000) has exploited the amenity of the aurora borealis or northern lights. This phenomena is of special significance to Korean and Japanese visitors. This niche group is accessed by an air link to Calgary, one of the major winter sports transit points for Asian visitors to the Alberta ski resorts. It is estimated to bring an annual revenue of $1.5 million to the community.

2. The **linkages between amenity and craft production**. The marketing of unique products drawing on the cultural amenity of the Canadian North is exemplified by the development of Arctic Co-operatives Ltd. Among its many services, this organization links 37 community cooperatives (with a total of 9,967 members in 1992) to selected retail crafts outlets in urban areas throughout Canada, including eight of its own stores.

3. Heritage Canada (a national not-for-profit organization), for example, assists communities and local businesses to put to **use heritage and amenity resources as business resources** (Brown, 1996). The process of turning

scenery and tradition into saleable commodities has brought local people together with the aid of trained project officers to discuss, learn and act in partnership before setting up specific business projects. The role of an animateur (project coordinator) as a catalyst for local action, to help identify and develop niche products and services is vital to Heritage Canada's work.

4. Amenity is an important factor in encouraging **mobile retired persons to migrate to the countryside**. The example of Elliot Lake has already been discussed. Similar developments are occurring elsewhere and amenity is a key factor in this type of counter urbanization (La Greca *et al.*, 1985; Cossey, 1989).

5. **Migration to rural areas by small businesses**. Work in the UK and Canada suggests that amenity is important in attracting small urban entrepreneurs to rural locations (Keeble *et al.*, 1992). Improved telecommunications also play an important role.

There are three main implications for the niche marketing of rural amenities. First, development must not damage amenity. It may be in the producers' interests to seek conservation measures and to work closely with planning and environmental organizations to achieve long-term sustainability. Second, the use of amenity to create niche market jobs entails cooperation and collaboration among key players, usually requiring outside assistance or networking and partnership development. Finally, it seems that employment creation linked to amenity exploitation tends to be small scale. This may have relatively little effect in some areas but in small remote communities, even a few jobs can make a difference.

What is the role of entrepreneurship and management skills for rural niche market producers?

The research (Chassagne, 1995; Chassagne *et al.*, 1989; Sylvander *et al.*, 1994; Joyal, 1994) has identified two major findings:

1. specific aptitudes are required for niche market development; and

2. there is no universal way to transfer niche market development skills to rural entrepreneurs.

Specific abilities are required for niche market entrepreneurship. These aptitudes differ fundamentally from those required for traditional rural economic activities. A carefully cultivated, rather than spontaneous, relationship between producer and consumer is essential. Innovation, development, production and marketing are all required, a mixture which makes working in partnership vital. In rural areas many local people are shy of innovation and rivalries between local people can make working in partnerships difficult. Marketing as a form of entrepreneurship is especially difficult: traditional rural activities do not require professional marketing. Enterprise failure is commonly due to a belief that a good product will sell itself. Furthermore the non-industrial background of rural producers could be a problem in achieving standardized, "industrial" quality control, where variations in size, shape etc. are not permitted. The acceptance of the idea of a life cycle for a niche product is difficult for many rural producers. A strategy of continuous development and change is not a tradition in the countryside. To be successful, techniques for anticipating changes in demand are necessary, along with the early search for new products based on the same resources. In short, rural niche producers need a range of non-traditional skills, and many of these skills are both hard to acquire and hard to teach quickly.

The second major finding is that there is no universal and simple way of transferring niche market development skills to rural entrepreneurs. Four different types of rural situations, each requiring different forms of intervention, may be delineated:

1. **Developed regions**, usually with highly efficient agricultural systems, but totally unfamiliar with marketing. In the past, entrepreneurship has been geared to intensive, cost effective production of basic commodities. Market knowledge and knowledge of marketing are essential new entrepreneurial skills. Perhaps the best approach to developing niche market entrepreneurship in these regions would be to use specially trained farm advisors. The advisors have the confidence of the farmers and are aware of their background and existing skills base. Typical areas of this type in Europe include much of northern France and some of the eastern farmlands of the Republic of Ireland.

2. **Diversified economies in decline**, often due to economic re-structuring and to changes in demand for products. These areas frequently have enterprising attitudes, but those attitudes need to be given renewed confidence and a new product mix developed. While local actors in this type of area usually quickly understand the niche market approach, advisors are necessary to stimulate imaginative new ideas and to bring new production and marketing techniques. One useful way forward can be to analyse the products of the past, see why they have declined and build on the experience of the past to provide new products and new ideas. The Tarn region of France exemplifies this type of area.

3. **Areas lagging in economic development over a long period**, typically due to outdated farm systems and craft production and where the population lacks innovation. Regions of this type are probably the most difficult to inspire to niche market success and thus need the most extensive and most sophisticated assistance from outside. A pre-requisite is to boost morale, to restore local identity and to regain pride based on past successes. However, there is a critical danger if too much reliance is placed on outside assistance. Outsiders may be ill-received in such areas or even rejected. Local "resource persons" — potential "movers and shakers" — should therefore be identified

and encouraged to animate the local community. The vast arid plain of the Alentejo in southern Portugal is one example of this type of area.

4. **Peripheral, or regions with special climatic difficulties**, typified by the northern parts of Scandinavia, often having few physical resources, but with strong human resilience and combativeness connected with their difficult environment. Powerful innovation capacities are needed to overcome the handicaps of site and situation. Networking with outside markets and agents is also typically important. Once new ideas are available, together with start-up funds, this type of area often proves very successful at niche market activity. Success stories include Caithness and Sutherland in northern Scotland and the MicMac Indians on Cape Breton Island in Atlantic Canada.

Additional entrepreneurial and management factors to be considered are:

1. the need to be cautious about both technology transfer and the transfer of approaches to change and development from one region to another;

2. the need to obtain community consent and to set up a "grass roots" discovery and learning process;

3. the danger of developing dependency on outside expertise and on a single product;

4. the importance of participatory SWOT (strengths, weaknesses, opportunities, threats) analyses rather than sterile inventories of resources;

5. the relevance of teaching negotiating techniques to encourage better partnership and network building. Successful negotiation is a positive sum game where each party gains something, rather than a game where victory is one sided;

6. the importance of clear communication procedures, between partners, between advisors and local people, between markets and producers. Listening to partners and to consumers is an acquired skill of great importance;

7. the need to develop individual aptitudes within a partnership team.

What is the linkage between niche products and territory?

Guerry (1995) identified a number of points to consider in achieving and maintaining a territorial association with a particular rural product or service:

1. Territorial branding is closely linked to both quality standards and quantity limitations. Alone, territorial branding could fail if quality is compromised or if mass production makes niche goods commonplace.

2. While territorial branding can be used to charge premium prices, and price differentiation is an important part of territorial branding, overpricing can lead to market failure.

3. Territorial branding is a complex area which requires careful consumer research. Only a few people recognize local names outside the local area: recognizable, regional names must be researched. In France a survey revealed that many French and foreign tourists were having difficulty locating the Midi-Pyrénées region. The region was obliged to change its name for tourism marketing purposes to Toulouse Midi-Pyrénées because the city was better known than the surrounding area in the minds of consumers.

4. Too many territorial labels can confuse consumers.

5. There can be political issues where regional names have great local significance, but are not known outside the area by consumers.

6. Partnership implications can arise if several communities need to unite to use a common regional brand name.

7. Legal protection may be required for certain regional names. EU law now recognizes two forms of protection:

● Protected designation of origin (PDO) applying to products closely linked to place of origin from raw material to preparation;

● Protected geographical indication (PGI) referring to products in which place of origin is less important but nevertheless is a feature in at least one stage of production or processing.

8. Designation protection cannot be used as a "customs barrier" to stifle competition.

Guerry (1995) recognized the importance of synergy between tourism promotion, tourism, product promotion and product production. Two concepts were put forward to develop this synergy. The first was to develop group sales to visitors by means of *Maison de Pays* (local produce centres) and/or *Maison de l'Artisanat* (local crafts centres). These developments freed producers from difficult and time-consuming retail activity, helped to develop the regional brand among consumers and could provide a channel to develop partnership among local entrepreneurs.

Secondly, he examined the new concept of Village Plus, a proposed network of 300 villages across the whole of France designed to market and enhance performance in the rural sector through tourism and local product promotion. Similar to ideas such as Country Village Weekend Breaks in UK (Lane, 1995a), and the Japanese One Village, One Product movement (*Isson Ippin Undo*), (Fujimoto, 1992), Village Plus takes territorial branding to a new scale, that of the entire countryside, to achieve economies of scale in promotion and development and to overcome the geographical ignorance of many consumers.

The key implications for niche market producers are three fold. First, it is clear that territorial linkage is important for niche market products. Second, great care is necessary in choosing names that are recognizable and meaningful to the consumer, that are protected and that guarantee quality. Third, there is valuable synergy between tourism services and niche market products, but that synergy is not easy to grasp and more research is needed to test the validity of various methods of achieving synergy.

The specific case of farm household diversification and niche product development

Important to this discussion is the recognition of the many different ways in which individual farm households may diversify their income. There may be farm diversification — producing different products, or services such as tourism. There may be farm income diversification, whereby off-farm income is earned by household members and that income may or may not be linked to agriculture. Farm households may seek to diversify their income sources in many ways and all could be connected to niche product development. A review of the Japanese experience is instructive (Goto, 1995; Chiiki Shakai Keikaku Centre, 1993; Sakata Tokio, 1989; Takahashi Masaro *et al.*, 1985; Fujimoto, 1992; and Hiramatsu, 1993).

The One Village, One Product movement originated in 1959 in Oita Prefecture in the town of Oyama. Local farmers came together to seek ways of adding value to their farm production by specializing in high value plums and chestnuts. In addition to measures to aid production, emphasis was placed on developing human resources and local people were encouraged to travel and study abroad. By the mid 1970s Oyama was recognized as a leader in niche marketing and in rural regeneration in Japan. Numerous other towns within the province and the nation began to emulate Oyama's self-help specialization: total sales from over 250 specialist rural products now amount to 120 billion yen per year across the country. Critical to success has been indigenous effort and innovation, assisted by education and study. In addition, the concept was backed and led by provincial governor Hiramatsu Morihiko:

> *I thought that if they made a speciality product symbolising their area and advertised the item nation-wide, their income would increase and more tourists would visit their town. (Hiramatsu, 1993)*

Complimenting the One Village, One Product concept has been a highly innovative and efficient direct marketing scheme. The Japanese wholesale/retail system is both complex and expensive. Direct marketing is therefore well suited to local conditions. It is estimated that 17 percent of all perishable farm products in 1989 were distributed by direct marketing. Central to the system is the *furusato* sales and parcel system, which links regular supplies of local products to urban households. Specific villages supply specific households and often develop a personal relationship between the parties, with urban people coming out to the village to help in crop planting and/or harvesting.

The Japanese experience provides a number of lessons. Most success was achieved in localities which were not advanced in modern agriculture and were forced to rely on traditional methods. This apparent weakness was converted into a strength by niche marketing. Greatest success has come where there were strong local partnerships and leadership. There is effective participation at the household level. Also, great stress is put on human resource development, reinforcing the findings of Chassagne (1995).

A second set of lessons concerns the increasingly important role of women in innovation and development.

Third, and again reinforcing the findings of Chassagne (1995), close links were established between consumers and producers, with the latter involving and listening to the needs of the former. Research also revealed that confidence and pride development measures were critical parts of the development process.

One of the key reasons for success in Japan has been the national nature of rural product development. The concepts discussed above are nationally known and they have captured the imagination of many urban consumers. The earlier discussion on the need for niche products to be fashionable is extremely relevant here (Lane, 1995a).

While Japan has successfully seen steady "grass roots" development of niche products, there remains a need to better coordinate the response of central government departments. Specific areas noted were the need for enforceable quality and territorial labelling schemes and better advice and information systems for farm households and communities.

Public policy frameworks to facilitate rural niche markets

Beyond doubt, the concept of niche market production has a valuable role to play in encouraging enterprise development within the countryside. It encourages a re-evaluation of rural resources, it can help raise female participation rates in both employment and decision making, it can lead to new forms of market responsive business and it can encourage new migrants into the countryside. Also, there is likely to be synergy with existing rural economic activity. All of these points are typical objectives of existing rural policies.

Why has niche product development been so slow to date? A number of reasons may be put forward. Farm price support has discouraged innovation. Rural society tends to deprecate change and distrust new ideas. Risk takers can have a hard time in rural society: there is little anonymity and failure is rarely forgotten. Partnership and negotiating skills can be rare. Contacts within urban markets are few. Above all, the art and science of product marketing is not a rural strength. While in theory public sector bodies could help, lethargy, sectoralism and fear of free market enterprise and new ideas has slowed public sector response.

Six areas of policy response require attention (Summarized from Clemenson, 1995b; Lane, 1995b):

1. **Human resource development**

   Training is necessary for both rural people in the private sector and for public officials. Critical areas include leadership training, general entrepreneurship, marketing, negotiation and partnership skills, networking and the use of information technology. Exactly how to carry out human resource development remains an area for further research. While there are great differences between regions and their requirements, there are common factors. In some rural areas the conventional education system could help, in others, distance learning may be a possibility, while both brokers and animateurs may have a special role.

2. **Research, information and communications**

   Market awareness and market research have been key factors in many successful niche product developments. Most rural entrepreneurs have little access to research findings, nor are they generally informed or have sufficient resources to commission special enquiries. Three issues of policy response arise. How much emphasis should government put on research into niche markets? How should research results be disseminated and made available? How much public money should be injected into research and dissemination?

3. **Regulations and finance for niche product development**

   The issues of territorial and quality labelling are areas of consumer confusion and, often, governments are the best regulatory body. Yet to devise territorial labelling legislation is no easy task and may be abused as a market distorting measure. There may be, on the other hand, a case for de-regulating some areas of activity: for example, laws designed for factory production relating to hygiene, sanitation and safety may be an unjustified restriction on home based business development. Special funding could be used directly as risk capital, or indirectly to finance advice services, or "one stop shops" to provide assistance to entrepreneurs needing financial, legal, technical or marketing aid.

4. **The balance between public and private sector involvement and the roles of central and local government**

   The role of the partnership is a linking thread. However, within partnerships, there are many variations on how they are devised and operated. Important policy issues emerge: Who should be responsible for setting up partnerships and for pump-priming their finances? Who should hold and disseminate information and expertise on how to set up and operate partnerships? Another issue concerns the balance of power within partnerships between the public sector, the private sector and the local community. Finally, there is the issue of the duration of partnerships: are they short-term innovations to oversee change, or are they long-term requirements?

5. Territorial differentiation and niche market development

Policy responses need to take into account differences among rural areas if success is to be achieved. The OECD (1993) typology of territory that recognizes economically integrated regions, intermediate regions and remote areas is instructive. Research (e.g. Chassagne, 1995) illustrates the need for territorial differentiation in policy responses.

6. Conserving rurality into the 21st century

Many niche products and services carry the potential seeds for the destruction of their own market. The possible overdevelopment of rural tourism, the potential population imbalance that retirement living policies can bring, the overproduction of speciality foods leading to loss of speciality: all call for a carefully developed policy towards the conservation of rurality to ensure sustainable development. There are many examples of conflict between job creation and conservation. Niche market development should therefore include land management and community planning policies at an early stage. Entrepreneurship should act responsibly for the public and private good despite the pressures of the market place. Only public policy responses can ensure this. Whether there are special ways of achieving that balance and whether the balance is best achieved locally or centrally are matters of debate.

Conclusion

The enquiry into the role of niche markets and marketing as a strategy for rural regeneration has initiated a solution-based discussion on rural policy, as opposed to a problem-based discussion. Also, niche marketing provides a cross-sectoral focus — another objective of rural development policy. How do rural producer networks best function? What are the keys to successful partnership creation? Can the information highway be used to disseminate new ideas, start new networks and develop new marketing methods? Is synergy a mirage, or are there real values in seeking synergy between producers in a rural region? Will niche products survive the stresses placed on the middle classes by white collar job restructuring, and equally, will new industrial manufacturing techniques seek to seize the initiative for niche products away from traditional rural producers? How can advisers and educators best act to develop the human resource to cope with all those issues? We remain convinced that a better understanding of niche markets and niche marketing will improve rural employment opportunities, and, with care, lead to sustainable rural community development.

References and further reading

Brown, V. (1996) Heritage, tourism and rural regeneration: the heritage regions programme in Canada. *Journal of Sustainable Tourism* Vol. 4, No. 3 (forthcoming).

Canadian Economic Advisory Council. (1992) *Eco-tourism in Canada*. Ottawa.

Chassagne, M.E. (1995) Entrepreneurship and management skills among rural producers. In *Niche Markets and Rural Development: Workshop Proceedings and Policy Recommendations*. Paris: OECD, pp. 29-50.

Chassagne, M.E., Gorgeu, Y. and Hirn, J.C. (1989) *Guide de la valorisation économiques des ressources locales*. SYROS, coll. Initiatives.

Chiiki Shakai Keikaku Centre. (1993) *Noson Fujin no Kigyo ni kansuru Chosahokokusho (Research Report on Entrepreneurship among Rural Women)*. Tokyo: Chiiki Shakai Keikaku Centre.

Clemenson, H. (1995a) Rural amenities, employment and enterprise creation. In *Niche Markets and Rural Development: Workshop Proceedings and Policy Recommendations*. Paris: OECD, pp. 51-66.

Clemenson, H. (1995b) How to build niche market capacity: policy issues. In *Niche Markets and Rural Development: Workshop Proceedings and Policy Recommendations*. Paris: OECD, pp. 21-26.

Cloke, P. (ed.) (1988) *Policies and Plans for Rural People: An International Perspective*. London: Allen and Unwin.

Coppack, P.M., Beesley, K.B. and Mitchell, C. (1990) Rural attractions and rural development: Elora, Ontario Case Study. In Dykeman, F. (ed.). *Entrepreneurial and Sustainable Rural Communities*. Sackville, New Brunswick: Rural and Small Town Research Studies Programme, Mount Alison University, pp. 115-128.

Cossey, K.M. (1989) *Rural Environments and the Elderly: Impact, Contributions and Needs Fulfilment*. Sackville, New Brunswick: Rural and Small Town Research Studies Programme, Mount Alison University.

Dickson, P.R. and Ginter, J.L. (1987) Market segmentation, product differentiation and marketing strategy. *Journal of Marketing* Vol. 4.

Fujimoto, I. (1992) Lessons from abroad in rural community revitalization: the One Village, One Product movement in Japan. *Community Development Journal*. Vol. 27, pp. 10-20.

Goto, J. (1995) Income diversification in the farm household. In *Niche Markets and Rural Development: Workshop Proceedings and Policy Recommendations*. Paris: OECD, pp. 111-134.

Guerry, P. (1995) The linkage between niche products and territory. In *Niche Markets and Rural Development: Workshop Proceedings and Policy Recommendations*. Paris: OECD, pp. 67-79.

Heritage Canada. (1991) *The Ontario Heritage Regions Programme Description*. Ottawa: Heritage Canada.

Heritage Canada. (1992) *Annual Report 1991-1992*. Ottawa: Heritage Canada.

Hiramatsu, M. (1993) One Village, One Product. *Farming Japan* Vol. 27, No. 3, pp. 10-34.

Joyal, A. (ed.). (1994) *Studies on Small and Medium Size Organizations in the Development of Rural Communities*. Trois-Rivières: GREPME (Groupe de recherche en économie et gestion des petites et moyennes organisations et de leur environnement), Université du Quebec à Trois-Rivières.

Keeble, D., Tyler, P., Broom, G. and Lewis, J. (1992) *Business Success in the Countryside: The Performance of Rural Enterprise*. London: HMSO.

La Greca, A.J., Streib, G.F. and Folts, E.W. (1985) Retirement communities and their life stages. *Journal of Gerontology* Vol. 40, No. 2, pp. 211-218.

Lane, B. (1994) Tourism strategies and rural development. In *Tourism Policy and International Tourism in OECD Countries 1991-2*. Paris: OECD, pp. 13-75.

Lane, B. (1995a) Creating niche markets in a growing sector: rural tourism. In *Niche Markets and Rural Development: Workshop Proceedings and Policy Recommendations*. Paris: OECD, pp. 80-109.

Lane, B. (1995b) Niche markets: their role and impacts. In *Niche Markets and Rural Development: Workshop Proceedings and Policy Recommendations*. Paris: OECD, pp. 15-19.

OECD. (1993) *What Future for Our Countryside? A Rural Development Policy*. Paris: OECD.

OECD. (1994) *The Contribution of Amenities to Rural Development*. Paris: OECD.

OECD. (1995a) *Niche Markets as a Rural Development Strategy*. Paris: OECD.

OECD. (1995b) *Niche Markets and Rural Development: Workshop Proceedings and Policy Recommendations* Paris: OECD.

Plog, S. (1991) *Leisure Travel: Making it a Growth Market Again*. New York: John Wiley.

Robinson, G. M. (1990) *Conflict and Change in the Countryside*. London: Belhaven.

Sakata Tokio (1989) *Chiiki Kasseika: Sono Senryaku (Strategies for Revitalising Local Areas)*. Tokyo: Gyosei.

Schnaars, S.P. (1991) *Marketing Strategy: A Customer Driven Approach*. New York: The Free Press.

Shih, D. (1986) VALS as a tool of tourism market research. *Journal of Travel Research* Spring, pp. 2-11.

Sylvander, B. and Melet, I. (1994) *La qualité spécifique en agro-alimentaire, marchés, institutions et acteurs*. Toulouse: Series 94-01 INRA.

Takahashi Masaro *et al.* (1985) *Mura o Ikasu: Chiiki Kako-sangyo no Atarashii Nami (Giving Life to the Village: New Waves in Local Processing Industries)*. Tokyo: Tsukuba Shobo.

Chapter twenty-nine:

Tourism: A Potential Source of Rural Employment

Jean-Claude Bontron and Nadine Lasnier
Études Géographiques, Économiques et Sociologiques Appliquées (SEGESA)
Paris, France

Abstract

Tourism contributes significantly to rural employment, although the impact varies greatly among rural regions. Tourism in rural areas employs relatively more females than urban tourism, partly because rural tourism is more seasonal and part-time. Also, due to seasonality factors, rural tourism capacity (e.g. accommodation capacity) generates fewer jobs than urban tourism capacity. Within predominantly rural regions, employment in tourism in all countries is growing faster than the overall employment growth.

Introduction

Although tourism has been affected by the recession that has swept through our economies, over the past thirty years tourism has emerged as a high-growth activity involving an increasing number of people and increasing capital investments. For an increasing number of countries, this has meant an increase in the number of both incoming and outgoing travellers.

In rural areas this expansion has been more modest slower to develop, except in some coastal regions, mountains, historic towns and outstanding cultural sites. But today rural tourism is demonstrating genuine economic potential based on local heritage resources (e.g. landscape, natural attractions local culture, gastronomy, etc.), on the development of reception facilities and on tourism expertise which is becoming increasingly specialized and better geared toward the new aspirations of urbanites.

Rural tourism is a growth sector and a means to diversify rural economies affected by a decline in agriculture and traditional industries. Local operators frequently view it as a way to develop new initiatives and create jobs, if not to restructure the entire economy.

A recent OECD report (OECD, 1994a) contends that tourism helps, *inter alia*, to preserve local jobs in marginal rural areas, to create new jobs where the activity prospers, and to diversify employment, but there are few hard figures to substantiate the claims. The objective of this chapter is to assess the importance and role of tourism-related employment in rural areas. The first step was to clarify the methodology and to obtain statistical data from OECD countries at a regional level. This work is experimental and represents a contribution to the OECD Rural Development Programme.

It should be noted that our approach differs from that taken by the OECD Tourism Committee (OECD, 1994a); we do not view rural tourism as a separate sub-category of tourism but as any tourism carried out in localities or regions classified as rural under the definition set forth by OECD's Rural Development Programme (OECD, 1994b).

Methodology: aims and options

An international approach to tourism-related employment raises numerous problems, involving a number of methodological options.

Problems involved

The problems involved in measuring the impact of tourism development on rural labour markets are threefold.

1. Tourism-related activity is inadequately identified in statistics

There is international consensus on the definition of tourism. It comprises, according to the United Nations,

> *The activities of persons travelling to and staying in places outside their usual environment for not more than one consecutive year for leisure, business and other purposes.*

> *The use of this broad concept makes it possible to identify tourism between countries as well as tourism within a country. "Tourism" refers to all activities of visitors, including both "tourists" (overnight visitors) and "same-day visitors". (United Nations, 1994)*

Such practices clearly generate economic activity and jobs in a large number of sectors, particularly services: transport, accommodation, catering, activity leadership, leisure activities, organization, marketing, etc. However, the tourism industry as a statistical concept is not used by any of the OECD member countries.

2. Tourism-related employment is, by its very nature, hard to identify

For several reasons it is hard to identify tourism businesses and measure their activity in terms of jobs:

1. The businesses involved rarely cater to the tourist trade alone but usually serve year-round residents as well.

2. Jobs may arise from tourism either directly (e.g. accommodation, catering, operation and maintenance of specific facilities, organization of tourism, promotion, etc.), in tandem (e.g. passenger transport, services and businesses catering for extra consumers, etc.) or indirectly (e.g. construction and civil engineering, agricultural produce for direct sales, etc.).

3. Employment in tourism is largely seasonal (and often insecure); for this reason it is often measured poorly by major population censuses (a census carried out in March, for instance, will take no account of summer jobs).

4. In some cases businesses and employees are mobile, and it is therefore difficult to pinpoint jobs (a certain proportion of workers in the catering trade, for instance, may successively spend the summer and winter season in different places).

5. Tourists by definition are away from home and therefore difficult to trace, which means they are absent from many major censuses.

3. International harmonization

These methodological problems are naturally compounded when the focus moves from the national to the regional level (as there are usually fewer statistics at the regional level), and from the national to the international level (owing to major differences among national statistical systems). Nevertheless, this should not preclude any attempt to compile indicators.

Methodological options

It seemed feasible, using the existing detailed nomenclatures for employment and activities, to identify at the regional level a sphere of activities fully or partly involved in tourism production. Three main methodological options, taking into account previous OECD recommendations (OECD, 1991) were selected:

1. Labour force at the time of the census

Several approaches have been proposed to measure the level of tourism-related employment, some based on special surveys, others on converting value-added or the wage bill into job equivalents. In this particular case, we decided to opt for a more pragmatic solution, i.e. the labour force at the time of census. While this has the disadvantage of poorly reflecting seasonal employment (censuses are usually conducted around March), it does offer the double advantage of reliability and comparability for many countries.

2. Three main sectors

The "tourism labour force" concept spans a number of different industries involving catering, accommodation, transport as well as recreational and leisure activities. After discussion in the OECD Steering Group on Rural Indicators, and bearing in mind the need to compile information for the regional level, the following representative tourism-related activities were selected from the ISIC international two-digit codes:

55	hotels, restaurants and cafes;
60–63	transport and travel;
92	recreational, cultural and sporting activities (market and non-market services).

Of course not all the jobs in these industries can be attributed to tourism. Discussions have been held on the subject within OECD, but have not yet produced any detailed weightings. We have therefore decided to count in full all three categories of activity, which are indisputably related to tourism.

We should point out that some countries have more detailed nomenclatures at the regional level, which gives a finer view of tourism-related employment, but the need to harmonize international data was felt to be more important.

3. Ten-year trend

For the trend in tourism-related employment and its comparison with overall employment, our approach has been to compare the last two available census years, corresponding roughly to the decade of the 1980s. The use of annual rates eliminates the impact of periodicity-related disparities. (Note that the data for Switzerland is for 1985 and 1990 and for France, the data are for 1982 and 1990.)

Collecting indicators

Based on experience gained in the OECD Steering Group on Rural Indicators, a questionnaire was sent to OECD countries to obtain indicators on tourism-related employment at the regional level within each country. The purpose was threefold.

1. To assess tourism's contribution to regional employment

Using the methodological options described above, it was possible:

1. to assess the proportion of regional jobs involved in tourism;
2. to analyse the nature of these jobs (e.g. employment sector, female employment, growing or declining industry, etc.); and
3. to relate these employment trends to overall labour-force trends.

2.   To study the salient features of tourism-related employment among different types of regions

The structural and development features of tourism-related employment were compared for the three types of region identified by the OECD Rural Development Programme: predominantly rural; significantly rural; and predominantly urbanized.

3.   To study the salient features of employment in rural regions identified as "tourist" regions

We thought it would be interesting to analyse employment in rural regions in which tourism was very important. The regions were identified on the basis of indirect indicators of tourism potential such as tourist accommodation capacity, the proportion of second homes, statistics on overnight stays, and the relative importance of certain types of tourism-related jobs.

Comparing the statistics raised a few problems, owing to the concepts used in each country. However, since the focus is on the differentiating impact of tourism rather than tourism-related employment *per se*, the work will conceivably produce some interesting comparisons.

Tourism-related employment in OECD countries and regions: the comparative approach

Our data cover nine countries and over 1,500 regions. In spite of the reservations outlined above, it has been possible to prepare a number of comparative tables, by country and by type of region, and these do provide a range of insights. Although intra-country comparisons are valid, international comparisons must be interpreted carefully.

Contribution of tourism to rural employment

Three basic trends emerge from an analysis of the contribution of tourism to rural development.

1.   A significant contribution to national employment

On the basis of our assumptions, the share of tourism-related employment in total employment varies substantially from one country to another but is always relatively important (Table 29.1). At the national level in 1990, tourism-related employment represents 4 percent in Germany, 8 percent in France, Finland and the United Kingdom, 10 percent in Canada, 11 percent in the United States, 12 percent in Spain, 15 percent in Switzerland and 22 percent in Austria. The differences among countries are partly due to differences in the content of statistical categories (in particular with regard to transport and recreational services). However, if we look solely at the hotels/cafes/restaurants category (the most homogenous group of activities across all countries), we find the same patterns, which confirms that tourism plays a very different role in the economy, depending on the country concerned.

Table 29.1.   In predominantly rural regions, employment in hotels/cafes/restaurants varies from 2.8 percent in France to 12.3 percent in Switzerland

	All 3 tourism sectors			Hotels-cafes-restaurants only		
	All regions	Predo-minantly rural	Relatively rural	All regions	Predo-minantly rural	Relatively rural
	Tourism-related employment as percent of total employment, 1990					
Germany	4.0	5.2	4.4	–	–	–
Austria	21.8	17.7	21.0	5.6	7.3	5.1
Canada	9.8	9.3	9.3	4.6	4.3	4.7
United States	11.2	10.5	11.3	3.4	3.0	3.5
Finland	8.3	11.0	4.2	2.8	3.7	1.3
France	7.9	6.5	7.4	3.0	2.8	2.8
United Kingdom	8.3	9.8	4.9	4.2	7.3	3.1
Switzerland	14.9	18.7	11.7	6.9	12.3	6.3

Source: OECD rural data surveys.

2. Profiles vary according to how rural the region is

The relative importance of tourism-related employment, depending on the extent to which a region is urbanized, varies from one country to another. In four countries (Austria, Canada, France and Spain), tourism-related employment as a share of overall employment increases in proportion to urbanisation (Figure 29.1). In another four countries (Finland, United Kingdom, United States and Switzerland), the lowest rates are found in the intermediate (significantly rural) regions, forming a U-curve. Germany, where tourism-related employment decreases with urbanization, appears as a case apart.

To some extent this can be attributed to the fact that, in the transport sector (a major industry only partly given over to tourism, and defined quite differently from one country to another), most workers are located in urban areas. But it is also clear that major cities attract numerous tourists, given the quality and diversity of their cultural heritage and the potential for business tourism. In some places too, growth in the tourist industry generates urbanization (as on the coast).

Figure 29.1. Tourism-related employment as percent of total employment

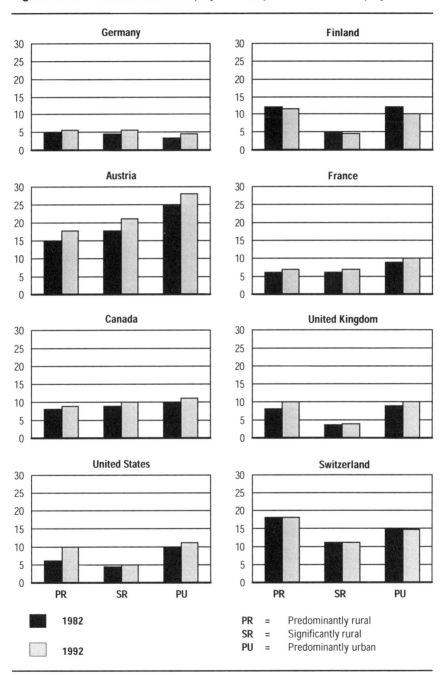

Source: OECD rural data surveys.

Taking the hotels/cafes/restaurants category separately, predominantly rural and significantly rural regions have a higher share of employment in this category relative to the national average.

Tourism-related activities and employment can develop in very sparsely populated rural areas, as demonstrated by the figures in the "predominantly rural regions" column for Canada (1 person/km²), Finland (8 persons/km²) or the United Kingdom (14 persons/km²), with tourism-related activities totalling some 10 percent of employment. Interestingly, for half of the countries in the survey, tourism-related activities already account for more jobs than agriculture in the predominantly rural regions (Figure 29.2).

Figure 29.2.   In predominantly rural regions, tourism-related employment is larger than agricultural employment for countries above the diagonal

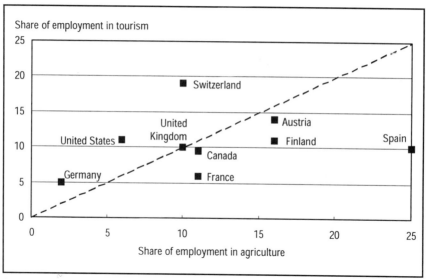

Source: OECD rural data surveys.

3.   A very uneven female participation rate

The participation rate of women in tourism-related employment differs widely from one country to another: one-third in France, 40 to 50 percent in Austria, Canada, Switzerland and the United States, nearly 60 percent in the United Kingdom and two-thirds in Germany. In the last two countries, women seem particularly drawn to tourism-related jobs, which probably offer more scope for part-time work.

The difference among countries is pronounced in all three types of region, and the most interesting feature is that women always account for a greater share of tourism-related employment in rural regions than in urban areas (Figure 29.3).

Tourism activities therefore constitute a particularly valuable source of employment for women in rural regions, many of which suffer from a shortage of jobs.

Figure 29.3. Women hold a larger share of tourism jobs in rural areas than in urban areas

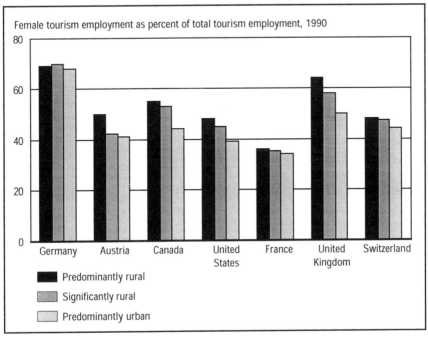

Source: OECD rural data surveys.

As in most sectors of the economy, the proportion of women in tourism-related employment increased almost everywhere (except in the United States) during the period under observation. But the relative increase in the female workforce was less noticeable in rural regions than in the national averages (Table 29.2).

Table 29.2. Change in female employment share in tourism-related employment, 1980 to 1990

	All regions	Predominantly rural regions
	Percentage point difference between 1980 and 1990	
Austria	7.9	6.3
Canada	3.1	3.6
United States	-5.0	-10.6
France	1.4	0.8
United Kingdom	2.3	-3.8
Switzerland	2.3	1.8

Source: OECD rural data surveys.

Rural tourism facilities generate less employment

If tourist-flow indicators (e.g. overall accommodation capacity, number of second homes, overnight stays, etc.) are set side-by-side with tourism-related employment, the comparison among the various types of region turns to the disadvantage of predominantly rural areas. In France, for instance, 100 tourist beds generate 33 tourism-related jobs in urban regions but only five in rural areas. By and large, the ratios show that the number of jobs generated by tourist flows in predominantly rural regions is lower than the national average, 40–50 percent lower in the hotels/cafes/restaurants sector and 60–85 percent lower in recreational services (figures based on five countries). One explanation may be that, taking the year as a whole, less use is made of tourism facilities in rural than in urban areas, and accordingly they generate fewer permanent jobs.

Role of tourism in rural employment trends

1. Tourism, a growth sector in terms of employment

Employment trends in "tourism" activities show that the sector is expanding almost everywhere. For the 1980–90 period, the annual rate of growth for tourism-related employment was approximately 1.5 percent in France, Austria and the United Kingdom, a little over 2 percent in Canada, 2.9 percent in Switzerland, 3.5 percent in Germany and around 6.5 percent in Spain (Table 29.3). It should be noted that the figures for Finland indicate a slight decline in the number of jobs in tourism-related activities, down 0.3 percent, but the breakdown by sector shows that the trend is due to transport activities alone.

Table 29.3.   Rural tourism employment grew substantially in Spain (3.9 percent) the United Kingdom (3.5 percent) and Germany (3.4 percent)

	Total employment change			Tourism employment change*		
	All regions	Predominantly rural regions	Significantly rural regions	All regions	Predominantly rural regions	Significantly rural regions
	Annual percent change in employment, 1980 to 1990					
Germany	1.5	2.1	1.7	3.5	3.4	3.5
Austria	0.4	0.2	0.7	1.9	1.8	2.3
Canada	1.6	1.4	2.6	2.2	2.2	3.0
Spain	0.7	0.7	-0.3	6.4	3.9	2.5
United States	1.8	1.4	2.2	..	..	..
Finland	0.5	-0.2	0.4	-0.3	-0.4	-1.2
France	0.8	0.5	1.0	1.5	1.6	1.9
United Kingdom	0.4	0.9	1.2	1.7	3.5	2.9
Switzerland	1.7	1.5	2.1	3.0	3.0	3.8

Source: OECD rural data surveys.
*   *All 3 tourism sectors.*

Part of the increase in jobs can be attributed to higher local demand for services, namely meals outside the home, and above all urban public transport. But the hotels/cafes/restaurants sector and recreational services, which are more tourist-related, do show very high annual rates of employment growth, usually 2 percent and more for the hotel trade and over 3 percent for recreational services (Table 29.4).

Table 29.4. Employment change in two tourism sectors

	Hotels-cafes-restaurants only			Recreational services		
	All regions	Predo- minantly rural	Rela- tively rural	All regions	Predo- minantly rural	Relatively rural
	Annual percent change					
Austria	2.0	1.5	2.0	3.3	5.8	4.3
Canada	3.8	4.4	4.2	3.8	5.5	3.5
Spain	8.1	6.2	4.4	..	..	..
Finland	1.8	1.5	.9	3.6	4.4	3.4
France	1.9	1.6	2.3	4.0	4.5	4.3
United Kingdom	2.5	2.6	3.1	1.9	5.3	3.3
Switzerland	2.4	2.2	2.8	4.1	11.9	7.6

Source: OECD rural data surveys.

In many countries (Austria, Canada, France, Switzerland, United Kingdom) growth was higher in rural than in urbanized regions. This was not the case for Spain, where the highest rates of growth applied to jobs in urban tourism (Table 29.3). In the United States, it was the intermediate (significantly rural) regions that obtained the highest score. It should also be noted that in Finland only urbanized regions have seen an increase in tourism-related employment.

The upward trend in tourism-related employment in rural regions can also be seen from a separate analysis of the hotel trade and recreational services (Table 29.4). There is a noticeable difference between the predominantly rural regions, which saw a sharp increase in jobs in recreational services (due no doubt to an earlier shortage of facilities), whereas in hotels/cafes/restaurants the expansion was more in intermediate (i.e. significantly rural) areas.

2. Faster growth rate than for overall employment

Tourism-related employment everywhere is expanding rapidly, with rates between two and ten times higher than for the labour force as a whole (Table 29.3). The difference is greater in predominantly rural than in significantly rural areas (Figure 29.4). In some countries (United States, Spain), tourism-related activity clearly has a decisive impact on broad employment trends in rural regions.

Figure 29.4.   Change in total labour force compared with tourism-related labour force, 1980–1990

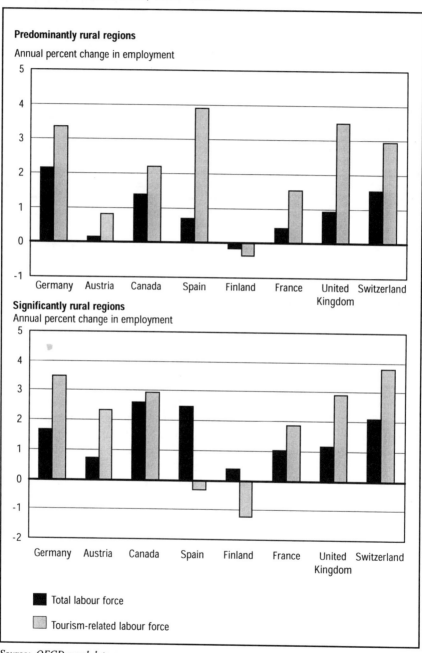

Source: OECD rural data surveys.

2. Features of employment in rural regions with a developing tourist industry

In our opinion, an examination of employment in the most popular tourist regions will bear out the above analysis. To this end, for each country in each group of predominantly rural and significantly rural regions, we have selected three or four regions (listed in the footnote to Table 29.5) showing signs of strong growth in tourism-related activities (in terms of tourist flows and/or employment), and then added up the figures for these regions to calculate a number of percentages (Table 29.5).

Table 29.5. Features of selected rural regions with tourism-intensive employment

	Austria	Canada	Spain	United States	Finland	France	United Kingdom	Switzer- land
Predominantly rural regions that are tourism-intensive								
Population density (1990) (persons/km²)	30.0	3.0	27.0	2.0	1.0	25.0	13.0	16.0
Tourism-related employment as percent of total employment	28.7	18.8	9.3	23.9	11.9	12.6	10.7	47.2
Hotels/cafes/restaurants as percent of total employment	15.8	7.4	4.2	10.1	5.1	5.9	8.5	36.6
Female employment in tourism (percent)	42.9	49.8	–	37.6	–	37.3	65.6	45.6
Annual change in tourism employment (percent)	3.1	4.0	10.0	1.8	-0.5	1.7	3.3	1.9
Annual change in hotel/cafe/ restaurant employment (percent)	1.3	4.9	12.4	–	-0.7	1.6	2.8	1.3
Annual change in total labour force (percent)	1.2	2.1	0..2	2.1	1.3	0.9	0.9	0.3
Significantly rural regions that are tourism-intensive								
Population density (1990) (persons/km²)	88.0	102.0	101.0	76.0	9.0	89.0	94.0	70.0
Tourism-related employment as percent of total employment	23.8	10.8	14.9	21.1	5.0	8.7	12.6	21.9
Hotels/cafes/restaurants as percent of total employment	8.3	6.0	9.2	7.0	1.7	4.5	10.0	16.8
Female employment in tourism (percent)	42.1	57.6	–	37.4	–	37.1	59.2	47.3
Annual change in tourism employment (percent)	4.3	1.9	2.6	2.1	-1.1	2.6	0.1	2.7
Annual change in hotel/cafe/ restaurant employment (percent)	1.3	2.9	3.5	–	0.1	2.7	-0.5	2.1
Annual change in total labour force (percent)	1.1	1.1	0.7	2.6	1.3	1.7	1.5	3.9

Source: OECD rural data surveys.

Notes:

The following predominantly rural regions were used to calculate the figures:

Austria: Landeck; Reutte; Zell-am-See; Kitzbühel.

Canada: Okanagan-Similkameen Region, British Columbia; Census Division No. 15 (Banff and Jasper), Alberta; Fraser-Cheam Region and Squamish-Lilloet Region, British Columbia.

Spain: Huesca; Lerida; Huelva.

United States: Regions 2102, 2199, 2101, all three located in Colorado; Region 2202, located in eastern California.

Finland: Kittilän; Föglön; Sodankylän.

France: Alpes-de-Haute-Province; Lozère; Savoie; Hautes-Alpes.

United Kingdom: Highland; Dumfries and Galloway; Powys.

Switzerland: Schanfigg; Davos; Oberengadin; Engadina-Bassa.

The following significantly rural regions were used to calculate the figures:

Austria: Bludenz; Villach; Bregenz.

Canada: Essex County, Ontario; Niagara Regional Municipality, Ontario; Saint Maurice Region, Québec.

Spain: Baléares; Gerona; Tarragona.

United States: Region 5201 (Hawaii) and 17801 (southern New Jersey).

Finland: Heinolan; Rovaniemen.

France: Pyrénées-Orientales; Var; Haute-Savoie.

United Kingdom: Cornwall; Gwynedd.

Switzerland: Sierre; Locarno; Nidwalden-Engelberg.

The popular tourist regions in the "predominantly rural" group all have in common a very low population density (1 to 30 persons/km²). Tourism-related employment plays an important part, with a share of total employment of up to 47 percent (Switzerland). In most cases the share of jobs in tourism is double that for rural regions as a whole. For example, employment in the hotel/cafes/restaurants category alone amounts to up to 37 percent of total employment in the four Swiss regions selected, which are regions with a large number of ski resorts. The female participation rate reflects the average already discussed above. Tourism-related jobs are expanding rapidly (by 2 to 4 percent a year), except in Finland, and are promoting the growth of overall employment in these regions, whose demographic and economic development is generally higher than that of other rural regions (Table 29.3). It should be noted that this does not hold true for Switzerland, where the rural plain regions are benefiting from peri-urbanization, whereas the traditionally popular tourist regions are seeing a levelling out of their activities. Spain does not, for the moment, appear to have translated into jobs its efforts to develop tourism in predominantly rural regions.

In the tourism-intensive regions in significantly rural areas, population densities are distinctly higher (Finland apart) and the share of tourism-related employment (with the exception of Finland) fluctuates between 9 and 24 percent, with rates that are slightly lower than those of the regions in the previous category, except the

United Kingdom and Spain. The growth in tourism-related employment confirms the trends already noted, and the increases in four of the countries are even higher (Austria, France, Switzerland, United States). In this group, the most popular tourist regions are also experiencing growth rates higher than those of less popular regions (except in Canada).

Rural regions are therefore directly concerned with the development of tourism, which consolidates and diversifies local employment and may become the main factor in its growth.

Employment in tourism activities at the regional level: the French situation

In France, tourism is an important sector of economic activity which justifies considerable investment in certain regions, leads to the creation of many jobs and contributes significantly to the equilibrium of the balance of payments. Furthermore, it must be kept in mind that France is first in the world for number of visitors. A particular aspect is its dependence on diverse local resources (e.g. historic cities, rural landscapes, cultural heritage, coastal areas and high mountains) which cause many regions, especially the most rural, to be concerned with its development. However, the impact of tourism activities do differ according to the type of region which justifies the OECD geographic typology.

Available data sources

In France, there are a number of data sources on tourism activity:

1. Concerning employment, infra-national statistics on the labour force are available for the years corresponding to the census of population (1975, 1982, 1990). They can be tabulated at the 4-digit level of industrial classification which allows one to identify most of the activities involved in tourism: the types of transportation, hotels/cafes/restaurants, various commercial services for recreation, culture and sports, and travel agencies (Table 29.6). These data are available for each region and département, both in terms of labour force classified by place of residence and in labour force classified by place of work.

2. Statistics are also available on business establishments, according to the same industrial classification, in terms of numbers of establishments, business starts and business closures plus indicators of their legal status and work-force, but not their sales figure.

3. Concerning accommodation, a count of secondary residences is made in each census, and an inventory was carried out at the communal level for the years 1970, 1979 and 1988. This makes it possible to evaluate accommodation capacity estimated as number of "tourist beds" (equivalent to persons) for the different types of lodging:

hotel	youth hostel
tourist room	vacation colony
rural shelter	vacation village
camping and trailer park	secondary residence

Statistics on overnight stays at hotels are also available.

Table 29.6.   Preliminary delineation of tourism activities, France

	Industry classification	Number of wage earners	Number of female wage earners	Percent female wage earners
54.02	Manufacture of sports equipment	10,584	4,624	44
54.03	*Manufacture and repair of pleasure craft	10,628	2,676	25
54.09	Photography and film development	11,584	5,324	46
64.44	Retail optical and photography	16,076	8,260	51
64.47	Retail sports equipment	16,476	8,056	49
67.01	Restaurants and cafes serving meals	506,492	88,708	18
67.04	Beverage sales	16,692	8,020	48
67.05	Cafe/tobacconists	8,048	4,852	60
67.06	Beverage sales with entertainment	8,624	2,900	34
67.07	Multi-purpose cafes	3,228	2,048	63
67.08	*Hotel restaurants	124,359	62,423	50
67.09	*Hotels	23,444	14,880	63
67.12	*Vacation hostels	28,804	16,800	58
67.13	*Vacation lodgings	9,408	4,300	46
70.01	*River transport for travellers	648	140	22
74.09	*Travel agencies	26,381	17,785	67
80.04	Car rental	8,404	3,584	43
84.07	*Health institutions (hot springs, sea therapy, etc.)	9,640	6,920	72
86.06	*Entertainment and recreational services	8,372	3,169	38
86.08	Services added to entertainment	7,324	2,644	36
86.09	Gambling establishments	10,516	4,196	40
86.10	Management of sports facilities	25,212	9,004	36
86.11	*Ski lifts	7,460	1,544	21
96.12	Public cultural heritage conservation	17,796	8,708	49
96.14	Management of public cultural facilities	612	300	49
96.21	*Private cultural heritage conservation	2,536	1,364	54
96.22	*Managing private cultural facilities	2,672	1,576	59
96.24	Managing private sports facilities	1,528	712	47
97.12	*Tourism offices	5,160	4,024	78

*   *Activities based mainly on tourism*

Tourism employment in France

If we keep the three main employment categories used earlier, activities related to tourism involve 2.0 million jobs, 9 percent of the national labour-force. Although overall employment growth is generally weak, these sectors are all growing (Table 29.7), with a particularly high rate for recreational services. These sectors increased 16 percent between 1982 and 1990, more than the national employment growth rate.

Table 29.7.   Growth in "tourism" jobs in France

Industrial classification code	Activity	1982	1990	Percent change
68/74	Transportation	880,812	938,047	6.5
67	Hotels/cafes/restaurants	622,820	745,145	19.6
86/96	Commercial and non-commercial services for recreation, culture and sports	200,344	297,208	48.3
	Total	**1,703,976**	**1,980,400**	**16.2**

Generally speaking, tourism in rural regions benefits from the significant capacity for accommodation (47 percent of the French tourist accommodation capacity). However, this accommodation capacity requires little or no specialized employment. In fact, the lodging consists mainly of secondary residences (60 percent). After this come camping grounds which represent half of all tourist accommodation, excluding secondary residences.

In rural regions, this accommodation capacity makes it possible to lodge a population that is slightly larger than half the number of permanent residents (compared with just 14 percent in urban areas). Thus, tourism is an important factor for employment and social life.

There is a strong seasonal variation in tourism activity in France, especially for "outdoor tourism", which reaches a peak during July and August. Mountainous regions enjoy a second tourist season from December to April based on winter sports. The existence of two possible periods for tourism explains the fact that mountainous rural regions are among those with the highest proportion of jobs in tourism, along with, of course, those of the coast. But there is no absolute correlation between the capacity for accommodation and the number of employed for two types of reason: the share of commercial lodging in the measure of accommodation varies from one region to another, as does the utilization rate for these accommodation structures throughout the year.

In all categories of region, there is a strong growth in the spaces available in tourist lodgings, but the period 1982–1990 saw a significant growth in occasional and secondary lodging in the large cities (Table 29.8).

Table 29.8. Employment in tourism-related sectors by type of region, France

Region	1982	1990	Employment per 1,000 persons (1990)	Percent change
Employment in the transportation sector				
Predominantly rural	192,804	214,629	12.5	11.3
Significantly rural	330,300	364,375	15.8	10.3
Predominantly urban	357,708	359,043	22.0	0.4
Total	**880,812**	**938,047**	**16.6**	**6.5**
Employment in the hotels/cafes/restaurants sector				
Predominantly rural	173,432	204,045	31.2	17.7
Significantly rural	227,870	284,124	31.8	24.7
Predominantly urban	221,518	256,976	37.2	16.0
Total	**622,820**	**745,145**	**33.5**	**19.6**
Employment in the commercial recreation and sport sector				
Predominantly rural	28,280	38,870	2.3	37.4
Significantly rural	42,512	59,556	2.6	40.1
Predominantly urban	68,948	93,102	5.7	35.0
Total	**139,740**	**191,528**	**3.4**	**37.1**
Overall capacity for accommodation (data for 1979 and 1988)				
Predominantly rural	7,626,094	8,973,093	521.2	17.7
Significantly rural	6,380,407	7,817,287	339.2	22.5
Predominantly urban	1,899,028	2,257,807	138.1	18.9
Total	**15,905,529**	**19,048,187**	**336.2**	**19.8**
Number of secondary residences				
Predominantly rural	1,266,803	1,316,557	76.5	3.9
Significantly rural	885,361	1,113,695	48.3	25.8
Predominantly urban	299,508	391,968	24.0	30.9
Total	**2,451,672**	**2,822,220**	**49.8**	**15.1**

Source: RGP 92-90 and communal inventory, 1988.

The proportion of jobs in the different tourism activities are systematically higher in urban areas than in rural regions. Nevertheless, rural tourism is in the process of becoming more professional and creating more and more jobs. This employment growth, female to a great extent, is important for rural areas where there is traditionally a job market deficit.

But the impact of tourism indirectly concerns a large number of activities. Thus, a comparative analysis carried out in a rural region which has little tourism (Mayenne)

and a very touristic rural region (Savoie) confirms that the three specific employment sectors used in the international-comparative analysis (above) are indeed directly linked to growth in tourism (Table 29.9). Note also that construction and retail trade benefit from tourism spin-off.

Table 29.9.   Employment in each sector per 1,000 persons

Industrial sector	Low tourism-intensive region: Mayenne	High tourism-intensive region: Savoie
	Employment per 1,000 persons	
Construction	29	32
Neighbourhood or specialized retail food stores	4	5
Non-food retail business	13	16
Super stores	5	5
Banks and insurance	9	6
Transportation	10	50
Automobile repair	8	7
Hotels, cafes, restaurants	9	64
Commercial recreational services	2	36

Conclusion

This study of tourism in rural areas leaves many methodological problems pending. International comparisons should be viewed with caution.

Tourist areas are usually economically specialized regions — an accurate picture of tourism cannot be gained from national figures. Accordingly, the region is a very good level at which to analyse the role of tourism in the development of new activities and employment.

Tourism is a powerful force of change in the economy and society. It plays a part in the globalization of the economy and access to a more universal culture, and its development is part of a shift in the balance between work-time and leisure-time which is bound to operate in its favour. As the shift occurs, rural areas must find which role can make the most of the natural and cultural assets they possess.

Appendix A: Method of data collection

Questionnaire content

The OECD Rural Development Programme mailed a questionnaire to OECD member countries who had agreed to participate. For each region, statistical information was requested on various categories of tourism-related employment and certain features of tourist accommodation, capacity and occupancy. This information was to be provided for 1980 and 1990 if possible, distinguishing between male and female employment to allow the necessary comparisons.

Questionnaire processing

Nine countries sent usable information: Austria, Canada, Finland, France, Germany, Spain, Switzerland, the United Kingdom and the United States. Not every country was able to provide all the information requested, but taken together they represent some 1,500 regions, thus constituting a sizeable database.

The Statistical Office of the European Communities (Eurostat) has sent a list of data available on the Eurostat base for the tourist industry. Although the data are extensive, covering such subjects as accommodation, visitor flows, tourism-related activities and employment and tourism expenditure, the geographical levels at which they are available (60 percent at NUTS II and 40 percent at NUTS I) make it difficult to integrate into the OECD regional classification.

Precautions for use

Only the first group (hotels/cafes/restaurants) seems relatively consistent in all the country statistics. The case of transport raises comparison problems, relating no doubt to factors such as whether the various types of transport are in the public or the private sector, whether or not certain automobile-related activities have been included (automobile trade, repairs, fuel), the relative importance of urban public transport, and the lack of any distinction between goods and passenger traffic. The third group (market and non-market recreational services) may also show substantial disparities from one country to the next, and there is no certainty that the same activities are included (gambling, leisure sports, paramedical or cultural activities, etc.)[1].

With respect to indicators on tourist facilities, there is a lack of detail on the types of accommodation included in the measurement of accommodation capacity, and on overnight stays (whether or not they include open-air accommodation, accommodation with local residents or relatives, etc.). Only one country indicated the number of second homes, although the figure should be readily available.

References and further reading

Anonymous. (no date) Tourisme rural. *Cahier Espaces No. 42.*

Ministère de l'équipment, des transports et du tourisme. (no date) *L'élaboration d'indicateurs territoriaux du tourisme.* Paris: Vademecum, Observatoire national du tourisme, July.

OECD. (1991) *Manual on Tourism Economic Accounts.* Paris: OECD, Tourism Committee.

OECD. (1994a) *Tourism Strategies and Rural Development.* Paris: OECD/GD(94)49.

OECD. (1994b) *Creating Rural Indicators for Shaping Territorial Policy.* Paris: OECD.

OECD. (1994c) *Tourism Policy and International Tourism in OECD countries, 1991-1992.* Special Feature: Tourism Strategies and Rural Development. Paris: OECD.

United Nations. (1994) *Recommendations on Tourism Statistics,* series M No.83. New York: UN.

---

1. *Activities are undoubtedly classified more selectively in Germany than in other countries.*

Chapter thirty:

Rural Employment and the Information Highway

John Bryden
Arkleton Centre for Rural Development Research, University of Aberdeen, Aberdeen, United Kingdom

Abstract

The Information and Communications Technology (ICT) revolution is having, and is expected to have, profound effects on employment. These effects arise both through the link between ICT and many facets of globalization and restructuring and because it opens up both new threats and new opportunities for economic activities in rural areas. The key element in both is said to be the abolition of "distance" which is associated with ICT.

The changing context — rural development prospects and the information economy

Rural areas in western Europe are vulnerable to the impact of globalization, free trade, deregulation and associated restructuring (Bryden, 1994a; Bryden, 1995). This vulnerability arises from their present employment structure, especially their relatively high dependence on the primary sector and associated processing, low value services, and public sector employment and social welfare support. In addition, privatization and deregulation, especially in the transport sphere, has had significant consequences. Finally, the consequences of the 1992 Rio Summit (Agenda 21) challenge recently developed patterns of mobility, especially commuting, which has been a major factor in the "population turnaround". Although rural Europe is very diverse, and these forces will have different effects in different areas, considerable restructuring is anticipated as we end the Millennium. In most cases, the future of rural areas and people, including members of farm and fishing families, will be determined not by agricultural policy, but by the development of non-agricultural activities and income sources.

At the same time, new hope has been offered to rural areas by the Information and Communications Technology (ICT) revolution. The most obvious impact of ICT is to reduce many of the effects of physical distance which challenges the logic of agglomeration or clustering of enterprises, public authorities, political and cultural life, and people. It is immediately evident that this is potentially of disproportionate importance to rural areas, especially those which are "remote" from main markets. Our attention is therefore drawn to both the positive opportunities which this opens up, and on the other hand, to the new threats which it poses.

One effect of economic restructuring, globalization and the changing labour market is the movement of low-skilled work, or low-skilled components in the chain of production to low-wage countries. Where it is not possible, there has been a downward pressure on the relative wages of unskilled and low skilled workers (Cox,1994; Gillespie, 1994). Also, within richer countries, there has been a shift towards low wage, often rural, areas. These factors, combined with the ICT revolution, has caused a number of enterprises to locate in remoter rural areas (Sociomics Ltd. and The Arkleton Trust (Research) Ltd., 1994; Bryden *et al.*, 1995).

ICT plays a key role in the information flows that facilitate trading into niche markets. ICT permits decentralisation and decomposition of production, just-in time manufacturing, CAD-CAM and rapid and frequent design changes. It is a key factor in the restructuring of the retail sector, and the growth of brand name products which implies new relations with associated manufacturing sectors. Therefore, one key issue for enterprises in rural areas is how they maintain competitiveness and innovate products and processes.

Although service occupations form a growing part of the European labour-force, indicating in a broad sense the growing significance of information flows, and hence of ICT for employment and economic activity, there is a general tendency for information services, and especially high-value services concerned with information (financial services, IT consulting, media, etc.) to be more represented in major cities, than in rural areas. On the other hand, in rural services there is a higher component of services related to persons (including visitors), which often involve lower skilled and lower paid occupations and a lower "information content". Within processes of globalization, it is in the more highly skilled areas of service provision that employment and income earning opportunities appear to be growing, and are likely to grow fastest in the richer countries. Indeed, projections in Finland estimate that by the year 2000, the "content of work in Finland will include: 93 percent information work, 5 percent industrial work and 2 percent in primary production" (Finland, 1995). Given the fact that employment structures in most rural areas appear to be more vulnerable to globalisation tendencies[1], and contain fewer high-skilled growth areas, a critical

---

1. *Because of the relatively high proportion of unskilled and semi-skilled jobs in traditional primary and secondary sectors, and the skewed nature of the tertiary sector, in particular the high proportion of public sector related jobs and the low proportion of jobs in higher level business and information/knowledge services.*

factor for the future will be the extent to which rural areas can "capture" a higher share of information and knowledge related work than has been the case in the past.

In principal, then, ICT opens new opportunities for rural areas and people, through the freeing of many elements in production processes from the constraint of distance, and the ability to access markets. Equally, it poses threats that enterprises formerly protected by distance are exposed to new competition, and activities formerly linked to place may move elsewhere. In practice, the evidence from a number of European countries suggests that both of these tendencies are occurring. The key question concerns the conditions that would favour rural areas in terms of income and employment and how public action (policy or local collective action) might "tip the balance" towards rural. Equally, questions arise about what regions and which people get left out — we do not expect the effects of ICT to be neutral.

What is the information highway?

The information highway (IH) arises from the computer chip and its impact on Information and Communications Technologies and particularly the **combination** of the information and communication technologies. What this combined technology does is to radically change the costs, speed and feasibility of moving large amounts of information about the globe. The IH has major economic, social and political significance, at the very least as great as the introduction of motorized transport at the end of the 19th century.

In infrastructural terms, the IH depends on the microchip and the optical fibre, the satellite and advanced radio communications, and digital switching systems. In software terms, it depends on networks and networks of networks able to communicate using common protocols. In market terms, it depends on information as a resource and as a commodity which can be exchanged for cash, improve the quality of life, or empower people and improve and extend democracy. It challenges hierarchies whose power depends on limiting access to information, whether in the public, social or private spheres. The IH is the medium which allows our credit cards to be checked, our spare parts to be ordered from just-in-time manufacturers, our home banking, our directory enquiries, our remote searches of libraries and databases, and which carries live TV pictures from the other side of the globe, buys and sells our futures options on the Tokyo market, and so on. Probably for the first time **social organization** is developing in the "cyberspace" of the Information Highway. These remote "societies" or "communities" develop norms, rules, trust and other elements of social organization across social and national boundaries, and without personal face-to-face contact. We have yet to imagine the eventual consequences of this.

There are many such networks and networks of networks, heavily exploited by the financial sector and the media, by researchers, by international companies, by governments, and increasingly by citizens. The best known is probably the Internet, itself a network of networks using common protocols for the exchange of information between host computers which are the link with users. For the academic and research establishment, the Internet is the global standard, and increasingly it is also the standard for community networks — freenets and so on — and also for various kinds of cyberspace associations and business ventures. Through the Internet we have services like WWW, Gopher, Mailbase, etc.

Allusions to telecommunications infrastructures which are able to deliver all kinds of electronic information and communications services commonly refer to the "Information Superhighway". The defining characteristics of this "superhighway" have been identified by Dutton *et al.* (1994b) as:

1. A broadband telecommunications service with the ability to carry enormous quantities of information at high speed; the capacity for two-way (interactive) communication; and the ability to deliver any media, including video, audio and text[2].

2. The infrastructure ... should ultimately be able to provide a seamless interconnection between many networks. It is unlikely to be a single homogenous network.

3. The network of networks would evolve by interconnecting many existing and new public and private information "highways, main roads and avenues". Some countries could evolve relatively quickly to more advanced capabilities because they already have many coaxial links as well as traditional copper wires at local levels, together with optical fibres for trunk routes. A more revolutionary leap forward from basic capabilities would be needed elsewhere.

4. Regulations and standards should promote an open environment in which any company could provide any service to any person.

These defining characteristics are important because they reflect the current state of thinking in academic and policy circles. However, I would suggest that the second sentence in point 3 above should start "Some regions in some countries". The point is that rural areas even in otherwise well-endowed countries are unlikely to be in the same position as urban areas, since they often do not have "many coaxial links", and are commonly served by twisted pairs of copper wire[3]. This has implications for the final point about regulations and competition. In sparsely populated areas the economics of providing the necessary infrastructure

---

2.　 *"Broadband" refers to the speed and data capacity of the links. The bandwidth required for digital telephony, high speed fax, and the videophone is 64K bits per second; that for uncompressed broadcast TV is between 1100 and 2200 times higher — i.e. 70 to 141 Mega bits per second, impossible on a twisted pair of copper wires, feasible on coaxial cable up to about 3 km, but beyond that requiring optical fibre links. See Dutton et al., 1994b, Figure 1.*

3.　 *Although new options are opening up through GSM mobile communications, digital radio, and satellite communications, these tend to be expensive at present.*

may require a (regulated) monopoly provider who can capture revenues from all information services. We would not expect rural concerns to dominate ICT regulatory decisions. Rural people must therefore be very vigilant indeed if they are to ensure that the overwhelming attention to urban and "national" issues does not have serious and adverse consequences for them. In this context, it is interesting to note that the recent commitment by Mr Blair, leader of the UK labour party, to wire every school, college, library and hospital to the "broadband network" did not extend to a commitment to a "universal service" extending to remoter rural areas (*Financial Times,* 1995a).

The present situation in rural Europe is very patchy. France has 100 percent digitally switched telecommunications, and Sweden and Finland are rapidly approaching this state. In Finland and Sweden, both very advanced in ICT, ISDN I (64kbps) is a reality in every commune centre. In the Scottish Highlands and Islands, over two-thirds of the population is covered by digital exchanges, although problems remain with lengthy copper links between exchanges in remoter areas, radio links between islands, and long copper links with customers remote from exchanges. In Ireland, some 63 percent of exchanges were digital in 1993. In southern Europe, however, digital communications in rural areas are less advanced, in some cases considerably so. In general, however, the current prospects of accessing the broadband network in rural areas of low population density and far from towns and cities anywhere in Europe are not good.

Information highway and rural employment

The most obvious new opportunity for rural areas has been in **telework**, which includes a range of activities where "information work" is produced at home and delivered electronically to the enterprise.

Such activities have been targeted by regional and rural development agencies in countries where new telecommunications infrastructure is in place. Also interest is coming from agencies and social movements concerned about urban congestion and pollution. Underlying this, of course, is a corporate concern to reduce costs. One study estimated average savings of $US 1,554–3,030 per annum in fixed costs per teleworker (European Foundation for the Improvement of Living and Working Conditions, 1994). However, much of the expansion in "telework" has occurred near towns and cities, rather than in "deep rural" areas. This is because it is "part-time" teleworking with some presence required each week at the office in the city.

A report for British Telecom (BT) in 1992 estimated that there were 594,000 teleworkers in the UK of whom 576,000 were self-employed, 13,000 were with major employers, and only 5,000 with medium or small sized employers[4]. In

---

4.   *This is based on a definition of teleworkers as those who "spend 3 days or more a week working from home producing work at their homes, at local centres or travelling." (European Foundation for the Improvement of Living and Working Condition, 1994).*

Europe, although data is scarce, teleworking is considered to be best developed in the UK. Work for the European Foundation for Living and Working Conditions estimates the costs and benefits (including environmental costs and benefits) of teleworking, concluding that a population of 500,000 teleworkers would have a direct net employment impact of +55,800 jobs. Road transport in general is responsible for a high proportion of noxious emissions contributing to poor air quality in urban areas and to global warming (Alberti *et al.*, 1994a, b).

In Scotland and Ireland at least, public agency support for rural telecommunications infrastructure has been based on expected increase in direct employment. For example, the prime argument for the Highlands and Islands Development Board (HIDB) (later, Highlands and Islands Enterprises (HIE)) "unusual" investment of £5 million in telecommunications infrastructure in the Scottish Highlands and Islands was based on the anticipated number of jobs to be created[5].

HIE are also involved in marketing advanced telecommunications to potential inward-investors. HIE targets the area of export services: "there is scope for growth based on utilisation of the new telecommunications network" (HIE, 1992, 5). HIE also hope to encourage back offices to locate in the region. Thus amongst the targets for its inward investment strategy are "large companies which, using the advanced telecommunications facilities available, are able to undertake administrative functions at locations remote from their main office or offices" (HIE, 1992, 27). In this respect the HIE network has also begun to develop speculative offices (e.g. RACE), and over the past year the region has started to attract a number of inward investment projects in this area.

A sample of six companies interviewed in 1993 as part of a European project had about 90 jobs associated with them, and consisted of all but four of the companies known to be major users of advanced telecommunications in the region at that time. Including these other four companies increased the numbers of jobs to 180, of whom some 30 are teleworkers working remotely from the main offices. One example from Scotland, Crossaig Ltd., now part of ISI (see below) uses over 15 teleworkers in the Highlands and Islands for extraction, indexing and compilation of medical abstracts for Elsevier's Embase on-line data base. Another example is AEA technology based in Thurso which employs 43 people administering six pension schemes for three employers. Taken overall, BT reckons that HIDB's five year target of 500 jobs created in the Highlands and Islands will be comfortably met and recent independent survey evidence points to significant net job creation (Bryden

---

5. *Overall, 500 jobs were projected to be created within five years as a result of the investment which was unusual in the sense that the HIDB did not normally invest in infrastructure projects. The investment was described by Sir Robert Cowan, then Chairman of the HIDB, as " ... without doubt ... the most important single investment we have made in the economic future of the Highlands and Islands" (Quoted in* The Scotsman, *June 3, 1989). The £16m investment did not include the costs of upgrading the trunk networks which accounted for an estimated additional investment of £30 to £35m. In total therefore almost £50m was invested in the development of the telecommunications infrastructure of the region.*

et al., 1995b). True, some of these will involve the "displacement" of jobs from elsewhere: for example, in one recent investment in Grampian region, jobs will be partly displaced from the headquarters of the Regional Council. On the other hand, a process of "displacement" of such jobs has taken place *from* rural to urban areas over many years. In addition to such companies, there were a growing number of independent teleworkers and self-employed people using telematics, and these would comprise most of the balance of 350 jobs (in full-time equivalents) related to the initiative as estimated by HIE in April, 1993.

In the Scottish Highlands and Islands, the largest project so far is the telework centre development by Hoskyns in Forres (200 jobs plus, and rising). Hoskyns processes local government tax demands and even London parking fines (*Financial Times*, 1995b). The latest additions to employment in telecommunications related companies in the Highlands include two firms based in Dunoon — Televisual Data (20 jobs) and Database Direct (50 jobs). In each of these recent cases, it is understood that a substantial package of property and training assistance was also provided. For Hoskyns this amounted to £1.5m from a variety of public sector sources including Grampian Regional Council, HIE and the LEC (*Glasgow Herald*, November 16, 1993). In addition, there has been an increase in employment by BT at Thurso of some 36 jobs which was announced in 1994. BT now has over 100 "distance workers" in Thurso, involved in document production, password validation, and a helpdesk for computer problems, servicing BT's internal (UK-wide) organization.

In effect this is an example of what is now called a "call centre", which is reckoned to be the fastest growing area of telecommunications based services in the UK. Similar examples can be found elsewhere in Europe. For example, Ericsson has a call service centre similar to BT's in Northern Sweden, and SAS (Scandinavian Airlines) has an operation also in Northern Sweden handling its reservations business (Bryden *et al.*, 1995a). Mail order firms and banks are making increasing use of such "centres" which can be far from head offices.

In Ireland too, the focus has been on direct employment in "tele-defined" and "tele-transacted" businesses[6]. Ireland has in many ways been more successful than Scotland in attracting tele-transacted kinds of business. For example, Worldscope Ltd. in County Clare, Ireland collates, analyses, updates and distributes information relating to public companies worldwide. The parent company is Disclosure Ltd. in Maryland, and telecommunications are used directly to transfer data to computers in Maryland. It employees 75 people, many of whom have tertiary educational qualifications. The quality of telecommunications was said to be critical to their location decision. Other significant factors were

---

6.   *"Tele-defined" products are value-added tele-communicated activities or transactions. "Tele-transacted" products are those where good communications networks and facilities are increasingly crucial to the transaction of work on-line between offices and sites. (Sociomics Ltd. and The Arkleton Trust (Research) Ltd., 1994).*

the availability of government grants, the availability of skilled labour, access to Shannon Airport and relatively low labour costs (Sociomics Ltd. and The Arkleton Trust (Research) Ltd., 1994). Another example from the same source is Neodata Services in Limerick, based in Limerick, but with three other sites in Ireland. They have 400 employees in Ireland, servicing the needs of the magazine industry for mailing labels, reader reply cards, subscription renewals, updating of subscriber databases, etc. Although present in Ireland before the upgrading of telecommunications infrastructure, the company has benefited greatly from advanced telecommunications services, enabling more and more work to be transferred from their main office in the US. Most employees are secondary school leavers, although some 30 have tertiary level qualifications. A third example, this time "tele-defined", is Dell Direct in Bray, County Wicklow, employing 300 people involved in telesales and technical support for Europe, of whom 87 percent have tertiary level qualifications. Other cases exist in various kinds of information processing — an example being ISI, a subsidiary of Thompsons International. ISI are publishers specializing in index products for researchers. They have 87 employees, mainly school leavers with commercial or secretarial skills, although six are secondary school graduates. As is common in this industry, a high proportion of employees are female.

In the Irish study, 12 case studies produced 1,359 jobs. In the three case studies which were "tele-defined", 87 percent of the 326 employees had tertiary level qualifications. This was in marked contrast with the "tele-transacted" cases which involved 1,033 employees of whom only 16 percent had tertiary level qualifications. Ten of the twelve companies were of US origin and involved inwardly mobile investment. The policy emphasis in Ireland (through IDA and Shannon Development) has been on the attraction of tele-defined and tele-transacted businesses, rather than on general adoption of ICT in all sectors and by domestic firms, and so far at least, it has evidently met with some success (Sociomics Ltd. and The Arkleton Trust (Research) Ltd., 1994, pp. 46–49).

Thus investment in ICT opens up new opportunities for employment activities in rural areas, as the examples from Ireland and Scotland show. Many of these are linked to inward investment, and although some involve the displacement of employment from urban to rural centres, most are tapping international markets and are new kinds of enterprise. Many kinds of jobs which are directly related to telecommunications investment involve information processing of one kind or another, and capitalize on the falling cost, increasing speed, and improved reliability of data transfer using digital telecommunications. The provision of the necessary infrastructure, whilst essential, is only one side of the coin, however. In principal, the associated work can, by definition, be undertaken anywhere where high speed digital communications are feasible. There is no natural monopoly in rural places, nor in the rural places of richer countries. Although the dominance of the English language in international commerce, finance, and information industries has to date given a competitive edge to countries where the English language is the mother tongue, the essence of this kind of work is that it is highly mobile by comparison with other kinds of work. In addition, it is clear that quality of life factors, access to a well educated labour force, cost factors, and access to government grants have been important in the location decisions of firms moving to such places as Ireland, Northern Sweden and the Highlands and Islands of Scotland.

Of course, ICT has brought with it job losses in rural as well as urban areas — through automated banking, remote monitoring, and digitalization of telephone exchanges, as well as through the associated restructuring of private enterprises and public authorities. These will happen anyway. The challenge is to identify and to take advantage of the new opportunities which are being opened up. This includes understanding the new rationale for choice of location of various enterprises.

In my view, the rather singular focus on direct employment creation through inward investment of tele-transacted and tele-defined enterprises is mistaken. Much more important for the future of rural areas is the impact of telecommunications infrastructure on the **competitiveness of rural firms in general**, and the impact on employment in these firms if a positive strategy on telecommunications is not adopted. There are also very serious implications for the quality of life, educational provision and democratic involvement.

In a recent survey of enterprises in the Scottish Highlands and Islands, most were surprised to find that over 20 percent had modems (Bryden *et al.*, 1995b). This is more than double the rate of modem use in rural firms estimated by the EU's SARBA project. In this respect, firms in the Highlands and Islands are not far behind and may well be ahead. Talking to a fish farmer in the Hebrides recently, I found he was using a modem for an information system directly connecting him with his customers. He had found the technology vital to improve information flows and to enlarge his market. He envisages adopting a video conferencing system in the future to cut the cost of travelling time which are considerable for remote enterprises. Similar stories are told in many other enterprises which are neither "tele-transacted" nor "tele-defined". Increasingly access to certain markets, to suppliers, to design and other services will be determined by the adoption of ICT. The link with competitiveness is thus increasingly clear.

Moreover, at least one new enterprise (Highland Trail) has been established in the Highlands and Islands to market "niche" products of small local firms on the World Wide Web. The process involves the creation of web pages for each firm, an ordering and payment system, and research on the web (called "web-weaving") to find appropriate people to target through relevant user-groups. In this way, small firms are gaining access to global markets.

Although rural development agencies must pay some attention to the possibilities for tele-defined and tele-transacted enterprises in rural areas, including various forms of telework, I would argue strongly that they should have a clear focus on, and strategy for, ICT in all sectors and activities in rural areas.

Some policy issues

Universal access to the information highway is a crucial issue, but what does it mean. There is almost universal access to the telephone, but this is no longer enough[7]. It is access to the high speed, high quality, low cost digital communications networks that will count. Ultimately this means optical fibre, co-axial cable (or their equivalents) to every home, business, and public, educational and voluntary body. Ultimately it means local call or no charges for access to these networks. Meantime, it means such links to a variety of local community facilities which are used by people for other purposes like schools, libraries, post-offices or village halls, etc. This should be a minimum requirement.

In an era of privatization and de-regulation, how can this be achieved? One recommendation is to permit telecom companies to carry broadcasting media (entertainment and infotainment) on the fibre links. It may be the only way that telecom companies can justify the investment required, and produce the low tariffs needed. This poses huge challenges not only because of the vested interests involved and the dangers of monopoly practices, but also because the forms of regulation in telecoms and broadcasting have been historically quite different. It is not clear whether, in remoter rural areas, competition will retard rather than advance provision of full access to the superhighway. There are arguments that only a single protected provider could justify the investment in fibre optic cable, although, on the other hand, opening up the use of a single infrastructure to a wide range of providers would almost certainly increase utilization.

Other regulatory issues concern intellectual property rights, privacy and security, editorial control and censorship (which raises huge concerns) and interconnectivity and inter-operability. This last is obviously easier in Canada and the UK, where there is a single national regulator (at least of telecommunications). In the US and Europe, each "state" has a regulator. The main problem, however, will be the convergence of telecommunications and broadcasting regulation.

I have argued that provision of the infrastructure and potential access is one thing, and encouraging use is quite another. I do not myself think that rural areas are backward in this respect, indeed many have been at the forefront of new uses of ICT. However, there is an urgent need for mass experience and exposure to the possibilities opened up for economic, social, cultural and political life. This needs local "champions" concerned with the range of business, community and educational applications, and local ICT forums, which need public encouragement and support.

---

7.   *Thus "'universal service' must be redefined. Canadians need access to more than telephone service in order to participate in the information age" (Angus and McKie, 1994, p. 118).*

A critical issue in this respect will be coping with those relatively disadvantaged groups in rural society, which may become even more disadvantaged as a result of ICT developments. A conscious effort will be needed to ensure that the mechanisms for mass exposure, the activities of "champions" and forums, reflect this requirement.

Left to itself, the market will produce highly unequal access to, and engagement in, the ICT revolution, largely dependent on the capital and human resources available. This situation may produce a few teleworking jobs in rural areas, but it will fail to capture the potential benefits. So far, I suggest that the private sector has led. There is a sharpening of divisions between those who can gain advantage from the ICT revolution and those who can not. This requires determined effort, including strategic planning, and changing practices, in the public and voluntary spheres. It is very important to collect, evaluate and communicate "case studies", for example the teleworking initiative of Grampian region, to avoid repetition of mistakes.

Summary and conclusion

The combination of Information and Communication Technologies (ICT) underlying the "Information Highway" is important for rural areas and people. It is not just about direct employment creation in the form of "teleworking". The long run competitiveness of all rural enterprises will depend on ICT in the context of globalization and Europeanization. Other important aspects concern quality of life issues including health, culture, educational access and quality, participation and democracy.

The public policy issues include issues of universal access and charging, the need for mass experience and avoiding disadvantage and "exclusion", the role of local champions, ICT forums and strategies and regulatory change. Regulatory issues include the importance for rural areas to obtain local call access to the Internet and the ability of telecommunications companies to carry entertainment and infotainment along fibre optic cables to rural homes. Such changes may be essential to ensure that rural people are not at the "end of the line" when it comes to investments which make access to the "superhighway" possible. Otherwise rural citizens may be at a serious disadvantage in the new economic and technological environment.

References and further reading

Alberti, M. *et al.* (1994a) *Urban Environment and Sustainable Development.* Discussion Paper 1 for the Conference Towards a New Development Approach, Brussels, November 24-25.

Alberti, M. *et al.* (1994b) *Environmental Impacts Caused by the Mobility of Passengers and Goods due to the Localisation of Administrative Activities in the Urban Area, and Analysis, on the Basis of Economic and Social Criteria, of the Cost Effective Solutions to Reduce Negative Impacts: A Case Study for Brussels.* Paper presented to the Seminar on Sustainable Development, Mens en Ruimte, Brussels, November.

Angus, Elizabeth and McKie, Duncan. (1994) *Canada's Information Highway: Services, Access and Affordability. A Policy Study for New Media Branch and Information Technologies Branch.* Ottawa: Industry Canada, May.

Black, John. (1986) *Reducing Isolation: Telecommunications and Rural Development.* Enstone, Oxford: The Arkleton Lecture, The Arkleton Trust.

Bryden, John. (1994a) Prospects for Rural Areas in an Enlarged European Union. In Thompson *et al.* (eds). *Proceedings of the 23rd seminar of the European Association of Agricultural Economists*, Aberdeen, June-July. [Also in *Journal of Rural Studies* Vol. IV, 1994.]

Bryden, John. (ed.). (1994b) *Towards Sustainable Rural Communities.* Guelph: University of Guelph.

Bryden, John.(1995) *A Future for Rural Europe?* Paper presented to the Institute of Social Studies Rural Economy Seminar Series, March.

Bryden, John and Fuller, Tony. (1986) *New Technologies and Rural Development.* Enstone, Oxford: Report of the 1986 Arkleton Seminar, The Arkleton Trust.

Bryden, John and Misener, B. (1991). Rurtel: A Rural Communications Network, Some lessons from a 3-year pilot project. In Kuiper, D. and Roling, N.G. (eds). *The Edited Proceedings of the European Seminar on Knowledge Management and Information Technology.* Wageningen: Agricultural University. [Summarised in a special issue of *Knowledge in Society* Vol. 3, No. 3, March, 1991.]

Bryden, John, Black, Stuart and Rennie, Frank. (1993) *Final Report on the Evaluation of the Pilot Teleservice Centres Project in the Highlands and Islands.* Enstone, Oxford: The Arkleton Trust (Research) Ltd.

Bryden, J., Bendixen, O.C., Gabrielsson, R. and Rintala, K. (1995a) *Joint Scotland-Scandinavia Study on the Scope for Establishing Collaborative Activities, based on IT, between the Peripheral Regions.* Report of the Coordination Group on Stage I, Highlands and Islands Enterprise and Nordic Council.

Bryden, J., Black, S. and Sproull, A. (1995b) *Evaluation of the Economic and Employment Impact of the Highlands and Islands Telecommunications Initiative.* Highlands and Islands Enterprise.

Canadian Information Highway Advisory Council. (1994) *Canada's Information Highway: Building Canada's Information and Communications Infrastructure. Providing New Dimensions for Learning, Creativity and Entrepreneurship.* Ottawa: Canadian Information Highway Advisory Council, Industry Canada, November. [Also available on Internet through Gopher at debra.dgbt.doc.ca port 70/Information Highway Advisory Council and the World Wide Web via http:/debra.dgbt.doc.ca/info-highway/ihohtwl]

Cox, Gabrirlle. (1994) *Priced into Proverty.* Glasgow: Low Pay Network (UK), Scottish Low Pay Unit.

Dutton, William, Bulmer, J., Garnham, N., Mansell, R., Cornford, J., and Peltu, M. (1994a) *The Information Superhighway: Britain's Response.* PICT Policy Research Paper No 29, December.

Dutton, William, Taylor, J., Bellamy, C., Raab, C. and Peltu, M. (1994b) *Electronic Service Delivery: Themes and Issues in the Public Sector.* Brunel University: ESRC Programme on Information and Communication Technologies (PICT). Research Paper No. 28, August, PICT Programme Office.

European Foundation for the Improvement of Living and Working Conditions. (1994) *The Potential for Employment Opportunities from Pursuing Sustainable Development.* Dublin: European Foundation for the Improvement of Living and Working Conditions, Working Paper, October.

Financial Times. (1995a) Blair wants £10bn information superhighway, p. 10.

Financial Times. (1995b) Scots transform London parking fines into profits. September, 29, p. 8.

Finland. (1995) *Finland's National Telework Development Programme.* Helsinki: Advisory Committee for Rural Policy, Association of Finnish Local Authorities, PT Finland Ltd, and the Ministry of Labour.

Gillespie, Morag. (1994) *Low Pay in Scotland, 1994.* Glasgow: Scottish Low Pay Unit.

Highlands and Islands Enterprises. (1992) *Strategy for Industrial Development.* Inverness, Scotland: Highlands and Islands Enterprise.

Industry Canada. (1994) *The Canadian Information Highway: Building Canada's Information and Communications Infrastructure. Spectrum, Information Technologies and Telecommunications Sector.* Ottawa: Industry Canada, April. [Also available on Internet through Gopher at debra.dgbt.doc.ca port 70/Industry Canada Documents and the World Wide Web via http:/debra.dgbt.doc.ca/isc/isc.html]

Newby, Howard. (1984) *Rural Communities and New Technology.* Paper presented to the 1984 Arkleton Seminar.

Sociomics Ltd. and The Arkleton Trust (Research) Ltd. (1994) *Employment Trends Related to the Use of Advanced Communications.* Nethy Bridge, Inverness-shire: Arkleton Research for the European Commission, D-G XIII.

The Teleworker Magazine.

Index